"Frank Gaffikin has produced a truly maj
breaking and page-turning book. He cou
political economic, social, technological :
human species during this period of profound change and existential uncertainty. Frank paints on a broad global canvas, asks uncomfortable questions, draws on wide academic reading and on his long experience both as a public intellectual and as a radical community activist. He writes incisively, persuasively and wittily. You will want to buy this and recommend and discuss it with friends and colleagues."

Professor Emeritus John Benington, CBE, *Warwick University*

"A masterful, connect-all-dots interrogation of our polarising and foreboding world. No political, economic, or cultural fault-line is left unexamined in this probing analysis of today's boiling points."

Scott A. Bollens, *Warmington Professor of Peace and International Cooperation, University of California, Irvine*

"*The Human Paradox: Worlds Apart in a Connected World* is a must-read book. It offers a critical, political, and intellectual discussion of our urgent global challenges namely social polarization and diversity as well as global and local injustice, and also analyses the power of the new world of information and its effect on culture, economy, and democracy. The book systematically analyses human development and progress and the ways these have been shaped by populism and authoritarian nationalism. Instead of looking at such issues as populism, climate change or geopolitical hegemony separately, the book offers an integrative understating of these challenges and further offers a radical approach for humanity, looking at the importance of the next generation's social improvement. This book will be of interest to researchers and students as well as for a wider audience interested in matters of political economy, sociology, and politics."

Professor Haim Yacobi, *The Bartlett Development Planning Unit, University College London*

THE HUMAN PARADOX

In *The Human Paradox: Worlds Apart in a Connected World*, author Frank Gaffikin probes widely and meticulously into our past and present to analyse the connections between the many acute polarisations that mark contemporary times. Addressing profound issues related to Trumpism, Brexit, the outbreak of Covid-19 and ensuing pandemic, and environmental change, the book argues that beneath all the present social tumult lies a fundamental dilemma for human stability and progress, namely how we can be estranged from what we refer to as humanity.

The book begins with an appraisal of populism and authoritarian nationalism, and later explores whether, in our human development, we are bound for enhancement or extinction. Interrogating these big ideas further, the book identifies three central challenges that confront us as a society: living on the planet, living with the planet, and living with one another on the planet. These challenges prompt a re-think of what it is to be human and social, and hinging on these key themes, the book thus concludes with consideration of a radical agenda for future social improvement.

Rather than peering through the conventional lenses offered by separate disciplines, this book argues for interdisciplinary appreciation and recognition, especially so if we are to address the dilemma at the center of its concern. *The Human Paradox* will appeal to readers interested in the major conflicts of our times, as well as students of subjects including sociology, politics, history, and economics.

Professor Frank Gaffikin, has been an academic for four decades, in the University of Ulster and Queen's University Belfast, and for periods at two universities in the United States, with a special focus on urban scholarship and, in recent years, on planning in contested space. He is a Fellow of the Royal Society of Arts.

He has been co-Director of the Urban Institute at the University of Ulster; a Senior Research Fellow at the Great Cities Institute in Chicago; and Director of the Institute of Spatial and Environmental Planning, at Queen's University.

THE HUMAN PARADOX

Worlds Apart in a Connected World

Frank Gaffikin

As we make sense of these strange times let's believe in better days!

Best wishes, Frank

Routledge
Taylor & Francis Group

NEW YORK AND LONDON

Designed Cover Image: © Getty Images

First published 2023
by Routledge
605 Third Avenue, New York, NY 10158

and by Routledge
4 Park Square, Milton Park, Abingdon, Oxon, OX14 4RN

Routledge is an imprint of the Taylor & Francis Group, an informa business

© 2023 Taylor & Francis

The right of Frank Gaffikin to be identified as author of this work has been asserted in accordance with sections 77 and 78 of the Copyright, Designs and Patents Act 1988.

Library of Congress Cataloging-in-Publication Data
Names: Gaffikin, Frank, author.
Title: The human paradox : worlds apart in a connected world / Frank Gaffikin.
Description: New York, NY : Routledge, 2023. |
Includes bibliographical references and index. |
Identifiers: LCCN 2022060295 (print) | LCCN 2022060296 (ebook) |
ISBN 9780367617929 (hardback) | ISBN 9780367617912 (paperback) |
ISBN 9781003106593 (ebook)
Subjects: LCSH: Social change. | Social policy. |
Polarization (Social sciences)
Classification: LCC HM831 .G344 2023 (print) |
LCC HM831 (ebook) | DDC 303.4–dc23/eng/20230316
LC record available at https://lccn.loc.gov/2022060295
LC ebook record available at https://lccn.loc.gov/2022060296

ISBN: 9780367617929 (hbk)
ISBN: 9780367617912 (pbk)
ISBN: 9781003106593 (ebk)

DOI: 10.4324/9781003106593

Typeset in Bembo
by Newgen Publishing UK

Dedicated to Paddy and Molly:
Wise Heads on Burdened Shoulders

BRIEF CONTENTS

DETAILED CONTENTS

ACKNOWLEDGEMENTS

Authorship of this book should really read: *Frank Gaffikin with Ryan Gaffikin*, because my son, Ryan, played a major part in its writing -- through our many discussions, his reading of various iterations, and his suggestions for incisive changes in the text. For me, the experience of this collaboration confirmed how important it is to talk across generations on these issues. I write as somebody who came of political age in the 1960s. Ryan brought invaluable insight into how the present world looks to somebody in their twenties, somebody very much engaged with, and knowledgeable about, the key concerns addressed here. This book could not have been written without him.

I'm also indebted to my daughters, Claire and Laura, who read much of the text, and made instructive comment. They brought the much-needed perspective of young women, who do not regard themselves as 'political', but who are very much astute observers of the world, involved in health and educational jobs that bring them into daily contact with the practical problems, and who are concerned to help make the world a kinder and more just place. I also want to thank my brother Patrick, from whom I've learned a lot over the years. He comes to these issues as a scientist. I appreciate that he doesn't agree with many of the positions I adopt here, regarding religion. But he offered a critical review of most chapters, and his assessment was most helpful. My sister Bernadette was a great inspiration. As a person of deeds, she has shown me the wisdom that comes through kindness. Always looking for the best in people, she walks the message of this book. My grandchildren: Daniel, Dawson, Emily, Willow, and Cohen, also played a part, because in thinking about the future, I've been mindful of the kind of world that they'll inherit.

Always to the fore, I want to express thanks to my wife, Colette. As partners in everything, we've been witnesses to each other's lives for more decades than we would care to count. Her selfless work with the home and family has allowed me the time to undertake this project. Her thoughts and honest feedback always give me a reliable basis for my writing. She is my main sounding board. It's through her social skills -- rather than mine -- that we have networked with people far and wide, contacts that have been crucial to us being open to the condition faced by people elsewhere. Notably, she was much quicker off the mark than me in recognising, and acting on, the 'green' challenge. As a creative person, she reminds me of the importance of arts & culture to societal improvement. She would not want me to say much more here. Suffice to say, without her guiding words and constant support, I would not have travelled the path that brought me to this book.

Many other people deserve my gratitude. For the sake of brevity, let me just mention: Brendan Boyle, Malachy McEldowney, Paul Sweeney, and Paul Toal, who read early chapter drafts, and made prudent comment. They are friends first and foremost. When it comes to my views written here, they have been 'critical friends'. Through many discussions with them -- out hiking the hills, having lunch in cafes, sharing holidays, and family occasions -- I've learned as much as from any books. It shows the importance of close friends -- in some cases, lifelong friends -- who can navigate the world together over the years, even if at times, using different maps.

What we come to know about anything, and the ideas we come to have, are shaped by all the exchanges and collaborations we have with many people over a lifetime. In that sense, this is not 'my' book. It's the result of engagement with, and learning from, many wise people -- with some of whom I've worked for decades -- and I reference just some here: James Anderson; Ralf Brand; Tovi Fenster; Sandra Griffiths; Liam Kennedy; Roger Kline; Judith Kossey; Monica McWilliams; Mike Morrissey; Paul & Honora Murphy; Brendan Murtagh; Andrew Nickson; David Perry; Derek Ray; David Rowlands; Scott Sinclair; Ken Sterrett; Socrates Stratis; Jackie Redpath; Michael Rosato; and Robin Wilson.

Finally, I stress that none of those mentioned are accountable for any views expressed here. That responsibility rests with me.

PROLOGUE

The 'cancel' concept used in this book refers not only to the current arguments around 'cancel culture', but also (a) the wider issues of identity politics and populism that deny or demote 'the other', and seemingly abandon the prospect of human solidarity (covered in *What on Earth?*, *All the Rage* and *Mistaken Identity* chapters); (b) the way some whole communities are 'cancelled' from society by being left behind in terms of inequality and exclusion (*False Economy* and *Power Play* chapters); (c) the risk of cancelling ourselves as a species in terms of either losing sense of our evolutionary human nature, or moving to self-extinction through nuclear proliferation, climate emergency, eco-injustice, etc. (the *Only Human* and *Dead End* chapters); and finally, the prospect of 'cancelling' our humanity with artificial intelligence, and the worst de-humanising features of social media and online abuse, instead of using the potential of high tech for greater human connection (the *Net Effect* chapter).

Despite the sombre nature of these times, public discourse can be reduced to sham exchange. Indeed, the many misfortunes facing our world are increasingly filtered through a performative politics, weak on requisite gravitas, while strong on farce. This is the faux buffoonery of authoritarian populism that attempts to tap into the present disconcerting mood and moment. Though credited with plain-speaking, many of the populist leaders actually talk humbug. Can we make sense of what seems to be the absurd? Is there method behind the madness of a contemporary politics that deliberately deploys the risible and preposterous as a tactic of disruption, designed to perplex and then to reset the dial for a new social reality?

Many books address one or more of these subjects. In insisting that they are all linked and only can be understood as a complete picture, I set about a project to join the dots. The result is a two-volume work, of which this book is the first.

Combined, the two books examine the extent to which there is such a thing as 'humanity' that can be summoned at this cusp of human existence to address, in mutual interest, pressing risks to civilisation. In the context of current social tumult, they examine whether this sense of the common good is being forfeited in a divisive politics of identity and nationalism. Each book is intended as a stand-alone publication. Basically, this initial volume addresses the issues and challenges facing us in these turbulent times. Its twin book explores how we struggle to shape a common future in a period marked by parallel universes when it comes to truth and reality, and to reach agreed definitions of the good society, at a time when traditional interpretations of social ethics from religion and politics are under strain, and when democracy itself can be a soft touch in hard times.

The following gives an outline of the structure and chapter content of the book:

In structure, there are two main sections:

1. *understanding the convulsion of contemporary times*: This deals with current controversies in politics and economics, including resurgent nationalism; populism; culture wars; identity politics; immigration; 'wokeism'; and an economy dominated by high finance, productive of great inequality, and alienation of those left behind. (All Shook Up);
2. *the story of human origin, and possible human extinction or enhancement*. This follows from the tribal contests covered in Section 1, and probes the origins of this partisan belonging; human evolution; nature versus nurture; limits of human intelligence; whether humans are headed for self-extinction with climate change etc in the Anthropocene; or whether instead we're headed into post-humanism, and the surveillance society, led by artificial intelligence. In essence, it examines the extent to which we're bound for doom or bloom. (Hello, Goodbye).

In all this, the book analyses the links among the many acute polarisations that mark contemporary times. While acknowledging the limits of progressive politics in the last half century in addressing social issues such as inequality and diversity, it examines how the new world of information can infect as well as enrich culture, economy and democracy itself. In doing so, it suggests that beneath all the present social tumult lies a fundamental dilemma for human progress, namely how we can be estranged from what we call humanity. With this in mind, the book concludes with an outline radical approach toward social improvement, an agenda that is elaborated in the second volume.

The content addresses populism and the politics of identity, within a context of diversity and demands for social equality, and the economics and politics that have dominated our world in recent times. It proceeds to examine our understanding of what it means to be human beyond any social difference, and whether we can escape the delusional appeal of human centrality in the natural world. Looking at demography and migration in human destiny, and threats such as climate change, nuclear proliferation, and new pandemics, it asks whether we can avert self-extinction. In the digital age of robotics, artificial intelligence and social media, it explores benefits of big tech, alongside its economic and democratic deficits.

This prepares the way for the companion second volume (*Resolving The Human Paradox*), in which people's empowerment is seen within the uncomfortable reality of contested reality. What is the human cognitive capacity to separate fact from fiction, to discern reason from revelation and change minds with evidence? In appreciating the role of consciousness in perception, can we distinguish the lens of faith and science in determining truth? And how do we understand principles of goodness and justice in an increasingly complex world? Within this analysis, what is a feasible agenda for a better, if never perfect, world, one that aligns us with our own limitations as humans?

In outline, the following indicates chapter content of this book within this structure:

A. All Shook Up

Chapter One: What on Earth?

This chapter opens with a summary review of the contemporary challenges facing the world and introduces the book's key arguments.

Chapter Two: All the Rage

How do we account for a resurgence in populist nationalism and related angry culture wars? How did this high octane political invective arise, whereby issues of sovereignty and identity manifest in populist nationalism with an authoritarian pose? Outrageous exchange that is indignant and brazen evokes outrage among the affronted. Fears are incited in order to tap into subsequent acrimony. In this way, the new political landscape is deliberately designed to keep discourse off balance by interventions that confuse, distort, and distract. Culture wars, deploying militarist idioms of treachery, coup and surrender, embolden adherents of nativism and nationalism to erect borders and boundaries against their perceived threat of a more globalised world. But different variants of populism must be acknowledged.

A key paradox underpinning this rancorous politics is that people's *economic* impulse to shelter inside a big trading bloc in a pitiless world economy is offset by their *political* impulse to recapture self-determination from distant bureaucrats in those very same blocs. What is the 'self' to be determined here? How does the individual self align with tribal belonging? Where is the blueprint for the human mould? This leads into the next chapter about self and group identity, and how far such provide an anchor in stormy political seas.

Chapter Three: Mistaken Identity

In an age where politics seems more devoted to addressing competing identities based on nationality, gender, race, sexuality etc. the issues of growing wealth inequality, inequities around gender and race, and between global north and south, are being relatively neglected. In turn, these disparities are linked to the prevailing model of world economy. Have culture wars around diversity displaced class wars around inequality? Are the two factors related in what some see as a rigged system privileging those from a well-heeled background, with racial, ethnic, gender and class markers?

One problem with present emphasis on diversity and its rights is that the issue of equality can be inadvertently marginalised. This is not to be reductionist and determinist about class. It is simply to acknowledge that the growing gap in social inequality is not being seen sufficiently in terms of its serious causes and ramifications. To mind this gap – and its relevance to rights and opportunity in the contemporary world -- implies wariness about the focus on diversity and related identity politics, however much social mix itself should be commended within a culture of cosmopolitanism.

The complicated intersection of culture and class dislocates the conventional political axis of left and right, and makes it highly problematic to align policies geared to social inclusion and cohesion. Amplified through the information net, all of this is reshaping politics and economics, which are the concerns of the next two chapters.

Chapter Four: False Economy

More than a decade after the financial crash, those who caused it have seen their wealth and status largely reinstated, while those who bore the cost in terms of austerity have seen their wages largely stagnate, and work conditions deteriorate, as part of a general transfer of wealth and power from labour to capital in the last four decades. Whatever the supposed hegemony of neo-liberalism, there has pertained a prevalent economic model that elevates the market over the state and accepts inequality and uneven development as the price of efficiency and reward for enterprise. As a result, a sizeable section faces the insecurity of precarious work in the gig economy.

At the same time, assumptions about ever-increasing economic globalisation can be challenged by data suggesting that the global movement of people, capital and trade has been stalled. Following the financial crash, the pandemic, and Putin's adventure in Ukraine, the pattern has been disturbed, but is far from defunct. While banks maintain their grip on the economy, world indebtedness is bigger than it was in the aftermath of the financial crisis, and responses to that crisis, such as quantitative easing, have had the effect of distorting productive investment and boosting asset values. Meanwhile, fundamental weaknesses in infrastructure, education and productivity beset sustainable economic development.

Across the world stage, titan monopolies like Google, Meta, and Amazon generate enormous profits that escape proportionate taxation, and 'big brother' surveillance capitalism has transformed the very nature of production, whereby consumers of many high tech services essentially produce privacy data that is harvested by these companies to make their money. In this process, their unbridled power grows, evident in acquisition of Instagram and WhatsApp by Meta, and Twitter by Musk.

In western societies given to the clutter of over-consumption, fixation on speed, whether in the form of jet propulsion, fast food, speed dating, smart phone, or such, has not always freed time for more consequential pursuits. Rather, it has captured some people in frequent traffic jams, pressured schedules and harrying demands and pace of work. Habitual fast-paced multi-tasking leads some to be hyper-stimulated, over-stressed and potentially less productive. Less time to reflect is not conducive to creative thinking, whatever the clichéd claims about the rise of the 'smart' economy.

Alongside this dysfunction, the limits of carbon-based economic growth merits greater consideration if care for the planet is to rise above rhetoric. How can we re-register the life-work balance, and in the process classify activities we regard as important, like care for children and elderly, as valid 'work' with high social dividend? Gaining greater social control over what is predominantly a private economy worldwide demands for democracy to be re-thought and reclaimed. Put simply, many seek greater control over their lives, but are put off by what passes for politics, the issue of the next chapter.

Chapter Five: Power Play

There is some sense that democracy isn't working for many people; that the world of big business, high finance, distant government, 'spinning' media, unregulated markets, trimmed social protection, digital divides, and greater people migration, is one that leaves sizeable populations voiceless on the margins. In turn, this can induce revolt against conventional politics in a surge for a more authentic and representative form. Equally, it can produce disaffection, apathy, and fatalism. Beyond any such disenchantment, there is a basic dilemma in Western democracy. In many countries, long-standing choice between social democracy and conservatism has been replaced by either semi-permanent managerialist technocracy, or what some see as the enduring 'shadow government' of the 'Goldman Sachs'.

Much of populist politics seems to offer the chance for 'real' citizens to take back control from the 'elite'. It contains a vague idea of closely-tied personal and national sovereignty. This chapter unpacks the ambiguities and contradictions involved. It takes a comparative perspective on relevant features such as loss of trust in government that favours politicians who do not sound like politicians. Priority for public compliance and social stability in an uncertain world can undervalue basic tenets of democracy, which ultimately rely on a well-informed electorate. Debate about such values is blighted by escalation of disinformation, blurring the lines between knowledge and belief, and between truth and fiction.

Alongside political disenchantment by some, democracy is stirring across the world, often expressed in angry reaction to political orthodoxy, and challenge to conventional wisdom, in forms that confound pundits and polls. This has been evident in the Occupy Movement in the aftermath of the financial crisis, in resistance movements in Hong Kong, Belarus, and Myanmar, and in Extinction Rebellion. In the important arena of gender politics, there has been the MeToo movement, and in the struggle against racism, the Black Lives Matter movement, and both have set new agendas. However, these shifts can be fickle and fluid, reflecting the very volatility that derives from the social fragmentations underpinning them. In the West itself, this can assume remarkable and maverick displays such as: the sudden prominence of Trump; the rise of nationalism; and Brexit. Of course, all such tumult cannot be explained by a single cause.

Amongst many, there is disenchantment with the way democracy is actually working. In Europe, with the exception of the 'island of contentment', that takes in Denmark, Switzerland, Norway and the Netherlands, this dissatisfaction is quite pervasive. Specific shocks such as the Iraq War, the 2008 financial crash, the 2015 refugee crisis, and the EU Referendum in the UK can cause dips in democratic legitimacy. But over the last quarter of a century, there has been a more durable loss of trust in the capacity of democratic institutions to deal with corruption, economic crises, and climate emergency.

Addressing democratic deficit can be tied up with recovery of sovereignty -- taking back control. Like all holy grails, sovereignty is an elusive ambition. For instance in the case of the UK, where does sovereignty rest: with the sovereign monarch; government, parliament, judiciary, or the people? Indeed, some parse 'the people' further, and distinguish what they see as the 'real people', who are regarded as the genuine constituency, and thereby the true political contest is between such people and parliament. In short, confusion reigns about who exactly reigns. Given this complication about where control lies, democracy itself is on trial. It's facing a disruption with many dimensions.

Overall, in this first section, the shifting axis between the *local* and *global* is addressed. Under rising globalisation, it has been argued that scope for local decision-making has been curtailed. But it is more than that. Even within the local sphere, privatisation has squeezed the public realm, and thus democratic space and jurisdiction have been compressed between a deflated national state and an inflated international dominion. Alongside this, there is an *ideological* re-alignment. Traditional contest between left and right has been intersected with other binaries about identity and nationality, thereby splintering political allegiance into a more complex composite that can be internally contradictory.

Given the impact of growing *urbanisation worldwide*, ever larger cities congregate greater diversity and pluralism, a mix which can be uncontainable within usual party affiliation. In turn, this is complicated by changing *demography*. For instance, the growing share of young people at one end and with improving life expectancy, the growing share of elderly at the other, give scope to a starker clash between radicalism and conservatism.

There are the variable *boundaries of debate*. To what extent can free speech be compromised by political correctness, or to what extent is use of the term 'political correctness' a deliberate ploy to infer illiberal tendencies on the part of those advocating rights and protections? Debate itself can be distorted by wider processes of *electoral manipulation*. This includes the capacity for misusing private data to profile the electorate into distinct strata, which then can be subject to customised political messages that influence voting or non-voting intention in hidden and deceptive persuasion. Such manoeuvring can exploit the use of the *loud soundbite*. Attention grabbing in the busy age of the 24 hour news cycle can reduce complex issues to simplistic appeal, particularly through exploitation of the provocative and controversial, not to say sheer disinformation. This creates echo chambers of counterfeit exchange that seek affirmation rather than examination.

Beyond political content there is reshaping of *political style*. The importance of optics in the new media age, combined with disaffection from orthodox politics, can rapidly mobilise global movements geared to inventive and confrontational political expression, such as civil disobedience. Such new movements face the permanent *power of lobby*. The age-old pressure from the high and mighty can be reinforced now with supersize donations and financial inducements, in an age when money can tip the balance in electoral campaigning. This scale of lobbying is a 'swamp' not so easily drained.

Found deep in the swamp is the *durable patriarchy*. Presumptions that favour 'toxic masculinity' in conceptualising strong leadership still bedevil both the style and substance of debate, and political priorities. In similar vein, the influence of 'angry white guys' on the rise of the populist right, while over-simplified, has some purchase in explaining a global pattern. Partly, this is reflected in the macho-politics of people like Putin. His assault on liberalism chimes with the autocratic impulses far and wide. These are incarnated in domineering male figures, but not exclusively so. Sarah Palin, Kari Lake, and Marjorie Taylor-Greene in the US; Marine Le Pen in France; Giorgia Meloni in Italy; and Alice Weidel in Germany etc. all show that far-right politics is not restricted to a patriarchal chauvinist ideology.

These issues of controversy and contest lead us into the second section, which first returns to our earliest beginnings as a species, and explores our understanding of what it is that makes us human, and maybe inevitably tribal. It then proceeds to examine the proposition that we may now be at a point of possible self-annihilation through various factors of demography, climate damage, nuclear proliferation, and pandemics. The section ends with an alternative scenario – that high tech may transform us into a post-human, maybe even a super-human form, but with accompanying risks for the basics of what makes us human in the first place.

B. Hello Goodbye

Chapter Six: Only Human

In addressing the confused, chaotic and crisis-ridden state of the world, we have to go back to the basic question; what does it mean to be human? The Ukraine war has reminded us that we are a species of both feuding and fellowship.

Modern science has probed the once assumed unique design of our universe, never mind our planet, and space programmes continue to redefine human relations with the extraterrestrial. Meanwhile, the emerging science of genome editing and genetic modification, as part of a new biotechnology, has raised alarmist concern about people in the future claiming a right to 'designer' children. Following the trail from early hominids through to Cro-Magnon to modern man, and speculatively beyond, can we ascertain that what constitutes the human involves a linear narrative from the primitive to the perceptive?

This takes us through new understanding about old arguments of nature versus nurture; the role of culture; the distribution and testing of intelligence; the degree to which humans operate on animal instinct; and the possibilities and risks of 'human enhancement'.

These core questions inform our subsequent assessment of our changing demography's imprint on the planet in the Anthropocene. Has the rendition of the human era gone from human centrality to cosmic insignificance to planetary dominance to transhumanism in the form of homo deus? In essence, what kind of species are we, and is there a universal presence known as 'humanity'? The latter carries benign association with virtues such as compassion, mercy, sympathy, civilization etc. But this concept of our 'better angels', extolled by scholars like Stephen Pinker, is countered by others like John Gray, who remain sceptical of the utopian projects that can accompany such human exaltation and the pretension of their scientific underpinning.

Paradoxically, just at a time when humans have the means to live longer and stronger, does human abuse of the planet show a sub-conscious death wish, or is it more likely due to the blinkered quest for immediate gratification? This leads us into the next chapter, which addresses the sources and prospects of existential risks to us as a species.

Chapter Seven: Dead End

For millennia, humans attained more understanding and control over natural disasters, such as earthquakes, tsunamis, volcanic eruptions, and various diseases – to, at least, mitigate their worst effects. Now, we're faced with myriad threats of our own making, such as the climate emergency, nuclear proliferation, and food insecurity. In addressing these, the main obstacle may be the divisions of various kinds that hinder our collaboration. Phenomena like droughts, changing jet streams, wildfires, and related events that are literally 'earth shattering', are inexorably on the rise. Given the precedent for species extinction, including those close to Homo *sapiens* like the Neanderthals, the prospect is not fanciful. But is the risk exaggerated as part of an 'end of days' tenor of apocalyptic times?

Do we face an increasingly uninhabitable earth? The crisis is one of environmental justice, whereby the poorest parts of the world will be most negatively impacted the quickest. Yet, paradoxically, some of these same populations in places like China, India and Africa seek to escape their poverty through rapid industrialisation that strains the planet's viability.

The rabid global networking of resistance to carbon-based living, such as Extinction Rebellion, speaks to an extensive, if not necessarily intensive, concern. What is the relationship between what individual humans can do and what requires collective response by people across the globe? This involves a massive package of measures that hinges on global commitment: clean rather than fossil-fuelled energy; new ways of agriculture away from intensive farming; changed human diet; less food waste; protecting tropical forests; ending land degradation; dispensing with plastic; and addressing growth in population and consumerism, amongst other interventions.

Alongside this pressing issue, we have the realignment of geopolitics, with persistent ethno-nationalism, growing powers like China seeking to extend their sphere of influence, resurgence of militarist Russia, and many more countries seeking security shelter in nuclear weapons. Consequent instability, not helped by the apparent erosion of authority in bodies like the United Nations, augurs a different kind of existential threat. Before Putin's invasion of Ukraine in 2022, it seemed as if the new geopolitical axis principally concerned the US and Pacific powers like China. Recently, we've have a re-visitation of the Atlantic-based Cold War, with Russia accorded pariah status and the West characterised by the Kremlin as both triumphalist and decadent. As with climate change, these big risks can only be abated by a new system for international cooperation. In turn, this presupposes a world which sees a common interest and destiny. Yet as noted earlier, we have pushback against this mutual perspective, with the rise of identity politics that polarise and balkanise. Whether new information networks and social media can bring us together or tear us further apart is the subject of the next chapter.

Chapter Eight: Net Effect

The exponential upgrade of technology and the improvement in Artificial Intelligence (AI) pose great opportunity and challenge to conventional ideas about the economy in particular and society in general. Whole sectors such as bio-engineering and telecommunications are set to be re-made. While offering to network and connect us as a species, the 'smart' age of big data also holds prospect for exploitation in the short term and radical redefinition of what it means to be human in the longer term. In one area, we have seen its role in disseminating disinformation and promoting surveillance, both posing severe threat to democracy.

Some argue that the net holds a mirror to human nature, and reveals starkly its range from the caring to the cruel. But can it refract rather than reflect human nature? We're at the cusp of an historical transformative technology, whereby smart machines may be created to have superior intelligence to humans. In developing a more cultivated understanding of the world, this hyperintelligence may bypass human cognition and in effect demote humans. We have no precedent for a species creating a higher form of intelligence to its own.

At present, Alexa responds to human directive. But one day, might it be reversed? More insidiously, it can be speculated that over time this enhanced processing power and algorithmic calculation can recode, and thereby trigger control over, human behaviour. The difficulty faced in confronting any such prospect is that we can hardly conceive of machine learning and linked 'artificial' consciousness, when we still struggle to grasp human consciousness. Our very ignorance renders us susceptible to robotic aptitude.

Enhanced computational power will likely concentrate economic power unless socially regulated. In many parts of the world, the last four decades have witnessed increasing de-regulation in the economy, and Big Tech corporations, as powerful players in the new information economy, can be expected to resist restraint on their global supremacy. What does this kind of transnational clout augur for the prospect of an economy working for all?

Such misgiving is not to deny that Big Tech offers many opportunities for human development. Yet vexed issues about individual privacy rights abound in an increasingly surveillance society, facilitated by the internet. Every time we undertake a Google search, Google probes us. Digital rights also feature when, for example, Facebook can make a product *from* their consumers, who are supposedly accessing a free platform to globally network, but whose confidential information is being sold commercially. Moreover, this monetising of personal data to develop lifestyle profiles of distinctive sections of the electorate, who can then be targeted furtively with customised political messages, can corrupt people's democratic right to fair elections. Since internet platforms are not treated legally as publishers, slander and falsehood can be transmitted without liability.

Facebook and TikTok can present themselves as a fifth estate within the democratic system. Nonetheless, a societal future permeated with manipulative disinformation, while alarmist in its dystopian depiction, is not implausible. Outcomes are simply not predictable. The very technologies explicitly designed to 'bring the world together' have been adapted by populists to advance national, not to say xenophobic, agendas over global connection. Presently, while this on-line viral danger to democracy is off-limits to social scrutiny, other novel developments are emerging fast, such as facial recognition, drone imaging, brain implant technology and deep fake audio/video. As we're left struggling to catch up, subsequent public distrust may prompt unhelpful 'techlash'.

This brings us to the themes of the second volume, which addresses how we agree on common truths and values, sufficient to allow us to act together as humankind for a kinder humanity, or whether such faith has shown itself so often in the past to be dangerously delusional.

PART I

All Shook Up

This first section comprises five chapters, addressing the tumult of these strange times. Beginning with an overview of recent crises, it then gives an appraisal of populism and authoritarian nationalism, and how rooted they are to the discontent of those who feel abandoned by the global economy. Thereafter, it proceeds to assess the politics of identity. In the context of controversy over immigration, religious fundamentalism, race, and patriarchy, it examines whether wokeism, cancel culture, and the wider culture wars are distracting from redress of inequality.

In turn, these troubling issues are set within a framework of a changing world economy, dominated by high finance, and a deceptive politics that offers the illusion of taking back control. Exploration of this landscape reveals the spirit of our times, and central themes that thread through the book: the tendency for humans to think in binaries; the enduring basis, yet enigma, of human nature; limits of progress; fixation on rights over values and responsibilities; and the set of paradoxes that confound us. One such that emerges from contemporary culture is that for all the politics of fear, loss of confidence in the public realm, and wokeist concern about 'safe spaces', we are far from risk averse when it comes to pressing threats that beset humanity.

DOI: 10.4324/9781003106593-1

PART I

All Shook Up

1

WHAT ON EARTH?

Living in Strange Times

Consider this century to date. In the decade preceding, a new world order took shape. The Soviet system collapsed. Germany united. An expanded liberal democratic Europe emerged. For a brief period, the US dominated geopolitics, until the emergence of China as an important economic power in the context of accelerated globalisation and apparent capitalist hegemony. Then came the millennium, since when we've had: in 2000, the dotcom bubble burst, as the inflated promise of high tech investment was unrealised; in 2001, the 9/11 assault on the US and the consequent War on Terror; invasions of Afghanistan (2001) and Iraq (2003); the financial crash in 2008/9 and ensuing era of austerity; the pro-democracy Arab Spring in the Middle East and North Africa, starting in 2010; the following year, the fall of Gaddafi and beginning of Libyan civil war, alongside opening attempts to topple the Bashar al-Assad regime in Syria; the rise of nationalism and discontent of those who felt left behind, exemplified by the Brexit vote; growth of authoritarian populism, manifested in the election of Trump, both in 2016; and then the pandemic that locked down much of the world for much of a two-year period, starting in late 2019.

Most recently, we have witnessed the pitiless assault on Ukraine. Arguably, this has been Putin's war – not Russia's, since its people have been long captured by an autocracy, rooted in oligarchic support, nostalgic militarism, and klepto-capitalism, and deprived of a pluralist media, independent judiciary, and basic rights such as protest and dissent. However, there remains a question of what resistance to this adventurism should come from Russian people, as some at least gain insight from global media. Though an unprovoked act of aggression, meriting unequivocal censure, sections of the Left in places like the UK were slow to denounce it in these clear terms. With such failure, they gave an impression that they shared with sections of the Far Right an ambivalent attitude to

DOI: 10.4324/9781003106593-2

this criminal invasion. For some on the Right, it was to be commended as a nationalist strike by a strong leader, one of the last true defenders of white Christian Europe, and who in Trump's terms was 'smart', 'savvy' and 'genius'. But contradictions abound for the Far Right. For example, Alternative for Germany (AfD) has traditionally supported Putin, as has Marine Le Pen. Yet some on the Right, like Giorgia Meloni, see it as a violation of national sovereignty. Still others continue to associate Russia with communism, and were confirmed in their reservations about Putin's offensive when he pitched it as an anti-fascism crusade.

For some on the Left, it was to be understood primarily as an inevitable outcome of NATO's expansionist project. Some of the same people, quick to march in outrage against the illegal invasion of Iraq, could not bring themselves to do likewise when American imperialism was not their direct target. It represented inconsistency of principle – by default, if not intent, giving succour to the despotic Putin and his 'useful idiot' in the client state of Belarus.

With NATO encirclement, and false claims of genocide, his bullish pretext for *casus belli*, Putin has pulverised Ukrainian cities in an asymmetrical war. Within three months from its start in February 2022, 6.7 million refugees had fled the country and 8 million in total were displaced from their homes. It's difficult to give an accurate up-to-date picture on this movement because as the war has proceeded some left to later return. As of October 2022, over 14 million border crossings from Ukraine to other countries were documented.[1]

Simplistically characterised as a struggle between democracy and autocracy, this ignores how the Greek Colonels in the past have been, and Erdogan's Turkey and Orban's Hungary at present are, part of NATO, thereby indicating its compromised democratic credentials. NATO has not been a consistent font of peace. For instance, the long-standing Greek-Turkish conflict over Cyprus has not been resolved by their current shared membership. Most markedly, given their blame for the onslaught against Iraq, the US and UK, as two leading NATO members, struggle to explain the probity of one invasion and the iniquity of the other. When George W. Bush denounced the 'decision of one man to launch a wholly unjustified and brutal invasion of Iraq....I mean of Ukraine', the gaffe only confirmed his reprehensible immunity.

The Atlanticist alliance has always been US-led and overwhelmingly US-funded. As this war has become protracted, a process of attrition that depletes Russian military and economic capacity – even if it achieves ultimate partial victory in regions like Donbas – it may suit the US, whose primary focus in the medium-term is on Indo-China. But such a scenario would not suit Europe. Its strategy would likely fragment, not only with Hungary resisting full sanctions on Russian energy supplies, but also with Poland bearing the heavy cost of the refugee crisis, and Germany and France pushing for a quicker diplomatic compromise that might be unwelcome to the UK, the Baltic countries, and Ukraine itself. Thus, the Russian aggression that initially reinvigorated NATO may succeed in the longer term in fracturing Europe internally and causing a rift between it and the US.[2]

Despite NATO's own flaws, and Macron's diagnosis of its brain dead status in recent years, Sweden and Finland, with their impeccable pedigree of peaceful behaviour over many decades, received an open door for their membership application. Whatever of such moves, any concern held by contemporary Russia about being hemmed in by NATO does not validate Putin's land grabs.

All member states together cover an area of 24.59 million km^2 and about 949.06 million people. This is 16.27 percent of the world's habitable area and 12.11 percent of the world's population.

In general, opportunity for a more de-militarised Eurasia that might have followed the implosion of the Soviet system was forfeited in the early 1990s. In 1949, NATO had 12 founding members. By 1990, its membership numbered 19, compared to its present 30. This accounts for 949.06 million people, over 12 percent of the world's population.[3] Now, the Ukraine tragedy has spurred plans for increased defence spending in Europe, including in Germany, which had been purposely non-militaristic since 1945. Moreover, the crisis illustrates how vulnerable the planet remains to the triggering of extensive nuclear confrontation, even if such escalation is based on bluster or blunder rather than measured risk assessment. Putin's thinly-veiled threat to deploy nuclear retaliation for any direct Western military intervention re-opened the nuclear debate. Would Ukraine have been invaded if it had retained nuclear weapons? Does NATO's hesitancy to face down Putin militarily confirm the deterrence of 'mutually assured destruction'? Does the continued existence, and indeed proliferation, of nuclear weapons portend ultimate catastrophe someday for humanity, given a perennially unstable world? And what about the menace of chemical and biological weapons?

Global consistency about the ethics of war remains nonexistent. By 2022, the war in the Yemen was into its seventh year. According to a United Nations report,[4] the Saudi/UAE-led coalition, the Yemeni government, the Southern Transitional Council (STC), and the Houthi rebel militia all 'continue to commit egregious violations of international humanitarian law and international human rights law, including indiscriminate attacks against civilians, enforced disappearances and torture'. Yet, the US, UK and other Western powers persist in licensing weapons and military hardware sales to the Saudi-UAE-led alliance.[5] In decrying Putin's war crimes, the West has been unable to see the contradiction in their arms exports to this war zone. Nor does the West hold a consistent line against brutal dictatorships. In November 2022, Mohammed bin Salman was granted US immunity, despite the finding by US intelligence that he was implicated in the torture and murder of Mr Khashoggi in the Saudi consulate in Istanbul in 2018. No wonder the secretary general of Amnesty International saw it as immunity that amounts to impunity. Essentially, the US was never going to trouble a leading figure in Saudi Arabia, its strategic partner in the Middle East, an important source of oil, a lucrative customer for US arms, and a country that could always switch allegiance to Russia and/or China.

We're faced with the brutal question as to whether we in the West can manage attention and sympathy only for those who look like us. It goes to the heart of the issue of *identity* that troubles many aspects of domestic and global relations. For instance, countries in Eastern Europe that did not show much empathy with refugees from places like Syria and Afghanistan have shown remarkable generosity to the plight of Ukrainian refugees. Of course, no one knows how long that will endure, if their presence becomes protracted and involves social strain on the poorest parts of Europe.

This war underlines other concerns addressed in this book. For instance, we have Putin's disinformation campaign, whereby he has tried to convince the Russian public that they're waging a necessarily ferocious battle against fascism in general, and genocide of Russian-speaking eastern Ukrainian regions in particular, that echo Hitler's onslaught in the Great Patriotic War, when in reality he is the more recognisable Hitler tribute act, given his repugnant record in Grozny and Aleppo. Unfortunately, Putin's symbol of the Z is the new swastika. Referring to the warped version presented by Kremlin-controlled media, the *Economist* notes:[6]

> In state television's distorted mirror, Russian shelling did not destroy Mariupol but 'liberated' it. The atrocities of Bucha were not perpetrated by Russian soldiers but staged by Kyiv. Russia did not attack Ukraine, but was attacked by the West. No explicit mention is made of Russian losses....Propaganda and repression are intertwined. Any truthful information about the war is branded 'fake news'; spreading it, not just as a journalist but also as a private citizen, is punishable by up to 15 years in jail.

To what extent does this propaganda of 'de-nazification' epitomise a new era of fake news, or simply a new tech version of the normal 'fog of war'? Or is it a faint improvement on ancient barbarity, that an aggressor in a modern world that at least rhetorically avows human rights and humanitarianism, feels obliged to justify invasion. After all, the deception in the US/UK-led offensive against Iraq involved fictional claims about weapons of mass destruction.

The assault on Ukraine also exemplifies a theme that will be further developed in the second volume of this book: the interweaving of religion and ultranationalism. Kirill, Patriarch of the Russian Orthodox Church, bestowed his blessing on Putin's aggression, casting it as a defensive action to resist immoral Western influence. He endorsed Putin's claim that Ukraine shares an inalienable link to Russia's culture, history and 'spiritual space'. This inference of a 'holy war' to protect the God-given Motherland, even when it involves fratricidal conflict, is hardly new to human affairs. God is conscripted to ensure, in the words of Kirill,[7] that 'Russia's sacred borders may be impregnable ... and that God grant that by the end of the century, our country will be like this – strong, powerful and at the same time have God's love'. In turn, the Patriarch's readiness to sing from the same hymn sheet as Putin is entwined with the schism within the Orthodox church, with the Ukrainian constituent opting for independence from their former Moscow master.

Sanctions on Russia have highlighted the global character of the financial system. Similarly, moves to cut Russia's main economic artery through phasing out Western dependency on its oil and gas illustrate the quandary of maintaining *national* energy security, while resolving to *globally* reduce fossil fuels for a decarbonised world. Will the alternative to Russian energy supply be a speedier switch to clean energy, or more intensive investment in Western hydro-carbon sources, including fracking? In turn, will the latter's more national emphasis on energy independence be inhibitive of zero-carbon targets? Such economic nationalism, added to anti-Russian trade and investment embargos, certainly disturb the drive toward modern globalisation. Meanwhile, Putin's war hiked up oil and gas prices, which, in turn, helped to bankroll his military complex. His is not the only petro-state to have accrued the financial dividend of war. But this showed the paradox of sanctions. If one of the effects is to reduce supply of oil and gas, then it pushes up their price, and in this case Russia can actually see its petro coffers increased even while its export volume is decreased.

Given his close ties with Putin, unsurprisingly, Hungary's prime minister, Orban, objected to the EU's proposal to close down Russian oil supply to the bloc as too swift and containing inadequate remedial measures for viable energy security. He also rejected specific sanctions against Patriarch Kiriil as violation of religious freedom.

In the harrowing immediacy of the Ukrainian upheaval, some corporations keenly virtue-signalled disapproval in strange ways. For instance, Meta announced that its normal ban on violent speech on its platforms like Facebook would be temporarily suspended to allow those impacted by the war to express enmity to the invaders, and even, for a brief period, advocacy for the demise of Putin and Lukashenko. Would the same latitude to convey passionate loathing and lethal harm to Western illegal warriors, apply? That seems as likely as having such leaders summoned before international courts for war crimes, an indictment that appears applicable only to those from weaker nations.

Such moral inconsistency is standard. Former Prime Minister Johnson condemned Russian imperialism. At the same time, he waged a cultural war against critics of Britain's imperialist past. While finally taking overdue action against those who essentially committed grand larceny against the Russian people in the giveaway sale of public assets in post-Soviet privatisation, Western leaders have shown breathtaking hypocrisy – none more so than Truss, when she was UK Foreign Secretary:[8]

> *Today's sanctions show once again that oligarchs and kleptocrats have no place in our economy or society. With their close links to Putin, they are complicit in his aggression. The blood of Ukrainian people is on their hands. They should hang their heads in shame'.*

In fact, the British government should hang its head in shame for offering over decades sanctuary to Russian tycoons and crooked money in London, as elaborated in Chapter five. Putin's repressive regime has been long hiding in plain sight. Having inherited from Yeltsin an economy significantly annexed by bandit moguls, who swindled billions in the rigged auctions of public assets and the country's overall market transition, he, together with old KGB cronies, sought to bring this new elite under his control. This concentrated power involved the establishment of a security state. Essentially, it combined a conspiracy to defraud the Russian people economically and democratically, while playing the patriotic card of reclaiming a Greater Russia that would redeem the Motherland from alleged post-Soviet humiliation by the West. Indeed, the West played its part. Initial market reforms that impoverished many Russians were influenced by advice from, among others, American economists. Havens for oligarchic money were offered in places like London, happy to turn a blind eye to these ill-gotten treasure troves in the interests of swelling their own financial and property sectors.[9] If Putin's assault on Ukraine brought us to the brink of World War III, a good part of the explanation lies in the old adage: follow the money.

Aggression against Ukraine underscores recurrent contradictory features of human conflict. In the short-term at least, it has achieved the opposite of what Putin intended, pushing his neighbours more toward NATO; prompting growing support for an EU army;[10] enhancing European and nationalist identity in Ukraine itself; revealing vulnerabilities in his supposed military might; and exposing the fragility of the Russian economy, heavily reliant on fossil fuel exports. However, Europe is not totally united on the issue. More than 70 percent of people in Scandinavia, the UK, Poland and the Netherlands attribute most blame to Russia. Conversely, a majority in Bulgaria and Greece regard either NATO as culpable, or NATO and Russia as sharing equal responsibility. Also, most people in Slovakia and Hungary do not consider the war as mainly Russia's fault.[11]

At the same time, the West was ready to cheerlead Ukrainian valour against the odds, while careful not to risk NATO involvement in a global and possibly nuclear showdown. The tension between these two positions highlighted a central dilemma. Was further Western arming of Ukraine and applauding its resilience from the sideline, in effect urging it to fight on against overwhelming opposition, thereby enduring more death and destruction in glorious defeat? At what point was it in Ukraine's interest to negotiate peace in preference to a prolonged war prone to wreck and desolate the country? Ukrainian resistance has been notable, capturing back territory gained by Russia, most notably in the liberation of Kherson. But unless the West really upgrades its support with air defence capacity, the country is set to endure prolonged pounding by what is still a superior military force. If the West does so raise the stakes, how close does that take NATO's direct involvement? When an apparent Russian-made missile was responsible for two fatalities in Poland in November 2022, and early assumptions drawn about Russia's deliberate strike, there was high risk that NATO could be pressured to invoke Article 5 of its charter that sees an assault on one member as equivalent to an assault on all -- a solidarity whose only precedent was the reaction to September 11th, 2001. It would not have been the first time that an attack on one small country became the trigger for a more global catastrophe.

The war has also highlighted the geopolitics of food insecurity. In the global context of where 44 million people are 'teetering on the edge of famine',[12] and with 60 percent of the world's hungry themselves in conflict zones like Yemen, Syria, Libya, Ethiopia and Afghanistan,[13] export interruptions in the Black Sea and Azov Sea ports carry considerable impact. Russia and Ukraine rank among the top five exporters in the global market for wheat and maize, and in addition are important exporters of sunflower and barley, accounting for over three-quarters and one third of global supplies respectively. With household budgets of the poorest squeezed by rising energy prices, and related general inflation, the rising cost of food due to the war's disruption puts countless millions in peril of hunger. It pinpoints the concentration of certain basic food production, and its fragile supply chain in a globalised economy.

Some see this war in terms of a humiliated post-Soviet Russia replicating some behaviours of a vanquished Germany, dishonoured by the Treaty of Versailles, and seeking recovery of Lebensraum (living space) through territorial expansion. But any such analysis has to also pay regard to the complicated demography that now pertains. With the collapse of the Soviet domain, 25 million ethnic Russians resided outside their homeland, many in ex-Soviet republics, forming significant minorities, with affinity toward Russia.[14] Meantime, Russia itself has been experiencing population decline, and related need for immigrant labour from Central Asia, about which it feels ambivalent. Accordingly, some are concerned to tilt their population toward a Slavic Christian composition, relative to 'Muslim' peoples of Central Asia and the Caucasus.[15] For a military superpower with an undersized economy, capturing the people and resources of Crimea and Ukraine may seem to auger restoration of geopolitical status and clout, while extending the Slavic character of a re-fashioned Russian Federation.

This raises the question for both Ukraine and the West regarding what constitutes victory. If, for instance, Ukraine was encouraged to pursue the restoration of all of its recently lost 'sovereignty', that could be taken to include Crimea. But this shows the contested nature of nationalism, as explored in later chapters. Crimea was tied to Tsarist Russia since 1783, and was passed over to the Ukrainian Soviet Socialist Republic by Stalin in 1954, hardly the basis of democratic self-determination. Yet without clarity about what is legitimate and negotiable, wars can continue until attrition induces one side to yield.

Arguably, a possible diplomatic package to save lives, horrific injury and plight of refugees was always likely to include some permutation of the following: the relationship of a section of the eastern region with Russia is settled, with the consent of the people in the separatist part of that region, ratified by objective observers; Ukraine forsakes any intent to join NATO, and instead has its neutral status endorsed in international agreement; Ukraine receives substantial funding from the West to assist its economic development, with suitable safeguards against corruption blighting this effort; its consequent development is tied to social redistribution and the strengthening of democratic culture; its progress opens up the prospect of its EU membership; procedures for greater disarmament -- particularly, though not exclusively, nuclear – follow in the wider geopolitics; and as part of a Green New Deal in Europe, dependency on Russian gas and oil is systematically reduced.

In realpolitik, China has been well-placed to put appropriate pressure on the Kremlin to take the 'golden bridge' of a compromise at an early stage to forestall further catastrophe. Hard questions arise about any helpful Chinese intervention. What would China want in return? Would any concession amount to appeasement? Would Putin be content, or would he bank any gains as a stopgap before being emboldened for his next adventure in the region? For peaceniks like me, it's a key dilemma. Do bullies always need to have their violence answered in kind? Does the related retaliation produce the escalation beloved of the military-industrial complex, and endured by civilian populations? In this particular instance, does Putin's unilateral belligerence endorse his rejection of liberal universalism, and with what impact?

In addition to reawakening the world to the nuclear threat, the Ukraine war has highlighted how energy sources can be weaponised. Hydrocarbons make for 56 percent of Russia's export earnings. The West's attempt in the medium term to cut off, or at least substantially reduce, that income by curtailing its energy demand on Russian supply has two major geopolitical consequences. First, in the medium term at least, it makes the West dependent on supply from other despotic regimes, such as Saudi Arabia; and second, it throws Russia further into the embrace of China, as its main energy customer, thereby cementing an autocratic axis from the Baltic to Pacific in contest with a re-structured Atlantic alliance, in complement with a recently enhanced American-Pacific pact. Altogether, it generates a new world 'order', geared at best to uneasy stand-off, and framed in a vast military build-up.

Each major event – the financial crash, rise of China, escalation of climate crisis, prevalence of populism, the pandemic, and aggression against Ukraine – was heralded by many as a seismic shift that changed the world. Individually, that isn't the case. But collectively and cumulatively, it is. These shocks demonstrate that for all our clever risk management models, so many key events are unknowable and unpredictable in a complex, volatile, and unruly world. We are at what German Chancellor Scholz has dubbed a *Zeitenwende* – an historical turning point. Against all this momentous background in the first two decades of this century, contemporary public debate abounds with a set of disputed terms: sovereignty; populist nationalism; culture wars; wokeism; ecocide; extinction; AI; big data; surveillance capitalism; neoliberalism; fake news; and such like. Moreover, debate is beset with caricatures of adversaries. For instance, 'snowflake' is used pejoratively to infer that young people are prone to melt when faced with hard truths. Similarly, it is suggested that red-faced angry old conservative men resemble 'gammons'. In such stridency, disagreement is reduced to slur, with nuance of difference lost in infantile abuse.

The 2021 United Nations Report, *Our Common Agenda*,[16] highlights the blunt dilemma facing us as a species:

> *We are at an inflection point in history. In our biggest shared test since the Second World War, humanity faces a stark and urgent choice: a breakdown or a breakthrough.*

For the UN, viable response lies in rediscovery of common purpose as a global family, rooted in mutual trust and camaraderie. But this value contains its own tension:[17] 'In the absence of solidarity, we have arrived at a critical paradox: international cooperation is more needed than ever but also harder to achieve.' Widespread disquiet and trepidation prompt a yearning for solidarity, but solidarity cannot flourish amid so much mistrust. In a 2022 United Nations report, *New Threats to Human Security in the Anthropocene,* people's sense of unease in the contemporary period is acknowledged:[18]

> *We are faced with a development paradox. Even though people are on average living longer, healthier and wealthier lives, these advances have not succeeded in increasing people's sense of security.*

Just over half a century ago, I sat with my father in our working class Belfast home, watching avidly on our black & white television the amazing human achievement of the moon-landing. Not that long before, talk of people on the moon was dismissed by many as moonshine. For some, the whole space venture was an extravagance for humankind, when it had failed to address the time's pressing earthly priorities, related to inequality, racism, and war. For some others, the 'one giant leap for mankind' seemed to spellbind us as a species, set on a common purpose towards further extra-terrestrial adventure. For a few ultra-optimists, this shared ambition even offered hope that we could see ourselves as belonging to the one planet, and in time abandon the nuclear threat of self-destruction. Now we have space adventure headlined as the indulgence of billionaires in a very unequal world, and reawakened possibility of nuclear devastation posed by Putin's aggression.

In that very same summer of the moon-landing back in 1969, violence spilled onto the streets of Belfast, my home town, in what was the start of a long war about a small piece of earthly territory. The contrast between global and parochial could hardly have been more stark. While space travel was boding well for humans to go boldly to 'infinity and beyond' in a bright scientific future, the dark ancient quarrel back home was set to bring us to insanity and beyond. In the three subsequent decades of our violence, the conflict's barbarity was matched only by its futility. For some at least, the pull of tribe and nation outbid the pursuit of any universal human mission.

Interestingly, my father did not believe that the moon-landing was real. Rather, he insisted that it was a Hollywood-filmed stunt to make good President Kennedy's pledge to land men on the moon by the end of the 1960s. For him, it was what we would call today 'fake news', and his dismissal of it as conspiracy was not altogether strange. Born in the late nineteenth century, he saw the early development of air flight, starting as a child in 1903, when the Wright brothers operated the first powered aircraft, and then as a young man, when in 1924 there was the first round-the-world flight. While appreciating the human progress of us being creatures not only of land and water but also of the sky, he could not accept the truth of humans walking on the moon within such a short time-span.

In a way, these same issues face us today. What is the relationship between the local and global? What sense of common identity and purpose do we have as a species inhabiting this planet? Why is it so difficult to deal with human inequity and conflict? Can we avoid the prospect of self-annihilation through nuclear proliferation or climate emergency? How do we come to see things as 'real' and 'unreal' and agree on what is true, particularly at a time of widespread disinformation?

I come to these issues as a beneficiary of Prime Minister Attlee government's welfare reforms, and of the preceding Education Act. For people from my background, great hope was invested in education as a civilising force and as a source of equal opportunity. Yet despite society's educational advance, many people of my vintage with whom I engage express a sense of despondency about the current state of the world.

This two-book project grapples with this conundrum. As humans, we've come so far in knowledge, and yet it is clear that reason and logic cannot necessarily outbid the impact of prejudice and fear. We've come so far in appreciating the benefit of collective social improvement. Yet any such progress is not a forward march that can't be readily halted, and indeed reversed. The project brings together my research, thinking and activism, stretching over half a century. For some time, I've been studying conflicted cities like Jerusalem, Nicosia and my own Belfast. These appeared to be places set apart, caught in a time warp and locked in ancient quarrels around religion and nationalism. Now it appears that much of the rest of the world has caught up.

The Power of Paradox and the Paradox of Power[19]

Bette Davis cautioned that old age was not for cissies. But despite its vagaries, it's not without its compensations. When you've more memories of the past than dreams of the future, it grants the chance to take the long view on life. Thus, while this book addresses many contemporary social dilemmas, it does so with a long view of history. In doing so, it identifies a set of paradoxes that humans face.

I'm defining *paradox* here as an apparently contradictory, inconsistent, or even absurd, statement that may still make sense upon reflection. Some paradoxes are familiar as aphorisms: empty vessels make most noise; you have to be cruel to be kind; the only constant is change; less is more; youth is wasted on the young; the child is father to the man; and the best thing to say is nothing at all.

Sometimes, the seeming contradiction can be stark. Socrates is supposed to have said: 'I know one thing, that I know nothing'. Strictly speaking, one of those two statements seems to be a falsehood. (The second volume looks at the way humans tell themselves lies -- or at least are economical with the truth.) But the term *paradox* as used here is more akin to the concept of dialectics, which holds that contradiction lies in the essence of everything, including humans themselves.

In moral philosophy, questions containing apparently irreconcilable ideas can be posed to test the relationship between ethics and logic. Can you tolerate intolerance, if that intolerance risks ending tolerance? If God is defined as omniscient, he knows in advance how we will decide. But if he does, can there be free will? Similarly, is not the existence of evil incompatible with an omnipotent, morally flawless God?

Similar dilemmas are found in political philosophy. In his *Social Contract*, in which he argues about people's sovereignty over monarchs' divine right, Rousseau talks about the idea of forcing people to be free. Again, this seems a contradiction in terms. But as with the example I was given in my undergraduate philosophy course, it can be very sensible. If you're bad at early-morning rising, and insist at night, in the full freedom of your will, that you want to be woken in the morning, regardless of your protests, you're requesting that you be forced to be free.

Humans have developed a conflicting mindset to cope with the contradictory, the incompatible and the incongruous. Sometimes we do that through metaphor. When we say 'the pen is mightier than the sword', we don't mean it literally. Rather, we're suggesting that the soft-power influence of words, argument and diplomacy – represented by a small pen – can overcome the hard-power influence of military might, represented by the sword.

When we look at the strange and unexpected way the world works, we can see hidden logic, even as it appears nonsensical. For instance, the Sorites (Greek for *heap*) Paradox suggests that we can designate 100,000 grains of sand as a heap. Minus one grain, it's still a heap. Logically, how many grains have to be removed to the point where it's no longer a heap? If there is a dividing line, it might come down to one particular grain. This conveys the idea that small change can bring big effect. A different example given is that when a grain of sand falls, it makes no sound. When a thousand grains fall, they do. So a thousand of nothing is something. Given these cited examples of how the granular can exhibit global consequence, little wonder that in Blake's poem *Auguries of Innocence,* he talks about seeing the world in a grain of sand.

In everyday life we encounter frequent paradox, such as: social media that claims to link us across divisions can more disconnect us; globalisation, which suggests greater integration of everyone, can end up concentrating wealth and power in the hands of the few; and so on. That is not to say that we don't experience cognitive dissonance, the discomposure of holding two or more opposing positions simultaneously. But it is to see that when facing awkward juxtaposition, dualism or inversion, we can learn to trust more in the counter-intuitive. We need such skill now more than ever. Even before the tumult of COVID-19 and Ukraine, it seemed to many that we lived in strange times. Foroohar[20] expressed the disoriented feeling many have at present:

> *We know on some level how out of control things have gotten, but we can't even imagine living any other way….Life feels off. People feel stressed, behind, out of sorts, disconnected, lost. It's not just the whacked-out politics of the current presidential administration, not just the political polarisation, not just job anxieties, not just the upheaval of industrialism giving way to the computer age.*

Testing Times

Interrogating these ideas further, this book argues that beneath the surface politics of fragmentation and upheaval, three core challenges confront us:

1. **living *on* the planet:** including how we deal with the conundrum of relentless pursuit of economic growth on a finite earth with intrinsic growth limits;
2. **living *with* the planet:** including how we co-habit the world in balance with the wider eco-system and animal kingdom; and
3. **living *with each other* on the planet:** including how we find peaceful democratic means to manage not only inequality and diversity, but also conflict, as a feature inherent to humankind.

While we retain the individual impulse for self-preservation, we seem to have little collective will for our preservation as a species. The current period cannot be understood simply in terms of a rise in nativist nationalism and its political expression in authoritarian populism. Thus, talking about Trumpism in the US, Brexit in Britain, or the widespread presence of autocratic rule in Putin's Russia, Xi's China, Modi's India, Orban's Hungary, Erdogan's Turkey, etc. can often miss the point. For one thing, these phenomena are not all the same, and should not be lazily lumped together. Second, they are best thought of as symptoms rather than causes. But what are these causes?

If we look at them through a set of paradoxes, we can see the following:

In terms of *culture* -- we're burdened with information overload, yet it's getting harder to tell truth from fiction. A glut of 'reality TV', which is often fake, can produce reality TV stars like Trump as real Presidents. Zelensky played an eccentric Ukrainian leader for comedy television and then became the actual leader. And in 2022, in Shakespearian scale, the comedian came to face the tragedy of his homeland's fate. The selfie generation lives in a connected world, but in divisive times, many can feel cut adrift from 'the other'. Indeed, the very technology that makes association easy also permits micro-targeting of small slices of the electorate with customised messages, designed to fragment. As the globe gets more urban, many big cities come to embody the global, in terms of their population diversity. However, in many of these great cities of social and cultural mix, this human variety gets re-sorted into separation and segregation.

This sense of people living close to each other, and yet living worlds apart can be found in highly charged encounters between those who differ with each other. For instance, in response to centuries of repression, some social activists commend a 'woke culture', by which they mean that people should be awake to social and racial injustice and call it out. To others, this vigilance is seen as moral grandstanding by the self-regarding thin-skinned, who succeed only in shutting down conversation with those who do not conform to their purist ideas about the way the world should be. In this view, those policing political correctness are at best 'virtue-signalling' with their smug 'holier-than-thou' posture. Such exchange is part of a wider democratic dilemma about how people's human rights include the 'right' to be insulted and how far free speech should include a tolerance of the intolerant.

In terms of *politics* – the more complex the issue, the more it risks being reduced to a simplistic catch phrase: Get Brexit Done; Make America Great Again; Build Back Better; Putin Must Fail. Despite the apparent promise of ever greater secularism and rationalism, we seem to face resurgent religious fundamentalism and its doctrinaire mission to proselytise the heathen. Enlightenment assumptions about persistent progress fail to impress many who endure social and environmental decline. Those keenest on national legislatures taking back control can be the biggest critics of those self-same assemblies. Parties of the left appeal to social liberals and cosmopolitans, while haemorrhaging support in their working class base. Parties of the right offer an individualist disruptive capitalism at odds with their platform to preserve family and tradition. While phenomena like Trump and Brexit may disenchant, they can also enrage and engage, and thereby, present-day politics can induce both cynicism and activism.

Amidst all this churn, what has become marked is the widespread dissatisfaction with democracy over the last quarter of a century. Whereas in 2005, 38.7 percent of citizens across the world registered dissatisfaction, more recently the figure is 57.5 percent. Before the financial crash, over three quarters of the US electorate were satisfied. Now 55 percent are dissatisfied. In a similar vein, three out of five of the UK electorate are discontented with their democracy.[21] In 1950, the year of my birth, the UK General Election had a turnout of 83.9 percent. In 2001, it hit a low of 59.4 percent. Decline in trust in many places can be traced to the mid-1990s. At the very time when some declared the supremacy of liberal democracy as the upshot of the Cold War, faith in that system was actually starting to ebb.

When it comes to *economics* – culprits of the financial crash get off scot free, while victims bear the cost. Rising employment is accompanied by growing in-work poverty. As fluidities of identity and tempo of change increase, many 'left behind' communities feel stranded in fate and time. Apparently free services such as social media platforms come with the hidden cost of people's privacy. After decades of elevating the role of private consumers and privatising many parts of the economy, the new surveillance capitalism has intruded into the very privacy of the individual.

Supposed benefits of speed in the modern economy, for releasing more free time, not only contribute to slowing time, as with greater traffic congestion, but also to instruments like smart phones, which can be used to extend people's working day. More generally, growth is understood in terms of price rather than value, when it is clear that there is a big price to pay for under-valuing a finite planet. But that price is not evenly spread. Climate change most impacts those places with least resources.

This book is about understanding these and similar paradoxes. In examining the links among them, it shows how all this dislocation has distorted our ways of seeing and being. It argues that instead of the traditional study of these issues via conventional silos of psychology, politics, economics, theology, and such like, unravelling the confusion demands inter-disciplinary appreciation. The *central paradox* it proposes is that humans are at odds with what they call humanity, even as we live in what has been labelled the 'human age' – the so--called *Anthropocene* – a term used to describe the current geological epoch, which is set apart from previous epochs by being mostly shaped by human impact on the planet.

Maybe this estrangement has always been there. Christianity used the term 'original sin' to infer that humans had come to feel that this world was not their home due to their quest for forbidden knowledge copyrighted by their Creator. From this perspective, restlessness and unease are inherent human conditions because Homo *sapiens* is the only earthly species, some of whose members await their true dwelling-place in a celestial rather than material space. Marx used the term *alienation* to refer to the de-humanising of people in an impersonal class stratified society, in part because workers were separated from the products of their labour, itself owned by exploitative employers. Durkheim used the term *anomie* to refer to the imbalance between the individual and wider society in circumstance where there was a breakdown of clear norms to frame social order, leading people to lack worth and purpose. Contemporary estrangement embraces a deeper sense of individual isolation from the world at large at the very time technology offers chance for greater global connection.

Take just a few of these issues in more detail. Population change is going to have great bearing on the world in ways few consider. For instance, when I was born in 1950, of the top ten countries in the world in population terms, three were in Europe – Germany, the UK, and Italy. Now, there are no European countries in the top ten. Looking ahead to the end of this century, five of the countries with the largest populations will be from Africa, with Nigeria in third place, holding 733 million people, pushing the US into fourth place with 434 million.

The 'Eastern' side of the world – India, China, Pakistan and Indonesia – will become a more significant site of geopolitics and the global economy. China will be a central player, even though in population, it will be over-taken by India. The big population expansion will be in Africa, which is expected to see more than a three-fold increase from 1.3 billion to 4.3 billion. The continent, which cradled *sapiens*, will once again house the largest single share of the species.

On a recent visit to South Africa, I saw in glaring terms the vast economic gap between black and white, despite over twenty years of a post-apartheid regime. In one township I visited, the squalor and deprivation starkly contrasted with nearby affluence of mainly white neighbourhoods. Notably, the white opulent houses were ring-fenced with elaborate defences. Plainly, the price of severe inequality is severe insecurity. Even the poorest dwellings in the townships were linked to the world by satellite dish. The world's most deprived can be huddled together and cordoned off from the privileged. They cannot be prevented from seeing how the rich live, and believing that they have a right to their share. If we think that the immigration push from Africa into Europe in recent years has brought disturbance, we've only witnessed the beginning.

Rival Explanations

Attempts to understand the present tumult see it in terms of different clashes:

- There is that between detached *establishment elites* and *the people*, a demo-cratic severance depicted as being conspiratorially suppressed in the deep state and mainstream 'fake news' media;

- Conflict also exists between the *global* and *local*, between left-behind communities rooted to place and cosmopolitans whose world is evermore their oyster;
- Others emphasise the resurgence of a *white supremacist nationalism*, often portrayed as tied to a 'Judaeo-Christian' culture, that conjures prospect of a 'great replacement' by migrant people of colour, tied to 'alien' religions such as Islam. People attached to this belief see a complacent *liberal system* ready to ignore this demographic shift, thereby betraying western civilisation to a doomsday 'white genocide';
- Then, there's a synthetic *nostalgia* invoked about an illusory past, counterposed to a *present that is broken* for that resentful part of the electorate, with the related pledge to take back control and to make the country great again;
- On the gender side, *toxic masculinity* offering 'strong man' leadership is contrasted with a politics of *equality and rights* that challenges 'alpha male' impunity and its assumed sense of entitlement;
- Finally, there's reference to *rebellious youth* who feel their future is being embezzled by '*OK Boomers*', some of whom in turn regard claims about inter-generational inequity as the gripe of ungrateful 'snowflakes'.

For each in turn, these six 'explanations' concern dislocation of power, space, race, time, gender and generation. Of course, they inter-penetrate. Common to all six, the usual political axis of left and right – of ideological argument between advocates of an interventionist state for distributive justice and those acclaiming the liberating force of unregulated markets in a minimalist state – is now intersected by another axis. This is one of strident cultural hostilities, marked by a politics of identity and belonging. Seen in these terms, culture, rather than class, is presently the decisive dividing line. If so, it flies in the face of Marxist certitude that class is the driving force of history, and that anything which distracts from its primacy is down ultimately to false consciousness.

Much of the insurgent politics worldwide has witnessed *escalation* of stakes; greater *polarisation* of sides; *amplification* of discourse into theatrics if not pantomime; and *acceleration* of events. Vladimir Lenin once said that there are decades where nothing happens, and there are weeks where decades happen. In a similar vein, Prime Minister Harold Wilson once remarked that a week was a long time in politics. Little did they know. Particular manifestations of this tumult are easily evident. For instance, within six years since 2016, the UK has had five Prime Ministers: David Cameron, Theresa May, Boris Johnson, Liz Truss and Rishi Sunak, a turnover reflective of deep political commotion.

This all poses a more fundamental and durable issue beyond episodes like Brexit or Trump, or the piracy of Putin: what does it mean to be human? At least since the industrial revolution, humans have actually become more disconnected with other living creatures and their wider environment, presuming they can exercise dominion over nature. One expression of this rift is a crisis of over-consumption, which together with what can be seen as a crisis of capital's over-accumulation, are contributing to an existential crisis for the planet, linked to factors such as the climate emergency.

And beyond that await other big dilemmas. These include: the interweave of social diversity and equality, and the related public policy tensions between social inclusion and social cohesion; the economic dislocations of a digital divide, involving transformative technologies of artificial intelligence and robotics; the commodification of personal data in an emerging surveillance society that threatens democracy itself; and the capacity for gene editing to bio-engineer the 'new human'.

Let-down

This is all a long way from the best hopes of my childhood. My father left school when he was ten and my mother's experience of formal learning was not much different. She worked in a textile mill, and he in a pub. As a friend from similar circumstance put it, I was an Attlee child, benefitting from the first opportunity of free secondary education, and was later the first generation in our family to go to university. Like many working class families, we were invested in the transformative power of education. Not only was it going to be an avenue for personal social mobility, it was also going to be a democratic force for greater civilisation. The latter has not happened as expected, and it has to be asked why not.

The opportunity I experienced caused me to hope for further radical change through democratic politics from the optimistic 1960s onward. In the 1970s, I channelled most of that effort into community activism. In the early 1980s, I worked in the trade union movement in the West Midlands, England's indus-trial heartland, that was experiencing economic devastation under Thatcher. As a Labour Party member, I placed hope in the Bennite intent to socially control the commanding heights of the economy in the interests of working people. Even by the late 1980s, as Labour continuously failed to win central power, I was excited by the pre-figurative possibilities manifest in municipal socialism in places like Sheffield.

In the wider world, I rooted for Mugabe in the promise of radical post-colonial change. In a visit to Yugoslavia, I thought I'd get an insight into its alternative form of communism that seemed to have succeeded in pacifying long-standing ethnic hostilities among its component regions. At the early stage of the Nicaraguan revolution, I was in Managua to see firsthand how its social change was progressing. Right on through subsequent decades, I was searching for examples of social transformation that brought democracy and development. Having studied social and racial divides in many US cities, it was an historical experience to be present in Chicago's Grant Park on the election night Obama spoke to a jubilant crowd as the first black US President.

Ultimately however, many parts of the West Midlands were to join those 'left behind' places. Bennite radicalism did not deliver. Anticipation of the wider gains of municipal socialism was inflated. Mugabe's despotism was disastrous for Zimbabwe. Yugoslavia, by the 1990s, descended into a series of civil conflicts around ethno-nationalism, and its apparent socialist solidarity proved to be threadbare. Ortega became a long-standing leader in Nicaragua, more as mini-despot than great democrat, with his repressive strategy of preventing the most viable opposition candidates from contesting presidential elections. For all his achievement and under-achievement, Obama was succeeded by Trump. Back home in Belfast, the two most successful political parties that emerged from thirty years of violent sectarian conflict were those representing the most partisan positions of the two tribes.

My personal search for sustained democratic social progress has proved to be largely elusive.

Echoing words of Chesterton speaking of Christianity, some on the political left will say that Marxism hasn't been tried and found wanting. It simply hasn't been tried properly. That is a cop-out. For all of Marx's useful insights into history and the nature of capitalism, government in the name of Marxism has given us the crimes of Stalin, Mao, and Pol Pot, among others, and those crimes are intrinsic to the regimes' totalitarianism.

Moreover, those crimes cannot be offset in some strange audit with those of capitalism and its long-time twin, imperialism, as in a contest about which system has overall behaved more badly. For one thing, the former system presented itself as morally superior to the latter. It offered liberation *from* the latter, based on science of all things. Instead, what it really offered was a false science that professed grasp of the total nature of humans and society. Its dogma declared that for society to be free of exploitation, there was need not just for structural change, but also for the creation of a 'new human'. Since the masses were unconsciously blinded by their very exploitation, a politically awakened vanguard was needed to lead them out of their current quagmire into the light of liberation. Unfortunately, in many cases this elite all too readily became the new oppressor.

Rights and Values

Currently, class wars have been often overtaken by culture wars, and featuring eminently in these are terms such as *sovereignty* and *identity*. They speak of a yearning for control in a confusing world. Faced with this splintered discourse, some seek sanctuary in the concept of universal and inviolable human rights. Long prominent in democratic political discourse, this notion of basic legal entitlement contains related ideas of freedom, justice, and good governance. It is rooted in attempts to get to the heart of being human.

The classical liberal position has tended to emphasise an individualistic perspective that focuses on prerogative to certain social goods – the *right to* free speech; to assembly; to self-determination and such like (**liberty**). The socialist perspective, on the other hand, tends to underscore collectivist solidarity as the basis for the *right from* – the right to be secure from poverty, homelessness, etc. (**equality**). Alongside these traditions, is a civic/republican stance that proposes bridging this sometimes contradictory or competing set of rights with social empathy, affinity, and reciprocity, rooted in rapport, fellowship, and bonds of common purpose (**fraternity**). Such latter attributes are seen as the 'social glue' that fastens society as it grapples through what can be rival priorities of liberty and equality.

Apart from the problem that 'rights' often apply to people as citizens rather than as humans, the persistent conundrum consists in the reconciliation of these three distinct tenets. Some see such resolution as unachievable since they are inherently incompatible. For instance, they argue that to secure equality demands the oppressive power of the big state that ultimately diminishes liberty. In these terms, espousal of equality is a denial of individual freedom to be different – richer, cleverer, prettier, luckier, and such like – traits that are innate to the human condition. Conversely, others propose that protection of effective liberty for vulnerable groups demands removal of inequalities that sustain their disadvantage.

While a *human rights* approach plays an important role in advancing social progress, it has to be complemented by one that embodies *human values*. In short, a more productive pathway towards the good society involves engagement with philosophical concepts such as eudaimonia and empathy. The former concerns the nourishing of human potential for well-being and happiness, rooted in the human drive for meaning, autonomy, attachment, competence and continuity. The latter concerns people's ability to appreciate the feelings of fellow humans as though those emotions were their own, a trait necessary for humans as social animals.

But the interesting aspect of empathy is whether capacity for affinity in human nature is restricted to tribe, and is protective of the similar and familiar by erecting boundary and bias against 'the other' – the different, the strange. A telescoped world that throws diverse people and values together demands not only the bonding capital of tribalism, but also the bridging capital of commonwealth, without which violent human conflict can thrive. These issues are considered more fully in the second volume.

As Fritz argues,[22] democracy doesn't engender equality. Rather, equality engenders democracy. In advocating this social contract, he disavows a view of human nature as involving perennial struggle between passion and reason, but rather sees both as essential to our two-sided moral character. Moral justification can be found in human cooperation and competition, in egalitarian values of humans' equal worth and in the discriminatory filters to arbitrate good and bad; in the individual personality capable of empathy and altruism, and in collective societal frameworks based on ethics and solidarity.

In practical terms, this means a fundamental shift in key human activity such as the economy: a shift whereby value determines price rather than the reverse, and the added public value is a vital metric. In all this, morality concerns relationships, not only of humans to each other, but also of our species to the wider bio-system, moving from estrangement to engagement. In such a shift, it is well to pay regard to what Wrangham[23] calls '*the goodness paradox*'. From years of anthropologic study, particularly of our primate cousins such as chimpanzees and bonobos, he became fascinated by the human capacity for both violent aggression and peaceful tolerance. Through evolution, the former was nurtured through domesticity in social community, and yet all the while becoming more peaceful, cultured and civilized, humans have retained capacity for the most cruel and calculated violence. This apparent paradox is down, he thinks, to our simultaneous tendency for both social bonding and conflict. Whereas the former can involve disagreement, it can usually be managed through the force of argument, while the latter favours the argument of force.

We face the plausible prospect if not of human extinction, then of human contraction and withered civilization. In this Anthropocene time, the cause is more likely to be of our own making, through global warming, nuclear and chemical weapons, artificial intelligence (AI) and such like, rather than natural disaster. In this regard, we are on what Ord[24] calls 'the precipice', from which we can either flourish or flounder. Highlighting another paradox, he notes how the very democratisation of high tech, in terms of its access, creates more chance for abuse of AI and for contrived pandemics in biological warfare.

Gone Viral

Speaking of pandemics, COVID-19 casts light on many of these issues troubling our times. It started in one locality – Wuhan in China – and spread globally, showing that in a globalised world, borders may trouble humans. They don't deter those things most lethal to humans, like climate change, nuclear winter, or a humble virus. Yet attempts to restrict the reach of this particular virus involved countries trying to protect their borders by limiting travel, particularly from countries with perceived high risk. Key to tackling the virus was transparency about its threat, and this tested democratic credentials, particularly those of China, where it proved wanting. By the same token, authoritarian regimes like China's were able to impose a command and control over its diffusion, with an apparently effective result on the immediate crisis, a coercive process not so easily replicable in democratic countries.

Interestingly, in the first wave of the virus, there was no neat divide in outcomes between democracies and autocracies. As expressed by Baldwin:[25] 'competence and compliance were closely connected. Where the state delivered, it continued to be trusted'. In such circumstances, democracies secured citizen buy-in to self-curbing of liberty to a great extent. By late spring 2020, around one third of the world's people 'was effectively in house arrest', showing that in extreme emergency 'freedom means being our own jailers'.[26] But sustained lockdowns cannot be totally policed even in totalitarian societies.

Important to its control were facts based on scientific evidence. However, in a social media age of disinformation, some depicted public concern as being deliberately stoked, for instance to cause economic problems for Trump in election year. To offset such talk of conspiracy, governments, such as in the UK, made much of their reliance on experts, even though a leading UK government figure, Michael Gove, had been previously dismissive of them. Reinvesting faith in specialists did not stop some questioning the expertise, pointing out that in the last quarter of a century alarm about avian flu, BSE, SARS, and swine flu had been proven to be alarmist. The fact that an estimated 36.3 million people have died from AIDS/HIV-related illnesses seems to have by-passed their radar.[27] But can we rely on this number as 'fact'?

There is real difficulty in science offering us accuracy when it comes to the most basic outcome of the pandemic: the number of fatalities. By March 2022, official data put the COVID-19-related deaths worldwide slightly in excess of 6 million. Though accounting for only 4.25 percent of the world's population, the US – the world's richest country – accounted for around 16 percent of these global deaths,[28] nearly four times what might be expected. One factor that may explain some of this disproportion is obesity. According to 2017–2018 data from the US National Health and Nutrition Examination Survey (NHANES), over 73 percent of US adults are overweight or obese – 42 percent of adults had obesity, while 10 percent were severely obese, and another 30.7 percent were overweight.[29] In countries where under half of adults are overweight, the probability of pandemic-related death is about one-tenth of the level in countries where over half of adults are overweight.[30] Yet, can this connection be talked about openly without accusation of 'body-shaming'?

An alternative estimation of global 'COVID' deaths,[31] after two years of the pandemic, put it at over 18 million people – three times higher than official data suggested. This is calculated from records of 191 countries and territories, in terms of the number of deaths above what would be normally expected. This research indicates that in descending order, the countries ranked worst in excess mortality rates per 100,000 were Russia, Mexico, Brazil and the US. A different estimate of excess mortality – between 1 January 2020 to 31 December 2021 – comes from the World Health Organisation (WHO),[32] which puts it at 14.9 million. Of these deaths, the over-whelming share (81 percent) comes from middle-income countries, compared to 15 percent and 4 percent for high and low-income countries respectively. Though it may be thought that a disease associated with poverty would have had a greater impact on the poorest parts of the world, it's not that simple. Other variables are at play, such as a country's elderly share of population. According to the WHO figures, of excess deaths per 100,000, the 10 countries ranking worst were: Peru (437);

Russia (367); South Africa (200); India (171); Brazil (160); Turkey (156); US (140); Italy (133); Germany (116); and Spain (111). With the global average being 96, the UK comes out at (109), while Sweden, which took a relatively light touch to lockdown, comes out much better (56).

Yet another estimate, given by the *Economist* in May 2022,[33] sets the total toll at 21.3 million. The truth is that we'll never know for sure. Such differences in research assessments illustrate the problem of getting reliable comparative data, when countries estimate differently. We may long for definitive data to afford an evidence-based understanding of our planet. But the world cannot be reduced to numbers. A different kind of problem for science in addressing the pandemic concerns the absence of agreed definition for certain features of the disease. For instance, Long-COVID lacks a globally-agreed definition about nature and symptoms. Accordingly, we have no precision about its pervasiveness and duration.

In respect of the contribution of science, it arrived at an agreed analysis of the make-up and diffusion of the virus, and in a positive aspect of globalisation, it shared that knowledge readily in global cooperation. But given the universal threat and this degree of medical agreement, why was there such variation in policy response across the world? Baldwin notes:[34]

> *Despite a common etiological understanding of the virus and its spread, nations marshalled different preventative strategies ....Nations' political complexions and the preventative strategies they applied did not line up in any evident correlation.*

Amongst health advisors to government, some argued the need to get a grip by moving 'ahead of the curve' through taking drastic action to curtail people's movement and social contact. Other colleagues preferred a step-by-step approach that they thought would avoid peak demand on health services already strained with the seasonal pressure of winter illnesses. Many behavioural scientists argued for a similar incremental approach since they thought that this gradual nudging of the public to a state of restricted social exchange stood the best chance of securing their full cooperation. Two years on from the onset, countries across the world took different approaches about 'returning to normality', each claiming that policy was science-based. In short, getting public agreement about the facts of best prevention proved to be problematic – even among scientists.

It would be cheering to say that science triumphed. Rapid discovery of a vaccine was certainly an achievement. But in the early stages, disputes within science about the efficacy of face masks and border controls, and about strategies for herd immunity, and then subsequent limitations of test and trace, and different assessments about the timing and duration of lockdown, all brought some confusion. The mantra that took hold – follow the data rather than the dates – has proved to be sensible. In a switch from recent disrespect for experts, politicians in some democratic countries became keen to stress that they were battling the virus by listening to 'the science'. But in fact, there isn't one agreed 'science' in this sense. This is highlighted in varied models, data analysis, and processes about testing, tracking and tracing to minimise transmission. In other words, there will be debate within the scientific community about how best to tackle a virus, even when that science is agreed about its nature. Analysis will change with cumulative data. And that is good, even if it makes for less certainty for a public anxious for definitive answers.

Unsurprisingly, amid this anxiety, the pandemic has given rise to conspiracy stories, and quack cures, such as Trump's perilous notion of ingested disinfectant. In the end, this sham can only be countered by a scientific approach that favours critical questioning and evidence. But amidst the noise, many are left confused about what to think, understand and believe. The cliché that truth is the first casualty of war holds good in many circumstances of today's embattled world.

All this has underscored for the public, the significance and shortcomings of science. In my lifetime, use of science has harboured both hope and harm. For instance, the seminal decade of hope – the 1960s – yielded a celebrated film called *The Graduate*. The lead part, Ben Braddock, is taken aside at a family party to toast his graduation by a neighbour, who shares with him the confidential path to lucrative prospect: 'I want to say just one word to you, just one word: plastics!' In other words, great commercial future lay in plastic. Now, we're advised that there may not be a future, partly *because* of plastic. In science, we need to distinguish between hope and hype.

One thing for sure – the recent pandemic has shown the significance of inequality in stark terms. Before locking down the whole country, Italy first tried to cut off the rich northern region, particularly Lombardy, a place which has tried in the past to cut *itself* off from the generally less affluent rest of the country. This made for a strange turnaround in the normal Italian contest about secession and sovereignty. Also evident in the rich-poor divide were features such as panic-buying, whereby stockpiling was a more readily available option to those who could afford it. As state benefits were offered in many countries to those made redundant, the precarious status of those operating in the 'gig economy' was exposed, as was the poor rate of statutory sick pay in some places like the UK. Certain particularly vulnerable groups, like the homeless, and institutions like over-crowded prisons, were relatively ignored. The slogan to '*stay safe…stay at home*' doesn't resonate for the homeless, the refugees, or for those facing domestic abuse.

While the World Health Organisation emphasised the need to 'test, test, test', many national governments, particularly in the poorest countries, had limited capacity for such comprehensive testing. At the same time, there were reports of some rich people paying for private testing, raising the question of whether at a time of such emergency, private health capacity should be socialised for collective benefit.

Another aspect of inequality was the factor of age. Since the virus had its most lethal impact upon the elderly, in countries with stretched health capacity, there was an implication that treatment might have to be rationed to those best able to recover, thereby 'dispensing' with at least some of the older and most frail patients. For some, this underscored a wider societal problem, wherein if society was increasingly reduced to the economy, the elderly, as economically inactive, would be increasingly seen as a drain rather than a blessing. Arguably, the ongoing 'epidemic' of loneliness suffered by some isolated elderly has been highlighted by the call for them to distance themselves from others considered a health hazard.

Collateral Damage

This highlights the wider repercussion of drastic interventions like lockdown. For some, it's the big issue of governments finding emergencies a useful chance to exercise very centralised and draconian control. Those critics are concerned that this could be a practice run for governments to adopt more authoritarian rule. Indeed, some governments find a global crisis offers local opportunity. For instance, China's extensive monitoring of their people's health and movement during the crisis may be used to enhance their surveillance state beyond the crisis. Non-compliance with belated government action against the virus by a discontented public in Iran allowed Ayatlollah Ali Khamenei to pursue more coercive state control. Crown Prince Mohammed bin Salman in Saudi Arabia used global distraction to make further moves against his rivals, and Putin advanced his aim to install himself as effective president for life. The viral threat also risked endorsing the autocratic tendency in some of today's world politics, as people become convinced that, in crisis times, security is to be valued over liberty, and only 'strong men' can ride to the rescue. Even in robust democracies, this trade-off is real:[35] 'In emergencies, democratic procedures must paradoxically be temporarily side-stepped in order to preserve democracy'.

Unquestionably, government restriction on social contact, national and international travel, and the opening of schools, shops, restaurants, bars, and workplaces in general, represents major intrusion on civil liberty. Also, it has serious knock-on effect on healthcare.[36] By the start of 2022, just over 6 million people were on the waiting list for pre-planned NHS treatment in England, more than one-tenth of the population, and representing an increased figure 'by around a third since the start of the pandemic due to the disruption that Covid-19 has wrought on the NHS'.[37]

Economic fallout has been immense. The International Labour Organisation (ILO)[38] projected a deficit of 52 million full-time equivalent jobs for 2022, compared with pre-pandemic figures, adjusted for population growth. Extreme poverty levels, which had fallen by more than 1 billion between 1999 and 2019, have risen again, with World Bank estimates of the increase between 2019 and 2020 put at 77 million.

Against these damaging economic effects, there have been some mixed outcomes. As growth has shrunk, so also has air pollution. With lockdown, heavily polluted urban centres, like Delhi, saw their harmful levels of nitrogen dioxide reduce significantly. Given that the WHO estimates that 7 million premature deaths annually can be ascribed to exposure to ambient and household air pollution, this decline carries benefit.

Globally, road traffic collisions produce around 1.35 million deaths annually, with a cost of around $1.8 trillion annually. Overwhelmingly, these fatalities occur in low and middle income countries. With reduced traffic volume attending various forms of pandemic lockdown, there was a drop in annual road deaths in 2020 compared to 2019, in 33 out of 42 countries studied by one source.[39] This benefit was not universally shared. Despite its reduction of vehicle driving on the roads during the early period of the pandemic, the US saw an increase of fatalities in 2020 of about 7 percent, compared to 2019, while traffic fatalities in the first half of 2021 rose by 18.4 percent since the first half of 2020, according to the National Highway Traffic Safety Administration. Explanation for this strange paradox – fewer cars on the road, yet more deaths – was that though there were less drivers, among those who did drive, there was more risky behaviour, such as speeding, failure to use seat belts, and driving under the influence of alcohol or drugs.[40]

The pandemic also both highlighted and impacted other public health hazards. For instance, the opioid epidemic in the US saw its worst fatality rates in 2020, with over 100,000 drug overdoses, 76,000 of which were opioid-based, a rise of about 30 percent on 2019. While the pandemic crisis may have accentuated the problem through supply-side problems with medicines such as naloxone, or the interference with treatment courses, the basic predicament can be traced to the mid-1990s, particularly associated with the approval granted by the US Food and Drug Administration (FDA) to OxyContin, and its deceptive promotion as a relatively non-addictive extended-release opioid painkiller.[41] While synthetic opioids like Fentanyl also play a part in this crisis, the story of OxyContin carries a distinctive warning about the corporate power of Big Pharma, particularly in health systems where profit is a key determinant.

Members of the Sackler family, who owned and operated Purdue Pharma – the firm that sold OxyContin – are estimated to have profited by over $10bn from the analgesic. On two occasions, Purdue has pleaded guilty to felonies in respect of the drug. In 2007, it related to its unlawful marketing, while in 2020, it concerned inducement of doctors to prescribe it, and being mendacious about the addiction risk. Despite such culpability, in 2021, a bankruptcy arrangement for Purdue would grant those Sackler members extensive legal immunity, thereby protecting a great deal of their riches. In 2022, they settled for a payment of $6 billion, not a sum that would impoverish the multi-billionaires.[42] Notably, the Sackler name is well-known in the arts and academic worlds for receipt of a sizeable donation, leaving some to question whether such philanthropy can be used to de-contaminate unethical profit.

Krelle and Tallack[43] debunk three myths advanced about the pandemic's effect in the UK. First, those who died from COVID-19 would have died shortly anyway. In the first year (5 March 2020–5 March 2021), each of the 146,000 victims lost on average 10.2 years of life. Altogether over this period, 1.5 million potential life-years were lost to the virus in the UK. Second, it was similar to a bad flu season. Not so. In such a scenario, about 30,000 individuals on average in the UK expire from flu and pneumonia, accounting for a loss of around a quarter million life-years, a mere sixth of that attributable to the much more lethal pandemic. This loss was more for men than women. In England and Wales, women 75 years and older, forfeited about four-times more life-years than typical of a bad flu break-out. With men, it was five-times. Third, the virus didn't 'discriminate' on the basis of income. Again, not so. Residents in the most deprived quintile (fifth) areas of England were twice as likely to die from the virus than those of the same age in the least deprived quintile. This disparity 'is also seen in numbers of deaths, which are 35 percent higher in the poorest areas than in the wealthiest. This is despite the fact that more deprived areas tend to have younger populations, so would be expected to have fewer deaths'.[44]

From Local to Global

And then with respect to social diversity, the origin of the virus in China caused some who were or looked Chinese to be subject to abuse in parts of the world, emphasizing how selected 'others' can be grouped together in such crisis situations as existential threats. Trump made a point of naming it the Chinese Virus, a reference that some took to be deliberately racist. At the same time, the risk of xenophobic inference or heightened geopolitical friction, shouldn't stop us properly investigating the possibility that a human-engineered virus escaped from the Wuhan Institute of Virology. Short of any conspiracy about bio-warfare, there is an issue of bio-security. Global competition to find solutions to pandemics may help accelerate the search. But it also may prompt higher-risk experiment. How then can we operate global supervision over such research, or as John Gray has argued,[45] must we 'accept and deal with the reality that the planet is an extremely unsafe place'?

If we take the Coronavirus as a test case of how the world deals with a pressing world problem, not all aspects of human behaviour augur well. However understandable it may be for countries to adopt a barrier to travel from countries with perceived high risk, decisions about travel access were largely taken without due multilateral discussion. We've also seen the problem of vaccine nationalism, whereby there has been contest within the rich world and between it and the poor world, about fair and affordable distribution. Proper strategic collaboration across the world would have involved dispensing with normal ideas about intellectual property; waiving patents; and engaging in technology transfer – all to ensure the vaccines became available globally at low or no cost, and at speed. Only through such measures could multiple sites be set up promptly to secure the most efficient logistics for vaccine production and allocation.

The vaccine should be seen as a global public good, a people's vaccine, not a profit vaccine. One way to minimise monopolies on vaccine production is by contractually tying public funds for research to the free share of data and knowledge so derived.[46] Instead of equal distribution, we witness the awful spectacle of unused vaccines in the West having to be discarded, while so much of the world awaits the first jab. By Autumn 2021, the target of having 70 percent of the world vaccinated was far off the mark. The actual figure was only 48 percent.[47] Only 3 percent of people in low-income countries had received at least one dose. By mid-February 2022 – a full two years after the global spread started – 61.9 percent of the world's population had received at least one dose of a vaccine. However, the figure for low-income countries was only 10.6 percent, and it was pitifully low in the very poorest countries. In Chad, for example, it was 1.51 percent. At this same time, the share of people with complete vaccination in the world was 54 percent, with great variation: United Arab Emirates (94 percent); China (85 percent); Canada (80 percent); Brazil (71 percent); UK (71 percent); US (64 percent); India (54 percent); Russia (49 percent); and Nigeria (2.6 percent).[48]

Inevitably, the failure to get a genuine global response, despite it being in everyone's interests, raises questions about the clout and reach of agencies like the World Health Organisation (WHO). Data from COVAX – the global initiative aimed at equitable access to COVID-19 vaccines – shows very poor levels of vaccine donation from the rich world, particularly when it comes to doses actually delivered, compared to those donated but not yet delivered, and especially compared to those simply announced, but not yet even donated. Stockpiling by rich countries and vast profits by Big Pharma sit together. Just in COVID vaccine revenue, Pfizer forecast $31 billion in 2022, a year that the company was also set to add about $17 billion in sales of Paxlovid, an antiviral drug.[49] For some, global disaster brings big business.

All in all, this has not been the world's finest hour. Instead of a global response, it has generated distinctive national reactions. Does this show the limits of human solidarity, or does it attest to durable cultural difference that makes customised antidote appropriate? If anything, does it bolster rivalry and division across the world, over priority access to protective equipment and vaccine? In an interdependent world, global collaboration is the only viable remedy to global malady. Both markets and nationalism have been exposed for their limitations. Beyond that, there's the question of what kind of politics is appropriate at national level. Arguably, social democracy is insufficiently radical to address a radical age of pandemics, climate emergency, and other major challenges, an issue to which we'll return more fully in the second volume.

Within all countries, the viral threat has raised interesting political questions that will endure. To take some instances: public open space, which has come under duress from economic maxims of privatisation over many decades, has come into its own as a 'safe space' relative to crowded private spaces. Whether the UK's National Health Service, providing cover for all, offers a better health model than less inclusive systems in such times of major health crisis is now a matter of valid debate. The question about whether to protect physical health by social isolation even if such seclusion yields mental health problems, throws up again the relative priority attached to each.

While responses to the pandemic have emphasised hunkering down into self-isolation for the public good, the crisis has generated many examples of altruistic generosity to the vulnerable at local level, a rediscovery of so-called 'eclipsed community'. Public assets, such as the National Trust in the UK, have made their spaces open to the public for free. All this shows that *social capital*, as well as the *natural capital* of the biosphere, are crucial components of human habitat.

For all the negatives of high tech, it has been shown to offer the chance for schools, colleges, and workplaces to carry on in virtual connection even when 'locked-down'. Nevertheless, there is likelihood that long periods of school closure worsen educational inequality, with better-off families better able to provide a home education substitute. On another issue, emergency isolation procedures can afford time for family members to re-encounter each other after a period of economic life being so relentless as to crowd out time for family. It may suggest that contrary to contemporary political wisdom, a work-driven society doesn't make for a well-balanced one. The crisis challenges us to rethink the way we work and commute and work-life balance, offering the chance to explore how protection of life, livelihood, and lifestyle can be harmonised. Dramatic change can raise new possibilities of hybrid work patterns, with more working from home, and new approaches to social security such as basic universal income.

It has led to the third economic crisis this century (following the dot.com crash and the financial crisis). In each case, the tenets of neoliberalism have been temporarily abandoned in favour of Keynesian intervention. This has tended to socialise the debts of the rich and to privatise the debt burden to the wider public in the form of austerity. It has failed to ask fundamental questions about the nature of the economy itself. Yet the pandemic highlights a new definition of 'key workers', and the gap between their contribution and remuneration.

Nor can we just discard the role of orthodoxy and ideology at such terrible times, as referenced by the UK Chancellor, when the orthodox ideology of market primacy has been long projected as offering no alternative. Markets can have virtues in terms of efficiency, innovation and supply. But in times of acute crisis, their jittery nature is exposed in a world economy marked by casino capitalism, a deficiency further impaired by the way in which they can be manipulated by unscrupulous traders to exploit share price and currency fluctuation. Also, the economic pressure exerted by something like a pandemic shows how the virtues of Keynesian stimulus can be re-discovered even by die-hard free-marketeers. Suddenly, magic money trees came into bloom. But as we'll see in later chapters, the cumulative national debt burden generated by a series of crisis interventions has produced its own fiscal dilemma that can be used to justify a new round of austerity.

In 2021, the UK's Conservative Chancellor increased taxes by around £40 billion, pushing the tax take to surpass 36 percent of national income, 2.7 percent of GDP higher than in 2019–20.[50] One official study[51] noted that: 'current estimates of the cost of Government measures announced so far range from about £315 to £410 billion'. At the same time, tax receipts were down due to recessionary pressure. 'The Government accounted for this shortfall by increasing borrowing to £323 billion in 2020/21'. Britain's total public debt of £1.95 trillion in 2020 was greater than the size of its economy for the first time since 1963. Also in 2020, the American Rescue Plan provided another tranche of pandemic relief, estimated at $1,844 billion – around 8.8 percent of 2020 GDP.[52]

The biggest question thrown up by the virus is whether, across the world, humans can act in unison for each other in time of great need, and whether this political will can be tapped to address other existential threats. All this has been the outcome not merely of human over-population, but more particularly of the global north's over-consumption. In such a context, animal infection can be readily contagious to humans – a process known as *zoonosis*. It's not just that such a virus does not respect sovereign borders, it does not respect species' borders. As Quammen[53] points out, ecological disturbances are transmitting animal pathogens into humans, while human behaviour and technology are then extending these pathogens broader and faster than ever before. He notes:

> *When the trees fall and the native animals are slaughtered, the native germs fly like dust from a demolished warehouse. A parasitic microbe, thus jostled, evicted, deprived of its habitual host, has two options -- to find a new host, a new kind of host ....or to go extinct. It's not that they target us especially. It's that we are so obtrusively, abundantly available.*

Thus, care for the planet in the widest form is crucial not just to cope with the climate emergency, but also with other threats to human existence. The 'green' politics that derives from that imperative cannot be separated from addressing the injustice of deep social inequalities around categories such as class, gender, race, ability and age. We cannot credibly claim at moments of crisis that 'we're all in this together' when society is based on unwarranted disparity of worth and care.

Even in its confusion, the recent pandemic offers this kind of revelation. It shows the speed at which 'normal' life can be upended. It reminds us of how thin the veneer of civilisation can be. If we were to encounter a virus with the lethal potential of an Ebola and the infectious capacity of COVID-19, the prospect for a disordered selfish response is great. Also, it shows that our welfare is tied to that of other animals and indeed the entire ecosystem. The speed at which many species have been decimated in the last century, relative to millions of years before, has led some to talk of the prospect of the Sixth Extinction in the 700 million year story of complex earthly life.

This suggests the need to better understand the links between us humans and other animals, and indeed between humans and biodiversity – the array of Earth's life. In an Anthropocene age, when humans try to dominate the planet, long-standing human activity such as logging, de-forestation, road construction into previously undisturbed landscape, chemical pollution, mineral extraction, urban sprawl, nuclear leaks, plastic diffusion, and so on, are cumulatively breaking down the ecosystems that make Earth habitable. In his analysis of the decline of the Roman Empire,[54] Harper notes that it wasn't just particular elements like pandemics and environmental vandalism that were the cause. More fundamentally, it was human failure to appreciate that all creations of *sapiens* are inherently impermanent. He talks about 'a great act of self-deception....that the Romans had tamed the forces of wild nature....the fall of their empire was the triumph of nature over human ambitions'. Has this pandemic cautioned us about hubris?

Or is it the case that unlike the Romans, we live in an age of science that will offer us reprieve? Certainly, some have extolled the power of technology to monitor and manage with contact apps, etc. Others have expressed reservation about outcomes of such surveillance capacity for citizen privacy and state power. What government can introduce in an emergency measure for a benign purpose may by stealth creep into the political culture as a more permanent curtailment of human rights. Thus, mobilising people's consent for what is near to house-arrest shows the potential of people choosing security over liberty if they are fearful. The varied success in managing the virus spread between democratic and authoritarian government systems may suggest to some the appeal of strong centralised leadership and the contrasted weakness and indecisiveness of democratic processes. Crisis times stress-test the degree to which civic culture is embedded.

The pandemic can be depicted in biblical terms of pestilence and plague. As always in these perturbing circumstances, some will read it as a sign from God about the end of times, an eschatological theme that plays into the mistaken impression that pestilence, wars, and environmental degradation are new to the world, and augur Armageddon. For other religious observers, faith brings consolation. The spiritual offers repose in the serenity of a non-material dimension. For non-believers, it can confirm that there is no benign interventionist God that can intercede on the basis of prayer. If such a divine presence existed why did the devout close their places of worship as places of risk, as if their God would punish those coming to beseech deliverance. For them, the fact that a merciful God would stand idly by in the face of such global disease is close to the plea: 'where was God in the Holocaust?'

The massive change the world has experienced in the intensive first two years of the pandemic has shown that government can take huge steps quickly, and that what everyone thought was impossible was actually doable. Indeed, it has created surreal urban scenes of desolation that would normally be associated with far-fetched sc-fi movies. In this vein, it has opened up a new canvas of what the world could be – both bad and good. Thus, some insist that things will never be the same again. This shows that government has the power, if it has the political will, to mobilise in response to other crises such as climate change. This 'new normal' isn't a given. The crisis of the First World War together with the 1918/19 Flu was supposed to transform societies like the UK into 'homes fit for heroes'. It didn't happen. Instead, depression and fascism took hold. On the other hand, the Second World War did deliver social welfare transformation in many developed countries.

In short, the pandemic has revealed many aspects of our world. With all the sophisticated modelling of risk-assessment, why were we still caught out in preparation for the calamity? With all the great benefits and insights of science, why are we not able to calculate precisely the fatality data, or determine the comparative efficacy of specific approaches such as mask mandates, school closures, herd immunity, or 'zero-COVID'? What it has revealed in broad terms is the importance of health systems; public health; mental health; the significance of schools in both children's educational development and in community life; the need for trust in robust evidence over disinformation; the role of social inequality in vaccine access and hesitancy; identification of who are the 'essential' workers; and the beneficial impact of proactive government in the public interest, supported by much greater fiscal latitude than normally assumed.

The pandemic has also brought a salutary reminder of human vulnerability and focus to many of the issues addressed in this book. It has shown how quickly simple social tenets we take for granted can be over-turned in emergency. Whereas we used to think of giving someone the elbow as shoving them away, it became the safe form of greeting. Whereas we used to think that being social was about getting close to people, the responsible act was to keep social distance. Whereas we once associated masks with either harmless Halloween dressing, or with harmful criminal behaviour, we came to see their purpose in protecting others. And whereas we used to associate lockdown with a strategy to contain prisoners, we have had to understand it as a measure imposing restriction on our movement and gathering, designed to contain a deadly virus. In so many ways, it has prompted re-think of what it is to be human and social. These are the central themes of this book.

Notes

1 Statista (October 2022) Number of Border Crossings Between Ukraine and Central and Eastern European (CEE) Countries After Russia's Invasion of Ukraine from February 24 to October 11, 2022, by Selected Country. *Statista*. www.stati sta.com/statistics/1293403/cee-ukrainian-refugees-by-country. Accessed on: 17 October 2022.

2 Tooze, A. (20–26 May 2022) The Second Coming of NATO: Will The Revived Alliance Survive In The New World Order? *The New Statesman*.

3 World Data (2022) Members of the NATO. *World Data*. www.worlddata.info/allian ces/nato. Accessed on: 17 October 2022.

4 United Nations (2021) *Final report of the Panel of Experts on Yemen*. United Nations Security Council. 3. https://reliefweb.int/sites/reliefweb.int/files/resources. Accessed on: 10 March 2022.

5 Human Rights Watch.www.hrw.org/world-report/2022/country-chapters/yemen. Accessed on: 10 March 2022.

6 The Economist (May 4th 2022) Putin is Failing in Ukraine But Succeeding at Oppressing Russia. *The Economist*.

7 Quote of Kirill's Sermon on 3 May 2022 (4 May 2022) Kirill's Provocative Statement: Russia Has Never Attacked Anyone. *Orthodox Times*. https://orthod oxtimes.com/kirills-provocative-statement-russia-has-never-attacked-anyone. Accessed on: 9 May 2022.

8 Quoted in *The Times* (11 March 2022).

9 Belton, C. (2020) *Putin's People: How the KGB Took Back Russia and Then Took On the West*. London: William Collins.

10 Smith, M. (5 May 2022) Support for EU Army Grows Across Europe Following Russian Invasion of Ukraine. *YouGov*. https://yougov.co.uk/topics/international/ articles-reports/2022/05/05/support-eu-army-grows-across-europe-following-russ. Accessed on: 11 May 2022.

11 Stolle, D. and McGill, J. (5 May 2022) Support For Ukraine is Strong in Europe, but Nations Are Not As United As It Looks. *YouGov*. https://yougov.co.uk/topics/ international/articles-reports/2022/05/05/support-ukraine-strong-europe-nati ons-are-not-unit. Accessed on: 11 May 2022.

12 World Food Programme (2022)*Food Security Implications Of The Ukraine Conflict*. Rome: WFP. 1.

13 Tisdall, S. (27 May 2022) Running On Empty: Five Ways Food And Security Overlap. *The Guardian Weekly*.

14 Diamant, J. (24 July 2017) Ethnic Russians in Some Former Soviet Republics Feel a Close Connection to Russia. *Pew Research Center*. www.pewresearch.org/fact-tank/2017/07/24/ethnic-russians-in-some-former-soviet-republics-feel-a-close-connection-to-russia. Accessed on: 11 May 2022.

15 Tertrais, B. (14 February 2022) Why Ukraine Matters to Russia: The Demographic Factor. *Institut Montaigne*. www.institutmontaigne.org/en/blog/why-ukraine-matt ers-russia-demographic-factor. Accessed on: 11 May 2022.

16 United Nations (UN) (2021) *Our Common Agenda – Report of the Secretary General.* New York: UN. 3.

17 *Ibid.* 14.

18 United Nations Development Programme (UNDP) (2022) *New Threats to Human Security in the Anthropocene: Demanding Greater Solidarity.* New York: UNDP. iii.

19 I've adapted this from the book title of: Therborn, G. (1980) *The Ideology of Power and the Power of Ideology.* London: Verso.

20 Foroohar, R. (2019) *Don't Be Evil: How Big Tech Betrayed its Founding Principles - and All of Us.* New York: Currency. 121–122.

21 Foa, R.S., Klassen, A., Slade, M., Rand, A. and R. Williams (2020) *The Global Satisfaction with Democracy Report 2020.* Cambridge UK: Centre for the Future of Democracy. This study involved the biggest global dataset on attitudes to democracy ever undertaken, using a dataset of over 4 million people that included over 25 international surveys covering 154 countries, over the 25 year period of 1995–2020.

22 Fritz, S.M. and edited by Morel, D. (2019) *Our Human Herds: The Theory of Dual Morality.* Indianapolis: DogEar Publishing.

23 Wrangham, R. (2020) *The Goodness Paradox: How Evolution Made Us Both More and Less Violent.* London: Profile Books.

24 Ord, T. (2020) *The Precipice: Existential Risk and the Future of Humanity.* London: Bloomsbury Publishing.

25 Baldwin, P. (2020) *Fighting the First Wave: Why the Coronavirus Was Tackled So Differently Across the Globe.* Cambridge: Cambridge University Press. 8.

26 *Ibid.* 7.

27 World Health Organisation (2022). See: www.who.int/data/gho/data/themes/hiv-aids. Accessed on: 16 February 2022.

28 www.statista.com/statistics/novel-coronavirus-2019ncov-deaths-worldwide-by-country. Accessed on: 9 March 2022.

29 Note: This is calculated as body mass index (BMI), meaning a person's weight in kilograms divided by the square of height in metres, with those overweight falling between 25 and 29.9, with those between 30 to 39.9, categorised as obese.

30 World Obesity Federation (March 2021) *COVID-19 and Obesity: The 2021 Atlas: The Cost of Not Addressing the Global Obesity Crisis.* www.worldobesity.org. Accessed on: 9 March 2022.

31 Wang, H. et al (10 March 2022) Estimating Excess Mortality Due to the COVID-19 Pandemic: A Systematic Analysis of COVID-19-Related Mortality 2020–2021. *The Lancet.* www.thelancet.com/journals/lancet/article. Accessed on: 11 March 2022.

32 World Health Organisation. (5 May 2022) www.who.int/news/item/05-05-2022-14.9-million-excess-deaths-were-associated-with-the-covid-19-pandemic-in-2020-and-2021. Accessed on: 5 May 2022.

33 *The Economist* (5 May 2022) The Pandemic's True Death Toll. www.economist.com/graphic-detail/coronavirus-excess-deaths-estimates. Accessed on: 8 May 2022.

34 Baldwin, P. (2020) *op. cit.* 9.

35 *Ibid.* 12.

36 Spiegelhalter, D. and Masters, A. (13 June 2021) What Were Some of the Collateral Effects of Lockdowns? *The Observer.*

37 Stoye, G., Warner, **M.** and Zaranko**, B. (February 2022)** The NHS backlog recovery plan and the outlook for waiting lists. *Institute for Fiscal Studies.* https://ifs.org.uk/publications. Accessed on: 9 March 2022.

38 International Labour Organisation (ILO) (2022) *World Employment and Social Outlook Trends 2022*. Geneva: International Labour Office.

39 Yasin, Y.J., Grivna, M. & Abu-Zidan, F.M. (September 2021)Global Impact of COVID-19 Pandemic on Road Traffic Collisions. *World Journal of Emergency Surgery* 16, 51. https://wjes.biomedcentral.com/articles. Accessed on: 16 February 2022.

40 National Highway Traffic Safety Administration (June 2021) *Fatalities Data Show Increased Traffic Fatalities During Pandemic.* www.nhtsa.gov/press-releases/2020-fatality-data-show-increased-traffic-fatalities-during-pandemic; and US Government Accountability Office (January 2022) *During COVID-19, Road Fatalities Increased and Transit Ridership Dipped.* www.gao.gov/blog/during-covid-19-road-fatalities-increased-and-transit-ridership-dipped. Both Accessed on: 16 February 2022.

41 Editorial. (5 February 2022) Managing The Opioid Crisis in North America and Beyond. *The Lancet.* 399 (10324). 495.

42 McGreal, C. (5 September 2021) Opioids Have Killed 600,000 Americans. The Sacklers Just Got Off Basically Scot-free. *The Guardian*; and BMJ (9 March 2022) Opioid Lawsuits: Sackler Family Agree Final $6bn Civil Settlement with US States. *BMJ* 2022; 376 doi: https://doi.org/10.1136/bmj.o616. Accessed on: 8 May 2022.

43 Krelle, H. and Tallack, C. (23 March 2021) *One Year On: Three Myths About COVID-19 that the Data Proved Wrong.* The Health Foundation. Note: 'life-years lost' is estimated from the difference between the age the person died and the life expectancy of someone that age. The authors acknowledge that people who died from the virus were more likely to have experienced co-morbidities than their peers, with implication for their lower life expectancy. Accordingly, data for lost life-years may be over-estimates. However, their calculations excluded the excess deaths that happened during the pandemic, but were not directly caused by it.

44 *Ibid.* 7.

45 Gray, J. (11–17 June 2021) China's Covid Cover-Up? *New Statesman.*

46 Note: this is a central point made by The People's Vaccine campaign.

47 Mathieu, E., Ritchie, H., Ortiz-Ospina, E. et al. (2021) *A Global Database of COVID-19 Vaccinations.* Nat Hum Behav. Our World in Data.

48 Our World in Data. https://ourworldindata.org/coronavirus. Accessed on: 16 February 2022.

49 Lauerman, J. (8 February 2022) Merck's Covid Pill Fumble Gives Pfizer Potential $17 Billion Win. *Bloomberg.* www.bloomberg.com/news/newsletters/2022-02-08/coronavirus-daily-merck-covid-pill-fumble-gives-pfizer-big-win. Accessed on: 13 March 2022.

50 Institute for Fiscal Studies (2021) *Autumn Budget and Spending Review 2021*: https://ifs.org.uk/budget-2021. Accessed on: 9 March 2022.

51 Brien, P. and Keep, M. (7 December 2021)*Public Spending During the Covid-19 Pandemic.* House of Commons Library. 4. Accessed on: 9 March 2022.

52 U.S. Department of the Treasury (September 2021) *American Rescue Plan: Treasury's Progress and Impact After 6 Months.* https://home.treasury.gov/system/files/136/American-Rescue-Plan-Six-Month-Report.pdf. Accessed on: 9 March 2022.

53 Quammen, D. (2013) *Spillover: Animal Infections and the Next Human Pandemic.* London: Vintage. 41.

54 Harper, K. (2020) *The Fate of Rome: Climate, Disease, and the End of an Empire.* Princeton, N.J.: Princeton University Press. 4.

2

ALL THE RAGE

Fear and Loathing in the Politics of Resentment

A key paradox underpinning this rancorous politics is that people's economic impulse to shelter inside a big trading bloc in a pitiless world economy is offset by their political impulse to recapture self-determination from distant bureaucrats in those very same blocs. What is the 'self' to be determined here? How does the individual self-align with tribal belonging? Where is the blueprint for the human mould? This leads into the next chapter about self and group identity, and how far such provide an anchor in stormy political seas.

Many observers depict the current unsettling period as exceptionally fractious and fraught, and traceable most immediately to the financial crisis in 2008–09. Pervasive volatility of events and erratic behaviour by some world leaders confound convention and prediction. They seem to portend relentless political turbulence. For some who feel unease at the perplexing form and pace of change, their exasperation spills over to rage on social media and in the street. In short, we are experiencing widespread *dislocation*, whereby we seem off-key with both planet and fellow humans, and left wondering about what is happening to the world we thought we knew.

This unmooring is manifest in increased disorder within post–Cold War geopolitics; disruption of traditional boundaries of government, parliament and judiciary that may betoken more autocratic rule; displacement of people from their sense of attachment, evident most distressingly in refugee plight; and unravelling in party political affiliation and support structures for social solidarity. In total, this precariousness represents a 'new normal' in which the principle of social contract has been cumulatively dislodged. While the extent and reach of the imbalance can be argued, confusion about how to cast it is evident in the various labels used to define it: the age of uncertainty, impunity, anxiety,

DOI: 10.4324/9781003106593-3

rebellion, and the like. Collins dictionary selected *permacrisis* as their word of 2022, signifying the year's unremitting upheaval and insecurity.

Clearly, these intemperate times have not come out of the blue. When I was coming of age in the late 1960s, social disturbance was auguring a 'new age' of Aquarius, promising humankind peace and harmony. Thirty years ago, some speculated that we lived in a 'terminal' age: post-Keynesianism, Marxism, Fordism, Modernism, and indeed the end of history itself. In the case of some at least, these mortalities have proved to be exaggerated. But even though the long view cautions against claims of seismic paradigm shifts, it's hard to deny that we live at one of those historic moments of makeover.

At the same time, this book argues that the prevailing picture of an optimistic past that is fast disappearing is too simple. The 1960s decade was not only about peace and love. It also hosted the Cuban nuclear crisis amid a perilous Cold War; assassinations of the two Kennedys and Martin Luther King; racial animosity associated with civil rights struggles; persistent anti-colonial conflicts; the Chinese Cultural Revolution, and war in Vietnam.

Adopting a wider canvas for our current tumult, we can picture humans in the present period – referred to, by some, as the *anthropocene*, meaning an era of the Earth's domination by human activity – being cast adrift from humanity itself. At a time of supposed hyper-connection, many experience the bond of common ancestry and earthly abode as fragile, and fear further fracturing of social fellowship.

Indeed, as we'll discover in later chapters, some argue that we live at a time of social atomisation, which thins the connective tissue between the individual human and humanity. We may ask whether 'humanity' itself really exists as a unit. Do people have a conscious tie with wider humankind to the extent that we all share a sense of the common good? Can this awareness be activated to address collective threats such as climate change? Or are we hardwired to see the world mainly through self or tribal interest?

You may think that such deep questions demand calm consideration. However, the digital age is inconducive to tranquil reflection. Darroch,[1] the UK ambassador to the US before he offended Trump, has written that the politician who can dominate social media directs the world, because it is a world in which outrage is highly transmittable. Since the centre ground has become less inhabited, electoral success entails riling up the political base, to optimise your side's turn-out. A related growth in illiberal democracy seems to follow.

Even leaving aside authoritarian regimes like China and Russia, by 2020, five of the most populous *democratic* countries had populist leaders installed, accounting for just over 2 billion people. Four of these were disposed to right-wing authoritarian nationalism: India; United States; Brazil; and the Philippines. In the case of the latter, Duterte was replaced in 2022 with Marcos, son of the former dictator, while Duterte's daughter was installed as vice-president. Autocracy likes to keep things in the family. Even with Trump's unruly dispatch from the Oval Office, populism's appeal in the US is markedly resilient, with Trumpism having captured the Republican Party. And here it's important to note that while populist leadership is rooted in the cult of personality, you can have Trumpism without Trump himself necessarily remaining the figurehead. The US mid-term elections did not deliver the 'red wave' that Trump predicted. Many candidates he endorsed proved too dud for the electorate. Conversely, DeSantis, who many republicans see as a preferable challenger for their party's choice for Presidential candidate in the 2024 contest, secured victory as Governor of Florida by an impressive margin of 19.4 percent. When asked in advance of the electoral count, whether Republican results – good or bad – should be attributable to him, he replied: *'Well, I think if they win, I should get all the credit. If they lose, I should not be blamed at all, OK?'*. In his unabashed vanity, it's always heads I win, tails you lose.

He declared his third-bid candidacy for President in a rambling address, replete with the usual deluded achievements, and was immediately greeted with a swathe of pessimistic prognoses about its outcome. It was said that his time was done. His signature conceit had become tiresome. He had lost the blessing of Murdoch. Campaign funders were fighting shy of his disruptive brand. His electioneering would be haunted by the special prosecutor established to investigate his alleged misuse of government documents and his suspected involvement in subversive attempts to nullify the 2020 Presidential contest. But, at the time of writing it is not clear that Trumpist appeal has significantly abated. Yes, republicans only narrowly won the House and failed to win the Senate. However, around 300 of their mid-term candidates – the majority – seeking various offices of state affirmed totally or partially the Big Lie that Biden wasn't the legitimate President. In turn, this reflects various polls showing that around 70 percent of republican supporters believe that the 2020 result was a cheat. So even though Trump zealots in key states like Pennsylvania and Michigan, and high-profile devotees like Kari Lake in Arizona, lost in the mid-terms, the Republican Party remains in the grip of an anti-democratic conspiracy story.

A much less noticed frailty of American democracy is the persistent low voter turnout, despite some recent improvement. A Pew Research study,[2] contrasting franchise use by the voting-age population in the 2020 presidential election with that of recent national elections in 49 other countries, graded the US as 31st. Such patterns amplify the importance of riling up the base to motivate their electoral participation.

In the other America, despite his evident incompetence, and depraved cannibalism boast, Bolsonaro's firm support base made the 2022 Brazilian Presidential election close-run. His rival, Luiz Inácio Lula da Silva, won on 50.9 percent, a mere 1.8 percentage point lead. On that narrow victory, he faces a deeply divided country, with millions of disaffected *bolsonaristas*; a Congress controlled by Bolsonaro's allies; the legacy of graft that thrived under the previous regime of his Workers' Party; a tight fiscal squeeze in a listless economy; and the formidable challenge to restore the extensive deforestation in the Amazon sponsored by his predecessor. Even within the comfort zone of a widespread leftist shift in Latin America, Lula has not escaped the embedded influence of his far-right opponent.

Turning to the limited democratic space in the Middle East, Netanyahu's renewed parliamentary majority following the 2022 election – the fifth in less than four years –depended on his right-wing party securing support from various Religious Zionist groupings even further to the right, or a compromise coalition with centrist blocs. The former option involves accommodation not only with the ultra-Orthodox, but also with ultranationalist interests like the Jewish Power party, under the leadership of Ben-Gvir, who is keen to support Jewish settlements in the occupied West Bank, and to impose strict loyalty tests on Arab Israeli citizenship.

In short, millions of people across even the democratic world affirm the redemptive power of 'saviour' leaders, whose calling card is an unrepentant relish in being the bruiser, imperious and bombastic. Thus in this chapter, focus is on this brand, with due recognition of the political intelligence behind its seeming imbecility. To start, let's pause to inspect core ideas behind standard 'explanations' for growth in populist, nationalist and autocratic politics, exploring how they may relate to each other. First is the view that a lot of current political debate is being pitched in terms of establishment elites versus the people.

Disestablishing the Global Elite

The idea of an untainted people, kept in check by a crooked select few at the top, lies at the heart of the way populism is discussed in the current period. For instance, Mudde and Kaltwasser define populism as:[3]

> ....a thin-centred ideology that considers society to be ultimately separated into two homogeneous and antagonistic groups, 'the pure people' and 'the corrupt elite', and which argues that politics should be an expression of the volonté generale (general will) of the people.

In this view, populism is not in itself one clear set of ideas about how the world works. It can be associated with a radical right or left view, both agreeing in their own way that liberal democracy, with its many factions and lobbies, hides the basic divide between two main rivals. In identifying heroes and villains, moral distinction is drawn.[4] The *people* are exalted as innately righteous, while the elite are irredeemably iniquitous. The people no longer connect with what they consider as the out-of-touch political class, and their cronies in the legal, academic and bureaucratic professions. It is an age of anti-politics.

With radical right populism, 'the people' are further parsed into the 'real' people and those who don't belong, outsiders like migrants who can be taken to pollute the purity of proper citizenry. Something of this moral match between the common people and social virtue is captured in Nigel Farage's speech, delivered as a narrow Brexit win was in sight:[5] 'this will be a victory for real people, a victory for ordinary people, a victory for decent people'. The inference is that nearly half the voting British public was not only deviant, but also disreputable. It's the reverse side of Hillary Clinton's reference to 'the basket of deplorables'.

In populist rendering, the big moral tale features an ignoble establishment ever keen to subvert the general will of the real people. Then into this crusade steps the valiant leader, honoured to wear the mantle of the 'little guy', in a gladiatorial combat with corruption and betrayal. He, and it's usually he, is decidedly on the side of 'regular folk', to whom he is saying, in effect, 'you may be thought of as untutored and unrefined by those on top. But I hear your voice. Indeed, I *am* your voice!' And this is a key paradox in populism: the strong leader posing as merely the instrument of a mass movement.

To many, the idea that ultra privileged figures like Trump, Johnson, or Berlusconi are best placed to champion the masses is absurd. This actually misses the point. It's more important that the followers believe that their leaders *like* them than for the leaders *to be like* them. People side with those they think are on their side, value those who claim to share their values, especially when those values appear to be derided by mainstream opinion. Trump captured this fellow-feeling well in an electoral speech in 2016:[6]

> *While my opponent slanders you as deplorable and irredeemable, I call you hardworking American patriots who love your country and want a better future for all of our people....Above all else, you are Americans - and you are entitled to leadership that honours you, cherishes you, and defends you.*

Similarly, Marine Le Pen, in her Presidential campaign launch in 2017,[7] proclaimed that '....against the candidates, either left wing or right wing, but both guided by financial interests, I am the candidate of the people'. In fact, populist leadership goes further. It proclaims a special bond, as if leader and people are one and the same. They don't need to feel the pulse; they *are* the pulse. The former Irish head of government, Eamon DeValera, expressed this sense well when he reflected on how he had ruled: 'when I wanted to know what the Irish people wanted, I had only to examine my own heart....'[8]

The pitch of global against the local or national is a second facet of populism. Often, it is presented in three distinct, though linked, aspects: economy; culture; and security. There is the argument that the welfare of global interests, such as high finance and international corporations, is privileged over that of the national economy. Hence this process will include uncompetitive trade deals, and the export of jobs to foreign locations where labour is cheaper and regulation lighter. Next is rampant immigration, a process that is seen in terms of stealing jobs from native workers, but perhaps even more insidiously of whittling away cultural identity and national values. Finally, there is the import of what is depicted as the barbaric ideology of Islamic fundamentalism through the ill-controlled flow of Muslim refugees and migrants.

One example of how these aspects are woven together in the doomsday messages of populist leaders is Marine Le Pen's representation of globalisation as 'social dumping':[9]

> *It is called the global economy ....(which has) weakened the natural defences of our nation and deprived it of all these descending attributes: borders, national currency, the power over its laws, economic policymaking, and it allowed the birth of a new form of globalisation which is rapidly growing: Islamic fundamentalism....*

In her portrait, French leaders have betrayed their people by opting for a lop-sided globalism that profits the few; robs the many of livelihood and dignity; promotes individualism over national solidarity, and opens the door to outsiders, who far from embracing the values of their host nation, exploit the western concept of freedom to wage terrorist war on their streets. In the latter regard, she is warning in effect: 'beware those enemies who bite the hand that feeds them'.

The first round of the 2022 French Presidential election saw Macron on top with 27.84 percent to Le Pen's 23.15 percent, with the latter narrowly edging the radical-leftist Mélenchon (21.95 percent) to make the dual one between herself and Macron in the final round. Adding Le Pen's tally with that of an even more extreme candidate, Zemmour, the total far-right share of the vote was around 30 percent, an unprecedented showing for the bloc. The far left and right vote together came to over half (52 percent). Ejected decisively from the race were the two traditional rivals: the Socialist candidate received a derisory 1.8 percent, coming 10th in a field of 12, while the Republican contender achieved 4.8 percent – a measure of the political transformation that the once dominant parties were reduced to less than 7 percent in total. In the runoff between Macron and Le Pen, the former secured 58.54 percent to the latter's 41.46 percent. Though apparently commanding, this lead was notably less than in 2017, with the two-thirds over one-third advantage Macron achieved against Le Pen. Indeed, it's worth recalling that her father attained only 18 percent in the 2002 runoff.

Given the final stark option, it could be said that many French electors were left with Hobson's choice. That may explain the high abstention rate for France of 28 percent – the worst since 1969. Polls suggest that 42 percent of Mélenchon's

7.7 million voters switched to Macron in the second round, 17 percent of them went for Le Pen, while the rest abstained. The geographical spread of the votes reflect France's political rupture:[10]

> Fully 85 percent of the electorate in Paris backed Mr Macron. In the village of Auchy-les-Mines, in the former mining basin of the north, 69percent voted for Ms Le Pen. Thanks to campaign promises to ease the cost of living and stand up for the downtrodden, Ms Le Pen pushed out of the rustbelt of the north and east, and her party's old stronghold in Provence and the Riviera, into many rural and semi-rural parts.

Former banker, Macron – labelled *le président des riches* by opponents – drew high support from the business and professional classes, and the beneficiaries of higher education, both concentrated in large urban areas.[11] Le Pen pitched herself as the champion of the socially neglected and the culturally scorned. Importantly, her rhetoric of foreboding is offset with an assurance that France is rediscovering its national consciousness, a revival that nevertheless demands vigilance – western tolerance can be taken as weakness. What is needed is an economic patriotism that includes forms of trade protectionism, but also involves preference for French-made goods and French workers. Public procurement, for instance, should prioritise French companies and jobs. Correspondingly, French nationals should take precedence in the allocation of national social services and housing, since charity begins at home. At the same time, there should be zero tolerance of crime, and fortification of national security. All this demands restoration of state authority. But it is that very sovereignty that is compromised by the domineering European Union.

This antagonism to global institutions and their perceived thwarting of national will was evident in Bolsonaro's address to the 74th General Assembly of the United Nations in September 2019: 'We are not here to erase nationalities and sovereignties in the name of an abstract 'global interest'. This is not the Global Interest organisation. It is the United Nations organisation. And so it must remain'!

While boasting about Brazil's recovery from the stagnation and corruption of the preceding socialist regime, he talked of liberating business from bureaucracy and regulation, and of installing the free market and privatisation. Importantly, these steps were linked to restoration of family and religious values, which he saw as central to Brazilian traditions. Since this agenda was within Brazil's domain, part of its 'sacred sovereignty', he was saying in effect, 'while we mind our business, you mind yours'. Thus, for example, he did not accept environmentalist 'interference' in the Amazon: 'It is a fallacy to say that the Amazon is the heritage of humanity, and a misconception, as scientists certify, to say the Amazon, our forest, is the lungs of the world'.[12]

Prophets of Populism

Similar concern to protect 'spheres of influence' in the 'new global' is found in the views of Russian philosopher, Alexander Dugin. In summary, his position is that while Russians were happy to discard totalitarian communism, the implosion of the Soviet Union and its satellites by 1991 had created what the Americans took to be a unipolar world. As leader of western liberal democracy and its assumed twin, capitalism, the US behaved as if it had unchallenged supremacy in a new world order that demoted Russia as a bit player. Moreover, there was even western intellectual speculation about whether this was the 'end of history' in the sense that if history was understood to involve the clash of ideologies about the best form of society and humanity, the contest was over, with liberal democratic capitalism the last man standing.

Since then, Dugin argues, 'traditional' societies like Russia have been subject to an ideological offensive, based on the boast that West is best. This has led to an attempt to universalise beliefs held dear in the West, concerning secularisation, scientific rationalism, social liberalism, human rights, and the like. Such a messianic mission to proselytise does not respect cultural difference. In Dugin's view, it fails to appreciate that truth is often a matter of belief, and fact is often about interpretation.

For Russia and other 'traditional' societies to push back on this conceit, they had to regain geo-political influence by a new alignment that might include the Russian Federation, China, India, the Baltic region, and at least parts of eastern and central Europe. Seen by Dugin as strategically placed between East and West, Russia is well-positioned to help forge this Eurasian bloc. To support its greater collaboration, and act as a counter-weight to American domination – or hegemony – it would be useful to develop a common ideological frame.

So far, this has been tentative. It does seem to chime with some key tenets held dear by right populism in the West: hostility to globalism and cosmopolitanism; reservation about international institutions; belief in a world of sovereign, culturally distinct nations; respect for Christian tradition and the importance of both faith and reason. Dugin slates Atlanticism, which he sees as American power masquerading as defender of the 'free world', an ultra-liberalism in terms both of the economy and moral principles. While Dugin's direct influence on Putin's thinking is subject to dispute, his credo chimes with that of the Russian president, as evidenced in the ideologue's hard-line acclaim for Putin's militarist expansionism. In August 2022, Dugin's daughter, Darya, was murdered just outside Moscow in a car bomb, thought to be intended for him.

Putin's territorial ventures – the second Chechen war, invasion of Georgia (2008), annexation of Crimea in 2014, leading to his subsequent assault on Ukraine, and attempted annexation of the Donetsk and Luhansk People's Republics, Zaporizhzhia and Kherson regions into the Russian Federation – manifest this ambition of Greater Russia. Having climbed to the top of the power pyramid in Russia, he wants to restore Russia's place near the top of geopolitical power pyramid.

This kind of argument about power and spheres of influence in today's world can be set within Huntington's frame of 'a clash of civilisations'.[13] Briefly, his argument is that in modern history, distinct periods can be discerned. Over centuries, nation-states emerged in the West, and cooperated and fought with each other, and then those among them with imperialist ambition colonised large parts of the world. The onset of the Cold War saw bipolar conflict between communism and capitalism, represented primarily by the Soviet Union and the US, often played out in 'proxy' wars in parts of the global south. In the post-Cold War world, conflict is destined to be less about ideology and economics and more about culture, and its associated aspects such as ancestry, religion, heritage, language, history, values, and such like. These 'civilisation identities' will manifest themselves in symbols of crosses, crescents, head coverings, flags, etc. and whatever of western assumption about the universalist nature of its system, global politics will be multi-polar.

Far from coming out on top, the reshaping power structure is seeing the West lose ground, as Asian civilisations expand and resurgent Islam ascends in terms of demography and influence. Societies with a common cultural bond will collaborate, and assemble round the lead states of their civilisation. Given that the West's universalist conceit will intensify enmity with other civilisations, particularly Islam and China, its endurance hinges on Americans prioritising their western affinity; westerners seeing their civilisation as distinctive but not universal; and western societies banding together to face challenges from non-western societies.

Through all this shift and sift, comes real prospect that that part of humanity once belittled as the Third World will see the global power axis tilt in their favour. We were raised to see somewhere like China as an un-developed peasant society, knowing next to nothing about its philosophers like Confucius (551–479 BCE) and his thoughts on the cultivated human, distinguished by virtues of filial piety, humane benevolence (jen), authenticity (Xin), and rectitude and propriety (li). Similarly, we were uninformed about the country's previous prestige in the Han Dynasty (206 BCE–220 CE), and particularly in the Tang Dynasty (618–907 CE), an acclaimed 'golden age' of cosmopolitanism, marked by educational and cultural advance. Now China is set to take centre-stage again, and such geo-political realignment is disconcerting for those whose western sensibilities lets them see the world only in their image.

Radical Right

For some on the Radical Right, it's too late for the West. Faye,[14] one of its leading theorists, sees humanity at breaking point, due to a 'convergence of catastrophes' that is pushing places like Europe back to the Middle Ages. In his ominous narrative, 'colonisation' of the Northern hemisphere by peoples of the global south, and the failure of multi-racial and multicultural societies, will likely ignite ethnic civil war in Europe. Against such prospect, there must be recognition of 'bloodlines', and of nativism – a belief in the priority that must be accorded the native-born over migrants.

In this view, economically, much of the global north suffers from an ageing unproductive population that is welfare-dependent in an economy that on the one hand invests faith in speculative financial markets, and on the other, resembles the 'Third World' because of unrestrained immigration of unskilled people. Meanwhile, the global south is generating social chaos by displacing their traditional cultures through rapid industrialisation. Ecologically, we are faced with uninhibited and rising pollution that threatens human, though not earthly, survival. Such environmental vandalism is the outcome of universal industrialism, one of the myths of egalitarian progressivism.

For Faye, the answer lies in what he coined as 'archeofuturism' – not simply a 'back to the future' approach, but a bringing together of technoscience and archaic – that is foundational – European values. Social and cultural decay in Europe is reflected in the growth of crime and drug abuse; disintegration of the family within the permissive society; decline in quality education in favour of progressive education; and reappearance of poverty.

In his telling, all these assumed calamities are in part the outcome of colonisation by American culture, but are aggravated by the ascendency of zealous religious cults, especially those within Islam:[15]

> *The rise of radical Islam is the backlash to the excesses of the cosmopolitanism of modernity that wanted to impose on the entire world the model of atheist individualism, the cult of material goods, the loss of spiritual values and the dictatorship of spectacle. In reaction to this aggression, Islam has radicalised, just as it was already becoming once again a religion of domination and conquest, in conformity with its tradition.*

Faced with this supposed upheaval, it's pointless to look to the elite and their experts. They are the authors of the misfortune. For Faye, their deceitful utopian optimism operates within a system of democracy, which itself is inherently lethargic, indecisive and weak. Any chance of renewal demands a new strong form of government – shorthand for right-wing authoritarianism, within not nationalism, but European nationalism, which in his terms, means white nationalism.[16] Faye belongs to the French tradition of the Radical Right, often referred to as the New Right (*Nouvelle Droite*). Perhaps its key figure is Alain de Benoist, who, in 1999 with colleague Charles Champetier, brought together the thinking behind the New Right that goes back to 1968. Published in English in 2012 as *Manifesto for a European Renaissance*, it champions rediscovery of what it sees as authentic values and customs, and the related right of people to resist imposition of 'sameness' under the guise of multiculturalism and global markets.

Identifying this historical moment of crisis as a turning point, the 'manifesto' sees modernity as a convergence of five processes: *individualisation*, involving rejection of what was considered outdated communalism; *massification*, through embracing homogenised lifestyle and conduct; *desacralisation*, through shedding the great religious chronicles for scientific understanding; *rationalisation*, through the supremacy accorded to reason, technicality, and the free market; and *universalisation*, through holding up a model society applicable worldwide. It sees some of these processes rooted in Christian thinking about being, the nature of the universe, and ultimate reality (metaphysics).

It traces individualism to the tenet of individual salvation and personal relation to the divine. Egalitarianism is seen as derivative from ideas of redemption available to all humanity, not just a chosen people. Progressivism can be sourced to the idea of history as having a planned beginning and end, and universalism to the idea of a revelation that directs all along the same path. In this framework:[17]

> *Humanity is understood to be the sum of rational individuals who, through self-interest, moral conviction, fellowship or even fear are called upon to realise their unity in history. In this perspective, the diversity of the world becomes an obstacle, and all that differentiates men is thought to be incidental or contingent, outmoded or even dangerous....(modernity) attempts by every available means to uproot individuals from their individual communities, to subject them to a universal mode of association. In practice, the most efficient means for doing this has been the marketplace.*

Essentially, they contend that this modernist system betrays the liberation and equality it promises. Freedom at best is just formal, since people are under domination from both techno-science and market. Equality has been unattained, due both to Communism's tyrannical regimes and liberal capitalism's inequity, through which all aspects of human existence are commercialised. Liberalism and Marxism essentially share the same worldview embedded in the Enlightenment, with its belief in progress, rationality, egalitarianism, and primacy of economics. Given its fundamental flaws, modernity is imploding. Like all aspects of social life, politics has been demeaned to a marketplace. Voters have become consumers. Offered a false impression of choice, they're stuck with parties whose convergent policies and programmes amount to slight variations of welfare capitalism. The competitive 'political market' is in reality a monopoly.

For the Radical Right, the answer lies in the founding of 'sovereign spaces' freed from this control and its attendant void and disenchantment. This involves giving people back their identity in a specific time and place – their roots – within a particular culture. Without this anchor in the singular – that is a distinctive historical period, country, way of life, sense of ancestry – people can be made subject to absolute, universal, and eternal laws, a process that augurs totalitarianism. Time does not work in a progressive line, since a people's past and future inform their present. Thus, origins, heritage, and memory are crucial to being and becoming. From this standpoint:[18]

> ....man as such does not exist, because his membership within humanity is always mediated by a particular cultural belonging. This observation does not stem from relativism. All men have in common their human nature, without which they would not be able to understand each other, but their common membership in the species always expresses itself in a single context.

The argument here is that the individual is always contextual, that each of us is formed and fostered in a particular community to which we belong, with certain rights and duties. This distinctive association, with its grounding and bonding, is held to be under-appreciated by both modern individualism and universalism. Paradoxically, far from liberating the individual from parochial constraints of familial, tribal and religious adherence, modernity has created the isolated individual, feeling disconnected in an inhospitable world that is increasingly materialist, mechanistic and uniform. Real diversity has been sacrificed on the altar of homogeneity. We've gone from personal identity to the identical.

Absurdly, though often portrayed as xenophobic, the Radical Right poses as the true defender of diversity in the world, respecting its plurality of races, ethnicities and cultures. It claims that Modernism, with its universalist pretensions, has reduced people to what they have in common, thereby suppressing the richness of difference. In particular, the West has been engaged in a long-standing imperialist project: converting people on the basis of: religion (the Crusades); political model (colonialism); socio-economic model (capitalist development); and moral principles (human rights). Westernisation has become globalisation, with its ethnocentric notions of excellence and progress.

From this critique, the Radical Right project is about replacing this failed model with a multipolar world containing many civilisations – European, North American, South American, Arabic-Muslim, Chinese, Indian, Japanese etc. Rather than supplanting old tribal, provincial or national roots, these civilisations will provide a collective basis with which each individual can identify together with their shared humanity, to support collaborative responses to issues such as ecology. Power in this new world arena will be exercised rightly to resist meddling from, but not to encroach upon, another civilisation:[19] 'The main enemy of this pluriverse will be any civilisation pretending to be universal and regarding itself entrusted with a redeeming mission ('Manifest Destiny') to impose its model on all others'.

In the view of this Radical Right 'manifesto', accusations about its links with nationalist bigotry, racism, and anti-immigrant sentiment, are missing the true target. The real culprit behind deformed expression of belonging and loyalty, such as chauvinistic nationalism, is the globalist ideology that imposes uniformity and denies the primacy of difference.

Similarly, it suggests that its position is not racist, if racism is to be understood, separately or together, in three main claims: a racial hierarchy that allows for designation of races as superior and inferior; individual worth that can be construed from the race to which the individual belongs; and the view that race is the key determinant in human history. All three are dismissed as untrue. Indeed, they see the source of such contentions in scientific positivism that upholds inter-racial qualities and aptitudes to be measurable, and in social evolutionary theories about a single unified human history that can be broken into stages of development and advancement.

Likewise, they say their opposition to immigration is not down to prejudice. Rather, they dispute a world economic system that uproots people largely from poor to rich countries, often for their labour benefit to rich corporations, and propagates mass consumer advertising that creates an alluring picture of Western lifestyle to the world's impoverished. Subsequent big population shifts are seen to damage the stability and traditions of both vacated and host countries.

In a similar vein, the 'manifesto' acclaims anti-sexism, insisting that the real challenge to women comes from those who don't acknowledge feminine and masculine qualities, and see women as deficient men, a manipulative expression of male domination. With regard to labour and remuneration, it says it's on the side of the socially sidelined:[20]

> *In today's society, the attraction and promise of goods grow ever larger, but increasing also is the number of people whose buying power is stagnating or even diminishing. Thus, it is imperative to gradually disassociate work from income. The possibility must be explored of establishing a fixed minimum stipend or income for every citizen from birth until death and without asking anything in return.*

It's saying in effect that we've drifted from market economy to market society. To get back on track, we have to decouple the idea of human progress from economic growth, which itself is propelled by advertising devised to convince us that our happiness is found in commodities. An alternative agenda involves: being against big corporations and cities; returning to community and the human scale; controlling technology as part of a return to 'sound ecology' that uncovers nature as partner, rather than enemy or object; and protecting free speech, within rekindled critical thinking, all as part of a more participative democracy. Read as a whole, the central case is that there is a natural order, which is being subverted by liberals, leftists and globalists. Human debasement is fated when humans depart from their nature.

It's interesting how this right-wing thinking can present itself as the authentic defender of the normal constituency of the left – including opponents of big capital, advocates of environmentalism, marginalised workers, women, and so forth. They also share with a strand of the left, like Morris and Ruskin, a nostalgia for an arcadian, pastoral idyll, wherein humans could commune with nature and each other in a genuine way. This is not the only aspect that left and right populism share in common. Left populism also rails against an elite establishment, and its promotion of globalism, and the related financialisation of the economy. It also offers a version of economic nationalism that speaks to protecting home manufacturing, markets, trade, and blue collar labour. In France, as in the UK, this agenda can be traced from Mitterrand to Benn to Corbyn – socialism in one country; wariness of not only being subject to a market-driven bloc like the EU, but also of free trade, and big business. A lot of this rhetoric resonates in both political camps, though the end goal is very different.

Democratic illiberalism appears to most on the left to be an oxymoron. But its advocates are railing against what they see as the actual outcomes of undemocratic forces, such as supranational institutions, international legal systems that champion minority rights, and political creeds that promote cosmopolitanism. Instead, they favour the assumed harmony of ethno-nationalism and majoritarianism. While traditional mainstream conservatism has pitched itself as a critical friend of the Enlightenment and modernism, and valiant foe of fascism, this new brand of right-wing politics exhibits more ambivalence towards these tenets. By contrast, critics of liberalism on the left are prone to decry its hypocritical practice in the established hierarchies inherent in racism, sexism, colonialism, and the like. For them, it can be domination dressed up as liberation.[21]

Both left and right recognise the importance of political culture. With respect to the right, figures like Faye and de Benoist see themselves in the business of metapolitics. This goes back to Gramsci's emphasis on the importance of infiltrating ideas into political discourse to a point that they become 'the common sense' of how society is and should be. Metapolitics is about creating big narratives about social reality that gain command – or hegemony – and shift the terms of debate, thereby opening political space for great change. So it is that we can see how their ideas have come to frame Radical Right thinking about the supposed crisis of identity, leading in turn to populist talk about 'the great replacement'.

The Great Replacement

This concerns the view that the white Christian tradition of Europe is being supplanted by a massive influx of migrants from the Middle East and North Africa, mostly people of colour and of Muslim faith. It represents both desecration and cultural erasure.

One person prominently associated with this premonition is Renaud Camus. What he terms 'the great replacement', concerning the substitution of 'native' Europeans with populations of a different race, colour and creed, is part of a wider set of proxies imposed by a global elite he calls the Davocracy —named after the Swiss resort, Davos, which hosts an annual get-together of the Western world's movers and shakers. In short, this threat to white civilisation has to be seen as part of a global 'replacism', a fakeness whereby imitation is privileged over authenticity.

It's important to grasp this overall argument as being about a harmful shift from the natural to the unnatural. This elevation of the former is found in fascism as in the Nazi exaltation of the Volk, and their cultural expression, as embodying the true spirit of the nation. It links into a longer tradition of associating the urban as corruptive of good rural values – the decadence of the Sodom and Gomorras.

In the contemporary world, we have lots of examples of this alleged debasement. We have virtue-signalling for genuine virtue; fake news for real news; artificial hearts and intelligence for human hearts and intelligence; sprawling suburbia for distinctive town and country; shopping mall for traditional shopping; PVC for proper wood; tar and cement for earth, and so on. As I mentioned, these concerns about the inauthentic are not peculiar to the right. The left too has reservations about the shift to the 'false'. Camus insists that many of the modern replacements are 'faux'. They are forgeries. And further indication of the pervasiveness of this transplant lies in the replacement of:[22] '....residents by tourists, natives by non-natives, Europeans by Africans, White Anglo-Saxons by Afro-Americans and Latinos, mothers by surrogate mothers, men by women, women by inflatable dolls, men and women by robots....'

This counterfeit world of one big amusement park is making life itself unnatural, and its ultimate destiny is one in which humans are replaced by posthumans. In this understanding, Camus disowns much of the standard meaning of identity politics:[23]

> *Identity, always, is already a way of mourning the thing or being, a way of acknowledging their loss. Being* identical *is being exactly* like *something or somebody else: that is,* not *being it. Such is precisely the reason why, although I have much sympathy and admiration for them, I am not an* 'Identitarian'.

From his viewpoint, what makes places and cultures genuine and what we appreciate or disapprove about them, derives from the people and elites who moulded them and continue to imbue them with their essence. When under pretext of 'equality' and 'anti-racism', you challenge or change that essence, you destroy the integrity of the original and leave behind an inferior copy. Thereby, paradoxically, the very thing that attracts migrants to a particular place becomes corrupted the more migrants that are attracted, because their presence crowds out the uniqueness and lure of the 'real thing'. Taken to its ultimate conclusion, this process descends into what Camus refers to as 'Undifferentiated Human Matter'. This is where there are:[24] 'no races, no sexes, no cultures, no nationalities, no origins, no discrimination and no defining borders either, in short a general reversion of history and evolution of human society, to what biologists call *the Primeval Soup*'.

The intended appeal of this argument is clear. It is saying to those who feel dislocated in the contemporary world that the source of *displacement* lies in deliberate *replacement* at all levels. From the multitude of 'little replacements', such as elevation of popular over high brow culture, globalists have conspired to create a synthetic habitat that has robbed humans of the ability to distinguish and value the authentic over the bogus. It is a message that can tag conventional leftist agendas of environmentalism, and markets that work for workers, with rightist defence of heritage and culture and ethnic independence. Taken together, this agenda is deemed to be the natural order.

Yet, in the current sham world to which we have supposedly degenerated, mass movement of 'alien' people proceeds into Europe and North America, once seen as the innate domain of white people. In these terms, these migrants and refugees are 'inauthentic'. Together with worthless mass consumer culture designed to standardise and atomise, these processes are chipping away at distinctive European identity.

According to those who buy the replacement idea, this is not simply an immigration crisis. It is nothing less than invasion of white people's native soil. Interestingly, though the Radical Right disown the idea of universal human rights, they adopt the idea of 'rights' for their own purpose. They see it as the denial of the right for European peoples to their own history and homeland, an assault that justifies resistance. A distinctive slant on this perspective comes from Bat Ye'or (real name: Gisele Littman), who sees a pervasive conspiracy, involving a jihad strategy of world conquest, with its driving force, the Organisation of the Islamic Conference, based in Saudi Arabia. The plot is seen as being underpinned by Wahhabi ideology, which is a conservative purist form of Islam within the Sunni tradition, demanding a strict literal read of the Quran. All non-subscribers, including fellow Muslims, are tagged apostate.

For Bat Ye'or, one immediate project on the journey to universal caliphate – that is a worldwide Islamic state – is about creating a Euro-Arab Mediterranean civilisation – Eurabia – designed among other things to check American power and to destroy Israel. The specific instrument for achieving Eurabia is deemed to be the Euro-Arab Dialogue (EAD), set up in the 1970s in the context of the Oil Crisis, when Western powers were concerned about improving relations with Arab countries to ensure reliable oil supply.

Derivatives of these narratives are found in the work of others. For example, addressing what she considers to be detrimental change in the UK, Melanie Phillips attributes it to the legacy of lost empire and postcolonial guilt. Britain's establishment came to see the country's values as burdened with racist and nationalist bigotry. Reparation involved adjusting national culture and population makeup into a multicultural society. Traditional moral standards, the basis of Western civilisation, and rooted in Judaism and Christianity, had been discarded in favour of individualist lifestyle choices supported by indisputable rights:[25] 'The outcome has been the creation of a debauched and disorderly culture of instant gratification, with disintegrating families, feral children and violence, squalor and vulgarity on the streets'.

Phillips insists that whereas in the US at least there are culture wars, in Britain there has been only defeat and concession. Minorities demanding particular entitlement get used to capitulation from a flinching liberal elite, anxious not to be seen as reproachful. Those who protest this moral lapse are cast as intolerant, while prejudice is considered to be exclusively a problem of those with power. In this critique, multiculturalism, particularly involving an expanding Muslim constituency, has run alongside moral decadence, deliberately designed by a 'progressive intelligentsia' that is both national and global in its reach:[26]

> *As religion has retreated and morality becomes privatised, individual conscience has become universalised. The nation and its values are despised; moral legitimacy resides instead in a vision of universal progressivism, expressed through human rights law and such supranational institutions as the European Union, the United Nations or the International Criminal Court, and revolving around multiculturalism and minority rights.*

Douglas Murray echoes this theme in a wider framework. In his estimation, Europe is committing suicide. It is forfeiting its moral foundations, as exemplified in principles such as the Rule of Law, and replacing them with a relatively thin self-definition based on 'respect', 'tolerance' and 'diversity'. Indigenous Europeans are set to lose the only place they can call home. Manifestation of this change is to be found in 'streets in the cold and rainy northern towns of Europe filled with people dressed for the foothills of Pakistan or the sandstorms of Arabia'.[27] The scary bit for him is that at the very time Europe has been the recipient of a mass population movement, it has been losing confidence in its own convictions:[28]

> *The world is coming into Europe at precisely the moment that Europe has lost sight of what it is. And while the movement of millions of people from other cultures into a strong and assertive culture might have worked, the movement of millions of people into a guilty, jaded and dying culture cannot.*

Murray spells out the immigration pattern in the UK since the 1948 British Nationality Act, through to the Notting Hill riots a decade later and subsequent Race Relations Acts in 1965, 1968, and 1976, which came to make it illegal to discriminate against a person on the basis of colour, race, ethnicity, or national origins. Over a period of seventy years, what was thought of originally as a modest influx became a more considerable one.

It can be argued that migrants, largely from former colonies, have been returning the 'favour' of Empire, though they come wanting to be lawful citizens rather than illicit subjugators. Murray acknowledges this link to Empire, though, for him, whereas Empire was in the end temporary, this population shift seems permanent. The guilt about colonial history has been a key factor in what he calls Europe's 'existential tiredness', a resignation that perhaps the best way to elude an objectionable past is to dispel the identity and values that can be taken to underpin it.

Arguments that support immigration include: its economic benefits, since many who risk geographic mobility also seek social mobility through diligent enterprise; its corrective to an ageing society, since migrants are typically younger and can swell the working population to support the older economically inactive indigenous population; its cultural enrichment; and its creation of a more globalised society that in turn is best placed to thrive in a globalised world. While considering many such arguments, Murray remains unconvinced. Rather, he stresses the downsides in terms of: strain on a welfare state to which migrants may not have made full contribution; competition for jobs and related pay squeeze that impacts mostly on lower skilled workers; and expanded demand in the housing market, with possible extra pressure on the greenbelt. Such issues of advocacy and contest that feature prominently in the immigration debate are complicated, and merit detailed analysis.

Beyond these considerations, there is in the positions of authors like Phillips and Murray, a deeper sense of unease about what they see as the great pace and scale of cultural and religious transformation, and concern about possible security implications. Murray contends that if you allow entrance to the world's people, you're inviting intrusion of the world's problems:[29] 'Events that happened anywhere else in the world now had an impact inside Europe'.

This notion about immigration and its attendant multiculturalism eroding distinctive British customs and provoking discord is nothing new. Addressing similar themes in April 1968, the senior Tory, Enoch Powell, gave what has since been dubbed somewhat mistakenly as the 'Rivers of Blood' speech.[30] Quoting a constituent who felt that 'in fifteen or twenty years time the black man (would) have the whip hand over the white man', and then, quoting a more classical source, he warned that those whom the gods destroy, they first make mad. British people must be mad, he said, to let this happen. 'It is like watching a nation busily engaged in heaping its own funeral pyre....As I look ahead, I am filled with foreboding. Like the Roman, I seem to see *the Tiber foaming with much blood* '. Significantly, the language of 'whip hand', 'destroy', 'mad', 'funeral', 'foreboding' and 'blood' is carefully chosen to convey prophetic revelation of conquest and doom.

Deplorably, a very tiny extreme minority hearing these alarmist opinions see the scenario depicted as catastrophe that validates violent response. A few within that tiny cabal go on to translate hate into harm. The gunman responsible for the Christchurch massacre in New Zealand is held to have left what passes for a manifesto called: 'The Great Replacement: Toward a New Society', which contains many echoes of this deluded threat of incursion and takeover. Evident here is the confused message of these self-appointed defenders of white people. The 'manifesto' speaks of the need to foment racial, cultural and political conflict in the US so as to weaken its capacity to side with Muslims against Christian Europeans, as they supposedly did in Kosovo. Ebner[31] sees the killing of 77 people by the Norwegian Breivik in 2011, the Quebec city mosque shooting, and the Christchurch slaughter, as acts by radicals who see themselves as prescient 'inspirational terrorists' or 'invader crusaders' in the impending showdown race war, in which their heroic role is to expose the threat and incite division to bring the inexorable collision to a final reckoning.

Birds of a Feather

Unavoidably, an important factor in many 'takeover' narratives is the perceived impact of a rising Muslim population in places like Europe. No question, there is evidence of growth. It has nonetheless been highly exaggerated. Though it cannot be dismissed as a non-issue, as some on the left are inclined, it also can be subject to deliberate distortion by the right for their own political ends. Populist misuse of statistics triggers fear, and distorts the complexity behind migration patterns and projections.[32]

As can be seen from the table below, the basic trend in recent times has been an increase in Muslim population, alongside a relatively slight decrease in that of non-Muslim. Based on the zero migration scenario, Europe would see the share of Muslim population grow from its 2016 figure of 4.9 percent to 7.4 percent. In the medium migration scenario, Muslim population share

TABLE 2.1 Migration Effects on European Population

	2010	2016	2050	2050	2050
			Zero migration	Medium migration	High migration
Muslims	19,520,000	25,770,000	35,770,000	57,880,000	75,550,000
Non-Muslims	495,280,000	495,060,000	445,920,000	459,070,000	463,040,000
Total	514,810,000	520,830,000	481,690,000	516,950,000	538,600,000

Source: Pew Research Center: Europe's Growing Muslim Population. Estimates and Projections. 2017. Note: Europe is defined here as the 28 nations of the EU as then, plus Norway and Sweden.

grows to 11.2 percent, over double its 2016 share. But even under the peak scenario of high migration, Europe's population would be 14 percent Muslim by midcentury, hardly an impending Islamist conquest.

This is not to underplay the increasing factor of migration in Europe and across the world. As expressed by Norris and Inglehart:[33]

> The United Nations estimates that in 2015, 248 million migrants lived outside their country of birth. This figure has doubled since 1960 and continues to rise. Many migrants move to high-income European societies, which now contain 74 million or around 30 percent of the world's migrants. Europe now hosts more migrants than any other region. In absolute numbers, however, the United States has a larger immigrant population than any other country, with 49.7 million immigrants in 2017.

Yet this has to be put in perspective. Migrant numbers have doubled since 1960. But since then, the global population has increased over two and a half times, from 3 billion to what will become by the end of 2022, 8 billion. Nevertheless, some scholars frame the change in terms of a significant shift from white majorities in a number of western countries.

Kaufman projects that in a century, people of mixed race will constitute the largest group in places like Britain and America, and in two centuries from now, the vast majority of urbanites in Western societies will have mixed racial background. He recognises that for some, this transformation will be a disturbing process:[34] 'Many people desire roots, value tradition and wish to maintain continuity with ancestors who have occupied a historic territory'. Pinpointing likely impact, he says:[35]

> Together with New Zealand, North America is projected to be 'majority minority' by 2050, with Western Europe and Australia following suit later in the century. This shift is replacing the self-confidence of white majorities with an existential insecurity channelled by the lightning rod of immigration.

What do people make of immigration? A 2016 survey[36] involving 10 European countries explored outlooks on Muslims in general, and on refugees in particular. It found that negative attitudes toward Muslims were linked to belief that they were disinclined to take part in wider society. In every country surveyed, the main opinion was that, rather than espouse the country's traditions and culture, Muslims sought to be distinct from wider society, an opinion shared by six-in-ten or more in Greece, Hungary, Spain, Italy and Germany.

Similar attitudes prevailed about refugees. In half the 10 nations, 50 percent or more considered refugees a burden since they would take their jobs and social benefits, a view expressed by 82 percent in Hungary and 75 percent in Poland; by 46 percent in the UK; and by just under one third in Germany and Sweden, the only two countries where at least half thought refugees were an asset because of their diligence and aptitude. While most respondents – a median of 59 percent –regarded the refugee surge at the time as posing potential risk of more terrorism, there was less concern about support of current European Muslims for violent radical Islamists.

Regarding the worth of cultural diversity, relatively few felt that it brought benefit to their country, with Sweden (at 36 percent) registering highest agreement with the proposition that racial, ethnic and national mix made for a better place to live, with over half of Greeks and Italians and about four-in-ten Hungarians and Poles stating that ever more diversity worsened their society. In many countries, most saw diversity making no difference to quality of life.

Overwhelmingly, however, people in every country considered it very important that residents be able to speak the national language, a median of 77 percent expressing this view. While a median of 86 percent felt that it was important that people share national culture, a third felt that to be regarded as a national, it was very important for the persons to be born in the country, with a median of 58 percent considering this important.

Generally, religion was less seen as key to national identity, though in Greece, 54 percent felt that to be fully Greek, it was very important to be Christian. Significantly, views about what are essential to national identity – language, customs, native birth, and religion –varied across nations, with more exclusionary views expressed in southern and eastern Europe, in places like Greece, Italy, Hungary and Poland, with the least such views evident in Sweden, Germany and the Netherlands.

While concern to control immigration – essentially meaning to reduce it – was seen as a central driver of the Brexit vote, attitudes in Britain to the issue have mellowed. Having conducted a tracker survey on the topic since 2015, IPSOS has recently reported[37] that support for cutting immigration levels is at its lowest level since then. Alongside the 42 percent who preference reduction, 26 percent favour it staying the same and 24 percent approve its increase. More believe that immigration has had a positive return for Britain (46 percent) than a negative one (29 percent). For certain occupations – doctors, nurses, care workers, and seasonal fruit and vegetable pickers –less than one in five back reduction in numbers, and for others like construction workers and hospitality staff, less than one in four. Such attitudes may indicate enhanced appreciation that economies like Britain's need a stronger labour force base for much needed improvement in tax base and productivity, if only to support an increasing economically-dependent population of elderly.

Alongside this data, which invite nuanced appraisal, alarmist portrayal of Europe's supposed conversion to Eurabia raises many problems. It infers wrongly that migration to Europe is almost exclusively Muslim. For instance, between mid-2010 and mid-2016, an estimated 43 percent of migrants to the UK were Muslim. Migration within the EU tends to involve people with similar religious profile to that of Europeans overall. Rather than its characterisation as one united bloc, the Muslim population itself is diverse, with varied levels of religious conviction and identity. Apart from not distinguishing migrants in general from those that are Muslim, little distinction is drawn between those who are short-stay compared to long-term and permanent, between those of recent arrival, and those of Muslim background.

It should be noted that recently the refugee component of this migration is coming from the Middle East and Afghanistan, conflict zones in which leading western powers have been implicated. Moreover, some countries, like Poland and Hungary, whose leaders speak ominously about threats to Christian heritage, have actually miniscule Muslim populations. Finally, the implausible idea of a plot by Europe's governing elite to promote a Muslim 'takeover' is proclaimed rather than proved.

The evidence presents a more complicated picture that falls far short of one showing invasion by an alien culture and religion set to supplant white Christian heritage. For Ebner,[38] this 'replacement' narrative contains four elements that, combined, risk being inflammatory. First, it implies contamination of a once pure people; second, it conjures a dystopian outcome; third, it suggests that the gravity of the infiltration involves threat to the very existence of white Europeans; and finally, it attributes root cause to an insidious conspiracy by a reprehensible elite.

Interestingly, while nationalism *within* Europe has sought to rediscover borders and boundaries to mark distinctive virtues of particular European countries, nationalist exceptionalism goes hand-in-hand with an 'identitarian' movement *across* the continent that emphasises common historical, cultural, and religious bonds that can only be protected internationally against a mutual Muslim foe. In the 2022 travails following Putin's invasion of Ukraine, countries like Poland and Hungary suspended any reflexive xenophobia, and welcomed refugees. Was that in any way because they were white and Christian?

Confusion intensifies when you consider 'replacement' stories in places like the United States. For instance, Jared Taylor propagates an apparently intellectualised concern about white extinction and demoted importance, a process he attributes to 'racial egalitarianism'.[39] He wants to be understood as a 'white advocate' not a white supremacist. But there is nothing refined about his racist views. For him blacks and whites are not just different. Rather, he claims that when Blacks are left to their own ways, not only western civilisation, but all civilisation, perishes.[40]

Preference for one's own kind, he argues, is intrinsic to human nature, indeed to all nature. To have this special regard doesn't necessitate hostility to another race.[41] But it does mean that it is reasonable to expect 'whites to love, first and foremost, the infinite riches created by European man'.[42] This, he insists, is just 'race realism'. Here, he presents partisan views as being in everyone's mutual interest. In these terms, white liberal guilt about oppression of blacks actually disempowers blacks since it enfeebles their responsibility and resilience. Racial diversity not only destroys trust between people of different races living in close proximity, it also makes for an unstable society, since affirmative action and anti-discrimination laws bring their own contest. So he insists on the 'right' to have his tribe and culture persist against what he takes to be the false orthodoxy of enforced diversity:[43]

> We're building a society on a mistaken premise, and we're reaping the conse-
> quence, and unfortunately it is whites who as they become a minority and not just
> a minority, but a despised minority, who are suffering the most from this mistaken
> assumption about human nature ....

While opposed to many notions of 'civil rights', he exploits the concept of right to free assembly to argue for voluntary segregation of the races, preferably in the end in the form of different homelands for different racial groups. As developed more fully in the second volume, part of the problem in achieving human agreement about universal morality, is that opposing political and religious perspectives define terms like rights, justice, and fairness differently.

A uniting logic for many rightist proponents is that each race should have its own space. They don't accept that you can be other than white and be fully American or European. Race is tied to nationality. The model needed is that of the ethnostate. Indeed, in their characterisation, this is true diversity and pluralism – what we might call a biblical Babel, a scattering of the world's tribes to their own 'proper' place. In this view, nations are natural.

Rising Nationalism

Before we try to understand explanations for the growth of nationalism, it is useful to acknowledge that there are different types of nationalism. As Wimmer states,[44] they can attach to varied ideologies and thus take specific form in liberalism, fascism, liberation movements, and in theocracies and dynasties. Civic nationalism is democratic and pluralist and is invested in values of tolerance, inclusion and co-habiting diversities. It values all citizens, regardless of cultural background, as equals.

Ethnic nationalism exalts linguistic and cultural distinctiveness. It tends to favour those of 'blood' origin as natives of the sacred soil; see nation as a refuge from the abstraction of vast humanity and what it depicts as rootless cosmopolitanism; is prone to populist calls for protectionism and isolationism, in the name of putting the country first; and looks for emotional rather than just procedural attachment to the nation-state. In its worst manifestation, it boasts of exceptionalism, to the point of disrespecting other countries.

For Hobsbawn,[45] the former is associated with the French Revolution, whereas the latter links to German Romanticism, and it's to the latter that people are prone to turn in times of crisis and unease – in other words, times like the present. In practice, many actual 'nationalisms' contain elements of both civic and ethnic. What matters is the degree of each in the mix.

Accounts of how nationalism came to be are many, as Smith[46] demonstrates in his excellent book. He refers to the *primordial* explanation, which has biological and cultural varieties. For some, it derives from the genetic. It's about organic shared ancestry, stretching out from kinship and clans. However, such a biological view can't stand the test of history, tending to underplay complicated patterns of population resettlement, conquest, intermarriage, and assimilation. The cultural version stresses not just the ties of blood, but also of tradition, religion, language and land, assuming some indefinable sense of common belonging and loyalty develops with such long-standing special affinities.

A second main explanation is *perennialism*, and suggests that for a long time, nations have been either fairly permanent or recurrent as human constructs that can be historically contextualised. Some are quite ancient, others come and go in new formations, while others are recent outcomes of post-colonialism, whereby nationalism was a rallying ideology for anti-imperialist struggles.

Smith goes on to address the view that nations are the outcomes of *modernisation*, dismissing as overly deterministic the idea that as societies modernised and brushed off traditional cultures with the growth of big anonymous cities, shared language through formal state education produced cultural homogeneity for larger sets of people. This, in turn, provided the basis of how concocted traditions could be manipulated to manage the increasingly emancipated industrial masses (as examined by Hobsbawn[47]) or how an 'imagined' sovereign, fixed and restricted political community could take different formations in varied historical contexts (as elaborated by Anderson[48]).

While acknowledging that our modern sense of 'nation' emerged with the American (1775) and French (1789) Revolutions, Smith thinks these accounts tend to stress how national identity comes to be fashioned by elites, thereby underplaying the genuine emotional appeal of nationalism for the masses. He defines nation as:[49] 'a named human population sharing an historic territory, common myths and historical memories, a mass, public culture, a common economy and common legal rights and duties for all members'.

He sees most nations as emerging from an ethnic core, a dominant population whose solidarity derives from at least the myth of shared descent and destiny, historical memory, values, sentiments, rituals, anthems, symbols and emblems, and homeland, that all serve to unify. From this, many have spread in terms of ethnic composition, and maybe territory. But no matter how much these founding features evolve from perception, they become more structural as successive generations are socialised into ancestral narratives. In a sense, having been defined as real, whatever the actual truth, over time they become real in a simpler definite edition.

One interesting version of nationalism that holds relevance for our present period is one rooted in a covenant between a chosen people and its deity that offers divine protection in return for adherence to certain moral rules. Such reciprocal understanding permeates the Old Testament. Conceivably though, the New Testament globalised the 'elect' to all peoples who would hear and heed the Word. This contrast echoes some of the local versus global slant evident today. Amid this tension, in Smith's view, the local and national are not departing anytime soon:[50]

> ....*the continuing power of myths, symbols, and memories of ethnic chosenness, golden ages and historic homelands has been largely responsible for the mass appeal of ethnic nationalism in the aftermath of the Cold War and the demise of the Soviet empire; and that we are therefore unlikely to witness the early transcendence or the supersession of nationalism.*

Resurgent nationalism in the past three decades takes many forms. You have moves by big powers like the US, Russia, China, India, and the UK to boost their global ranking. You have moves in places like Scotland, Catalonia, Kashmir, Hong Kong, and Taiwan for some form of separatism and independence. Often these two processes are in conflict because just at the time when separatists want to depart a state, that state wants to stress its sovereignty. Each process feeds off the other. Catalan rebellion assists a Spanish nationalist party like Vox; the Brexit strategy can be seen as a populist English nationalist project that is contrary to Scottish interests, thereby helping the Scottish nationalist cause; and stirrings in Kashmir, India's only majority-Muslim state, allows Modi to parade his Hindu nationalism by curbing Kashmir's special status, which he depicts as a separatist threat. At the same time, separatist movements in certain places like Ukraine allow the big neighbour to claim their affinity and ultimately their territory.

Ancient history is littered with the ashes of empire: Egyptian, Assyrian, Babylonian, Greek, Carthaginian, Roman, Persian, and so on, and they brought with them contest about group identity, sovereignty and legitimacy.[51] While today, it's easy to associate nationalism with xenophobia, secessionist conflict and ethnic cleansing, it's worth considering how modern nationalism – that is from the late eighteenth century – can be seen as progressive for its time. By the middle of the eighteenth century, much of the world was subjugated by multinational imperialist powers – Britain, Austria, Russia, Ottoman, China and Spain. Nationalism helped to dissolve those oppressive empires.

That is not to deny that legacy of empire remains strong in today's world. Evidence of this lies in the multi-ethnic nature of places that may appear totally homogeneous. China's population is 91.5 percent Han. But it has 55 other minority groups, 302 living languages, and four official religions. India has over 2,000 ethnic groups and four main languages, though it mainly comprises two genetically differing populations, which mixed in ancient times: Ancestral North Indians, largely the Indo-Aryan speaking population of northern India, which is genetically close to Middle Easterners, Central Asians, and Europeans, and Ancestral South Indians, mainly the Dravidian speaking population of southern India.[52]

At the start of the last century, just over a third of the earth's surface was under nation-state government. By 1950, the share was around 70 percent, and now, only a handful of dynastic and theocratic countries remain.[53] Some see this shift as a necessary though insufficient precursor to democracy. Theoretically at least, sovereignty was being vested increasingly in a wider public rather than in nobility, monarchy or religious hierarchy. Moreover, nationalism that is generously encompassing can include room for cosmopolitanism, within nested identities. Belonging to a locality or region does not preclude identifying with a continent, like Europe or Asia, and beyond that to the wider world. You could argue that effective cosmopolitanism demands something like nationalism. As noted by Appiah:[54] 'What's distinctive about modern cosmopolitanism is its celebration of the contribution of every nation to the chorus of humanity. It is about sharing. And you cannot share if you have nothing to bring to the table'.

Tamir[55] argues that if the political left is to retrieve nationalism from right wing chauvinism, it would do well to appreciate its appeal and how it can be channelled for social democratic purpose. Specifically, civic nationalism has democratic and egalitarian potential that can bring 'strangers' together within a demarcated frontier of the nation-state. In fact, it can bring people at large together behind beneficial projects like the National Health Service in the UK. Still, she argues that to keep people together in a sense of unison – what is called social cohesion – each country has a threshold on the extent of diversity it can accommodate.

Evidently, there is a problem if migration is mostly experienced by the poorest countries and the poorest in rich countries. For instance, as the EU, US, UK, and Australia 'secure' their borders, extra pressure falls on nearby countries such as Turkey in the case of the EU. As old industrial areas decline, suffer population loss and house price deflation, they can attract migrants, who are then seen as threats to those 'left behind'.

Often, resentment to immigration can be seen as right-wing xenophobia, though concern about scale and pace of immigration is not always down to just white racism. For instance, as I saw for myself in protests by Namibian and Zimbabwean migrants in Cape Town concerning their treatment, some South African black people have reservation about how their persistent poverty may be aggravated by the influx of low-income labour. Arguably, such black South African concern about black migration from nearby countries is as racist as similar sentiment would be regarded by the western left. The left, on the other hand, tends to argue that racism only manifests itself fully when you have *both* prejudice and power. My own view does not preclude the possibility of racism by people of colour, though they are overwhelmingly the victims rather than perpetrators.

What is unfair is the scope given to people who are white and/or rich to move around the world in privileged manner. The comedian John Cleese complains that London is not an English city anymore, while residing as a white Englishman on a Caribbean island. Harry and Meghan can depart from England to Canada and then to the United States. It's funny that when Westerners go to live abroad, they tend to refer to themselves as ex-pats, not migrants. About 100 countries have 'golden visa' schemes in return for large investment. Some essentially sell passports, a gift for tax dodgers, and even in some cases, money launderers. Meanwhile, at the poorer end of the global tracks, the 'undocumented' in countries like the US struggle for citizenship. Yes, indeed, it is a rich man's world.

Masculine Toxicity

Man is the operative word here. That's one reason why populism has a gender slant. Within the Radical Right, feminism can be seen to threaten the family, and along with homosexuality, to jeopardise reproduction of the nation itself. Furthermore, being anti-immigration can be presented as shielding women, since stereotypes of non-white men as sensual and brutish feed into scare images of stalked white women. In such ways, white and male supremacism intertwine, and sexism can assume two faces: that which demeans women as manipulators of men through feminist edicts or sexual temptation; and that which misrepresents women as morally chaste but physically fragile.[56] At the same time, women and feminist positions can be misused to support nativism:[57]

> *Women (and girls) are portrayed as vulnerable, threatened by 'aliens' (domestic and foreign), and dependent upon the protection of 'their' (masculine) men. It is only within the context of Islamophobia that far-right groups defend gender equality and women's rights, juxtaposing an egalitarian 'West' against a misogynist 'Islam'.*

Liberals and leftists can reveal their own ambivalence around the issue of masculine toxicity. An apparent trivial, but nevertheless telling, indicator of this showed up recently in showbusiness. The 2022 Oscars was marked most by the mark left by Will Smith on compere Chris Rock, an assault that followed Rock's injudicious humour about Smith's wife. Though the Oscar Academy tried unsuccessfully to persuade Smith to leave the ceremony, it proceeded later to award him an Oscar, and the assailant's acceptance speech was received with a standing ovation by a crowd normally associated with disapproval of macho violence. What was the message being conveyed here – that male aggression in defence of female honour was tolerable, maybe even noble, or that black on black violence was acceptable in a way that white on black violence in a similar circumstance would not be?

In the political realm, male leaders, who present themselves as strong, charismatic, ebullient and irrepressible, dominate the global stage. Employing laddish vernacular and mercurial posture, they brag about being maverick rulebreakers, prepared to brave the hostile arena of the politically correct. In their hyper-masculinity, they present themselves as Masters of the Universe. Despite their often crass behaviour, what is notable is their resilience. Authoritarian right figures, whatever their competence, apparently benefit from what David Miliband has dubbed 'the age of impunity'.

Some stark examples present themselves with respect to combative rightist resistance to democratic government. There was the case of an open letter,[58] signed in April 2021, by about 1,000 active and retired French army personnel, in challenge to the Macron government's supposed lenience in addressing liberal and immigrant risk to French culture and history. The letter warned that the country, already in chaos, was headed for civil war. The hour was grave and the nation was in peril. Danger came from Islamism and 'the hordes of the banlieue' (the deprived suburbs of some French cities, populated mainly by immigrants). Other threats came from fanatic 'anti-racists', who challenged public statues and French colonial history. Such 'military' criticism of civil government is menacing.

Despite the undertones of anti-democratic manoeuvrings from army members, the populist impulse remains pervasive. After a decade of Tory austerity, Johnson's party gets re-elected with a substantial majority in 2019; Orban is re-elected in 2018 with over 50 percent of the vote, and then achieves a landslide victory in 2022, giving him a fourth consecutive term as Prime Minister, with a two-thirds super-majority in Parliament; Modi, despite India's many problems, gets re-elected in 2019; Netanyahu continues to dominate politics in Israel, despite his presiding over a peace process impasse and facing corruption charges; and this is not to mention many others like Putin, Duterte, and Xi Jinping. In his victory speech in 2022, Orban expressed confidence about the durability of his mandate, given his two-thirds Parliamentary majority against a coalition of six opposition parties:[59]

> *The entire world can see that our brand of Christian democratic, conservative, patriotic politics has won. We are sending Europe a message that this is not the past—this is the future.*

A notable feature of these leaders is that they're easily miffed at the slightest slight. Orban's petulant style, his party's paranoid conspiracy story about a Jewish billionaire intent on subverting the will of Hungarians, his influence over the media and judiciary, and the alleged gerrymandering of the electoral system, all compromise the democratic culture:[60]

> *Hungary has shown once again how well fearmongering works. Voters are never more attentive than when hearing about threats, even phoney ones. Because of social media, unscrupulous politicians can easily spread vivid, viral footage that appears to support their scare stories. If such types win power, they are likely to abuse it. Even in a liberal democracy, as Hungary once was, a determined would-be strongman can chip away at independent institutions, such as the media or the courts, until his voice drowns out every other.*

In populist politics, swagger and bombast seem to triumph, if tied to an external threat, such as Mexican or Islamic migrant 'invasion'. Trump, the venal poster boy for the brand, born with a golden spoon in his mouth, offered himself as saviour to the economically bereft; a draft dodger reincarnated as Commander-in-Chief in a national emergency of COVID-19, which he initially dismissed as a hoax, and then as a Chinese infiltration that would be miraculously routed. Consider the sense of entitlement as he boasted in a tweet about the 'sport' of getting round tax payment: developers 'were entitled to massive write offs and depreciation which would, if one was actively building, show losses and tax losses in almost all cases'. He carried on:[61] 'You always wanted to show losses for tax purposes....almost all real estate developers did -- and often re-negotiate with banks, it was sport'. Clearly, it was ludicrous to have ever seen him as a reformer of Washington's corrupt lobby system, from which he had long prospered, and a drainer of the government 'swamp', into which his family members had waded deep. This display of blatant hypocrisy and nepotism may be thought by many to be mortifying – but populist leaders can't be embarrassed because an essential part of their political armour is shamelessness.

In politics, it's crucial to distinguish substance and style. This is particularly so in populist politics, where the theatrical is implanted into the extravagant rhetoric. Witness the ludicrous spectacle of Trump in June 2020 getting Lafayette Square near the White House cleared of protesters with brutal force to ease his ceremonious walk for a photo opportunity of himself outside a church holding a bible, sending a clear if crude message to his evangelical base, while turning holy ground into a battleground.

For white conservative Christians, mortal life *is* a battleground, and he was God's intrepid warrior defying the heathen foe with biblical shield. Having berated governors for failure to 'dominate' the streets, he wanted demonstrators ejected to make way for him to demonstrate. It is politics as outlandish performance, a form of designed bedlam contrived to flummox opposition as much as to rouse devotees. Next day, the pantomime is moved on to some other outrageous stunt or statement before critics can catch their breath. In this way, constant controversy makes it hard to fact-check or pin down any particular provocation.

This high octane discourse is fuelled by spiralling rage more than sober reason. In suggesting that the people face a clear and present danger, it is designed to inflame and unnerve, channelled as it is through trolls, memes, rallies, political ads, and such like. Yet by trying to sensibly engage with lunacy you have to grant it some degree of sanity. This is a basic paradox of populism confronting its opponents. If they dismiss its claims, they can be seen to confirm the charge that they treat 'the people' with disdain. If instead they try to show respect and understanding for the claims, explanation readily can become legitimation.

Some critics will end up saying in effect: 'I don't want to dignify that drivel with a response'. By doing so, they silence themselves. In the political rumpus kicked up by populists, you either take sides or get sidelined. Space for nuance becomes ever squeezed. When moral positions are cast as absolutes, everything gets seen through a lens of 'us versus them'. You're either part of *our* solution, or you're part of *the* problem. Compromise corrupts and principled compromise corrupts principally. Opponents are enemies to be crushed rather than conciliated. In this way, culture wars demand relentless provocation rather than progressive pacification. This is the politics of the constant campaign, and is considered more fully in the next chapter.

Even when in government, populist leader and party are in opposition, partly because they relish the role of victimised outcasts in a rigged system run by, and for, a narrow powerful clique. Also though, it is because this in-group out-sources some of its power to a deep state, conspiratorially seen as a secret administrative state within the official one. So even when populist leaders win an election, it is implied that they face sabotage and defiance from within, from the 'permanent government' of various illuminati, including career bureaucrats, bankers, globalists, and such like. This stealthy 'enemy within' is seen as being in cahoots with the globalist power elite that disenfranchise honest working people, a ploy Trump claimed to 'expose' in a 2016 campaign speech in Florida:[62] '....Hilary Clinton meets in secret with international banks to plot the destruction of U.S. sovereignty in order to enrich these global financial powers, her special interest friends and her donors ....'

Some features can be summarized at this stage: figures like Trump, Putin, Duterte, Duda, Erdogan, Orban, Modi, and Bolsanaro seem to delight in flaunting chauvinism in a defiant tone. They speak plainly, with repetitive slogans and mantras, an untamed directness that deliberately discards 'political correctness' and nails their credentials as authentic ventriloquists of plain people. They are the unique curators of the people's will. Despite driving a political project, they pose as counter-politicians, or at least hipster politicians, in an age when politics can be a by-word for sleaze and deceit. Though operating *through* a political party, they are ultimately *above* the party, relying on their own unique antenna to detect and express the popular will.

Firebrand style fuels two important facets: it keeps the debate heated, and it energises supporters. Cronyism is decried as inherent to the corrupt character of present-day government. Yet populist leaders are not shy about indulging in nepotistic behaviour. While speaking in high rhetoric, they portray themselves as men of action not words. They promise: 'to make America great'; 'to build the wall'; 'to drain the swamp'; 'to get Brexit done', and such like.

Such throwaway comments are so madcap as to suggest flippancy. Nevertheless, they succeed in setting the media story. They hearten believers, since shock and awe are key to a disruptive agenda, which demands continuous chaos. The more crackpot the comments, the more it helps to make mainstream rightists appear restrained, thereby re-setting the dial of what is politically acceptable. And they can throw traditional opponents off-beam since contempt for conventional wisdom can appear counter-intuitive to conservativism. Perhaps most of all, they want to trumpet their power by daring rivals to laugh at them, since such scorn may only serve to insult their loyal base. In retaliation, the base rewards its leader with even greater approval, further exasperating opponents. The whirlwind continues.

Nostalgia: Not What it Used to Be

A strong dimension of populist nationalist appeal lies in nostalgia – the rosy-hued picture that the good old days were better because our country was then great, foreigners were few, things like gender and religion were simpler and fixed, and we were in charge. Now all that we took for solid has melted into air.

But a much wider version of this wistfulness comes from Evola (1898–1974), who locates decline and malaise back to the desertion of ancient traditions for the lure of the decadent modern world. His writing rejects the idea of progress since the Enlightenment. Rather, he argues that we must again appreciate two natures: the physical and metaphysical, the mortal and immortal, and the observable and material compared to the invisible and intangible. We have forfeited the transcendent element of being for the materialistic. Ensnared by pointless consumerism, the false god of technocracy, erroneous values of egalitarianism, and selfish individualism, humans have strayed from their true core:[63]

> *The division of individuals into castes or into equivalent groups according to their nature and to the different rank of activities they exercise with regard to pure spirituality is found with the same traits in all higher forms of traditional civilizations, and it constitutes the essence of the primordial legislation and of the social order according to 'justice'.*

Hierarchy is not an outcome of human will, but of human nature. While liberals today renounce slavery of the past, they don't see the 'slavery' of the great masses, fated to execute petty routine jobs in what is an ever more collectivised society. Old artisan expertise created the genuine article. Today, in an impersonal economy, we have the copy, the artificial. In numbing the spirit, this programmed world corrodes the higher ideals and behaviours derived from Tradition, the bedrock of western civilisation. Again, like some others of the Radical Right, he locates these moral convictions in paganism rather than Christianity. Heroic values include: truth, purity, fidelity, valour, chivalry, audacity, steadfastness, and discipline. Reaching for those standards deepens the inner absolute individual, a process of deification, whereby the human can rise above their nature toward affinity with God. Authority in the traditional society stemmed not from power based on force, but rather power and veneration based on the leader's nonhuman quality, a natural or attained superiority. In this way:[64]

> ....*Evola took issue with the concept of the nation, since this was determined merely by biological and cultural parameters; instead, he advocates a spiritual-monarchical empire....(this means) opposition to democracy, since this depended on quantity not on quality, and lacked the spiritual element.*

You can see how much of this 'paradise lost' narrative echoes that of other Radical Right thinkers, like de Benoist and Dugin. But Evola goes further than most. He attributes the restlessness and resentment that he says marks the modern period to a loss of mystery, simplicity, independence and balance, with people forced to find their meaning in things. Endorsing the Hindu concept of time as cyclical rather than linear, he asserts that we are in a Dark Age (Kali Yuga) that summons revolt:[65] '....the West can be saved only by a return to the traditional spirit in the context of a new unitary European consciousness'.

Evola's writings, that speak to the hollow and inconsequential character of modern life, offer what is mostly an obscure alternative, a re-awakening to imprecisely drawn lost values. If God is dead in the Nietzschean sense, for those of upright and higher character – 'the aristocrats of the soul' – they may be best to 'ride the tiger', to ride out the tempest of this collapsing world, ignore its jaded tedium and prepare for a redemptive alternative:[66]

> *The natural place for such a man, the land in which he would not be a stranger, is the world of Tradition....a civilisation or a society is 'traditional' when it is ruled by principles that transcend what is merely human and individual, and when all its sectors are formed and ordered from above, and directed to what is above.*

Such esoteric vagueness allows his work to be adopted by those on the Right who wish to evoke apocalyptic Armageddon before a new world order can be created, and who believe this deliverance is the destiny of Europeans as a superior civilisation. Also, it can be taken to infer the need for superhuman 'priest-king' leaders to usher people through troubled times.

Evola's script can be linked to Guenon (1886–1951), often cast as lead thinker of Traditionalism, which in its broadest meaning concerns how metaphysical insight is set within material reality and revealed through primal spiritualism, found in 'pure' creeds like Hinduism, Islam, and medieval Catholicism. For Guenon too, this is a time of spiritual rot, during which this era will collapse to be reconfigured into a better heroic world. This chimes with the Hindu doctrine of *samsara* – the constant cycle of birth, mortality and reincarnation. People like Evola and Guenon continue to influence the Radical Right and alt-right, evoking as they do a soulless drift in current times that can be put down to loss of civilisation, a by-word for 'white' civilisation:[67]

> *By indulging in myths that recast whiteness as a remnant of superior or semi-divine origins, followers of the alt-right can vicariously credit themselves, through their alleged ancestors, to be the architects of the world's great civilisations, from ancient India to Egypt, Rome and Persia. Claiming Indo-European-Aryan heritage excuses the appropriation of Eastern cultures by Western racists as a revival of their own tradition.*

It's Complex

Up to this point, the case has been made that we live in particularly discordant times. But there is a counter-narrative. And it's often neglected. Surveys over recent years, undertaken by YouGov-Cambridge Globalism Project, suggest a contrary reading:[68]

> *Academic theorists of 'authoritarian populism' may perceive a new, mass disdain for liberal pluralism, but we found little evidence of this in public sentiment. Instead, majorities around the world maintain a determined belief in the superiority of democracy, with little partisan difference on the issue.*

That's not to say that partisan splits are undetectable. When asked about how they position themselves with regard to broad labels like right/left, feminism, and Black Lives Matter, very opposing views are expressed by those describing themselves as rightwing or leftwing. However, when drilling down to specific views about the need for equality between the sexes and races, or about the urgency to decarbonise the economy, there is much common ground – in favour of progressive goals. What appears to be acute aversion between rival camps around identity markers turns out to be significant similarity around specific agendas of social change. The overall pattern of opinion, revealed in these global surveys, suggests that 'far from being poles apart, people tend to cluster somewhere in between'. In this interpretation, people's shared views about their preferred society outstrips their differences, provided you penetrate beyond 'labels and loyalties'.[69]

Taking this finding further, the Project[70] posits that public endorsement of populist beliefs is on the wane. Across the twenty-two countries surveyed, support dropped for such populist sentiments as: 'the will of the people should be the highest principle in this country's politics'; 'my country is divided between the ordinary people and the corrupt elites who exploit them'; 'the power of a few special interests prevents our country from making progress'; and 'a lot of important information is deliberately concealed from the public out of self-interest'. The figures do indeed demonstrate a fall in support for such populist sentiment – but in some countries, it's a fall from three-quarters to two-thirds, or from two-thirds to a half or just over. In other words, the discernible decline, in the period 2019–2021, in such espousal is starting from a high base. Even if we take the main message to be that populism has peaked, decline in 'anti-establishment discontent' does not hold for the data from the US, which demonstrates little shift over those three years, and similar trends are evident in places like India and Thailand.

Nevertheless, some insist that European populism has reached a turning point, sparked by Trump's electoral defeat, the pandemic emergency, and Putin's aggression. In the case of the pandemic, 'their incessant denunciation of the experts and scientists also falls short because, ultimately, the experts are listened to, even if they sometimes deliver divergent and debatable analysis'.[71] But even some[72] who detect chinks in the armour of those they cast as European populists, from Le Pen and Salvini to Meloni, and Melenchon, acknowledge that the underlying dynamic that has nurtured this political breed persists – public distrust; yearning for strong leadership at a time of crises; inadequate government intervention to ameliorate social inequality and economic distress; and the persistent challenge of migration, particularly if subject to inflated association with militant Islam.

In response to these genuine concerns, interesting research,[73] analysing 150 elections across 17 Western European countries from 1970–2017, argues that mainstream parties are faced with three potential responses: dismissive, accommodative, and adversarial. While it is unwise to write off the apprehensions, it is also counter-productive to adapt to the far-right agenda. This only serves to standardise and legitimate it, and those parties which capitulate tend to haemorrhage voters to right-wing challengers, who can present themselves as 'the real deal', rather than the pale imitation. As argued earlier, the most viable alternative is to challenge them.

This implies taking the issues seriously, if not slavishly. This chapter has concentrated on the contemporary strategy of the right and its intellectual underpinning. If the left are to understand why they keep losing, it is important to interrogate these views. Knee-jerk leftism has failed, by failing to examine their opponents at their highest intellectual expression. Simply dismissing them all as evil, racist, *etcetera* doesn't cut it.

How do we make sense of all this so far? Asked to abbreviate the defining aspect of current politics and social discourse, many will distil it into 'authoritarian populism'. Asked to elaborate on this phenomenon, responses will include well-worn facets: charismatic leaders, combative, deceitful without qualm, presenting themselves as both providential and the personification of people's will, appealing to the angry crowd by playing on legitimate grievance, with menacing polemics rather than evidence; shrewdly mingling a bit of populist leftism with traditional rightist themes; normalising the extreme; leaders incapable of critical self-reflection, and given to over-simplification of a complex world; deployment of scapegoating and conspiracy tales about secretive global elites; dismissal of criticism as 'fake news'; designation of enemies within and without, who imperil native interests; the trumpeting of hyper-patriotism that is the last refuge of the scoundrel; juxtaposition of peripheral province and wealthier metropolis; and so on. The debris of this tenor is said to be pervasive in its rant and cant, and its lethal mix of genuine gripe and feigned righteous indignation. But however tiresome the swagger, the infectious sanguinity in dark times can appeal beyond its immediate far-right orbit. By contrast, more sober leadership can appear lacklustre for eventful times.

While all this offers a partial take on current times, it commits its own sin of simplification. Assessing the current state of populism, Mudde[74] sees it as a plural rather than a singular. There are populisms, comprising variants in ideology, influence, and background. As culture has come to overshadow class, populist ideas around nativism and white nationalism have spread from political margins, and shifted debate. With mainstream parties moving into once forbidden terrain like immigration, the line between the traditional conservative right and far right has blurred in places, whether this has been down to the former's conversion or opportunism. The idea that the key political divide is between elite establishment and wider public has become normalised, and thereby difference between standard right parties and those on the far-right has become more a matter of degree than of absolute.

While electoral fortunes of the far-right are irregular and can falter, the impact of its agenda is more durable. In that regard, its 'metapolitical' mission over many decades has yielded some success. Its reach has been international, since no country, whether long-term social democratic like Sweden or short-term liberal democratic like Greece, has been totally immune to its appeal. The rise of the Sweden Democrats and the Danish People's Party has been swift, but not sudden. Compared to merely 12 years ago, when the former achieved modest representation in the Riksdag, the 2022 election saw them attain over 20 percent of the vote, and significantly bolster the right-wing presence in a parliament once known as a haven of egalitarian social democracy. Their appeal, rooted in a blame game of crime and gang violence on migrant communities, is not geographically uniform, but rather quite skewed, particularly in the southern region of Skane, where they achieved nearly a third of the vote in rural areas, compared to a tenth in Stockholm.[75]

Such patterns show that populist right-wing influence needs to be contextualised, in particular in locality and history. Because it is a diverse phenomenon, no single counter-strategy is viable. However, liberal and social democracy will have to re-discover their own convictions rather than just reacting to those of the populists, and this recharging will include finding better ways to deal with the strain between majority rule and minority rights.

In his appraisal, Muller agrees with a lot of this. Democrats are ill-advised to either abandon debate with populist opinion, or to chase after its tail:[76]

> There is no alternative to engaging with populists. But talking with populists is not the same as talking like populists....At the same time, it is important to recognise that a whole range of policy positions that liberals find highly problematic are nevertheless permissible in a democracy -- and that one has to argue against them with the best arguments and evidence available, not with the polemical charge of 'populism'.

He's saying that rather than dismiss populism as a passing malaise, recognise it within democratic politics as an enduring presence that must be challenged. Understand that populists are not simply anti-elitist, but are also anti-pluralist, particularly in their claim to be the sole authentic voice of the people. Watch out for their sleight-of-hand in dividing 'real' people against the rest, as they set about defining 'common sense' and the people's will. Note how in government, they are keen to capture the state and marginalise critical voices in civic society, while shoring up their base through mass patronage.

In all this disapproval of populist polemics and practice, we should acknowledge that it finds political space and echo because of democratic deficit. If democrats suppress discussion of issues that concern many people, the vacancy can be occupied by those who claim that democracy itself is flawed. In circumstance of democracy's failure to listen to citizens, it's not that populism is remedial. But it can reveal the extent to which some groups and ideas are unrepresented. Of course, that in turn raises difficult questions about whether 'democracy' is obliged, or able, to be all inclusive, even if it means granting recognition, if not validity, to values that many find abhorrent.

In exploring Radical Right thinkers, we have seen that contradictions abound. Some see the current crisis in terms of economic displacement. Others see it in terms of cultural replacement. In response to the latter, some affirm restoration of Christian heritage. Others suggest that the deeper spiritual roots of places like Europe lie in paganism.

Some see the broader issue in terms of blatant white supremacism. Others insist that their emphasis on ethnic distinction and separation does not imply belief in racial hierarchy. Some are happy to talk directly about race, while others, perhaps more wary about being considered racist, sanitise their ideas with code words like 'culture'. Some are anti-Semitic. Others take Judaism and Christianity as important partners. Some take their anti-materialism to the point of anti-capitalism. Others strongly endorse the free market. Some attribute supposed cultural decadence to 'alien' migration, while others locate the same problem in a wider frame that includes western secularisation and mass consumerism of sameness.

Some are unapologetically part of a Radical Right, while others insist that their political position is beyond right and left, and involves a complex composite, including support for environmentalism and scepticism of free markets. Some see the US as lead champion of resistance, backed by important allies like Israel, while others include the US as part of the problem when it comes to loss of European cultural integrity, and have less focus on the Middle East. Then, when it comes to action, some want to ship back those they see as foreign intruders on their soil, without asking whether that principle would apply to whites in places like North America and Australia. Some characters like Putin and Xi, cast as populist, are not purely populist, since they *are* the establishment. In short, the Radical Right and its associated tenets of cultural and economic nationalism, is a bewildering political landscape.

Consequent disorientation is understandable. Shocks to the global system like the financial crash, austerity, the Brexit/Trump phenomena, the pandemic, and the crisis of Ukraine are accelerators of history. Amid the disruption, one word recurs as a call to anchor us humans: the word '*natural*'. It professes an understanding of 'true' human nature, and argues against a world of racial mix, migration, multiculturalism, liberal values, cosmopolitanism, modern bureaucracy, and global agencies as an unnatural order. Some older thinkers add concern about the human estrangement that attends mass consumerism and techno-science. This search for the authentic human society can rail against the hollowness of modernity. But that position doesn't hold for all autocrats. Xi's China embraces modernity in its quest for geo-political supremacy, while paying suitable regard to Chinese tradition. Of course, Xi is critical of the West, while wanting to imitate its economic prowess and consumer lifestyle. Meanwhile, the West is critical of the autocracy of China and Russia, while itself imitating some of that illiberal behaviour.

Across this juxtaposition, certain white Christian nationalists see themselves in a strange global alliance with fellow devotees elsewhere. The puerile, but vile, rhetoric of the latest far-right celebrity in the US – Nick Fuentes – speaks to this connection. Exposing far-right admiration for Putin's militarism, he invited applause for him from attendees at the America First Political Action Conference in 2022. It would be mistaken to dismiss this as fringe inanity. By outflanking the US Conservative Political Action Conference, it permits the latter to test the wilder waters of extremism. Whereas the latter was once fringe, it is now a leading presence in the Republican Party, which itself indulged the mutual flirtation between Trumpism and Putin's Russia, despite constantly parading its gung-ho patriotism in hollow boosterism.

Individuals like Trump and Putin may come and go. The ideas and conditions that lie behind them are set to endure much longer. One feature that unites both is their disdain for what they cast as a weakened West. In Trump's case, that meant elevating the US interest over that of NATO or Europe. America's greatness was not to be compromised by being fettered to the enfeebled and parasitic West. For Putin, it is the effrontery of a corrupt dissolute Western imperialist project, given to disrespect the proper global prominence of Greater Russia. Both want to project themselves as powerful, yet paradoxically are prone to whine about their victimhood.

For some, the tribulations of the last few decades validate eschatological scenarios. Within Judeo-Christian tradition, an apocalyptic strain sees this as a showdown time with forces of evil, ending in a rapture to heaven or at least an earthly liberation with a Second Coming. Those of us deprived of this consolation have to wrestle with an awkward truth. Great divides around religion, race, gender, and nationality have left us inhabiting different social universes, whereby we struggle to find a common language. We could be in the midst of one of those big gaps in history between one era and another, as in the deeply disturbed periods leading into the Agrarian and Industrial Revolutions. Adrift, we're navigating common social storms in separate dinghies without an oracle or map.

Of course, since antiquity, humans have dwelled in their own small settlements, bound with each other and against outsiders by their distinctive customs, beliefs, cults, and conspiracies. The difference today is that these rival truths are revealed as divergent realities because we're all networked globally. So, although these sobering times might be thought to merit serious leaders, they also give scope to hucksters and charlatans, ready to exploit division and disaffection. Given the economic fallout of the crash, pandemic, and Ukrainian war in terms of stagflation and fiscal stress, the discontent of the socially abandoned provides plentiful opportunity for persistent populism.

In terms of the rise of rage, as addressed in this chapter, one of its blatant manifestations was the startling scenes of rioters breaching the security of the US Capitol Building on 6th January 2021, to prevent certification of a Presidential election that Trump had told his followers had been stolen. In the preceding rally, Trump had bid the crowd, which included militia like the Oath Keepers and Proud Boys, and conspiracists like the QAnon Movement, to 'fight' to take their country back. The House Select Committee, established to determine the causes and culprits of this anti-democratic insurrection, has focussed on whether Trump and his inner circle were engaged in a criminal conspiracy, which the Justice Department could pursue to prosecution. While the world had wondered at how America had come to this, Trump's shameless mendacity epitomised the key trait of the autocratic populist. Though subject to the Mueller inquiry into his links with Putin, two attempted impeachments, and official investigations of his business and tax affairs, his domination of the Republican party endures. To date, he has resisted democratic constraint with impunity.

His disciples in the Republican party persist with his deceit. For instance, Congresswoman, Marjorie Taylor Greene, in a text on 17 January 2021 to Trump's White House chief-of-staff, Mark Meadows, pressured for Trump to resist the electoral outcome, even after the Capitol attack:[77]

> *In our private chat with only Members, several are saying the only way to save our Republic is for Trump to call Marshall [sic] law....I just wanted you to tell him. They stole this election. We all know. They will destroy our country next.*

Clearly, democracy doesn't die a quick death. It wanes and withers.

At this stage, let me suggest that there is a space-time dimension to how the pressing issues of our time are seen. In terms of space, some see the important unit as being nation, while others emphasise a wider 'family' we can call civilisation. In terms of time, some see the saga of decline and decadence in terms of the last half century. Others see its origins in modernity and related amnesia about ancient values. Each dimension affects the other. If your perspective is going back centuries, you may be inclined to see nationalism as a product of modernity, and thus suspect. Whereas if your focus is on change since the 'peak white' era of the 1950s, you may be more inclined to think in terms of nationalism than of civilisation, or at least to blur the distinction between white nationalism and civilisation.

The next chapter unpacks issues of identity, equality, and culture wars, tied into the populism, authoritarian nationalism, and anti-immigrant sentiment explored here.

Notes

1 Darroch, K. (2021) *Collateral Damage: Britain, America and Europe in the Age of Trump.* London: William Collins.
2 www.pewresearch.org/fact-tank/2022/11/01/turnout-in-u-s-has-soared-in-rec ent-elections-but-by-some-measures-still-trails-that-of-many-other-countries. Accessed on: 17 November 2022.
3 Mudde, C. and Kaltwasser, C. (2012) Populism and (liberal) Democracy: a framework for analysis. in Mudde, C. & Kaltwasser (eds) *Populism in Europe and the Americas: threat or corrective for democracy?* New York: Cambridge University Press. 1–26. 8.
4 Muller, J-W. (2017) *What is Populism?* London: Penguin Books.
5 Nigel Farage, Leader of the UK Independence Party (UKIP), speaking in anticipation of a referendum victory for Brexit, as covered by CNN, 23 June 2016. Accessed on: 2 June 2020.

6 Quoted in: Lamont, M., Yun Park, B. & Ayala-Hurtado, E. (November 2017) Trump's Electoral Speeches and His Appeal to the American White Working Class. *The British Journal of Sociology.* Vol. 68. Issue S1. S153–S180. S164.

7 Carrie Chapman Catt Centre for Women and Politics, Archives of Women's Political Communication. Iowa State University. Speech of Marine Le Pen in her Presidential Campaign Launch, on 9th March 2017. sourced in https://awpc.cattcen ter.iastate.edu/2017/09/01/presidential-campaign-launch-march-9-2017. Accessed on: 8 June 2020.

8 Knowles, E. (ed.) (1999). *The Oxford Dictionary of Quotations.* 5th ed. Oxford: Oxford University Press. 259.

9 Carrie Chapman Catt Centre for Women and Politics. *op. cit.*

10 Leader. (30 April 2022) France's Re-elected President Prepares for a Tough Second Term. *The Economist.*

11 Fourquet, J. (28 April 2022) What the Presidential Election Really Revealed About Fractured France. *The Guardian.*

12 UN News (24 September 2019) *Brazilian President Speaks Out Against 'Media Lies' Surrounding Amazon Fires.* New York: United Nations.

13 Huntington, S. (1997) *The Clash of Civilizations and the Remaking of World Order.* London: Simon & Schuster.

14 Faye, G. (2012) *Convergence of Catastrophes.* United Kingdom: Arktos Media Ltd.

15 *Ibid.* 14.

16 See also Francois, S. (2019) Guillaume Faye and Archeofuturism in Sedgwick, M. (ed) *Key Thinkers of the Radical Right: Behind the New Threat to Liberal Democracy.* Oxford: Oxford University Press. 91–101.

17 de Benoist, A. and Champetier, C. (2012) *Manifesto for a European Renaissance.* London: Arktos. 12.

18 *Ibid.* 18.

19 *Ibid.* 30.

20 *Ibid.*42.

21 Laruelle, M. (22 October 2021) Disillusioned With Democracy: A Conceptual Introduction to Illiberalism. *Institut Montaigne.* www.institutmontaigne.org/en/blog/disillusioned-democracy-conceptual-introduction-illiberalism. Accessed on: 11 May 2022.

22 Camus, R. (2018) *You Will Not Replace Us!* 14–15.

23 *Ibid.*12.

24 *Ibid.*193.

25 Phillips, M. (2006) *Londonistan: How Britain is Creating a Terror State Within.* New York: Encounter Books. xx.

26 *Ibid.* xxiii.

27 Murray, D. (2018) *The Strange Death of Europe: Immigration, Identity and Islam.* London: Bloomsbury. 2.

28 *Ibid.*7.

29 *Ibid.* 329.

30 Quoted from Marr, A. (2007) *A History of Modern Britain.* London; Macmillan. 303–304.

31 Ebner (2020) *Going Dark: the Secret Social Lives of Extremists.* London: Bloombury.

32 Pew Research Center (2017) Europe's Growing Muslim Population. Estimates and Projections. 2017. Note: Europe is defined here as the 28 nations of the EU as then, plus Norway and Sweden. Three scenarios were projected about changes in Europe's

Muslim population, beginning with a baseline of just under 26 million in 2016. The first assumed zero future migration, and allowing for fertility and age profile. This saw the Muslim population increase by 10 million (+ 39 percent) by 2050. A medium scenario allowed for previous levels of regular migration to persist, but without addition of further asylum seekers, and this trajectory would bring the Muslim population to almost 58 million (+ 125 percent) by midcentury. A high migration scenario involved continuation of both regular migration levels and the elevated refugee intake of recent times, and this would see numbers rise to 75 million (+193 percent). Alongside all three settings, the non-Muslim European population, which was 495 million in 2016, was anticipated to contract: by 6 percent in the high scenario; by 7 percent in the medium; and by 10 percent in the zero option.

Taking the period mid-2010 and mid-2016, around 60 percent of the rise in Muslim population was due to migration. Overall in this period, not considering religion or immigration status, an estimated 7 million migrants came to Europe (excluding 1.7 million asylum seekers who were not anticipated to have their asylum applications approved). The majority of refugees over this time were Muslim (78 percent), while the majority of regular migrants were non-Muslim (54 percent), making the share of the total just over half (53 percent) Muslim. Between 2014–2016, about one-quarter of immigrants to Europe were refugees, a notable surge that drew political attention to 'the migration crisis' that was linked to conflicts in Syria, Iraq and Afghanistan.

Based on the zero migration scenario, Muslim share of 7.4 percent would vary among countries: in France, from 8.8 percent to 12.7 percent; in Belgium from 7.6 percent to 11.1 percent; in Sweden from 8.1 percent to 11.1 percent; and in the UK from 6.3 percent to 9.7 percent. In most countries of eastern and central Europe, the share would remain very low: Hungary (0.4 percent); Czech Republic (0.2 percent); and Poland (0.1 percent); as would some western ones: The Republic of Ireland (1.6 percent); Portugal (0.5 percent). This growth in a zero migration situation stems from the fact that half of all European Muslims are under the age of 30, compared to just under a third of non-Muslims, and Muslims currently have higher fertility.

In the medium migration scenario, Muslim population share grows to 11.2 percent, over double its 2016 share. Given that the UK was the top host country for regular Muslim migrants between 2010–2016, it would have the highest numbers – 13 million by 2050 (16.7 percent), overtaking the two countries with the highest numbers in 2016, France and Germany. The former would have a projected 12.6 million (17.4 percent), while the latter would have 8.5 million (11 percent). Muslim shares of both Sweden and the UK would increase by over 10 percentage points. Belgium would have 15.1 percent; Norway 13.4 percent; and Italy 12.4 percent.

In the high migration scenario, at 17.5 million, the highest Muslim numbers would be in Germany, a projection that comes from its recent reception of many Muslim refugees. This would take its share from 6 percent to about 20 percent. Sweden's population (8 percent Muslim in 2016) could rise to 31 percent Muslim, taking it from 810,000 in 2016 to nearly 4.5 million, a fivefold increase, and the most marked in Europe. But even under this peak scenario, Europe's population would be 14 percent Muslim by midcentury, hardly an impending Islamist conquest.

33 Norris, P. and Inglehart, R. (2019) *Cultural Backlash: Trump, Brexit, and Authoritarian Populism*. Cambridge: Cambridge University Press.

34 Kaufmann, E. (2019) *Whiteshift: Populism, Immigration and the Future of White Majorities*. London: Penguin. 1.

35 *Ibid*. p. 2.

36 Pew Research Center. (2016) *Global Attitude Survey*. For a good summary, see Wike, R., Stokes, B. and Simmons, K. (11/07/2016) *Europeans Fear Wave of Refugees Will Mean More Terrorism, Fewer Jobs*. www.pewresearch.org. accessed 23/06/2020. The ten European countries polled were: France, Germany, Greece, Hungary, Italy, Netherlands, Poland, Spain, Sweden, and UK.

37 IPSOS (11 October 2022) Public Attitudes to Immigration Shows Public Take a Balanced Approach. *IPSOS*. www.ipsos.com/en-uk/immigration-tracker-october-2022. Accessed on: 19 November 2022.

38 Ebner (2020) *op.cit.*

39 See Anti-Defamation League (2013) Jared Taylor/American Renaissance. www.adl.org. combating-hate/jared-taylor-extremism-in-america.pdf. Accessed on: 26 June 2020.

40 Taylor, J. (2005) *American Renaissance website*, quoted by the Southern Poverty Law Center. www.aplcenter.org/fighting-hate/extremist-files/individual/jared-taylor. Accessed on: 26 June 2020.

41 see Nieli, R. (2019) Jared Taylor and White Identity. in Sedgwick, M. (ed) *op.cit.* 137–154.

42 Taylor, J. (July 3, 2008) *op.cit.* quoted by the Southern Poverty Law Center. www.aplcenter.org/fighting-hate/extremist-files/individual/jared-taylor. Accessed on: 26 June 2020.

43 Quoted from: *A Conversation with Jared Taylor*. Streamed live on August 6th 2018. American Renaissance website. www.amren.com

44 Wimmer, A. (March/April 2019) Why Nationalism Works and Why it isn't Going Away. *Foreign Affairs*. 98(2). 27–34.

45 Hobsbawm, E. (1990) *op.cit.*

46 Smith, A.D. (1999) *Myths and Memories of the Nation*. Oxford: Oxford University Press.

47 Hobsbawm, E. (1990) *Nations and Nationalism since 1780*. Cambridge: Cambridge University Press.

48 Anderson, B. (1991) *Imagined Communities: Reflection on the Origins and Spread of Nationalism*. London: Verso.

49 Smith. A.D. (1999) *op.cit.* 11.

50 *Ibid.*, 19.

51 Puri, S. (2020) *The Great Imperial Hangover: How Empires have Shaped the World*. London: Atlantic Books.

52 Reich, D., Kumarasamy, T., Patterson, N., Price, A.L., & Singh, L. (2009) Reconstructing Indian Population History. *Nature* 461. 489–494. www.nature.com/articles. Accessed on: 6 July 2020.

53 Wimmer, A. (March/April 2019) *op.cit.*

54 Appiah, K.A. (March/April 2019) The Importance of Elsewhere: in Defence of Cosmopolitanism. *Foreign Affairs*. Vol.98. No2. pp.20–26. 24.

55 Tamir, Y. (2019) *Why Nationalism?* Princeton, NJ: Princeton University Press.

56 Mudde, C. (2019) *The Far Right Today*. Cambridge: Polity Press. 150.

57 *Ibid.* 173

58 It was published in the right-wing magazine *Valeurs Actuelles* on 21 April 2021 – not accidentally on the 60th anniversary of a failed putsch against de Gaulle's government over its handling of Algerian independence.

59 Quoted in: Portella, M.A. (10 May 2022) Orbán's Challenge to Uphold Christian Democracy. *Hungarian Conservative.* www.hungarianconservative.com/articles/politics/orbans-challenge-to-uphold-christian-democracy. Accessed on: 12 May 2022

60 Leader. (9 April 2022)Fearmongering Works. Fans of the Truth Should Fear It. *The Economist.*

61 Trump quoted from his tweet in: Buettner, R. & Craig, S. (08/05/2019) Decade in the Red: Trump Tax Figures Show over $1 billion in Business Losses. *New York Times.* www.nytimes.com/2019/05/07/us/politics/donald-trump-taxes.

62 Quoted in: Choksi, N. (13 October 2016) Trump Accuses Clinton of Guiding Global Elite Against U.S. Working Class. *The New York Times.* www.nytimes.com/2016/10/14/us/politics/trump. Accessed on: 8th June 2020.

63 Evola, J. (1995 edition) *Revolt Against the Modern World.* Rochester, Vermont: Inner Traditions International. 89.

64 Hakl, H. (translated by J. Godwin) (2019) Julius Evola and Tradition, in Sedgwick, M. (ed) *op.cit.* 54–69. 61.

65 *Ibid.* 358.

66 Evola, J. (translated by J.Godwin & C. Fontana) (2003 edition) *Ride the Tiger: a Survival Manual for the Aristocrats of the Soul.* Rochester, Vermont: Inner Traditions International. 2.

67 Hermansson, P. et al. *op.cit.* 238.

68 Shakespeare, S. and de Waal, J.R. (26 November 2021) Be Reassured: the World is Not as Divided as We Might Think. *YouGov.* https://yougov.co.uk/topics/international/articles-reports/2021/11/26/be-reassured-world-not-divided-we-might-think. Accessed on: 11 May 2022.

69 *Ibid.*

70 de Waal, J.R. (18 November 2021) European Support For Populist Beliefs Declines. *YouGov.* https://yougov.co.uk/topics/international/articles-reports/2021/11/18/european-support-populist-beliefs-declines. Accessed on: 11 May 2022.

71 Lazar, M. (11 December 2020) 2020: A Turning Point for European Populists? *Institut Montaigne.* www.institutmontaigne.org/en/blog/2020-turning-point-european-populists. Accessed on: 11 May 2022.

72 *Ibid.*

73 Abou-Chadi, T. and Krause, W. (July 2020) The Causal Effect of Radical Right Success on Mainstream Parties' Policy Positions: A Regression Discontinuity Approach...*British Journal of Political Science.* 50 (3) 829–847; and Krause, W. et al (2019) Does Accommodation Work? Mainstream Party Strategies and the Success of Radical Right Parties. www.almendron.com/tribuna/wp-content/uploads/2019/09/krause-cohen-abouchadi-2019.pdf.

74 Mudde, C. (2019) *op.cit.*

75 Mac Dougall, D. (Updated: 16/09/2022) Sweden election: Why the far-right were the biggest winners and four other takeaways. *EuroNews.* www.euronews.com/my-europe/2022/09/16/sweden-election-why-the-far-right-were-the-biggest-winners-and-four-other-takeaways. Accessed on: 19 November 2022.

76 Muller, J-W. (2017) *op.cit.* 113.

77 Lowell, H. (26 April 2022) Marjorie Taylor Greene Texted Trump Chief of Staff Urging Martial Law to Overturn 2020 Election. *The Guardian.*

3
MISTAKEN IDENTITY
Pushing People into Rival Camps

The complicated intersection of culture and class dislocates the conventional political axis of left and right, and makes it highly problematic to align policies geared to social inclusion and cohesion. Amplified through the information net, all of this is reshaping politics and economics, which are the concerns of the next two chapters.

Across the world, great attention is paid to identity politics, as if it was new. It isn't. Essentially, it involves mobilising group power around common identity – in terms of nationality, ethnicity, gender, sexuality, religion, and the like – to promote policies favourable to that special group interest. In democratic societies that role has always been played by *pressure groups*. Similarly, in sociology, distinction has been long drawn between *ascribed* and *achieved* status, whereby some aspects of a person's identity were regarded as assigned and fixed, whereas others were alterable and attained. Group identity was often seen in terms of *subculture*, the idea that within society's mainstream norms lay sub-sets attached to particular groups, who had different ways of seeing and being. Politics has always entailed people *identifying* with sectional interest. So what, if anything, is new?

Some see current focus on identity as traceable to movements associated with the 1960s, such as student protest, civil rights campaigns, second-wave feminism, environmental and anti-nuclear struggles, and later gay rights. All these suggested that radical left politics had to go beyond class to a politics of resistance around multiple forms of injustice, which generated particular 'identities' of people facing distinctive discrimination. Back in the 1980s, Brunt[1] praised such politics as helping each of us understand our many selves. In the spirit of liberation, she saw it as an escape from boxed-in convictions about the primacy

DOI: 10.4324/9781003106593-4

of class to what is 'a very welcoming kind of politics because everyone can have a go at defining it in their own terms'.

Expressed like that, it seemed to offer a broad politics of inclusion that went beyond a mainly white, male-dominated labour movement concerned about work and wages. Then how did we get from this all-embracing approach to an identity politics that can be used now to typecast and contain? And let's not mistake its presence on both sides of the political aisle. Presently, the right focus mostly on identity based on race, nationality, culture, whereas the left focus on identity based on race, gender and sexuality.

Race Ahead

If we take the issue of race, what does it tell us about the discourse and politics of identity? From the previous chapter, it can be seen that a key source of current racial identity is anti-immigrant sentiment. To determine how far discussion about immigration is coded with xenophobic bigotry, we must first examine key terms that now dominate the debate about racism. As indicated in the previous chapter, the right has projected immigration into Europe in terms of a *replacement*. UK Home Secretary, Suella Braverman has referred to those arriving in Britain by dinghies operated by criminal gangs as an *invasion*. Data from the 2021 Census show that 16.8 percent of people in England and Wales (10 million) had been born outside the country, an increase from 13.4 percent (7.5 million people) in 2011, and nearly double the 8.9 percent figure in 2001. Some see this as too much too fast, a rate and pace likely to transform particular communities if settlement is concentrated geographically. Others see it positively in terms of younger migrants balancing an ageing population. Indeed, net migration comprised 2 million of the total 3.5 million population increase since 2011.[2]

From a general liberal-left 'progressive' perspective, *systemic racism* is taken as an interwoven practice, whereby racial discrimination in law, education, housing, health and so on can bolster each other to form and keep racial inequality in nearly every important facet of life. Societies like the US, where once black people could be regarded as the property of white people, are regarded as having racism built into their very establishment.

From this origin, racist ways of seeing the world have been used to validate white advantage and power. Racism here is distinguished from racial prejudice, which is taken as belief and attitude. It occurs when such bias is turned into detrimental action, and involves prejudice plus power. Reference to *structural* and *institutional* racism concerns how these embedded systems show themselves in policies and practices that become experienced as routine injustice by people of colour. In Britain, the Macpherson report into the police investigation of murdered black British teenager Stephen Lawrence in 1993 defined racism as consisting of 'conduct or words or practices which disadvantage or advantage people because of their colour, culture, or ethnic origin', and institutional racism as:[3]

> *the collective failure of an organisation to provide an appropriate and professional service to people because of their colour, culture or ethnic origin. It can be seen and detected in processes, attitudes, and behaviour which amount to discrimination through unwitting prejudice, ignorance, thoughtlessness, and racist stereotyping which disadvantage minority ethnic people....Without recognition and action to eliminate such racism it can prevail as part of the ethos or culture of the organisation. It is a corrosive disease.*

Forms of domination may have adapted over time to outlast the legal and cultural frameworks that gave rise to them. Racial hierarchy persists, through which people are typically valued less for their individual quality than for their classification and rank on the basis of factors such as skin tone. Racism is mostly seen as a 'white' problem, and is based on assumptions derived from legacies of empire and slavery, that white is standard, or is superior and 'ideal'.

Even outside the extremes of white supremacism, racial divisions are created through behaviour that distinguishes white as normal and non-white as abnormal, or at least different – the way, in some quarters, before rock n roll, rhythm & blues used to be called 'race music'. In short, the problem goes beyond individual racist acts. Rather, it refers to the workings of the whole social arena that takes 'whiteness' as the natural state, a presumption that white experience is universal, or that white is right, and for some right is might.

From this racial inequality is said to come *unjust enrichment* for white people. If housing supply is restricted for blacks, as happened under 'redlining' in the US, this grants greater housing choice for whites. If police prioritise 'street drugs' under the so-called 'war on drugs', this may not only criminalise some in black neighbourhoods, but also minimise attention to white middle class abuse of drugs like cocaine. Whites can gain 'unearned' benefit – what has been labelled *white privilege* – where black disadvantage can create white advantage. This pattern has played out over a long history of exploitation, the culmination of which can be seen in present day privilege, an inequality that is the consequence of European colonialism, the Atlantic slave trade, and in the US, Jim Crow laws, which, after the abolition of slavery, took the form of local and state legal statutes to uphold segregation and discrimination in housing, schools, and public facilities. All this was further secured by suppression of the black vote.

White privilege does not mean that white people have never been burdened, or that their accomplishment has all been unearned. It's not saying that whites have everything going for them, while blacks have nothing. No, it suggests instead that white people enjoy an inherent head-start gifted to them, relative to non-whites with similar income level and diligence.

Another term is *de-colonising space*, and involves the removal of symbols that venerate an imperial past, intending to make that space welcoming to people of colour. This has been evident in protests against statues of colonialists, slave traders, and owners. Such actions speak to how the past is not 'another country', but very much alive today, as evident when in July 2020, the US senator, Tom Cotton, unashamedly referred to the mass enslavement of Africans in North America as 'the necessary evil upon which the union was built'.[4] That a senior US law-maker could seek to excuse such crime is not only beyond human decency, but also shows the currency such wicked views still command. In his abysmal conceit, he missed the cruel irony of his surname.

Another aspect of this is where big corporations jump on the bandwagon of events such as global protests about George Floyd's killing in Minneapolis, to exploit a marketing opportunity to parade the virtue of their brand under the guise of empathy with the oppressed.

Wilkerson[5] prefers to talk about an American caste, rather than race, system. Distinguishing between *caste* as a firm and constant category, and *race* as an adaptable one that could be demarcated at the convenience of the dominant power, the clear dividing line became that between black and white, with black as permanent inferior caste. Black people were subordinated and degraded not simply by individuals or companies, but by the very law. American slavery, enduring as it did for a quarter of a millennium, beginning with Virginia colony's first African arrivals in 1619, and ending in 1865, over time embedded its legality and enforcement. Its brutal system penalised the enslaved not the enslaver.

By the late seventeenth century, as English and Irish indentured servants were gradually granted concessions over their African co-workers, a stark polarity emerged between those who could be blended into a European white category, with Anglo-Saxon Protestants at the top. Descending rank was tied to relative resemblance to this upper tier, with those captive on the lowest rung of the hierarchy cast as black. Subject to horrors of torture, whipping, branding, rape, mutilation, and even death, for perceived impertinence, they were essentially de-humanised as a means of justifying their total privation of rights and dignity. And it has always been easier to inflict this on a minority that is visually distinct from the in-group.

They were products, not people. They were owned, shackled, and useful only at the absolute discretion of their masters. Over centuries, the appalling depravity of this order became normalised, so that an established ranking took hold on the basis of appearance, particularly colour. Wilkerson refers to race in America as the visible decoy for caste. Everyone is conscripted into its 'silent war-game' of contrived division, and assumption about relative worth. The very imperceptible nature of caste bestowed it with authority and durability. Wherever there remains white resentment about surmised black 'disobedience', offhand attitudes about blacks getting uppity can resurface.

Hence, it's inaccurate to talk about the 'legacy' of American slavery. To take William Faulkner's famed quote: 'the past is never dead. It's not even past'. The deep imprint of caste leaves its persistent impression, complicating race relations in the US, and its relationship to identity. While some white conservatives have tended to be open to the appeal of the alt-right on racism, white liberals have tended to move in the opposite radical direction of greater resistance to racism and greater support for racial diversity. This has been called the *Great Awokening*[6] that can be traced to the 2014 protests in Ferguson, Missouri. One outcome was the withdrawal of racially conservative Democrats from the party, leaving them open to Trump's appeal. This shift gave a false impression of a major surge in white nationalism, when the latter was being highlighted rather than newly invented. White racial resentment may have been emboldened by Trump, but it wasn't simply summoned by him.

Both forces – radical anti-racism and white nationalism – have reaffirmed each other in a highly polarised politics. For decades up until recently, many white Democrats thought that a key source of racial inequality lay in African American lack of drive for self-advancement. Today, white liberals not only see systemic racism as the principal cause, but are also more fervent about the virtues of migration and diversity than are generally blacks and hispanics.

At the same time, the share of Democrats who identify as liberal rose, to make up about 40 percent of the party, a significant pressure for a socially liberal identity politics. Whereas Democratic party policies in the Clinton years of the 1990s talked about tightening borders and chasing down 'rampant' illegal immigration, by 2008, though there was still emphasis on curbing the undocumented and unchecked, there was also a modest move to creating citizenship pathways for unauthorised migrants.

The Matter of Black Lives

What is the current evidence about racial attitudes in the US, given the prominence of the Black Lives Matter movement?[7] Two-thirds of adults register support for the movement, with nearly four in ten saying they strongly support it. While this view is noticeably strong among black Americans, some support level is found in most white (60 percent), Hispanic (77 percent) and Asian (75 percent) Americans.

Nevertheless, it is a partisan issue. Ninety-two percent of white Democrats express support, while only 37 percent of white Republicans feel the same. In relation to protests following George Floyd's death, black adults reference durable complaint about their treatment (at 83 percent); rage at Floyd's killing (81 percent); and tensions between police and black people (76 percent). The figures for white adults for each of these factors respectively were 62 percent; 68 percent; and 67 percent.

Party affiliation makes a big difference. While white and black Democrats mostly agree about the extent to which each of these factors played a part in the protests, 84 percent of Democrats as a whole attribute longstanding concerns about treatment of black people, but only 45 percent of Republicans agree. In terms of Trump's impact on race relations, 80 percent of Democrats say he made things worse, with 40 percent of Republicans agreeing, meaning a high share of his base were more honest than him about his position on race, even though he shamelessly claimed: 'I did more for the black community than anybody, with the possible exception of Abraham Lincoln'!

The Black Lives Matter protests in Britain became highlighted by the tossing of the statue of slave trader, Edward Colston, into Bristol Harbour in June 2020. It showed how race was seen by some as inextricably tied to empire. Critics of the act varied in their alarm: it mistakenly judged history by contemporary values; it needed to be seen in the wider frame of Cultural Marxism, according to the then attorney general, Suella Braverman; and it was part of a more general attack on western culture by a Taliban-like movement, which claimed that black people were inevitable victims of a white society tainted by colonialism.[8]

> *The establishment is effectively standing back from, or even condoning or actively assisting, a sustained and organised onslaught which is taking place against not just a number of stone images but a culture's historic memory....On Twitter, the malevolent, the moronic and the mentally unhinged are out in force similarly seeking to intimidate, smear and ruin any who stand up to this cultural totalitarianism.*

Diversity of race, ethnicity and religion in England and Wales has been increasing. As indicated earlier, preliminary data released from the UK's 2021 Census offers only a broad picture: about one in six people in England and Wales were born outside the UK. Of these, over a third (36.4 percent) were born in the European Union (EU), an increase in the 2011 share (32.7 percent), representing a longer-term trend of a rising share coming from the EU. More comprehensive data of the 2011 Census by the Office of National Statistics reveals the following:[9] the share identifying with a White ethnic group has fallen from 94 percent in 1991 to 86 percent in 2011, with 8 percent Asian/Asian British and 3 percent Black/African/Caribbean/Black British. Contrary to some impressions, almost half (46 percent, 3.4 million) of the foreign-born population identified with a White ethnic group.[10]

In terms of religious identity, 59 percent of total residents were Christian, 5 percent were Muslim, and 25 percent had no religion. Of the foreign-born population, nearly half (48 percent) identified as Christian, compared to 61 percent of those UK-born; a fifth identified as Muslim (19 percent), compared to

3 percent who were UK-born; and 14 percent had No religion, compared to 27 percent of those UK-born.[11] The largest single share of foreign-born residents (3.6 million) were Christian, with 53 percent of these arriving in the previous decade. The second largest share was Muslim (1.4 million). So the racial, ethnic and religious composition of residents has been changing toward a greater mix. But images suggesting that this has all been about influx of non-white, non-Christians do not accurately encapsulate the complexity of this churn.

Data update on these categories for 2019,[12] showed the White group reducing to 84.8 percent. While 78.4 percent of the total population self-identified as White British, the Other White category was an estimated 5.8 percent. Around half (51 percent) of people recorded their religion as Christian, a drop of nearly 8.3 percent since the 2011 Census. The share registering No Religion increased from 32.3 percent in 2011 to 38.4 percent in 2019, with Muslims accounting for 5.7 percent and Hindus, 1.7 percent.

Britain's migration pattern has been moulded by both Empire and relationship to Europe. In the 1950s, labour demand drove immigration from both colonies and Europe. Since the 1948 Nationality Act, immigration policy has often seen citizenship in racialised terms, evident clearly in the Windrush scandal. Following EU expansion since 2004, migration from Europe has increased. Yielding to pressure from an adverse politics around immigration, government has created a 'hostile' or 'compliant' environment since 2010, designed to curb net migration.[13] The politics of anti-migration has been long embedded, and, as a reflection of this, the British government came under international criticism for its early ungenerous response to Ukrainian refugees in 2022.

In general terms, public policy around 'race relations' in Britain has shifted over the last seventy years from vague assumptions about integration and assimilation of long-term settled migrants, to slow appreciation that 'assimilation' could unfairly suppress cultures, onto a period of validation of multiculturalism, and then by the 1990s, to questioning whether multiculturalism produced separatism. When attacks in New York in 2001 led to the 'war on terror', attention switched to the risk seemingly posed by fundamentalist religious groups. At the same time, race was being placed within a wider frame of identity politics. This is captured well by Byrne et al:[14]

> While questions of race and racism largely fell off of the policy and political agenda, issues of religion, ethnicity and identity moved centre-stage, with evocations of 'parallel lives' and 'community cohesion' conjuring familiar and well-worn tropes of cultural difference and incompatibility that resonated strongly with the earlier 'race relations' framework, but now with a sense of global urgency and threat – both external and 'homegrown'.

But given these changes in migration and policy, what is the evidence from recent government data of racial inequality in Britain? The following summarises key features:

Asian and Black households and those in the 'Other' ethnic group were more prone to be poor and were the most liable to be in enduring poverty. Around 1 in 4 children in Asian-headed households or those in the 'Other' ethnic group were in persistent poverty, as were 1 in 5 children in Black households, compared to 1 in 10 White British households.[15] People from Pakistani and Bangladeshi ethnic groups are over 3 times as likely as white British people to reside in the most income-deprived 10 percent of neighbourhoods.[16] Similarly, all Black ethnic groups were overrepresented in these neighbourhoods in England.[17] A report by the Social Mobility Commission[18] noted that 46 percent of the Muslim population live in the 10 percent of the most deprived local authority districts.

Poor educational achievement in the UK is closely connected with economic disadvantage. A more complicated relationship exists between attainment and ethnic background. In England, White British and White Irish pupils who are ineligible for free school meals (FSM) – a proxy for those from low-income families – are around twice as likely to attain A★- C in maths and English GCSEs as those who are entitled. In contrast, Black Caribbean pupils experience very low overall attainment, with less difference between pupils eligible for free school meals and those not.

The McGregor-Smith review (2017)[19] into the role of race in the workplace reported that while in 2015, 1 in 8 of working age population came from a Black and Minority Ethnic (BAME) background, they comprised only 1 in 10 of the workforce and only 1 in 16 of top managerial posts. Those BAME individuals in work tend to be disproportionately in lower paid jobs. The unemployment rate of the young Black group (30.3 percent) was more than double that of the young White group (13.3 percent).

In the Criminal Justice system in England and Wales,[20] most staff come from an ethnically White background (93.4 percent of police officers; 93.2 percent of court judges; 89.6 percent of tribunal judges and 94 percent of prison officers). With stop & search, Black groups faced a rate eight times that of white people in 2016/17. The Lammy Review (2017) addressing treatment of minority groups in the criminal justice system found that many from such backgrounds experienced it as one loaded against them. It found that though they comprised 14 percent of the population of England and Wales, BAME people accounted for 25 percent of prisoners, and over 40 percent of those in youth custody. Black people specifically, though constituting around 3 percent of the general population, made up 12 percent of adult prisoners in 2015/16, and over 20 percent of children in custody. The Report sets this data in an international context:[21]

In France, Muslims make up an estimated 8 percent of the population and between a quarter and a half of the prison population. In America, one in 35 African-American men are incarcerated, compared with one in 214 White men. In Canada, indigenous adults make up 3 percent of the population but 25 percent of the prison population. In Australia, Aboriginal and Torres Strait Islander prisoners make up 2 percent of the population, but 27 percent of prisoners. In New Zealand, Maoris make up 15 percent of the population, but more than 50 percent of the prisoners.

The government's Race Disparity Audit[22] reports that most people across all ethnic groups feel a very or fairly strong sense of belonging to their neighbourhood and to Britain. Of course, questions about 'belonging' are subject to interpretation. For example, Ali,[23] writing about the Muslim experience of belonging in Britain distinguishes between a cultural sense (feeling at ease) and an affective sense (feeling attached).

Two points are worth making at this stage. First, such data show that although there is a persistent divide between whites and people of colour, variation within and between ethnic groups is significant and interesting. Second, racial difference in wealth and poverty must be set within the overall context in Britain. The Social Mobility Commission in 2020[24] noted the following: In the UK today, 8.4 million working age adults live in relative poverty; an increase of 500,000 since 2011/12. Almost one in three children and one in six pensioners face relative poverty in what is the sixth richest country in the world. Despite myths to the contrary, this can't be attributed to wholesale fecklessness. Almost three-quarters (72 percent) of children living in poverty are in households where at least one adult is in work. When you move from income to the issue of wealth, the gap is severe:[25]

The disparity in wealth clearly shows this: the top 10 percent of people hold almost half of the total wealth, and average wealth has increased by 11 percent for the richest compared to 3 percent for the poorest. Similarly, incomes for the top 5 percent of households have pulled away from the bottom 10 percent, whose incomes have largely stagnated over the previous two decades.

A UK government report in 2022, *Inclusive Britain*,[26] identifies a range of social inequalities. One of the most impactful is how deprivation influences longevity. For example, males in the most deprived decile have close to 10 years' lower life expectancy than males in the least deprived decile. Within the general pattern of social disadvantage, the report emphasises the spatial concentration of ethnic minority populations in large urban areas in de-industrialised regions like the North West, Yorkshire and the Midlands. This was reflected in Black, and Bangladeshi and Pakistani people having the highest unemployment rate out of all ethnic groups (8 percent), twice the rate of White people in 2019. In turn, the experience of living in areas beset by poverty can carry added risk of violent crime. Young black people are 24 times more likely to be murdered than their white counterparts. Nationally in 2021, black people were 7 times more likely to be stopped and searched than white people. Does that mean for many young black people that they suffer the dual adversity of being more subject *to* crime, while also being more suspected *of* crime?

Despite such sharp divides, the UK government is keen to stress that racial disparities are complicated, and are not always reducible to white versus people of colour. So, for example, black African pupils are less likely to experience exclusion from school than white British pupils. In terms of university access, in 2021, 72.1 percent of pupils from the Chinese ethnic group in the UK achieved a higher education place – the highest entry rate out of all ethnic groups, whereas the figure for white pupils was 33.3 percent – the lowest entry rate. With regard to home ownership, rates varied from 74 percent of Indian households to 68 percent of White British households, to the lowest rates found in the Black African (20 percent) and Arab (17 percent) ethnic groups.[27] Such variations invite careful consideration about the specific aspects of discrimination, without denying the general feature of its racist character.

Against these backgrounds of income inequality; differential educational attainment and treatment in the Criminal Justice System; and immigration patterns, particularly with respect to the changing demography of Muslims, where sit two particular aspects of prejudice and discrimination – Islamophobia and Antisemitism?

Islamophobia

Some claim that Islamophobia and anti-Semitism cannot be considered under racism since Muslims and Jews are not races – their mistreatment is best categorised as religion-based rather than racist. Others believe that it sits properly within debate about racism, because the term is apt wherever a group is considered inferior, even if it's down to its culture and heritage rather than assumptions about 'biological race'. This is complicated by the fact that most Muslims across the world are black or brown, and for those who see skin colour as 'race', it's easy to see how Islam can be racialised. Undeniably, negative portrayal of Muslim emblems is pervasive. Prior to becoming Prime Minister, Johnson derogated women in burqas as resembling letter boxes and bank robbers.

However, some dislike the very term 'Islamo*phobia*' because it sets the main problem as fear and anxiety felt by non-Muslims. Some critics of the term insist that *phobia* means an irrational or undue fear, whereas for them, concern about the theocratic character of particular forms of Islam is well justified. Still others reject measures addressing prejudice and harm against specific groups, which can lead to a victim hierarchy, preferring a single clear law against hate crime. In the UK, this is defined as: 'any crime or incident where the perpetrator's hostility or prejudice against an identifiable group of people is a factor in determining who is victimised'.

In such disputes, there's difficulty getting agreed definition. In the case of Islamophobia, from the UN[28] to various Muslim organisations[29] to agencies like the Runnymede Trust[30] to the UK All Party Parliamentary Group on British Muslims,[31] attempts to pin down the term cite the following factors: unfounded and irrational alarm and hostility regarding Islam; representation of Islam as irreconcilable with Western values; prejudicial enmity that demonises most or all Muslims; discriminatory behaviour that produces unequal treatment, and social and political exclusion; depictions of Muslims as one uniform group defined by a unified essence; and supposed Muslim failure to show a sense of belonging to their Western society of residence.

In particular places like Britain, it's easy to refute some stereotypes Muslims face. They are not all the same; they do not speak with one voice. A third are below the age of 15, compared to just under a fifth of UK population, and half are under 25 years old, and young Muslims carry distinct opinions compared with older Muslims to some degree on many matters. Similarly, differences in viewpoint exist between men and women, between the less and highly educated, and between those living in London, compared to those outside the capital.

In Britain, the Muslim community is ethnically and religiously diverse. The 2011 Census shows 68 percent are of Asian or Asian British descent (Indian, Pakistani, Bangladeshi), 10 percent come from Black ethnic groups, 8 percent from White ethnic groups and 6 percent from Arab ethnic groups. Major differences in religious affiliation are evident, not only that between Sunnis and the Shi'as, but also involving other subgroups such as the Barelwi, the Deobandi/Tablighi Jama'at, and the Jama'at-i Islami. Despite these distinctions, Muslims tend to be cast as a uniform collective.

Overwhelmingly, Muslims say that they have a strong sense of belonging to Britain.[32] Nearly all feel it is a place where they can practice their faith freely,[33] and 72 percent disagree that Western liberal society is ill-suited to Islam, unlike the widespread view among Britons in general that Islam and British values are incompatible.[34] But then the British public mistakenly think that Britain's Muslim population is about three times the share of the reality.[35] Because Muslims are concentrated in particular places, it can make for their high visibility in those areas. In England, 47 percent live in London; 15 percent in the West Midlands; 11 percent in West Yorkshire; and 10 percent in Greater Manchester.[36] Religion plays an important role for the great majority of Muslims in both their daily lives and identity. Related to those religious values, many hold traditional ideas about family. When faced with the proposition that homosexuality should be legal in Britain, 52 percent disagree, although young Muslims are slightly more liberal. Moreover, nearly half of Muslim men and a third of Muslim women agree that 'wives should always obey their husbands'.[37]

This social conservatism raises problems for a liberal society. Anti-Islamophobia should oppose anti-Muslim hatred, without censoring itself on valid criticisms of Islam. Too often today the two are mutually exclusive. As anti-Muslim sentiment is typically associated with the right, some on the left fail to voice warranted censure. If anti-Islamophobia equates to an inability to call out *any* aspect of Islamic creed that is at odds with democratic values, for fear of seeming racist, such moral relativism prevents many progressives defending their own self-claimed principles. Wary of failing victims of racism, they end up abandoning those who suffer at the hands of sexism and misogyny. This illustrates the dilemma of competing rights. There should be no equivocation in condemning the repression of women by the Taliban or Iran's morality police, at whose callous treatment a 22-year old women ended up dead in custody in September 2022, an outrage that sparked persistent dissent, and the killing of at least 185 protesters, including 19 children, within the first three weeks of street resistance. Unfortunately, such policing zealotry is not restricted to a few places. Going back a decade, similar constabulary was present in a third of countries in the Middle East and North Africa. Two decades ago, 15 Saudi girls died in a school fire, because the so-called guardians of morality there considered it unfitting to permit their escape since they weren't wearing the deemed modest attire of abayas.[38] Such barbaric behaviour cannot be excused in the name of religious freedom or cultural relativism.

When Qatar hosted the world cup soccer tournament in late 2022, critics of FIFA's location decision lamented the country's human rights record, its theocratic response to sexual identity and certain social behaviour, and its exploitation of migrant workers. An anti-imperialist perspective might charge that such condemnation was hypocritical in ignoring the historical role that the British played in the Gulf and their specific influence when Qatar was a British protectorate from 1916 to 1971. Such critique holds challenges for both right and left. Yes, it shows the importance of the West remembering its colonial record. But such record should not become a pretext for contemporary repression. The old saying holds true: two wrongs don't make a right.

For too many contemporary liberals/leftists, some groups' rights are more important than those of others. It should be possible to respect Muslim's right to live, work and practice religion in the West, while at the same time expecting them to respect democratic norms around such basics as gender equality. Rights come with responsibilities. Morality is, after all, a two-way street. Being subjugated does not absolve you from all moral responsibility.

Any censorship that closes debate and proper theological and social dispute, including feminist opposition to Islam's patriarchal and sexist elements, is wokeism at its worst. This highlights the democratic right to criticise any belief system, even if it upsets cultural or religious feeling, a point the previously mentioned UK All Party Parliamentary Group affirms: 'criticism of religion is a fundamental right in an open society and is enshrined in our commitment to freedom of speech'. Having considered definitions from varied sources, this body ended up with a simple version: 'Islamophobia is rooted in racism and is a type of racism that targets expressions of Muslimness or perceived Muslimness'. Even more terse is Runnymede's rendering: Islamophobia is anti-Muslim racism.

If combating Islamophobia should not be used to justify an uncritical appraisal of illiberal Islam, where is the dividing line between criticism and hate? The right to subject ideas to appraisal is fundamental to democracy, though critique can be readily *felt* as insult where religious beliefs are devoutly held. It's important to distinguish feeling from fact. Moreover, bigots can hide behind such critique to propagate hatred of, and fear among, all adherents of a particular faith. Since even far-rightists these days are guarded about being cast as racist, they may resort to cultural criticisms as a cover for their hateful intent. This sleight-of-hand is unconvincing, and should be exposed for its deception:[39]

> *Yet all forms of racism have contained a cultural element, symptomatically by attributing pathological, dangerous or aberrant behaviours to groups ranging from black to Chinese to Jewish people. Nonetheless, the focus on culture as a key component of current forms of racism is useful for understanding why racism and its effects persist even as essentialist biological claims about race have become unfashionable.*

Furthermore, where religion penetrates every aspect of life, it can be argued that it is hard to separate religion and culture. Religious affiliation can be associated with generalised cultural attributes, such as depiction of all Muslim women as repressed by a misogynist and patriarchal system. Where this happens, women are pictured as all pitifully submissive and men as all prone to sexist domination – classic stereotyping.

At the same time, critics of Islam, coming from inside that religious upbringing, merit attention, as with Ayaan Hirsi Ali.[40] She agrees that Muslims are not all alike. Yes, Islam has a central creed, derived from the Qur'an, which claims to be God's word as revealed by the Angel Gabriel to the Prophet Muhammad, and from the hadith, which gives account of Muhammad's life and ideas. From both sources, there is the affirmation of all Muslims – the Shahada: 'I bear witness that there is no God but Allah; and Muhammad is His messenger'. Within this fellowship, she identifies three sets that she calls: the Mecca Muslims; the Medina Muslims; and the dissident or reformist Muslims.

The first two she relates to mission stages attributed to Muhammad, whose birth is generally thought to be 570 years after that of Jesus, and his death in 632. From the Banu Hashim clan of the Quraysh, an influential mercantile tribe that commanded the Arabian trade path via Mecca, and one linked to Ishmael and thus distantly back to Abraham, he is credited with bringing Abrahamic monotheism into the prevailing polytheism of his milieu. In his early period as a preacher in Mecca, he proselytised about a one true divinity and the spiritual value of good works, a message that saw him exiled with his modest group of believers to Medina in 622. It was here that he developed association with other clans, knitting them into a faith community through the Constitution of Medina, a set of religious and political protocols that became the basis of shari'ah.

This Medina period is said to have seen him head a large military force that conquered the Quraysh, whose leader's daughter he married before proceeding to extend his reach across the Arabian peninsula, thereby forming the first major Islamic grouping. In Hirsi Ali's telling, these two stages marked the move from what now may be thought of as religious Islam (in the early Mecca phase) to religious-political Islam in the Medina phase. Muhammad's military adventures were accompanied by brutal treatment of the vanquished, and it is this mix of the military, patriarchal, political and religious that she sees as problematic for any Muslim dissident seeking to reform Islam:[41]

> *The Qur'an emphasises that all Muslims form one community of believers, the ummah (2.143). Although this community superseded prior tribal allegiances, the new religion retained many traditional tribal customs and enshrined them as religious values. These values pertain especially to honour, male guardianship of women, harshness in war, and the death penalty for leaving Islam....What had been tribal raiding now 'became sanctified as an act of religious duty': holy war, or jihad.*

In this characterisation, Mecca Muslims constitute largely religious Islam, whereas Medina Muslims are various shades of religious-political Islam. For all Muslims, reverence for bloodline is critical. Here, Hirsi Ali distinguishes between *shame* and *guilt* cultures, with the former based on the disgrace that comes from actions which dishonour the tribe, and which must be met with retribution or expulsion; and the latter based on self-awareness of, and remorse for, culpability through personal conscience and atonement.

Whereas the Western world over a long history transitioned from a shame to a guilt culture, the Islamic world, she says, remains stuck in the notion that discreditable behaviour, including internal dissent, is grave treachery to the 'sacred' bloodline. Hirsi Ali proceeds in her book, *Heretic*, to detail at length a series of religious-sanctioned practices in many Muslim-majority countries that I would consider shocking and obnoxious for any age, never mind the twenty-first century. Though she holds out hope for Islam's reform, she appreciates the obstacle of its central scripture.

The Last Word

For Islam, since Muhammad is God's last prophet, the Qur'an is God's final word, and as such, to be treasured in its literal, perfect and unalterable form. Despite this rigidity, Maajid Nawaz, prominent Muslim reformist, sees adherents divided into three concentric circles: a core of jihadists, who use coercion to spread Islamism; a larger group of Islamists, who seek to impose Islam on society at large, most obviously through the diffusion of shari'ah as law, and then a wider constituency that itself is split into sects. He designates groups like Islamic State and al-Qaeda as global jihadists, compared to regional ones like Hezbollah and Hamas.

A leading light in Quilliam, a global think tank focused on citizenship, religious freedom and anti-extremism, his big gripe is against some Western liberals who he refers to as the 'regressive left' and 'reverse racists'. These are people who are at the forefront of championing democratic and egalitarian values, and yet refuse to apply the same standards to Islam, or to support liberal Muslim dissenters, for fear of being regarded as racist or giving comfort to racists:[42]

> They have a poverty of expectation for minority groups, believing them to be homogeneous and inherently opposed to human rights values. They are culturally reductive in how they see 'Eastern' – and in my case, Islamic – culture, and they are culturally deterministic in attempting to freeze their ideal of it in order to satisfy their orientalist fetish.

Those he rebukes can retort that it is counter-productive, and indeed unjust, to add fuel to the fire. Having been extensively subjected to Western wrath and prejudice, Muslims don't deserve further criticism. After all, the geo-political context has been so unfavourable to them: the 1991 Gulf War; the War on Terror that followed the 2001 World Trade Centre bombing, including the illegal invasion of Iraq; use of counter-terrorist strategies like PREVENT in Britain, designed to stop 'radicalisation', but which can be seen as putting whole communities on watch; and thinly-veiled dog-whistling from figures like Trump.

Undoubtedly, all these and more contribute to a perception among some Muslims that they are being tarred with one brush, and that their identity is being treated with disdain. It has been argued that since the 'war on terror', they have been seen unjustly as a risk population that imperils the West:[43]

> An understanding of Muslims as a 'suspect community' has taken hold within contemporary popular and political conceptions. Muslims are widely viewed as a 'threat' to the nation (whether through associations with terrorism, criminality, grooming, sharia law and so on), as not, or only contingently belonging to the

nation, and as bearers of sets of values deemed irreconcilable with the values of Britain's asserted status as a liberal democracy. These established tropes work to deny the heterogeneity of Muslims in terms of nationality, ethnicity, religious practice, place, social and economic positions, and gender.

In turn, any such stereotyping has negative impact on Muslim sense of belonging. And then, any such reservation feeds into portrayal of their 'contingent' belonging and segregation. As the Casey Review[44] noted in the case of Britain, relative to other minority faith groups, Muslims tend to congregate in higher residential concentrations. For example, Blackburn, Birmingham, Burnley and Bradford have wards with between 70–85 percent Muslim population. Segregation in highly deprived areas, combined with poorer English language and labour market performance, make for much less opportunity.

For women in such communities, there may be a harmful blend of gender inequality, as well as religious and cultural obstacles that limit access to citizen rights. Other criminal practices that may confront women in particular include female genital mutilation, coerced marriage and 'honour' violence. A similar double-bind hits those whose sexuality faces hostility from both mainstream society and their particular culture. Also endangered is children's welfare when they are 'taught' in illegal and unregistered faith schools.

Where these practices exist, values of equality, rule of law, and tolerance are infringed. Moreover, we should remember that before any 'war on terror', in 1989, the non-Muslim world was shocked by the free speech implications of the fatwa calling for Salmon Rushdie's death for authoring a book, *The Satanic Verses*. Since then, there's been Islamist terror attacks, organised grooming, videoed executions for social media, a massacre in 2015 at the centre of Charlie Hebdo, a French satirical magazine, followed by an attack on a Paris Jewish supermarket, and later a suicide bomb attack on the Bataclan concert hall, murdering 130 people. Then, in August 2022, Rushdie was seriously stabbed while speaking on stage. All these, and similar events, are real, and represent a fundamental assault on democracy. Casey makes no bones about the need for democratic push-back:[45]

> *The prevalence and tolerance of regressive and harmful practices has been exploited by extremists, both 'Islamists' and those on the far right, who highlight these differences and use them to further their shared narrative of hate and division. These extreme ideologies feed on fear and suspicion, peddle hatred and prejudice, and seek to turn communities against each other in a vicious circle....Too many public institutions, national and local, state and non-state, have gone so far to accommodate diversity and freedom of expression that they have ignored or even condoned regressive, divisive and harmful cultural and religious practices, for fear of being branded racist or Islamophobic.*

Such harmful practices penalise their immediate victims, and prompt some among the general public to see a basic clash between Islam and liberal democratic values. This negative appraisal in turn leads some Muslims to experience hostility because of their religious identity, and this then prompts some to look to the global Muslim community for affirmation.

An illustration of how values and rights can themselves clash comes from the case of Anderton Park primary school in Birmingham, England in 2019. The public media picture was of a persistent protest/picket at the school gates, representing resistance by some Muslim parents about the school's LGBTQ-inclusive curriculum. In apparent conflict was the school's deemed obligation to cover the complicated relationships in modern British families, while respecting parents in the school, 90 percent of whose pupils came from a Muslim background, with roots in socially conservative Mirpur culture in Pakistan. Rival legitimacies were more complicated than typically portrayed. Did parents have legitimate concern about sensitive issues of sexuality, given the children's age? Should they have been consulted, or should the school have had authority to interpret its compliance with national curriculum guidance? Was the protest's leading public face, who was not a parent, but a pupil's relative, a democratic representative or self-nominated gatekeeper? Was this a simple case of theocratic Muslim culture, out-of-step with secular and pluralist values?

Actually, it was all much more complex.[46] The head-teacher regretted how the controversy was dogged with misinformation. They were not teaching about sex, gay sex, or gender reassignment, but simply using books that depicted diversity in British family life in all aspects – race, religion, and varied parenthood. The leading protest spokesperson denied homophobia and recognised LGBTQ rights, but claimed that he, and by inference parents, had the right of dissent. Some emphasised that while this was portrayed as a Muslim versus gay quarrel, similar sentiments were likely in other primary schools, with an equally deprived socio-economic catchment. Still others found those holding counter-protests, favouring liberal values, to be signalling a colonial outlook of 'white saviours', unnecessarily intruding into the education of non-whites, whereas more effective resolution needed fine-tuned dialogue within the Muslim community.

Meanwhile, Education Department guidance encouraged primary school coverage of LGBTQ issues at their discretion, paying regard to issues like age-appropriateness. Such scope for local judgement may seem sensible. But this imprecision leaves teachers holding the can. Would greater clarity be achieved through its compulsion under the Equality Act?

Then some may say that teachers are meant to be in loco parentis, not to override parental will about something sensitive to early child learning. Moreover, if parents come to believe that aspects of a curriculum offend their convictions, they may be induced to form a faith school alternative, which may only segregate identities further. There is a general principle that parental participation in the schooling of children is a good thing. If this crosses the line into an attempt to impose Shari'ah Law on British education, it is unacceptable.

Also, it can be said that those who want to defend their idea of liberal values have the right of expression, without being cast as 'white saviours'. What comes through this and similar disputes, is that 'identity rights', if pressed by any side without sensitivity or concession to alternative views, can trigger culture wars of attrition. Battles are won not by merit of argument as much as by who is worn down first.

Anti-Semitism

Similar definitional problems afflict anti-Semitism. The International Holocaust Remembrance Alliance (IHRA) adopted a working definition, which has been widely espoused:[47]

> *Antisemitism is a certain perception of Jews, which may be expressed as hatred toward Jews. Rhetorical and physical manifestations of antisemitism are directed toward Jewish or non-Jewish individuals and/or their property, toward Jewish community institutions and religious facilities.*

Imprecision is apparent – what does 'certain perception' mean? Terms like 'may be' and 'non-Jewish' raise further confusion. Definitions should seek to be definitive. Ambiguity invites interpretation, and interpretation invites easy labels of racism against political opponents. Is it a 'working definition', which means it's open to amendment, or does it have to be endorsed in full and forever?

Criminal attack on individuals and/or property because of their Jewishness or perceived Jewishness is straightforward. Navigating beyond that, however, the IHRA produced eleven 'illustrations' that gave examples of what could be considered anti-Semitic, having regard to the overall context, including: Holocaust denial; summoning, assisting, or justifying the harming or killing of Jews in the name of an ideology or religion; reference to 'blood libel' and Jesus killers; myths about global Jewish conspiracies, or Jewish control of media, finance, government, and similar tropes about the power of Jews as a collective.

Importantly, many have some reference to Israel: reproaching Jewish citizens about having greater allegiance to Israel than to their home countries; seeing the State of Israel as a racist endeavour, thereby denying Jews the right to self-determination; holding Israel to higher standards than other democratic countries; comparing Israeli policy to that of the Nazis; and regarding Jews as collectively answerable for Israel's actions. At the same time, it does acknowledge that criticism of Israel comparable to that directed against any other country cannot be considered anti-Semitic.

The Anti-Defamation League (ADL), founded in 1913 in reaction to rising anti-Semitism, advances the following definition:[48]

> *The belief or behavior hostile toward Jews just because they are Jewish. It may take the form of religious teachings that proclaim the inferiority of Jews, for instance, or political efforts to isolate, oppress, or otherwise injure them. It may also include prejudiced or stereotyped views about Jews.*

Again, they offer examples of common tropes such as: Jews are too powerful; disloyal; and greedy. Of course, some bigotry is easily recognised: 'perfidious Rothschild Zionists run world governments'; and variations of 'wicked Jewish financiers and moneylenders who defraud the common people'. These characterisations carry currency beyond the right to those leftists who see global capitalism in these conspiratorial terms. Where it becomes even more difficult, and is also included by the League, is anti-Zionism. Hatred of, hostility to, and persecution against, Jews as a collective are tied by some to anti-Zionism, which in turn is linked to negative attitudes to Israel. That shouldn't mean that Zionism isn't held to the same standards of critique as other ideologies and religions. Similarly, it must be possible to criticize Israel's government without placing the burden on such critics to prove their motive is not anti-Semitic. Proving a negative is always problematic.

All this requires historical context. Persecution against Jews has a long inglorious pedigree:

* the First Crusade in 1096, following Pope Urban II's call for holy war to assist Eastern Christians and reclaim the Holy Lands, led to Jerusalem's capture and slaughter of thousands of Muslim and Jewish residents;
* Edward I's killing of 269 Jews and expulsion from England of the rest (about 3000) in 1290, for Jews not to be able to return until the 1650s, when then invited by Cromwell;
* the systemic violence visited upon Jews in Europe in the mid-fourteenth century, particularly when cast as scapegoats for the Black Death, with myths about them causing the pestilence by poisoning the wells – despite several Papal decrees from Clement VI pleading for an end to anti-Jewish slaughter;
* the Spanish Inquisition from 1478, based on permission from Pope Sixtus IV, leading to expulsion from Spain in 1492;
* Martin Luther's vitriolic denunciation of Jewry in his book *The Jews and Their Lies*, in which he spoke of their conceit and blasphemy, and urged that their synagogues, schools, and even houses, be razed, their wealth be confiscated, and that they should be put into forced labour or expelled, in a treatment that should be merciless and without legal protection;

- the anti-Jewish pogroms in Russia in the nineteenth century;
- and all this and more culminating in the unique horror of the Holocaust.

Given this long litany, and today's rising anti-Semitism,[49] it's unsurprising that the notion of a safe haven, embodied in Zionism, finds appeal. Furthermore, it can be said that while there are many countries with majority Christian or Muslim character, there is only one for Jews.

A recent report[50] charts increased incidence of physical assaults and other hate crimes inflicted on Jews across the world. While much of it comes from radical right groups, it also includes state-sponsored versions, as in Belarus. The report argues that the pandemic has generated anti-Semitic conspiracies, holding Jews in general, and Israel in particular, responsible for disseminating the virus. Moreover, related lockdown periods have provided more time for people to consume toxic anti-Semitic tropes online.

So how can clearer markers be set for what constitutes anti-Semitism? Certainly, the Israeli government can be criticised. But all Jews can't be held accountable for its behaviour, and it's useful to acknowledge that Israel is a very flawed democracy in a region of non-democracies, and often under local threat. Distinction between anti-Semitism and anti-Zionism is more complicated. With respect to Zionism as understood as Jewish people's right to self-determination, this offers Jews anywhere the right to the same home somewhere, namely Israel. Though most Jews will never live there, it is marked as the Jewish homeland.

In language of the previous chapter, this can create an ethno-nationalist state, with which all Jews are expected to identify at some level. While the state accepts non-Jews as citizens, it accords special status to Jews. To be anti-Zionist can be seen as depriving Jews of this fundamental right to self-rule. Clearly, an anti-Zionism that singles out Israel's ethnic nationalism as unique, or that demands its extinction, is anti-Semitic, whereas an argument for self-determination on behalf of both Jews and Palestinians in Israel/Palestine is not.[51] Care has to be taken with the argument that Jews have the right to define their own identity, and if that includes a 'homecoming' to Zion, then Zionism is part of who Jews are, and if anyone criticises it, they are criticising who Jews are, and as such are patently anti-Jewish. This confuses right of identity with assured destiny.

If Israeli nationhood is seen in terms of a divinely preordained promised land for a chosen people, of which non-Israeli Jews constitute a diaspora with a right of return, contest over 'sacred' territory will be unhelpfully tied to identity. The 'Holy Land' is special to Jews. But it's also so for Christians and Muslims. And what about secularists who don't see it in religious terms? Hence, exclusive claims by any side guarantees perpetual insecurity for all sides.

In this regard, Beinart's position[52] is compelling. He notes that when addressing other ethno-nationalist conflicts, no one suggests that it is bigoted to prefer a Spanish identity that embraces Catalans or an Iraqi identity that accommodates Kurds, rather than splintering these multiethnic states into separatist ethno-states. Taking the model of the new South Africa, he extols how it has swapped Afrikaner ethnic nationalism and white racial nationalism for a pluralist and equal belonging for all. By contrast, in the context of Israel's nine million population, which includes nearly two million Palestinians, or 'Arab Israelis', and another five million non-citizen Palestinians under Israel's power, prioritising Jewish demography and privilege to protect the state's existence, turns that state into one based on inequality.

Beinart observes that just as not all anti-Zionists are anti-Semitic, so not all those favouring a 'national home for the Jewish people' are free of anti-Semitism. The so-called Balfour Declaration in 1917 was forwarded by someone who seemed happy to see this outcome as a way to free 'western civilisation' from a Jewish presence long considered as alien and hostile. Correspondingly, some rightwing American Christians, not always renowned for their pro-Jewish sympathies at home, can be Christian Zionists, because they see the end-time for Christ's Second Coming as demanding the re-gathering of Jews in Israel. Beinart concludes:

> *Antisemitism isn't wrong because it is wrong to denigrate and dehumanise Jews. Antisemitism is wrong because it is wrong to denigrate and dehumanise anyone. Which means, ultimately, that any effort to fight antisemitism that contributes to the denigration and dehumanisation of Palestinians is no fight against antisemitism at all.*

Plainly, these issues around race, religion and nationality are controversial, as are other identity contests around gender, sexuality, body shaming, ability, and such like. Accordingly, some want to frame how they can be discussed, and regulate who has validity in discussing them. Essentially, they want to set rules of engagement in the culture wars.

Mind Your Tongue

From the right, many are affronted by what is seen as a deliberate cultural war waged by the left. Jupp[53] captures this indignation when he affirms that there are two genders, not multiple. They are biologically fixed, not elected. Men and women are equal, but not the same. Branding masculinity as innately noxious undermines an important role model for stable families. Western heritage, rooted in Christianity and Greek culture, is to be valued not defamed. Virtue and malice are not exclusive traits of any particular race. Society cannot be reduced to a grievance story of oppression of women by men, of blacks by whites, of gays by straights, of the transgendered by the gendered, and of the global south by an avaricious West, led in modern times by the US, and in history by European colonialists. In his view, centres of learning, particularly universities, should not capitulate to doctrines of political correctness to the effect that they change curriculum by way of literary or historical revisionism, or censor free expression of 'non-woke' opinion.

This introduces the key term of *cancel culture*, which has gone through a series of iterations. It can refer to a backlash against what are considered hateful statements, or to various forms of no-platforming speakers or events considered to exclude or offend groups on the basis of their gender, race, sexual orientation, or ability. Most recently, it relates to removal of statues and symbols that are taken to glorify domination of the persecuted. In his July 2020 address at Mount Rushmore – a contentious monument on land revered by Native Americans – Trump spoke of the culture war in a comprehensive speech, worth quoting at length:[54]

> *In our schools, our newsrooms, even our corporate boardrooms, there is a new far-left fascism that demands absolute allegiance. If you do not speak its language, perform its rituals, recite its mantras, and follow its commandments, then you will be censored, banished, blacklisted, persecuted, and punished....Against every law of society and nature, our children are taught in school to hate their own country.... The radical ideology attacking our country advances under the banner of social justice. But in truth, it would demolish both justice and society....We declare that the United States of America is the most just and exceptional nation ever to exist on Earth....Our opponents would tear apart the very documents that Martin Luther King used to express his dream, and the ideas that were the foundation of the righteous movement for Civil Rights....We are proud of the fact that our country was founded on Judeo-Christian principles, and we understand that these values have dramatically advanced the cause of peace and justice throughout the world. We know that the American family is the bedrock of American life. We recognize the solemn right and moral duty of every nation to secure its borders. And we are building the wall....We believe in equal opportunity, equal justice, and equal treatment for citizens of every race, background, religion, and creed. Every child, of every colour — born and unborn — is made in the holy image of God. We want free and open debate, not speech codes and cancel culture. We embrace tolerance, not prejudice....We are the nation that gave rise to the Wright Brothers, the Tuskegee Airmen, Harriet Tubman, Clara Barton, Jesse Owens, George Patton — General George Patton — the great Louis Armstrong, Alan Shepard, Elvis Presley, and Mohammad Ali. And only America could have produced them all.*

In this, you have good summary of US right-wing identity politics: political correctness as new religion; America's exceptionalism and championing of global justice; 'natural' nationalism; invocation not only of God, but of Judeo-Christian heritage; family values; protective borders; heroes and villains; pervasive liberal indoctrination; and cultural threats from 'justice warriors'.

Resistance to cancel culture has not been restricted to the right. Obama rebuked judgemental attitudes that failed to appreciate the world as a complex, messy and ambiguous place, and humans as a flawed species. The American liberal comedian, Bill Maher, for a long time has reproached those liberals who he thinks have policed language to a point of needlessly goading potential allies for the sake of their own virtue-signalling. One example he takes relates to those who dig into what someone has written or said in the distant past that appears appalling by current standards. Just like technology, people can change and improve:[55]

> *Liberals are funny. They believe in evolution, except when it comes to people.... Wokesight is not 2020. And you don't have ESPCP (Extra Sensory Politically Correct Perception)....You're not morally better than your grandparents. You just came later. You're the next upgrade. You're the iPhone 11.*

Taking another example, a series of campus conflicts in Yale, Wesleyan, Oberlin, and Evergreen, have raised concern about freedom of inquiry, and speech suppression, in some US universities. In the University of Chicago, John Ellison, dean of students, wrote a welcoming letter to the class of 2020, making clear:[56]

> *Our commitment to academic freedom means that we do not support so-called trigger warnings, we do not cancel invited speakers because their topics might prove controversial, and we do not condone the creation of intellectual 'safe spaces' where individuals can retreat from ideas and perspectives at odds with their own.*

This statement had followed a report[57] outlining the university's principles around these issues, proclaiming it to be improper for the university to shield individuals from views and ideas that they consider disagreeable or even acutely offensive. Speech restriction may arise only in specific circumstance, for example where it breaches the law, wrongly defames an individual, poses a real threat or harassment, and unduly infringes significant privacy or confidentiality interests.

In similar sentiment, *A Letter on Justice and Open Debate*, signed by 153 high profile liberal authors and academics such as Martin Amis, John McWhorter, Noam Chomsky, Gloria Steinem, and JK Rowling, was published in *Harper's* magazine in July 2020.[58] While applauding protest for the 'needed reckoning' around racial and social justice, it deplored patterns 'that tend to weaken our norms of open debate and toleration of differences in favour of ideological conformity'. The democratic threat represented by illiberals like Trump called for resistance, but not one that settled into its 'own brand of dogma or coercion', limiting free inquiry and expression:

> *While we have come to expect this on the radical right, censoriousness is also spreading more widely in our culture: an intolerance of opposing views, a vogue for*

public shaming and ostracism, and the tendency to dissolve complex policy issues in a blinding moral certainty. We uphold the value of robust and even caustic counter-speech from all quarters. But it is now all too common to hear calls for swift and severe retribution in response to perceived transgressions of speech and thought.

In their opinion, stifling debate tends to hurt most those with least power. A preferable alternative is to counter bad ideas with better, more persuasive, ones. Similar argument has come from other 'progressive' sources that see this so-called cultural revolution more as an attack on intellectualism, with punitive reprisal for those who depart from the permitted narrative around justice. In retort, their progressive opponents insist that it is not about empty moral indignation, bullying or opinion curtailment, but is instead a pushback against those who misuse privileged positions to foster bigotry and harm. As stated by Giorgis in reaction to the *Harper's* letter:[59]

> *There's something darkly comical about the fretfulness of these elite petitioners. It's telling that the censoriousness they identify as a national plague isn't the racism that keeps Black journalists from reporting on political issues, or the transphobia that threatens their colleagues' lives.*

The complaint here is that this defence of free speech by powerful people shows little appreciation of how power determines who gets to say what, and who gets heeded, in public platforms. In not engaging with the history of discriminatory censorship, it takes refuge in a fanciful version of 'free speech' supposedly open to all. Certainly, it's hypocritical of that part of the media, owned by a few moguls and prone to analysis that legitimates their interest, to parade themselves as champions of pluralist comment.

A different objection to those criticising erosion of free thinking and open discussion comes from those who see it as deliberately exaggerated. For instance, Bollinger, President of Columbia University, has affirmed that at his university and 'at thousands of other schools across the United States, controversial ideas are routinely expressed by speakers on both the left *and* the right, and have been for decades. In fact, Columbia University is something of a magnet for provocative speakers'.[60] But for many on the right, wokeness, political correctness, and no-platforming for the purpose of protecting a 'safe space' for exploited or vulnerable groups, all stem ultimately from the same pernicious source – Cultural Marxism.

Cultural Marxism

The term *Cultural Marxism* is used to suggest that the far left's deliberate agenda is to erode faith in western values as a prelude to tearing down capitalism. Often, this is traced back to the late 1920s and the Frankfurt Institute of Social

Research, under Max Horkheimer, what came to be known as the Frankfurt School of Marxism. Today's Radical Right see the School's mainstay framework, known as Critical Theory, as offering a means of cultural revolution.

The story goes something like this: by the 1930s, it was clear to Frankfurt School theorists like Adorno and Marcuse that standard Marxist analysis of stages in history, whereby feudalism gave rise to mercantilism, which led to capitalism, which would in turn inevitably transform to communism, was wrong. Assumption about predestined history was considered too 'determinist'. History didn't have a plan. Despite the Russian Revolution, and the economic travails following a devastating World War triggered by monarchies, but fought by the masses, there was little sign of worker revolutions in places like industrial Europe. Thus, liberation towards a classless society as the fated outcome of class war between the owners and workers was far from assured.

How could Marxism be revised to make sense of this letdown? The answer was that its traditional version gave too much weight to the economy – the so-called 'base' of society, upon which was built the 'superstructure' of social institutions, culture, and the rest. This materialist emphasis reduced everything to class interest. If the working class did not rebel against exploitation by bosses, their passivity must be due to 'false consciousness', a misguided contentment with their lot.

But why this submissiveness? Critical Theory suggested that it was largely down to how power worked manipulatively to make the oppressed 'consent' to their oppression. To understand power, you had to grant separate significance to culture, rather than see it play second-fiddle to the economy. In this view, the ruling class exercises cultural hegemony – a fancy way of saying that the rules, principles and worldview validated as being in society's interests really serve to advantage those on top, and to keep the rest in their place. This notion about how vested interest is presented plausibly as natural and indisputable, indeed as *common sense*, is associated with the Italian Marxist, Gramsci.

He understood that power was not always about brute coercion. It was frequently about averting opposition ever arising in the first place because the dominated were 'domesticated' into the system by capitalist ideology. This exploitation of political consciousness could only be overcome by resolute spread of counter ideas that would seep into the routine everyday experience of the masses. In Gramsci's words:[61] '....every revolution has been preceded by an intense labour of social criticism, of cultural penetration and diffusion'.

The link here between the Frankfurt School and Gramsci is clear. Both were against managerialist welfare capitalism, which for them had a facade of liberal democracy and meritocracy that blinded workers to the reality of their subjection. Ideas most associated with Critical Theory come from: its cultural focus; perceived limitations of 'scientific socialism'; doubt about universal social laws of how the world is run; the enslavement involved in both authoritarian communism and standardised modern capitalism that relegates individuals to cogs in the machine, one-dimensional humans, and engenders a bland sameness in mass culture; the fabrication of 'needs' that only consumer capitalism appears able to meet, even if at the price of political docility; and an agenda for fuller human emancipation.

Postmodernism

Postmodernism shares common ground with Critical Theory. Both are concerned about how knowledge is entangled in power relationships between dominant and dominated. Both are sceptical about certitude and permanence of meaning, particularly as rooted in big picture explanations of social reality – so-called grand narratives about how the world works and history moves. Indeed, Lyotard[62] identifies incredulity toward metanarratives as the essence of the post-modern. Both seek to reveal hidden values and assumptions that underpin what passes for rationality, causation, and objective reality. Both are keen to uncover how language conceals the process by which reality is perceived. In other words, both claim that knowledge isn't a fixed thing out there waiting for discovery. Rather, it is embedded in, and mediated through, belief-systems. To a large extent, it is socially made, influenced and referenced by history and culture, and thus subject to interpretation and contest. It is relative rather than absolute. On this basis, rationally-determined knowledge does not dispense universal 'facts' and 'laws'. Rather, knowledge is conditional on perspective, contingency and context, which in turn relate to specifics like time, place, and power.

No wonder that some see in this a retreat from Enlightenment concepts of reason, actuality, truth, and progress, toward moral relativism that can no longer distinguish good and evil, and cultural relativism that no longer dare judge the worthiness of one set of cultural values over another. In particular, Cultural Studies, and its off-shoots like Gender and Race Studies, challenge social meaning 'at face value', interrogating how it is produced, validated, conveyed, and debated, always searching for sub-text that gives the game away about power domains.

Concerns about how we produce and confirm knowledge are not peculiar to Critical Theory and postmodernism. It's widely accepted in sociology, for example, that the discipline is not value-free, since it involves people studying society of which they are a part. Being both subject and object in any study can make for 'conflict of interest'. Nevertheless, my presentation here is over-simplified, as is that of many today who want to make a neat link between Marxism and Critical Theory, between Critical Theory and postmodernism, between all these and Cultural Studies, and finally between the latter and political correctness and wokeness.

First, not all Critical theorists are fans of postmodernism. Habermas isn't. He sees postmodernists trapped in the contradiction of using reason and logic to belittle reason and logic. Second, many Critical theorists, going right back to

Adorno and Horkheimer, have been critics of conventional Marxism, which is wedded to its own objective 'truths' based on science. Third, Critical Theory at best is what it says on the tin: being contrarian, it questions received wisdom. Postmodernism acclaims nuance, paradox and satire, and values the eclectic. These stances are a far cry from the absolutist, right-on, holier-than-thou cheerleaders of debased political correctness, who suffer from irony-bypass and wilt at controversy.

Reservation about Critical Theory and postmodernism can be shared by both left and right: its obscure language that sometimes makes little sense; its partiality toward personal sentiment and anecdote over at least attempted objectivity; its dismissal of debate that doesn't mainly defer to someone's lived experience. Pluckrose and Lindsay[63] lament this dismissal of objective investigation, based, as they see it, on an assertion that truth and ethics are framed by power and language games deployed by the privileged to protect their position. They are concerned about an ideologically driven scholarship that sees reality, knowledge, and truth as culturally constructed – what Foucault referred to as power-knowledge, embedded in discourses legitimated by the beneficiaries of domination.

Pluckrose and Lindsay argue that what they term in capital letters, 'Social Justice Warriors', who problematise language as irredeemably value-laden with Eurocentric assumption, render all argument invalid, because there is no universal normative form of exchange. Conveniently, they also put themselves beyond critique. Since the powerful and powerless are not singing from the same hymn-sheet, those who self-identify as exploited are entitled to their own truth, based on their experience. A person's personal experience is beyond valid dispute by others, and thus can be seen to be protected from any criticism. This in turn, risks feeding right-wing identity politics, furthering tribalism and polarisation.

Interestingly, elements of this Social Justice scholarship are to be found in the seminal book *Pedagogy of the Oppressed* by Paulo Freire,[64] dating back to 1970. I remember it being very influential as part of the spirit of emancipation at that time. He advocated a liberation pedagogy that did not assume a docile and resigned subjugated people. The poor's humanisation depended on them being able to critically appraise the 'truths' embedded in an education system established by a repressive order: 'To surmount the situation of oppression, people must first critically recognise its cause, so that through transforming action they can create a new situation, one that makes possible the pursuit of a fuller humanity'.

But Freire saw the poor trapped in a paradox. They wanted freedom. Yet they also feared it, because they were at once the oppressed and oppressor, 'whose consciousness they (had) internalised'. As the foundation of what's been called 'epistemic injustice' – the deliberate creation of knowledge that validates an unequal status quo – this idea of the oppressed as 'hosts' to their oppressors is a variation of the Marxist concept of false consciousness.

While sharing some similar analysis, perhaps a big difference between Freire and some contemporary scholar-activists dealing with identity and hierarchy, is that he believed that the injustice de-humanised both oppressor and oppressed. The liberation he sought was for everyone in an improved common humanity.

Roots of Culture Wars

In the early 1980s, I was a research economist for the trade union movement in Birmingham, centre of the industrial heartland of Britain, then under-going massive deindustrialisation. Part of my research involved understanding corporate strategies of domestic contraction, alongside expansion in newly developing countries, an important forerunner to modern globalisation. Basically, this became known as the new international division of labour, whereby big companies could decompose their production process to ensure that the most labour-intensive part was located where labour was cheapest. I recall addressing a mass gathering of workers in the Dunlop factory – known as Fort Dunlop – one of the city's industrial landmarks. My advice that they needed to prepare for the company's likely strategy to relocate much of its pro-duction overseas, and maybe even ultimately close its Birmingham operation, was greeted with scepticism, if not derision. After all, the clue was in the name. This was Fort Dunlop. It would be defended by circling the normal trade union wagons. Of course, Dunlop did eventually pack up shop.

Nonetheless, the incredulity of the workforce to any such prospect was understandable. This was a well-organised mainly white male staff, who had felt immune to the vagaries of a rapidly changing economy. Many, I'm sure, considered themselves indispensible. But they weren't. Under Thatcher's stand-back policy, private corporations took harsh decisions based on the bottom line. During her show-down with 'aristocratic' labour in the Miner's strike of 1984/5, we helped Welsh miners organise financial and political support in the city, all ultimately in vain as the Mining union went down to humiliating defeat, and eventual extinction. They were ill-served by leaders, whose reluctance to democratise the union helped seal its fate.

At the same time, I was a member of the Labour Party in the Handsworth area, where given its majority minority-ethnic composition, the local branch was dominated by an uneasy alliance between an Afro-Caribbean faction and its Asian counterpart, who had carved up respective spheres of influence. Their leaders apparently offered the local Labour MP guaranteed delivery of block community votes, and were accorded consequent legitimacy. On the sidelines, were those working in places like textile sweatshops, mainly Asian women who were unorganised and highly exploited. I recall participating in a long-standing picket of one such plant with these women, demanding trade union recognition, a hard ask amidst growing mass unemployment.

In many ways, these four stories encapsulate the dilemma for the British left in the 1980s. The mainstay of the labour movement – its white, male-dominated and somewhat macho-style trade unions – were being emasculated by a combination of disempowering legislation and wholesale manufacturing job loss. While this massive incapacitation of working class security was underway, parts of the Labour Party were becoming sites for fragmentation around issues like race. Struggling to be heard were other voices, such as women, and other campaigns such as the anti-nuclear movement, alarmed at Thatcher's contribution to Reagan's arms race with the Soviets. Other elements of the progressive 'family', like the barely visible environmental movement, could hardly be expected to be enthusiastic allies of industrial stalwarts like coalminers, who produced the very fossil fuels to which they were opposed. In short, in the battle between capital and labour, the latter's forward march was not only being halted, but reversed, and much the same was happening elsewhere, like in the United States.

Amid such disturbance, organising politics around a splintering working class became ever more problematic. Disenfranchised interests like black rights organisations, feminists and gays were seeking their place in the sun at the very time when it was the winter of discontent for the working class. The so-called New Left that emerged in the 1960s had hoped to include these groupings within a broad progressive front, whose foundation was still the organised working class. In the United States, forces like the Civil Rights Movement still sought to get black rights within social improvement for all. It was an integrative project, increasingly connecting the black condition to wider concerns about economic inequality and the morally corrosive impact of the Vietnam War.

I recall undertaking an undergraduate thesis on the theme of Black Power in summer 1971 in New York. The city was a cauldron of racial animosity, and for a poverty-stricken student like myself, compelled to encamp in a Bronx tenement, the place was dystopian. The American Promised Land, on which I'd been reared through music, film and television since the 1950s, looked more like Eliot's waste land in many forsaken parts of the city. A lot of my study was in Harlem, at that time practically a no-go place for a white person like myself. Though a poorly structured and naive study, it found little traction for a separatist politics based around 'black nationalism'. A decade later, under Reagan's America, things changed. Since then, the universalist aspirations of Roosevelt's New Deal, Johnson's Great Society, and British Labour's welfare state have been vulnerable. Ideas about the collective good in places like America have been cornered between white nationalism on the right and Black Lives Matter on the left, even if the two are not morally equivalent.

In October 2022, the US Supreme Court started consideration about the constitutional authority of forms of affirmative action that permit universities to use racial background as a criterion that might benefit applicants of some races compared to others, even if only part of a 'holistic admissions' procedure. Such concern about racial preference is not echoed by unease at the class bias evident in the skewed student intake by US elite universities like Harvard and Princeton. Over half of Harvard students hail from families in the top 10 percent of the income distribution, and over two-thirds from those in the top 20 percent.[65] Expressed more generally, offspring of parents who are in the top 1 percent of the income distribution are 77 times more likely to enrol at an Ivy League college than those whose parents are in the bottom 20 percent.[66] Yet, such glaring class inequities, reflective of a lack of 'economic diversity', do not generate the requisite attention.

This loss of social solidarity based on the common good may be lamented by scholars like Mark Lilla in his book:[67] *The Once and Future Liberal*. Although, it's also true that these supposedly inclusive agendas of progressive social advance paid scant regard to the most oppressed groups, who were still of marginal concern to mainstream liberalism/labourism. Groups that felt abandoned or neglected by political parties have been increasingly prone to rely more on their own steam, separate from the party vehicle, or as with white identitarians, to hitch their star to bandwagon candidates like Trump. In part, this offers explanation for identity politics. But some see it running deeper and for longer.

In the early 1990s, Stuart Hall[68] spoke about the remaking of identity from the Enlightenment period, which had viewed the individual as unified, cognitive – *I think therefore I am* – rational, conscious, and possessed of an inner core that persisted throughout life, even as the full person was developed in social interaction with significant others. Shaped between self and wider cultures over time, identity was the blend of the personal and public character of each of us. It was always partial and in process. Then, major social change over the last half century upset this coherence between subjective and objective worlds. Identity became more splintered and contested, with its fragments internally at odds. In turn, this created the post-modern person, whose identity is seen as fluid rather than fixed, complicated rather than elementary, and mutable rather than enduring.

Politics as Personal

Even more fundamentally, Fukuyama[69] sees current identity politics as driven by *Thymos*, that part of our inner being that sources our pride or rage. By early-nineteenth century, this inner self, by then valued more than the outer self, yearned for social recognition on the basis of inherent human dignity, equality and moral freedom. For him, this universal impulse for affirmation is an essential part of how we build self-esteem. Even for the socially sidelined, it goes beyond material needs. People's interiority – the authentic self deep down – becomes particularly significant as society modernises. In small traditional communities, made up mostly of identical populations, in terms of things like ethnicity, religion, and language, identity does not arise. For most, position is ascribed and conformity is expected. They are meant to know, and content themselves with, their place within a time-honoured social hierarchy. Since the modern era though, with its greater complexity, social layering and secularisation, individual freedom to define and express one's own moral universe increases.

Paradoxically, this new choice to stamp your individuality amidst the crowd, can bring with it isolation and alienation, which in turn can push those who don't want to stick out like a sore thumb to rediscover the hand of fellowship with the similar and like-minded. There's only so much individualism that humans can take as social animals. They also seek affinity and bonding. Nationalism and religion can offer that attachment. But how can such collectivities enrich rather than enclave individual autonomy?

In Fukuyama's telling, from the French Revolution to World War I, two readings of dignity and identity were in rivalry: one tended to be national, and concerned about the rights and liberation of particular oppressed peoples, while the other was universal and concerned about human rights everywhere, though an early version of the Universal Rights of Man has a giveaway sexist exclusion in its title, never mind its racial qualification. The former tended to stress collective ties as expressed in nationalism and religion, which can be illiberal, while the latter exalted liberal thought about individual uniqueness within the global family.

Identity politics may be taken to be about achieving visibility and recognition as an individual and as part of a group on the basis of intrinsic dignity and worth. Obviously, you can accord recognition without approval. You can accept that under the current American definition, scientology and Mormonism constitute religions. But you can still think it madcap to believe Hubbard's idea of a god Xenu, from a faraway galaxy, who 75 million years ago, landed billions of his subject thetans to Earth, or that Joseph Smith had divine revelation that an early Israelite diaspora interbred with indigenous tribes of the Americas.

If you start with the principle that each group gets to define itself on its own terms, and these terms are beyond challenge from anyone outside the group, it opens prospect for myriad 'identities' that fragment society into multiple rival camps. In elevating a mix of subjective individualism and group exceptionalism, it splits and salami-slices. Each group feels entitled to protect its integrity against intrusion by adversaries or corruption by heretics. Within such identity protectionism, questions arise about who guards the gates of each identity boundary, and what mandate such 'gatekeepers' are granted. The idea that only members of a particular community can define its essence, values and boundaries comes ultimately from an epistemological argument. It suggests that experiential knowledge tops any other kind, and those outside that group's lived experience cannot know anything of substance about the group. Empathy isn't enough. Hence, from this view, a man transitioned into a woman isn't fully a woman.

This has become a hotly-contested issue. Some natal females have adopted a position, labelled *gender-critical feminism*, which disputes whether trans women are women in the same terms as those born and reared as female, with the lived experience throughout their lives of sex-based subordination, and the material reality of menstruation, menopause, and possibly childbirth. For them, sex is factual and immutable, and should not be confused with gender, which being more of a social construction, is fluid and changeable. From this perspective, transsexuals have a right to gender reassignment and recognition, based on their self-identification and statutory declaration, and the human right to be protected against discrimination. But they do not have a right to discount the distinctive category of womanhood, based on biology. Among the concerns raised by those of this disposition is that gender segregated spaces, designed to provide safety for women, may be undermined in some instances if access becomes open to self-identified women, who were once male.

Opponents of 'gender-critical' viewpoints are concerned that these opinions are essentially transphobic. In creating a hierarchy of womanhood, they subordinate trans women as not fully real women, an inherently discriminatory and exclusionary depiction. In failing to appreciate the interconnection of sex and gender, the 'gender-critical' position is said to emphasise a medical rather than social version of the female/male essence. While it is possible that spaces reserved for cis-women (those whose sex given at birth and gender identity match) may come under harm from a minority of trans women, it's argued that this potential small threat has to be set against the definite harm and humiliation visited upon trans women by their exclusion.[70]

This dispute has tended to pit one group, long subject to prejudice and inequity (women), against another, currently vulnerable to hostility and marginalisation (trans women). It raises many of the awkward questions attached to identity. Can self-perception be accorded the same weight as an objective category? In the complicated spectrum of sex and gender, what is authentic? How can competing ideas about rights, genuinely held, be arbitrated? How can debate about such raw and core quarrels be conducted with respect and civility, rather than via nasty trolls that are conversation stoppers prone to embitter more than enlighten?

For some, it has come to a sorry state if we can't classify one of the most basic human distinctions – male and female. For others, it is regrettable that into the third decade of the twenty-first century, people can't be recognised for who they are. In 2022, JK Rowling slated the UK's Leader of the Opposition,[71] when he offered the following definition: 'a woman is a female adult, and in addition to that, trans women are women….' If this designation is endorsed, some women are offended by their loss of distinctive identity. If it isn't accepted, most or all of trans women are left feeling that they are not fully able to identify with, and live, their self-assigned sex/gender, different to that given at birth.

Self-identity also comes into racial categories, as in the case of Rachel Dolezal, an American woman who passed herself as black, and later changed name to Nkechi Amare Diallo. In 2015, she was 'exposed' by her parents as white. Was her self-imaging an offensive fabrication of identity, an interesting boundary-crossing, an exaggerated or delusional affinity with African-American culture, or valid representation of how claims about racial purity are nonsensical? Or is it simply another instance of failure to distinguish feeling and fact? Since race has become less regarded as a fixed biological entity, can Dolezal claim that she was 'transracial'? In September 2020, a university teacher of African American history, Jessica Krug, also admitted to assuming a 'false identity' of blackness.

For some who berate these assumed identities, this is *black-fishing*, cosmetically changing appearance to seem to have black heritage, particularly when the badge of diversity may bring benefit in a context of positive discrimination. Yet if we say that self-identification lacks authority, it implies that identity can only be bestowed in line with broadly agreed societal definition. This idea that we need others' validation to authenticate ourselves can foster constant craving of approval from public spectators to our lives. In turn, this can deform into narcissistic self-absorption, a dependency on affirmative feedback, evident in anxious quest for 'likes' in social media.

Some identities we can readily appreciate as socially constructed. For instance, in my childhood, teenage identity emerged due to prolonged schooling, delayed working, extended adolescence, new music, mass media and consumer-driven styles that promised you could be yourself by being like everyone else of your ilk. It was sub-group conformity masquerading as individuality. For sure, within this category, you had teddy boys in the 1950s, mods and rockers in the mid-1960s, hippies in the late 1960s, glam and metal rockers in the 1970s, punk in the 1980s, and so on. I remember them all with varied degrees of delight and distaste.

These subcultures may have each looked unique, with their own aesthetic and image, but really they shared a general inclination to appear weird and to hold that being hot was being cool. Their music was intentionally ear-splitting to their elders. They all had at least pretension to be subversive. Though, for all of them, their very trendiness gave them commercial appeal that lured them to the corporatist trough, whatever their renunciation of the 'capitalist pig'. In the end, the line between identity being 'owned' by the subculture and being moulded by dictate of marketability became blurred. Once again, that elusive trait of *authenticity* makes its ambivalent appearance.

Authentic approaches to identity need to respect language. It's not just that words that were common parlance in my youth are now clearly inappropriate. Many were always so, in respect of their racial and sexist slur. But even in more recent decades, certain terms have been revised. For instance, even second-wave feminists were prone to use the term 'sexual preference', whereas now the apt expression is 'sexual orientation', because the latter recognises that it is not about 'lifestyle' choice. Such distinction is properly drawn. Inconsiderate use of language is a significant contributor to micro-aggressions that hassle and bully people on the basis of identity.

Nonetheless, some identity semantics are ill-advised. For example, DiAngelo's concept of *white fragility* casts all whites in similar mode. Their thoughts, if not their words, are taken to be innately racist. Their implicit bias is internalised through socialisation. Lacking 'racial stamina', whites are given to stress-induced avoidance around the issue of race, which triggers discomfort for those used to entitled cultural privilege. To cleanse themselves, the first step is to acknowledge their sin. While this public self-shaming is intended in part as atonement, it seems more like affected contrition that is more truly self-congratulation. Underlying assumption about black delicate sensibility smacks of snooty gesture politics that is devaluing rather than ennobling your intended beneficiary. Surely, that's the basic problem with racism?

Within this broad analysis, it's said that some whites, feeling unease about the challenge of an equity agenda, can get defensive. In turn, such injured response can inhibit candid conversation around racial inequality, and thereby disarm victims who want to avoid causing bother. A different, but also unhelpful, approach can come in the form of *whitesplaining*, where white people condescendingly pronounce their expertise about racism when they might better serve the situation by listening more to its victims. Belief that white people are best placed to define what is racist is patently impudent.

This form of anti-racism, in its negative generalisation of a whole group, pigeonholes each individual member as holding all the group's assumed flaws. It is guilt by association rather than action. Similar imprudence lies behind Applebaum's[72] concept of *white complicity*. In her take, white people, through the 'practice of whiteness', contribute to perpetuation of systemic racial inequality. Again, the first step is to acknowledge the sin, though she goes further. Those who try to be, and see themselves as, morally good may paradoxically encounter the greatest frustration in recognising themselves as accomplice.

You can see the similarity here to the tautologies of a religious cult. You are evil. Your failure to confess and repent is a sure giveaway of your malevolence. You cannot disagree because this means you're in denial, self-deceptively taking comfort in 'white moral innocence'. Moreover, you're weaponising that denial to discomfort people of colour when they raise the issue of race.

However well-meaning, such mindless self-flagellation is no more redemptive than the mortification practiced in medieval Christianity. Those who argue in this way put themselves beyond any possible falsification. If you disagree, you can be dismissed as not listening properly, or of being defensive, or of having such moral or mental disability that 'you just don't get it'. I consider racism as deeply-embedded and pervasive, and I think we need to decode its subtle forms that are designed to offer plausible deniability when confronted. But if you want the admirable things that these authors seek: accountability, 'racial literacy', and racial justice, alongside laws that empower people of colour, you need conversation, and you can't get engagement on the back of blanket reprimand that demands perpetual purification.

In deeply divided societies, it is generally a good principle that before you assume moral authority to criticise the 'other', first stand up to the shortcomings of your own background. Clearly, people like DiAngelo and Applebaum are trying to do that, particularly in a society based on separate and unequal development. But if you caricature rather than characterise, it defeats your purpose.

Even more so, serious aspects of the issue get lost when celebrities prostrate themselves in apparent mortification and penitence about being white. In a tweet (7 August 2019),[73] the film star, Rosanna Arquette declared: 'I'm sorry I was born white and privileged. It disgusts me. And I feel so much shame'. Such public self-debasement is pathetic platitude. What is meant to be the atonement? Who is being implored to grant pardon? Who benefits from someone's self-loathing about her skin-colour? It's an example of how these terms can be rendered senseless.

Reid's book *The Good Ally*[74] attempts to distinguish performative white allies, who want to make a show of their anti-racism, from genuine white supporters, who realise that their best contribution is to work alongside oppressed groups. She offers a staged method for white allies of first listening, then unlearning, then relearning, before moving into responsive action. Wisely, she acknowledges that this is an uncomfortable and non-linear process. While her book is informative, and her objective of improving everyone's humanity commendable, she makes a critical mistake early in the book by claiming that social injustice around race is increasing in frequency. In many parts of the world, that simply isn't true. Racism persists in the US. But it is not the same as in the era of slavery and Jim Crow. To imply that little or nothing has changed is do a great disservice to past campaigners for emancipation. Contemporary racism is bad enough. It doesn't need to be exaggerated to merit redress.

That is not to diminish the vile hatred intrinsic to white supremacism, still very evident in many white-majority societies. Ultimately, it's impenetrable what brings an 18-year-old white male in 2022 to slaughter ten people in a grocery in a black neighbourhood in Buffalo, New York state, all the while dressed in body-armour, heavily-armed, and livestreaming his military-style attack. In the immediate aftermath, questions emerged. How was he able to execute this when he had previously posted online a white supremacist manifesto? Would he have been given the chance to surrender if he was black? Beyond the usual prayers, candles, and marches that follow such tragedies, what will be done to really deter such mass killing?[75] Even in a society with 40,000 firearm-related deaths a year, the brutal carnage in such assaults shocks to the core. But it has to be seen as an extreme incident in a wider embedded pattern of hate crimes, where people are targeted for their particular identity. FBI figures – most likely an under-estimate – record 10,000 people reporting offences connected to their gender, race, religion, sexuality or disability in 2020, a 12-year high. In some aspects of human behaviour, there is no incremental improvement.

A reminder of the brutal horror of the worst of American racism is found in Barndt's[76] book, which is concerned to understand and dismantle it. He concludes that we are all harmed and diminished by racism. Charting its American beginnings from the initial colonial invasions and suppressions, he explains how racial distinction and discrimination were embedded in the power structures of the US from its origins. While taking individual, institutional and cultural expression, it is fundamentally rooted in white power. Though primarily a white problem, its solution lies in recognition 'that the goal of freedom is for all people'.[77]

The positive thing to recognise in all this is that science has helped us understand better the nature of, and solution to, racism. Psychology and neurobiology have pinpointed the basis of implicit bias in our cognitive processing that produces prejudice and discriminatory behaviour. It is not a disposition peculiar to bigots. We are all prone to generalisation and shortcuts in thinking and reasoning that prompt stereotypes, and neuro-imaging techniques can illustrate how specific parts of the brain – the amygdala, the prefrontal cortex, and the posterior cingulate – are activated in response to stereotypes. The good news is that these reactions are not permanently hardwired into us. They are learned behaviours that can be changed.[78]

Similarly, science helps us appreciate the psychological impact of daily micro-aggressions experienced by people of colour; the falsehood of genetically distinct races; the sociology of effective social activism; and the impact of anti-racism training. At the same time, science itself can highlight the sexist and racist bias that can operate *within* science and the bias that can be written into supposedly 'neutral' algorithms.[79] In short, we can benefit from an informed approach to this issue – that may be challenging to both political left and right.

For instance, a different view from the standard progressive stance comes from John McWhorter, a black American professor. He examines the persistence of black educational underachievement in the United States, and concludes that three main factors are at play: *victimology*, by which a key marker of 'cultural blackness' is to handle victimhood not as a predicament to be remedied but as an identity to be fostered; *separatism*, which sees black people as an 'unofficial sovereign entity', within which standards applicable to other Americans are deferred because their victimhood makes them more morally excused; and *anti-intellectualism*, which sees scholarship as something questionable and foreign to the genuinely black person. For him, these three forms of 'self-sabotage' link in mutual reinforcement:[80]

> *When a race is disparaged and disenfranchised for centuries and then abruptly given freedom, a ravaged racial self-image makes Victimology and Separatism natural developments. Victimology makes mediocre scholarly achievement seem inevitable. Separatism, casting scholarly achievement as 'what white people do', sanctions mediocre scholarly achievement. It is a short step from inevitable and sanctioned to 'authentic' and authentic is just another word for 'cool'.*

This view echoes educational debate in the sixties between those who saw educational under-attainment as rooted in structural social disadvantage, and those who emphasised cultural deprivation, a way of life supposedly given to immediate rather than deferred gratification, or that had restricted rather than elaborated language codes. The left favoured the first, and the right, the second. I was on the side of the former, considering that cultural explanations were convenient means of blaming the victim. But over time, I've come to conclude that it is a complicated interplay of the two, a process elaborated in chapter six.

In the US, for example, context is critical. As Noam Chomsky has remarked, America was built on two unspeakable crimes: quasi genocide of Native Americans, and enslavement of African Americans. McWhorter recognises the grave imprint of this bondage. He simply questions whether it needs to be indelible to the point of defeatism, thereby relinquishing the defiance behind the anthem *We Shall Overcome*.

Cultural Theft

Similar complexity besets other identity concepts, such as *cultural appropriation*. Take the case of Elvis and rock 'n' roll. Did he invent it? Most definitely he didn't. Nor did he ever claim to, always attributing its origins to strong influence from gospel and rhythm n' blues. But was he a musical pioneer? Most definitely he was. His first record was originally a blues number by Arthur Crudup, *That's Alright Mama*, backed by Bill Monroe's country song, *Blue Moon of Kentucky*. But both were done by Elvis in his own unique style. They weren't copies. They went in as a particular genre and came out Elvis. His genius was rooted in his special time and place. Born into grim poverty amidst the Great Depression, his early years were spent in proximity to the black community in Tupelo, Mississippi, and later in highly diverse, though segregated, Memphis. While imbued with country music and white gospel, he frequented the black music haunts on Beale Street and black Gospel Halls.

Infusing all these influences with his own take, his mishmash encouraged his devotees to sample blues and gospel artists they otherwise would have bypassed. In racially divided 1950s America, he was one of the few who opened rather than closed doors. That's how all culture progresses, not in cul-de-sacs, but in awkward spaces of crossbreeding and hybridity. Did he benefit from being white in a white-dominated society? Yes. But did he help break down racial barriers by leading a new popular culture that in time recognised black artists, whose work had been previously segregated into 'race music', but whose value he himself always acknowledged? Yes. That's why the great Little Richard praised the Lord for Elvis, James Brown called him soul brother, and Bob Dylan talked about hearing him for the first time as akin to busting out of jail. He was a liberator. I was in Memphis in 1977, days after he died. You just have to experience firsthand the city that at once gave birth to a new culture and brought death to Martin Luther King, to appreciate the boundaries Elvis crossed. He helped turn a black-and-white world that people like me still inhabited in the 1950s into one of Technicolor. Like his friend, Mohammad Ali, he shook up the world.

So distinction needs to be drawn between *takeover* and *makeover*, between commandeering a culture for exploitative purpose, and up-heaving cultural idioms to create a new cultural form that respects its ancestry. The latter brings added-value. The former is plain theft. Between these two, there can be *imitation* of a culture as mockery, and that's objectionable, i.e. old minstrel shows performed by white men with black face. But imitation, presented as the 'sincerest form of flattery', and intended as cultural appreciation rather than appropriation, can offer ambiguity and scope for debate. Ultimately, the general principle is that culture is not well-served if captive in strict copyright.

Right On

Issues of immigration, refugees, citizenship, border control and national sovereignty, amplified by misinformation, conspiracy stories, and social media noise, all relate to identity. The last chapter addressed the contested nature of nationalist identity and its distinction with citizen rights. For many parts of the world, two main 'brands' of citizenship have operated:[81] the right of *soil* (*Jus Soli*) that is citizenship as birthright, accorded to all born in the country; and the right of *blood* (*Jus Sanguinis*), whereby citizenship is 'inherited' from one or both parents, who are already citizens. As mentioned earlier, the more identity politics gets entangled with contested ideas about what constitutes a nation, the more identification with particular features such as shared history, heritage, pedigree, and collective cultural awareness, become enmeshed with definitions of legitimate citizenship – who are 'real' Americans, British, etc.?

By the mid-twentieth century, the US claimed its capacity for accommodating both multiculturalism and the melting pot. Supposedly, you could have a hyphenated identity as Italian-American or Irish-American, and still be regarded as fully American. Of course for some, this was a veneer of inclusivity since White, Anglo-Saxon, Protestant (WASP) lineage had long been the passport to being accepted as a 'real' American. More recently, amongst white identitarians, the emphasis is a little broader. It's now about European extraction.

But this question about who governments identify as 'real' citizens is global – Israel, China, India, Myanmar, and so on – where religious and racial minorities struggle even for second-class citizenship.

Back in the 1960s, Northern Ireland was thought to be a place apart, immune to 'normal politics'. I was a member of the Northern Ireland Labour Party, a minor political force, wondering why it was so hard to get both Protestant and Catholic working class to forge mutual interest in a more class-based rather than sectarian politics. Now many parts of the world have caught up with our culture wars. Based on tribal allegiance, these tend to operate as a zero-sum game. If the other side are for it, we're against it. Flags, statues, emblems, wall murals all offer markers of territory and tradition. Blind bigotry it isn't. It's very much alert to rules of tribal loyalty, and it's riddled with the problem of competing identity rights, where according rights to some appears to involve withdrawing them from others.

However, sometimes these clashes are not directly about parochial ethno-national issues, but about identity contests with global ramification. The case of Northern Ireland's Asher's Bakery, which refused to inscribe a message favouring gay marriage on a cake, highlights the limits of 'self identity'. While not refusing to bake a cake for gay customers, they stopped short of imprinting a view they considered contrary to their identity as devout evangelicals. Ultimately, the UK Supreme Court ruled in their favour. Included in the gay rights argument, was the special justification for gay marriage affirmation, since heterosexuals were automatically accorded such right. Many questions posed by the case are difficult to arbitrate.

Was this an instance of religious prejudice leading to discrimination? Are businesses which convey a message – through whatever medium – obliged to agree with its content? Does this clash of 'identity rights' show how some identities are privileged over others?

For myself, I think the final judgement was right. Two things need to be distinguished. Restriction on free expression – unless it incites violence – should be treated warily because if the right to offend is conceded in the name of tolerance and reverence, challenge to the powerful can be also compromised.[82] This case was less about *free* speech as about *forced* speech. This is where people are required to say things with which they disagree, a situation that some may take as a violation of free speech. The latter should carry a notion of 'protected speech', which should safeguard the individual from being legally compelled to use particular expression.

A wider illustration of this debate has arisen recently with an amendment to the Canadian Human Rights Act and the Criminal Code (Bill C-16, 2016), which adds gender identity and expression as prohibited ground of discrimination. Some, like Jordan Peterson, have interpreted this to mean that under legal sanction he could be obliged to use non-gendered pronouns when addressing non or transgendered people. Contrary legal interpretation suggests that it is not unlawful to continue using standard pronouns, but that those who don't identify as 'he' or 'she' are protected from discrimination, a fine though important difference. But this whole area that moves from forbidden words – that are hateful or inflaming – to mandatory words that tell us how to talk, is a minefield in the culture wars.

Using another example, under what, if any, circumstance should an anti-monarchist UK citizen be obliged to express an oath of allegiance to the British King? Monarchy in the twenty-first century ranks alongside papal infallibility in their shared absurdity. That is my belief, and I appreciate that its expression may be offensive to devotees of either tradition. But it's a considered rather than gratuitously offensive view. I don't think that I should feel compelled to express otherwise. The protracted period of mourning, accompanying pomp and pageantry, and blanket media coverage that followed the death of the British Queen Elizabeth illustrated the sycophancy and deference accorded an institution that helps legitimate a UK class hierarchy still heavily weighted in favour of hereditary privilege. Yet some peaceful protesters against this prolonged parade of grief, and the accession of King Charles, based on assumed entitlement through bloodline, found themselves arrested. Now that is a clear example of 'political correctness' and 'cancel culture' threatening free speech.

Intersectionality

Another aspect illustrating the complexity of identity rights comes in the concept of *intersectionality*, first coined in 1989 by Crenshaw,[83] who mainly concentrated on the overlapping and 'crossroad' experience of race and gender by black women. She argued that racism and sexism, as mutually supporting systems of discrimination, meant that black women were 'multiply burdened' in their subordination. Thus, they experienced this in forms that could be similar to, or different from, both white women and black men, in ways that black liberation or feminist politics didn't accommodate. This recognition of how multiple identities interact with compound effect is very important in appreciating the unique combinations of possible disadvantage. In recent decades, further identity categories have been added, including ethnicity, religion, sexual orientation, gender identity, age, and ability.

The practical problem is how you calibrate and audit multi-dimensions like this. How would you assess the social disadvantage gap between a professional black woman, a working class white man, a disabled mixed-race older lesbian, a transitioning black middle class man, and so on? Further complication comes when *colourism* is considered. This refers to the varied levels of discrimination encountered by people of the same 'race', dependent on the social meaning attached to skin colour, with dark-skinned people of colour most disadvantaged. With all these various layers more than the sum of their parts, difficulty in calculating degrees of domination is clear, without invalidating the concept.

In essence, critics of this approach see it as a divisive hierarchy of victimhood, where you earn 'credit' depending on the number of disadvantaged categories you can claim, and reversely, accumulate 'debt' based on the dimensions of privilege you have accrued. These credit/debt ratios, they argue, bring special allowances, and also determine who has greatest legitimacy to speak about oppression. Victimhood accords insight and moral authority.

On this reckoning, the white, able, male, straight person has to 'shut up and listen'. It's for those enduring hardship the most to best expose privilege and power. Conservatives view these dogmas as declared rather than propositions that are proven; the scholarship that supports it as doctrinaire and self-referential. Every relationship is problematised in terms of dominator and dominated. Since it is seen as insidious and persistent, and not redressed by standard equality measures, some people are positioned in permanent fault and mortification, whatever their intent or action.

It's hard to assess the accuracy of this representation of left identity politics and intersectionality. Undoubtedly, the risk of their malpractice is greater in North America than elsewhere, and within North America, the university campus is where they purportedly most ferment. Interestingly, Crenshaw did not intend it to be some grand theory about how all reality could be seen in terms of oppressive relationships. Her sensible critique was about how American black women could fall through the crack in legal protection against racism and sexism. But then the list of unearned disadvantage and privilege lengthened. It was not just about white and black; male and female; gay and straight; but also socially-considered attractiveness and non-attractiveness; average size and non-average; traditionally educated and self-educated; healthy and less healthy; vegan and non-vegan, etc.

With such proliferation, auditing adversity, virtue, and privilege becomes ever more complex. Which of these are imposed and which chosen? What metrics are valid to give extra weight to the most significant categories? And if each identity alone can understand itself, then a small, black, bi-sexual, disabled man can only possibly be 'understood' by that small minority who can also tick those boxes. That way lies lunacy.

Nevertheless, it does highlight how identity politics can involve a set of paradoxes. In the case of intersectionality, a reasonable idea was 'appropriated' by some, who are likely the first to decry 'cultural appropriation'. By acknowledging that identity is not singular, but rather a composite of many categories, their logic is ultimately towards individuality rather than group solidarity. They're saying that the bits and pieces of our attributes, experiences and backgrounds make us each unique. That's fine. But where is the commonality that binds? We are not completely defined by specific traits. Otherwise, there'd be no role for human agency. Also, there's little space for a credible politics of liberation if the discourse divides much more than it unites. Mostly, the politics of grievance encourages self-pity more than empowerment.

Insofar as any part of the left becomes evangelist on these questions, it falls into a contradictory position. On the one hand, it disclaims objective truth, since its most valid source is subjective self-witness of victims, a view that comes from Standpoint theory, which claims that knowledge derives from social standing. Still, leading advocates give every impression that they know the universal truth about domination. Of course, if you think you know the truth, you don't do debate. You only need the pulpit and pew. Scholarship based on edict rather than evidence is as reliable as electoral outcomes in Lukashenko's Belarus.

The right too has its own contradictions. Conservatives depict the 'woke generation' as snowflakes, unable to deal with creedal dissent, and reluctant to engage in critical exchange with opponents. They also rail against what they see as propaganda passing for scholarship in some courses in the academy. But when faced with calls to re-examine their own articles of faith, their wish to shield from contrary opinion is as stark. Recall former Prime Minister Johnson's reluctance as he responded to news that the BBC's Proms programme in 2020 would see performance of *Rule Britannia* and *Land of Hope and Glory* without lyrics, which some take to carry imperialist tinge: 'I think it's time we stopped our cringing embarrassment about our history, about our traditions and about our culture, and we stopped this general fight (sic) of self-recrimination and wetness'.

This line on culture wars was deliberately drawn by the Johnson government, and was influenced by among others, Munira Mirza, until 2022 head of Downing Street Policy Unit.[84] The essence of the strategy was to rail against the victim narratives of a grievance culture attributed to an unpatriotic metropolitan left that was out of touch with ordinary people. Such summoning of culture wars was further developed in negative government comments about the English soccer team 'taking the knee'; the few students removing the Queen's portrait in a small common room in one college in Oxford University; and any moves by public institutions like museums and universities to look back in shame at British history. Former UK Culture Secretary, Oliver Dowden, outlined a strategy that would ensure that the boards of heritage organisations would be 'genuinely diverse and not solely governed by people from metropolitan bubbles'. The broad inference is clear. A strident minority is intent on trashing our history, through policing thought and language about understanding the past:[85]

> *I will not look on as people threaten to pull down statues or strip other parts of our rich historic environment….confident nations face up to their history. They don't airbrush it. Instead, they protect their heritage and use it to educate the public about the past….And as national institutions, heritage organisations should take into account the views of the entire nation: the people for whom they were set up, and whose taxes pay for them….any account of the past should start from a commitment to telling a balanced, nuanced and academically rigorous story — one that doesn't*

automatically start from a position of guilt and shame or the denigration of this country's past....The pressure on our heritage is part of a worrying trend – a cancel culture whereby a small but vocal group of people claim to have the monopoly on virtue, and seek to bully those who dare to disagree. But the world is too complicated for that kind of totalitarian moral certainty – and we must resist it at all costs.

The study of history and heritage should be based on intellectual honesty, and critical appraisal of the past, rather than submission to any party-line. Such a stance is disconcerting for sections of both right and left. Many on the right see all that is associated with intersectionality as coming from Marxism, and as such, dangerous by that association alone, even though orthodox Marxism has always been that ruling ideas come from a ruling class, and thus are rooted in material rather than cultural reality. They think that if you want to get shot of ideas that underpin various manifestations of oppression, you need revolutionary change of the capitalist system. In that regard, some on the left think that leftist identity politics mistakenly puts the cart before the horse, privileging culture before class. The latter, which is often marginal to 'woke' discussion of intersectionality, is central to them, and demands a solidarity that is jeopardised by factional movements around identity. It's class not classification. Granted, some of this gets confused in the mix, and, for instance, some elements of Black Lives Matter locate their struggle within anti-capitalism.

In a wider sense, it's foolish to think of 'culture wars' as a distraction from economic inequality. Both are often tied together. Injustice around race and gender can be presented as prejudice that can be remedied by awareness, rather than as an outcome of systemic inequality requiring not just personal change, but also transformation of the social system. Pledges for diversity, as for education, are necessary but insufficient. Moreover, success in such anti-discrimination programmes could legitimate poverty by suggesting that with better legal protection around racism and sexism, and improved educational opportunity, those still deprived are more likely the authors of their own misfortune. It is mistaken to think identity is the be-all and end-all of inequality.

America First

Whether or not contemporary culture wars first emerged in the US is arguable. Certainly, it is there that their presence is most acute. Fascinating insight into current public opinion relevant to evolving identity in that country can be found in the 2021 American Values Survey.[86] The general context is the widespread belief in American exceptionalism. About three-quarters (74 percent) of respondents agree that 'America has always been a force for good in the world', a view shared almost unanimously by Republicans (92 percent), but held also by two-thirds of Democrats. It is a strongly held conviction by people of faith, particularly by white Christians (80 percent plus), though less so by

Black Protestants (69 percent). Holding this belief the least (58 percent) are the religiously unaffiliated. In turn, this is tied to the idea that there is 'a divinely ordained role for America' in human history, though adherence to this special claim has reduced significantly from 64 percent in 2013 to 44 percent in 2021.

When asked whether American culture had changed for the better since the 1950s, only 29 percent of Republicans agreed, a significant drop from 46 percent in 2020, with most (70 percent) registering a view of its deterioration. Most Democrats (63 percent) think the reverse. For them, American culture and way of life have improved. This gap marks the big gulf between the two political aisles. At the same time, there is overwhelming unity of opinion that a key indicator of what makes someone a 'true American' is acceptance of people of diverse racial and religious heritage (up from 86 percent in 2018 to 92 percent in 2021). And less than one in five Americans hold that being of Western European background is important in this regard, with little difference between the parties. On other indicators of what constitutes being truly American, difference is pronounced: belief in God (78 percent of Republicans, and 45 percent of Democrats); being Christian (63 percent of Republicans, and 35 percent of Democrats); belief that capitalism is the best economic system (77 percent of Republicans, and 50 percent of Democrats); and being born in America (62 percent of Republicans, and 43 percent of Democrats).

Division is also apparent when it comes to preference for the US to comprise people belonging to a wide variety of religions. While 55 percent of Democrats agree, only 17 percent of Republicans do. Similarly, in response to a question about the country's diversity, whereas 82 percent of Democrats think that it makes America stronger, only 47 percent of Republicans agree. A majority of Americans (59 percent) say that it doesn't matter that the white population in the US has decreased for the first time in its history, according to the 2020 Census. But while Democrats believe that it's mostly positive rather than negative (39 percent to 9 percent), Republican opinion goes in the opposite direction (6 percent vs. 33 percent).

In response to the statement: 'things have changed so much that I often feel like a stranger in my own country', 41 percent agreed, and 59 percent disagreed. Again, the partisan dimension is clear. Three in ten (31 percent) Democrats agreed, compared to 56 percent of Republicans, and 78 percent of Republicans, who most trust far-right news sources. Just over half (52 percent) of all Americans agree that 'today, America is in danger of losing its culture and identity', while 45 percent disagree. But there is a huge gap between Republicans (80 percent) and Democrats (33 percent) in their agreement with this proposition. With regard to immigration, a majority of Americans (56 percent) think that immigrants strengthen their society. Again, significant political divergence appears. Whereas Republicans have become more inclined to think that immigrants threaten American values (71 percent in 2021; 65 percent in 2018; and 55 percent in 2011), Democrat views have been going in the opposite direction in favour of the idea that immigrants strengthen the country (78 percent in 2021; 76 percent in 2018; and 62 percent in 2011). Anti-immigrant sentiment among Republicans is also reflected in the way two-thirds (65 percent) of them say that immigrants pose a burden as they press for jobs, housing, and health care.

Killings of Black Americans by police are considered by 79 percent of Republicans to be isolated episodes rather than part of a wider pattern of how police behave towards Black Americans, a view shared by only 15 percent of Democrats. While the US is split 50–50 on whether Islam is at odds with American values and culture, Republicans (74 percent) are more than twice as likely as Democrats (35 percent) to agree with that standpoint. In respect of the above views about cultural change, immigration, policing the black community, and Islam, it's telling that those Republicans who most trust far-right media and Fox News register even higher percentage figures.

If we take *critical race theory* as one current touchstone issue of culture wars in the US, only one in five say that they've heard a lot about it. Just over a third (34 percent) claim complete unawareness. Despite all the controversy about how it's supposedly permeating the school curriculum with the view that race determines nearly every social outcome, the term gets only modest recognition. Instead, a notable survey finding is that overwhelmingly (84 percent), Americans agree with the statement: 'we should teach American history that includes both our best achievements and our worst mistakes as a country'. Only 13 percent affirm the view that 'we should teach American history that focuses on what makes this country exceptional and great'.

A decade ago, Senator Lindsey Graham (Republican, South Carolina) warned the Republican Party:[87] 'The demographics race we're losing badly.... We're not generating enough angry white guys to stay in business for the long term.' It looked like increasing diversity in the US was inexorably delivering a durable foundation for the Democrats' electoral pre-eminence. Since then, Republicans have responded on two fronts. They've adopted a populist economics that has largely ditched fiscal rectitude for a readiness to deficit-spend, and at least appear to champion 'national' workers over 'foreign' ones. In that regard, they're competing with their rival's traditional appeal to the blue-collar constituency. To out-compete their rival, the political space they want to capture, centres around crime, immigration, and culture wars.

In relation to crime, mantras like 'defund the police' are a gift to Republicans, who understand that the communities needing most protection against violent crime are the poorest. The latter want police reform, not the abolition implied by the ill-considered catchword of 'de-funding'. Similarly, those who advocate a dutiful role of parents in public education cannot be properly cast as infringing on teacher professionalism. Other messaging such as 'open borders' can convey the same dismissal of those with reservations about unmanaged immigration as irredeemably reactionary. Thus, analysis by the Democratic Congressional

Campaign Committee (DCCC) suggests that many 'natural' Democratic voters are turned off by what they perceive as the 'preachy' tenor of some 'progressive' rhetoric.

All told, this is not a time of measured political exchange. For some, the contest between cultural liberals and conservatives is a fundamental showdown between good and evil that has to be engaged to the ultimate victory of one over the other. Nothing short of civilisation itself is at stake. On the Democrat side, these people see the Republican party as having been captured by racists and those intent on subverting American democracy. Conversely, their counterparts depict the Democrats as unpatriotic, self-appointed guardians of justice for every conceivable group except white Christians, ever-ready to rob true Americans of their freedoms, whether it be their speech, guns, or values. The pandemic has brought a new proxy for these portrayals: are mandates around masks and vaccines to be considered undue Federal imposition or proper citizen solidarity? Greater ambivalence attends the invasion of Ukraine. Since the contest is between two white Christian leaders defending national sovereignty, not all Republicans feel easy applauding Trumpist affinity with Putin.

The important thing to note is that this has been a long time coming in America. Nixon and Ford appreciated that conservatives could not, with electoral impunity, turn back the tide of social interventionist government, traceable to the New Deal, as some in their party, like Barry Goldwater, wanted. Reagan disagreed, and campaigned successfully around the idea that post-Vietnam America could recover its world standing with a combination of reduced social state and an enhanced military complex. By 1992, conservatives had achieved presidential power for 20 of the previous 24 years. In their seminal report, *The Politics of Evasion*, in 1989, Galston and Kamarck[88] addressed this repeated failure with a blunt lesson for Democrats: too many Americans had come to view the party as 'inattentive to their economic interests, indifferent if not hostile to their moral sentiments, and ineffective in defence of their national security'. This distance from the public stemmed in part from 'liberal fundamentalists' imposing 'ideological litmus tests' on a range of social and cultural issues.

In response to such critiques, Clinton rebranded the party as New Democrats, and presented it as tough on crime, immigration, and habitual welfare claimants, while liberal on economic regulation and global trade. Progressive Democrats today blame this realignment for the mass incarceration of young blacks, alongside an economic strategy that accelerated globalisation, while abandoning the rustbelt, leaving the country susceptible to Trumpist economic nationalism and culture crusades.

In 2022, Galston and Kamarck[89] re-entered the discourse with *The New Politics of Evasion*, which laments how 'too many of the most vocal Democrats have adopted stances on fraught social issues – policing, immigration, public schools, and others – that repel a majority of Americans'. This represents 'the new politics of evasion, the refusal to confront the unyielding arithmetic of electoral success'. They emphasise that Trumpism, however bizarre its manifestation, is not an aberration. Trump obtained 11 million more votes in 2020 than in 2016, including many from African American and Hispanic communities. So even though Biden won by securing over 15 million votes more than Clinton, Trump's support far from collapsed, and was not restricted to his assumed cultural base.

Galston and Kamarck advocate for Democrat activists to understand better the country as both *deeply* and *closely* divided. Because they get the first bit – the intensive polarisation – they mistakenly think that electoral success hinges on rallying the base with a radical partisan platform. They ignore the second bit – how close the parties tie in the electoral count. Accordingly, they underappreciate the significance of swing voters in a small number of swing states, on whose persuasion rests electoral outcome. Geographic concentration of Democratic votes means that some states are won with big surpluses, undermining the correspondence between the overall popular vote and that of the decisive Electoral College. Activists within such geographies of confirmation may be blind-sighted to their unrepresentative character, relative to the rest of the country. In short, they can trapped in their own culture bubble and echo chamber. They need to spend more time looking for converts rather than traitors.[90]

In their current miscalculation, they have been self-deceived by three political fictions: first, that people of colour think and act the same; second, that it's always the economy stupid that wins over culture; and third, that they are on the right side of demography for a 'progressive ascendency'. In the case of the first, this ignores diversity within the Hispanic community and divisions between it and the African American community, with the latter, for example, more favourable to Critical Race Theory, but less hawkish on defence. Among Hispanic voters, national support for Democratic presidential candidates has been dropping dramatically: 71 percent in 2012; 66 percent in 2016; and 59 percent in 2020. A small, but perhaps telltale example of divisions within Hispanics comes from the use of the term Latinx, as a gender-neutral or inclusive expression rather than Latina or Latino, one that encompasses gender-expansive people and gets beyond the gender binary. But it is known and used by a relatively few people, and as even some who can see merit in its selective use, acknowledge:[91] '....Latinx as a gender-neutral pan-ethnic term fails to represent many people of Latin American origin or descent, particularly those at the intersection of other – mostly marginalized – positions (e.g., immigrants, people with lower educational attainment)'.

In the case of the second myth, the convergence of economic policies between the two parties has highlighted the significance people attach to their identity and sense of belonging. Biden's success in Georgia, Arizona, and Wisconsin – key to his ultimate triumph in the Electoral College – rested a great deal on his appeal to white non-college voters, wary of the competence and trustworthiness of government, but responsive to recognition of, and respect for, their more conservative values.

In the case of the third misapprehension, the electoral 'reality' of the country remains rooted in an overall culturally conservative populace, but one that does not offer an overwhelming majority to either political brand. As Galston and Kamarck note:[92]

> *Of the 17 presidential elections between 1920 and 1984, 10 were settled by margins of 10 percentage points or more in the popular vote, and five yielded landslides in which the winner's margin exceeded 20 points. But in the nine elections between 1988 and 2020, no candidate has come close to a 10-point victory margin, and five of the past six have been settled by margins of less than 5 percentage points. In five of these elections, the winner failed to secure a majority of the national popular vote; in two, the candidate who lost the national popular vote prevailed in the Electoral College. During this 32-year period, neither political party has been able to establish a stable national majority, and the White House has changed hands between the parties five times. Of the roughly 1 billion votes cast for the major party candidates in the past nine elections, Democrats received 51.2 percent compared to 48.2 percent for Republicans.*

On this analysis, one of the reasons why culture wars have become so intense in the US – and the same holds in other places like the UK – is that the electoral split is so knife-edge. In such close calls, culture can be both an expression of conviction and a politics of fabrication, whereby unscrupulous leaders and media foment division by exaggerating difference and resentment, and distorting the motive of those who simply want justice. A discourse arena where people find it difficult to disagree, without descent to unforgiving hatred, bodes ill for democracy. In particular, the online environment is deliberately designed to facilitate squabbling and shaming that by-pass the demanding alternative of nuance and empathy. Humans benefit from humility, but not from humiliation.

Instead, some see these issues in terms of uncompromising moral choice. An example, which has re-emerged in the US is the issue of abortion. When a highly sensitive matter is contested in terms of child murder versus the reproductive and health rights of women, a categorical dividing line is drawn. When this is politically arbitrated between a deadlocked Congress and a Conservative-majority Supreme Court, there is every prospect of a protracted and visceral dispute that accentuates a battle-line cast between progressives and traditionalists, however much this edits the complexity.

In the US, a potential extreme outcome of the cultural divide is a segregated space that has become known as the American Redoubt – the idea that a combination of groups, such as white Christian conservatives, survivalists, certain types of self-reliant ecologists, and those keen to flee urban corruption and degradation are best to frontier their own territory that allows them to 'live off the grid'. It is suggested by some that a geography embracing much of Idaho, Montana, Wyoming, and Oregon may make for such a retreat. For some advocates, it represents a necessary protective zone against the coming societal breakdown with the 'end of days'. Such a scenario reveals the extent to which some combatants on both sides of contemporary culture wars feel they can no longer share the same space.

Beyond Identity

So is much of this a case of mistaken identity? Appiah[93] talks about three facets of identity: labelling; norms; and treatment. For him, it involves a set of markers, and tenets for ascribing them to people. While these labels bear meaning for those to whom they are attached, sometimes influencing their conduct and emotions, they also carry implication for how their bearers are handled by others. In other words, he sees identity as having subjective and objective aspects. For each of us claiming an identity, it has *normative* significance: 'since I'm this identity, I should think and act this way'. For others, including those who share that identity, they're prone to say: 'because you're that, we can see and treat you this way'. But people can break norms. Categories and treatment can be disputed. Identities of imposition and choice need to be distinguished. In addition, Appiah regards essentialism about identities as usually off-beam. Given this complexity and contest, holding an identity does not give you the right to speak for others of that identity. I agree, and am thus wary of gatekeeping.

But this view of tolerant pluralism, of live and let live, is not the norm in this partisan age. For many, identity involves absolutes, though paradoxically it can be based on cultural relativism. If you deal in absolutes, your claims tend to be non-negotiable. Even when identity is nourished within well-intended concepts like multiculturalism,[94] it can end up as bonding capital (solidarity within the group) over social capital (wider solidarity). This has been aggravated by surging nationalism. Paradoxically again, advocates of ethno-nationalism are internationalised. Borderless networking of these advocates is evident in Generation Identity, a mainly European grouping, but with contacts in the US, through message-board sites like 4 Chan and 8 Chan. Facebook, Twitter, and YouTube also offer meeting spaces. The right is happy to mobilise globally for nationalist purposes.

Does the same apply to the left – have culture wars around diversity displaced class wars around inequality? Fukuyama thinks so:[95] 'Identity politics for some progressives has become a cheap substitute for serious thinking about how to reverse the thirty year trend in most liberal democracies toward greater socio-economic inequality'. Of course, *equality* of treatment is not necessarily *uniformity* of treatment.

Marginalised groups, wanting to distinguish their pronounced disadvantage, may want that redressed by special 'affirmative action', since an overall rigged system based on class, also generates specific disadvantages, with racial, ethnic, and gender markers. In slowly recognising these identities, the most radical sections of the left have underplayed the de-industrialised fate of the working class.

Its social progressiveness has elevated identities around race, gender, sexuality, and the like, while at least appearing to downplay others, such as old-style patriotism, traditional families, the religious, rural and suburban residents, and those who want controlled immigration, but who do not consider themselves bigots.[96] At times, the left has seemed to think that if you gather all the diverse identities associated with socially progressive politics into a grand rainbow coalition, you have assured electoral fortune. In fact, the evidence is that there is no guaranteed bright political future over that particular rainbow. Instead, the left has usually got itself stranded on a roundabout: power without principle is a sell-out; but principle without power is a cop-out.

When I was young, there was a familiar saying parents taught children to boost resilience against taunts: 'sticks and stones can break my bones, but names will never harm me'. But names can harm. Words do matter. It is not indulgent political correctness to address codes that language can hold. Certainly, what is considered 'correct' can be unpredictable. There was a time that the term 'coloured people' was replaced by 'black'. Now, we talk about 'people of colour', even though not considering 'white' as a colour serves to give it distinctive label. Once, 'queer' was a term of abuse. Now, it's 'owned' by its adherents, and adds 'Q' to LGBT. Recently, we've had new identity labels that keep extending the acronym. Now it's LGBTQ2. The 2 stands for 'two spirit', a term used by US Native American and Canadian First Nation peoples to acknowledge that some people contain both feminine and masculine spirits. We might add NB to the list to recognise non-binary people, who do not identify absolutely as either male or female.

No doubt some will query whether these kind of additions ever stop. Others will welcome them as recognition that gender and sexuality are each multiple and fluid. All this is proper debate. The problem is that while acronyms are very useful ways of distilling complicated categories, the continual addition of new items can play into the critique of opponents, who dismiss it all as a never-ending litany of competitive victimhood.

In the UK in 2022, an Employment Tribunal found that for a factory supervisor to have called a worker 'bald' was an act of sexual harassment:[97]

In our judgment, there is a connection between the word 'bald' on the one hand and the protected characteristic of sex on the other.....(it was) a violation of the claimant's dignity, it created an intimidating environment for him, it was done for that purpose, and it related to the claimant's sex.

I think that such legal findings trivialise the seriousness of sexual harassment, to which women are overwhelmingly subject. At what point do 'micro-aggressions' become indistinguishable from robust exchanges that are part of human engagement? What does discredit the decorum of language use is when some take speech propriety to ridiculous levels, as when Gwyneth Paltrow described her split with her partner as 'conscious uncoupling'. There is good and bad PC, and the baby needs to be distinguished from the bathwater. When people adopt an over-zealous interpretation of a sound idea – that we should be sensitive to others, particularly those that have been long mistreated – and use the idea to parade their exemplary purity, it only dishonours the virtue of civility. What is needed is more engagement across divides. You can't achieve that if people feel they're walking on eggshells, and watching every word they utter. Such apprehension stifles natural conversation, and makes everyone involved inclined to avoid repeat encounter.

War of Attrition

Since we wrap much of this discussion in terms of 'culture wars', let's sustain that metaphor to see where it leads. Zealots, of left or right, who weaponise identity into a Trojan horse for their wider political project, can fire salvos that actually bring collateral damage to that very project. The left thinks it is fighting an asymmetrical culture war. Asymmetrical warfare is understood to mean a David and Goliath contest between a resistance movement and a large well-equipped professional army, with battleground skewed in favour of the latter. Thus, the left can feel its war chest is so depleted, relative to the powerful establishment, that its best tactic is relentless cultural skirmish in a war of attrition. While 'justice warriors' expect that this can bring pyrrhic victories and glorious defeats, they hope to triumph in the long-term.

If combat is already lop-sided, you need more than 'allies'. You need unity in your ranks, even if in many battalions. Ultimately, it's not helpful to have some who feel they're 'no longer talking to white people about race'.[98] It is true that key liberation events for black people in the past happened at their own behest rather than were gifted by 'white saviours'. Slavery wasn't ended by exclusive efforts of the Wilberforces of the world. The Haitian Revolution, 1791–1804, the slave rebellion in Demarara in 1823, and in Jamaica in 1831, were examples of successful revolt against colonial domination by slaves themselves. However, other radical mobilisations, like the US Civil Rights Movement, did benefit from white people joining the black-led campaign to proclaim racial equality as a mutual interest for ethical human beings.

Just as today's big problems demand an inter-disciplinary approach, informational diversity – opinions, experience, and expertise coming from a wide range of racial and ethnic backgrounds – yields special dividend. Working together socially and cognitively across diverse milieus may be harder than doing so in a more homogeneous environment, but it renders better results.[99]

However understandable the exhaustion and frustration felt by some black people about what they see as white indifference to, or collusion with, racial injustice, separatism of any kind isn't a clever battle plan. In the UK, around 13 percent identify as Black, Asian or minority ethnic. In the US, a similar percentage is African-American. Those shares don't offer the numbers. You're engaged in unilateral disarmament if you dismiss recruits in what could be a broad-based coalition of the willing. Besides, the notion that it is an asymmetrical culture war is held also by some on the right, who feel they've been in retreat, or at least under siege, since the 'permissive' 1960s. This is another paradox. Each side fighting over *identity* can have an *identical* take on their respective casualties and victimhood. Others, who do not feel easy about the war itself, see themselves as caught in the crossfire.

Some identities struggle to attract commiseration. For instance, incels (involuntary celibate males) lament how, in their view, the women's movement has disfigured sexual relations to the point where their 'rightful' access to sex has been frustrated. How can such misplaced prerogative, and its attendant sexism, be best addressed – through ridicule of such 'sad sacks', or appreciation that they can only be disabused of their warped sense of injustice through public challenge to the media sources of their delusion? As Manavis says:[100]

> *It should be possible to remain unsympathetic to the violent, misogynistic, entitled lines of thought without maligning the lonely people who frequent the nefarious sites where such thinking thrives.*

The point here is that some 'identities' cannot be readily granted 'recognition' on the basis of a group's self-definition. But perhaps they can be best countered by humanising the individuals entrapped by exploitative forces that dehumanise relations.

More generally, we're faced with one of the key paradoxes of our time. At a stage when we need optimum global solidarity to tackle common problems such as climate emergency, nuclear proliferation, and pandemics, we risk atomising into ever-increasing number of separate identity groups, each keen to out-bid others with their grievance.

Nevertheless, it's hard to see 'identities' going away. It's useful to remind ourselves of two things: first, some people who have lived in a clan-based society regard it as inherently tyrannical; second, many atrocities have been executed in the thinly-veiled guise of seeing some 'identities' in dehumanised terms: settler colonialism in North America and Australia; Amritsar massacre; Armenian treatment by Ottoman Turkey; Bengal famine; the Holocaust; the onslaught on Rwanda's Tutsis; Serbian-directed ethnic cleansing; Iraqi suppression of Kurds; Myanmar military's brutal campaign against Rohingya Muslims. The list goes on.

The next chapter explores something that affects all tribes, even if in different ways – the global economy – and in particular, the elevated role accorded high finance. And over the next two chapters, it invites examination of how far economics and politics in the contemporary world would benefit from seeing identity issues in a different context – replacing culture wars with wars on poverty and inequality.

Notes

1 Brunt, R. (1989) The Politics of Identity, in Hall, S. and Jacques, M. (eds) *New Times: the Changing Face of Politics in the 1990s*. London: Lawrence & Wishart. 150–159. 151.

2 www.ons.gov.uk/news/news/census2021demographyandinternationalmigratio nstatistics. Accessed on: 20 November 2022.

3 Macpherson, W. (February 1999) The Stephen Lawrence Inquiry Report. Cm 4262-I. 6.34. https://assets.publishing.service.gov.uk/government/uploads/system/ uploads/attachment_data/file/277111/4262.pdf.

4 Graham, B. (26 July 2020) Tom Cotton Calls Slavery 'Necessary Evil' in Attack on New York Times. 1619 Project. *The Guardian*.

5 Wilkerson, I. (2020) *Caste: The Lies That Divide Us*. London: Penguin Books.

6 Yglesias, M. (Updated Apr 1, 2019, 9:25am EDT) The Great Awokening: A Hidden Shift is Revolutionizing American Racial Politics — and Could Transform the Future of the Democratic Party. www.vox.com/2019/3/22/18259865/ great-awokening-white-liberals-race-polling-trump-2020. Accessed on: 20 July 2020.

7 Parker, K. Horowitz, J. and Anderson, M. (12 June 2020) Amid Protests, Majorities Across Racial and Ethnic Groups Express Support for the Black Lives Matter Movement. Pew Research Center. www.pewsocialtrends.org/2020/06/12/amid-protests-majorities-across-racial-and-ethnic-groups-express-support-for-the-black-lives-matter-movement. Accessed on: 18 July 2020.

8 www.melaniephillips.com/taking-knee-destroyers-worlds. Accessed on: 21 July 2020.

9 Office of National Statistics (2015) 2011 Census Analysis: Ethnicity and Religion of the non-UK born population in England and Wales: 2011. Last updated: 18 June 2015. www.ons.gov.uk/peoplepopulationandcommunity/culturalidentity/ethnic ity/articles/2011censusanalysisethnicityandreligionofthenonukbornpopulationin englandandwales/2015-06-18.

10 Note: Indeed, more than 1 in 8 foreign-born residents (13 percent, 949,000) saw themselves as White British. A third identified as Asian/Asian British (33 percent, 2.4 million) and 13 percent (992,000) identified with Black/African/Caribbean/ Black British. Just over a third of the foreign-born population was born in Europe (37 percent), with the top country of birth being Poland (with 579,000 people). Of those who were European, 74 percent identified with Other White. Just under a fifth of the foreign-born population was born in Africa (17 percent).

11 Note: The largest single share of foreign-born residents (3.6 million) were Christian, with 53 percent of these arriving in the previous decade. The second largest share was Muslim (1.4 million).

12 Office for National Statistics (ONS) (2019) Population estimates by ethnic group and religion, England and Wales: 2019. London: ONS. www.ons.gov.uk/peopl epopulationandcommunity/populationandmigration/populationestimates/artic les/populationestimatesbyethnicgroupandreligionenglandandwales/2019. Accessed on: 14 March 2022.

13 Byrne, B. and Shankley, W (2020). in Byrne, B., Alexander, C., Khan, O., Nazroo, J. and Shankley, W. (eds.) (2020) *Ethnicity, Race and Inequality in the UK: State of the Nation*. Bristol: Policy Press. 35–50.

14 Byrne, B., Alexander, C., Khan, O., Nazroo, J. and Shankley, W. (eds.) (2020) *Ethnicity, Race and Inequality in the UK: State of the Nation*. Bristol: Policy Press.

15 Race Disparity Audit (October 2017. revised March 2018) Summary Findings from the Ethnicity Facts and Figures website. Cabinet Office. 2.9. 9. Data for Scotland, Wales and Northern Ireland is only included if it pertains to policy areas that are not devolved and remain the responsibility of central government departments. www. gov.uk/government/publications/race-disparity-audit.

16 Department for Equalities (17 March 2022) *Inclusive Britain: Government Response to the Commission on Race and Ethnic Disparities*: Presented to Parliament by the Minister of State for Equalities. Command Paper number: CP 625.

17 Note: Pakistani and Bangladeshi people and all Black ethnic groups were overrepresented in the most deprived 10 percent of neighbourhoods in England. *Ibid.*, 6.10.

18 Stevenson, J., Demack, S., Stiell, B., Abdi, M., Clarkson, L., Ghaffar, F., and Shaima Hassan, S. (September 2017) *The Social Mobility Challenges Faced by Young Muslims*. London: Social Mobility Commission.

19 McGregor-Smith Review (2017) *Race in the Workplace*. https://assets.publishing. service.gov.uk/government/uploads/system/uploads/attachment_data/file/594 336/race-in-workplace-mcgregor-smith-review.pdf.

20 Shankley, W. and Williams, P. (2020) Minority Ethnic Groups, Policing and the Criminal Justice System in Britain. in Byrne, B., Alexander, C., Khan, O., Nazroo, J. and Shankley, W. (eds.) (2020) *op.cit.*, 51–71.

21 Lammy Review (September 2017) *An Independent Review into the Treatment of, and Outcomes for, Black, Asian and Minority Ethnic Individuals in the Criminal Justice System*. Gov.UK. 4. https://assets.publishing.service.gov.uk/government/uploads/system/ uploads/attachment_data/file/643001/lammy-review-final-report.pdf.

22 Race Disparity Audit (October 2017. revised March 2018) *op. cit.* Note: While Asian adults were most likely to agree (85 percent) that their local area was a place where people from different backgrounds had good relations, only 77 per-cent of Black adults held that view. When it comes to a sense of power in ability to shape local decisions in 2016–17, Black adults felt most able (44 percent) and White adults, the least at 25 percent. While this contrast may not be expected, the concerning feature is that such a small share in each group felt such influence. Finally, around 85 percent of White and Asian adults, and around 80 percent of adults from Black or Mixed backgrounds felt that they belong to Britain, though the share of adults from Other ethnic backgrounds who felt this was lower, at 68 percent.

23 Ali, S. (2013). *Identities and Sense of Belonging of Muslims in Britain: Using Survey Data, Cognitive Survey Methodology, and In-Depth Interviews*; DPhil. University of Oxford. Available online at https://ora.ox.ac.uk/objects/uuid:2f83a760-1090-406a-bb59-5478c90c5954

24 Social Mobility Commission (June 2020) Monitoring social mobility: 2013–2020: Is the government delivering on our recommendations? London: Social Mobility Commission. https://assets.publishing.service.gov.uk/government/uplo ads/system/uploads/attachment_data/file/891155/Monitoring_report_2013-2020_-Web_version.pdf.

Note Relative poverty figures are assessed at a household income below 60% of median income in the current year. Relative poverty after housing costs assesses this household income after housing payments. Poverty after housing costs rather than before housing costs is reported here, as a clearer picture of what families have to live on.

25 *Ibid.* 19.

26 Department for Equalities (17 March 2022) *op. cit.*

27 Such data can be obtained from: www.ethnicity-facts-figures.service.gov.uk. Accessed on: 17 March 2022.

28 UN Special Rapporteur on Contemporary Forms of Racism, Racial Discrimination, Xenophobia and Related Intolerance. UN Human Rights Council Document No. A/HRC/6/6, 21 August 2007. Available at: www.oicun.org/uploads/files/articles/ UNHRC-rep.pdf.

29 For example, Organization of the Islamic Conference (2008) 1st OIC Observatory report on Islamophobia. Kampala, Uganda: OIC. Available at: http://ww1.oic-oci. org/ uploads/file/Islamphobia/islamphobia_rep_may_07_08.pdf.

30 Runnymede Trust (2017) *Islamophobia: Still a Challenge for Us All*. London: Runnymede Trust.

31 All Party Parliamentary Group on British Muslims (2019) *Islamophobia Defined: The Inquiry into a Working Definition of Islamophobia/Anti-Muslim Hatred*. London: UK House of Commons. This report covers the many arguments around definition mentioned in this chapter.

32 Ballagan, K., Mortimore, R., and Gottfried, G. (2018) *A Review of Survey Research on Muslims in Britain*. London: Ipsos Mori Social Research Institute.

33 ICM Survey of Muslims for Policy Exchange (2016) *Interviews with 3,040 Muslims aged 18+, conducted face-to-face across Great Britain between 19 May -23 July 2016*.

34 ComRes poll for the BBC *Today* programme: Interviews with 1,000 Muslims aged 18+, by telephone, 26 January-20 February 2015.

35 Ballagan et al (2018) *op.cit.*

36 Hussain, S. (2017) British Muslims: An overview in Runnymede Trust. *op. cit.* 17–24.

37 Ballagan et al (2018) *op.cit.*

38 The Economist Explains (26 September 2022)Who Are Iran's Hated Morality Police? *The Economist.*

39 Runnymede Trust (2017) *op. cit.* 8.

40 Hirsi Ali, A. (2015) *Heretic: Why Islam Needs a Reformation Now*. New York: Harper.

41 *Ibid.* 85.

42 Harris, S. and Nawaz, M. (2015) *Islam and the Future of Tolerance: a Dialogue*. Cambridge, Massachusetts: Harvard University Press. 49.

43 Shankley, W. and Rhodes, J. (2020) Racisms in Contemporary Britain. in Byrne, B. et al *op.cit.*, 214.

44 Casey, L. (2016). *The Casey Review: A Review into Opportunity and Integration.* Department for Communities and Local Government. Available online at: www.gov.uk/government/uploads/system/uploads/attachment_data/file/575 973/The_Casey_Review_Report.pd.f

45 The Casey Review (December 2016) *A Review into Opportunity and Integration. Executive Summary* Department for Communities and Local Government. 15–16.

46 Igbal. N. (21 Sep 2019) Birmingham School Row: This is Made Out to Be Just Muslims v. Gays. It's Not. *The Guardian.* www.theguardian.com/uk-news/2019/ sep/21/birmingham-anderton-park-primary-school-row-parents-teachers-demonstrators. Accessed on: 24/08/2020.

47 International Holocaust Remembrance Alliance (IHRA). (2016) https://web.arch ive.org/web/20180825032144/https://www.holocaustremembrance.com/sites/ default/files/press_release_document_antisemitism.pdf.

48 See Anti-Defamation League (ADL) www.adl.org/who-we-are.

49 *The ADL Global 100: An Index of Anti-Semitism.* (based on a 2014 survey, with follow-up surveys in 2015, 2017, and 2019, tracked attitudes in 102 countries and territories, claims 1.09 billion people harbour anti-Semitic attitudes). https://global 100.adl.org/map/global survey of anti-Semitic views. Accessed on: 19/08/2020.

50 The Center for the Study of Contemporary European Jewry. Faculty of Humanities. Tel Aviv University (2022) *The Anti-Semitism Worldwide Report 2021.* Tel Aviv University.

51 Malik, K. (24 January 2019) Antisemites Use the Language of Anti-Zionism: The Two are Distinct. *The Observer.*

52 Beinart, P. (07/03/2019) Debunking the Myth that Anti-Zionism is Antisemitic. *The Guardian.* www.theguardian.com/news/2019/mar/07/debunking-myth-that-anti-zionism-is-antisemitic. Accessed on: 19 August 2020.

53 Jupp, D. (2019) *A Gift for Treason: The Cultural Marxist Assault on Western Civilization.* Daniel Jupp.

54 Celebration: Keystone, South Dakota. Issued on: 4 July 2020 www.whitehouse. gov/briefings-statements/remarks-president-trump-south-dakotas-2020-mount-rushmore. Accessed on: 12 July 2020.

55 Maher, B. (10 August 2019) Past & Furious. Real Time with Bill Mayer. *HBO.* www.youtube.com/watch?v=efbm3JS0J04. Accessed on: 30 July 2020.

56 www.insidehighered.com/news/2016/08/25/u-chicago-warns-incoming-stude nts-not-expect-safe-spaces-or-trigger-warnings. Accessed on: 17 July 2020.

57 https://provost.uchicago.edu/sites/default/files/documents/reports/FOEComm itteeReport.pdf

58 https://harpers.org/a-letter-on-justice-and-open-debate.

59 Giorgas, H. (July 13, 2020) A Deeply Provincial View of Free Speech. *The Atlantic.* www.theatlantic.com/culture/archive/2020/07/harpers-letter-free-speech/ 614080.

60 Bollinger, L.C. (June 12, 2019) Free Speech on Campus Is Doing Just Fine, Thank You.
   Norms about the First Amendment areEvolving—but Not in the Way President Trump Thinks. *The Atlantic.* www.theatlantic.com/ideas/archive/2019/06/free-speech-crisis-campus-isnt-real/591394/

61 Gramsci article for socialist newspaper Il Grido, quoted in: Boggs, C. (1976) *Gramsci's Marxism*. London: Pluto Press. 59.

62 Lyotard, J-F. (1984) *The Postmodern Condition: A Report on Knowledge*. Manchester: Manchester University Press.

63 Pluckrose, H. and Lindsay, J. (2020) *Cynical Theories: How Activist Scholarship Mae Everything About Race, Gender, and Identity - And Why This Harms Everybody*. Durham, N.C.: Pitchstone Publishing.

64 Freire, P. (1970. 1993 edition. translated by Ramos, M.B.) *Pedagogy of the Oppressed*. London: Penguin Books.

65 Bolotnikova, M. (19 January 2017) Harvard's Economic Diversity Problem. *Harvard Magazine*.

66 Chetty, R., Friedman, J., Saez, E., Turner, N., & Yagan, D. (July 2017) Mobility Report Cards: The Role of Colleges in Intergenerational Mobility. Paper. https://opportunityinsights.org/wp-content/uploads/2018/03/coll_mrc_paper.pdf. Accessed on: 20 November 2022.

67 Lilla, M. (2017) *The Once and Future Liberal: After Identity Politics*. New York; HarperCollins.

68 Hall, S. (1992) The Question of Cultural Identity, in Hall, S., Held, D., and McGrew, T. (eds.) *Modernity and its Futures*. Cambridge: Polity Press. 274–323.

69 Fukuyama, F. (2018) *Identity: Contemporary Identity Politics and the Struggle for Recognition*. London: Profile Books.

70 Note: for an elaborated analysis, see Zanghellini, A. (May 2020) *Philosophical Problems With the Gender-Critical Feminist Argument Against Trans Inclusion*.Sage Journals. https://journals.sagepub.com/doi/full. Accessed on: 17 March 2022.

71 Wheeler, C. (13 March 2022) JK Rowling Rounds on Keir Starmer Over Gender. *The Sunday Times*.

72 Applebaum, B. (2010) *Being White, Being Good: White Complicity, White Moral Responsibility, and Social Justice Pedagogy*. New York: Lexington Books.

73 Henderson, C. (Updated 5:36 AM EST Dec 18, 2019) 'Rosanna Arquette slammed for saying she 'feels so much shame' over being white, privileged'. *USA Today*. https://eu.usatoday.com/story/entertainment/celebrities/2019/08/08/rosanna-arquette-feels-so-much-shame-over-being-white-privileged/1962475001/ Accessed on 30/07/2020. It was also referenced in Mayer, B. (28 September 2019) White Shame. Real Time with Bill Mayer. *HBO*. www.youtube.com. Accessed on: 29 July 2020.

74 Reid, N. (2021) *The Good Ally: A Guided Anti-racism Journey: From Bystander to Changemaker*. London: HarperCollins.

75 Helmore, E. (15 May 2022) Buffalo Shooting: Teenage Accused of Killing 10 in 'Racist' Supermarket Attack. *The Observer*.

76 Barndt, J. (2007) *Understanding & Dismantling Racism: The Twenty-first Century Challenge to White America*. Minneapolis: MN: Augsburg Fortress.

77 *Ibid.* 7.

78 Agarwal, P. (2021) *Sway: Unravelling Unconscious Bias*. London: Bloomsbury Sigma.

79 See: The Science of Overcoming Racism: What Research Shows and Experts Say About Creating a More Just and Equitable World. (Summer 2021) Special Edition of *Scientific American*.

80 McWhorter, J. (2000. 2001 edition) *Losing the Race: Self-Sabotage in Black America*. New York: HarperCollins. 162–163.

81 Malik, K. (4 November 2018) Myths About Shared Culture Have No Place in the Citizenship Debate. *The Observer*.

82 Malik, K. (2017) Fear, Indifference and Engagement: Rethinking the Challenge of anti-Muslim Bigotry, in Runnymede Trust. *op.cit.* 73–77. 74.

83 Crenshaw, K. (1989) Demarginalizing the Intersection of Race and Sex: A Black Feminist Critique of Antidiscrimination Doctrine, Feminist Theory and Antiracist Politics, *University of Chicago Legal Forum*: 1989 (1). Article 8. 139–167. Available at: http://chicagounbound.uchicago.edu/uclf/vol1989/iss1/8.

84 Note: she resigned in 2022 because of what she took to be Johnson's slur on the Leader of the Opposition.

85 Dowden, O. (15 May 2021) We Won't Allow Britain's History To Be Cancelled. *The Telegraph Website.* www.telegraph.co.uk/news/2021/05/15/wont-allow-brita ins-history-cancelled.

86 Public Religion Research Institute (PRRI) with the Brookings Institution (2021) *Competing Visions of America: An Evolving Identity Or A Culture Under Attack? Findings From the 2021 American Values Survey.* Washington: PRRI.

87 Helderman, R.S. andCohen, J. (29 August 2012) As Republican Convention Emphasizes Diversity, Racial Incidents Intrude. *The Washington Post.* www.was hingtonpost.com/politics/2012/08/29. Accessed on: 18 March 2022.

88 Galston, W. and Kamarck, E. (September 1989) *The Politics of Evasion.* Progressive Policy Institute (PPI). 2. www.progressivepolicy.org/wp-content/uploads/2010/ 01/Politics_of_Evasion.pdf. Accessed on: 19 March 2022.

89 Galston, W. and Kamarck, E. (February 2022) *The New Politics of Evasion: How Ignoring Swing Voters Could Reopen the Door for Donald Trump and Threaten American Democracy.* Progressive Policy Institute (PPI). www.progressivepolicy.org/wp-cont ent/uploads/2010/01/Politics_of_Evasion.pdf. Accessed on: 19 March 2022.

90 Note: this final sentence is a point well-made in: Perry, L. (2–8 July 2021) The Jess De Wahls Debacle Shows That You Can Only Really Be Cancelled By Your Friends. *New Statesman.*

91 del Rio-Gonzalez, AM (June 2021) To Latinx or Not to Latinx: A Question of Gender Inclusivity Versus Gender Neutrality. *American Journal of Public Health.* 111(6): 1018–1021.

92 Galston, W. and Kamarck, E. (February 2022) *op. cit.* 17.

93 Appiah, K.A. (2018) *The Lies that Bind: Rethinking Identity: Creed, Country, Colour, Class, Culture.* London: Profile Books.

94 Parekh, B. (2000) *Rethinking Multiculturalism.* Basingstoke: Palgrave.

95 Fukuyama, F. (2018) *op.cit.* 115.

96 *Ibid.*

97 Agencies. (13 May 2022) Calling a Man 'Bald' is Sexual Harassment, Employment Tribunal Rules. *The Guardian.*

98 Eddo-Lodge, R. (2018) *Why I'm No Longer Talking to White People About Race.* London: Bloomsbury Publishing.

99 Phillips, K. (Summer 2021) How Diversity Works in: The Science of Overcoming Racism. *Scientific American.* 19–21.

100 Manavis, S. (27 August-2 September 2021) The Problem With 'Incel' Discourse. *New Statesman.* 18.

4

FALSE ECONOMY

The Great Recession and the Ghost of Neoliberalism: Easy Money and Hard Times

Plainly, we're living through momentous economic change in both scope and speed. The pace is staggering. When I was growing up, transistor radio was considered a marvel of modern electronics. Now we have the continuing miniaturisation in the semiconductor sector toward the 1-nanometre chip – a micro that augurs further macro change.

The First Industrial Revolution, starting roughly mid-eighteenth century, developed hydro and steam power to mechanise production, and this technology, translated into printing, produced mass communication, and over time with public schooling, mass literacy. The Second, starting roughly in the 1870s, deployed electrification and oil-powered combustion engine to create factory mass production, with mobility and communication extended by the automobile, railroads and telegraph. By late twentieth century, digital technologies of information and communication augured the Third, which further automated production, and brought the personal computer and internet. Currently, a Fourth Industrial Revolution is debuting, marked by advanced collaboration between humans and machines, as explored in Chapter eight.

For most of us, this transformation is most manifest in the mobile devices that allow us to access, process and store massive amounts of data, and communicate internationally at ease. Although, as mentioned earlier, megatrends behind this change operate at the *physical* level in such features as smartphones, robotics, autonomous vehicles, drones, wearable sensors, and 3-D printing; at the *digital* level in the internet-of-things, social media platforms, cloud and cognitive computing, and big data analytics; and at the *biological* level in gene editing, and wider bio-engineering.[1] Importantly, these are linking together, via such instruments as nanotechnology, and this blend is said to engender greater prospect of intelligent production, consumption, and mobility, and with

DOI: 10.4324/9781003106593-5

these improvements, higher global income, alongside smart homes and cities, and personalised education and healthcare.

Rifkin conflates the last 250 years into three industrial revolutions, each one involving a 'convergence of communication technology and energy regimes'.[2] Others conflate it further, into two, the first and second machine ages, with the latter penalising workers with ordinary over digital skills, but rewarding consumers with improved goods and services in terms of volume, variety and quality.[3] For Rifkin, the current economic makeover is marked by: accelerated digitisation; shrinkage of space and eradication of time; shift to renewable energy; retrofitting of buildings into dual-purpose habitats and micro-power plants to harness renewable energy on site, use hydrogen and other storage technologies, and share surplus via an energy internet; and vehicle electrification, generated via a 'green grid', from sources such as solar, wind and hydro-power, biomass, and geothermal energy.

Whereas the first revolution spawned dense polluted industrial cities and multi-storey factories, the second gave rise to flat suburban sprawl of low-density residence, shopping malls and industrial parks, connected by multi-lane highways. The third will reshape cityscape as a decarbonised integrated biosphere, with more mixed-use downtowns beyond office and retail, re-designed housing for more home-working, more urban farming and public parks, and the reappearance of the wild within urbanism.

Rifkin is optimistic about how the new era will democratise energy utility, and bring collaborative networking that will see power relations as lateral rather than hierarchical, in what he calls 'distributed capitalism'. 'Carbon' industry – oil, automotive, utilities, telecommunication, construction – is big in capitalisation; vertical in economies of scale; marketised in exchange; centralised in command and control; and highly unequal in distribution.

By contrast, this new economy offers niche and customised over mass standardised; micro-financing and crowdfunding over big banking; networks to compete with markets within a more generous public domain: in short, 'a more distributed and collaborative industrial revolution (that), in turn, leads to a more distributed sharing of the wealth generated'.[4] This theme is developed in a companion book,[5] which decries the trend toward ever greater privatisation, whereby knowledge in general, and the earth's gene pool specifically, get cast as intellectual property, patented and copyrighted for commercial gain.

He argues that effective response to these profit-driven 'enclosures' doesn't lie in old forms of command socialism, but rather in reclaiming the social Commons, a shared universal heritage of public space, atmosphere, knowledge, culture, renewable energy, and genetic information, held in human trust for stewardship of nature, our species, and fellow creatures. Current integration of communication technology and new energy systems, via the internet-of-things, facilitates this rediscovery of individual agency within mutual support. Growth in personal computer power, extended transmission networks, and tumbling costs of data storage, green energy, software, and bio and other technologies, all hold potential for democratising research and turning consumers into their own producers – *prosumers*.

This new economic actor – the prosumer collaboratist – sharing produce in globally connected Commons at near zero marginal costs,[6] transforms relationships of production, ownership and exchange. Such reinvention offers a hybrid selling-sharing economy, with expansion of social, relative to market, capital. Enhanced scope for *commonwealth* sees a shift from free-market zones to market-free zones, including: more open-source licensing; vehicle, tools and skills sharing; exchanging clothes, books, furniture, and music at low or no cost; shared vegetable gardens; house-swaps for holidays; and so on. This is sometimes referred to the *circular* economy, involving repair, re-use, recycling and replenishing.

Thereby, over-production and consumption give way to less wasteful trading patterns that comprise swapping, partaking, bequeathing, and bargaining. Even outside the non-profit version of the new exchange, ownership is redefined. Airbnb owns no accommodation. Uber owns no cars.

As more productive economic activity reaches near zero marginal cost, profits dip as scarcity disappears, and profusion deflates exchange value. This undermines the traditional capitalist business model. In Rifkin's view, this in turn takes politics beyond conventional left and right to a contest of autocratic, privileged, sheltered, and proprietary thinking, versus an inclusive, open, lateral, nodal, and mutual approach, involving less machismo and more mediation. The change brings a new 'class' division, between new collaboratists and old capitalists, and a new political geography. Logistics and viable regulatory jurisdiction for delivering a Commons model, are more likely to favour pan-continental economies, like the EU, over national or global economic frameworks, regardless of how much either remain essential for networked governance.

The vision is of radical change from Capitalist *excess* to Commons *access*. But even if some or all of this sounds plausible, there are cautionary notes. Rifkin's idea of continental scale raises an intriguing paradox of opposing pulls between economics and politics. Economically, it seems groups of countries are prepared to pool into large unions – the EU for Europe; ASEAN for Asia; the African union; and the Union of South American Nations – for scale and protection. By the same token, these large formations seem beset by bureaucratic rather than democratic structures, and thus politically to many citizens, are remote and unresponsive. In the case of Europe, whether Brexit was a one-off response to that democratic deficit remains to be seen.

In addition, modern economies require agility and decisiveness to keep pace with rapid innovation, whereas modern polities require slow deliberation to do justice to the complexities of contemporary problems. Economic imperatives will trump political ones only if people's faith in their own agency is wilted by the maxim that there's no alternative. Besides, in a world facing existential threats as explored in Chapter seven, old-style geopolitics that is planet-bound must accommodate biosphere politics that positions us in a wider universe. As the world gets smaller, we need more focus on this bigger picture.

However precisely understood, if this new economy yields net job loss, it may strengthen capital relative to labour, or at least skew the clout *within* labour towards the more digitally competent, leaving the low-skilled with increasingly precarious service employment, and depressing the labour market's middle tier. This new division of labour between the human and digital, whereby tasks with rule-based logic can be increasingly undertaken by machines,[7] would have significant implication for inequality, social stability, and democracy. Moreover, since 1.3 billion people lack ready access to electricity, they've yet to fully experience the second revolution, and since 4 billion people have no easy internet access, they've yet to undergo the third revolution.[8] These 'under-developments' bring to mind Joan Robinson's wry observation[9] to the effect that the only thing worse than being exploited by capitalism is not being exploited by capitalism.

Nobody denies that this stage of capitalism is radically different from its predecessors. Even for its optimists, it presents stark choice. It could 'robotize humanity, and thus compromise our traditional sources of meaning – work, community, family, identity'.[10] Or it could 'lift humanity into a new collective consciousness based on a shared sense of destiny'.[11] Best scenarios see digital connectivity improving the world of work, while extending transparency, civic engagement, and global common purpose. In these projections, it can equalise and democratise.

Such confidence is not universally shared however. Reservation about the new economic order has been expressed by Zuboff.[12] In her blistering critique, she sees us subject to 'surveillance capitalism', which covertly extracts our privacy from our online activity as free raw material for predictive behavioural analysis, distributing this surplus to commercial interests for behaviour modification and profitable commodification. Fundamentally, the knowledge economy concerns knowledge *from* and *about*, rather than *for*, us. Our behavioural surplus – data about us beyond that needed to improve service to us – is sold to other corporate clients in what is a behavioural futures market. Zuboff contends that the division of labour has been replaced by a division of learning. As our browsing traffic is tracked, the inequality of learning favours tech companies over us as info-searchers.

This new logic of accumulation is invasive of intimate realms of social life, a 'coup from above' that threatens our democratic right to agency and sanctuary. Our individual sovereignty faces incursion and capture by corporations who seek habitat in lawless space outside any national sovereignty. For this take-over, the free market needs not just an invisible, but a free, hand.

All told, 'surveillance capitalists take command of the essential questions that define knowledge, authority, and power in our time: Who knows? Who decides? Who decides who decides?'[13] The 'attention merchants' in this new capitalism are conditioning us 'to spend so much of (our) waking lives not in concentration and focus but rather in fragmentary awareness and subject to constant interruption'.[14] Unremitting connection asset-strips us of a vital human trait: intermission to ponder, to be in communion with nature, and to engage in purposeful dialogue. In this telling, we may marvel at our remote controls for various gadgets. But it is we who are being remotely controlled. Overall, this kind of digital economics further empowers capital, while debilitating labour's ability to organise effectively. More casual and quiescent labour is the consequence.

For example, in Chapter eight we'll examine the lobby power of big tech, together with its furtive hold on democracy, evident in the use of surveillance in Trump's election campaigns. It's important to emphasise though that it didn't begin with Trump. The 2008 Obama campaign gathered data on over 250 million citizens. Obama presented himself as chum to leading big techies, and an influential 'revolving door' operated between personnel from his government and those from the sector. Another shortcoming of the centrist Obama administration came with its acquiescence to the financialization of the economy.

Funny Money

Since the 1970s, a new international division of labour has emerged, as first, production processes were recomposed, with labour intensive components increasingly relocated to countries with low labour costs. This meant over a few decades that traditional industrial zones in developed economies became, to varying degrees, rustbelts. Extension of world trade, greater capital mobility, and technological upgrade at once narrowed inequality *between* countries, while widening it *within* some countries.[15] In this new world, global finance assumed economic dominance.

The oft-told story of the financial crash 2008–09 is worth recapping for the insight it offers about today's political economy. It started in the US, where the then Bush presidency, when it wasn't fighting war on terror abroad, and tax-cutting and privatising at home, was intent on expanding home ownership to low-income and minority communities. Though this was sold as a means of giving excluded groups greater stake in a property-owning society, other agendas were in play as well. By allowing the less well-off access to private assets that were appreciating in value, it was hoped that they would rely less on government welfare. Politically, it served to broaden Republican Party appeal to Hispanics and blacks in a country whose electoral demography was becoming more diverse. Furthermore, the real estate and financial interests set to be beneficiaries of any housing boom were among the significant donors to the Bush re-election coffers.[16]

Home loans became available with low or no deposit and seemingly attractive repayment conditions, as this so-called subprime mortgage market invited predatory lending practice. In a society where big can be thought better, some families were induced to purchase larger houses than their incomes could support. Three obvious drivers were active once this housing boom took off. First, many deemed it prudent to jump on board promptly. Otherwise, they'd miss the boat, and prices would soar beyond their reach. Second, at a time of stagnant average wages, real estate seemed to offer a sure-fire way to make money, as house-price value rose much greater than average earned income. Between 1997 and peak value in 2006, US house prices increased by an astounding 152 percent.[17] Housing became an investment commodity, as many anticipated exchange as well as use-value. Finally, the era of unusually low interest rates provided cheap money, and made borrowing more attractive than saving.

Those with savings were tempted to take higher risks to achieve better return than that offered by traditional savings accounts. Speculative property investment, either directly or through investment banks, seemed a good bet. The frenzy took off. When the reliable mortgage market became saturated, selling turned to the subprime sector, where households had a high debt to income ratio. In the worst cases, this involved 'ninja' (no income, job, or assets) loans. As a share of personal disposable income, household debt rocketed from 80 percent in 1993 to nearly 130 percent by mid-2006, with over three-quarters of this being mortgage debt. By mid-2005, nearly one-quarter of new loans were interest-only, postponing payment of principal.[18] Truly, this was immediate gratification based on deferred pain.

Amid the giddy optimism, some borrowed on the assumed equity in their key asset – rising house value – to finance a more extravagant consumerist lifestyle than their regular income would warrant. Bigger houses needed more stuff to fill them. And in such a credit-driven economy, big banks wanted in on the act. They purchased bundles of mortgages from the direct lenders, and re-packaged them into mortgage-backed securities. To obtain good grading from credit rating agencies – whose job it was to assign the calibre of such financial products – the investment banks bundled them into tranches that mixed the loan quality from assured payback to basically junk that was likely to face payment default. This newfangled blended parcel was called a Collateralized Debt Obligation (CDOs), and could be graded Triple A on the basis of its best constituent. In its entangled complexity, the junk part could be hidden. We might call this a case of grade inflation that gave false confidence to institutional investors like pension, mutual and insurance funds. By late 2007, signs of an overheated housing market loomed. Those who had bought adjustable rate mortgages, initially set at 'teaser' levels, were faced with repayments re-set at less affordable charges.

For some, this meant they had to re-finance, a euphemism for borrowing more to re-pay existing debt. As house values fell, even re-financing became no longer an option for some, whose de-faulting led to foreclosure, a nice word for eviction. As these houses were dumped onto the market, the glut helped depress it further. Investment banks, and the funds with which they traded, were left vulnerable. Their collateral for mounting unpaid mortgages was the depreciating asset of relinquished houses that might only yield fire-sale price. With the party stopped, the headache began. One local manifestation was abandoned homes and related neighbourhood blight. In these forsaken places, the bubble had turned to rubble.

Alongside this frenetic activity, complicated financial instruments, expressed in banking gobbledygook, seemed designed to bamboozle even insiders. Most people have no idea precisely what are securities, derivatives, credit default swaps, hedge funds, and so on.[19] All these and more were summoned to advance speculative opportunities and hedge bets in a rampant housing market, thereby helping the entangled Finance, Insurance and Real Estate (FIRE) sector to tower over the economy. Strange money created an unreal world for real estate.

The first sign of potential meltdown came in March 2008, with Bear Stearns revealing they had a 'liquidity' problem. Having prospered from mortgage-backed securities, they reeled as their risky investments tottered. JP Morgan offered to buy it if the Federal Reserve (the US Central Bank) put in $30 billion to ring-fence its toxic part – and government rode to the rescue to assist purchase by JP Morgan, in what was effectively the first bailout.

Then in summer 2008, Fannie Mae and Freddie Mac faltered. These were the major house loan agencies, whose supportive role in promoting public policy of home ownership, and designation as government-sponsored enterprises (GSEs), carried assumption that however dire their performance, government would guarantee their survival. But they were in fact private profit-oriented companies, with a $5 trillion mortgage exposure.

Market turmoil reached critical point in mid-September 2008, with Lehman's bankruptcy, Merrill's takeover by the Bank of America, and government rescue of American International Group (AIG). Lehman's collapse wiped $700 billion in value from government pension funds, retirement and other investment portfolios, and impacted around 8,000 subsidiaries with $600 billion in assets and liabilities, over 100,000 creditors, and close to 26,000 staff. Despite this fallout, government refused to act as if it was too big to fail, forsaking it to its fate. By contrast, the imminent crash of AIG brought state assistance of over $180 billion.[20]

As this downturn rippled, it roused wider market unease, triggered tighter credit, slammed brakes on much trading and new investment, and shook stock markets to near the brink. Paulson, the US Treasury Secretary, and Bernanke, chairman of the Federal Reserve, were concerned to contain the panic, thereby averting contagion that could tank the economy. Interestingly, Paulson had produced a blueprint for a 'Modernized Financial Regulatory Structure' in March 2008,[21] saying that globalisation and innovation in capital markets had contributed to domestic and global growth, but now needed a regulatory framework that was more 'flexible'. Though more regulation was not the answer in his view, capital markets competitiveness had to be offset with market stability and consumer protection.

Clearly, this faint-hearted nod to better oversight was too little too late. Government light-touch regulation to boost 'competitiveness' had encouraged excess in lax lending, bloated portfolios, and so-called distressed assets. Amidst ensuing credit panic, and in flustered urgency to fend off economic collapse, Paulson pressed a pressured Congress to pass The Emergency Economic Stabilization Act in October 2008. It followed initial rejection of the plan, seen by many legislators as moral hazard, since it sought to rescue a reckless Wall Street. But Paulson recognised that in a stand-off between politics and the market in the US, the market prevails.

Cajoled into accepting that these institutions were 'too big to fail', without toppling the whole house of cards, and that crisis demanded obedience to 'market reality', Congress relented. It had to cave to save. The Act set aside $700 billion for a Troubled Asset Relief Program (TARP) that gave Federal Government wide discretion to 'relieve' banks of their toxic debt, and re-establish liquidity and trust in financial markets.

Top executives of the top nine US financial institutions – holding over $11 trillion in assets – were summoned by Paulson and told they had to accept TARP capital, because if they rejected, and regulators subsequently were to find them under-capitalised, they would not like his terms, if compelled to come back to him cap in hand. All nine signed the deal. This was semi-nationalisation that kept private business in charge. Apart from such 'crisis' lending, the Fed poured about $2.3 trillion into the economy up to late 2010. Designed for stimulus, and purchase of mortgage-backed securities and government bonds, while keeping interest rates low, it was sold under the wily name of 'quantitative easing'.[22]

A 2011 report[23] from the National Commission on the Causes of the Financial and Economic Crisis in the United States noted the aftermath at that point: 26 million Americans jobless, or unable to get full-time employment, or resigned to not finding work; about four million families who had been evicted and an additional four and a half million who either were near foreclosure or had fallen badly behind on mortgage re-payment; and around $17 trillion of net household wealth that had evaporated, including retirement funds and life savings, and with $5.6 trillion attributable to falling house prices, which dropped a third between their peak in 2006 to their trough in 2009. For perspective, US GDP in 2008 was $14.4 trillion.

The report asked why it had come down to two grim options: either risk implosion of not only the financial system but also the whole economy, or heap massive amounts of taxpayer dollars to save a system that still left many citizens forfeiting jobs, homes and savings. It concluded that this predicament was long in the making. Although the immediate trigger was the bursting of a housing bubble, puffed up by low interest rates, relaxed and accessible credit, poor transparency of financial products, negligible regulation, and trillions of dollars in dodgy mortgages implanted in the financial system as multiply-packaged 'securities', off-loaded to investors around the world. Big global finance houses had huge exposure to these dicey assets and indeed had borrowed imprudently against them. The calamity was aggravated by the opaque nature of derivatives such as synthetic securities, for which safeguards were few, and involved serial refinancing that piled debt upon debt.

In reviewing corporate blame among leading firms, the Commission repeatedly charged them with: weak governance and risk management; inadequate liquidity; unjustified leverage; poor transparency; and indulgence in a remuneration system that rewarded quick return on equity. AIG, with its massive use of credit default swaps and insufficient capital reserves, exemplified defective practice.

This disaster, however, had a thirty-year backdrop. Between 1978–2007, total debt held by the financial sector rocketed from $3 to $36 trillion, over doubling as a share of gross domestic product (GDP). In the process, the business became more concentrated. By 2005, the 10 biggest US commercial banks accounted for 55 percent of the sector's assets, over double the share held in 1990. This combination of growth and domination yielded high returns, with the sector's profits comprising 27 percent of total US corporate profits, a rise from 15 percent in 1980.[24] The report noted: 'as demand for all types of financial products soared during the liquidity boom at the beginning of the 21st century, pre-tax profit for the five largest investment banks doubled between 2003 and 2006, from $20 billion to $43 billion; total compensation at these investment banks for their employees across the world rose from $34 billion to $61 billion.'[25]

For a time, riskier trading brought greater profits. As a result, key figures like long-standing Federal Reserve boss, Alan Greenspan, advocated minimal interference in markets that he thought would naturally self-adjust. Effectively, the sector was allowed to self-regulate for over three decades, as it became ever-more powerful. When the crisis came, 'the sentries were not at their post'.[26] As expressed by the Commission's report:[27]

> *financial institutions made, bought, and sold mortgage securities they never examined, did not care to examine, or knew to be defective; firms depended on tens of billions of dollars of borrowing that had to be renewed each and every night, secured by subprime mortgage securities; and major firms and investors blindly relied on credit rating agencies as their arbiters of risk. What else could one expect on a highway where there were neither speed limits nor neatly painted lines?*

Banking executives later confessed to being in the dark with regard to major holdings. For instance, Citigroup's CEO explained to the Commission that a $40 billion stake in highly rated securities would 'not in any way have excited my attention'. Senior executives of AIG, the top global insurance company, were unaware of the gamble involved in their $79 billion derivatives exposure to mortgage-related securities. Similar stories were recounted for Merrill Lynch and others. Ignorance was bliss. Unsurprisingly, the Commission rebuked this neglect: 'too big to fail meant too big to manage….Too often, risk management became risk justification'. It was a system that rewarded the quick return on a 'big bet', rather than deliberation about downstream outcome.[28]

A bank's 'capital' is the sum of its assets over its debt and other liabilities, a measure of what it owns over what it owes. The extent of under-capitalisation was remarkable. The five big investment banks – Goldman Sachs, Morgan Stanley, Merrill Lynch, Lehman and Bear Stearns – in 2007 had leverage ratios up to 40 to 1, leverage being the degree to which a firm finances its assets with loans rather than equity. So a leverage ratio of 5:1 denotes that for every $5 of assets bought, it involved $4 of debt and $1 of capital.

At this stage, Lehman's stockpile of $111 billion in housing and commercial property and securities was nearly double its holding of two years previous, and over four times its total equity. Given such indebtedness, these firms' vulnerability to even a modest fall in asset values was obvious. Of course, households were also beholden in this binge. Between 2001–2007, there was near doubling of US mortgage debt.[29] Between 2001–2006, total value of issued mortgage-backed securities hit $13.4 trillion.[30]

It might be thought that the unlikely viability of this burden amidst sluggish wage growth was hiding in plain sight. However, the poor visibility of commitments, wrapped up in complex interconnected financial products across the global market, disguised the investment's thinly protected status. Deliberate obscurity seemed expedient for all concerned, and the lucrative blinded some to the ludicrous.

Far from risk being spread, it was clustered. Essentially, in a deceitful business culture, guaranteed to come to grief, it was a game of pass the parcel. Mortgage brokers did the reconnaissance by identifying home loan candidates. They passed contenders on to lenders, who arranged the mortgages. They sold these on to financial companies, which re-packaged them into a variety of mortgage-backed securities and collateralised debt obligations (CDOs), to be dispatched to investors down the line.

In addition, with house prices skyrocketing, speculators bought property to sell for quick yield. There were even so-called synthetic CDOs, which held credit default swaps that referenced rather than held mortgage assets, allowing investors to wager for or against those referenced assets. In this way, the same product could be sold over and over again. Each transaction in this circuit brought fees and profits, and hopefully a quick getaway. Nobody in the chain wanted to be left holding the parcel when the music stopped. And in high frequency finance trading – what we may call speed betting – the music can stop abruptly. And it did.

Resulting crisis revealed the smoke and mirrors. With greater use of securitisation, it was hard to trace the original loan and its credit-worthiness. And in this maze, the mighty AIG had not been obligated to hold capital reserves that could cover the indemnity it was vending. AIG's credit protection offers on various assets, including mortgage-backed securities, expanded from $20 billion in 2002 to $533 billion just five years later. In 2005, the firm's triple-A rating was forfeited when auditors discerned that its earnings had been contrived.[31]

Ultimately, to prevent the conglomerate's collapse, the US government had to commit $180 billion. The world's biggest insurance company couldn't ensure its own survival. And one obvious question arises: where in this crazy credit bubble were the credit rating agencies? Well, the Commission's report sees the big three – Moody's, Standard & Poor's, and Fitch – as 'key enablers of the financial meltdown' since 'mortgage-related securities at the heart of the crisis could not have been marketed and sold without their seal of approval'.[32]

Masters of the Universe?

By mid-January 2009, the four largest financial institutions in the US had lost half their value.[33] Importantly, it wasn't only particular banks that were considered too big to fail. The sector itself was thought of likewise. For about two decades, beginning in the early 1980s, the US financial sector expanded faster than the rest of America's economy – growing from about 5 percent of GDP to about 8 percent early this century. But an interesting aspect of this growth was the country's increasing dependence on international capital flows in the context of its sizeable current account deficits. A country like China, with its fast-growing financial system and domestic consumer market, was keen to transfer a good share of its expansive wealth into the US dollar, by for instance buying US government bonds. This liquidity in the US financial system allowed government and public to mount debt, yet keep long-term interest rates quite low. The housing bubble in the US, and indeed in parts of Europe, was funded to a large extent by big global capital streams.

Ironically, countries in the rich world that were seeing a rise in anti-foreigner sentiment, expressed as threats to their lifestyle, were becoming increasingly reliant on foreign capital to indulge that lifestyle. As they were finger-pointing foreigners, the question of how these transfers would one day be reimbursed was put on the long finger.

Meantime, the 'masters' – the finance executives, dealers and brokers – were being paid handsomely. Their remuneration is best thought of not in terms of salary, but rather of 'compensation packages', that involved topping their base earnings with generous bonuses and stocks. Many big investment firms typically devoted around half their revenue to such compensation. Moreover, this pay was not necessarily commensurate with the company's long-term security. Merill's CEO received $91 million in 2006, a short period before its needed takeover. In 2007, Fuld, head honcho of Lehman, collected around $34 million,[34] and as we know, a short time after, Lehman was toast.

So what exactly did these people master? Some of the clever behaviour involved playing both sides with clients, like trading subprime mortgage securities with buyers, while using that inside information to wager against those same products that it knew likely to default – what in the jargon is known as 'shorting' them. Evidently, this grand casino lacked supervision.[35]

One form of regulation was meant to be the credit rating agencies. But they were found to have privileged their own business opportunity above the honesty and quality of their appraisals. The system rewarded such prioritisation. If an investment bank selected a particular agency, which didn't give its product favourable rating, it could turn instead to a more acquiescent competitor agency for a better outcome. In this model, the investment bank is the customer, and in such a relationship, there is a trace of the maxim that the customer is always right.

Since Triple-A ratings not only offered marketing appeal, but also allowed banks to hold less capital against their securities, such incentives required better oversight of the ratings agencies. True, they added a rider to potential investors in these products that their evaluation was opinion, not fact. But the effect of over-generous estimation could be to reinforce collective fantasy among agencies, banks and investors, compromising the principle of due diligence, and minimising preclusion of unforeseen risk. Simply put, you can't have a corporation picking its own regulator.

In general, regulators such as the Securities and Exchange Commission, the Office of Thrift Supervision, and indeed the Fed itself, proved to be more push-over than pushback. If they weren't willing or able to police proper underwriting standards, they should have been addressing, at minimum, the overall lack of transparency, which left many market players on all sides unsure about what precisely they were trading and buying. This game was more blind men's bluff than blind man's buff. It prospered in a political culture rigged for deregulation, and which rewarded the finance sector's power to buy influence. Between 1999 and 2008, the sector 'expended $2.7 billion in reported federal lobbying expenses; individuals and political action committees in the sector made more than $1 billion in campaign contributions'.[36] If Bob Dylan is right that money doesn't talk, but swears, this amounts to a stream of expletives.

In short, the whole system was defective. The banks, regulators, and rating agencies all acted in cosy mutual understanding to produce the calamity. The consequent devastation in many people's lives would not have happened if those responsible did not abuse their position of power.

Hard Lessons Hardly Learned

In the midst of the financial crisis, there was complaint about government inconsistency: resuscitate Bear Stearns and the GSEs, abandon Lehman's, yet save AIG. It could be taken that this variation reflected confusion in a fast-moving crisis. But what have been longer-term lessons? Critics of the financial sector may point to how a relatively small entity – the housing bubble – can have contagion impact on a larger entity – the global economy, a bit like the small Covid virus having huge bearing on humans across the planet.

They may point to the paradox that a monopolistic US banking sector, which coerced government to cushion firms deemed too big to fail, has become now even more concentrated, given subsequent takeovers and bankrupt-cies. Looking at the link between the crisis, rises in housing negative equity, reductions in consumption, and the subsequent recession in a country where consumer spending accounts for over two-thirds of GDP,[37] they may revisit the Keynesian *paradox of thrift*. This posits that over-protective saving by households and firms in hard times can cut overall investment and expenditure – aggregate demand – which in turn leads to reduced gross production and economic growth, which then will diminish total saving.

Essentially, the bailout was a great heist, whereby the private debt of institutions most responsible for the problem was 'socialised' with public money, and consequent public debt was borne as private austerity by individuals and families. In American lingo, though the real crime scene was in Wall Street, it was Main Street that took the hit. The cavalry of big government, that had long been dismissed as a hindrance to a buoyant economy, rode to the rescue. But people at large ended up saddled with the bill. This regressive distribution of costs was reflected not only in the pain absorbed by workers and firms, but also in service cuts in state and local governments, whose reduced tax base meant they were hard-pressed to deliver the extra support residents needed in the downturn.

Estimates of the cost of the 2008 US bailout vary from zero, because the money was repaid, to trillions of dollars. One study that comes in between these accounts is by Lucas,[38] who deduced that the total direct cost was around $500 billion, representing 3.5 percent of GDP in 2009, with the biggest direct bene-ficiaries being the unsecured creditors of financial institutions.

Americans refer to borrowers who fail to meet timely mortgage payments as 'delinquents'. But the real delinquents here were the various lenders and their insurers and ratings endorsers. Little of this delinquent behaviour was totally new. Back in 2000, the dot-com and telecom bubble collapsed. Inflated investor expectation about the emerging tech economy's surging value weren't realised, based as they were on prospects talked up by the very banks and securities firms that underwrote the original public sale of equity shares in these tech firms. Similarly, when the ignominy of Enron's sudden fall came and it filed for bankruptcy in 2001, big name Wall Street firms like Citigroup and JP Morgan doled out billions for their part in assisting Enron to play down its debt, fabricate earnings, and indulge high leverage. Despite the disgrace, such fiascos failed to dent complacency about the finance sector's vim and vigour.

Many perceptive books have been written about the financial crash, such as Tooze's *Crashed*[39] in which he charts the underlying features. Deep globalization is driven less by national economies and more by connecting 'value chains' of oligopolies. Also, it is marked by growing pressure on interbank credit, based on dollars, within an over-leveraged financial system. Its wider geographical frame is being realigned, with Asia rising and Europe declining.

In particular, China's export-led growth is facilitated by deliberate undervaluation of its currency relative to the dollar, which impairs US competitiveness. America's persistent twin deficits of budget and trade expose it to volatilities in the bond market, since its imbalance is being rescued by foreign purchase of its government bonds. For all the American indebtedness to China:[40] 'by far the largest foreign lenders to the United States prior to the crisis, were not Asian but European. Indeed, in 2007, roughly twice as much money flowed from the UK to the United States as from China'.

Disguising its debt dilemma, capital flows into the 'safe haven' of the dollar, keeping interest rates low and American governments and households spending. Real estate sucks in a lot of the latter, since it is seen as a source of future wealth and collateral for current borrowing. In this freewheeling folly, proper democratic debate about these vulnerabilities is curbed, to avoid spooking the market.

For the low-down on the finance sector's shenanigans, and how its under-disclosure meant over-exposure, it's worth wading your way through 662 pages of the US Commission's Report. It should be essential reading in every Business School in every reputable university. That includes its dissenting minority report, in which a conservative analysis identifies the main culprit to be government housing policy, between 1997–2007, that created a bubble that contained 27 million high risk loans – half of all outstanding mortgages – vulnerable to default once the bubble burst.

On this reckoning, it was not too little government, by way of deregulation, but rather too much government interference in the housing market, creating artificial demand that promoted subprime lending, excessive speculation, inflated house prices, and a belief that government would always ultimately cushion penalties for the prodigal. The conservative view was that the disaster wasn't down to private sector negligence by way of weak risk management or Wall Street greed, though there was a factor of global capital flows into the US and parts of Europe that reduced the price of borrowing. But, the market, left alone, could have adjusted for this. This is an example of how people who have faith in a system find ways to explain a systemic debacle, without blaming the system.

Certainly, US public policy since the 1960s has promoted home ownership, which since then has been above 60 percent, peaking in 2005 at 69 percent. Initiatives like the 1977 Community Reinvestment Act (CRA) were designed to redress biased lending and redlining, which discriminated against people of colour, added to the racial household wealth gap, and reinforced race-based residential segregation. While the Act obliges regulated banks to reinvest in communities from which they get deposits, and has helped expand provision of affordable housing, the CRA was not implicated in any significant practice of irresponsible credit.

Global Problem

As already indicated, while the financial crisis seemed to originate in the US, similar patterns of credit-fuelled booms emerged elsewhere, such as Europe, now facing its own challenges. A disruptive union between West and East Germany has been added to by rapid absorption of former Soviet satellites into the EU. An economic union that embodies very uneven development across northern, southern and eastern Europe, and a monetary union under the Euro, without a common economic policy or tax rates, burdens the European Central Bank to oversee viable interest rates, budget deficits, and debt ceilings for diverse economies.

Relatively prosperous Germany, with its own problems such as an imbalanced demography that increases social dependencies while reducing its youth labour market, is not keen to be lumbered with other members' debts. At least rhetorically, it promotes an anti-inflation priority and tight fiscal discipline, increasingly at odds with 'social Europe':[41] '... Europe has 7 percent of the world's population and 25 percent of global GDP. But it is responsible for 50 percent of global social spending'.

Overall, however, the Eurozone crisis that followed in 2010 was rooted more in private than public debt, again reflected in hollow property booms. As Tooze explains:[42] 'In modern finance, credit is not a fixed sum constrained by the 'fundamentals' of the 'real economy'. It is an elastic quantity, which in an asset price boom can easily become self-expanding on a transnational scale'.

The run on the banks came about because banks encouraged people to lose the run of themselves. The Republic of Ireland is a case in point. Its banks' liabilities totalled 700 percent of its GDP. Despite generous subsidies it has received from the EU, it has tried to out-compete its European friends with low corporation tax and lax regulation. On the back of this liberal globalist business model, it has drawn in foreign investment and nurtured a financial centre in Dublin. This apparent buoyancy of the 'Celtic Tiger', in turn, induced many farmers to see land for housing as a great 'cash crop', and many householders to see house purchase as a guaranteed bet. Between 1994 and 2007, house prices quadrupled. Between 2008 and 2012, they halved, crashing household wealth at the very time government was imposing austerity to pay for bank bail-out, unilaterally guaranteeing E 440 billion in liabilities. Irish citizens were not consulted. Nor were European partners.[43] Public security was surrendered to secure private debt.

The UK experience was also interesting. In 1986, Thatcher unleashed the 'Big Bang' – a deregulation of the financial sector. Given that her government had largely stood back and let traditional manufacturing decline in the name of weeding out inefficient and over-unionised sections, dependence on the services sector correspondingly increased, particularly the top end like high finance. In the 1990s, the Blair government made an unspoken bargain with the sector, that it would yield substantial taxation receipts to help pay for New Labour's social programmes, in return for light touch supervision. The stage was set for hubris.

An early warning was sounded in September 2007 with the near collapse of Northern Rock, a former building society that had demutualised to become a bank ten years previously. Large queues of anxious depositors outside its branches intent on fund withdrawal, represented the first run on a British bank in 150 years. With credit markets tightening globally, Northern Rock had to turn to the lender of last resort – the Bank of England – and the substantial government rescue money meant the bank was essentially nationalised in early 2008. It was later sold to Virgin Money, with the bad debts – mainly mortgage-based – removed.

A UK Parliamentary Treasury Committee inquiry into the debacle[44] found the bank's directors to be the main culprits, in their adherence to a reckless business model that involved rapid growth in assets, based on short and medium-term loans from the wholesale money markets. In its high risk strategy, the bank had insufficient insurance and standby facility for addressing liquidity stresses once global capital markets started to seize up with the crisis.

Having ditched the cautionary culture of building societies, the bank had seen its assets rise six-fold from £15.8 billion in 1997 to £101 billion by 2006, with nearly 90 percent of those assets comprising secured lending on residential property. To maintain this momentum, it had to depend evermore on securitisation – packaging the mortgages as collateral for extra funding by selling on the loans to investors.

The main regulator, the Financial Services Agency (FSA), was guilty of dereliction of regulatory duty. At best, it was reliant on measures of solvency, and paid scant regard to liquidity. Given the poor contingency planning for any congestion in credit supply, when emergency struck, liability was transferred to the public purse, as government felt obliged to guarantee security of bank holdings to restore confidence among the money markets and general public.

Also under question was the role of the auditors, PricewaterhouseCoopers, with the Committee expressing concern that there seemed to be a conflict of interest between the auditor's statutory role and any non-audit consultancy undertaken for the same financial institution. The report concluded that a bank's shareholders and creditors should bear the risk of failure, not the general public via government or small depositors. But was this lesson learned, as the drama moved from the dress rehearsal of Northern Rock to the tragedy of the Royal Bank of Scotland (RBS)?

Particularly since the noughties, RBS had gone on a whirlwind acquisition drive, stretching throughout Europe and the US, buying up NAT West, Ulster Bank, Isle of Man Bank, Greenwich Capital, Mellon Financial Corp., and Coutts, among others. The bank was headed by Fred Goodwin, known as Fred the Shred, an uncomplimentary reference to his reputation for abrasive management cost-cutting. In 2002, he was awarded businessman of the year by Forbes, and in 2004, he was knighted, as a doyen of British enterprise in an age when Chancellor Gordon Brown promised that government had delivered an end to boom and bust.

By late 2008, RBS was a global player, the 5th largest bank in the world by capitalisation, and the largest by assets, totalling $3.5 trillion, with operations in 27 countries. Its own sense of self-importance was witnessed by its extravagant £350 million new headquarters, and private corporate jet for the boss. It led a consortium that successfully bought ABN AMRO, funding it chiefly with short-term debt rather than equity. Yet come October 2008, it needed what the Treasury Department hailed as 'the biggest bail-out in history', with government input of £45.5 billion of equity capital and public money exposure through the Asset Protection Scheme of £282 billion.

Despite this abysmal failure, the FSA decided in December 2010, that following its study of the causes behind the calamity, that no enforcement action was necessary. At first, it declined even to make its report public, spuriously citing commercial confidentiality. It only released an account when pressed by the Parliamentary Treasury Committee, an extraordinarily cavalier approach to public accountability. The FSA report acknowledged its own multiple shortcomings in proper oversight, including its lack of appreciation of the bank's risk exposure in capital, liquidity and asset quality; and its passivity about the bank's over-reaching acquisition of parts of ABN AMRO. In response to this negligence, the Treasury Committee commented curtly:[45] 'The failures described in the FSA's Report amount to a serious indictment of senior management not only at RBS but also at the FSA'.

Interestingly, the FSA sought to mitigate its own blame by claiming to operate 'within the context of a widely held, but erroneous, view about the inherent stability of the global financial system, and of political pressure to maintain a 'light touch' regulatory regime to support the competitiveness of the UK financial sector'.[46] It is true that the Labour government took great pains to virtue-signal to business that it was on its side. In an amazing speech to the Confederation of British Industry in November 2005, Gordon Brown spoke about his keenness to take economics out of politics; to make planning more responsive to business; to minimise 'regulatory concerns' and their 'burdens'; and to encourage more risk. A sample of the speech conveys the concession that Brown was prepared to offer:[47]

> *The better, and in my opinion the correct, modern model of regulation – the risk based approach – is based on trust in the responsible company, the engaged employee and the educated consumer,....not just a light touch but a limited touch....And more than that, we should not only apply the concept of risk to the enforcement of regulation, but also to the design and indeed to the decision as to whether to regulate at all.*

To trust that the private sector will self-impose social responsibility is naive beyond belief. The clue is in the name. They prioritise private over social interest. It took him until 2010 to admit his mistake in bowing to bank pressure to de-regulate.[48] But that is no excuse for the FSA. It was supposed to be an independent agency. Failure to act robustly was either cowardice or complicity. In its account of the RBS fiasco, it identified the derisory regulatory capital framework; over-dependence on chancy short-term wholesale funding; reservations about the bank's basic asset quality; weak liquidity oversight; defective corporate management, governance and culture; and deficient intervention by the FSA.

In retrospect, the agency recognised the potential for systemic crisis in the bank's imbalance between risk and growth, particularly when Goodwin's management style deterred the probing essential for probity. Significantly, remuneration systems that rewarded good revenue, profits and earnings per share led to neglect of fundamentals around capital, liquidity and asset quality. Pre-tax profit figures seemed impressive – in 2004: £6.9 billion; in 2005: £7.9 billion; in 2006: £9.2 billion and in 2007: £9.9 billion. But these disguised its real condition. When it undertook capital raising of £12 billion in 2008, it soon saw its share price fall by 35 percent, with further falls following, amidst downgrading of its credit ratings, so that it had no option but to seek emergency liquidity assistance from the Bank of England.[49]

The Treasury Committee reprimanded the regulator for its 'insufficient focus on prudential issues', and it expressed its 'considerable surprise' that essentially nobody had been held 'meaningfully accountable for the failure of RBS'.[50] Generalising this pattern for the whole sector, it concluded:[51] 'In financial institutions senior executives reaped large rewards, much of it paid as bonuses inflated by taking on what proved to be unsustainable risks. Yet when the crash came, they proved to be insulated from many of the risks on the downside'.

The National Audit Office later reported[52] that the sum total of openly pledged assistance to the banks was £456.33 billion as of March 2011, down from the March 2010 figure of £612.58 billion, and the peak of some £1.162

trillion. That this burden should fall on the public is a testament to the grotesque incompetence of many players, and to the low standards in high finance.

Because blame can be spread wide does not mean the fault doesn't run deep. In the settled dust, it still comes down to the way a preposterous financial system, skewed to reckless gambling, undergirds the whole economy. As a former government minister said later, it wasn't about saving the banks, but rather saving the economy *from* the banks.[53]

Hedging Bets

A silly example of this persistent malaise came in 2021 in the unlikely form of GameStop, an American video game retailer. Its business profile was dire – outcompeted by online rivals; shutting shop on 450 outlets; and suffering tumbling share value. As such, it was a suitably dud candidate for 'shorting'. Thus, some leading hedge funds thought they were on to a winner by betting its asset price would dive. But a bloc of 'amateur' investors, communicating together in an online forum, purchased shares all together, thereby inflating their value. Once underway, the artificial surge was further propelled by others globally getting a piece of the action, driving its share price skyward, much to the shock and sorrow of experienced investment traders. It was presented in places as the growing might of retail over institutional investors.[54] Of course, this is overhyped nonsense.

In the short term, it did seem to bring retribution to overweening Wall Street pros, and a rare market triumph for the small guy through the good graces of big tech. This reminds me of the story about Beatles' manager, Brian Epstein, buying massive amounts of the group's first record to get it in the charts, from where its popularity would self-boost. At least in that case, it was a good record. However, the crazy nature of the stock market means that firms can buy their own stock to lift its value, and potentially get better return than if they'd invested that same sum in improved production.[55] In short, the various indices we see on nightly bulletins – Dow, FTSE, Nasdaq, etc – are far from reliable barometers of an economy's health. Indeed, the opportunity for 'gaming' the system, built into the stock market, can invite the short-term speculative investor over the financier committed to long-term outcome. Why bother with manufacturing when you can make much more from stock manipulation?

It is true that investor dividends in the technology sector quadrupled in the decade following the 2009 downturn. Overall in that period, dividends almost doubled, with shareholders gaining $694 billion more in 2019 than in 2009, to a record total of $1.43 trillion. Across that decade, shareholders were paid an amazing $11.4 trillion.[56] For some, it was business as usual. Resilient capitalism had restored the good times.

As Good as Gold

Whatever the surmise about the new industrial revolution auguring more personal autonomy within a shared commons, current reality is still about big: big corporations in big sectors such as high tech, finance, energy, automobiles and pharma. Their value is insufficiently distinguished from their price, and their price largely relies on what we mean by money.

To achieve greater stability in currency exchange value, the 1944 Bretton Woods Agreement pegged one troy ounce of gold to 35 US dollars – the world's reserve currency. In 1971, Nixon switched the US from this 'commodity' money – valued on the basis of a commodity, gold – to FIAT money – government-issued currency, which is now the basis of money across the world. Governments, through their Central Banks, decree the value and print and hold an amount of 'legal tender' money for their economies, granting them greater charge of their money supply, liquidity, and interest rates. Hence, global confidence in any currency rests on the dependability of its political and economic system.

By the early 1970s, there had been many bouts of deficit spending in America, linked to major post-war infrastructure; military expenditure; Korean and Vietnam wars; Space Race; and various social programmes. Given that this involved more money than that backed by gold reserves, it could make some countries keen to swap their dollars for gold, a process that were it to take hold, would see a run on US gold.

Notwithstanding, this removal of cast-iron convertibility to gold and related ability of a Central Bank to create money, were seen by some to license government squandering. Since currency value was less reliably solid and more related to exchange rate with the dollar, FIAT money was also thought to induce some countries to effectively devalue their currency to boost export trade with rich economies like the US.

As its economy has deindustrialised, the US makes less of the products that it still consumes. Rather, it imports more from countries such as China. But these countries don't wish to turn all these earned dollars into their own currency, as that would raise its value, thereby reducing their trading competitiveness. So much of these dollars, a good deal of which have been borrowed in the US as individual or government debt, are transferred back to the US as purchased US government bonds. Basically, this process involves borrowing from countries that are increasingly selling you their goods. In turn, it induces more factories in American industrialised heartlands to relocate overseas for cheaper production, creating a rustbelt in places like the Mid-West. These three facets – fiscal integrity; trading imbalance based on 'artificial' exchange rates; and industrial loss – are for fiscal conservatives predictable outcomes of making money less real.

These critics charge that if, say, the American government wants to fund a big spending programme, it can borrow from the Federal Reserve, which prints whatever is needed. For collateral, government gives the Fed acknowledgement of this debt in the form of government bonds, which can be sold to foreign governments and investors. Very easily, these loans to government can be used to mainly pay off previous principals plus interest, and over time, such a cycle amasses substantial sovereign debt. Since much of this liability can be owed to other countries, it raises the question of how truly 'sovereign' are the countries dependent on this borrowing to finance their lifestyle.

This fiscal sleight-of-hand has been likened to a massive Ponzi scheme, which is a swindle that attracts investors on the assurance of swift lucrative returns. Although, as a good part of 'Ponzi' money is being creamed off in the scam, the organizers need to lure an increased cadre of new investors, some of whose cash is tapped to pay yields to the initial investors, and so on in a stacking house of cards. No genuine wealth creation is involved, just a cash grab at each transaction by the fraudsters. So is this similar to government getting into more debt to pay off previous debt? When your hands are on the till, is it too tempting to keep them out of it?[57]

Of the world's 195 countries, 37 are in the rich bloc of the Organisation for Economic Cooperation and Development (OECD). Following the financial crash, gross borrowing requirement in the OECD area flattened to around $10.5 trillion between 2010 and 2019. During that decade, 80 percent of that loan went on debt redemption – borrowing new money to repay debt. In 2020, its members' expansionary monetary policies to cope with COVID caused them to borrow $18 trillion from the markets, about 29 percent of their collective GDP, nearly double the loan upsurge registered during the 2008 crisis. Public finances were hit by reduced economic activity, lowered tax revenue, and increased social expenditure. Accordingly, marketable debt for OECD countries rose from $47 trillion in 2019 to near $56 trillion in 2020, with expected increase to $61 trillion by the end of 2021.[58]

Such patterns sit alongside a new monetary instrument used by government – Quantitative Easing (QE).[59] This involves Central Banks purchasing bonds – government and corporate – on the open market, and paying by creating new bank reserves on their balance sheets – effectively 'printing money'. At a time of crisis, when credit flows tighten, this new money supply is designed to stimulate lending to consumers and business, and thereby boost economic growth, while retaining low interest rates and low stable inflation. Supposedly, this extra liquidity permits financial institutions to maintain confidence in the investment market.

With such easy money what could possibly go wrong? For one thing, increased money supply may ratchet up demand that over time fuels inflation. Its low interest cost and apparent Central Bank security may encourage speculative investment that produces bubbles, particularly since low interest returns on savings induces investors to focus on higher returning assets. In turn, the wealth gap between those in a position to invest in financial and property assets, and benefit from their price increase, and those with no assets, or negative assets (debt), widens.

In the intensive period related to the financial crash −2009–2012 – the Bank of England undertook seven rounds of QE, totalling £375 billion. Then, in response to the economic impact of COVID-19, it purchased £450 billion of government bonds and £10 billion in corporate bonds. Altogether, by early 2022, the Bank owned £875 billion of government bonds and £20 billion in corporate bonds – equal to about 40 percent of UK GDP. But where does all this money land, and with what benefit for the real economy? The House of Lords Economic Affairs Committee concluded in its July 2021 report:[60]

> available evidence shows that quantitative easing has had a limited impact on growth and aggregate demand over the last decade. There is limited evidence that quantitative easing had increased bank lending, investment, or that it had increased consumer spending by asset holders. Furthermore, the policy has also had the effect of inflating asset prices artificially, and this has benefited those who own them disproportionately, exacerbating wealth inequalities.

The report noted that other main Central Banks had also raised their rates of quantitative easing, with QE programmes in the US, Eurozone and Japan now totalling around 30 percent, 32 percent and 106 percent of GDP respectively. According to US thinktank the Atlantic Council,[61] from 2020 to April 2022, together, the four largest central banks in the world (the US Federal Reserve, the Bank of Japan, the European Central Bank and the Bank of England) had put over $11 trillion into the global economy just to address the economic fallout from COVID-19.

True, the record-low interest rates up to recently have cut borrowing costs. Moreover, healthy demand for government securities curbs the debt service burden and thus lowers the risk to sovereign bond markets. But when these debts 'mature,' what new borrowing will be required to refinance them? From 2022 looking ahead this decade, the world faces a grim period of high inflation – the highest for three decades – demanding increased interest rates to restrain big asset purchases. This will increase the cost of government debt, thereby affording rationale for reduced public spending. Together with higher energy costs and the impact of trade sanctions, related to Russian aggression in Ukraine, greater national protectionism, and supply bottlenecks, this could be a harbinger of stagflation that will hit the poorest hardest. A direct line can be traced from the bad behaviour of the money banks to the sad necessity of food banks.

Since the financial crisis, there has been some move to greater bank regulation. For instance, the 2010 Dodd-Frank Act in the US requires lenders to certify that borrowers are sufficiently solvent to repay home mortgages. In the UK (Vickers Commission 2011), and in the EU (the de Larosiere Report 2009 and Liikanen Report 2012), ideas for the separation of basic banking services from risky investment have been forwarded.[62] The Third Basel Accord,[63] covering 27 jurisdictions (such as the US, China, Russia, UK, Germany, France, and Japan), introduced in November 2010 to increase minimum capital requirements for market risk, improve credit valuation and risk assessment, enhance transparency via disclosure frameworks, and to raise leverage ratios, among other measures, was set to take full effect by early 2022. Delay in the finalised version of the reforms to early 2023 has been attributed to the disruption of COVID-19. Given the five-year phase-in allowed, this will bring it up to 2028. We await a long time to test whether these complete provisions will be robustly applied.

It remains the case that the whole world economy is dependent upon proper control of a relatively small number of financial institutions. The Financial Stability Board recorded at the end of 2021 that a mere 30 establishments constituted the category of Global Systemically Important Banks (G-SIBs). Presently, the top four of world banks are Chinese.[64] That's another indication of the shift in the world's economic axis. The first industrial revolution involved about one-third of the world's people. Currently, emerging economies account for about 80 percent of the world's people, a share likely to increase. But while the global south now plays a significant part in the world's economy, the key international reserve currency remains the dollar. Yet American debt is in 14 digits. The 'national debt clock' calculated it at $31,293,953,000,000 at approximately 10.30am (UK time) on 21 November 2022, or a daunting $247,882 per taxpayer. An indicator of the trend is the US Federal Debt to GDP ratio: in 1960 it was 52.19 percent; in 1980 it was 34.70 percent; in 2000 it was 55.54 percent.[65] Usually, government debt as a share of the national economy is a metric deployed by investors to assess risk of government default on debt and accordingly influences borrowing charges and government bond yields. In the recent period, the US debt has been at or above its national economy.[66]

The Congressional Budget Office's 2022 report[67] on the long-term budget outlook paints a gloomy picture. Over the next three decades, Federal deficits are forecast to nearly triple, from 4 percent of GDP in 2022 to 11 percent in 2052. Taking the average over this time, deficits will be 7.3 percent of GDP, over double the average of the past fifty years. During the last century, the deficit has hit such height only through the Second World War and the pandemic's tough years of 2020 and 2021. A big factor in this growth is the rise in interest costs. Net interest expenditure more than quadruples over this projected time, to amount to 7.2 percent of GDP in 2052. This is in the context of real potential GDP (the most sustainable economic output, amended to eliminate inflation effects) rising more slowly throughout the 2022–2052 cycle than it did on average over the previous three decades. Consequently, the accumulated deficit spend in this economic circumstance sees debt stretch to 185 percent of GDP in 2052. The report warns that such big and growing indebtedness could itself depress growth, raise interest costs paid to overseas investors in American debt, accentuate the prospects of a fiscal crisis, and thereby curtail government policy scope.

In its previous report,[68] the Budget Office affirmed conventional understanding about the risks generated by public spending outpacing tax revenue and persistent reliance on borrowing. It argued that when debt was big and surging as a percentage of GDP, not only government, but also business borrowing costs rose; high government borrowing 'crowded out' loans for the private sector; investor assurance about government capacity to service and repay its debt declined; private investment plummeted; mounting inflation and related interest rate rises could also attend high debt levels. In such a scenario, costs of servicing public debt increased, squeezing fiscal space for stimulus. Economic production and productivity became negatively impacted; worker remuneration and consumer capacity suffered; interest payments to foreign holders of US debt swelled; and confidence in the US dollar as a reliable international reserve currency faltered, making it harder and more expensive to finance business and public activity in global markets.

The pattern of high borrowing is, of course, not peculiar to the US. Particularly, in the aftermath of the financial crisis and the pandemic, many countries have operated budget deficits. In the UK, borrowing hit a post-World War 11 high at £322 billion – 15 percent of GDP – in 2020–21. With the spike in inflation, and related hike in interest rates, this legacy of borrowing contributed to what the UK Office For Budget Responsibility reported in 2022 as record-high debt interest payment of £83 billion.[69]

The general pattern of Central Banks building new reserves to buy bonds and stimulate the pandemic-hit economy all seemed to be about creating free money in an era when interest rates were low and appeared destined to remain so. By 2022, that scenario changed. Combination of supply chain problems and the fuel insecurity and price hike, linked to the war in Ukraine, boosted inflation across the world, and despite sluggish growth, Central Banks came under pressure to raise interest rates, and thereby the cost of servicing public debt.

According to Modern Monetary Theory (MMT), we shouldn't get too worked up about any of this. Essentially, it insists that in monetary sovereign countries – that is those where the government has monopoly authority to issue a FIAT currency – deficit spending need not be a problem. In her recent book, *The Deficit Myth*,[70] Kelton spells it out. First, despite all the folksy admonition that governments should live within their means just like responsible households, this myth misses the point: households are different to governments, which have their own Central Bank. Households can't print their own money, whereas it isn't true that governments have no money of their own, only that of taxpayers and market sources of loans. In simple terms, she argues that Uncle Sam can never go bankrupt because he's in sole charge of the main bank. He can issue more dollars, including 'digital' dollars – or reserves – that are no more than electronic entries on the national balance sheet. Another 'myth' she challenges is that deficits are always problematic and evidence public over-spending. No, she says. It depends on the spending. If it is allocated to improve economic capacity or social well-being, it's more likely a positive investment.

Third, there is the flawed belief that current borrowing transfers the debt to the next generation. The US national debt, as a share of GDP, was at its highest in the immediate aftermath of the Second World War. Yet, the generation that followed in the 1950s and 1960s experienced improved lifestyle, based on the rapid rise of median family income, without raised tax rates. The fourth myth is that deficit spending contains an opportunity cost, because it 'crowds out' private investment since it subtracts from a limited money supply, thereby reducing what could otherwise be spent by business for future prosperity. Related to this critique is the argument that 'excessive' borrowing invariably produces a *fiscal* crisis that translates into a *financial* crisis that in today's global system of investment and trade, readily becomes a contagious *economic* crisis. Instead, properly targeted deficits – whether through tax cuts or public spending – put extra spending capacity, and thus demand, into the economy.

The final myth is that rich countries like the US are like compulsive consumers with a foreign credit card, allowing rivals like China to buy up their debt, and consequently to hold them in dependency. Kelton's different slant is that the US is furnishing countries like China with dollars and facilitating them to trade that same currency for savings in a protected interest-bearing asset, known as a US Treasury. In that sense, from its own self-interest, China is invested in a stable and prosperous America. So persistent US deficits could be looked upon negatively as debt, or positively as wealth held by domestic or foreign savers.

She is not implying that government can magic a continual free lunch. Constraints exist. For one thing, countries without the authority to issue credible currency cannot operate this way. That is why some European countries, like Greece, got into acute difficulty after the crash. Being in the euro, they weren't free to affordably finance themselves by 'creating' their own money. As currency users rather than issuers, those countries seeking loans, but lacking monetary sovereignty, offered government bonds that carried higher risk of default, and thus had to be tied to a higher premium. They paid high yields for their loans on the international finance market. For example in the case of Greece, with recessionary pressure on its economy, and related reduction in tax revenue, it faced the dilemma of having to increase social spending and debt interest payment, while borrowing at high rates, thereby raising its budget deficit to over 15 percent of its GDP in 2009.

By contrast, a currency-issuing government is not obliged to borrow to spend. Even when it borrows, it exercises a big say on what interest it pays on those securities, which always tend to be oversubscribed by investors, because they're a safe bet. The story is different for countries like Argentina when they do not borrow in currencies issued by their own government. For them, borrowing in a foreign currency – typically, the US dollar – does carry a heavy price tag.

In those countries with monetary sovereignty, deficits are only indicative of over-spending if they kindle inflation because there is insufficient productive economic capacity to absorb the spend. Finding the 'fiscal space' for productive public spending is about optimising all the resources of the economy. By the same token, you could have an *insufficient deficit* if the effect is to underuse economic potential for the public good. For Kelton, the real deficits in American society include: high poverty rates; low educational attainment; stagnant real wage growth; accentuated wealth inequality; forty-five million Americans tied to over $1.6 trillion in student loan debt; 87 million with their health care uninsured or under-insured; unclean environment and dilapidated infrastructure.

Those unconvinced by this new take on monetary and fiscal policy can wonder about how real this thing we call 'money' actually is, given such remarkable levels of global debt. In a country like the US, that wants to spend big and tax small, the borrowing that fills the gap, aided and abetted by 'over-printing' of currency, is seen by fiscal conservatives to degrade purchasing clout, a loss that can be considered as a closet tax. Such concerns triggered the populist Tea Party in 2009 within the US Republican party, where the name harks back to the Boston Tea Party in 1773, a remonstration against Britain's tax on tea that involved chucking British tea off ships into the Boston harbour. The 'tea' in the modern movement also stood for 'taxed enough already', and signalled a platform for: low tax and public spending, within limited government; reduced deficits and debt; reclamation of US sovereignty, including tighter border and immigration controls; and restoration of free markets, that meant no more bank bailouts or subventions for 'losers' mortgages'. In many respects, it prefigured Trump.

The world at large has skin in this game, if only because many countries' reserves are in dollars. Even for those who see a world economic system based on credit and debt, and 'unreal' money, piling problems for the future, electoral time-spans are more immediate, enticing politicians to constantly defer sweating the big stuff. When plentiful supply of cheap money circulates in the private sphere, it can create 'gold rush' fever. Those who can borrow substantially think of asset acquisition for future exchange value. Unlike the goods market, when asset prices are soaring, demand can follow. All this remains premised on the presumed virtue of unlimited economic growth and agreed definition of wealth. By the 1980s, the edict that wealth creation precedes its distribution had taken hold. Bake a bigger pie, and even if slices remain unequal, all at the table get a better bite. Thus far, has such simplistic trickle-down economics had its political comeuppance?

Interpreting this chapter's account of how the real economy works in such surrealist ways suggests the following bold propositions: capitalism dominates the world; capitalism runs on consumerism; consumerism runs on debt; and thus, debt runs the world. If that is so, how do we ever stand a chance of bringing this unruly system under some measure of public control? The next chapter considers the relationship between the economy and democracy in today's disordered geopolitics.

Notes

1 Schwab, K. (2017) *The Fourth Industrial Revolution* (2017) London: Penguin Random House.
2 Rifkin, J. (2011) *The Third Industrial Revolution: How Lateral Power is Transforming Energy, the Economy, and the World.* New York: St. Martin's Griffin. 36.
3 Brynjolfsson, E. and McAfee, A. (2014) *The Second Machine Age: Work, Progress and Prosperity in a Time of Brilliant Technologies.* New York: W.W.Norton & Company.
4 Rifkin, J. (2011) *op. cit.* 115.
5 Rifkin, J. (2014) *The Zero Marginal Cost Society: The Internet of Things, The Collaborative Commons, and the Eclipse of Capitalism.* New York: St. Martin's Griffin.
6 *Ibid.*
7 Levy, F. and Murnane, R. (2004) *The New Division of Labour: How Computers are Creating the Next Job Market.* Princeton, N.J.: Princeton University Press.
8 Schwab, K. (2017) *op. cit.*
9 Robinson, J. (1962: 2006 edition) *Economic Philosophy.* London: Aldine.
10 Schwab, K. (2017) *op. cit.* 114–5.
11 *Ibid.* 115.
12 Zuboff, S. (2019) *The Age of Surveillance Capitalism: The Fight for the Future at the New Frontier of Power.* London: Profile Books.
13 *Ibid.* 175.
14 Wu, T. (2016) *The Attention Merchants: From the Daily Newspaper to Social Media. How Our Time and Attention is Harvested and Sold.* London: Atlantic Books. 344.
15 Bourguignon, F. (2015) *The Globalization of Inequality.* Princeton, N.J.: Princeton University Press.
16 Becker, J., Stolberg, S.G., Labaton, S. (20 December 2008) White House Philosophy Stoked Mortgage Bonfire. *The New York Times.*
17 National Commission on the Causes of the Financial and Economic Crisis in the United States (January 2011) *The Financial Crisis Inquiry Report: Final Report of the National Commission on the Causes of the Financial and Economic Crisis in the United States.* Washington, DC: US Government Printing Office.
18 *Ibid.*
19 In banking parlance, *securities* are tradable mechanisms to raise capital in markets, through equity, loans, or mixes of equity and borrowing. *Securitisation* is about pooling debt assets like mortgages and credit card debt into a financial product or security for purchase by investors. Based on a contract between parties, a *derivative* is a financial security, which derives its price from the value of a core asset, rate or index. The asset could be a commodity, precious metal, currency, bonds, or stock. So, derivatives come in different forms. For example, 'futures' are contracts

that oblige the contract's purchaser to procure an asset at a pre-settled price on a designated future date, whereas 'options' accord the buyer the right, though not the requirement, to buy or sell the underlying asset at a predetermined price. A *credit default swap* (CDS) is a kind of insurance policy, whereby under legal agreement, a lender purchases a CDS from another party, who pledges to compensate the lender should the borrower fail to pay, or should the value decline. A *hedge fund* is a privately offered investment instrument, available to richer clients, and generally freer from regulation.

20 National Commission on the Causes of the Financial and Economic Crisis in the United States (January 2011) *op. cit.*
21 See: US Treasury (31st March 2008) *Remarks by Secretary Henry M. Paulson, Jr. on Blueprint for Regulatory Reform,* and accompanying Fact Sheet and Press Release.
22 National Commission on the Causes of the Financial and Economic Crisis in the United States (January 2011) *op.cit.*
23 *Ibid.*
24 *Ibid.*
25 *Ibid.* 132.
26 *Ibid.* xviii.
27 *Ibid.* xvii
28 *Ibid.* xix.
29 *Ibid.*
30 *Ibid.* 22.
31 *Ibid.*141.
32 *Ibid.* xxv.
33 Kelton, S. (2020) *The Deficit Myth: Modern Monetary Theory and How to Build a Better Economy.* London: John Murray.
34 National Commission on the Causes of the Financial and Economic Crisis in the United States (January 2011) *op.cit.*
35 Sinn, H.-W. (2010) *Casino Capitalism: How the Financial Crisis Came About and What Needs to be Done Now.* Oxford University Press, Oxford.
36 National Commission on the Causes of the Financial and Economic Crisis in the United States (January 2011) *op. cit.* xviii.
37 See: US Bureau of Economic Analysis (BEA). US Department of Commerce.
38 Lucas, D. (2019) Measuring the Cost of Bailouts. *Annual Review of Financial Economics.* 11: 85–108. *doi:10.1146/annurev-financial-110217–022532.*
39 Tooze, A. (2018) *Crashed: How a Decade of Financial Crises Changed the World.* London: Allen Lane.
40 *Ibid.* 76.
41 *Ibid.* 96.
42 *Ibid.* 106.
43 *Ibid.*
44 House of Commons Treasury Committee (24 January 2008) *The Run on the Rock. Fifth Report of Session 2007–08. Volume I.* London: The Stationery Office Limited.
45 House of Commons Treasury Committee (October 2012) *The FSA's Report into the Failure of RBS. Fifth Report of Session 2012–13.* London: The Stationery Office Limited. 3.
46 Financial Services Authority Board (December 2011) *The Failure of the Royal Bank of Scotland: Financial Services Authority Board Report.* 254.

47 Gordon Brown's speech to the annual conference of the Confederation of British Industry in London November 28 2005. The full speech can be found at: www.hmt reasury. gov.uk/better_regulation_action_plan.htm

48 Bonsignore, T. (14 April 2010) I was Wrong to Let the Banks off the Leash, Gordon Brown Admits. *Citywire*.

49 Financial Services Authority Board (December 2011) *op. cit.*

50 House of Commons Treasury Committee (October 2012) *op. cit.* 30.

51 *Ibid.* 35.

52 See HM Treasury, *HM Treasury Annual Report and Accounts, 2010–11* (July 2011) Certificate and Report of the Comptroller and Auditor General, HC 984, July 2011, p89. The peak figure of £1.162 trillion is the sum of the cash spend (e.g. for purchasing shares in RBS and Lloyds) and the maximum assistance guaranteed by government (e.g. through such measures as the Credit Guarantee Scheme and the Asset Protection Scheme), including sums that went unused. The £1.162 trillion sum was not accessible at a single point in time.

53 Burley, L. (Producer & Director) (2018) *The Bank That Almost Broke Britain*. STV Productions. BBC.

54 Brignall, M. (5 February 2021) How Did a Call to Buy Shares in an Ailing US Games Retailer Became a Finance-shaking Mass Movement? *The Guardian Weekly*.

55 Malik, K. (31 January 2021) An Uprising Against Wall Street? Hardly. GameStop was about the Absurdity of the Stock Market. *The Observer*.

56 Janus Henderson Investors (17 February 2020) *Global Dividends Rose to New Record in 2019, Though the Pace of Growth Slowed Compared to Last Year*. www.janushenderson.com/en-gb/media/press-releases/global-dividends-rose-to-new-record-in-2019-though-the-pace-of-growth-slowed-compared-to-last-year. Accessed on: 30 March 2021.

57 Spencer, J. and Delmastro, T. (authors); Delmastro, T. (director). (2017) *End of the Road: How Money Became Worthless*. A documentary by 100th Monkey Films.

58 Organisation for Economic Co-operation and Development (OECD) (February 2021) *Sovereign Borrowing Outlook for OECD Countries 2021*. Paris: OECD.

59 Forbes Advisor (19 January 2022) *Quantitative Easing Explained*....www.forbes.com/advisor/investing/quantitative-easing-qe. Accessed on: 4 April 2022.

60 House of Lords Economic Affairs Committee (16 July 2021) 1st Report of Session 2021–22 HL Paper 42 *Quantitative Easing: a Dangerous Addiction?* 5. https://committees.parliament.uk/publications/6725/documents. Accessed on: 4 April 2022. See also: House of Lords Library (11 November 2021) *In Focus: Quantitative Easing*. House of Lords Library.

61 Atlantic Council (April 2022) *Global QE Tracker*. www.atlanticcouncil.org/global-qe-tracker. Accessed on: 6 April 2022.

62 Field, J. (2018) *Is Capitalism Working?* London: Thames & Hudson.

63 Basel Committee on Banking Supervision (October 2021) *Progress Report on Adoption of the Basel Regulatory Framework*. Bank for International Settlements.

64 LexisNexis (September 2021) *Top 50 Banks in the World*. LexisNexis.

65 www.usdebtclock.org. Accessed on: 21 November 2022.

66 https://tradingeconomics.com/united-states/government-debt-to-gdp. Accessed on: 21 November 2022.

67 Congressional Budget Office (July 2022) *The 2022 Long-Term Budget Outlook*. www.cbo.gov/publication. Accessed on: 21 November 2022.

68 Congressional Budget Office (March 2021) *The 2021 Long-Term Budget Outlook*. www.cbo.gov/publication. Accessed on: 11 April 2022. See also: Committee for a Responsible Federal Budget (4 March 2021) *Analysis of CBO's March 2021 Long-Term Budget Outlook*.

69 Office For Budget Responsibility (March 2022) *Economic and Fiscal Outlook*. https://obr.uk/efo/economic-and-fiscal-outlook-march-2022. Accessed on: 12 April 2022.

70 Kelton, S. (2020) *op. cit.*

5

POWER PLAY

Are Markets Our Masters?

This chapter concerns how power works, or doesn't, to make the economy and society work for citizens. In its annual review of the state of democracy across the world,[1] the Economist Intelligence Unit bases its estimation on 60 indicators within five categories: electoral process and pluralism, the functioning of government, political participation, political culture, and civil liberties. On these measures, it classifies countries into four regime types: full democracy, flawed democracy, hybrid, and authoritarian.

For 2021, only 21 countries were accorded status of full democracy, 12.6 percent of the 167 countries examined, accounting for a mere 6.4 percent of the world's people – down from 8.4 percent for 2020. Interestingly, 12 of the 21 so classified comprise West European countries. The Nordics (Norway, Finland, Sweden, Iceland, and Denmark) top the democratic rankings. Less than half (45.7 percent) of the world's people inhabit some kind of democracy, compared to 49.4 percent for 2020. Well over one third (37.1 percent) live under authoritarian government, particularly in China and Russia. In late 2022, the 20th Congress of the Chinese Communist Party affirmed the uncontested power of President Xi Jinping, who while intent on extending China's global reach and influence, is pressing down on dissent at home.

Illegal invasion of Iraq didn't bring the promised democracy. Together with a Taliban-run Afghanistan, it joins countries such as Belarus, Cuba, Syria, Zimbabwe, Cambodia, North Korea, Palestine, and Myanmar as 'authoritarian'. Also faring badly are the Middle East and Africa, particularly West Africa, given the presence of absolute monarchies, autocratic and corrupt government, military conflict, and retreat from the hopes of a democratic 'Arab spring'. Latin America does not fare well, given illiberal populist rule in Bolsonaro's Brazil, Lopez Obrador's Mexico, Bukele's El Salvador, Ortega's Nicaragua, and

DOI: 10.4324/9781003106593-6

Maduro's Venezuela. And notably, despite its assumed leadership of the free world, the US is ranked as a 'flawed democracy', a category covering nearly four in ten of the world's population.

The prevalence of OECD (Organisation of Economic Cooperation and Development) countries among democracies indicates some correspondence between economic and democratic advancement. But this match is not guaranteed. Since 1990, the Chinese economy has expanded at almost triple the rate of the US economy in nominal GDP terms. Similarly, despite its economic improvement, India has experienced democratic retreat under Modi's premiership, which has embraced Hindu nationalism and incited anti-Muslim sentiment. Regression to ethno-nationalism is reflected in its 2019 Citizenship (Amendment) Act, which invalidates India's claim to be a secular state by introducing a religious aspect to citizenship status. At the other end, 2021 saw the first transfer of power in Niger between two democratically elected Presidents since independence from France in 1960. Maybe the incumbent's 'leadership prize' of £3.5 million helped to prise him from the leadership.[2] The United Nations ranks Niger as the world's poorest country.

Even in the more democratic countries, the tendency to technocratic management of society is indicative of a general democratic regression. Many protest about losing say and sway over what most impacts their lives. The pandemic has afforded opportunity for some governments to disguise their inclination towards more autocratic rule within the constraints of a public health emergency. Together with disinformation from social media, stark social inequality, repression of dissent, erosion of trust, spread of corruption, and major blemishes by democratic governments, such as the invasion of Iraq, the financial crisis, and violent challenge to a Presidential election result in the US, this toxic litany has cumulatively contributed to the malaise. Another recent assessment[3] suggests that the over-a-quarter of the world's people living in 'democratically backsliding countries', taken together with those living in varying forms of autocracy, constitute over two-thirds of humanity.

In short, across the world, democracy is in short supply. Mistrust of government and fraying social cohesion have prompted extensive literature that questions whether democracy faces revolt,[4] siege,[5] decline,[6] retreat,[7] death,[8] or at least, hollowing,[9] all challenges requiring defence[10] of democratic principles.

Disconcerting signs of this disenchantment came in the treatment of Greece amidst the Eurozone crisis. Recently mandated in an election, the Greek government sent Varoufakis, its finance minister, to negotiate with the EU. He sought to present a strategy to reform the country's public and tax administration, its public assets, and flawed banking system, without imposition of fiscal restriction that would deflate demand, thereby stifling recovery from its deep debt. In response, Schäuble, Germany's pro-austerity finance minister, retorted: 'Elections cannot be allowed to change an economic programme of a member state!' In its brutal bluntness, it exposed the difference between sovereignty and power.[11] Greece had the former without the latter, and in the end, it was compelled to relent. The power of money and market outbids the power of people. The 'economy, stupid' quashed any political dissent.

Thus, Gordon Brown's promise to business to take a lot of the politics out of economics was bizarre. The dismal science of economics comes down a great deal to the art of politics. For instance, the financial crash in 1929 ushered in the depression years in Europe and America. In the US, Roosevelt's New Deal would bring stimulus through public works, greater regulation of finance, and social relief that moderated the devastation depicted in Steinbeck's *Grapes of Wrath* and songs like *Brother, Can You Spare a Dime?* For many industrious citizens, the American dream had been smashed to smithereens by the financial elite's economic duplicity, and the New Deal represented a radical shift toward the Federal government assuming accountability for the public's social and economic well-being. Importantly, it was intended to foil revolutionary tendencies and show that liberal democracy was a more viable response to social distress than zealous alternatives of fascism or communism. Meanwhile, in many parts of Europe, the centre and left proved to be impotent in halting the forward march of fascism and war.

A New Social Contract

In post-war Europe, consensus emerged around the principle, if not the degree, of welfare capitalism. The economy would be best served if the public was protected against disease, ignorance, squalor, want, and the idleness of unemployment. So greater state support for health, education, housing, social security and economic management achieved wide endorsement. For the left, it represented a step in the direction of greater equality. For the right, it was a practical way to reproduce stable capitalism that relied on healthy, educated labour. Together with a more mixed-economy, greater government regulation, and some degree of trade union power, this seemed to offer a more humane and pluralist capitalism. It was underpinned by core ideas of Keynes, and broadly social democratic politics.

For example, there was the idea that full employment needed a certain level of demand, and this came from four main sources: government; consumers; business; and exports. Thus, if exports fell and/or business cut investment, jobs would go and this would likely see total consumer spend decline, which in turn would reduce demand further and lead to more job loss, which would further deflate demand, and so on. The only agent that could halt this cycle was government, which could stimulate demand with more public spending, even if this required borrowing. With a stimulated economy, confidence would return to the market, and government could lower its share of aggregate demand, and with future growth and tax revenue pay back debt accumulated through any years of deficit budgets. Such tweaking seemed to offer prospect of managing the inherent boom and bust cycles of capitalism.

For thirty years, this welfare-Keynesianism presented compromise upon which social democrats and liberal conservatives could broadly agree, leaving political contest to be largely about type and extent of government intervention. But this 'consensus' was within a wide bandwidth of political ideology in the period, stretching from communism to socialism to social democracy to liberal capitalism to more laissez-faire traditions. By the late seventies, critics of this ideologically-light, technocratic government came from left and right. Traditional left, and New Left that emerged in the 1960s counter-culture, dismissed it as managerialist legitimation of capitalism, indeed as facilitation of how capitalism could continually reproduce itself more sustainably. Its offer of equality of opportunity and social mobility through mass education was a mirage. Educational research had conclusively shown that school success hinged largely on class background. Hence, significant social inequality, as a hallmark of capitalism, impeded fair opportunity. But the pretence of meritocracy permitted the blame to fall on individual rather than systemic failure.

That said, the left itself was divided. Its traditional working class base largely saw the labour movement in terms of white, male, urban, industrial workers, represented by what were largely undemocratic trade unions. Mostly, they accepted the realpolitik of capitalism, but wanted a collective bargaining arrangement in the workplace that strengthened organised labour, alongside a reformist government that alleviated social inequality. By contrast, the New Left wanted a more liberal, pluralist socialism that challenged the basic tenets of individualist consumer capitalism that it saw as corrosive of human values of international solidarity. This did not need extension of statism as much as democratisation of society, centred on worker, women's and community organisations. Wedged between these two was a radical leftism, like the Bennite wing of the UK's Labour party, that saw the state as a valid public instrument for taking greater social control over the commanding heights of the economy, in an age increasingly dominated by multinational capital.

Into this crisis of confidence in national Keynesianism steps the Thatcher-Reagan revolution of the 1980s. The 'revolution' didn't start with a finished script, but rather was emboldened as it advanced. Its basic premise was that government was the problem and not the solution, except when it came to domestic law and order and militarism abroad. In particular, instead of putting up with the Soviet Union, the 'evil empire' had to be faced down. Western interests had to prevail, whatever arms race had to be run. Economic growth was to be facilitated by globalisation. However, this global order was no longer to be based on Kissinger's 'realistic' geopolitics of continuously resetting spheres of influence to create power balances that secured the West. This was unapologetically ideological. The West had to win.

As such, the Reagan Doctrine proactively backed insurgency movements against leftist governments that the US interpreted as extending Soviet influence. Under the banner of freedom, this meant supporting autocratic rule in places like Latin America. But this was deemed at worst to involve authoritarian governments that were morally preferable to totalitarian ones. For Reagan personally, and his evangelical support-base, this mission against godless communism had divine imprimatur. It justified a Keynesian boost to the US military-industrial complex, though this ran counter to his supposed supply-side economics.

Economics: Right and Wrong

This economics was based on the stimulus of substantial tax cuts, reduced social spending, and market deregulation. It would create greater consumer spending, whose demand would be more efficiently met by business freed from red tape – all generating a wider tax base that could deliver larger tax revenue, even though it was based on lower tax rates – the so-called Laffer curve. Economic benefit, while most obvious at the top in the early stages would over time trickle down to wider society. In fact, little evidence of trickle-down emerged. Tax cuts not only reduced government income, but validated shrinkage of the Federal welfare state, and off-loaded social programmes to state and city level.

In the canon of classical economics, Say's Law claims that creation of one product opens a market for other products, since the means to buy depends on production of something else which, when sold, yields an income that is used for purchase. Sometimes crudely translated as supply creates its own demand, this is a key principle underpinning supply-side economics. Policies designed to incentivise production (for example, by reducing costs through tax cuts or deregulation) will automatically generate demand for consequent output. People and companies will work more if the extra effort brings proportionate bonus in post-tax income. That extra income, in turn, gives greater scope for spending and investment.

But all this assumes that actual individual or firm behaviour translates into real macro-economics; that markets are free in terms of ideal competition; that prices and wages are adaptable; and that consumers rule supreme. None of this 'pure' market model can be presumed in an age of monopoly capitalism, which can rig markets with all kinds of cartels and restrictions. Moreover, it infers that income is spent on consumption or investment, sufficient to keep resources such as labour profitably employed. Income may not be fully spent to sustain stable aggregate demand.[12] Besides, this stimulus model of tax cuts and Keynesian spending on defence comes into conflict with those, such as monetarists, concerned that relaxed money supply stirs inflation and indulges budget deficits.

Such tension highlights contrasting conservative positions. *Fiscal conservatives* advocate free trade, privatisation, and the virtue of competition in efficient capital allocation. In particular, they want government to 'live within its means', and avoid budgetary shortfalls that foster national debt and inflationary pressure. Thus, they're wary of what they deem grievance culture, whereby disadvantaged groups become supplicants to big-spend government for social programmes that positively discriminate in their favour. *Neoconservatives* commend interventionist foreign policy that promotes a globalisation in the image of western interests and values, which they think have been threatened by a pacifist counter-culture since the 1960s. Indeed, the latter has been indicted for whittling away at traditional moral standards and authority, a decadence that enfeebles western civilisation.

Neoliberal conservatives stress the self-corrective nature of markets that function best with small government, low taxes and minimal regulation. They can be more sceptical of the military-industrial complex if it violates these central precepts. By contrast, *Liberal conservatives* can buy into modest versions of welfare capitalism, acknowledging that adequate social cohesion supports capitalist stability, and that markets can fail, creating disruptive uneven development and social costs – negative externalities – that need government rectification.

Within such varied economic perspectives, some may be more relaxed about deficits and size of state – neoconservatives wanting a strong security state, with military spending that supports foreign adventurism; and liberals who endorse enough welfare to ensure a compassionate capitalism. By contrast, neoliberals and fiscal conservatives seek to curtail public policy and spending. Thus, they consider the crash to have been a consequence of government largesse and failure to let the market punish corporate imprudence. Cagey about government bailout, they saw it as the state embezzling money from the thrifty public to pay profligate or unwitting losers. To their mind, propping up failing business diverted resources from more efficient enterprises.

Of course, these slants can be further crisscrossed with *social conservatism*, rooted in religious beliefs of groups like Christian evangelicals, whose priority is to resist permissiveness and uphold the exceptionalism of the West as a God-chosen force against global evil. Alternatively, *libertarian conservatism* privileges individualism over public authority, upholding the free market and property rights, while championing individual sovereignty over a nanny state. Conservative governments across the world comprise uneasy alliances among permutations of these strands.

As covered in Chapter two, the re-emergence of populism as a major political force, has complicated these constituents further. In its authoritarian style, it magnifies binary divisions between the common people and privileged elite at home, and between nationalist protectionism and the threat of foreigners and free trade in a globalised world. Some scholars have emphasised the appeal of this *economic* nationalism to precarious 'left behind' sectors and communities, which have endured manufacturing loss, low wage growth, and persistent educational under-achievement. A different slant has stressed *cultural* displacement, due to social liberalism; and demographic and political change that have reshaped power relations around race and gender. While it's possible to see patterns of deprived people and geographies aligning with pro-Brexit and Trump agendas, growth of populism in places like Poland, Sweden and Austria is less easily captured within a framework of increasing stagnancy and inequality. In any case, it's over-simple to see the common popular sentiment behind populism as the cry of the herd to be heard. The idea of 'herd' is itself pejorative.

Politics Now: Same Old, Same Old?

Lind[13] argues that contemporary politics in western democracies involves a three-sided contest, involving: mostly white, native, metropolitan, college-educated overclass elites, who benefit from a divided working class. The latter comprises immigrants and some people of native minority background, often in rivalry with a mostly white native grouping, who regard their economic position, political influence, and cultural esteem imperilled from above and below. Both these subdivisions consider the system to be rigged, though their response to the stitch-up differs somewhat. The native grouping attached to place, tradition, and pressured manufacturing sectors is most likely to support economic nationalism, though it is a travesty to depict them all as bigoted fascists or white supremacists. Of course, many once supported centre-left platforms 'before 'leftism' and 'progressivism' were redefined to mean a combination of open-borders globalism, anti-nationalism, and radical race-and gender-based identity politics'.[14]

Overclass elites occupy business-managerial-professional positions. They can be liberal about mass immigration, from which they can benefit in terms of low-cost domestic or corporate labour, without facing competition from immigrants for housing, health or education services. Illegal immigration actually offers a pool of untaxed and unprotected labour, potentially open to greater exploitation. Conversely, the native working class is inclined to see such unorganised 'surplus' labour as threatening jobs, depressing wages, and competing for already stretched social services.

Likewise on internationalism, the overclass can see trade liberalization as opening global business opportunity, whereas workers in traditional industries see it as flooding the domestic market with cheap foreign goods and inducing job export. On climate, those living in a high-income hub, may well favour strict environmental controls that tackle pollution, traffic congestion, or other degradation of pleasant environs. But if your livelihood depends on carbon-based mining, manufacturing or agriculture you may be less keen on production restrictions.

Then there's what Lind calls 'asymmetrical multiculturalism', whereby the privileged present a two-faced approach to cultural diversity:[15]

> ....*appreciation of minority and immigrant traditions is often coupled with elite contempt for the ancestral traditions of white native and white immigrant subcultures, which are alleged by overclass intellectuals to be hopelessly tainted by white supremacy or colonialism.*

Within polarising populism, there are permutations of various discontents. White reaction against civil rights, of male resentment to feminist politics, and traditionalists' opposition to what they see as permissive sexuality, are certainly to be found. In Lind's view, however, there's no evidence to suggest that these are sole or even main factors. Rather, there is a genuine basis for grievance against 'oligarchic misrule'. Those sections of the working class, who want the political dial reset, cannot therefore be all cast as a 'basket of deplorables', credulous simpletons, ready to be duped by Russian manipulation or domestic demagoguery.

In the US, they understandably grew tired of the Bush-Clinton dynasties that held senior office every year between 1981 and 2013, and tried to have a run-off with each other in 2016. Their stewardship saw the stagnation of working class incomes, massive deindustrialisation alongside drives for greater globalization, financial crisis and the Great Recession, as well as catastrophic invasions feeding perpetual wars. Similarly in the UK, many are disaffected by what they claim to be the limited choice offered by varied shades of technocratic-neoliberalism that connect Blair, Brown, Cameron and May. Taking a view over the last four decades, Lind notes:[16]

> *It is no coincidence that Reaganism-Clintonism and Thatcherism-Blairism flourished in an era of prolonged asset bubbles. For a time, it is possible for stock market booms and real estate bubbles to fund public services and redistribution while allowing the wealthy to keep most of their gains.*

Two reservations are worth making about this overall analysis. First, whatever the convergence between Reaganomics and New Democrats, it is mistaken to lump Blair-Brown with Thatcher-Cameron. The former were centrist-left in a way that the latter weren't. Second, though these can be seen as particularly partisan times, there is nothing new about working class division. It's been long understood that some hold a deferential attitude to establishment rule, regarding the elite as an entitled class, whose background and education equip them for leadership. Another section, who aspire for social mobility, can adopt the values and voting preference of those further up the social ladder, in preparation for their own ascent. Other factors behind working class conservativism include nostalgic patriotism and religious traditionalism.

What is new is the breakdown of collective organisations that once gave cultural underpinning to a labourist, or at least civic, sense of solidarity – working men's clubs, mass membership political parties, and trade unions. Interestingly, Corbyn's leadership of the British Labour party saw massive increase in party membership to near half a million. But many of these new members seemed tied to cultural wokeism and ultra-leftism that were turn-offs to some traditional party members and voters, a paradox for a party leadership intent on prioritizing class politics.

With regard to trade unions, membership in the US peaked in the 1950s, at around one-third of the workforce. In the UK, union membership peaked in 1979 with 13.2 million, when around half of workers were unionised, and declined dramatically in succeeding decades. Over the last quarter of a century, as a share of workers, membership dropped from 32.4 percent to 23.5 percent. In the private sector, less than one in seven are unionised. Interestingly, membership rate of those with higher education qualification is around 30 percent, whereas it's just over half that rate for those with no or poor qualification.[17] The 'gig' economy may sound very rock n roll. But for many, being cast as 'self-employed' can erode their protection in terms of worker rights and benefits.

Generally, there has been a shift from labour to capital in the relative share each has in advanced economies. From the 1980s, the labour income shares trended downwards, 'reaching their lowest level of the past half century just prior to the global financial crisis of 2008–09, and have not recovered materially since'.[18] Amongst the factors behind this are: deindustrialisation; globalisation; technological advance, including automation of both routine and cognitive tasks; market concentration, whereby 'superstar' firms are capturing higher global market shares; a rising volume of available labour from emerging market economies like Russia and China; and growth of disorganised labour, particularly in the informal and gig economies. In charting this declining share, bodies like the International Labour Organisation (ILO), the OECD, and the International Monetary Fund (IMF) attribute this pattern in good part to the gap between growth in labour productivity through improved technology and average labour compensation. Particularly for the least educated, it is 'a race against the machine'.[19]

Consequently, labour income share in the world, compared to the percentage of national income accruing to holders of capital, dropped from 54 percent in 2004 to 51 percent in 2017, a decline that has been most marked in Europe, Central Asia and the Americas. While development in China and India has helped reduce labour income inequality globally over the last 15 years, wage inequality *within* countries has tended to increase. For 2017, the world's highest-earning 10 percent of employees obtained nearly half (48.9 percent) of total pay, and the next 10 percent got 20.1 percent, leaving the bottom 80 percent with only 31 percent.[20]

In 2022, the ILO's Employment and Social Outlook report[21] speculated whether the continued pressure on labour, due to pandemic patterns of reduced working hours, employment, and workforce participation, was likely to be temporary, or rather indicative of a structural trend of labour-saving renovations and inequities of a widening digital divide.

Two key explanations for this gap relate to the labour type and organisation that still predominate. Of the 3.3 billion employed worldwide in 2019, over 470 million have inadequate access to paid work. They are unemployed or under-employed. Moreover, about 2 billion workers (61 percent of the global workforce) are informally employed, meaning that they have limited worker rights and access to social protection.[22] Given such disparity across the world, in what way does globalisation help or hinder redress?

Globe Trotting

It's hard to pinpoint the start of globalisation. Was it the foundation of the Roman Empire with Augustus Caesar in 31 BC; the Silk Road, a trade route connecting East and West, starting in 130 BC; the Mongol Empire of Genghis Khan and family, in the thirteenth and fourteenth centuries; or the Columbus 'discovery' of the Americas in late fiftteenth century, and subsequent era of European empires?

More clearly, modern globalisation can be traced to the mid-nineteenth century, when changes such as the shift from sail to steamship made the world smaller for labour, capital, and trade flows. In more contemporary times, combined factors such as: improved transport and communication; less protectionism; growth of multinational corporations and global finance; technological diffusion; and specific changes such as containerization, all played a part in extending and accelerating global connections. These cover not just economic exchange, but also political, cultural, and ecological links.

In general, current globalisation receives a bad press from much of the left and part of the right.[23] Concern has been expressed about a 'race to the bottom', whereby governments compete for foreign direct investment on the basis of low tax and light regulation. For some, it's not just about hyper-exploitation of labour by capital, but also about rapacious plundering involved in resource extraction, waste and pollution, and distorted development of the global south in the image of the western economic model. In this view, little regard is paid to a finite world's limits to growth.[24] This critique is complicated by a new geopolitics. Immediately following the Soviet collapse, the triumph of western capitalism and liberal democracy seemed to augur a new world order. If history is a story about contesting social ideologies, we were at history's end-point, because only one was left standing.

We had western expansion, with the absorption of Eastern Europe and the Baltics, in which humiliated Russia felt hemmed in by an extended NATO. More recently, China's emergence as an economic competitor to the US is accompanied by increased tensions in the Pacific, where China is surrounded by myriad American military bases. Alongside this, we have a perpetual 'war on terror' that has seen barbaric political Islam countered with illegalities, such as kidnapping (rendition), torture (enhanced interrogation), and civilian killing (collateral damage with drone and other bomb strikes). In short, combination of technologies, such as robotization and containerization, increased populist demands for protectionism, and New Cold Wars are disrupting the assumed settled order post-1989.[25]

Rodrik[26] recognises the unparalleled prosperity brought by globalisation, including to very poor people in China and other parts of Asia. But he argues that it is faced with a trilemma, choosing among democracy, state sovereignty, and economic globalisation. You can't have all three together. Pure national self-determination will veer toward protectionism. Too much power to global markets will destabilise the world economy and disrupt democracy by offering too little social protection. Thus, the process faces a paradox. For it to work for widespread socio-economic benefit, it requires national government regulation within international rules. Yet the enterprise and flexibility of dynamic globalisation arguably demands free flow of trade, capital and labour, with minimal restriction. Smart, rather than maximum, globalisation is needed, he insists. China and India have advanced their form of it by balancing markets with state intervention, and controlling their reliance on international finance. Economic growth, social redistribution, and sustainability have to be considered together. Still, the practical difficulty with this calculus is how each is evaluated.

Take economic growth. In the US, critics of globalisation may argue that recent growth rates are worse than during what they regard as the heyday of American industrialism, before a lot of domestic manufacturing was eroded by globalisation. In the first half of the 1950s, average annual GDP growth was near 5 percent, translating for what was then around 160 million people as an additional $3,500 per capita. For the period 2011 to 2015, it averaged annually at only 2 percent. But this was growth of a bigger base. So it swelled income by about $4,800 per capita for a larger population of around 317 million, representing almost 40 percent more than sixty years previous. What appears to be a worse performance actually contributed more to average 'individual betterment', but within a period when we are more aware of competing claims to human well-being by material growth and biospheric conservation.[27]

Then take the issues of democracy and national sovereignty. In a more globalised world, there is a case for getting inside a bigger economic bloc for enhanced collective leverage, though in the case of the EU, this potentially entails a forfeiting of democratic self-determination and accountability. In the 2005 French referendum to ratify a proposed Constitution of the European Union, 55 percent of voters rejected it, and a month later, the Dutch did the same by 61 percent to 39 percent. For some, this signalled a reluctance of national electorates to give more power to a Brussels-based centralized bureaucracy. Yet when the Irish rejected the Lisbon Treaty in 2008, with 53.2 percent against, the referendum was re-held a year later, this time achieving a 67.1 percent vote in favour. This seemed to suggest the Union was pressing ahead on greater political unity, regardless of any reservation, and if the wrong verdict on this project was delivered by the electorate, one that was unacceptable to European political elites, then voters would be urged to reconsider.

One pernicious aspect of contemporary globalisation can be the 'contagion' effect of what appears to be a local difficulty. The collapse of Silicon Valley Bank and Signature Bank threatened a wider financial crisis when Credit Suisse had to be rescued, via purchase by UBS. In reality, behind these specific cases, lay global patterns. With higher world debt levels, the rapid switch from low to high interest rates by Central Banks to curb inflationary trends, triggered vulnerabilities in some loans, and with it, reduced the value of some long-term securities. Such strains were exacerbated by the economic 'detriment' attributable to the Ukrainian war and to post-pandemic bottlenecks. In turn, these banking problems risked accentuating a credit squeeze, with potential to suppress sustainable growth. Alongside these traditional woes, the much less regulated virtual global network of de-centralised digital money-crypto-currencies-witnessed the startling bankruptcy of crypto exchange company, FTX, whose founder, Sam Bankman-Fried, was charged with directing depositor money to his hedge fund, Alameda Research, which was alleged to have devoted some of that capital to US politicians, apparently to lobby for policy favourable to its business interests. The weakness of global regulation over global finance was once again exposed.

Many examples can be cited of the 'dark side of globalisation'.[28] Against that, Potrafke[29] offers a comprehensive review of multiple empirical studies addressing different aspects of the process. On a composite index, scaled from 1 (minimum globalisation) to 100 (maximum globalisation), it was estimated to have risen from 36.2 to 56.6 in the period 1970–2010. Overwhelmingly, the evaluation is positive. Open trade, free flows of capital, exploitation of specialization and comparative advantage, and competitive innovation were considered to have enhanced economic performance without harming the welfare state, particularly in developed economies. Nor did globalisation impact negatively on tax returns or public spending. Absolute poverty decreased.

Social globalisation – increased connection of people across the world via travel, internet, and information exchange – improved human development, and advanced gender equality and tolerance of diversity. Overall, human rights and social justice improved. Yes, there was evidence of greater within-country inequality, even as cross-country inequality declined, which, as Potrafke notes, may be because the poor were improving their position. All told, there is much to be welcomed.

Global Harming

Nonetheless, this priority attached to growth raises other social costs. For Rifkin, the politics and economics of the limitless pursuit of growth are tied, with both linked to energy. We have enshrined a moral imperative of diligence over indolence in the belief that economic activity is intrinsically good, yielding unlimited material progress. Wealth-creation is seen to derive from humans imposing order and design on raw nature. Such thinking underpins utopian projection of human perfection. Specifically here, it relates to how we politically treat economic growth, as advancement that upgrades rather than degrades our finite living environment:[30]

> ....*every civilisation inevitably ends up sucking more order out of the surrounding environment than it ever creates and leaves the Earth more impoverished. Seen in this way, the gross domestic product is more accurately the gross domestic cost, since every time resources are consumed, a portion becomes unavailable for future use.*

Other reservations about current globalisation come from the Social Justice Index. This uses 46 quantitative and qualitative criteria to measure six dimensions of social justice: poverty, education, the labour market, intergenerational justice, health, and social inclusion and nondiscrimination. The 2019 edition covers the 41 countries within the EU and OECD.[31] In summary, social justice has deteriorated since the financial and economic crisis ten years previously.

Among the top ten countries doing best in terms of social justice, five are from Northern Europe – Iceland, Norway, Denmark, Finland and Sweden. Germany, the UK, and France are ranked 10th, 11th, and 15th respectively. Apart from Portugal, countries in Southern Europe – Italy, Spain and Greece – continue to struggle. For instance, Greece registers a high unemployment rate of 19.5 percent, with the second-lowest employment rate of 54.9 percent. With its excessive debt levels – 183 percent of GDP – and untenable pension systems, it has problems with intergenerational justice.

In overall grading, Eastern Europe is not a monolith. Czechia and Slovenia are in the top ten, while Bulgaria and Romania rank at the bottom. Similarly, North America is divided. Canada ranks 12th, while the US does very poorly at 36th, and the difference between the two is most notable with regard to poverty prevention. The US has the second-highest population share at risk of poverty, at 17.8 percent, barely changed over the decade that covered the Obama administration. While social justice is inclined to be enhanced in stronger economies, it is not always so, as is the case with the richest.

Though 40 of the 41 countries have many more people in work since the crisis, they have been unable to cut their relative poverty rates. This is taken as indicative of increasing dual labour markets – secure well-paid jobs alongside casualised, flexible, and part-time jobs. Unsurprisingly, US high-poverty levels are tied to its workforce, almost one-quarter of which is low-waged, and its tax base, perennially under pressure to be cut.

The World Justice Report 2021[32] assesses and ranks 139 countries and jurisdictions on eight factors: constraints on government powers; absence of corruption; open government; fundamental rights, order and security; regulatory enforcement; and civil justice and criminal justice. The basic principles it emphasises are just law; open government; and accessible and impartial justice. For the fourth consecutive year, it found that rule of law practice in most countries deteriorated rather than enhanced – 74.2 percent declined, comprising 84.7 percent, or 6.5 billion, of the world's people, while 25.8 percent improved. Notably, the countries ranked as the best were largely Nordic: Denmark (1); Norway (2); Finland (3); Sweden (4); and Germany (5). In the Anglosphere, the UK at 16th and the US at 27th didn't fare well compared to New Zealand (7); Ireland (10); Canada (12); and Australia (13). Some of those countries that have boasted of their left revolutions for greater social justice performed dreadfully: Zimbabwe (127); Bolivia (129); Nicaragua (131); and Venezuela (139). It's easy to excuse these latter countries as victims of imperialist pressure, obliged to exercise various levels of repression to protect their position against external threat and internal subversion. That kind of let-off does a great disservice to genuine campaigners for social justice in those distressed places.

Taxing Problem

To tackle inequality and poverty, never mind key challenges like climate change, you need a progressive tax system. Tax-shy corporations disown that social obligation. For instance, the 'silicon big five': Meta (Facebook), Alphabet (Google), Amazon, Apple, and Microsoft 'earned income of about $197 billion on revenue of more than $1 trillion in 2020, while their market cap rose to $7.5 trillion by year's end'.[33] In 2021, Google's total revenue amounted to $256.7 billion, while Amazon's net revenue was $469.8 billion.[34] These corporations are truly tech titans. Yet one study into the top six such firms[35] found that over the period 2010–2019, the difference between expected headline tax rates and the cash taxes actually returned was $155.3 billion. Such shortfall is explained in good part by profit transfer to tax havens such as Ireland, Bermuda, Luxembourg and the Netherlands. Shamefully, a dozen small EU countries, including Ireland, thwarted a European move to compel multinationals to disclose the profits and tax they pay in each member state.

The Irish Fiscal Advisory Council reported[36] that the country's economy would be hard hit should there be any global crackdown on tax avoidance, such as the OECD's Base Erosion and Profit Shifting (BEPS) proposal. Half of corporation tax receipts, upon which the country has become increasingly dependent to fund spending, are paid by just ten companies, reckoned to include big tech firms such as Apple, Facebook and Google.

There was the ludicrous situation, wherein the Irish government, while imposing austerity on the public to pay for bank misconduct, at the same time refused to accept the gift horse of a €13 billion tax receipt from Apple, imposed by the EU for its 'unpaid' Irish taxes. If countries want to compete on the basis of offering the best tax haven, it's a race to the bottom. That can only be halted by serious global accord to operate a common minimum tax rate and to tax economic activity where it's generated, based on gross sales revenue and jobs, rather than profits, which can be located for tax convenience.[37]

In October 2021,[38] a step in this direction was taken by 136 countries and jurisdictions, accounting for over 90 percent of global GDP, under an OECD deal to get a global minimum corporation tax of 15 percent, due to be operable by 2023. Some hesitant countries like Ireland did eventually join the international tax agreement, which it's estimated will add around USD (US dollars) 150 billion in new annual tax revenue. It applies to those multinationals with global sales over €20 billion, and profit rates above 10 percent, and allocates some of their profit above the 10 percent threshold to the markets where they operate business and accrue profit. Clearly, the rate is low, and covers only the big players, and we have to wait to see how rigorous will be its implementation. The Tax Foundation sounded a note of caution in April 2022:[39] 'with both the U.S. and EU hitting roadblocks in their respective legislative processes, it is unclear when, or even if, the agreement will be implemented. If implementation fails, a return to a world of distortive European digital services taxes and retaliatory American tariffs could be on the horizon'.

Tax-shy multinationals have three main means to profit shift: transact debt through loans across corporate branches; transfer price to ensure their highest earnings are in those subsidiaries sited in places of lowest tax or best loopholes, while expenses are recorded in high tax regimes; and similar choices regarding intangible assets such as copyright and intellectual property. It's about location. In a globalised world, locality retains a premium.[40]

For instance, in his book *Treasure Islands*,[41] Shaxson shows how financial assets secreted offshore contaminate economies onshore. Taking the example of Britain, he describes how it operates at the centre of a global labyrinth of tax havens, or what some prefer to call secrecy jurisdictions, such as Crown Dependencies of Jersey and Guernsey, and Overseas Territories, such as the Caymans, and even to an outer ring of places like Hong Kong, which suck in trillions globally and subsequently channel capital through the City of London.

Banks and business scarper offshore for three main reasons: secrecy; tax reduction; and less regulation. In many such places, Britain still holds clout. For instance, the monarch appoints governors to the Dependencies. But when convenient, Britain can stress their independence and feign frustration at being unable to interfere. These fiscal paradises offer escape routes for paper trails of hot money, of dubious and devious origin, what Shaxson and others see as a form of financial Omerta. In normal rule of law, if you help or hide a criminal, you're regarded as an accomplice to the crime. Insofar as these hideaways offer sanctuary for tax dodging and money laundering, they should be regarded as rogue states, and places such as the City of London should be monitored robustly to ensure they are not facilitators in any such looting.

The *State of Tax Justice 2021* report[42] calculates the global revenue losses that year, attributable to tax manipulation by big corporations and individuals secreting their assets and income offshore, to total US$483 billion. Multinationals – accounting for about one third of world economic output, a quarter of the world's workforce, and half of all exports – carry the can for most of this loss: they 'are shifting US$1.19 trillion worth of profit into tax havens a year, causing governments around the world to lose US$312 billion a year in direct tax revenue'.[43] Taking into account indirect losses, such as the result of governments reducing corporation tax to keep competitive with this tax abuse, adjusted total losses may be around US $1 trillion. Then taking financial wealth, the US$171 billion attributable to offshore tax evasion per annum, and 'the UK spider's web' is answerable for half this.

Both types of tax manipulation – involving multinationals and individuals' financial wealth – is a feature mainly of rich countries and their dependent territories. OECD member countries account for 78.3 percent of this combined loss.[44] Campaigners for tax justice argue for the 4Rs of proper taxation:[45] *revenues* sufficient to finance good public services; *redistribution* to curtail deep inequalities; *repricing* to cover negative externalities, such as carbon-based energy and tobacco use; and *representation* – allowing for political accountability over tax generation and application. These principles would imply a new global tax regime that would, for example, include a wealth tax and an excess profits tax on those companies, such as in Big Pharma and Big Tech, that saw their earnings increase substantially with the pandemic, and energy companies that saw theirs increase with events such as the Russian invasion of Ukraine. To achieve this redirection, they argue that responsibility for global rule-setting on tax should be switched from the OECD to the United Nations.

Without this progress, we're likely to see continued expansion of tax havens, which have facilitated the kind of evasion that many Western governments have been relaxed about, or even resigned to:[46]

> *Rich-world governments have long tacitly encouraged certain types of avoidance for fear of otherwise being branded uncompetitive and turning off big investors. They may be less keen on billionaires dodging tax in personal property deals, but also reluctant to target plutocrats who make generous political donations.*

A different estimation sees the global public purse robbed of between $500 billion and $600 billion of corporate tax money annually due to profit shifting via tax shelters, with about one-third of this revenue loss coming from low-income countries, which are hit hardest in terms of GDP share.[47] Indeed, they lose more from this than they gain from foreign aid. When we wonder why a continent like Africa, with its bountiful mineral endowment, ends up being in dire economic straits, we can certainly attribute it in part to corrupt leadership, though, in doing so, we forget how much wealth is still diverted from it to the rich world. While elite private interests in these places generate capital flight to rich countries, their public sector borrows from the rich world, accruing debt burdens borne by their poor.

This is what is called the paradox of poverty from plenty. Money from resources like oil and diamonds can feed bribery, war and repression domestically, while accentuating hardship of the poorest by raising local prices; creating greater inequality; and draining skilled people from industry and government towards the lucrative sector. All told, many can end up worse off than if the valuable resource was never extracted in the first place. The process becomes part of the wider 'finance curse', whereby money flows surreptitiously through corrupt banking via secrecy jurisdictions.[48] In Bullough's telling,[49] this financialisation of the real economy has carved a special domain he calls 'Moneyland', the virtual place where shadowy nomadic capital goes to hide. It's a global jurisdiction for stashing dodgy money. It flourishes because, unlike money, law enforcement ends at national borders.

Among multiple examples of fraudulent behaviour, he cites a wide-ranging money-laundering ruse run by disreputable Paul Manafort, election campaign chairman for Trump in 2016. In a previous incarnation, Manafort had been consultant to pro-Russia Ukraine President, Yanukovich, who swindled his country via 'industrial scale corruption', enriching himself and his cronies. In a little over two decades after its independence from the former Soviet bloc, 'just forty-five individuals owned assets equal in value to half the country's economy'.[50] Convicted of tax and bank fraud, Manafort was pardoned by Trump.

This story of sleazy networks, linking political lobbying, state corruption, massive social inequality, and offshore finance, is all too common. As Henry says:[51] 'there's no interest group more rich and powerful than the rich and powerful'. He estimates, as of 2010, that between $21 and $32 trillion was invested nearly tax free through over 80 secrecy jurisdictions. That's just private financial wealth, never mind assets. Opacity and dissimulation make it problematic to be precise.

Although others estimate these figures somewhat lower, even with that, Africa's share of financial wealth held offshore is put at around 30 percent, while it is above half for Russia and the Middle East oil economies.[52] This goldmine is managed by big global banks, which are essentially robbing the same taxpayers they relied upon to rescue them after the crash. Other enablers include respectable professionals in legal, accounting, investment, PR and lobbying sectors. Of course, such well-remunerated elites have vested interest in resisting regulation, tax justice, and limits on electoral campaign financing.

When Dave Hartnett headed the UK's tax office (HMRC), he signed off on tax settlements with companies like Vodaphone and Goldman Sachs, details of which were secret for reasons of 'taxpayer confidentiality', but which observers saw as 'sweetheart deals'. In 2012, activists arrived uninvited to New College, Oxford, where he was addressing tax lawyers and accountants. In mock commendation, they bestowed him with a 'lifetime achievement award for services to corporate tax planning' before chorusing *For He's a Jolly Good Fellow* – swapping the refrain 'so say all of us' with 'so say Goldman Sachs'. In 2013, after leaving HMRC, he took up positions with tax consultancy Deloitte and with HSBC.[53]

Another UK scheme that allows the rich to elude their full tax liability is the concession bestowed on those living, but not 'domiciled', in the country – so-called 'non-doms', who, though they may in practice be resident mostly in the UK, claim their permanent residence to be overseas. Basically, this special status legally frees them from tax, including inheritance tax, on their foreign income and capital gains, if that wealth is not 'remitted' to the UK. Such non-doms are not even obliged to divulge to the tax authorities where they do pay tax on those funds, which may be off-shore located investments. A recent study[54] examining these non-doms, from 1997–2018, found that they constituted: a global rich elite, geographically concentrated in the ritzy parts of London; hailing mostly from the Anglosphere and the EU, with a rising number this century coming from Eastern Europe and Asia, particularly India and China, and former Soviet republics; three in ten earners of £5 million or more; over one- in-five high-income bankers; and one in six high-earning sports and film stars. Also included in their ranks were establishment figures, like members of the House of Lords, Mark Carney, a recent governor of the Bank of England, and Zac Goldsmith, a failed Conservative candidate for Mayor of London, later 'elevated' to a Lord.

While this public largesse to privileged individuals is an affront at the best of times, amidst a cost-of-living crisis, frozen tax thresholds and tax hikes in 2022, it was revealed that Akshata Murty, wife of the then UK Chancellor of the Exchequer, Sunak, was a substantial beneficiary of the scheme. Owning a stake valued at around £710 million in the corporation, Infosys, founded by her father, she would have gained close to £11.6 million in dividends in the previous tax year. Without her tax immunity, 38.1 percent of that – over £4 million – would have gone to the coffers of the Treasury, headed by her husband.[55]

Estimated to total 75,700, these non-doms' special tax status has deprived the public purse of almost £8 billion in taxes and national insurance.[56] Meanwhile, the burden falls on those who dutifully contribute. When UK Chancellor, George Osborne cut corporation tax from 28 percent to 19 percent, it did not deliver the assured boost to inward investment and economic growth. Alongside agreement reached by the G7 in mid-2021 for a global corporation tax rate of at least 15 percent, this failure of tax cuts to spur widespread prosperity should move the tax-and-spend debate in a more sensible direction.[57] But the proof will be in the practice. Furthermore, these steps stop short of a serious wealth tax, which has a high degree of UK public support.[58] The UK Wealth Tax Commission[59] has proposed a broad-based levy on ownership of net wealth.

Levied at 1 percent a year for five years on individual wealth over £500,000, it would generate the substantial sum of £260 billion.

The investigative journalist group ProPublica[60] undertook a recent analysis of taxes paid by the 25 richest Americans. Between 2014–2018, their wealth increased by a collective $401 billion, on which was paid $13.6 billion in federal income taxes, a 'true tax rate of only 3.4 percent'. By the close of 2018, that rich group was worth $1.1 trillion, a wealth equivalent of 14.3 million ordinary American wage-earners. Yet the personal federal tax paid by the super-rich 25 was $1.9 billion, compared to $143 billion due by the wage-earners.

When Russia and China dispensed with communism, their combination of autocratic politics and liberal economics facilitated the burst of billionaire beneficiaries of the handover of public assets to private interests. The age of Russian oligarchs was born. Amongst their devices to move and hide their money was the promiscuous purchase of luxury property, under the cover of unidentified companies of convenience, in what came to be dubbed as the 'laundromat' of Londongrad. In 2022, Transparency International UK[61] put the global figure for dubious investment in Britain's property market at £6.7 billion since 2016. Of this, £1.5 billion was purchased by corrupt or Kremlin-linked Russians. Nearly half (47.1 percent) was concentrated in the City of Westminster, and to its west, Kensington and Chelsea. Over half (55 percent) of the property value was in the name of companies in Britain's Overseas Territories and Crown Dependencies, noted for their opacity. In addition, the study pinpointed '2,189 companies registered in the UK and its Overseas Territories and Crown Dependencies used in 48 Russian money laundering and corruption cases. These cases involved more than £82 billion worth of funds diverted by rigged procurement, bribery, embezzlement and the unlawful acquisition of state assets'.

Summarising the scandal of Russian dicey money in the UK, the *Economist* noted in 2022:[62]

> *As well as owning mansions, oligarchs from the former Soviet Union own British football clubs (Roman Abramovich) and newspapers (Evgeny Lebedev), pay to have university departments named after them (Len Blavatnik), send their children to the swankiest schools, and cosy up to political parties, particularly the Conservatives, with donations. Oligarchs are among the heaviest spenders on British law firms, PR consultants and other reputation-launderers.*

Some see this in terms of a transnational transaction with kleptocracy, whereby post-Soviet elites are facilitated by Western professionals and institutions in laundering their finances and reputations, starting in the 1990s, with the convergence of Soviet collapse and the further development of financial deregulation under globalisation. In the case of the UK, such elites have employed exclusive lawyers to daunt investigative journalism or academic research with libel actions, and public relations companies to enhance their philanthropic image – and other tactics, designed to thwart intervention by under-resourced regulatory agencies. Glimpses of the problem cross the public's screen, like the £16 million splurged in the seminally up-market London store, Harrods, by the spouse of an Azerbaijani banker. But the wider Azerbaijani 'laundromat' involved, over a two-year period, $2.9 billion channelled through four UK shell firms, 'some of which was used on lobbying activities, including the bribing of European politicians'.[63] Between 2010 and 2012, the daughter of Karimova, then president of Uzbekistan, lavished investment in the UK property market to the sum of £35.2 million, small beer relative to the $865 million the US Justice Department claims she acquired from bribes given by global telecom corporations, keenly seeking admittance to Uzbek markets.[64] Such handling of dishonest money is paralleled by financial institutions. For example, 'much of the illicit wealth of Nigerian dictator Sani Abacha ended up in UK banks, while Riggs Bank in Washington DC held millions of dollars belonging to former Chilean president Augusto Pinochet and President Teodoro Obiang of Equatorial Guinea'.[65]

Other respectable institutions can play their part. UK universities, in contrast to their American counterparts, are not obliged to divulge the source and amount of, or strings attached to, donations they receive.[66] When in 2019, a 1980s amendment to the US 1965 Higher Education Act was fully implemented, it exposed $6.5 billion in previously unrevealed donations, many coming from autocracies. The influence of suspect funds goes to the heart of British politics. The then governing party, the Conservatives, accepted £3.5 million 'from donors with a Russian business background, including from former arms dealer Alexander Temerko'.[67] Summarising this sorry state of affairs, the authoritative and blistering report comments:[68]

> *The key allies of kleptocratic presidents merge into UK society and sometimes acquire British citizenship following receipt of a 'golden visa'. They settle down, donate to charities, threaten journalists with legal actions and make political connections. As government has failed to address this problem, British professional services provision to kleptocracies is undermining the fairness and efficiency of the legal system.*

Another dimension is the role of places like the British Virgin Islands in the complex money transfers that can be involved. A recent official report[69] on the country concluded that 'almost everywhere, the principles of good governance, such as openness, transparency and even the rule of law, are ignored'. Denouncing the discretionary decision-making and lack of public accountability, it called for a radical overhaul of the island authority. This critique was highlighted by the arrest in 2022 in Miami of the country's leader for alleged drug smuggling and money laundering.[70]

Consider the implications of this pattern: the global nature of the suspect transactions; the ineffective regulation and enforcement; reputable Western institutions turning a blind eye to corruption; a governing party taking money from an ex-arms dealer, while now railing against Russian militarism; visas granted to dubious characters, while anti-immigrant sentiment is subject to political exploitation; major assets like football clubs, precious over generations to working class communities, bought by wealthy elites; house prices inflated by affluent purchasers, thereby accentuating the housing crisis, which hits the poorest the hardest; and unknown influence over research and media, when they are sponsored in some way by sources that lack transparency. And processing it all, the money flows through banks.

Bankers and Banksters

Some say that reforms introduced by Obama and other governments have tamed the risk and rogue behaviour of banks, which now operate with more contrition and less swagger. Still, even when wolves of Wall Street appear silent as lambs, the public still gets fleeced. Unfortunately, 'banking scandal' is *not* an oxymoron.

In 2020, Goldman Sachs paid nearly $3 billion in fines for its central role in a massive Malaysian corruption scandal, wherein prime minister Razak and other high-ranking officials were involved in siphoning off billions of dollars raised supposedly for public development projects. Amongst its institutional 'failures' was its use of a $1 billion plus bribe to win work to raise capital for this sovereign wealth fund, about which it misled investors. In short, a deal was struck that let the bank off lightly for its association with a venal mix of politics, business and graft. This settlement to 'defer prosecution' allowed Goldman to avoid criminal conviction,[71] even though the United States Department of Justice acknowledged that 'Goldman Sachs participated in a sweeping international corruption scheme', and berated 'the Company's failure to voluntarily disclose the conduct to the department'.[72] Given the seriousness of the offence, this amounted to yet another 'sweetheart deal'.

Such let-offs are far from unusual. In 2012, the Department entered into a deferred prosecution agreement with the global giant, HSBC, which 'agreed' to pay $1.9 billion in penalty to settle charges that it helped launder proceeds of Mexican and Colombian narcotics trafficking. In the Department's own 30-page Statement of Facts about the deal, it acknowledged that 'if this matter were to proceed to trial, the Department would prove beyond a reasonable doubt, by admissible evidence, the facts alleged....'[73] It went on to say: 'at least $881 million in drug trafficking proceeds, including proceeds of drug trafficking by the Sinaloa Cartel in Mexico and the Norte del Valle Cartel in Colombia, were laundered through HSBC Bank USA without being detected'.[74]

In other words, the bank admitted the wrongdoing. Department senior officials were keen to pursue criminal charges. But Eric Holder, Obama's

Attorney General, chose not to, in part because a conviction could see revocation of the bank's US Charter, with economic 'collateral consequence'. Critics of this leniency claimed that this showed that not only were some banks 'too big to fail', but that some senior corporate figures were 'too big to jail'.

Consider the context. The US has boasted of its relentless War on Drugs. In one of the most punitive criminal justice systems in the world, it packs its penal institutions with young black men with drug convictions. Many other citizens have lives ruined by drug-taking and drug gang violence. The Mexican cartels, who are a prominent source of drugs into the US, exercise barbaric retribution on anyone who crosses them. Yet, despite all this death and detriment, a bank that facilitates this affliction gets its wrist slapped. In 2015, Holder returned to the corporate law firm, Covington & Burling, which serves Wall Street clients. As one commentator put it starkly:[75]

> For six years, while brilliantly disguised as the attorney general of the United States, he was actually working deep undercover, DiCaprio in The Departed-style, as the best defence lawyer Wall Street ever had....HSBC laundered money for guys who chop peoples' heads off with chainsaws. So we can dispense with the 'but no one broke any laws' thing.

Of course, this can be seen as part of long-standing hypocrisy about drugs in America. The 'war on drugs' was launched by Nixon. In an interview, Ehrlichman, Nixon's counsel and Assistant for Domestic Affairs, revealed the deceit behind their drugs policy:[76]

> The Nixon campaign in 1968, and the Nixon White House after that, had two enemies: the antiwar left and black people. You understand what I'm saying? We knew we couldn't make it illegal to be either against the war or black, but by getting the public to associate the hippies with marijuana and blacks with heroin, and then criminalizing both heavily, we could disrupt those communities. We could arrest their leaders, raid their homes, break up their meetings, and vilify them night after night on the evening news. Did we know we were lying about the drugs? Of course we did.

Deceit about public policy on drugs and related selective incarceration continues, as do banking scandals. Take JPMorgan, fined $13 billion in 2013 for misrepresenting residential mortgage-backed securities to unwary investors.[77] In February 2014, Senator Elizabeth Warren at a Senate Banking committee, asked why the bank's CEO, Jamie Dimon got a 74 percent pay rise, bringing his annual compensation to $20 million, in a year the firm faced penalties for illegal activity. Well, despite the malfeasance, the firm's stocks actually rose by over 30 percent that year. Maybe that's why. The apparent hefty fine was more than offset.

Did the reprimand at least act as deterrent against further financial crime? It seems not. In 2020, it had to pay nearly $1 billion to settle what it admitted to be illegal trading in precious metals, Treasury notes and futures, designed to create artificial price adjustments favourable to it, while distorting the market to other participants' disadvantage. Again, this deal involved a 'deferred prosecution agreement'.[78] Similarly in 2020, HSBC, supposedly under 'probation' for misdeeds with drug cartels, came under scrutiny by the US Financial Crimes Enforcement Network (FinCEN) for its movement of dirty money from a massive Ponzi network.

All this is power for the course. In 2014, the Luxembourg leaks focused on how PricewaterhouseCooper helped multinationals attain hundreds of advantageous tax rulings in Luxembourg between 2002–2010. Jean-Claude Juncker had been Prime Minister of the country when it passed many of its tax avoidance directives, and inconveniently was appointed European Commission President shortly before the leak.[79] In 2015, Swiss leaked papers were analysed by the International Consortium of Investigative Journalists (ICIJ), who noted how: 'secret documents reveal that global banking giant HSBC profited from doing business with arms dealers who channelled mortar bombs to child soldiers in Africa, bag men for Third World dictators, traffickers in blood diamonds and other international outlaws'.[80]

The 2016 Panama Papers revealed further offshore activity by prominent people, including politicians. As UK Prime Minister, David Cameron, was talking big about tackling tax avoidance and evasion, it emerged from these leaks that his father had run an offshore investment fund that had evaded ever having to pay a penny of tax in Britain. The Paradise Papers in 2017, based mostly on documents from offshore law firm, Appleby, drew in celebrities, but also the late UK Queen's private estate. Then in October 2021, came a massive set of material, known as the Pandora Papers, which unveiled hush-hush financial transactions of 35 current and former world leaders, and more than 330 politicians and public officials in 91 countries and territories:[81] 'The leaked records reveal that many of the power players who could help bring an end to the offshore system instead benefit from it – stashing assets in covert companies and trusts while their governments do little to slow a global stream of illicit money that enriches criminals and impoverishes nations'.

Such inter-penetration of global politics and concealed money movements shows that there's a long way to go to get to grips with the problem. In 2020, the OECD[82] reported that information exchange among nearly 100 countries in 2019 yielded data on 84 million financial accounts of their residents, held off-shore, and involving total assets of €10 trillion. In short, many global banks are implicated in tax cutting, money laundering and financial crime. Whatever the rhetoric from governments, banks' pursuit of hyper-profits seems worth the risk of regulator fines. Evidently, there is one decree for financial institutions, and another for ordinary citizens. While it may be a cliché that there is one law for the rich and another for the poor, it doesn't invalidate its truth. Such immunity invalidates the rule of law, the cornerstone of any democracy. Potential for corruption is not helped by the relationship that can develop between top politicians and high finance.

The Revolving Door

It's been said often that those in politics for business gain have no business being in politics. But if we examine why US sectors like finance get Washington's receptive ear, one explanation lies in the 'revolving door', whereby leading lights in Wall Street move into prominent government positions concerned with finance, and then sometimes later move back to their former profession.

And it's not just under Republican Presidents. Robert Rubin was co-CEO of Goldman Sachs, then became Treasury Secretary under Clinton, and later chairman of the Executive Committee at Citigroup's Directors' Board. Summers was a senior economist at the World Bank, also Treasury Secretary under Clinton, during which time saw the de-regulation of the financial system, including effective annulling of the 1933 Glass-Steagall Act, which had separated investment and commercial banking. Subsequently, he was a managing partner of a hedge fund and freelance speaker at institutions such as Goldman and Citigroup, and then under Obama, he was back in government as Director of US National Economic Council.

During the financial crisis, the Treasury post was held by Poulson, who had just been boss of Goldman Sachs, where he had accrued riches in the form of equity in the firm, valued between $600–700 million. He was able to avail of a tax provision that allowed deferral of capital gains levy on assets that had to be sold to avoid conflict-of-interest.[83] As CEO of Goldman's, he had presided over its involvement in mortgage securities. His fingerprints were all over the problem that landed on his then government desk. Under Obama, the Treasury Secretary was Geithner, who had served under Clinton, became President of the Federal Reserve Bank of New York, and after being boss of Obama's Treasury, he later became president and managing director of a private equity firm. Bernanke, the recent recipient of a Nobel Prize, chaired the Federal Reserve under Obama, and later became involved with a major hedge fund and a global investment management firm.

This kind of revolving door is sometimes justified in terms of the public being served best by senior people in government who understand best, and are respected by, the market. The counter-argument is that if they've imbued the ethos of the market, and are intent on returning to it for private dividend, they are not best-placed to challenge its assumptions and authority. This issue also applies to those working in regulatory and credit ratings agencies, who later may seek a position in the financial sector. Are they inclined to bite the hand that one day may feed them?

Other countries evidence similar patterns. For instance, in the UK, former Conservative Chancellor, Javid, previously worked as a vice-president in Chase Manhattan and as a senior managing director in Deutche Bank. After his Treasury stint, he became a senior adviser to JP Morgan, while remaining a Member of Parliament. His successor, Sunak, used to work at Goldman Sachs, after which he worked in two hedge funds, and was a director of an invest-ment firm. Osborne, a previous Chancellor, was an advisor to an investment firm, and became a partner in an Investment Bank. Former Prime Minister, Cameron, when in office had talked about reforming 'the far-too cosy relation-ship between politics, government, business and money' which he thought had 'tainted our politics for too long'. Out of office, he lobbied Sunak for millions in emergency COVID loans for Greensill Capital, a £5 billion financial ser-vices company that went bust in March 2021.[84] Cameron was reported to have earned $10 million (£7.2 million) as a lobbyist for Greensill[85] – a small fortune for a part-time job.

These moves between politics and finance are not exclusive to the Conservatives. In 2015, former Labour Prime Minister, Gordon Brown was appointed to the advisory board of the global investment firm, Pimco, where he joined Bernanke, and Trichet, former President of the European Central Bank. (Brown uses his fees for charity). In the same year, Darling, Chancellor during the financial crisis, joined the Directors' Board at Morgan Stanley. More recently, former Labour politician, Umunna, was appointed to lead JP Morgan's European environmental, social and governance unit.

All these issues that we've just covered – technocratic politics that by-passes de-industrialised communities; institutions like the EU that have democratic deficits; disputed distributional impact of globalisation; legacy of the financial crisis in terms of social justice; off-shoring; tax-dodging; business and political corruption; and revolving doors – all these and more are prompting people to see a hopelessly rigged politics as not only beneath their contempt, but also beyond their control.

Taking Back Control

Nominally, countries like the UK are marked as democratic and accountable. Yet when it comes to democracy, what are we to make of secret jurisdictions like the City of London Corporation? It appears like a local council for the Square Mile of Britain's financial heartland. But in 21 of its 25 electoral wards, votes are cast by corporations, mostly financial, and the bigger the firm, the more the votes.[86] It's not simply undemocratic. It's antiquated. In contemporary UK planning, local plan strategies are meant to be complemented by neigh-bourhood plans, devised in cooperation between local authority and neigh-bourhood forums. But the Corporation notes in its local plan:[87] 'at the time of preparation of City Plan 2036, no neighbourhood forum has been established in the City of London and no neighbourhood plans are in preparation or have been adopted'. That's certainly convenient.

Often with great pomp, the City presents itself as a place of propriety. Its autonomy is partly reflected in having its own police force. Indeed, without a trace of irony, it boasts about its leading national role in tackling economic crime. Others, less impressed by its anti-criminal credentials, regard it as an offshore island within Britain that protects a rich elite. It's been said that there are two significant island tax havens: Manhattan and the City of London.[88] The latter's capacity to compromise democracy is captured in former Prime Minister Attlee's telling remark:[89]

> *Over and over again, we have seen that there is in this country another power than that which has its seat at Westminster. The City of London, a convenient term for a collection of financial interests, is able to assert itself against the Government of the country. Those who control money can pursue a policy at home and abroad contrary to that which has been decided by the people.*

And yet it persists as an essentially brazen lobby for financial services, with an official advocate in the House of Commons, called the remembrancer, there to safeguard City privileges. Such a 'rotten borough' adds insult to the injury of Britain's democratic deficit, as manifest further by the fusty House of Lords and monarchy. It's no surprise that the tone-deaf privileged British monarchy, with their multiple palaces, and their wealth traceable to colonisation, received a cool reception in their 2022 Jubilee Caribbean tour, as they were pressed to support reparations for slavery. If you voted for Brexit in Britain to 'get back control' from foreign institutions, you must surely ask what control you exercise over these unaccountable domestic institutions.

Truly, what new control did the public acquire of finance after 2008? Very little. Instead, the narrative of the crash is revealing. Corporate wounds were bandaged in socialist dressings. Nobody was punished. Leading executives walked away with generous pay-outs. Within a year, the big bonus culture resumed. In a reprehensible speech in London's St Paul's Cathedral in 2009 on the theme of markets and morals, Lord Griffiths – note the 'lord' bit – vice-chairman of Goldman Sachs International and former adviser to Thatcher, sanctioned this disreputable culture. He declared that the public should 'tolerate the inequality as a way to achieve greater prosperity for all'. Lucrative remuneration should not be subject to shame when, without it, banks would move abroad.[90]

This then is the morality. Big banks can browbeat government to do their bidding, threatening economic collapse should they not. When bailed out by taxpayers, they can offer them the callous choice of brooking bountiful reward for bankers or risk their relocation. That way lies political capture, as plutocracy instigates its silent coup on democracy.

A tell-tale sign that a particular sector has captured society is its arrogant prerogative. For instance, it was with some gall that Bob Diamond, then the new Barclay's boss, pronounced to a UK House of Commons Committee that:[91] 'there was a period of remorse and apology for banks and I think that period needs to be over'. Sackcloth and ashes are just not their thing. For many, the enigma is why people submit to this sophistry. For example, why did the fool's gold exposed by the crash not expose a golden opportunity for the left? Or are we now doomed to submit to capitalism's golden rule – whoever owns the gold, rules?

Amid this pattern, people look to government to take control, including oversight and regulation of how the financial system works for society as a whole. They have been badly let down. Yet it was recently revealed that staff at the UK's Financial Conduct Authority (FCA) were rewarded with bonuses that from 2016 totalled £125.5 million, a payment that flies in the face of what critics take to be a poor performance of public supervision.[92]

In the wider political landscape, erosion of respect for the highest office in some democracies is hardly surprising. Former UK Prime Minister Johnson was a serial rule-breaker, whose notoriety for mendacity became so settled that it was said to have been 'priced into' his premiership. Under his watch as London mayor, a publicly-funded payment of £126,000 was granted to businesswoman, Jennifer Arcuri, who later alleged to have been his lover. During a discordant political period in finalising Brexit in 2019, he prorogued Parliament, an act subsequently ruled illegal. His brand of English nationalism undermined the unity of the UK, just as he was wrapping himself in the flag as valiant defender of that union. While originally claiming to have personally paid for expensive refurbishment of his apartment in Downing St., it was later revealed that payment came through an undeclared donation. When he bypassed the finding that his Home Secretary was responsible for bullying staff, this led to the resignation of the ethics adviser, who had delivered that verdict. In a 2021 sleaze scandal involving paid advocacy by one of his MPs, he tried to alter existing Parliamentary disciplinary arrangements, only to be forced to retreat and admit the MP's serious breach of lobbying rules.

After his multiple denials in Parliament that pandemic lockdown regulations were contravened by himself and others in 10 Downing St., he received a police fine for doing so, and an official report, in May 2022, attributed the culture of regular parties there to failures of senior political and administrative leadership – in other words, in good part to him. While still faced because of this 'partygate' with prospect of being found to have misled Parliament, and to have broken the Ministerial code, based on the Seven Principles of Public Life, including openness, integrity, honesty and accountability, he conveniently thought it appropriate to change that very code. The revised version reserves the penalty of resignation for serious infraction, and in his rewrite of the foreword to the code, he erased reference to honesty, integrity, transparency and accountability. Critics charged that it was a cynical case of when the rules don't suit, change the rulebook.

Nor did Johnson's cavalier disregard for bothersome directives stop in the domestic realm. He threatened to unilaterally breach international law by ditching parts of a protocol he agreed with the EU in relation to Brexit. Though posing as champion of the global rule of law in respect of Ukraine, he was ready to act unlawfully in a 'specific and limited way' with an international treaty he voluntarily signed. Eventually, the combination of his incompetence, lying, and impervious behaviour led to mass resignation of government ministers and sufficient rebellion of Tory MPs to cast him from office. The Economist dubbed it 'clownfall'. Even facing ignominious exit, he discredited his office. Ungracious to the last, he departed whining about the injustice of it all. When the leader of a democracy acts persistently in this brazen way, when a lawmaker becomes an habitual law-breaker, the edifice of trust crumbles.

Into this broken governance stepped yet another Tory Prime Minister – the fourth in less than six years – with a cabinet even more right-wing than the previous, and with a reckless intent to depose 'Treasury orthodoxy' with economic innumeracy. Liz Truss had long-held risibly simplistic libertarian views about shrinking what she saw as a bloated public sector and over-reaching nanny-state. In fact, though government revenue was set to be 40 percent of national income, the highest share since the early 1980s, the size of the UK state is about average for OECD countries, while smaller than most of its European neighbours.[93]

Almost concurrently with the instalment of a new unelected head of state – King Charles – she assumed the premiership on the basis of 81,326 votes from Tory party members. Together with an unelected legislature in the House of Lords, these represented the democratic credentials of the UK in 2022. It's unthinkable that the Chartists would have imagined this sorry outcome, when they fought to attain British democracy and parliamentary reform nearly two centuries ago.

And so without any mandate, she and her Chancellor, Kwarteng, set about offering £45 billion of unfunded tax cuts, designed to mostly benefit the rich and big corporations on the invalidated 'trickle down' theory that this would incentivise a flat-lining economy towards an early growth rate of 2.5 percent. First, there was a massive spend to cushion the burden of soaring household energy bills (£60–100 billion annually), poorly targeted based on need, so that half the subsidy would be donated to the top half of the income distribution.[94] Alongside this, the biggest tax giveaway in half a century amplified the already astronomical public debt accumulated under the pandemic lockdown. In 2021–22, such debt amounted to 97 percent of national income, the highest level since the early 1960s, and three times the level at the turn of this century. Though low debt interest eased this liability, borrowing, at 5.6 percent of national income in 2021–22, was over twice the long-term average of 2.5 percent.[95]

In this context, announcement of permanent tax cuts produced immediate mayhem. The financial markets took fright. The pound dived to near parity with the dollar, and public debt-interest rate on ten-year debt surged to 4.5 percent. The International Monetary Fund (IMF) and US President weighed in with criticism, with implied pressure for policy reversal. With the Bank of England already raising interest rates to dampen demand and curb rising inflation, this ill-considered 'dash for growth' had fiscal and monetary policy pointing in opposite directions, a conflict that unnerved investors. Interest rates for mortgage-holders and business would have to increase further. Rising inflation would push up the cost of outlays like state pensions. In short, though billed as a supply-side revolution to unleash market-driven enterprise, the hare-brained move was punished by the bond markets with higher borrowing costs and a related slump in the value of sterling, which served to import higher inflation, accentuating an existing cost-of-living crisis.

The Institute of Fiscal Studies estimated[96] that it would lead to government borrowing of £194 billion in that current financial year, and debt interest payment even in 2026–27 of £66 billion. All told, filling the black hole in government finances would necessitate annual savings of £62 billion in 2026–27, with at least £35 billion of this coming from a 15 percent current spending reduction across public services, assuming exemption for Health Service and Ministry of Defence budgets. These are the very public services already squeezed after the austerity years of 2010–2019. Even this estimated shortfall assumed the indexation of working-age benefits to earnings growth rather than inflation, a further hit on working-age households in the bottom half of the income distribution. Subsequent figures from the Office for Budget Responsibility suggested an even worse picture, with £72 billion of a black hole in public finances.[97]

Yet the Truss government initially denied that the package would compel public spending cutback. In short, rises in inflation, debt interest payments, mortgage rates and rents, all against the background of a run on sterling, augured lower growth, and persistent market turmoil. In desperation to hold onto her job of less than 6 weeks, Truss sacked her Chancellor, effectively for executing her wishes, and his replacement – the fourth in as many months – quickly reversed her strategy, signalling tax rises and spending cuts to fill a remaining gap of £30–40 billion, and thereby rendering her mortally wounded. The humiliating retreat – scaling back the energy price support, and revising tax and spend to ensure that debt would fall as a share of the economy – left Truss with her platform completely dumped, and her credibility trashed. I never experienced a UK government, which created such mess and domestic harm in such a short time. Amazingly, the UK was once again in search of a new Prime Minister.

Subsequently, the re-cycled Tory government under Sunak flagged a new era of austerity to come mainly after 2025 in an effort to appease the markets, alarmed at the country's budget gap. Essentially, the package involved £25 billion in tax rises and £30 billion in spending cuts, bringing the tax take to a post-war high of 37 percent of GDP. After 12 years of Tory rule, the UK was in recession; burdened with a deficit of 7.1 percent of GDP in 2022; facing raised interest rates to curb inflation; low prospects for growth; on-coming fiscal contraction; a decline in average disposable income that between 2019–20 and 2023–24 amounts to triple that endured in the four years following the financial crash; and interest payment due on government debt projected to be over £100 billion (over 3.4 percent of GDP) by 2027–28.

Alongside these measures, the government returned to the mission of deregulating finance, as a hopeful source of future tax revenue. The Chancellor told Parliament that the lesson to be drawn from a previous Tory Chancellor, Nigel Lawson, in Thatcher's administration in 1986, was that 'smart regulatory reform' could boost global investment, and similar impulses now would render the UK 'the world's most innovative and competitive global financial centre'. Once again, blind to the warning of the financial crash, a government in economic distress put its faith in a less regulated finance sector. To bolster this signal, he cut the tax surcharge on bankers' profits, to the cost of £1.4 billion annually, and endorsed the removal of the cap on bankers' bonuses, that had been imposed across the EU since 2014.[98]

In short, a government promising low taxation, fiscal efficiency, and robust private-sector growth, presided over the opposite, having failed to address fundamentals like poor skills and infrastructure, low productivity, feeble public and private investment relative to other G7 countries, and acute social inequality. It grappled with a series of contradictions, between: ambitions to be Singapore-on-the-Thames, yet with taxes as a share of GDP being at their highest in almost four decades; a monetary policy designed to dampen inflation and a fiscal policy that could not over-dampen demand amidst a recession; improving its trade and earning capacity, while battling with its nearest and biggest trading partner, the EU, post-Brexit; playing the culture wars with anti-immigrant rhetoric, while needing immigration to plug a hole in its weak labour market; and facing a despondent electorate, paying more for worse public services.

In such dire circumstance, it would be hardly unreasonable for those who pay their fair share to think that they are being taken for fools by a system that accords exceptional benefits to the uberwealthy. But since public spending retrenchment is scheduled to kick-in mostly by 2025, when it is probable that Labour will be in government, this poses its own challenge for that party. Is it going to accept these targets and frameworks to placate the market that can always be expected to test its business credibility? Or is it is going to be bold in taxing property, dividends, inherited wealth, housing capital gains, private education, and off-shore tax scams in a distributive re-balance between capital and labour?

That ineffectual people like Truss and Johnson were ever considered eligible for the role is testament to the bizarre politics of this period. Truss came to the premiership openly boasting about her intent to be a disrupter, echoing Facebook's early motto: *move fast and break things*. She certainly succeeded in both, to the cost of many. Amid the discomfort of the mutinous Tory Party, and its shattered reputation for fiscal discipline, it was tempting for the Labour Party to rejoice in the debacle. That was the wrong lesson. In essence, the havoc showed who was boss. And in his attempt to placate the financial system, the new Chancellor acknowledged this commanding power, declaring that politicians could not, and should not try to, control the markets. But if the markets are in ultimate control, and yet they often operate out-of-control, what becomes of the Brexit promise of taking back control?

Truss and Kwarteng saw themselves as servants of the markets, and yet the markets turned on them. Clearly, those that live by the markets can die by them. For many, it reaffirmed the idea that in global capitalism, there is no alternative to such subjugation, whatever your democratic mandate to the contrary. For a country that prides itself on stability, it was internationally humiliating for the UK to have four prime ministers in six years, each one less competent than their predecessor. Together with four finance ministers in four months, this unprecedented upheaval speaks volumes about the chaotic state of contemporary times and the fatuous leadership it can generate. Moreover, Labour's sums didn't add up either. To avoid accusation that they were incorrigibly addicted to tax and profligate spending, they foolishly supported aspects of the Truss package, such as a cut in the basic rate of income tax. That left them properly embarrassed when this measure was reversed.

While the UK is in undeniably dire straits, facets of the malaise are universally manifest. Partly as an aftermath of bail-outs, stimulus programmes and supply-side snarl-ups, we have double digit global inflation. As the Federal Reserve responds to this, its rising interest rates have boosted the dollar to its highest value in nearly twenty years, while its constrictive monetary policy has impacted negatively on other trading countries, in tandem with their similar retrenchment. Central banks in major economies have for some time been purchasing bonds to keep the show on the road. According to the *Economist*, just preceding the pandemic, the central banks in the US, Europe and Japan 'owned a staggering $15 trillion of financial assets'. Addressing this dismal picture in late 2022, it noted:[99]

> *Global shares have dropped by 25 percent in dollar terms, the worst year since at least the 1980s, and government bonds are on course for their worst year since 1949. Alongside some $40trillion of losses there is a queasy sense that the world order is being upended as globalisation heads into retreat and the energy system is fractured after Russia's invasion of Ukraine.*

Left Behind

The very opacity of this erratic system makes it seem that nobody is in charge. The real crisis of confidence stems from the elusive solution to the turbulence. Along with bereft communities, the politicians have been left behind the curve of high-speed finance. If there is an answer, it lies buried in a complex web of socio-economic change stretching back decades that have eroded social cohesion and trust in the most unequal societies.[100] Where these have democratic credentials, the democracy has become more 'unequal', as the wealthy lobby to protect their position.[101] Persistent deep inequality can normalise it as inevitable, with the most privileged finding it easy to convince themselves that their status is deserved. Such entitlement contrasts with the scorn assigned to the 'undeserving' poor, juxtaposing strivers and skivers – a 'divide and rule' tactic well-practiced in the conservative handbook. Given the time-lessness of these tactics, this can't be the immediate cause of the left's poor showing.

No question, the fall of communism by the late 1980s supported the maxim that there was no alternative to markets and privatism. It squeezed the political space for radical substitutes. There's also no question that communism deserved to fall. Politically totalitarian, while economically incompetent, its self-regard was in inverse proportion to its social achievement. Paradoxically, those countries with 'workers', 'people's republic' or 'democratic' in their name proved to be the least worthy of any of those titles.

Some years ago, I visited Budapest's Momento Park, where removed statues of communist icons like Lenin are assembled together in all their vainglory. You can see in one desolate place the tyranny of false heroes, as monumental in their disastrous legacy as they are in their outsized physicality. For all its championing of the common people, the system was a leadership cult. Looking now at this politburo in stone, you're reminded of its awful hubris.

And now we can only despair at the death, or at least near-death, experience of European social democracy – the genuine variety, not the deformed managerialist incarnation. Blame has been attached to the loss of a solidarity culture with the decline of blue-collar jobs; the reshaping of progressive politics with the advent of 'green' perspectives; and the role of identity politics around gender, race, and sexuality in distracting from issues of class inequality. Beyond that, politicians like Blair, Clinton, Schroder, and Hollande have been censured for compromising with neo-liberalism as a 'third way' between capitalism and socialism, thereby distilling social democracy to some extra crumbs from the table of the new super-rich.

In terms of principled ideology, they are seen as having committed suicide to avoid being murdered.[102] They colluded, at least inadvertently, with a de-politisation of social inequities, inferring that problems can be redressed in a technocratic managerialism, stripped of ideology. As such, they departed from the core social democratic impulse of liberating citizens from being dehumanised, by having every aspect of their lives commodified and monetised.[103]

Most recently, it seems sometimes that we're in a period of political 'cross-dressing'. Leftist parties participate in coalitions that impose austerity. At the same time, Boris Johnson's government talked more about tax rises than cuts; operated a Keynesian stimulus in response to COVID-19; employed a rhetoric about 'levelling up' as a signal of allegiance to his party's new-found friends in northern working class constituencies; and did not demur automatically from state-assistance to ailing industry. As such conservative politics appears to move left on economics, it ups the ante to the right on culture. Ministers are decked by union jacks on television interviews. Stricter law inhibiting protests is introduced. Reclaiming imperialist history, as a source of pride rather than apology, includes severe penalty for those defacing statues glorifying this disreputable past. The supposed 'woke' bias of the BBC is subject to attack, and so on. By contrast, the liberal left is depicted as a self-righteous, snooty, privileged elite, that is derisive of large parts of the working class as bigoted and brainless.[104] Unsurprisingly, some turn to the Tories as their true defenders.

Something similar is apparent in the US.[105] Yes, Trump won the electoral college narrowly in 2016, and was defeated badly in both the national vote and electoral college in 2020. While this defeat was due in part to his relative loss of non-college educated white men, he secured the largest share of non-white voters by any Republican since 1960. Moreover, Biden's platform stole elements of Trump's economic nationalism to appeal to rustbelt states. Bill Clinton's boast about New Democrats seeing off the era of big government has been reversed with Biden's super-big government. Assuredly, the political dial is wobbling.

In the case of the US, is this because the right have won the economic argument? Or is the left – such as it is in the US – moving with the grain of demographics that favour an urban, educated, socially liberal, and culturally diverse electorate, inherently sympathetic to Democrats, but hidden from full view at present because of a distorted electoral system, aided and abetted by voter suppression? If we were to 'follow the money' on this one, we can see how the botched sedition by Trump supporters induced many big corporations to distance themselves from such unseemly scenes. We can note James Murdoch's belated repudiation of the disinformation propagated by elements of US media, and most recently companies like Delta and Coca-Cola railing against Georgia's new restrictive electoral legislation. Is this sign that big firms know what side their bread is now buttered? Leading Republican, Mitch McConnell, warned corporations against becoming a 'woke parallel government' intent on 'taking cues from the Outrage-Industrial Complex', whereby they 'amplify disinformation or react to every manufactured controversy with frantic left-wing signalling'.[106]

Well, let's not be fooled by performative over-reaction to corporate hollow rebukes. McConnell was a leading light in getting billionaires like the DeVos family to finance a case before the Supreme Court that ended with the

Citizens United decision facilitating unrestricted, and sometimes undetectable, campaign-finance from business donors – a boon to Republicans.[107] Indeed, what about the corporate contributions to Trump's campaign, long after it was obvious that he lacked the decency and decorum for high office? What about the corporate lobbying for his agenda of tax cuts and deregulation? As Reich notes:[108] 'they change sides with the electoral wind to keep their place at the table'. Similarly, James Murdoch's anguish about distorted media contaminating democracy represents a late conversion from a leading player in the Murdoch empire for so long.[109]

All this has to be seen in the way the world shares its 'spoils'. In many parts of the industrial world, and in emerging economies like China and India, the three decades up to 1980 showed reduction of inequality, and accompanying improvement in productivity and prosperity. But in their association of welfare capitalism with the tribulations of stagflation by the late seventies, conservatives like Reagan and Thatcher argued that high taxes, regulation, over-generous social programmes and benefits, and bolshie unions, penalised enterprise and hindered growth. Their prescription for market liberalisation gained global traction and augured widespread rise of inequality. So, in 2021, with global income amounting to €86 trillion and global net wealth at six times this value, €510 trillion, the distribution of this fortune was badly divided. The poorest half of the world, comprising 2.5 billion adults, accounts for just 8.5 percent of global income. The middle 40 percent – 2 billion adults – earn 39 percent of the share. But the top 10 percent – 517 million adults – receive 52 percent of the total. When it comes to global wealth, the situation is even more stark, with the world's poorest half owning just 2 percent of global net wealth, leaving the richest half with the treasure trove of 98 percent. Breaking this down further, the middle 40 percent owns 22 percent of total wealth, while the top 10 percent owns 76 percent. In summary, 'the world is marked by a very high level of income inequality and an extreme level of wealth inequality'.[110]

Unsurprisingly, the most equal area (Europe) holds attraction for many from the most unequal, Middle East and North Africa (MENA). While the income share of the European top 10 percent is about 36 percent, in MENA, it stretches to 58 percent. Great disparities can prevail in high income countries, for example between the acutely unequal US and the fairly equal Sweden. This contrast sits within a general pattern of reduced inequality *between* countries and widened inequality *within* countries:[111]

> *The gap between the average incomes of the top 10 percent and the bottom 50 percent of individuals within countries has almost doubled, from 8.5x to 15x.....This sharp rise in within country inequalities has meant that despite economic catch-up and strong growth in the emerging countries, the world remains particularly unequal today. It also means that inequalities within countries are now even greater than the significant inequalities observed between countries.*

As Piketty and colleagues argue, inequality is always a political choice, reversible through alternative public policy. A small wealth tax on the concentrated affluence of the global rich could make a big difference. They suggest that one redistributive scenario, raising 1.6 percent of global revenue, could have transformative impact on investment in health, education, and ecological transition.

Out of Order

So where are we with finding a viable democratic way of addressing how the world makes and shares wealth, in the context of a global economy dominated by capitalism for the foreseeable future? Search for a stable, equitable and prosperous outcome for capitalist economics has seen a long political journey from laissez-faire (non-government intervention) to Keynesianism (managing aggregate demand) to Monetarism (controlling money supply) to flexible managerialism, mainly by Central Banks, via modulation of short-term interest rates. In response to the financial crisis, and subsequently to the pandemic's economic disruption, the Central Banks have tried to stimulate demand by lowering interest rates and printing money. Despite such substantial effort to reinvigorate financial supply, and thereby economic activity, growth has been lethargic. Is it because the mass of consumers, as labour, have seen their purchasing power fall with widening social inequality, due to factors such as weakened labour organisation and inadequate state-based social protection? Is it related also to the way fiscal stimulus has been used to buy government and corporate bonds, a process which has contributed to inflated value of stocks and shares, and thereby to the increased share of wealth held by the already rich, who are more prone to save than spend most of their money?[112]

Demand driven by debt – both public and private – seemed to be feasible within a certain capitalist logic. The debt is owned by wealthy investors, whose high savings rate has helped to keep interest rates low. Low cost borrowing has, in turn, continued to make public and private deficit spending appear viable, maybe even sensible. De-regulation of finance further helped to flood the market with accessible loans. But over time, this process of feeding 'indebted demand' shifts more wealth from borrowers to savers, thereby increasing structural inequality. This very long-term pattern of entrenched inequality, and related factors such as reduced social mobility, itself becomes a drag on economic development. Consequent modest growth rates provide further inducement for Central Banks to suppress interest rates. However, to service high public debt, government is pressed to raise taxes and/or cut public services, both of which act as 'austerity' in depressing demand. This contributes to what has been called 'a debt-driven liquidity trap', which causes the economy to underperform to its potential, in capitalist terms. This may just about be manageable in a low interest rate environment. But with external global shocks – the pandemic and Ukrainian war, both disrupting supplies of basics like energy and food – inflationary pressures have mounted rapidly, pushing up the price of borrowing.[113]

Indeed, this came to pass in 2022. The perfect storm erupted. Populations, pummelled by long-term patterns of industrial contraction, rising inequality, and the austerity programmes that followed publicly-funded bank bailouts, were further battered with the economic fallout of the pandemic and Russian aggression. Meanwhile, the scope for government social compensation was compromised by the use of higher interest rates to curb inflation, a monetary move that made servicing public debt more expensive, and contributed to deflation of the economy. Low to no growth, with high inflation, augured the mire of stagflation, which in turn squeezed fiscal space for public intervention. This sorry scenario was dubbed a 'cost of living' crisis. But it was really the cost of a failed system of finance, underpinned by a flawed energy policy, misdirected criteria for economic success, and a corrupt use of money to subvert not only tax justice and social protection, but democratic government itself. In many countries, the social safety net is so threadbare that any shock – internal or external – impacts the poor very badly, since they've no reserves for hard times. As history reminds us, a gilded age for the rich and powerful proves to be a rusted cage for the impoverished and marginal.

An alternative agenda – examined in outline in the conclusion, and in further detail in volume two – would include: prudential and regulated finance; redistributive policies to reverse deepening inequality; application of technology to redefine meaningful work; and conversion to sustainable energy. The real bind here is the 'democratic deficit' that springs from the failure of a left/liberal coalition to offer a viable vision of such a programme.

In recent decades, the left has achieved power in most places very conditionally. Either, it's had to concede to austerity policies. Or, it's had to adopt fiscal measures to rein in the debt accumulated by the previous conservative administrations. Because the left tends to be mistrusted on how to run a capitalist economy, it tends to only get a chance at government when conservative administrations really foul up. Hence, left governments, inheriting the mess, and under pressure to prove their economic competence, feel obliged to adopt fiscal rectitude. This, in turn, disappoints their natural base, whose subsequent disillusion deters some from voting to return the government. This pattern partly explains why conservative parties can boast about being the 'natural' party of government in many western societies.

Taking the UK as an example, I've seen in my lifetime 11 leaders of the Labour Party. Only two were elected as Prime Minister, Wilson and Blair. Two others – Callaghan and Brown took over the premiership mid-term. Going back further to 1918, Labour has won only 8 out of 28 general elections. This abysmal record is offset somewhat by acknowledging that of the more than 700 million votes cast in such elections from that time, around 300 million were for Labour – in other words, the electoral contest was closer than the first-past-the-post system reflected in Parliamentary seats.[114] The devastating defeat in 2019 left Labour with less than a third of the 650 Commons seats, the worst performance since the mid-1930s.

For the Opposition to lose so badly, after nine years and four elections in that role, is historically unprecedented. In Scotland, once a heartland for Labour, the party had a meltdown, winning just half its 2017 vote, and only one out of the 59 seats. Recently, Peter Mandelson[115] expressed the dismal state of the British Labour party in the immediate aftermath of the 2019 debacle in terms of its electoral failure: '....the last 11 general elections read: lose, lose, lose, lose, Blair, Blair, Blair, lose, lose, lose, lose'.

Paradoxically, Labour is being hit badly in the most depressed regions, from where young people are moving for work and study. This is because there's now a clear age divide in party affinity. In 2019, Labour achieved 62 percent of the under-25 vote, and 51 percent of the 25–34 age group voters, whereas amongst the over-65s, the Tories had a huge 47 point lead. This older cohort, benefiting to some extent from pension protection and the asset of home ownership, was also particularly prone to favour Brexit and the conservative side in the culture wars. The party's review of the defeat recognises that the cultural divide has left some voters thinking that Labour no longer represents, or is listening to, them. With a simplistic slogan about getting Brexit done, Tories mobilised around 2 million who were non-voters in 2017, accounting for almost two-thirds of their increased vote in 2019. Labour were left with only a third of its Leave-inclined voters.[116]

The lesson for the British Labour Party is one for all progressive movements. The left gets left behind when its bonds loosen with those who feel left behind. Undoubtedly, Brexit crossed cultural and economic issues, complicating the political landscape. In 94 percent of places in Britain, where foreign-born populations more than doubled between 2001–2014, people opted to leave. This is despite the fact that the immigrant share in those areas was still relatively low. Yet most areas where foreign-born populations accounted for more than 30 percent, voted to remain. One deduction is that it's not the high migrant numbers that perturb people, but rather the high rate of change in those numbers.[117] People feel unmoored amid rapid tides.

This section has addressed these troubled times, in terms of their cultural, political and economic fallout. Promises about 'taking back control' have proved to be deceptive. Rather, marked social inequality and disturbance have splintered society further into rival groupings, prone to accentuated conflict and mutual misunderstanding. To what extent is this familiar story part of the human condition? Next we move into the second section, which overall looks at the *roots* of, and *routes* from, tribal belonging. It takes a long view of where we've come from as a species, and where we might be headed. The opening chapter explores what it means to be human; whether from their origin, humans have been inherently clannish and competitive; the role of culture in societal development; the nature versus nurture debate in the context of much greater understanding about genes; and indeed whether human nature itself is set to undergo what is called *human enhancement*.

Notes

1 The Economist Intelligence Unit (EIU) (2022) *Democracy Index 2021: The China Challenge*. London: EI.
2 www.economist.com/middle-east-and-africa/2021/03/08/nigers-president-wins-the-ibrahim-african-leadership-prize. Accessed on: 5 April 2021.
3 Institute for Democracy and Electoral Assistance (IDEA) (2022) *Global State of Democracy Report 2021: Building Resilience in a Pandemic Era*. IDEA.
4 Eatwell, R. and Goodwin, M. (2018) *National Populism: The Revolt Against Liberal Democracy*. London: Pelican Books.
5 Furedi, F. (2021) *Democracy Under Siege: Don't Let Them Lock It Down*. Hampshire: Zero Books.
6 Diamond, L. and Plattner, M. (eds) (2016) *Democracy in Decline?* Baltimore: John Hopkins University Press.
7 Luce, E. (2017) *The Retreat of Western Liberalism*. London: Little, Brown.
8 Levitsky, Steven and Daniel Ziblatt (2018) *How Democracies Die: What History Reveals About Our Future*. New York: Penguin.
9 Mair, P. (2013) *Ruling the Void: The Hollowing of Western Democracy*. London: Verso.
10 Fuller, R. (2019) *In Defence of Democracy*. Cambridge: Polity Press.
11 Varoufakis, Y. (5 April 2016) Why We Must Save the EU. *The Guardian*.
12 Abramovitz, M. and Hopkins, T. (1983) Reaganomics and the Welfare State, *The Journal of Sociology & Social Welfare*: 10 (4), Article 4. Available at: https://scholarwo rks.wmich.edu/jssw/vol10/iss4/4
13 Lind, M. (2020) *The New Class War: Saving Democracy from the Metropolitan Elite*. London: Atlantic Books.
14 *Ibid*. 81.
15 *Ibid*. 23.
16 *Ibid*. 123.
17 Department for Business, Energy and Industrial Strategy (27 May 2020) *Trade Union Membership, UK 1995–2019*. Statistical Bulletin 27. UK Gov.
18 Chi Dao, M., Das, M., Koczan, Z., and Lian, W. (July 2017) *Why Is Labor Receiving a Smaller Share of Global Income? Theory and Empirical Evidence*. IMF Working Paper. 17/169. 5.
19 International Labour Organization; Organisation for Economic Co-operation and Development; with contributions from International Monetary Fund and World Bank Group (2015) *The Labour Share in G20 Economies*. Geneva: ILO.
20 International Labour Organisation (ILO) (2020) *World Employment and Social Outlook: Trends 2020*. Geneva: International Labour Office.
21 International Labour Organisation (ILO) (2022) *World Employment and Social Outlook: Trends 2022*. Geneva: International Labour Office.
22 International Labour Organisation (ILO) (2020) *op. cit.*
23 Stiglitz, J.E. (2002) *Globalization and its Discontents*. London: Penguin Books.

24 Galbraith, J. K. (2020) Economics and the Climate Catastrophe. *Globalizations.* DOI: 10.1080/14747731.2020.1807858. Accessed on: 5 April 2021.

25 Tooze, A. (2 June 2020) The Death of Globalisation Has Been Announced Many Times. But This is a Perfect Storm. *The Guardian.*

26 Rodrik, D. (2011) *The Globalisation Paradox: Why Global Markets, States, and Democracy Can't Coexist.* Oxford: Oxford University Press.

27 Smil, V. (2019) *Growth: From Microorganisms to Megacities.* Cambridge, Massachusetts: MIT Press.

28 Heine, J., and Thakur, R. (Eds.) (2011). *The Dark Side of Globalization.* Tokyo/New York/Paris: United Nations University Press.

29 Potrafke, N. (2015) The Evidence on Globalization. *The World Economy* 38(3) 509–552.

30 Rifkin, J. (2011) *op. cit.* 202–203.

31 Hellmann, T., Schmidt, P., and Heller, S.M. (2019) *Social Justice in the EU and OECD: Index Report 2019.* Germany: Bertelsmann Stiftung.

32 World Justice Project (2021) *World Justice Project Rule of Law Index 2021.* Washington: WJP.

33 Beard, A. (January-February 2022) Can Big Tech Be Disrupted? Extracted from *Harvard Business Review.* https://hbr.org/2022/01/can-big-tech-be-disrupted. Accessed on: 15 May 2022.

34 Statista (February 2022) *Market Capitalization of the Largest U.S. Internet Companies as of February 2022.* www.statista.com/statistics/209331/largest-us-internet-compan ies-by-market-cap. Accessed on: 15 May 2022.

35 Fair Tax Mark (December 2019) *The Silicon Six and Their $100 Billion Global Tax Gap.* Manchester: Fair Tax Mark.

36 The Irish Fiscal Advisory Council (November 2019) *Fiscal Assessment Report.* Dublin: IFAC.

37 Cobham, A., Faccio, T. and FitzGerald, V. (October 2019) *Global Inequalities in Taxing Rights: An Early Evaluation of the OECD tax Reform Proposals.* A Preliminary Draft.

38 OECD (8 October 2021) *International Community Strikes a Ground-breaking Tax Deal for the Digital Age.* Paris: OECD. www.oecd.org/newsroom/international-commun ity-strikes-a-ground-breaking-tax-deal-for-the-digital-age. Accessed on: 16 October 2021.

39 Bunn, D. and Bray, S. (7 April 2022) *What's in the New Global Tax Agreement?* Tax Foundation. https://taxfoundation.org/global-tax-agreement. Accessed on: 15 May 2022.

40 Fair Tax. *How Do Companies Avoid Tax?* https://fairtaxmark.net/wp-content/uplo ads/2014/01/How-Companies-Avoid-Tax.pdf. Accessed on: 17 March 2021.

41 Shaxson, N. (2011) *Treasure Islands: Tax Havens and the Men who Stole the World.* London: Palgrave Macmillan.

42 Global Alliance for Tax Justice (GATJ); Public Services International (PSI); Tax Justice Network (TJN) (November 2021) *The State of Tax Justice 2021.* Bristol: GATJ; PSI; TJN.

43 *Ibid.* 6.

44 *Ibid.* 7

45 *Ibid.* 10.

46 The Economist Explains (4 October 2021) How Do People and Companies Avoid Paying Taxes? *The Economist.*

47 Cobham, A. and Janský, P. (2017) *Global Distribution of Revenue Loss from Tax Avoidance: Re-estimation and Country Results.* WIDER Working Paper 2017/55. Helsinki: UNU-WIDER.

48 Shaxson, N. (2018) *The Finance Curse: How Global Finance is Making Us All Poorer.* London: Bodley Head.

49 Bullough, O. (2018) *Moneyland: Why Thieves & Crooks Now Rule the World & How to Take it Back.* London: Profile Books.

50 *Ibid.* 11.

51 Henry, J.S. (July 2010) *The Price of Offshore Revisited: New Estimates for 'Missing' Global Private Wealth, Income, Inequality and Lost Taxes.* Tax Justice Network & James S. Henry.

52 Zucman, G. (2015) *The Hidden Wealth of Nations: The Scourge of Tax Havens.* Chicago: University of Chicago Press.

53 See: Guardian Editorial (28 May 2013) Dave Hartnett: One Sweetheart Deal Too Many. *The Guardian*; Syal, R. (29 April 2013) Revealed: 'Sweetheart' Tax Deals Each Worth Over £1bn. *The Guardian;* Murphy, R. (22 October 2010) Vodafone's Tax Case Leaves a Sour Taste. *The Guardian*; and Qdos Contractor (3 October 2012) Ex-Revenue Supremo's Party Hijacked. *Contractor's Weekly.*

54 Advani, A., Burgherr, D., Savage, M. and Summers, A. (April 2022) *The UK's 'Non-doms': Who Are They, What Do They Do, and Where Do They Live?* CAGE Policy Briefing, No. 36. CAGE Warwick University and LSE International Inequalities Institute.

55 The Economist Explains. (8 April 2022) What Are Non-doms, and Why Does It Matter that Rishi Sunak's Wife Is One? *The Economist.*

56 Editorial (15 April 2022) Britain's Non-dom Tax Laws: One Rule for the Rich and Another for Everyone Else. *The Guardian Weekly.*

57 Shaxson, N. (16 June 2021) Making Sure the 'Big People' Pay their Taxes Would Be a Boost to Democracy. *The Guardian.*

58 Rowlingson, K., Sood, A., and Tu, T. (2020) *Public Attitudes to a Wealth Tax.* Wealth Tax Commission Evidence Paper 2.

59 Advani, A., Chamberlain, E., and Summers, A. (December 2020) *A Wealth Tax for the UK: Final Report.* The UK Wealth Tax Commission. London School of Economics and Political Science; University of Warwick; UK Economic and Social Research Council; Atlantic Fellows for Social & Economic Equity; CAGE.

60 Eisinger, J., Ernsthausen, J., and Kiel, P. (2021) The Secret IRS Files: Trove of Never-Before-Seen Records Reveal How the Wealthiest Avoid Income Tax. *ProPublica.* See: www.propublica.org/article/the-secret-irs-files-trove-of-never-bef ore-seen-records-reveal-how-the-wealthiest-avoid-income-tax. Accessed on: 17 June 2021.

61 Press Statement (28 February 2022) *Stats Reveal the Extent of Suspect Wealth in UK Property and Britain's Role As Global Money Laundering Hub.* Transparency International UK. www.transparency.org.uk/uk-money-laundering-stats-russia-suspicious-wealth. Accessed on: 15 May 2022.

62 Leader (4 th February 2022:Updated May 13th 2022) Why Does So Much Dodgy Russian Money End up in Britain? *The Economist.*

63 Heathershaw, J., Cooley, A., Mayne, T., Michel, C., Prelec, T., Sharman, J. and Soares de Oliveira, R. (December 2021) *The UK's Kleptocracy Problem: How Servicing Post-Soviet Elites Weakens the Rule of Law*. Research Paper. Russia and Eurasia Programme.London: Chatham House. 9.

64 *Ibid.*

65 *Ibid.* 20.

66 *Ibid.* 35–36.

67 *Ibid.* 42.

68 *Ibid.* 44.

69 British Virgin Islands Commission Of Inquiry (4 April 2022) *Report Of The Commissioner The RT Hon Sir Gary Hickinbottom: Volume 1: Report*. Published on the Authority of the Governor of the Virgin Islands. 7.

70 Durbin, A. (29 April 2022) British Virgin Islands: Premier Andrew Fahie Arrested in US Drug Sting. *BBC News*. www.bbc.co.uk/news. Accessed on: 16 May 2022.

71 BBC (22 October 2020) *Goldman Sachs to Pay $3bn Over 1MDB Corruption Scandal*; and Wright, T. and Hope, B. (2019) *Billion Dollar Whale: The Man Who Fooled Wall St., Hollywood, and the World*. London: Scribe; and Masters, B. (27 July 2020) Goldman Has Done it Again with its Malaysia Deal. *Financial Times*.

72 The United States Department of Justice: Office of Public Affairs (22 October 2020) *Goldman Sachs Charged in Foreign Bribery Case and Agrees to Pay over $2.9 Billion*. The United States Department of Justice.

73 United States Department of Justice. Case 1:12-cr-00763-ILG Document 3–3 Filed 12/11/12. *Statement of Facts*.

74 *Ibid.*

75 Taibbi, M. (8 July 2015) Eric Holder, Wall Street Double Agent, Comes in From the Cold. *Rolling Stone*.

76 Baum, D. (April 2016) Legalize it All: How to Win the War on Drugs. *Harper's Magazine*.

77 United States Department of Justice: Office of Public Affairs (19 November 2013) *Justice Department, Federal and State Partners Secure Record $13 billion Global Settlement with JPMorgan for Misleading Investors About Securities Containing Toxic Mortgages*.

78 Shaban, H. (29 September 2020) JPMorgan Chase to Pay $920 Million to Resolve Illegal Trading Cases. *Washington Post*.

79 Reporting Team BBC Panorama (20 September 2020) *FinCEN Files*. BBC: www.bbc.co.uk/news/business-41877932. Accessed on: 21 March 2021.

80 International Consortium of Investigative Journalists (ICIJ) (8 February 2015) *Banking Giant HSBC Sheltered Murky Cash Linked to Dictators and Arms Dealers*. www.icij.org/investigations/swiss-leaks/banking-giant-hsbc-sheltered-murky-cash-linked-dictators-and-arms-dealers/ Accessed on: 21 March 2021.

81 International Consortium of Investigative Journalists (ICIJ) (3 October 2021) *Offshore Havens and Hidden Riches of World Leaders and Billionaires Exposed in Unprecedented Leak*. Washington: ICIJ. www.icij.org/investigations/pandora-papers/global-investigation-tax-havens-offshore. Accessed on: 16 October 2021.

82 OECD (30 June 2020) *International Community Continues Making Progress Against Offshore Tax Evasion*. Paris: OECD. www.oecd.org/tax/transparency/documents/international-community-continues-making-progress-against-offshore-tax-evasion. Accessed on: 16 October 2021.

83 Forbes (2 June, 2006) A Loophole For Poor Mr. Paulson. *Forbes Magazine*.

84 Neate, R. (31 March 2021) How David Cameron Got Caught Up in a Classic Lobbying Scandal. *The Guardian*.

85 See: Smith, R. and Pickard, J. (undated) Greensill Capital Paid Cameron Salary of More Than $1 million a Year. *Financial Times*; Courea, E. (13 July 2021) David Cameron Earned £29,000 a Day as Greensill Lobbyist. *The Times*.; and Chaplain, C. (9 August 2021) David Cameron 'Made £7.2m in Salary and Bonuses Lobbying for Greensill Capital' i:https://inews.co.uk/news/politics/david-cameron-made-7-2m-in-salary-and-bonuses-lobbying-for-greensill-capital. Accessed on: 23 August 2021.

86 Monbiot, G. (31 October 2011)The Medieval, Unaccountable Corporation of London is Ripe for Protest. *The Guardian*.

87 City of London Local Plan. Proposed Submission Draft (March 2021) *City Plan 2036: Shaping the Future City*. London: City of London Corporation. 9.

88 Shaxson, N. (24 February 2011) The Tax Haven in the Heart of Britain. *New Statesman*.

89 Quoted in: Bretherton, L. (2015) *Resurrecting Democracy: Faith, Citizenship, and the Politics of a Common Life*. New York: Cambridge University Press. 67.

90 Hopkins, K. (21 October 2009) Public Must Learn to 'Tolerate the Inequality' of Bonuses, says Goldman Sachs Vice-Chairman. *The Guardian*.

91 Treanor, J. (11 January 2011) Bob Diamond Stands Firm Against MPs' Calls he Forgo his Bonus. *The Guardian*.

92 Lingoed-Thomas, J. (10 October 2021) Outrage Over £125m Bonuses for Staff at UK's 'Failing' Financial Watchdog. *The Observer*.

93 Emmerson, C. and Stockton, I. (October 2022) *Outlook for the Public Finances*. Report R220. London: IFS.

94 IFS (8 September 2022) *Response to the Energy Price Guarantee*. London: IFS.

95 Emmerson, C. and Stockton, I. (October 2022) *op.cit.*

96 *Ibid.*

97 Wheeler, C. and Yorke, H. (16 October 2022) Hunt Takes Full Control As Plotters Circle Wounded PM. *The Sunday Times*.

98 Inman, P. (20 November 2022) A Big Bang for the City, A Damp Squib for the Country. *The Observer*.

99 The Economist (6 October 2022) A Great Rebalancing Between Governments and Central Banks is Under Way. *The Economist*.

100 Larsen, C. A. (2013) *The Rise and Fall of Social Cohesion: The Construction and Deconstruction of Social Trust in the US, UK, Sweden and Denmark*. Oxford: Oxford University Press.

101 Bartels, L. M. (2008) *Unequal Democracy: The Political Economy of the New Gilded Age*. Princeton, NJ: Princeton University Press.

102 This is paraphrased from an expression used in: Gouldner, A. (Winter 1962) Anti-Minotaur: The Myth of a Value-Free Sociology. *Social Problems*. 9 (3). 199–213.

103 Keane, J. (2016) *Money, Capitalism and the Slow Death of Social Democracy*. www.johnkeane.net/money-capitalism-and-the-slow-death-of-social-democracy. Accessed on: 7 April 2021.

104 Harris, J. (14 March 2021) The Conservatives are Now the Party of England. Changing That Will be Hard. *The Guardian*.

105 Hammond, S. (6 November 2020) Democrats Beware: the Republicans will Soon be the Party of the Working Class. *The Guardian*.

106 Levin, B. (6 April 2021) Mitch Mc Connell Doesn't Have a Problem with Corporations Getting Involved in Politics When He's Suckling at the Corporate Teat. *Vanity Fair.*

107 *Ibid.*

108 Reich, R. (24 January 2021) Don't Believe the Anti-Trump Hype – Corporate Sedition still Endangers America. *The Observer.*

109 Busby, M. (16 January 2021) James Murdoch Says US Media 'Lies' Unleashed 'Insidious Forces'. *The Guardian.*

110 Chancel, L., Piketty, T., Saez, E., Zucman, G. et al. (2022) *World Inequality Report 2022*, World Inequality Lab. 27.

111 *Ibid.* 11.

112 Economist Article (25 July 2020) The COVID-19 Pandemic is Forcing a Rethink in Macroeconomics. *The Economist.*

113 Mian, A., Straub, L., and Sufi, A. (24 January 2021) Indebted Demand. *Quarterly Journal of Economics.* 136 (4). 2243–2307. Publisher's Version. https://scholar.harvard.edu/straub/publications/indebted-demand. Accessed on: 17 May 2022.

114 Brown, D. & Barnes, P. (10 February 2020) Labour Leadership: A Century of Ups and Downs in Charts. *BBC News.* Source: House of Commons Library/BBC Research 2020.

115 Quoted in: Walker, P. (7 May 2021) Keir Starmer Under Pressure from Labour Left After 'Disappointing Night'. *The Guardian.*

116 Labour Together (2021) *Election Review 2019: Key Findings and Summary Recommendations.* https://electionreview.labourtogether.uk/ Accessed on: 7 April 2021.

117 Smil, V. (2019) *op. cit.*

PART II
Hello Goodbye

This second part of the book follows from the tribal contests covered in Section One, and probes the origins of this tribal belonging from our genesis. In exploring what makes us human, the relative importance of nature and nurture is explored, as are the limits of human intelligence. Given that in terms of Earth time, we've just really said 'hello' to the planet, the question is posed as to whether we're about to say 'goodbye' – whether humans are headed for self-extinction with climate change, and other mainly human-induced threats in the Anthropocene.

The section concludes with another scenario for the human story – that we're headed into post-humanism, and the surveillance society, led by artificial intelligence, and supervised by big tech. In essence, the following three chapters examine how, in our human development, we're bound for doom or bloom. Or is it all more complicated than such binaries suggest?

DOI: 10.4324/9781003106593-7

6

ONLY HUMAN

Making Sense of Sapiens

In Walt Whitman's remarkable poem, *Song of Myself*, he talks about how within 'the common air that bathes the globe', he sees himself in all people, since for every atom belonging to him 'as good belongs to you'. Regarding his being as 'untranslatable', he proclaims: 'I contain multitudes', a line that Bob Dylan borrowed for a recent song-title. Whitman was acknowledging that we're blends of many human mixes within a unity of the world. That's partly because we love to mix, and not only with each other.

We inhabit a planet reckoned to be 4.6 billion years old, in a universe about 13.7 billion years old. Lifeless Earth changed when its surface cooled and oceans formed, so that about 3.8 billion years ago, out of the primordial soup emerged self-replicating organisms, the first sign of life.

Not only does time take its toll. It's also on a roll. In other words, time changes over time. Back in the day, a day was different. This is because the earth once turned faster on its axis. Even fairly recently – between 250 million to 65 million years ago – when dinosaurs roamed, a day would be close to twenty-three hours. Of course for some, time is a matter of belief. I've often said to my students as we're climbing Belfast's Cave Hill that they're standing on 60 million years of basalt, unless they're Creationists, in which case it's 6,000 years. Recently, I revisited the Cliffs of Moher in Ireland's Wild Atlantic Way – sandstone and siltstone that layered into sediments of compact rock over 300 million years ago.

Around that time, the world's land mass was joined into one supercontinent, known as Pangaea, that over the Triassic (200 million years ago), Jurassic (150 million years ago) and Cretaceous (65 million years ago) periods broke up into the seven continents we know today.[1] In 1912, Alfred Wegener explained this process in terms of continental drift. One indication is how the eastern

DOI: 10.4324/9781003106593-8

border of South America and the western border of Africa look like a good fit in the Earth's jigsaw picture. Current understanding sees this pattern of continental joining and splitting as a cyclical process, dating back to the supercontinent, known as Kenorland, around 2.5 billion years ago. This rifting and shifting makes nonsense of any theory of nationalism that sees its integrity rooted in a permanent land formation.

All the Time in the World

Considering these timescales helps us appreciate how late in the day we arrived on the scene. We understand how bacteria, algae, and plants can reap sunlight and transfer that solar energy into chemical energy, through a process known as *photosynthesis*. This allows energy storage for future application, including creation of oxygen, which makes up a high share of the air that primates breathe. Primates arose a short time ago, around 55 million years, first from small terrestrial mammals, which adjusted to tree-living in tropical forests. It was some 66 million years ago that the great extinction of dinosaurs happened – thought to be due to a giant asteroid crashing to Earth. In April 2022, a fossil of a well-preserved dinosaur limb was discovered in Tanis, North Dakota, and it is purported that it was encased on the very day of the extinction.[2] Considerably after this catastrophe – between six to eight million years ago – the human and chimpanzee pedigrees took separate routes from the last shared ancestor.

We don't yet know that full story. But we do appreciate how more complex life forms like the ape took shape.[3] For example, Hominins are primates that comprise modern humans, vanished human species and all our direct forebears, such as those under the genus Homo, and Australopithecus and Ardipithecus. They are marked by certain traits: bigger brains, longer legs, upright bearing, bipedal movement, and conduct such as tool use, and possibly some primitive linguistic exchange.

For some time, it was thought that we were about 100,000 years old. More recently, the earliest remains of our species were designated as 195,000-year-old fossils found in Omo, Ethiopia. Thus, you'll often see our starting date put at around 200,000 years ago. Then in 2017, a find of skull fragments, jawbone and teeth in Jebel Irhoud, Morocco – over three thousand miles distant from East Africa, which had been considered the 'cradle' of our species – put the date at 315,000 years ago. A skull from Florisbad, South Africa, has been traced to 260,000 years ago. Debate remains over these latest finds. Are they *H-sapiens* or a very close subspecies? Do they represent the diversity of archaic and modern features at the earliest point of our emergence? If so, they suggest that the evolution of sapiens is associated with Africa as a whole, not just the traditionally assumed location of eastern and southern parts of the continent.[4]

Clearly, problems beset this timeline.[5] First, the literature offers different periods for different groupings within the Homo genus, which suggests how approximate we are about dates. Second, development was not linear. The famous picture in 1965, known as 'the march of progress', and depicting a gradual evolution to modern humans from earlier relatives, suggested steady chronology. Ongoing evidence shows its piecemeal character, depicting the human family tree as bushy rather than as a series of clean linked branches.

For instance in 2008, with the discovery of *Australopithecus sediba*, a two million year old hominin, and in 2015 with the revelation of a new find, *H-naledi*, that dates just before our assumed arrival, and in 2022 with another new unearthing of *H-boensis* in Bodo D'ar in Ethiopia dating back 500,000 years, some creatures show mixes of ape-like and human features, archaic and modern, that make them harder to locate in the transition to modern humans. Third, our lineage could go back further than we currently think. We may simply lack fossil evidence. Finally, interbreeding among ourselves and Neanderthals, and between the latter and Denisovans, complicate the picture further.

Interbreeding between two different human species involves what scientists dub: *introgression* – genetic fusion through admission of genetic material to one gene pool from another. One version has it that we came out of Africa around 60,000 to 80,000 years ago, and procreated with European Neanderthals to some extent. Neanderthals and Denisovans also mated. Indication of this has come with the recent discovery in Denisova Cave in Siberia's Altai Mountains of a girl's bone fragments, which evidence her Neanderthal mother and Denisovan father. Such cross-over is not so strange. Interbreeding between West Africans, such as modern Yoruba and Mende people, and unknown archaic hominins, started around 124,000 years ago;[6] and there is suggestion that Neanderthals and Denisovans interbred with 'superarchaic' ancestors of modern humans.[7]

All this leads some to speculate that, with respect to our lineage, instead of the metaphor of 'family tree', whether 'bushy' or not, we should be thinking more about a 'worldwide web',[8] that a good deal of hybridisation may have played a part in our speciation. Though traditionally we have thought about cross-breeding as a weakening process, or the concept of mongrel as negative, there is a view that hybrid offspring may benefit from enhanced biological attributes – hybrid vigour or *heterosis*.

In summary, at this point, our earliest ancestry is unclear, both in terms of date and location. Hominins make their entrance around six million years ago, in the Miocene epoch, which finished around 5.3 million years ago. From there, evolution stretched through Pliocene, Pleistocene and then Holocene, which began about 12,000 years ago, after the last Ice Age.[9] Amidst this flow, the genus *Homo* emerged around 2.5 million years ago, and within about half a million years, humans were living on, and traversing, African grasslands. Taken together, recent scholarship suggests that manifold early Homo groups had common features in physique, brain and teeth size, and adaptability in diet and living condition, to cope with changeable habitat as they spread out geographically and became globetrotters. Such traits were not all enveloped in any one 'brand' of early humans, but rather were permutated across them.[10]

In current scholarship, a lot of received wisdom for decades up until recently is being re-considered.[11] The break with chimps may have happened much earlier. Hominins may have become bipedal while still in trees. The notion that we all came out of the same stock in Africa – still the majority view – has been subject to revision. One alternative view sees us emerging in Africa, Europe, and Asia, all sprouting around the same time, from an earlier meandering species like *H-erectus,* reckoned to be the first hominin species to operate in groups larger than fifty, to use quite sophisticated tools, and to control fire.[12]

Portrayal of Neanderthals as significantly inferior to us is being corrected as indications surface regarding their cognitive capacity, reflected in such things as shelter-building, fire use, and burial. While it's still most likely that they did not morph into modern humans, but rather remained intact as a species until their extinction around 30–40,000 years ago, this may be contested if more evidence of interbreeding further clouds the picture. Discovery in 2003 of *H-floresiensis,* nick-named 'the hobbit' because of its small stature, on the Indonesian island of Flores, adds new complication. Now thought to be around 50,000 years old, the remains suggest a skull shape like *H-erectus* and a body shape more like the Australopithecines, another hybrid hard to pin on the Homo genus tree.

Alongside questions about lineage, further debate centres on how and when *sapiens* got to places like Europe, Australia and the Americas. Our distant relative, *H-erectus,* first arrived in Europe around 1.2 million years ago. Neanderthals evolved in Europe about 400,000 years ago. We have been thought to have come to Europe from the Middle East around 45,000 years ago. Fossil records of *H-sapiens* outside of Africa are 210,000 and 180,000 years ago, in southern Greece and the Levant, respectively. Discovery in 2020 of a set of seven footprints in a lake deposit in the Nefud Desert provided the oldest securely dated evidence for *H-sapiens* in Arabia, between 112,000–120,000 years ago.[13] But when we got to Indonesia and Australia is still subject to speculation. With respect to the Americas, did people known as the Clovis arrive first from Siberia to Alaska around 13,500 years ago? Well, in 2015, it was considered that Monte Verde in Chile may have had modern human habitat going back 18,000 years. In September 2021, the oldest human footprints discovered in North America were found in New Mexico, and dated between 21,000 to 23,000 years.[14]

Beyond these issues of entry dates and routes, there has been debate about first signs of sophisticated culture. We don't know when talk started, whether as recently as 50,000 years ago, or in basic form much further back. In short, big knowledge gaps, contested fossil analysis, speculation, and revision on the back of new evidence, mean that our origin story remains incomplete and subject to amendment. We do know that things that make us *sapiens* are not just bipedalism, digital dexterity, large brains, language, and sociability. We share such traits with close relatives like Neanderthals.[15]

It's our enhanced capacity to glean, process, store, and cultivate information, ideas and knowledge, and to pass these down generations. This gamut of 'collective learning'[16] underpinned our ability to develop conceptual language and to transmit sophisticated culture. It also improved our resilience and adaptability, out of which came our impulse for exploration, migration and mixing. With these patterns came greater diversity and complexity.

By ten thousand years ago, as the last Ice Age faded, bringing stable climatic warmth and wetness in the Holocene period, we were spread across most of the world, increasing in number, and on the cusp of a great transformation – the agricultural revolution. Through greater awareness of how to tap environmental energy and resources, farmers nurtured the most valued plants and animals, which in turn genetically adapted:[17]

> *More nutritious plants, such as domesticated wheat and rice, evolved, as did more helpful animals, such as domesticated dogs, horses, cattle, and sheep. Domesticated animals helped hunters, carried and hauled people and goods, or provided wool or milk. When slaughtered, they provided meat, skin, bones, and sinews.*

Settled communities intensively involved in tilling soil, weeding, harvesting crops, cutting forests, forging pathways, and directing irrigation, demanded greater social collaboration and seasonal organisation. Moreover, a new division of labour emerged, whereby surplus food supply allowed some to concentrate on other tasks, such as priestly and artisan crafts, and indeed philosophy. In the case of the latter, the opportunity and capacity for our species to grill itself about human drives, such as motive and purpose, set us on a distinct path as a living creature. Paradoxically, as this local closeness developed in village formation, rising sea levels due to global warming, undid connection between Afro-Eurasia and Australasia and the Americas, ties restored only about five hundred years ago. Clearly, matters of local-global links are nothing new.

We can still be startled by the capacity of our ancestors to live lives of order and ritual in trying circumstances. A simple example I visited recently is the megalithic Poulnabrone portal tomb, one of Ireland's archaeological landmarks, dated around 6,000 years ago. Another monument I found remarkable in its architecture and construction is the Parthenon, a dominant feature in the Acropolis, as a former temple dedicated to the goddess Athena, built in the mid-5th century BCE. A much more recent, but very impressive site is Angkor Wat, a massive mountain-temple complex in Siem Reap, Cambodia – claimed to be the world's largest religious site, and built in the early 12th century in homage to the Hindu god Vishnu. Experiencing these kind of places first-hand can't help but bring you to an appreciation of human development and its investment in the 'sacred' – the realm that is at once human and beyond human. At each stage of the human story, the evidence of ingenuity is compelling. But we've still a lot to learn about it, and maybe to unlearn the truths we thought we knew.

Leaps and Bounds

This creation story, derived from disciplines like archaeology, anthropology, paleontology, geology and ancient history, has been thrown into some doubt by the new science of ancient DNA, whereby since 2001, we can not only sequence the complete genome of people living today, but also relate it to DNA of ancestors going back into the deep past.

One source, which brings this together astutely, is Reich's 2018 book, *Who We Are and How We Got Here*.[18] In essence, he draws on up-to-date genetic studies to reach important conclusions. We today are mixes of past populations that were themselves the outcome of intermingling. Population blending is intrinsic to human nature, and that makes each of us interconnected. Such vast mixing of distinctive populations involved growth, substitution, interbreeding, and migration. Non-African genomes now are about 1.5 to 2.1 percent Neanderthal, with East Asians showing the higher number and Europeans the lower, even though Neanderthals lived mostly in Europe. Current geographic spread of world population is often deceptive about original location of our ancestors. Large numbers of living people come from hybrid populations.

The split between Denisovan and Neanderthal ancestral populations happened between 470,000 to 380,000 years ago, and between these common ancestors and us about 770,000 to 550,000 years ago. Interbreeding between Neanderthals and modern humans may suggest that the former were a sub-group of *sapiens* rather than a distinct species. H-*heidelbergensis*, ancestral to Neanderthals, Denisovans and us, was a species not only of Africa, but also of East and West Eurasia.

Taking all this into account, Reich and others emphasise the mix and spread of early humans. The co-existence of divergent human form 70,000 years ago suggests that the idea that we simply came out of Africa may be offset by the possibility that the ancestral population of Neanderthals, Denisovans and modern humans came from Eurasia, and derived from H-*erectus* that dispersed out of Africa, with a subsequent return from Eurasia to Africa, from whence came the originating population that developed into *sapiens*. Because our lineage can be traced to Africa before two million years ago and after 300,000 years ago, does not preclude an intervening period of ancestry in Eurasia.

Back in the eighteenth century, the world's peoples were classified into 'racial' clusters: west Eurasians as caucasoids; east Asians as mongoloids; sub-Saharan African as negroids; and those from Australia and New Guinea as australoids. Reich points out that if we go back 10,000 years to the early spread of farming, at least four distinct 'racial' populations existed in the Near East: farmers of the Fertile Crescent, that included Anatolia and the Levant; farmers of Iran; hunter-gatherers of western and central Europe; and hunter-gatherers of eastern Europe. Yet these classifications have not endured.

By the Bronze Age, technologies associated with domestication had helped spread the agricultural economy, and over time helped mix and fuse these different populations culturally and genetically in the process. Put simply, these supposedly fixed biological 'races' mutated, and this fluidity in genetic make-up means that '....today's classifications do not reflect fundamental 'pure' units of biology. Instead, today's divisions are recent phenomena, with their origin in repeating mixtures and migrations'.[19]

The mixing and moving of humans from their early foundations challenge fixed classification of race, ethnicity and other categories of geographical identity that tie people down to narrow notions of origin and belonging. It is a complex story, especially relevant to today's world, where populist nationalism offers a crude version of the 'native' and distinctive. The simplistic stamp of group identity, with attendant stereotypes, can stamp all over the intricacies of our common human story.

Genes and Genesis

The African base of human origins was spoken of authoritatively only in the last hundred years. Up to then, likely in part from a racial motive, widespread assumption had our origins in Eurasia. Robert Dart's discovery, in 1924 in South Africa, of the so-called Taung child, an ape-like creature identified as an early human ancestor, raised the probability of humans' African roots.

Throughout the twentieth century, more and more hominin fossils were discovered in Africa. Just as there was resistance to the Darwinian idea that we are part of, rather than apart from, the animal kingdom, there was reluctance among some to accept that we were of African descent. Could it really be that Africa was not the 'white man's burden' as much as his ancestral homeland? Did we hail not just from the 'wilds' of that 'dark continent', but also from its untamed killer apes? For some, such thoughts threatened certainty not only about race per se, but also about the human race.

And into this controversy steps Robert Ardrey, with his widely-read 1961 book: *African Genesis: A Personal Investigation into the Animal Origins and Nature of Man*. For him, the evidence now pointed to us not being born virtuous and special, but rather with a bestowed legacy of violent aggression from our immediate forebears, the big apes. We had inherited those animal instincts to acquire and protect territory and property. Also natural were predatory urges to dominate through social hierarchy, underpinned ultimately by lethal weapons, and later related drives of nationalism:

> *Is man innocent? Were we in truth created in the image of God? Are we unique, separate and distinct creatures from animalkind? Did our bodies evolve from the animal world, but not our souls? Is man sovereign? Are babies born good? Is human fault to be explained successfully in terms of environment? Is man innately noble?*

This version of African genesis is not biblical genesis. While the former is about an assortment of ape-like, then human-like, creatures that developed over millennia in admixtures we don't yet fully understand, the latter is about a definite creation of *sapiens*, as a specific chosen species in divine image, in gender sequence of man and woman, and in purposeful relationship with God. Naturally, there is greater spiritual appeal to a story with us as its centre.

Nevertheless, the idea that we may be just a higher form of animal, and that thus our animal instincts may be under-estimated, is long-standing. Pavlov's dog experiments supposedly showed how they were conditioned for automatic reflexes, triggered by cues and contexts of various incentives for dividends, and have been used to influence things like consumer behaviour. Lorenz's book *On Aggression*, published in English in 1966, argued that aggression in both animals and humans, directed against the same species, was an instinct that guaranteed survival of the individual and species.

The 1967 Morris book, *The Naked Ape*, claimed that a lot of our behaviour could be understood by understanding animal behaviour. We were simply a staged outcome in primate evolution. Contrary to lurid headlines about the book, Morris explained that our animal make-up was not reducing us to a species captive to base and beastly impulse, but rather recognising how our evolved resourcefulness had delivered our potential for loving and peaceful relationships. This chimed with one strand of the 1960s, the hippy notion that we needed to hang loose, and be liberated from artificial constraints of 'civilised' society to rediscover our fundamental essence as free spirits, who are present in the present.

I spent summers in London from mid to late-1960s, when the city was supposed to be 'swinging', and during that time, I encountered some 'way out' groups experimenting with new lifestyles, including one that embraced ape-ancestry to the point of regarding 'animals' as superior to humans, insofar as they remained true to their nature, whereas we had forsaken our biological roots. We had become inauthentic.

Nurturing Nature

Arguments about what constitutes the authentic modern human have been long entangled with dispute about whether we are determined more by nature than nurture. Since the start of this century, we've had new revelation from the Genome Project, questioning the extent to which genes are destiny. Plomin,[20] an expert in behavioural genetics, notes that for over 99 percent of our DNA, all modern humans are the same. But it is that under 1 percent that distinguishes each of us as individuals, accounting for about half the difference between us on all psychological traits, including school attainment, verbal ability and general intelligence. In the debate about whether nature or nurture is the greater influence, he opts for nature, and adds that even some of what look to be environmental factors have themselves genetic aspects:[21]

> *Genetics accounts for most of the systematic differences between us – DNA is the blueprint that makes us who we are. Environmental effects are important too, but they are unsystematic and unstable, so there's not much we can do about them. Moreover, what look like systematic environmental effects are often due to us choosing environments correlated with our genetic propensities.*

So, for instance, it may be thought that if you come from a high-income background, with parents of high educational attainment, that those advantages play a large part in your likely successful school achievement. But Plomin is saying that these factors are much less significant than genetic inheritance, and in any case involve overlap, since the parental school attainment has itself a genetic basis. Thus, he maintains that if you were adopted at birth, raised by different parents, attended different schools, made different friendships, you would be similar to the person you are now in personality, mental wellbeing, and cognitive ability. Despite this big claim, he insists that our fate is not preordained, but rather that 'genetic influences are probabilistic propensities, not predetermined programming'. Moreover, he is not talking about whole categories like 'races', but about differences between individuals.

To those who say that this weighting for nature conveniently chimes with a politics that sees inequality as naturally justified, he counters with two considerations. First, society can still decide for its general welfare that it compensates for this imbalance. Here, he quotes others like Bloodworth,[22] who decries meritocracy because it allows for a deeply unequal society, in which parental privilege is passed on to children. It penalises those with low ability, based on the accident of genetics, whereas a just society would be a more egalitarian one, prepared to ensure that all can live well. Second, those who politically invest in the power of nurture can also be in bad company, since regimes based on belief that people can be nurtured, by the same token believe they can be moulded at the behest of ideology – as in the gruesome Stalinist, Nazi and Maoist systems.

Studies continue to grapple with the comparative influences of genetic and environmental factors on our senses and behaviour. For instance, taking assumed genetic similarity of identical (monozygotic) twins to be close to 100 percent, while that of fraternal (dizygotic) twins to be close to 50 percent, a 2022 research paper[23] found that the former were closer to each other in their desire to be in nature spaces, such as rural environments and parks, and in their appreciation of such spaces, than the latter. In other words, there was a significant heritability factor in the orientation to, and experience of, nature. You could say that nature played an important part in human response to nature. But this heritability feature ebbed with age, and environmental aspects, such as access to green spaces, increased in significance.

Now that the 'gene' genie is out of the bottle with all the new genome research, these kind of studies are likely to proliferate. The old argument between nature and nurture isn't going away anytime soon. To take some further examples: James Watson, who along with Wilkins and Crick, first identified the double helix structure of DNA, sees our genes as the screenplay for our biographies. Controversially, he was quoted[24] as saying that while 'there are many people of colour who are very talented', he was 'inherently gloomy about the prospect of Africa'. He added: 'All our social policies are based on the fact that their intelligence is the same as ours — whereas all the testing says not really'.

Soon after, in response to overwhelming criticism, he released a statement to The Associated Press, saying:[25] 'I cannot understand how I could have said what I am quoted as having said. There is no scientific basis for such a belief'. While Watson's views about the relationship between race and intelligence were contested by most scholars in the field, a small number weighed in with support, including Rushton and Jensen, who insisted:[26]

> *The preponderance of evidence demonstrates that in intelligence, brain size, and other life-history variables, East Asians average a higher IQ and larger brain than Europeans who average a higher IQ and larger brain than Africans. Further, these group differences are 50–80 percent heritable.*

This echoes claims made by Herrnstein and Murray in their 1994 book *The Bell Curve*.[27] For them, intelligence is not only mostly genetic, but also unevenly split among races, with a 15-point gap in average IQ between American 'whites' and African-Americans. Moreover, in their view, a marked variance persists even when allowance is made for difference in cultural and socio-economic background, and this lower intellectual capacity is the key explanation for lower socio-economic achievement on average of African-Americans.

Critics pointed to the difficulty of comparing a population that had been long exposed to slavery and racial discrimination to a relatively privileged population. Moreover, where you have people from both populations with the same IQs undertaking various intelligence subtests, black children do better on aspects like recall and white children grade better on others like visuo-spatial capacity. Thus, if these 'sub-categories' are valued, and thus weighted, differently, you get a different overall measurement for 'general intelligence' (g). Mukherjee insists that the intricate crossing points between a person's biology and psychology on the one hand, and environment and context on the other, cannot be captured by a catch-all category like 'g':[28]

> *The tricky thing about the notion of g is that it pretends to be a biological quality that is measurable and heritable, while it is actually strongly determined by cultural priorities….a meme masquerading as a gene….Genes cannot tell us how to*

categorise or comprehend human diversity; environments can, cultures can, geographies can, histories can.

Alongside this critique, individual studies suggest that if you start from an even playing field, differences in development are insignificant. For instance, evidence from the University of Oxford's seven-year Intergrowth-21st Project,[29] based on a major international study of children's physical and intellectual development up to age two, shows that for all, regardless of race or ethnicity, who get a good life start in terms of habitat, nutrition, and quality education, achievement of neuro-developmental landmarks and related behaviours are likely inborn and worldwide.

Another dimension of this is the Flynn-effect, named after the scholar who revealed that worldwide, children perform better on old 'intelligence' tests than those taking the original test, an inter-generational enhancement of IQ over time that cannot be due to genes, but to other factors such as environmental health improvement, better nutrition and schooling, decreased behaviours such as in-breeding, and changed society that demands more abstract and conceptual thinking. On this basis, Flynn thinks 'evidence that inferior genes for intelligence handicap the developing world is suspect'.[30]

But for Flynn, 'nurture' is complicated. Family background is strong in early development, but withers to a low level by 17, and is inconsequential by maturity. Once it goes, 'the cognitive quality of your current environment tends to match your genetic quality. This is often called a tendency toward 'gene-environment co-relation'....High IQ people seek out more enriched environments'.[31] Also, there is chance circumstance in life, and he estimates that this accounts for about 20 percent of IQ difference. Importantly, he argues that it is emancipating for humans to appreciate that family impact fades, leaving individual autonomy open to improving cognitive performance. You can choose to improve yourself, whatever your start in life.

Yet Edward Wilson affirms that 'genetically based variation in individual personality and intelligence has been conclusively demonstrated, although statistical racial differences, if any, remain unproven'.[32] He says this, while accepting that human nature is neither the genes that stipulate it, nor the cultural universals, which are its outcome. Rather, genetic and cultural evolution are interwoven, whereby the former involves brain evolution happening in a social context, while the latter is predisposed significantly by biology. Determination of mental development involves interaction between culture and biology.

When referring to gender difference, he contends that even with women attaining the same education and access to all professions, men are likely to keep playing a disproportionate role in politics, business and science. Such 'natural' outcomes derive from his general view that however impressive are human languages, cultures, and subtle minds, 'the mental process is the product of a brain shaped by the hammer of natural selection upon the anvil of nature'.[33]

Amongst the many critics of such definitive conclusions, Lewontin[34] has resisted a biological determinism that sees a fixed human nature coded into our genes. He sees it as an ideological doctrine that moves seamlessly from supposed genetically-determined differences in health, ability and disposition, to assumption about the inevitability of society based on competition and hierarchy. If something is 'natural', it's regarded as largely unchangeable. Thus, a politics designed to improve teaching, home and school environment, and such like, will have marginal impact, other than on the public purse.

Enter Eugenics

Research claiming to have disentangled nature and nurture has often been based on twin and adoption studies. Joseph[35] forensically uncovers their bias, equal environment assumptions, flawed methodology and suspect theoretical frameworks. Elsewhere, he points to the problems of 'intelligence tests':[36]

> ....*assumptions about the genetic inferiority of lower classes and subordinated races are built into IQ tests. Thus, it is astonishing that anyone who knows how these tests are constructed could argue that the lower IQ scores of blacks versus whites, or working class versus upper class, are the result of genetic differences.*

Many scholars today refute the concept of race as a biological fixity, seeing it instead as a social outcome of historical and cultural processes, arbitrated by the powerful of any given period. Moreover, even accepting racial categories as presently attributed, there are bigger genetic variations between individuals of the same 'race' than there are between individuals of different 'races'.[37] Interestingly, as far back as my birth-year, 1950, UNESCO addressed the 'race question' in a remarkable statement that included the following:[38]

- 'The law sees in each person only a human being who has the right to the same consideration and to equal respect. The conscience of all mankind demands that this be true for all the peoples of the earth. It matters little, therefore, whether the diversity of men's gifts be the result of biological or of cultural factors'. p. 3
- '....the term *race* designates a group or population characterized by some concentrations, relative as to frequency and distribution, of hereditary particles (genes) or physical characters, which appear, fluctuate, and often disappear in the course of time by reason of geographic and or cultural isolation'. p. 5
- 'In short, given similar degrees of cultural opportunity to realize their potentialities, the average achievement of the members of each ethnic group is about the same'. p.7
- 'For all practical social purposes *race* is not so much a biological phenomenon as a social myth'. p.8

The document clothes human diversity in terms of the brotherhood of man, and the ethical imperative to be our brother's keeper – just over seventy years ago, the male *of* the species was still taken to be *the* species. Its content and tone are clearly influenced by the horrors of the recent war, fought by the Nazis in terms of their superior race. But it also addresses the longer strain of eugenics thinking, the idea of improving the human race by controlling which people make suitable parents.

It's usually traced back to Francis Galton in Britain. His 1869 book *Hereditary Genius*[39] suggested that intelligence had a genetic transmission, as evidenced in the likelihood that sons of high-achieving men would themselves become high-flyers relative to those from less distinguished backgrounds. Similar eugenics tracts emerged in the first quarter of the twentieth century, providing the basis of what came to be known as scientific racism. Schultz in his 1908 *Race or Mongrel: A Brief History of the Rise and Fall of the Ancient Races of Earth*, argued that the pure-bred stock that had built western civilisation was under threat from 'mongrelisation'.[40] Similar argument about racial purity is found in Stoddard's 1920 *The Rising Tide of Color against White World-Supremacy* and Grant's *The Passing of the Great Race*, which was praised by Hitler and influenced *Mein Kampf*, in its extolling of Nordic racial pre-eminence.[41]

In the USA, a leading figure espousing faith in biological heritage was Davenport, who as director of Cold Spring Harbor Laboratory, established the Eugenics Record Office in 1910. Its studies claimed to explain the heritability of many aspects of mental capacity and personality, including criminality, temperament, depression, and 'feeblemindedness'. Concerned about the way abolition of slavery had increased prospect of racial interbreeding (miscegenation), he co-authored the 1929 *Race Crossing in Jamaica*,[42] which asserted that such lineage-mixing brought disharmony that degraded human stock. The overall verdict from these kind of sources was that dilution of the 'white race' had negative mental and moral impact, producing deficient, troublesome people, prone to unstable behaviour. World improvement depended on selective breeding. Again, we can see the link between these kind of ideas and the scare stories about a 'Great Replacement' of the white race, that was covered in chapter three.

Anyone who has visited the Auschwitz labour and death camp, and has seen up close the remnants of its design for mass slaughter, and Mengele's 'medical experiments', might think that ideas associated with superior propagation would be consigned to history's trash-can. But eugenics in some form has never departed. In 1974, a senior British Tory, Keith Joseph, made an infamous speech,[43] in which he advocated fertility control for those he considered lower class unfit parents. He started by saying that, apart from promoting self-help, state aid to the poor harms them morally, while imposing unjust burdens on society. Then he continued:

> *The balance of our population, our human stock is threatened….a high and rising proportion of children are being born to mothers least fitted to bring children into the*

world and bring them up....Some (of these mothers) are of low intelligence, most of low educational attainment. They are unlikely to be able to give children the stable emotional background, the consistent combination of love and firmness which are more important than riches. They are producing problem children, the future unmarried mothers, delinquents, denizens of our borstals, sub-normal educational establishments, prisons, hostels for drifters. Yet these mothers, the under-twenties in many cases, single parents, from classes 4 and 5, are now producing a third of all births. A high proportion of these births are a tragedy for the mother, the child and for us.

In Joseph's view, together with the flight of enterprising talented people escaping Britain's semi-socialism, these tragic births were diminishing the country. Though increasing birth-control facility for 'these classes of people' might appear to pardon immorality, it might be the lesser evil, 'when already weak restraints on strong instincts are further weakened by permissiveness in television, in films, on bookstalls'. Linking this supposed debasing of the stock to 'worship of instinct, of spontaneity, the rejection of self-discipline', which mistake degeneration for progress, Joseph essentially taps into this idea that 1960s' counterculture was unwisely rooted in humans returning to nature to rediscover their animal instinct.

While Joseph was *talking* about a form of eugenics, using birth control, parts of the USA had been *practicing* it by sterilisation. In 1907, Indiana became the first state to enact forced sterilisation, and twenty years later, the Supreme Court in *Buck v. Bell* affirmed its constitutionality. With the 1970 Family Planning Services and Population Research Act, supported by increased Medicaid-funding, Nixon's administration extended the prospect of sterilisation of low-income people, particularly women of colour. Nixon himself is caught in one of his infamous tapes[44] telling his adviser Erlichman, that while people of their class were using birth control, those not 'are the people who shouldn't have kids'. Thus, between the 1940s and 1970s, the North Carolina Eugenics Board sterilised 7,600 women, held to be mentally disabled. Most recently, in May 2017, Judge Benningfield in Tennessee endorsed a standing order giving reduced sentences to inmates in White County, who undertook sterilisation, though a subsequent law abolished this practice.[45]

Most recently, scope for eugenics has expanded considerably with gene-editing that leads to a 'synthetic biology' of supposed human enhancement. This is considered further in Chapter 8. Of course, genetic modification is applicable to the crops that sustain human life, and such human 'interference' with nature has a deep past that delivered both advance and hazard:[46]

humanity's relations with the living world have seen three great transformations: the exploitation of fossil fuels, the globalisation of the world's ecosystems after the European conquest of the Americas, and the domestication of crops and animals at the dawn of agriculture. All brought prosperity and progress, but with damaging side-effects. Synthetic biology promises similar transformation.

With regard to eugenics, it's important to acknowledge its allure across the political spectrum. As Rutherford notes in charting its 'dark history and troubling present',[47] the notion of 'designer babies' is far from new, and some progressives saw selective breeding as a valid means of advancing human stock and well-being. H.G.Wells spoke in dismissive terms about what he saw as contemptible, stupid and inefficient people, given to unrestrained procreation. The world couldn't be changed for the better without curtailing this tendency. Such ideas mark a persistent fear among some of the 'enlightened' about the threat to civilisation posed by the differential fertility of certain races, and of the proletariat in general. Julian Huxley was another example of a learned mind promoting the virtue of 'scientific humanism' on the pretext of an indisputable calculus about what constitutes a commendable life. Moreover, these kind of arguments favouring the discarding, or at least disregarding, of 'defectives' have offered convenient cover for some colonialists throughout history.

Species and Specious

Who we are is linked to where we came from as a species, and to what we know about human nature. In what's been said here so far about both, it's clear that significant knowledge gaps remain. These are budging at the behest of very recent science. For a being that's been around for at least 200,000 years plus, scientific advance in the last twenty years has been eye-opening, but in a period of polarisation when minds seem more closed.

We've looked at how we came about through evolution, rather than from Adam and Eve in the Garden of Eden. Creationists insist that schools should teach the 'debate' about our origins rather than just the theory of evolution. This plays to a common take on the word 'theory' as no more than an inkling, impression, or even conjecture. Of course, in science that is not what theory means. Rather, scientific theory is a dependable explanation of a hypothesis or observable fact that can be continually tested for confirmation or falsification through rigorous methods of rational inspection, calculation and appraisal. So it's about evidence that bears out propositions, reveals new understanding, or at the very least offers plausible interpretation in the absence of alternative estimation.

Importantly, we can reassess explanations in the light of new knowledge. Evolutionary theory is based on abundant data from various disciplines that corroborate the general framework of species development over time. As shown here, we don't know every detail about our emergence as *sapiens*, our relationship to near 'cousins', our movement across the world, and our intermingling. Evolutionary theory itself can evolve. As Dawkins comments:[48]

> *We should not expect to draw a neat line between early Archaics and the Erects from whom they evolved, or between Archaics and the earliest Moderns who evolved from them....Evolution is a messy historical process, unlikely to proceed in straight lines.*

By the same token, we don't know everything about human nature, and about the relationship between our nature and nurture. While the genome revolution will be increasingly revelatory, we do know some important things from it so far.

Pinker says that to embrace the science behind studies of identical twins (monozygotic), which purport to show how much genes and heritability count, we have to discard three canons that have dominated western philosophy and theology. First is the idea of the *Blank Slate*, namely that we are born not with significant genetic imprint, but rather largely as a blank canvas, on which nurture through upbringing, culture and wider experience makes its mark. Second is Rousseau's exaltation of *primitive man as noble savage*, who was damaged by so-called civilisation, in contrast to Hobbesian man leading a solitary, poor, nasty, brutish and short life; and third, is the *Ghost in the Machine*, that sees us exercising free will through our soul, able to triumph over the biology of our 'machine' selves.[49]

While this importance of genes is now widely accepted, many refute the idea of their exclusive determinism. There is no such thing as 'the intelligence gene' or 'criminal gene'. In the case of something like intelligence, we have to distinguish between the 'heritable' (influenced by genes) and the 'inheritable' (handed down intact from one generation to next). Most human traits are outcomes of relationship among genes, environments and chance. Genes play a part in, but not an exclusive shaping of, human variance – even males and females share 99.688 percent of their genes. Genes determine sexual anatomy, but gender identity and sexual orientation derive from links between genes and environments, while slants on manliness and femininity are socially created.[50]

In distinguishing sex and gender, de Waal's recent book,[51] entitled *Different*, sees the former as a person's biological sex, sourced from genital anatomy and sex chromosomes (XX for female and XY for male), whereas gender refers to the culturally demarcated role and societal status of each sex. Gender identity, on the other hand, he takes as referring to an individual's inner awareness of being either female or male. As our genetic 'cousins', the anthropoid apes, chimpanzees and bonobos, exhibit very different conduct, with the former noted for male-dominated, combative and territorial behaviour, while the latter are more female-dominated and peaceful. Does that suggest that men and women are naturally different? He affirms that for most people, sex and gender are 'congruent', an alignment between natal-assigned sex and gender identity that is termed cisgender. But he identifies a small part of brain, known awkwardly as *the bed nucleus of the stria terminals* that seems influential in composing a person's gender identity. Thus, he argues that the brain, rather than genital anatomy, is a finer indicator of a person's gender self-identity. That's far from saying that gender is simply a social construct. For instance, being transgender he understands to be basic and essential to that person's very being.

Fuentes[52] maintains that sex/gender is a changing system of relations rather than distinctive biological (sex) and cultural (gender) elements. Gender, in particular, is best thought of as a spectrum rather than as a binary. Most presumed male–female variations in psychological and skill traits actually intersect a great deal. There is no evolutionary 'instruction' that only women care for young and only men bother with economics and politics.

He insists that DNA patterns and genetic variation do not endorse the idea of race, but rather of a human race that shares gene flow and African ancestry. While race is not a correct or useful category of human biological variance, as a cultural construct it has real consequence, such as inequality, that can in turn shape people's biology in terms of stress and ill-health. Far from being an inherent demarcation among people, ethnicity fluctuates and varies in social and historical context. Most genetic variation exists *within* rather than *between* populations.

We don't know what innate biological features impact on human aggressive behaviour. Most people are not regularly violent. Indeed, some insist that warfare is a fairly recent human phenomenon, 10–12,000 years old, and perhaps linked to more settled and organised approaches to property and territory, rather than to deep evolutionary history. Human aggression varies in form and degree across individuals, sexes, genders, social groupings, and time periods, and thus it is mistaken to think of humans as naturally aggressive at their core, or indeed selfish, but rather as a species capable of hyper-collaboration. Such cooperation was essential in developing from village to city, from foraging to agriculture, from limited exchange to trade and market, from small-scale rituals to vast religious organisations, from tribal decision-making to pluralist governance, and from limited travel to global reach. In busting what he sees as key myths about human nature, Fuentes notes:[53]

> As a human organism we are born into a suite of inherited ecologies, cultural patterns, and social contexts that immediately become entangled with our biological structures, initiating a process of biocultural development: we are naturenurtura'.

In a similar vein, Ridley talks of 'nature via nurture' as circular causality.[54] Behaviour and capacity are influenced by genes, which themselves are impacted by action, memory, senses and experience. Moreover, it's hard sometimes to say what form the 'genetic' and 'environmental' take. While racial distinction may have no sound genetic basis, it may be a marker that distinguishes the 'stranger' and we may have a 'natural' instinct to be guarded about those outside our customary environment and 'coalition' of friends and tribes.

Addressing the controversial issue of intelligence, Ridley interprets the evidence to show that IQ is about half 'additively genetic', a quarter effected by shared environment, and a quarter shaped by the individual's own special engagement with environment. More than personality, intelligence is receptive to family stimulus: 'living in an intellectual home does make you more likely to become an intellectual',[55] though the older you develop, your genes predict your IQ better, and family milieu less. On this take, the more we even the playing field of 'environment' for all, the more genes will account for different scoring between individuals in educational attainment. Ridley identifies this as a key paradox: the more equal we form society, the more relevance we accord genes.

That's not to say that family doesn't matter in personality forming. However, as long as that family is quite stable and happy, he says that it doesn't matter a great deal whether its well-off or deprived, small or big, out-going or reserved, and so on. Taking personality to be about a person's openness, conscientiousness, extroversion, agreeableness and neuroticism (OCEAN), Ridley summarises the data as showing high heritability in most measures, while appreciating that heritability is a measure of variation not determination. In terms of personality variation – and we're talking variation not absolutes – he says just over 40 percent is down to direct genetic influence, about 25 percent to unique environmental experience, and only just under 10 percent attributable to 'shared environment', which is largely the family (with about 25 percent taken as 'measurement error'). That's a big slice of 'error', and the other quite precise distributions make me wonder whether such calculation is as credible as it claims. Ridley does caution that this whole realm comes with qualification:[56]

> *To the extent that they can be teased apart, nature prevails over one kind of (shared) nurture when it comes to defining differences in personality, intelligence and health between people within the same society. Note the caveats.*

In stressing nature *via* rather than *versus* nurture, he sees the relationship as mainly nurture bolstering nature. Moreover, he acknowledges that it's hard often to distinguish what is instinct from what could be the outcome of logical deduction, imitative behaviour, or learned message. Despite such reservation, he talks about how certain cultural features may have developed from natural instinct, and how culture will often reflect rather than mould human nature.

Cultural Roots

Before we proceed though, we better define what we mean by culture. While we speak of someone being cultured to mean they are urbane and sophisticated, culture in its broadest sense is accumulated tradition of behaviour, values, rules and meanings, concerning: language; social, economic and political formations; customs; folklore; rituals; beliefs; and the arts, all of which are imparted, learned, pooled, assimilated, emblematic, and yet changeable. In other words, it covers a lot, and it's always a work in progress. In 1945, Murdock[57] listed universal features of every modern human culture across time and geography. They amounted to nearly seventy distinct practices.[58] Beyond these, Brown adds many further traits: from feelings such as fear, anger, pain, embarrassment, envy, and empathy to practices such as tickling, mourning, and gossip.[59]

Three things strike me about such a big list. First, if all this is common across time and space, there must be a lot about it that is natural to the species as a whole. Human nature is a strong constant in shaping how we live. Long-standing emphasis from anthropologists like Margaret Mead and Ruth Benedict in the 1930s about multiple varieties of customs, and the cultural relativism that came from that view, underplayed uniformities behind the human condition. Second, the diverse versions of many of these 'universals' in different places speak to how factors outside nature alone have also a big bearing on who we are and how we live. Third, the level of cognitive and social development involved in such intricate arrangements favours those who emphasise human exceptionalism – in other words, how much more advanced we are from the rest of the animal kingdom.

This last point is tied in with the idea of the 'Cartesian self', stemming from Descartes. His famed expression: *I think, therefore I am*, was acknowledging that human self-awareness and cognition allowed you to validate your existence, even when questioning it, because in the very deliberation of doubting, you had to exist as a thinking being to begin with. He saw this as his mind being detached from his body – mind–body dualism – that he could mentally contemplate his physical self, and have a conscious sense of selfhood.

This raises the hard problem of consciousness, and its evolutionary emergence, an issue tackled more comprehensively in the second volume. At this stage, it is useful to draw attention to Ginsburg and Jablonka,[60] who have developed a theory about how and when transition to the subjective experience not only of observation and comprehension of the world, but also of the self, happened. They refer to it as the Unlimited Associative Learning (UAL) framework. It builds on Ganti's 'hallmarks' of life,[61] namely capacity for: boundary maintenance (the bounded physicality of individuation); metabolism; inherent stability; information storage; internal regulatory and controlling processes; growth and reproduction; and ultimate mortality. In similar vein, they propose the basis of conscious life as: *global accessibility and broadcast* (where data from perception, recall and evaluation are integrated and 'broadcast' back); *binding/unification and differentiation* (whereby objects can be appreciated in their totality and distinction. A blue flower is not just about blueness or flowerness); *selective attention and exclusion* (capacity to distinguish some stimuli as more pertinent than others); *intentionality* (faculty to denote the world and one's self); *integration of information over time* (ability to repetitively perform such digestion); an *evaluative system* (aptitude for appraisal); *agency and embodiment* (awareness of being a contained entity with capacity for intervention); and *registration of a self/other distinction*.

Taking these cognitive capacities for tracing, connection, unification, association and perception of patterns, clustering, response to sensory stimuli, identification of the novel, flexible adaptation, and the rest, Ginsburg and Jablonka surmise that UAL is found in most vertebrates, some celhalopod molluscs (for instance, octopods, squid and cuttlefish) and some arthropods (such as honey bees and fruit flies). However, they acknowledge that this kind of consciousness is differentiated by those who espouse the higher-order thought (HOT) theory that holds that consciousness in its complete form entails a system being able to 'represent' its own mental conditions. How we might precisely distinguish and determine rudimentary and highly developed consciousness remains a disputed research terrain.

But if humans have such impressive capacity, and genes count for so much, how come we share between 98.6 percent to 95 percent – depending on which you accept in current debate – of DNA with chimpanzees? The Human Genome Project (HGP), 1990–2003, assumed about 100,000 protein-coding human genes. Analysis to date shows that it's actually between a fifth to a quarter of that number.[62] Though we don't yet know for sure how many genes we have, current estimates suggest that uniquely human genes are only in the hundreds, a small amount for such a big difference. Even more strangely, we're told that we share around 60 percent of our genes with chickens, fruit flies and bananas.

Nevertheless, it is not so strange when we consider that all living creatures have similarities because we all came from a rudimentary source, the single-cell organism, known as the last universal common ancestor (LUCA). Those stressing the role of genes remind us that our genome is our instruction handbook that comprises DNA that informs our organism on how to create protein molecules, which in turn play a big part in shaping us. Given the great difference in complexity between creatures, like ourselves and chimps, who share such a high amount of identical genes, some say it must be down to nurture. Yet those who play up genetic influence, can say that it is not about the number of identical genes, but rather about their sequence and configuration.

All this is made more complicated by consideration of the human-animal divide in a world where xenotransplantation – the exchange of cells, tissues, and organs between species – is becoming ever more sophisticated. Throughout history, we have had the notion of the human-animal as hybrid or metaphor. Think of Jesus as the lamb of God.[63] Now, a genetically-modified pig can be created to be killed for its heart to be transplanted into a human, who then comprises part of an involuntary donor animal. Does such procedure bring us closer to animals like pigs, or even more removed, as we slay them to prolong human life?

Decision and Destiny

The argument about nature and nurture is a question about how much our lives are determined by choice or fate. While we'd like a calculus that offered certainty about the weighting of each, we have to live with ambiguity about both. The language of complexity, interaction and likelihood that genetics is now using invites us to accept life as about both security and risk, consistency and deviation, durability and change, solidity and instability, the detachable and inseparable, and the nuanced and definitive. We not only contain multitudes, we also contain contradictions.[64] We are creatures of paradox.

> *Our genome has negotiated a fragile balance between counterpoised forces, pairing strand with opposing strand, mixing past and future, pitting memory against desire. It is the most human of all things that we possess.*

Present knowledge doesn't allow us to draw a precise border between the natural, instinctive, impulsive, automatic, and spontaneous on the one hand, and the considered, reflective, cultivated, and finessed on the other. In reality, such a border is a holy grail that doesn't exist. It's a false dichotomy. Rather, analysis that accepts the importance of genes, without considering them inactive and unchanging, and appreciating their dynamic interaction with environment, is more convincing. As summarised by Ridley, genes work through nurture, through reaction with experience. Rutherford[65] expresses it as gene-culture co-evolution, whereby each steers the other. Cultural diffusion relies on genetically-coded capacity to do so. Just as biology facilitates culture, culture alters biology. This subtlety disturbs some. But with its mix of exquisite order and random change, life is disturbing.

A lot of the literature concludes that nature and nurture are partners rather than rivals. Saying that doesn't free us from seeing life as about the determination and fortune of genes, environment, and happenstance. We don't get to choose our family, either for its genes or upbringing. As we age, how much is our later environment influenced by choice or chance? Granted, being human is too complex to be reduced to binaries. We're not hardwired to behave and achieve based on codes in our genes. Nor are we open books to be scripted by social engineering.

As someone out of his comfort zone when it comes to genetics, I'm struck by two things in reading through recent literature. First, there's no agreement among scientists about weighted influence of genes and various environmental factors. Second, while their command of genetic science is impressive, their knowledge of sociology is less so. Thus, some take the overwhelming commonality of family life to be fairly happy and secure, an assumption unsupported by data on domestic abuse and neglect.

When it comes to learning environment, Ridley, for instance, says most schools have pupil intake from similar background, and 'by definition' give them similar teaching, thereby minimising school environment as a factor. This is simplistic. Many schools have some social mix. Different subjects can have different class size. Particular teachers in a school have variant teaching skills. Teachers from a similar background to most of their pupils can have better affinity. School strategy to attain prestige varies, with some concentrating on selected pupils, excluding some from exams, and so on. Some schools will have strong relationships with parents as learning partners, with others less so. The 'hidden curriculum' will vary across schools. In other words, school environment is very complex and can't be captured by assumed simple characteristics.

Also, there's difficulty of definition and metrics for some human traits. Assessing cognitive capacity is more problematic than some on the right suppose. Moreover, intelligence isn't always what it's cracked up to be. Clever is as clever does. We've all met supposedly very bright people whose 'emotional intelligence' leaves a lot to be desired. When it comes to a trait like belligerence, the left would like to think that there is an 'evolutionary' truth about aggressive men not doing better than their milder counterparts. Notwithstanding that hope, we generally don't see the meek inheriting the earth.

Some on the left would like to hold on to idealised versions of the 'noble savage' that naturally behaves well without need for too much state restraint. But I remember Belfast going up in flames in 1969. Police in many conflict areas retreated to their stations. Tribal mobs were running amok. Many people living in working class areas, where violence was greatest, without protection from state or armed militia, were terrified by the prospect of being burned out of their homes. Believe me, when you face that mayhem as a threatening reality, you see the 'savage' rather than the 'noble', and you crave state security.

Robert Louis Stevenson's affable Dr Jekyll struggles in a losing battle with his baser self, personified as his alter ego, Mr Hyde, who in his violence and vice, lacks empathy and guilt. Again, this combat between our lesser and better angels is another take on how far life is chosen and thus changeable, or fated and thus fixed. It may be thought that the political left favours the former verdict, because the progressive project wants to think that most aspects of identity can be changed through reason and human agency. In contrast, the right tends to think that they work with the grain of nature and are consequently in the business of conserving over changing, and are often prone to confuse what they regard as *natural* with what should be *normal*.

They each have their contradictions. For instance, the left will think that sexuality can't be chosen as a lifestyle. It's not about sexual preference but orientation, and the reference point is fixed. Some on the right, particularly the Christian right, see 'deviant' sexuality as something that can be changed through education programmes that steer to 'normal' heterosexuality. The left can respond that such 'nurture' is misplaced since nature shows extensive practice of homosexuality in the animal world. Similarly, they'll resist the 'natural' state of patriarchy by pointing to matriarchal animal groups like killer whales, honey bees, bonobos and elephants. Both sides can play nature or nurture as and when it suits.

The right has tended to take human nature as inescapably programmed for self-serving ruthless competition, rooted in power hierarchy – what is called

Social Darwinism. In fact, this misconstrues Darwin. Perhaps unwisely, he was persuaded by his colleague Wallace to adopt Herbert Spencer's phrase 'the survival of the fittest' when referring to natural selection. Spencer used the term to infer that some were biologically endowed to be socially top-tier, and were thereby 'naturally' most likely to thrive in society. As a result, Darwin's ideas have become tainted with simplistic edicts, such as only the strong survive in a heartless world of winners and losers. But natural selection does not mean that you have to be the baddest ass in town to prevail. You simply need sufficient attributes, tuned to your environment, that permit survival and reproduction.

Dog-eat-dog does not ensure against canine extinction. Species survival may be more about mutual cooperation for common well-being. Nor can we square this circle by sorting between conscious rational collaboration and gene-based instinctive self-interest. The Nash Equilibrium in game theory – named after mathematician John Nash – assumed the possibility of reasonably deducing how actors would use their logic to optimise their position vis-à-vis others in a selfish, distrustful, scheming way. In real life, using reason to allow for instinct is not such an easy calculus.

Whereas animal instinct suggests life lived in the moment, the conscious rational *sapiens* is capable of imagination and memory, of understanding connection between cause and effect. For some, that extra brain-power only equips us to be more clever in disguising our bottom-line distinction between 'me' and 'others'. So even at my most altruistic, I'm still selfish, because it makes me feel and appear good, or it may earn me brownie points that I can cash in later. It's still all or mostly about me.

Others counter that there's nothing natural about egocentrism. Behold the selflessness behind collectivism and reciprocity in ant and bee colonies. Some even suggest that we have an instinctive moral sense rooted in our collective memory of fall from grace in the garden and a conscience guiding us back to paradise lost.[66]

Just as we can no longer think of the Earth as the centre of the universe, we can no longer assume that we're the centre of the Earth. Copernicus and Galileo debunked the former. And evolutionary theory has deposed humans from centre-stage in this planet. It would be comforting to believe that we're here for planned purpose. But genetic variation and natural selection are accidental, not predestined, processes. Evolution is fortuitous, not prophetic. For creatures who seem to yearn for meaning, attachment and continuity, this picture of random and aimless process, lacking intentionality and finality, can be perturbing. Without direction, where is progression?

The recent book, *The Dawn of Everything* by Graeber and Wengrow,[67] highlights the messy and fluid character of the human condition. They challenge the neat narrative of linear human development from simple non-hierarchal primitive hunter-gatherer society to the territorial, competitive and ranked society of feudal, industrial, and post-industrial times. Specifically, they contest the idea of a pre-agrarian society marked by egalitarian and collaborative social structure disturbed by systematic agriculture that brought private property and inequality. In their take, domination and subservience are constantly changing features of human relations, reflected in various forms of governance over time, rather than permanent traits. However, alongside this big claim, they confess that we don't have a clue about most of human history.

My Way

This chapter has argued the need to recognise human origins, even though we've changed unrecognisably from those origins. In the great expanse of time, we're a recent arrival, at the toddler and tantrum stage of development. We don't arrive in this world as blank slate. Nor do we exit as coherent novel. Rather, we become a book of short stories that capture our disjointed lives, or if we live long enough, a Netflix series with multiple episodes. Wordsworth talked about the child being the father of the man. Of course, I've been influenced by my early formative years. But I'm not the person I was as a child. We're not just the outcome of long evolution as a species. We're the outcome of short 'evolution' as individuals, because we're creatures of both essence and development.

And in this becoming, we're full of paradox. Our deep past is ever present in our biology and ancestral memory, whatever our desire to live in the moment. There is a constant self, and a changing self. We're restless in search of contentment. We're nesters who think faraway hills are greener. We favour familiarity, yet familiarity breeds contempt. We want what we don't have until we have it. We don't know what we've got until it's gone. Though we're creatures of migration, we problematise immigrants. We're a mongrel species in pursuit of purity. Each of us is both individual and collective, because we're also partly creatures of culture, which involves us all in constant mutual transmission. By teaching each other, we learn our selfhood.[68] Things that are most useful to us, like fire and rain, can also be the most destructive. Despite the contingency involved in our fluidity, hybridity and flexibility, we're prone to profess universal and constant principles of humanity.

We like the natural over the artificial. We endow it with inherent integrity, even though the maternal virtue of Mother Nature can be found wanting. In this view, contemporary genetic research risks stepping outside nature. Interference with the genes of humans, animals, or plants – in the name of enhanced intelligence, lifespan, or plentiful food supply – is seen by many as going against what makes us human. Conceivably, the search to escape our mortality, via gene modification or enhancement through human 'partnership' with machines, augurs a strange new inequality between humans and posthumans. For some, it is death that paradoxically gives life meaning. Tampering with this 'natural' order invites some version of hubris – of Icarus flying too close to the sun. Yet human agency includes a 'natural' impulse to explore new frontiers. It seems, for all our claims of self-control, we can't stop ourselves.

Both genes and environment constrain agency. Thinking of ourselves as in servitude to both has great moral implication. Can we be held totally responsible for our actions if they are heavily shaped by both nature and nurture over which we've had little control? In that sense, we don't have free will. But we can will to be more free from these constraints. They are about propensity, susceptibility and proclivity. They're not about mechanistic determinism. As Marx noted, people make their own history, but not in circumstances of their complete choosing. Trying to find total self-sovereignty, we lose the scope of being semi-autonomous.

Even those on a pedestal, in the end are only dust. As Shelley says in Ozymandias: 'think of my works, ye mighty and despair'! We may want to think of ourselves in terms of cognitive complexity. But even what seem to be the smallest and simplest organisms – like bacteria – have a greater record of avoiding extinction than any Homo genus, most likely including our own. Bacteria is 'simple', yet resilient. People are clever. But are we too clever for our own good? All these issues are re-visited in greater detail in the second volume. For now, the next chapter considers whether for all our assumed intelligence, we're on a fatal path to self-extinction.

Notes

1 See: www.gsi.ie/en-ie/education/our-planet-earth/Pages/The-Earth-through-time. aspx; and www.nationalgeographic.org/encyclopedia/Continent. Accessed on: 13 September 2021.

2 Amos, J. (7 April 2022) Tanis: Fossil of Dinosaur Killed In Asteroid Strike Found, Scientists Claim. *BBC News*. www.bbc.co.uk/news/science-environment. Accessed on: 8 April 2022.

3 In terms of timeline that became widely accepted: 5.8 million years ago (MYA), lived our oldest discovered human ancestor, named *Orrorin*, thought to have been bipedal in gait; an early 'proto-human', the *Ardipithecus*, was around 5.5 MYA; the *Australopithecines* appeared 4 MYA; the famed 'Lucy', categorised as *Australopithecus Afarensis*, was 3.2 MYA. The earliest member of the Homo (H) genus, *H-habilis*, or 'handy man', inhabited Africa around 2.4–1.6 MYA, and though with smaller face and teeth to previous hominins, is still nearer in appearance and capacity to the ape-like Australopitthecus than to us. More advanced in tool-use, and much taller, *H-erectus* (1.8–0.03 MYA), reckoned to be the first hunter-gatherer, migrated out of Africa to Asia in large numbers, and survived for at least one and a half million years. Bipedalism allowed better negotiation of diverse environments. Then 700-200 KYA, a close relative of ours, *H-heidelbergensis*, with similar brain size to modern humans, lived in Africa and Europe. Some evidence suggests they cared for their elderly. Between 500-280 KYA, we start to see purpose-built shelters, hunting with spears, and development of complex stone blades. The

H-neanderthalensis (430–40 KYA), lived in wide parts of Europe up to Siberia. We finally appear as *H-sapiens*.

4 Hublin, JJ., Ben-Ncer, A., Bailey, S. *et al.* (2017) New Fossils from Jebel Irhoud, Morocco and the Pan-African Origin of *Homo sapiens. Nature* 546, 289–292.

5 The timeline can vary with different sources. For instance: New Scientist. (Sept 2006) *Human Evolution.* www.newscientist.com/article/dn9989-timeline-human-evolution. Accessed on: 01/09/2020; New Scientist (2018) *Human Origins: 7 Million Years and Counting.* London: John Murray Learning; Roberts, A. (2018 edition) *Evolution: the Human Story.* London: Dorling Kindersley; and Roberts, A. (2010) *The Incredible Human Journey; the Story of How We Colonised the Planet.* London: Bloomsbury.

6 Durvasula, A. and Sankararaman, S. (Feb 2020) Recovering signals of ghost archaic introgression in African populations. *Science Advances* Vol. 6, no. 7, eaax5097. DOI: 10.1126/sciadv.aax5097. https://advances.sciencemag.org/content/6/7/eaax5 097. Accessed on: 01/09/2020.

7 Rogers, A., Harris, N., and Achenbach, A. (Feb 2020) Neanderthal-Denisovan ancestors interbred with a distantly related hominin. *Science Advances* (20 Feb 2020) Vol. 6, no. 8, eaay5483. DOI: 10.1126/sciadv.aay5483. https://advances.sci encemag.org/content/6/8/eaay5483. Accessed on: 03/09/2020.

8 The Economist (1 July 2021) A New Human Species May Have Been Identified. *The Economist.*

9 Smithsonian Institute. https://humanorigins.si.edu/research/age-humans-evolu tionary-perspectives-anthropocene. Accessed on: 01/09/2020.

10 Anton, S., Potts, R. and Aiello, L. (July 2014) Evolution of early *Homo*: An integrated biological perspective. *Science.* Vol. 345, Issue 6192, 1236828. DOI: 10.1126/ science.1236828. https://science.sciencemag.org/content/345/6192/1236828. Accessed on: 01/09/2020.

11 New Scientist (2018) *op.cit.*

12 Christian, D. (2018) *Origin Story: A Big Picture of Everything.* London: Allen Lane.

13 Stewart, M., Clark-Wilson, R., Breeze, P., & Janulis, K. (18 Sep 2020) Human footprints provide snapshot of last interglacial ecology in the Arabian interior. *Science Advances.* Vol. 6, No. 38, eaba8940 DOI: 10.1126/sciadv.aba8940.

14 Bennett, M., Bustos, D., Pigati, J., et al (24 September 2021) Evidence of humans in North America during the Last Glacial Maximum. *Science.* 373(6562). 1528–1531.

15 Finlayson, C. (2009) *The Humans Who Went Extinct. Why Neanderthals died out and we survived.* Oxford University Press.

16 Christian, D. (2018) *op.cit.*

17 *Ibid.* 190.

18 Reich, D. (2018) *Who We Are and How We Got Here.* Oxford: Oxford University Press.

19 *Ibid.,* 97.

20 Plomin, R. (2018) *Blueprint: How DNA Makes Us Who We Are.* London: Penguin Books.

21 *Ibid.* 186.

22 Bloodworth, J. (2016) *The Myth of Meritocracy: Why Working-class Kids Get Working-class Jobs.* London: Biteback Publishing.

23 Chang, C. et al (3 February, 2022) People's Desire To Be In Nature And How They Experience It Are Partially Heritable. *Plos Biology.* https://journals.plos.org/plosbiol ogy/article. Accessed on: 18 May 2022.

24 Hunt-Grubbe, C. (14 October 2007) The Elementary DNA of Dr Watson. *Sunday Times Magazine.* www.thetimes.co.uk/article/the-elementary-dna-of-dr-watson-gllb6w2vpdr. Accessed on: 14/09/2020.

25 Dean, C. (October 19, 2007) Nobel Winner Issues Apology for Comments About Blacks. *New York Times.* www.nytimes.com/2007/10/19/science/19watson.html. Accessed on: 14/09/2020.

26 Rushton, J.P. and Jensen, A.R. (November 2008) James Watson's most inconvenient truth: Race realism and the moralistic fallacy. Medical Hypotheses 71(5):629–40. DOI: 10.1016/j.mehy.2008.05.031 www.researchgate.net/publication/51429413_James_Watson%27s_most_inconvenient_truth_Race_realism_and_the_moralistic_fallacy. Accessed on: 14/09/2020.

27 Herrnstein, R. and Murray, C. (1994) *The Bell Curve.* New York: Simon & Schuster.

28 Mukherjee, S. (2016) *The Gene: An Intimate History.* London: Vintage.

29 For details on the University of Oxford's Intergrowth 21st Project, see www.intergrowth21.org.uk/

30 Flynn, J. (2012) *Are We Getting Smarter? Rising IQ in the Twenty-First Century.* Cambridge: Cambridge University Press. 32.

31 Flynn, J. (2016) *Does Your Family Make You Smarter? Nature, Nurture and Human Autonomy.* Cambridge: Cambridge University Press. 6.

32 Wilson, E. (1975. 2000 edition) *Sociobiology: The New Synthesis.* Cambridge MA: Belknap Press of Harvard University Press. vi.

33 Wilson, E. (1978. 2004 edition) *On Human Nature.* Cambridge, MA: Harvard University Press.

34 Lewontin, R. (1991) *Biology as Ideology: The Doctrine of DNA.* New York: HarperCollins Publishers.

35 Joseph, J. (2015) *The Trouble with Twin Studies: A Reassessment of Twin Research in the Social and Behavioral Sciences.* New York: Routledge.

36 Joseph, J. (2004) *The Gene Illusion: Genetic Research in Psychiatry and Psychology Under the Microscope.* New York: Algora Publishing.

37 See for example, Yudell, M. (2018) *Race Unmasked: Biology and Race.* New York: Columbia University Press.

38 UNESCO (1950) *The Race Question, including Text of the Statement Issued 18th July 1950.* Paris: UNESCO Publication 791.

39 Galton, F. (1869) *Hereditary genius: An inquiry into its laws and consequences.* London: Macmillan and Co.

40 Schultz, A. (1908) *Race or Mongrel: a Brief History of the Rise and Fall of the Ancient Races of Earth.* Boston: L.C. Page.

41 de Souza, V. S. (July 2016) Science and Miscegenation in the Early Twentieth Century: Edgard Roquette-Pinto's Debates and Controversies with US Physical Anthropology. *História, Ciências, Saúde – Manguinhos,* V.23, N.3. Available at: www.scielo.br/hcsm. www.scielo.br/pdf/hcsm/v23n3/en_0104-5970-hcsm-S0104-59702016005000014.pdf. de Souza discusses Grant, M. (1916) *The Passing of the Great Race.* New York: Charles Scribner's Sons. 1916; and Stoddard, L. (1920) *The Rising Tide of Color Against White World-Supremacy.* New York: Charles Scribner's Sons. 1920.

42 Davenport, C. and Steggerda, M. (1929) *Race Crossing in Jamaica.* New York: Carnegie Institution of Washington.

43 Joseph (Sir Keith) Speech at Edgbaston ("Our Human Stock is Threatened"). (19 October 1974) Grand Hotel, Edgbaston, Birmingham. Source: CCOPR 509/74. www.margaretthatcher.org/document/101830. Accessed on: 15/09/2020.

44 Conversation 700–10, 3 April 3, 1972, *Nixon Presidential Materials*, The White House Communications Agency Sound Recordings Collection.

45 Raterman, E. (March 29, 2019) Tracing the History of Forced Sterilization within the United States. *Health Law & Policy Brief.* www.healthlawpolicy.org/tracing-the-history-of-forced-sterilization-within-the-united-states. Accessed on: 15/09/2020.

46 The Economist (4 April 2019) The Promise and Perils of Synthetic Biology. *The Economist.*

47 Rutherford, A. (2022) *Control: The Dark History and Troubling Present of Eugenics.* London: Weidenfeld & Nicolson.

48 Dawkins, R. & Wong, Y. (2004. 2016 updated edition) *The Ancestor's Tale: A Pilgrimage to the Dawn of Life.* London: Weidenfeld & Nicolson. 51.

49 Pinker, S. (2002) *The Blank Slate: The Modern Denial of Human Nature.* London: Penguin.

50 Mukherjee, S. (2016) *op.cit.*

51 de Waal, F. (2022) *Different: What Apes Can Teach Us About Gender.* London: Granta.

52 Fuentes, A. (2012) *op. cit.*

53 *Ibid.* 66.

54 Ridley, M. (2004 Edition) *Nature Via Nurture: Genes, Experience and What Makes Us Human.* London: Fourth Estate.

55 *Ibid.* 90.

56 *Ibid.* 75.

57 Murdock, G. (1945) The Common Denominator of Cultures, in Linton, R. (ed) *The Science of Man in the World Crisis.* New York: Columbia University Press: 123–142. Quoted by Edward O Wilson. (1978. 2004 edition) On Human Nature. Cambridge, MA: Harvard University Press. 22.

58 These were: age-grading, athletic sports, bodily adornment, calendar, cleanliness training, community organisation, cooking, cooperative labour, cosmology, courtship, dancing, decorative art, divination, division of labour, dream interpretation, education, eschatology, ethics, ethno-botany, etiquettte, faith healing, family feasting, fire-making, folklore, food taboos, funeral rites, games, gestures, gift-giving, government, greetings, hair styles, hospitality, housing, hygiene, incest taboos, inheritance rules, joking, kin groups, kinship nomenclature, language, law, luck superstitions, magic, marriage, mealtimes, medicine, obstetrics, penal sanctions, personal names, population policy, postnatal care, pregnancy usages, property rights, propitiation of supernatural beings, puberty customs, religious ritual, residence rules, sexual restrictions, soul concepts, status differentiation, surgery, tool-making, trade, visiting, weather control, and weaving.

59 Brown, D. (1991) *Human Universals.* New York: McGraw Hill.

60 Birch, J., Ginsburg, S., & Jablonka, E. (2020) Unlimited Associative Learning and the Origins of Consciousness: A Primer and Some Predictions. *Biology & Philosophy.* 35(56) 1–23. This article distils key issues found in: Ginsburg, S. and Jablonka, E. (2019) *The Evolution of the Sensitive Soul: Learning and the origins of Consciousness.* Cambridge MA: MIT Press.

61 Ganti, T. (2003) *The Principles of Life.* Oxford: Oxford University Press.

62 Salzberg, S. (2018) Open questions: How many genes do we have? *BMC Biology* volume 16, Article number: 94 (2018) https://bmcbiol.biomedcentral.com/articles/ 10.1186/s12915-018-0564-x. Accessed on: 30/09/2020.

63 An example given in Bajaj, S. (12 August 2022) A Change of Heart. *The Guardian Weekly*.

64 Mukherjee, S. (2016) op. cit. 495.

65 Rutherford, A. (22 September 2018) Human League: What Separates Us from Monkeys and Dolphins - Language, Tool-Use, Non-Reproductive Sex? We Now Have an Answer. *The Guardian*.

66 Griffith, J. (2019) *Freedom: the End of the Human Condition.* Australia: Fedmex Pty Ltd.

67 Graeber, D. and Wengrow, D. (2021) *The Dawn of Everything: A New History of Humanity.* London: Allen Lane.

68 Rutherford, A. (2018) *op. cit.*

7

DEAD END

Is Our End Really Nigh?

From human origins and nature, we turn now to the prospect that the story of *sapiens* has a sad finale, when its sound and fury are brought to ruin by reckless self-harm. Since this existential threat has been raised repeatedly throughout history, it can be dismissed readily by some as doom-laden prophecy of 'end-of-days', associated with eschatology. Essentially, it posits that extinction or near extinction of our species is likely, given combined hazards of: over-population for a finite planet; fouling our own nest in a way that bodes ill for our wider habitat, extreme climate, and related needs like food security; nuclear proliferation; pandemics and biological weapons; acute social inequality; and the unprecedented peril of a species possibly creating a higher intelligence to itself, considered in the next chapter.

To begin with, we'll ponder whether the problem is population – the paradox that in over-breeding, humans harbour a death-wish – or whether our behaviour has been literally earth-shattering, particularly in carbon and radiation emission. *People say that time goes by; time says that people go by.* That Vietnamese proverb suggests we will likely perish before the planet. After all, it has bid final farewell to many species. In short, if we don't count in the risk of wipe-out, we risk being out for the count. Anyway, let's start by counting people.

Safety in Numbers?

Some 12,000 years ago – the end of the last Ice Age – world population was 4 million,[1] about half the size of present-day Switzerland. Today it is around 8 billion. But it is heavily concentrated. Just seven countries account for about half. In this uneven spread, the top two countries – China and India – account for over one third of world total, whereas the next country down, the US,

DOI: 10.4324/9781003106593-9

accounts for only 4.25 percent. Expressed differently, after China and India, the five next big countries (16 percent approximately) account for less than India (17.7 percent). In 2023, India is due to overtake China as the largest populated country.

Back in 1950, China's population was 543.98 million. By 2021, this had grown almost three-fold to 1.43 billion. Over the same period, India's population grew from 357.02 million to 1.41 billion; and the United States from 148.28 million to 337 million. More recently the global growth rate has declined. Since 2019, it has dropped below 1 percent, under half its peak figure of 2.3 percent in the 1960s. Though reduced fertility levels are slowing growth, United Nations medium-variant projections suggest that global population could grow to around 9.7 billion in 2050, and 10.4 billion in 2100. Already a 7-fold population increase within barely over two centuries has pressured the living environment to sustainably supply food, shelter, fuel and wellbeing for human habitat.[2] Will humanity come to agree with Sartre's comment: 'hell is other people'?

From 2.5 billion people in 1950, within my lifetime, there has been over a three-fold increase. It took all of human history up to 1804 to reach the first billion. The second billion took 123 years (1927); the third took 23 years (1959); the fourth, 15 years (1974); the fifth, 13 years (1987); the sixth and seventh, 12 years each (1999 and 2011). World population growth *rate* peaked in 1965–1970. As stated earlier, for the last half century, it has slowed, and further slowdown is expected to the close of this century. But projected *absolute* growth is unevenly spread. While sub-Saharan Africa's population is expected to double by 2050 (99 percent), accounting for just over half of the extra near two billion people, Europe and Northern America will likely see a small rise (2 percent). The world is shifting away from the West.

In the previous chapter, attention was drawn to our journey out of Africa. This century's big population story will be African growth. Up to 1995, people in Europe always outnumbered those in Africa, but Africa's population has nearly doubled in 25 years.[3] The UN foresees its present populace of around 1.3 billion as more than tripling to 4.3 billion by 2100, similar to the current Asian population, which is 4.6 billion, having risen from 1.4 billion in 1950. With just over 17 percent of global population today, Africa's share will increase to around 40 percent.

On these projections, Asia will rise to around 5.3 billion by mid-century to decline to under 5 billion by century end, and its share will drop from nearly 60 percent now to just over 40 percent. In other words, by 2100, eight out of every ten people will inhabit Africa and Asia. In 1950, of the top ten countries in the world in population terms, three were in Europe – Germany, the UK, and Italy. In 2020, there were no European countries in the top ten. The full import of this axis shift from Atlantic to Pacific has yet to be grasped.

Some of this pattern is well-set. For instance, population increase in Nigeria and Pakistan has more than doubled in the last thirty years. Across the next thirty, over half of global population increase will happen in just nine countries: India, Nigeria, Pakistan, the Congo, Ethiopia, Tanzania, Indonesia, Egypt, and the USA.[4] The poorest countries have been growing faster than the rest of the world. In the case of least developed countries (LDCs), numbers are expected to nearly double from the current one billion to 1.9 billion by mid-century, and then to 3 billion by 2100.[5]

This poses big challenges to sustainable development goals of ending poverty, hunger and malnutrition; improving quality and reach of health and education; and attaining greater social equality. At the same time, there is a 'demographic dividend' in many parts of sub-Saharan Africa, and parts of Asia and Latin America, where falling fertility rates means that working age population is growing faster than 'dependent' age groups, thereby stepping up economic development potential. Overall, the global population numbers are indicative of great social improvements: diminished infant mortality; improved longevity; and women getting more control over their fertility.

While the above data is from United Nations demographers,[6] an authoritative 2020 study by Vollset et al.[7] estimates population peak at 9.7 billion in 2064, declining to 8.8 billion by century's end.[8] Two things stand out in this alternative take. First, total numbers would be around 2 billion less in 2100, a significant decrease on what has been expected for some time, offering good potential for pollution reduction, food security, and response to climate change. Second, for one country within Africa to overtake the present largest country would be astonishing.

Both studies agree that changing age structure will be dramatic. The UN notes that in 2018, for the first time ever, persons aged 65 or more outnumbered the under-fives. Their share of global population is anticipated to increase from 10 percent in 2022 to 16 percent in 2050, at which time they will be more than twice the number of the under-fives. Ageing is most prevalent at present in Europe and Northern America, with 18 percent aged 65 or over. By mid-century, one in every four persons in Europe and Northern America could be in this older group. Those aged 80 or over numbered 143 million in 2019, almost triple the 1990 figure, and it is expected to triple again by mid-century to 426 million, and to double that by century end. This high share of older people bodes less tax revenue from income and consumer spending alongside greater pressure on state pensions, health and social care, and more emphasis on export-led growth. In 2019, global life expectancy got to 72.8 years, an enhancement of nearly nine years since 1990. But this improved longevity is uneven. The life expectancy gap between the least well-off countries and the global average was 7 years in 2021.[9]

How the politics plays out with this tension will be interesting, since this group's electoral importance is tied to their high voting rate. Notably, they're more inclined to be conservative in respect of issues like culture wars, immigration, and national sovereignty. As elderly numbers increase worldwide with social and health improvements, ageing population will become a global challenge. On one estimate,[10] by 2100, there will be 2.4 billion over-65s compared to 1.7 billion under-20s, and the over-80s, having risen six-fold to 866 million, will outnumber the under-fives by over two to one.

In 1950, for everyone turning 80, there were 25 births; in 2017 it was seven. By 2100, it is projected to be one. Relative loss of young people may augur well for less violent crime, smaller armies and less warfare, or it may simply mean high-tech wars fought with less boots on the ground. It's possible that with greater numbers of smaller families, the world will get less warlike, since parents will be even more conscious of losing children in mortal combat.[11]

Large population loss throughout the rest of this century for twenty-three countries, including China, Japan, Thailand and Spain, calls for decisive political response to offset economic consequence: incentives to raise fertility rates; less publically-funded contraceptive access; longer working lives and higher labour market participation rates; greater use of robotics and other means of higher productivity; and more net migration.

Between 2000 and 2020, the input of global migration to population growth in high income countries (net inflow of 80.5 million) surpassed the surplus of births over deaths (66.2 million). In essence, migration will be the lone propellant of population growth in those countries in the next period.[12] Paradoxically, rich countries presently face political pushback against immigration. Yet, when they come to rely on it to preserve their wealth, the poor countries that export their ablest as emigrants, may boost education and living standards to avert a brain-drain as they economically improve. So, when some countries need immigrants most, they may be available least.

People of Colour

Morland (2019)[13] captures demographic change in colour. We're getting more *grey* – between 1960 and 2100, the median-aged person will have doubled in age from just under twenty to just over forty. We can become more *green* if the rate of human innovation in addressing planet harm outpaces the slowing rate of population growth, such as better crop yields allowing for more land to return to nature. And we're becoming less *white*. In 1950, Europe accounted for around 22 percent of the world's people. Adding mostly white Northern America, Australia and New Zealand, it was 29 percent. By 2015, Europe's share was 10 percent, and the wider white geography was almost half what it was, at 15 percent. Such contraction helps fuel the foreboding behind vile ideas like 'The Great Replacement'.

UN median projections for century-end will see these shares drop to 6 percent and 11 percent. Moreover, these countries themselves are less pale. Morland notes that in 1965, US whites held an overwhelming 85 percent national share, which was cut to two thirds by 2005, and is set to go below half by 2050.

Meanwhile, Africa's ascent is astounding. Sub-Saharan Africa is predicted to go from being home to one in ten of humanity in 1950, to one in four by 2100.

Like genes, demography isn't destiny. But it matters a great deal. For instance, I'm part of the Western post-war baby boom that saw the share of young people rise by the 1960s. In turn, this gave rise to youth culture. In the 1960s, we had songs of 'my generation', expressing desire to die before getting old; of changing times in which parents were invited to get out of the new road if they couldn't lend a hand; of a strange vibration, in which a whole generation claimed a new explanation. In short, many Western youth had a sense of their size and significance, and shaped a radical politics of dissent, even if it translated by decade's end into many conservative governments.

Even today, population size can make a country economically and geo-politically significant, even if many inhabitants are poor, as in China and India. Going back in history, we can see this persistent social impact of demography. Population surge in the late-1700s, both fed off, and into, the industrial revolution. Expanding workforces in Britain and Europe manned factories, mills and mines. The steam engine, and later hydro-electric power, together with mechanisation allowed mass production and transport infrastructures for exports. Resultant higher wages raised domestic consumption. Improved living standards in the eighteenth-century increased longevity. But industrialisation also brought child labour, grim working conditions, pollution, and growth of cities, where densely-packed insanitary conditions produced a cholera outbreak in mid-nineteenth century Britain. Environmental health for the poor was slow in coming.

European expansion in people and power was linked to imperialism. Of course, we can forget that imperialism wasn't invented by the modern West. In ancient times, we had Greek and Roman empires. Thinking back to the Middle Ages, the Mongol Empire covered around a quarter of global population, 110 million people between 1270 and 1309, and about a sixth of world landmass. The Ming dynasty built a naval supremacy that supported their treasure voyages between 1405 and 1433 in the South China Sea and Indian Ocean, and later to East Africa. By the fifteenth and sixteenth centuries, the so-called Age of Discovery was led in Europe by Portugal and Spain, with later naval and land catch-up by the Dutch, French and British. If you ever visit the Cape of Good Hope and Cape Agulhas at the most southern edge of Africa, where Atlantic and Pacific oceans meet, you get a good vantage of the sea route taken by the Portuguese da Gama toward India in the late fifteenth century. Such expeditions gave rise in turn to systematic colonialism in Africa, Asia, Australia and Americas, under which European powers battled for command over global riches, labour and trade.

Particularly shameful was the religious validation of this colonial domination. For instance, following the West Indies landing by Columbus in 1492, empire-building rivalry between Spaniards and Portuguese led Spanish

Pope Alexander VI to issue papal bulls in 1493 to apportion 'legitimate' possession of newly discovered territories not already under Christian rule. These papal decrees influenced the 1494 Treaty of Tordesillas between Portugal and the Spanish monarchs, sharing out spoils, and approved by Pope Julius II in 1506. Obviously come the Protestant Reformation from 1517, such 'Catholic' arrangements were never going to hold the same sway. But religious sanctioning of colonialism in the name of spreading the faith continued for many to be an article of faith.

Over time, Britain's reign outreached all others. When I was in primary school, the dated world map used was overwhelmingly red, signifying Britain's once extensive domain. British seafarers – Francis Drake, Walter Raleigh, James Cook – ruling the waves with grand discovery voyages from 1570s to 1770s, were presented to us from childhood as adventurous heroes. Less was told about the exploitative nature of imperialism that ensued: privateer government/commercial enterprises in the colonies – for example, the East India Company and the Virginia Company; the infamous deportation of convicts to Australia's Botany Bay in 1788 that could be traced to the 1597 British Act legalising transfer of criminals to colonies; major disasters such as the Great Famine of Bengal killing over 10 million from 1769–73, due to both drought and failure of colonial rulers to waive land taxes, improve irrigation, and shift back from cash to edible crops; how little was learned, so that disaster repeated itself in the Irish famine in mid-nineteenth century, and in the Bengal famine in 1943; the European slave trade in the fifteenth century, with Portuguese and later others abducting West Africans to enslave in Europe; and then from the sixteenth century, the Euro-American slave trade that trafficked Africans as chattel, mostly to sugar and cotton plantations in the Americas.

From 1787, when Wilberforce's campaign to end slavery in British colonies started, it took nearly half a century to see some success. In 1807, conveying slaves in British ships or to British colonies was proscribed. But formal slavery abolition across the British Empire had to wait until 1833. Of course, it's wrong to think of human-bondage as a peculiarly modern white European sin. It's there in antiquity. It's in scripture, and not just the Hebrew bible. In the name of Apostle Paul, founder of Christianity, slaves are commanded to obey their masters in Ephesians 6:5–8. And it isn't always about white conquest and black affliction.

Davis[14] recounts the Barbary slave trade, concentrated in the sixteenth and eighteenth centuries that saw North African piracy of European merchant shipping, and coastal raids up to Italy and as far as the Netherlands, capturing around one million people for slave markets. When Ferdinand and Isabella expelled the Moors from southern Spain at the end of the fifteenth century, many fled to North Africa, where they rejuvenated a Muslim population, some of whom became intent on revenge with European Christendom. While this enslavement can be considered negligible compared to the trans-Atlantic trade of ten to twelve million black African slaves over four centuries, its victims still endured the yoke of cruel captivity. Nevertheless, the bigger stain of European colonialism both fed off, and into, a mindset about being a superior breed, evident in Winston Churchill's imperious comment to the Palestine Royal Commission in 1937:[15]

> *I do not admit for instance, that a great wrong has been done to the Red Indians of America or the black people of Australia. I do not admit that a wrong has been done to these people by the fact that a stronger race, a higher-grade race, a more worldly wise race to put it that way, has come in and taken their place.*

For such people, population was about quality not quantity. A minority could legitimately dominate a majority because they were both bulldog and top-dog. Imperialist conceit was premised on the immoral equation: *bright* plus *might* equals *right*.

Counting and Accountability

Shape of population *within* a state also impacts its politics and economics. For instance, Wyoming has a population of 580,000. Compare that to California's 39.8 million, which surpasses Canada or Australia. Despite this, America's out-dated government system accords each two senators. Moreover, while California is ethnically diverse, Wyoming is 91.4 percent white. In general, the former leans heavily to Democrats, while the latter pushes to Republicans.

Similarly, demography is at the heart of the Israel/Palestine conflict, with the Israeli government pursuing ethnocratic policies of illegal settlements in East Jerusalem and the West Bank as part of their policy to contain Palestinian population growth. Yiftachel calls it 'the long-term Zionist strategy of Judaizing the homeland'.[16] I have witnessed the cruelty of this subjection, particularly in and around Jerusalem, including meeting firsthand the distraught owner of a demolished Palestinian home amidst the rubble that Israeli security forces left him. Put simply, if your security depends on numbers, your future is precarious.

When I was a child in Northern Ireland, Protestant-Catholic proportions were two-thirds/one-third, and Protestant intent for continued unity with Britain seemed safe in that firm majority. In the 2021 Census, for the first time Catholics (45.7 percent) outnumbered Protestants (43.5 percent), and partly linked to that, Northern Ireland's destiny, whether with Britain or the rest of Ireland, is up for grabs. Population matters in great part because it shifts. It's reliably unreliable. And in its shift, it recalibrates ethnic power.

The role of ethnic hatred is evident in Africa's post-colonial civil wars. From the 3.8 million deaths in the Congo (1998–2002) to the UN-estimated 300,000 deaths in Darfur (2003-present), over eleven million fatalities have been estimated, covering thirteen major conflicts.[17] Ethnic cleansing, like 'collateral damage', are offensive euphemisms for brutality. For instance, the Rwandan genocide that involved Hutu militias and army members overseeing the slaughter of around 900,000 Tutsis, over a three-month period in 1994, testifies to the terror. Such atrocities can be attributed to colonial legacy, whereby artificial borders disturbed ethnic comfort, and in particular circumstance like Rwanda, the former Belgian masters favoured the Tutsi minority over the overwhelming Tutu majority, thereby stoking tensions for later eruption. Such colonial malice is hardly disputable. But many African states have been independent for as long as they have suffered European subjugation, and many leaderships have been guilty of divisive rule, motivated by personal corruption rather than revolutionary deliverance.

The Cold War bears witness to this cynical use of 'ideology'. Soviets and Americans fought each other in the name of communism versus capitalism in a series of proxy wars from Korea and Vietnam to Nicaragua, costing an estimated eleven million lives.[18] Take what happened in Cambodia's killing fields under Pol Pot's Khmer Rouge. Kiernan estimates that 'the 1975–79 death toll was between 1.671 and 1.871 million people, 21 to 24 percent of Cambodia's 1975 population'.[19] Longstanding ethnic hostility between Cambodia and Vietnam prompted the latter's 1978 invasion of Cambodia, effectively routing the Kymer Rouge by early 1979. This became a proxy battle between China as benefactor of the Khmer Rouge and Russia as sponsor of the Vietnamese. So much for America's domino theory that international communist solidarity was the basis for its global spread.

In effect, the Americans sided with China, which backed Khmer fugitives, against what both saw as the new Soviet-puppet regime in Phnom Penh. Throughout the 1980s, big-power geopolitics saw Pol Pot's regime flag fly over the United Nations, as they retained their seat in that august assembly until 1991, despite their genocidal crimes.[20] Adding salt to the wound, Kymer Rouge diplomats represented victims of their own regime. Simultaneously, much of the West refused aid to the 'illegal' Cambodian government. If you visit Cambodia even today, the trauma of American bombing and invasion, Pol Pot, and subsequent Western neglect, is evident in what remains a shattered society. Such duplicity exposes misguided banners that extol America as staunch champion of the free world, or figures like Mao as liberators of the oppressed. It's a reminder that often the world needs saving from its saviours.

Last century, wars took a big toll. While World Wars I and II, and later the Cold War, are usually seen separately, White treats them together, as what he calls the *Hemoclysm* ('blood flood'), costing altogether 150 million lives, over 80 percent of violent deaths in the twentieth-century. For him, Hitler, Stalin and Mao were key players in World War II, which was an upshot of the Great War, with its spin-off in the Russian Revolution. Similarly, overthrow of Chinese monarchy installed Chiang Kai-shek, who was confronted by Mao, and consequent chaos encouraged Japanese ambitions in China. Collapse of the Japanese empire, following 1945, left places like Korea as battlegrounds for contesting Cold War combatants.

In short, these were inter-connected events that followed the Ottoman demise in the West, leaving areas like the Balkans subject to rivalry between Russia and Austria-Hungary, whose conflict eventually embraced a wider world; and in the East, the downfall of the Chinese emperor, leading to four decades of civil strife that drew a Japanese expansionist drive, but ended with Mao's despotism from 1949–1976. Largely, the story is of falling empires giving rise to new empires. His study of human atrocities leads White to conclude that turmoil is deadlier than tyranny. Mass killings come mainly from collapse, rather than exercise, of authority. Moreover, since war tends to kill more civilians than military, the army can be the safest haven during combat. In summary, he says:[21]

> *By my calculation, around 3.5 percent of all deaths in the twentieth century were caused by war, genocide, or tyranny. This is certainly higher than the 2 percent who died of these causes in the nineteenth century, but less than the 15 percent that anthropologists and archaeologists have found to be average for tribal, pre-state societies.*

Presently, 'tribes' seem to be on the march again. Most organised violent conflicts are *within* rather than *between* states. In 2019, there were seven wars amid 54 state-based conflicts, 28 of which involved Islamic State, al-Qaida or linked organisations. With the routing of Islamic State in Syria and Iraq, 40 percent of the 31,200 global fatalities were in Afghanistan in 2019, and there was an increased share of transnational jihadist violence in Africa.[22] Conventional war continues to threaten humanity, but for now less so.

We have other ways of killing ourselves. It's true that a big killer of humans – an annual average of one million deaths – is from another species, namely mosquito-borne disease. It's also true that with our significant global hike in health and living standards, yearly death rates (deaths per 1000) have improved considerably. Back in 1950, it was 20.150, whereas in 2021 it was 7.645.[23] But if we add annual murders, suicides, traffic accidents, state executions, alcohol and drug abuse, and human-mediated disease, we can say that in some way humans are responsible for killing around six million humans on average each year. Let's never be blind to our gift as a species for self-harm. It is particularly poignant when young children are the victims. In the US, a country where there are over 390 million guns owned by civilians, there were 45,222 gun-related fatalities in 2020, a year which saw guns overtake vehicle crashes as the main cause of death for children and teenagers.[24] From 1970 to 2022, there have been over 1,369 school shootings,[25] with a particularly tragic incident in an Texan elementary school in May 2022, leaving 19 children and three adults dead, nearly ten years after the Sandy Hook elementary school massacre, which killed 20 children and six school employees. Such crimes by humans against humanity have been a constant feature of our species. The difference now is that we have much greater potential for self-inflicted detriment.

To avert prospect of serious annihilation, famed naturalist David Attenborough sees planned global population reduction as essential: "All our environmental problems become easier to solve with fewer people, and harder – and ultimately impossible – to solve with ever more people."[26] While accepting need for multiple policies: switch to renewable energy; less meat consumption; deforestation reversal; education investment; enhanced women's rights; end to poverty; and sustainable ocean management, he sees our numbers in, and consumption of, the planet as twin key factors. But it's important not to lump the two together.

As previously noted, world population growth rate has dropped from 2.3 percent per year in the 1960s to below 1.00 percent per year now. Conversely, global consumption rate growth is around 3 percent annually.[27] Per capita consumption rate in rich countries is around thirty times that in poor countries. Naturally, the latter are keen to catch up. For Monbiot, environmental footprint can be assessed as follows: impact = population x affluence x technology. But population growth is concentrated among the poorest, who lack affluence and technology.[28] While consumption and population are related, it's the former that should be of primary concern as threat to a habitable planet.

Concern about the planet being overrun by hordes of people as our numbers escalated has been perennial. It has included stories of Great Floods being deployed by various deities to tame the human surge, to Malthus in 1798 (when there were 800 million rather than 8 billion people on Earth), arguing that while unbridled population growth operated in geometrical ratio, survival capacity, in terms of basics like food, rose in arithmetical ratio.[29] Again, often these anxieties emphasised the differential fertility of 'lower classes' or particular ethnicities. Looking ahead, we don't know for sure whether the population projections are accurate. But it's safe to conclude that for the rest of this century, humans are going to have to deal with a massive populace trying to co-habit a vulnerable planet, where human footprint is omnipresent. It suggests an era offering stark choice of beneficial co-existence or existential calamity. But is it that simple?

The Human Age

In mid-twentieth century, Mumford[30] talked about the prospect of a doomed planet, with deforestation, over-exploited land, soil erosion, lowering of the water table, atmospheric and stratospheric pollution, and misused atomic energy. He was identifying the *Great Acceleration* of the postwar period that saw rapid expansion of population, industrialisation, urbanisation, technology, and energy use. Atomic bomb tests were increasing atmospheric radioactivity.

A few decades later, proliferating microplastics were becoming another source of environmental damage. For some, we were in a new era:[31]

> *By the end of the century, atmospheric CO2 levels were a third above pre-industrial levels and climbing steeply. Surface reactive nitrogen and phosphorus levels had doubled. Landscape was being reshaped, not least with half a trillion tons of concrete, and new chemical products such as persistent pesticides and plastics were becoming widely disseminated on land and in the sea. The biosphere, too, was being remoulded by increasing extinctions, myriad species invasions, and the increasing domination of domesticated over wild species.*

Recognition of human sway over earth goes back a few centuries, and in 1922, Russian geologist, Pavlov, used the term *Anthropocene* to signify this human-dominated age. The idea of human centrality on the planet was attuned to Christian theology, which saw *sapiens* as not only special and superior, but also accorded dominion over the natural world by God. In a more secular and humanist twentieth century, it also fitted Marxist assumption about people's power to remake themselves and their world.[32]

At the start of this century, Crutzen[33] argued the Anthropocene as a new planetary phase, distinctive from the Holocene, which refers to the geological epoch covering 10–12 millennia since the last Ice Age. Tracing Anthropocenic beginnings to late eighteenth-century, with rising levels of carbon dioxide and methane, and overlapping with emergence of the Watt steam engine, he identified environmental deterioration by 2000 in terms of many factors. They included: acidification, and photochemical pollution; 1.4 billion methane-emitting cows; 30–50 percent of earth's land surface and over half of available freshwater, under human exploitation; dam construction; vanishing rainforests; a 16-fold rise in energy use in the last century, discharging annually 160 million tonnes of atmospheric sulphur dioxide; and threatened ecosystems from, for example, increased use of nitrogen fertilizer, fossil-fuel and biomass burning. Thus, man-made chemical compounds, such as chlorofluorocarbon gases, accountable for the ozone patch, have made pervasive and pronounced geological imprint.[34]

Human reshaping of the Earth system, signatured in sediments and ice, is considered by some leading geologists, like Zalasiewicz,[35] sufficiently significant to merit designation of the Anthropocene Epoch in the Geological Time Scale. Rapid global spread of artificial new materials like microplastics – 'technofossils'; rising levels of polyaromatic hydrocarbons, polychlorinated biphenyls, and pesticide residues; rising nitrate and phosphorous levels; and radioactive fallout from thermonuclear weapons tests, all contribute.

With average global temperature increase of 0.6° to 0.9°C from 1900 to the present, changes have intensified since 1950.[36] This distinctive period can be cast in terms of excessive population growth, production and consumption, mineral extraction, intensive agriculture, militarisation, and globalisation. It can be regarded as a new geological epoch or a new part of an existing epoch. In terms of origin, it can be seen as 70 years, or centuries, in duration. Whatever way it's cast, the Anthropocene implies human's predominant imprint on the planet. It sees us as an overwhelming force *of*, and *in*, nature.

In considering the diminishing life-support system of the living world over his lifetime, Attenborough takes several indicators of decline. One is remaining wilderness. Whereas in 1937, it was 66 percent, by 1968 it was 59 percent; by 1989 it was 49 percent; and by 2020, it was 35 percent. This taming of nature involved humans overrunning the earth, evident also in the over-halving of wild animal populations since the 1950s. In changing temperature and chemistry in land and ocean, we are usurping the planet as ours alone to use and abuse:[37]

> *It took a million years of unprecedented volcanic activity during the Permian to poison the ocean. We have begun to do so again in less than two hundred. By burning fossil fuels, we are releasing the carbon dioxide captured by prehistoric plants over millions of years in a few decades....Our addiction to coal, oil and gas was on course to knock our environment from its benign, level setting and trigger something similar to a mass extinction.*

Hot Water

Five mass extinctions have afflicted the Earth in the distant past, due to *natural* events such as meteor collision; volcanic eruption; and oceanic toxicity from blue-green algae. While disasters such as landslides, earthquakes, droughts, flooding, tsunamis, hurricanes and tornadoes still threaten human life, it's speculated that the Toba catastrophe about 75,000 years ago – eruption of Indonesia's Toba supervolcano – saw air temperature plunge, bringing severe climatic change that nearly exterminated humans. Supposedly, it produced a genetic bottleneck, whereby only 10,000–30,000 people survived.

In the Anthropocene, over-drive *human* action has shaken and stirred the eco-system to a potential sixth mass extinction. Intensive agribusiness uses synthetic fertilizers for high-yield crops, emitting nitrous oxide, and methane emissions from ruminants and biomass burning, and with high dependency on irrigation water. At the same time, there's wastage of 25–30 percent of produced food. We have degradation of peatland, important for its high-carbon content storage. Forests that once offered carbon sequestration are commercially logged, or burned for palm oil production. Flora and fauna are lost as wilderness contracts with human migration. Wildfires rage with increased vegetation flammability due to warming. Alongside all this mainly rural depletion, we're experiencing increased riverbank and coastal erosion, nutrient diminution in floodplains, and delta subsidence.

Then you look to what we're doing with cities. Low density urban sprawl and mega-urbanisation, based on car-dependency and high-carbon energy, continue together with precariously placed informal settlements. More extensive industrialisation across the world has brought oil spills into waterways, consumer refuse, and the waste of built-in obsolescence, that pile landfill dumping. Also, it has seen excessive generation of plastic, concrete, and petroleum products, the latter used widely, from vehicle fuel and lubricants to road asphalt.

The natural environment has paid a heavy price. Extraction of minerals such as lignite and phosphate ore impairs nutrient-rich landscapes. Marine ecosystems are blighted with plastic pollution. In the endless drive for new sources of energy, fracking risks contamination by injecting chemicals underground to boost oil and gas flow. Total pollution deaths are at 9 million annually, one in six of all deaths, with a negative impact of $4.6 trillion. Three-quarters of these deaths are attributable to ambient air pollution. Deaths from the latter, together with toxic chemical pollution through lead, are related to expanding industrialisation and urbanisation, and have increased by over two-thirds since 2000.[38]

All this upheaval is now clearly associated with greater frequency and intensity of weather extremes such as dust storms, droughts, flooding, and heatwaves. Impact is also evident in expansion of arid zones, with enhanced desertification, shrinkage of polar zones, thawing of permafrost and sea-level rise, and erosion and bleaching of coral reefs, as ocean acidity increases with rising sea temperatures. Amongst the many effects are food insecurity, and species decline.[39]

A recent report[40] notes that the past fifty years have seen not only a little more than doubling of human population, but also an expansion of the global economy nearly fourfold and a tenfold growth in global trade. As a consequence, we have unprecedented decline in biodiversity, and related problems of pollination and pest control, with significant human repercussion. Since 1970, agricultural crop production has risen about threefold ($2.6 trillion in 2016); and raw timber harvest has risen by 45 percent, with the forestry sector accounting for about 13 million jobs.

Cropping or animal husbandry now cover over one third of the terrestrial land surface. Alongside massive urbanisation and related infrastructure, this expansion has disturbed natural habitats, impairing tropical forests, grasslands and wetlands. Such material output is unsustainable, with its adverse fallout in land degradation and pollinator loss. Wood fuel is the main energy source for over 2 billion people, and twice that number mainly depend on natural medicines for their health care:[41]

> Marine and terrestrial ecosystems are the sole sinks for anthropogenic carbon emissions, with a gross sequestration of 5.6 gigatons of carbon per year (the equivalent of some 60 per cent of global anthropogenic emissions)...diet-related disease drives 20 per cent of premature mortality, related both to undernourishment and to obesity. The great expansion in the production of food, feed, fibre and bioenergy has

occurred at the cost of many other contributions of nature to quality of life, including regulation of air and water quality, climate regulation and habitat provision.

Over 80 percent of global wastewater is being returned untreated to the environment, while every year, 300–400 million tons of heavy metals, solvents, toxic sludge and other industrial wastes are dumped into the world's waters.[42] All this imperils many animals and plants, with around 1 million species facing possible 'further acceleration in the global rate of species extinction, which is already at least tens to hundreds of times higher than it has averaged over the past 10 million years',[43] while 'the fraction of species at risk of climate-related extinction is 5 percent at 2°C warming and rises to 16 percent at 4.3°C warming'.[44] All told, the global Living Planet Index shows persistent decline between 1970–2016, with an average 68 percent decrease in population sizes of mammals, birds, amphibians, reptiles and fish.[45]

The scale and pace of human-induced blight on terrestrial, marine and freshwater ecosystems are extraordinary.[46] Since improving climate resilience needs substantial land for reforestation and bio-energy, such reclamation may vie with current land-use, possibly hiking food and housing prices, and prompting even more exhaustive use of remaining land, with negative implication for biodiversity, and air and water contamination. However, smart land management can upgrade carbon uptake, crop productivity, and soil nutrients. Adjusted consumer conduct can cut excessive food and energy intake. Ensuring reliable global access to nutritious food involves an 'equitable global diet' that addresses food waste; undernourishment of about 821 million people; and overconsumption linked to overweight problems of about two billion adults. A 2022 report[47] on the global food crises estimated that near to 193 million people were acutely food insecure, with critical support needing to be targeted to over half a million (570,000) at risk of starvation and death in Ethiopia, South Sudan, southern Madagascar and Yemen, showing how though multiple linked factors drive the problem, the key one is conflict/insecurity.

Breaking the Ice

Importantly, the challenge facing us is about land and sea. Some 71 percent of earth's surface is global ocean, containing about 97 percent of the planet's water. Around 10 percent comprises ice sheets and glaciers – the cryosphere. As the latter shrinks, sea levels rise and most immediately impact on low-lying coastal communities, currently around 680 million people, and projected to reach above 1 billion by 2050.

A 2019 IPCC report on these areas says that over the last fifty years, the global ocean has absorbed over 90 percent of the climate system excess heat, and ocean thermal rise has increased tropical cyclones and rainfall, raised sea levels and marine acidification, caused glaciers to recede, and aggravated coastal hazards.[48] Given that world trade by volume is still overwhelmingly ship-based, the impact of climate change and pollution on the oceans poses great problems.[49]

Greater urgency is suggested by the 2021 IPCC Report.[50] It notes that observed rises in greenhouse gas concentrations since about 1750 are attributable to human activity. Human influence has heated the climate at a rate that is unprecedented in at least the last 2000 years. Each of the past four decades has been increasingly hotter than any decade that preceded it since 1850. With medium confidence, the report assesses that warming of the global ocean has been faster over the past century than since the close of the last deglacial transition, about 11,000 years ago.

Averaged over the next two decades, global temperature is anticipated to hit or surpass 1.5°C of warming, bringing increased heatwaves.[51] Sea level rise will persist throughout this century, bringing more recurrent and perilous coastal flooding in low-lying districts and greater coastal erosion. With high confidence, the report notes that global mean sea level has risen faster since 1900 than over the preceding century in at least the last 3000 years. Repeatedly, the report stresses the role of human influence.

Impact will be global, but imbalanced. Even in one country – the US – we're already seeing the strange mismatch of drought and water supply problems in the western part, in places like California, alongside floods in the eastern flank. It raises the possible paradox that in a planet overwhelmingly made up of water, there could be a supply problem of useable water, echoing Coleridge's lines in the Rime of the Ancient Mariner: 'water, water everywhere, nor any drop to drink'.

In response to these threats, the last half century has seen common action for a fairer and more sustainable planet, including: the 1972 first Earth Summit in Stockholm; the second in Nairobi in 1982; the third in Rio in 1992 when 178 countries espoused *Agenda 21*, a global effort for sustainable development. These initiatives were followed by the 1997 Kyoto Agreement on preventative steps on climate change, and *the Millennium Declaration* adopted by UN member states in 2000 to tackle extreme poverty by 2015. The fourth Earth Summit in Johannesburg in 2002, emphasised multilateral partnerships for ending poverty and environmental neglect.

Significantly, in 2012, Rio+20 started a process of agreeing specific Sustainable Development Goals (SDGs), which led in 2015 to the UN Sustainable Development Summit adopting 17 SDGs. Then the Paris Agreement on Climate Change in 2015, set a collective framework to limit global warming to between 1.5°C and under 2°C. The UN 2019 Climate Summit committed to cut greenhouse gas emissions (GHG) to prevent the mean global temperature from rising by more than 1.5 °C above preindustrial levels. Leading up to the Glasgow gathering in 2021, the 26th UN Climate Change conference, the UN put the world on a 'red alert' about our imperilled state. The 2022 COP in Egypt was a dispirited affair, making strides in terms of authorising a 'loss and damages' fund to help poor countries redress the devastation visited on them by climate extremities, while back-peddling on stricter controls on fossil fuels, if the 1.5 °C commitment is to be meaningful. While the new fund is a breakthrough beyond the funding for adaptation, the size, source and distribution of the money remain unsettled, as does the extent to which it will really offer reparation by the countries who benefited most from fossil-fuel induced wealth to those that suffer most from the consequences. Future argument about appropriate donors and recipients is likely to create the impasse familiar to seasoned observers of this haggle. As the UK representative, Alok Sharma, noted, missing from the final text were: emissions peaking before 2025; follow-through on withdrawal from coal; and pledge to a full fossil fuel phase-out that, for example, doesn't let gas off the hook. The pervasive presence of the fossil fuel lobby at the conference told its own story about its resilience in the face of efforts to make the world more resilient.

Already, funding devoted to adaptation – such as relocation of the most vulnerable coastal communities, building effective sea-walls and flood defences – is patently inadequate. So a preventative strategy of addressing the cause of the crisis and helping the more immediate victims through mitigation and adaptation is preferable to prioritising a reactive compensatory programme that allocates modest redress when damage has been done. As can be seen from the COP process generally, making final agreement dependent on consensus, rather than on an over-whelming register of the world's population, holds obvious benefit and drawback. While it attempts to keep the reluctant, but important, players on board, it gives proportionately less voice to those most adversely impacted, and it can lead to the lowest common denominator. Sometimes mistakenly attributed to Stalin, the saying that quantity contains its own quality is important here. People on the frontline of the risk should be accorded a special standing.

Before the Deluge

While it would be easy to complain that the long list of pledges over many such events exemplifies the old adage that when all is said and done, there's a lot more said than done, by no means was all this effort in vain. Amidst the whole process, the seventeen SDGs pinpoint action links on environment, economy, education, equality, security, and intergovernmental collaboration.[52] In the case of particular countries, some progress can be identified. For example, UK total carbon footprint has fallen by 29 percent from its 2007 peak, quicker than any other big high-income country.[53]

But despite these efforts, GHG emissions are still rising.[54] Indeed, the UNEP Emissions Gap Report 2019[55] concluded that we were still set for a 3.2°C temperature rise, even if all Paris Agreement pledges were applied. Emissions would have to fall annually from 2020–30 by 7.6 percent for the 1.5°C objective and 2.7 percent annually for the 2°C objective in 2100. Hitting beyond 1.5°C will see greater recurrence and potency of devastating climate impact. Released in October 2021, the UN Emissions Gap Report,[56] revealed that new and updated Nationally Determined Contributions only took 7.5 percent off predicted 2030 emissions. Achievement of the 1.5°C Paris objective, would require a 55 percent figure, and effectively demand halving annual greenhouse gas emissions in the next eight years.

Glasgow's COP26 appeared to have delivered progress on *pledges* for deforestation and methane reduction, and though such moves are seen by some as more 'blah, blah, blah', they can also be seen as piling pressure for delivery. Interestingly, for all the criticism in the next chapter about the intrusiveness of high tech, we have with satellite technology, capacity to monitor actual performance. But even with such oversight, where is the ultimate regulator with meaningful sanction against those countries defaulting on pledges? Also, there is still the failure to follow the money. Insufficient kickback against the big banks, that continue to fund investment in fossil-fuel based activity, remains a telling deficit in the global response.

Critics of the COP process to date charge that many significant pledges have not been met, and this shortfall does not augur well for the credibility of future commitments, and for any hope of hitting the preferred target of 1.5°C. For example, the objective set in 2009 in Copenhagen to generate $100 billion a year by 2020 to distribute to poor countries to help pay for their decarbonisation has not happened. They also worry that some of the key medium-term objectives – such as countries having net zero emissions by 2050 – are too modest, given the urgency, and at the same time far enough in the future to allow many to kick the can down the road. Big cuts need to happen more immediately, and certainly by 2030. Climate emergency isn't about a predicted future. It's happening now. Particular initiatives, like phasing out coal-power, planting and saving more trees, switching to electric cars, converting to non-fossil fuel in the home, and infrastructural works such as coastal protection, need more urgent time-tabling and appropriate funding. Up to now, too often, promises have not been delivered.

Leaked documents in October 2021,[57] showing a range of countries pressing the UN's IPPC report authors to tone down some of the content, reveal a persistent strong lobby from countries with a stake in the carbon-based economy. Among concerns were those from some rich nations, challenging payment levels to poor nations to help with their climate action; Saudi Arabia, Japan and Australia, among others, expressing reservation about the speed of transition from fossil fuels; countries, dependent on oil and coal production, suggesting that the remedy of carbon capture and storage be emphasised; and Brazil and Argentina, as big exporters of beef products and animal feed crops, pushing back against the idea of a more plant-based, rather than meat-based, diet.

Unfortunately, the 71 countries and 11 regions that have targeted zero GHG and carbon emission, at some stage in the last half century, account for only 15 percent of global emissions. While G20 nations together account for 78 percent of total emissions, only five of them have time-lined long-term zero emissions. Environmental justice demands rich countries bear a bigger burden. Dissent by Trump, who withdrew the United States from the Paris Agreement, and by Australia's Morrison and Brazil's Bolsonaro boded ill, despite weather events such as rampant fires in California, New South Wales and the Amazon. Under Biden, the US signalled its aim to rejoin the effort. With new leadership in Australia, Albanese and his Labor Party claim to take climate emergency seriously, and Lula's comeback in Brazil augurs better prospects for the Amazon rainforest, with his commitment at COP27 to zero deforestation by 2030.

In descending rank, the countries emitting most carbon dioxide are: China, United States, India, Russian Federation, and Japan, and three of these have autocratic leaders given to economic nationalism. But five in the top 20 are European: Germany, UK, Poland, France, and Italy,[58] and reparation has to start with the rich.[59] The bottom 100 countries in terms of global greenhouse gas emission account for only 3.6 percent of total share.[60] These disparities make it hard to get international cooperation.

If the finger is pointed at China, it can offer three important mitigations. First, while its absolute contribution ranks top, its per capita share ranks 13th. Second, many of the goods produced by its worst carbon use are destined for the rich world. In a way, Western consumers are 'contracting out' their carbon footprint to China. Finally, it can reasonably claim that it has come late to the party. Whereas the UK may account for only 1 percent of total emissions now, it was in the forefront of industrialism and its related empires.[61] China has now simply joined the capitalist club.

Indeed, some position eco-spoilage within wider capitalist exploitation that abuses nature like it does humans, as material assets from which to draw most profit. For instance, Klein[62] quotes figures that almost half of global carbon emissions come from the world's richest 10 percent, and 70 percent come from the wealthiest 20 percent, who are effectively playing beggar-my-neighbour. The world's poorest, who spoil least, are most hard-hit and heard least, with 140 million in sub-Saharan Africa, Asia and Latin America likely to be displaced by mid-century due to climate strain, setting off new waves of migration upon which populists prey.

Inequity also comes in the developing world's role as dumping ground for hazardous and toxic pollutants, including electronic, industrial and radioactive waste. What has been dubbed 'waste colonialism' involves rich countries using poor countries as cheap waste-disposal sinks. Sale of outdated products is another version. Between 2015–18, Europe, Japan and the United States exported 14 million older poor quality vehicles, with 70 percent destined to developing countries, and with Africa taking the highest share (40 percent).

Most fail to meet minimum safety and environmental standards, and thereby risk higher rates of accidents, pollution, energy consumption, and climate change. Globally, light-duty vehicles are set to at least double by mid-century, and 90 percent of this growth is due in non-OECD countries.[63]

In such a context, some sceptics of the term *Anthropocene*, prefer *Capitalocene*, that acknowledges that the real trouble for the planet started with the Age of Capital that they trace back to mid-fifteenth century, well before the industrial revolution.[64] For them, it is capitalist logic of endless expansion and accumulation, involving the power relationship of capital and nature. It's not a dualism of humanity *and* nature, but rather humanity *in* nature.

Capitalism depends on competition in both labour and land productivity. For instance, the plantations that yielded cotton and sugar had to be exploited to their maximum, as much as the mills that refined sugar and cotton into marketable commodities. Later stages of capitalism, such as Fordist mass production factories, relied on cheap oil, steel and coal. Cheap food production through factory farming helped restrain industrial wages. In all these ways, labour and land are both 'property' to be rendered submissive to maximise profit. Cheap labour needs to be matched with Cheap Nature as an organic whole to be plundered.

So it isn't a case of humanity becoming separated *from* nature as much as a section of humanity – the capitalist class – connecting their enterprise *into* nature, organising nature into the commodity system, appropriating nature as an inexhaustible factor of production. The 1970s oil crisis was a shock to this conceit about Cheap Nature, and can be seen as one pressure for extracting more value from labour in compensation, thereby re-introducing more market 'discipline' that eventually led us to neo-liberalism and rising social inequality.

While abuse of nature and people hasn't yet wiped out the species, it impacts negatively on millions each year. In 1994, the United Nations introduced what it termed 'the human security approach', involving a shift in emphasis from security of territory to that of people. Nearly three decades later, it reports[65] persistent problems: about 2.4 billion people vulnerable to food insecurity, due mainly to inequitable socio-economic and environmental conditions, but exacerbated by the pandemic; a more than doubling of the number of the forcibly displaced in the past decade, even before the Ukrainian tragedy, bringing it to a new high of 100 million in 2022; sexual minorities in 87 percent of 193 countries deprived of full citizen's rights and recognition of their identity; and the scourge of femicide *within* the family, whereby in 2020, 47,000 women and girls are murdered by their intimate partner or a family member. In the face of these kinds of exploitation and cruelty, the 2022 UN report notes:[66]

> *We are faced with a development paradox. Even though people are on average living longer, healthier and wealthier lives, these advances have not succeeded in increasing people's sense of security.*

Unjust economic interactions are matched by unjust ecological ones. In the last third of the nineteenth century, dominant economies like Britain were driving a second industrial revolution based on chemicals, electricity, telecommunications, and motor vehicles. While self-reliant in energy and iron, their technologies depended on natural resources drawn from 'peripheral' countries in the modern imperialist world:[67]

> ....ores such as tin from Malaysia for the processed-food industry, as well as mineral oil; copper from the Andes and the Congo for electrification; gutta-percha for the telegraph network; rubber for mechanical industries....and then for automobiles.

Extraction of such raw materials involved not only abused labour in mines and plantations, but also exploitation of the 'natural capital' of the environment of countries trapped in economic dependency, bringing deforestation, soil degradation and disease. This hyper-development of empire is reflected in a widening wealth gap across continents. Between 1800 and 1913, per capita income in Europe increased by 222 percent, while it was 9 percent in Africa and a mere 1 percent in Asia,[68] during a time when European political control of the Earth's surface rose from 35 percent to 85 percent.[69] Empire was enemy to both ecology and equality.

Again, this grim picture should not underplay protective measures more recently undertaken. For instance, the United Nations Declaration of Rights of Indigenous Peoples, which received majority adoption in 2007, recognises historic wrongs of colonial dispossession, and affirms minimum standards for the welfare and dignity of such vulnerable populations. Importantly, it does so within a framework that sees claims and practices rooted in assumed superiority around national, racial or ethnic origin as unjust, illegal, scientifically false, and racist.

All this is good. But at the same time, it talks about 'their *right* to development in accordance with their own needs and interests',[70] confident that their indigenous culture will inherently uphold sustainable and equitable environmental management. Arguably, this may be wishful thinking. If you grant 'right' to any group to pursue their needs and aspirations in line with their tradition and judgement, there's no guarantee that self-interested calculation will not have global consequence in ecosystem abuse.

Two IPPC reports in 2022 suggest that for all the talk and pledges, the scale and immediacy of the problem are not being adequately addressed. For example, on basic needs like water, about half of the world's people presently have to cope with acute scarcity for at least part of the year because of climatic and non-climatic drivers. Increasingly, some of the damage done in terrestrial, freshwater and coastal and open ocean marine ecosystems is irreversible. Unequal experience of the detriment across the world remains evident. Between 2010–2020, the most vulnerable regions experienced human death from floods, droughts and storms at 15 times the rate of those with very low vulnerability. Arguably, such differential impact impedes the drive for the world to act as one. In the context of such urgency, sometimes these reports, for all their crucial worth for informed policy-making, can lapse into insipid exhortation, such as: 'climate resilient development is advanced when actors work in equitable, just and enabling ways to reconcile divergent interests, values and worldviews, toward equitable and just outcomes'.[71] Here, the spirit is admirable, but the flesh on the bones is weak.

Improvement in energy intensity has helped cut carbon emission, but such abatement has not counter-weighted emission rises from increased global activity in industry, transport, agriculture and buildings. It seems that we're still playing catch-up with rising energy demand. Such emissions will have to reach net zero in the early 2050s – that is where no further carbon is discharged to the atmosphere above that which is removed – to give the world a 50 percent chance of preventing more than 1.5°C of warming throughout the twenty-first century.[72] In turn, this entails all greenhouse gases peaking by 2025, and cutting by 43 percent by 2030. Furthermore, methane would have to be slashed by about a third. In short, it's now or never for big mitigation changes. This involves building on the heartening progress made to date, including the up to 85 percent drop in costs of solar and wind energy and batteries since 2010.

Starkly, the latest report[73] warns that the 'continued installation of unabated fossil fuel infrastructure will lock-in greenhouse gas emissions'. Yet, in the rush for national energy security in the context of the Ukrainian war, the UK, which hosted and 'championed' COP26, is intent on enhancing extraction of such deadly fuels. In October 2022, the North Sea Transition Authority opened a process of granting 100 licences to extract oil and gas. This was part of the Truss government's strategy for enhancing energy supply for supercharged economic growth, and included fracking and refusal to impose proportionate windfall taxes on excessive profits of oil and gas corporations, at a time when even the head of Shell acknowledged that governments needed to tax energy companies to help the poorest deal with soaring energy bills amid a general cost of living crisis. While her successor, Sunak, has walked back on the fracking aspect, it remains unclear as to how his formal rhetoric at COP27 about the urgency of the carbon-free target will square with his policy on further extraction of fossil-fuel.

Short-sighted strategies for energy independence, that fail to use the contemporary energy crisis as an opportunity for the more clean and green variety, bode ill for an already dire circumstance where total net anthropogenic greenhouses gas emissions have kept increasing between 2010–2019, with average annual emissions at their highest point in our history. This is on top of cumulative net carbon emissions since the mid-nineteenth century.[74] If countries like the UK adopt new fossil fuel projects, what chance is there to compel countries like Saudi Arabia, India, China, and Russia to take seriously any commitment to reduce their lethal contribution? COP28 is to be held in Dubai in 2023. As a previous visitor to the United Arab Emirates, I can vouch for three things about that country, relevant to this issue: it exemplifies the exhaustive heat due to be more universal and the attendant high-energy compensations used such as air-conditioning; its conspicuous wealth is tied to oil; and it is physically planned for the ubiquitous car. It is at once the kind of place that needs most to change in this regard, and that will be most difficult to change.

So at present, we're in a real conundrum. We're reminded of how important energy sources are in a geopolitics beset by accentuated ideological collision, and consequent incentive for home-based supply – even if that means more carbon-based stock has to be added to the mix. In addition, the downward pressure on growth due to the financial crash and pandemic, alongside the upward pressure on inflation, is producing an economic and fiscal strain that governments are likely to prioritise, even if that diverts them from targets on the climate emergency and inhibits international collaboration.

Concentrated in ten countries – China, Russia, US, Iran, Saudi Arabia, Australia, India, Qatar, Canada and Iraq – there are 425 'carbon bombs' – the largest fossil fuel extraction projects globally, that include 195 mega oil and gas extraction projects. Some 40 percent of these 425 had not commenced extraction in 2020, indicating how new schemes are continuing to come on stream. The term 'bombs' is deliberately applied to suggest how they would 'detonate' the supposed global commitment to curb carbon, and thus require 'defusing' as part of mitigation effort.[75] We have to keep in mind how immensely profitable the oil and gas sector remains. Over the last three decades, Exxon Mobile, BP, Shell, and Chevron have generated almost $2 trillion in profits, and Russia's assault against Ukraine has helped to boost profit levels. As expressed in a recent investigation: 'there was no mention of oil and gas in the COP26 final deal, despite these being responsible for almost 60 percent of fossil fuel emissions'.[76] Without a moratorium on new ventures, it's not credible to suggest that the world is serious about saving itself from a temperature rise no higher than 1.5C. Comments from the UN secretary general, Antonio Guterres, capture the urgency in the context of supply-side problems linked to Russia's war on Ukraine:[77]

> *Countries could become so consumed by the immediate fossil fuel supply gap that they neglect or kneecap policies to cut fossil fuel use. This is madness. Addiction to fossil fuels is mutually assured destruction.*

Some Hope

Official reports and literature cited here broadly agree about averting, mitigating and repairing harm to nature. Boosting natural eco-systems through conservation and restoration, the agenda is to: protect biodiversity; re-wild land;

enhance carbon capture and storage; specifically, impound carbon in soils and vegetation, including use of peatland and woodland restoration; improve tree cover and habitat linkage; cut methane and nitrous oxide emissions in agriculture; reduce food waste and promote less-meat diets; improve energy efficiency and shift from coal and other fossil-fuels to renewable energy in the power, buildings and transport sectors; decarbonise energy-intensive industry; retrofit existing buildings; recycle and repair; adopt longer-life materials; advance electric mobility and public and shared transport; minimise pesticides and pathogens to redress soil and air pollution; promote compact urban settlement; adopt low-cost energy and waste-water treatment technologies; and 'green' the city with trees, roof gardens, and greenways, and more locally-sourced food via urban agriculture. This list may seem exhaustive. But without adopting an integrative approach to all of it, we continue to exhaust a finite world.

This assumes rethinking *values* about what makes for the good life,[78] away from excessive individualist consumption and waste, and toward greater income and power equity, with regard to class, race and gender. Sharing costs and benefits of environmental stewardship, also involves major intergovernmental collaboration. We need not only new ways to measure success beyond gross national product, but also common education, regulation, monitoring, certification, taxation, and the like. In practice, many give short shrift to this tall order.

Increasingly in the rich world, we talk more about less materialism, a watchword about living simply that others may simply live. However, it doesn't always wash with the poorest, who can see movements like Extinction Rebellion as 'bohemian bourgeois' (bobo). The hard truth is that the poorest who benefit most long-term from eco-justice, may suffer most short-term from interventions that deliver high energy prices and job loss. It's a big ask to expect the dispossessed to forego 'possessions'.

This is where those that express reservation about Anthropocene and concepts like 'human footprint' have a point. It is not a simple case of humanity, as an abstract whole, subduing and ravaging the earth. Distinction between villains and victims would acknowledge that responsibility rests mostly with the main controllers and beneficiaries of how wealth is produced and consumed. Without this, we're left with an apolitical understanding that guilt and atonement have to be universally shared. At the same time, it can't be all about the exclusive evil of capitalism. If you think that countries once under Soviet communist influence were immune to such smash and grab, visits to places like Poland, Hungary, Czech Republic and former East Germany will quickly disabuse you of such fantasy.

Nonetheless, what is clear is that orthodox capitalist answers are highly suspect. The idea that we just need to trim a little and recycle a lot, to find more 'sustainable' ways to keep development within limitless economic growth, is fanciful. Another suggestion is that we can adopt market mechanisms to value and then price properly what was once considered the 'freebie' of nature. We can thus incentivise good environmental practice through subsidy and penalise polluters through taxation. In essence, this approach treats environmental damage as just another 'negative externality', to use the jargon of orthodox economics.

Seeing nature as 'external' to us is the problem, not the solution. When it comes to the problem's magnitude and momentum, fine-slicing won't cut it. Without popular buy-in, such measures are a cop-out. The market system in the past judged environmental degradation as a price worth paying for progress. We can see how resistance to petrol-tax increases in France sparked the *gilets jaunes* movement for economic justice, because the market system always seems to rely on getting the already hard-pressed to bear the big burden. Markets are used to dealing with private goods in the present. They have more difficulty with inter-generational public goods. As often said, you can't solve social-ills by thinking in the same mind-set that delivered them in the first place.

For others, calamity can be averted by clever geo-engineering. Dating back decades, suggestions abound about how techno-science can rescue the planet, though many early ideas sound more like science-fiction, such as orbiting a giant mirror to reflect sunlight back into space. More recently, several interventions have been proposed. Sulphate aerosol injection into the atmosphere – the planet's thermostat – could lower temperature by reflecting back solar radiation. Seeding clouds, particularly polar clouds, with sea salt could help re-freeze oceanic areas subject to severe defrosting. Thinning clouds with chemicals could also help lower warming. Veneering fresh ice with white sand could both stabilise ice sheets, while offering greater solar reflection. Injection of iron sulphate and similar nutrients into the ocean could revitalize algae growth that could sop up atmospheric carbon.

Even if such steps are viable and timely, they risk other pollutants and weather disturbance due to their inhibitions on solar energy.[79] While some argue that modest geo-engineering that seeks to halve anthropocenic warming, complemented by other steps to cut carbon emissions, could address this weather hazard,[80] more evidence is needed. In short, there's no easy fix for ecocide, particularly given the scary stuff that leaps off pages of reports and books, heralding imminent danger. The basic point remains: *sapiens* has not inhabited a planet as hot as this one now, and we're turning up the heat; we're now 1°C warmer than preindustrial level, and if we don't limit warming to at most 1.5°C by a decade's time, we're in deep trouble in terms of storms, floods, drought, extreme heat, climate refugees and poverty.

Even that target, hard as it may be, does not ensure against lasting imbalance. We could still get a big sea rise from melting land-based ice sheets in Antarctica and Greenland. Monsoons in Asia and Africa and the Atlantic's Gulf Stream could be disrupted.[81] Moreover, we can't guarantee against a runaway greenhouse effect, whereby unforeseen cascading facets and feedback loops magnify warming outcomes.

Faced with such disaster, it's an enigma why we all still don't get it. Maybe it's because it seems distant in time and space. The ultimate disaster is not happening tomorrow and it falsely appears to most impact faraway places. Maybe it's because we can't believe that minor changes in mean temperature can make such huge difference. It's hard to get your head round the thought that there is a third more carbon in the atmosphere now than at any time in the last 800,000 years, with over half fossil-fuelled carbon discharge occurring in just the last thirty years.

What we experience as gradual, is breathtakingly high-speed.[82] As shown here, that same period has seen a stream of papers and conferences stressing the crisis. Emergency demands agency and urgency. Individually, however, we feel helpless, and rhetoric about us all being in this together is as misguided as it is trite. At the same time, alarm stories of scorched-earth catastrophe can prompt fatalism or panic, and neither is constructive.

Beyond the Point of Rescue?

While there remain those who think the whole science is speculative rather than definitive, there are really two kinds of climate-deniers: those who ideologically resist the evidence, and most of us who casually resign to it. Does that leave us stranded on a receding shore?

Presently, there's minimal chance of the world acting as one. Despite various global accords, hard geopolitics stops common human agreement on culprit and cure. For instance, the US charges China with being 'the world's largest emitter of greenhouse gases; the largest source of marine debris; the worst perpetrators of illegal, unreported, and unregulated (IUU) fishing; and the world's largest consumer of trafficked wildlife and timber products'.[83] It claims China's total emissions are twice that of the US and almost one third of global emissions, while it is also the greatest emitter of mercury, and largest producer and exporter of plastic products, responsible for almost 30 percent of the global total.

In retort, China charges the US with being historically accountable for most greenhouse gas emissions, since between 1751 and 2010, emissions from US energy and industrial sectors accounted for 27.9 percent of the global total. Per capita carbon emission, the US is 3.3 times the global average and over twice that of China.[84]

While all such claims demand validation, they are designed in part to cause confusion. Fact-checking them found that from 1750–2018, China produced about 210.20 billion tonnes of CO_2, whereas over the same time, the US produced 404.77 billion tonnes. Currently, China's annual emissions are about double those of the US, and in 2019, China accounted for about one-third of global CO_2 emissions, while the US produced 13 percent. A high share of China's wood-product imports are from illegal harvests. As the world's biggest producer of plastic items, China is responsible for an estimated third of the world's total, though set within its huge volume of products and exports. On a per capita basis, the US produces more. With just over 4 percent of global population, it creates 17 percent of total plastic waste.[85]

It's tough getting big powers to accept objective findings that they find objectionable, and their war of words reflects rivalry rather than unity. Who can sanction great-again US? Who can rely on data from despotic China? Who can tell Putin's petro-state that climate change threatens, when its fossil fuels earn big bucks for a weak economy, and Russians might even welcome warming in Siberia? With what authority does the UK compel other countries to abide by climate change agreements when its Internal Market Bill legislated to break international law by reneging on the Withdrawal Agreement with the EU, within less than a year of its signing? All this testifies to how brittle global collaboration can be in practice, and thus confidence about surmounting human disaster by common action can't be blinkered about humanity's defects in this regard.

Given this weakness, and the way so many graphs suggest gloom and doom, it's tempting to seek refuge in the self-correcting resilience of nature. In study visits to the port city of Famagusta, Cyprus, I've been struck by this capacity. When the Turkish army advanced on the area in 1974, Greek-Cypriots fled southwards, abandoning their houses, and businesses such as beach hotels, carshowrooms, and such like. Since then, Cyprus has been partitioned, and the Varosha part of Famagusta has been reduced to ghost town, barb-wired and under Turkish military occupation. Yet as I saw up close, while the deserted built environment has decayed, nature has bloomed within and around it. And this buoyancy can deceive us into thinking that nature ultimately prevails over human folly. Not so.

A different delusion is a 'back to the future' nostalgic retreat to pastoral ideals of unblemished nature. In this view, maybe the answer lies in return to rural 'authenticity'. Whether in Dickens' 'bleak house' of grim industrial cities, or Wordsworth's romantic evocation of simple harmony with idyllic landscape, 'artificial' industrial life has had bad press. As referenced earlier, both political left and right hold narratives about corruptive modernity, bearing resemblance to biblical denunciation of decadence since exile from Eden, as in the fable about wicked Sodom and Gomorrah. Salvation doesn't rest in rustic sanctuary, no more than in sackcloth and ashes. For the first time in history, more people now live in cities than in countryside. True, within this new Urban Age, we can question the wisdom of mega-cities. We can re-design for 'smart' urban living. But as shown in the Khmer Rouge's mad reign of terror, we can't escape to bucolic utopia. Gaia offers no such easy getaway.

For some, we may be beyond the point of rescue. This is because we're taking steps, both forward and back. For instance, it's not that we're moving from wood to coal to oil to gas to nuclear to renewables. Rather, each is an extra to, rather than replacement for, the other. We're now burning 80 percent more coal than we were in the year 2000, and concrete production – the world's second most carbon-intensive process – is massively increasing,[86] with for instance, China's Belt and Road Initiative since 2013, a global infrastructure project that spans many countries. An optimistic take on all this comes from Lovelock, who doesn't see human pursuit of high-growth industrialism as transgression against nature, but rather as 'natural' evolutionary progression. As we'll discuss in the next chapter, he sees us now in a post-Anthropocene period he calls 'Novacene', when the wondrous computational power of robots will help us find guilt-free answers for a habitable planet.

A more sombre note is struck by Smil,[87] who argues that viable biosphere needs compatible levels of future material growth. In his view, we either check decay or concede to it. From antiquity to the early modern period, most people were subsistence peasants, and all aspects of life grew, if at all, slowly. Then, by the nineteenth-century, with railways, steamships, internal combustion engine, electricity, urbanisation, and longevity, vast change created expectation of endless accelerated growth. In many cases, people wanted not just to amass more, but saw bigger as better.

Smil gives many interesting statistics reflecting this. For instance, when Ford's Model-T car was released in 1908, it weighed 540kg, and global car sales were below 100,000, whereas a century later average weight of US cars was 1852kg, and global car sales had risen seven-fold. This makes the case that given the abundance in the rich world, we have much slack for less stuff. Even ample pruning doesn't have to mean frugality, and after all, surely it's better to feel the pinch than take the punch, better to have fewer belongings than to have nowhere to belong?

As stated earlier, this can't be a case of equal burden for unequal guilt. We have taken comfort in the deception of human exception, whereby for humans to be free *from* nature, we must exercise power *over* nature. In his book, *The Great Derangement*, Ghosch[88] laments the delusion that humans have liberated themselves from the elemental forces of nature, and hopes that they will 'be able to transcend the isolation in which humanity was trapped in the time of its derangement; that they will rediscover their kinship with other beings'. This call for a new Animism, an awareness of connection with other living beings across species, is partly reflected in a growing movement around animal rights.

Some go further. In 2019, the Lake Erie Bill of Rights was passed by Toledo voters, granting legal personhood to the lake as a living being. Thereby, citizens can act as legal guardians and sue polluters. In similar vein, New Zealand bestowed legal personhood to the Wanganui River in 2017. Such steps are part of a broader 'rights of nature' movement. Some countries are ahead of the game, at least in formal declaration. In its 2008 Constitution, Chapter Seven, Article 71, Ecuador recognises: 'Nature, or Pacha Mama, where life is reproduced and occurs, has the right to integral respect for its existence and for the maintenance and regeneration of its life cycles, structure, functions and evolutionary processes'.

The Nuclear Option

If climate emergency was the only risk to our extinction, we might stand a fighting chance. But as Ord's book *The Precipice*[89] details, humans now possess many means of mass self-destruction. A new world opened up with Hiroshima, and six years afterwards, one thermonuclear bomb comprised more energy than every used explosive in the Second World War combined. Beyond the direct killing power of such devices are aftermath effects of radioactive fallout and prospect of 'nuclear winter', whereby the massive smoke discharge injects soot into the stratosphere, darkening the sky, shading sunlight, cooling and drying the planet, and resulting in substantial crop failure and famine.

Of course, in the military jargon of Mutually Assured Destruction (MAD), we were told that the very enormity of such universal calamity was itself a surety against nuclear weapon use. I remember the tense days in October 1962 of the Cuban Missile Crisis, when Kennedy and Khrushchev faced each other down over Soviet installation of nuclear missiles in Cuba. We now know that of the 158 nuclear warheads already positioned, over 90 were tactical nuclear weapons, designed for first-use to resist any American island incursion, a strike that, in Kennedy's words, would have 'required' retaliatory response upon the Soviet Union. Unquestionably, this high stakes stand-off brought us to the brink, until Khrushchev blinked first. Ord remarks that even assuming that this chance of nuclear war did not in itself signal our complete wipe-out, the close call 'would remain one of the pivotal moments in 200,000 years of human history: perhaps the closest we have ever come to losing it all'.[90]

For me, it shows four reasons for the absurdity that parity of terror potential provides the symmetry to stabilise peace. First, it implies an endless arms race to keep in step and up-to-date. Second, MAD assumes no mad leaders – just think how that works when Trump was threatening North Korea's Kim Jong-un with 'fire and fury', before the two ended up exchanging deranged love letters. Third, rolling the dice on nuclear war also places blind faith in human immunity from error. In fact, as Ord explains, 'hair trigger alert' missiles in current Russian and American arsenals are very susceptible to accidental launch, or to intentional discharge during false alerts. Finally, the macho status accorded nuclear weapon states was always likely to encourage nuclear proliferation, as other states and even possibly terrorist groups sought the pull that attended that power. Consequently, the more countries that have such weaponry – particularly those in long-standing conflict like India and Pakistan – the greater the risk of use at some stage. All this suggests that in seeking ultimate defence in nuclear weapons, we've forgotten how defenceless we are against our own folly.

Of the total nuclear warheads in the world in 2022, around 90 percent are held by Russia and the US. Of the global total, over 9,400 are in military stockpiles for deployment by missiles, aircraft, ships and submarines, with the rest 'retired' and due for disassembly. Though the START 11 Treaty limits each major power to 1550 in active strategic deployment, both are way over that target. Russia's total nuclear warheads are estimated at 5977 to the US's 5,428. The other three in the top five, with available nuclear warheads, are: China (350); France (290); and the UK (225). NATO's combined total is 5943. Dating back to 1970, the Nuclear Non-Proliferation Treaty (NPT) has sought to stop the spread to 'non-nuclear' countries, though we know that Pakistan (165); India (156); Israel (90); and North Korea (50) have acquired them.[91] Taking the nine countries together, by 2022 they possessed around 12700 warheads. About 2000 US, Russian, French and British warheads operate on 'high alert' for rapid application.

Some will argue that massive as these numbers are, they at least represent significant reduction from the peak of 70,300 warheads in 1986. But three important factors need consideration. First, the drop is attributable largely to 'pensioning' off older weaponry. Second, contemporary weapons are immensely more deadly. The bomb responsible for around 140,000 deaths in Hiroshima was 15 kilotons, and that for the 74,000 deaths in Nagasaki was 21 kilotons,[92] whereas current nuclear warheads can be over 1,000 kilotons. Third, the trend in useable nuclear weapons is on the rise again. As expressed by the Federation of American Scientists:[93]

> *Instead of planning for nuclear disarmament, the nuclear-armed states appear to plan to retain large arsenals for the indefinite future. As such, they're in conflict with the objective and spirit of the nuclear non-proliferation treaty. All continue to modernize their remaining nuclear forces at a significant pace, several are adding new types and/or increasing the role they serve in national strategy and public statements, and all appear committed to retaining nuclear weapons for the indefinite future.*

None of this pessimism is to downplay the importance of continued efforts at arms control agreements. Certain steps have made their mark. For instance, in 1996, the Comprehensive Nuclear Test Ban Treaty aimed for no extra countries to be permitted to join the nuclear club, including South Africa, Ukraine, Belarus and Kazakhstan, former sites of such weapons. Despite the moves by North Korea, this has had some success.

The world has lived with the nuclear bomb for nearly eight decades. With the invasion of Ukraine, possibility of an escalation leading to World War III became present, if slight. Certainly, the risk of a militarily repelled Putin resorting to use of tactical nuclear weapons was real, if again improbable. Intended to keep NATO at bay, his threat that any country intervening directly would trigger 'consequences that you have never encountered in your history' was intentionally easy to decode. It illustrated the inestimable peril of an economically weak power, further humiliated on the world stage, launching its nuclear toy out of the pram. Perhaps even more so, it underscored the menace of a nuclear-armed North Korea, an economic basket case, with a deranged impetuous leader dominating a pliant people.

Given the increased global militarisation that is likely to follow Putin's Ukrainian venture, what is the increase in probability of more countries seeking a nuclear shield? If proliferation does resume, what is the probability of the world escaping a nuclear strike, by accident or design, over the next 80 years – in other words, for the rest of this century? We can't pretend it's low. On such flimsy fortune does our future depend. We live in a very unstable world with more nuclear powers. While the big share of this arsenal still lies with the US and Russia, some nuclear powers are caught in regional conflicts that could escalate to a nuclear component. Accidental and non-authorised use of such weapons is always possible. We have a recent example of where mishap can endanger retaliatory action, and subsequent escalation. On 9 March 2022:[94]

> *a mistake during routine maintenance saw a nuclear-capable (but in this case unarmed) Indian missile fired into Pakistan, its nuclear-armed neighbour. India's sheepish apology on the 11th would have been too little too late if tensions had been high.*

Such incidents between rival nuclear powers are prone to cause jitters at best and fatal miscalculation at worst. This is far from the first such incident. How many near-misses in nuclear Russian-roulette can the world survive? In my lifetime, there have been many close calls with nuclear weapons. Ord cities three by way of illustration: one in November 1979, when a training simulation of a Soviet strike was misread for awhile as a real and present danger of incoming missiles; another in September 1983 when Soviet early-warning systems mistook a screen image of sunlight twinkling off clouds as a US first-strike and nearly activated nuclear retort; and in January 1995, in a post-Cold War period, when Yeltsin briefly unlocked the Russian nuclear case before confirmation that what Russian radar misinterpreted as a nuclear missile was actually just a Norwegian scientific rocket surveying the Northern lights.

Coming into effect in 1970, the Nuclear Proliferation Treaty marked the hope that stockpiles would ultimately be reduced to zero. The agreement was about non-proliferation, disarmament, and peaceful application of nuclear energy. This prospect has been dashed in the recent period, which has seen increase and upgrade, when we already have enough of such weaponry for planetary destruction. In January 2021, the Treaty on the Prohibition of Nuclear Weapons came into 'effect', banning signatory states from developing, testing, producing, acquiring, holding, or stockpiling nuclear explosive devices; transferring or receiving them; and from using or threatening to use them.[95] It has 91 signatories. Strangely perhaps, Japan, the only country to have been victim to nuclear weapons, is not among them. They have to keep the US sweet, to remain under its nuclear 'umbrella'. None of the nine nuclear powers have signed.[96] Meanwhile, spending on such potential for human self-destruction is scandalously huge. Estimates in 2022 from the Congressional Budget Office see the US set to spend $634 billion over the following decade on upgrading its nuclear forces, while the Arms Control Association put a figure of $2 trillion on such spending over the next 30 years.

In September 2021, the US, UK and Australia announced a pact (AUKUS) that would include acquisition by Australia of a fleet of nuclear-powered submarines. As Tisdall[97] points out, such an initiative further nullified demands for non-proliferation, particularly in places like Iran and North Korea; raised the stakes in the emerging New Cold War with China; by-passed EU consultation, thereby compromising Western solidarity; and weakened the campaign to achieve a nuclear-free Pacific.

The nuclear threat remains real. That is not to under-estimate the long-term impact of 'conventional' war. For instance, I witnessed in Vietnam the persistent environmental and health legacy of Agent Orange, a 'defoliant' with highly toxic dioxin, deployed by the US military in Operation Ranch Hand to clear forest cover and destroy food sources that helped sustain the guerrilla campaign waged by the North Vietnamese. This use of deadly herbicide was complemented by Napalm-B in bombs, in what added up to intensive chemical warfare.

The contemporary world continues to nurture the military-industrial complex. With the arrival of AI, and autonomous weaponry that can operate without human agency – considered further in the next chapter – the stakes are being built ever higher.

End Game?

Combinations of conventional, chemical, and nuclear war; reckless environmental degradation; and drastic climate change may not separately, or even together, erase us totally from the planet. They do risk, *in extremis*, major civilisation collapse, a desolate world without books, culture, cities, and law.

What lessons may we draw from all this? Primarily, it's that it's hard to see humanity as a mutual unit, even when facing common existential threat. There is nothing new in this. As *sapiens* increased its numbers and spread its wings, there has been what I'd call the 'Babel effect'. In the biblical story, God's reprisal for human ambition to build a tower of Babel to the heavens was to scatter and diversify humans so they never could combine easily again to over-reach themselves through common purpose. Within this diversity, there's mostly been hierarchy. Historically, many categories of people have been considered short of being fully human, and thereby have been 'owned' in some way by privileged adult men: women; children; slaves; colonial subjects; infidels; and enemies. In Marxist thinking, they included the alienated worker, who was no more than 'cog in the machine'. One way or another, humanity has always stewarded selective membership to its club.

While we may fret about the future, most of us are short-sighted when taking the long view. The extent to which we're wired for immediate gratification makes us all inclined to put off till tomorrow what we should do today. And of course, tomorrow is a long time. While the Earth's fragility may be hiding in plain sight, we find it hard to contemplate our own death, never mind the death of our species, which to paraphrase Mark Twain, we trust is being greatly exaggerated. Maybe however many times we're told that as we lose the natural wild, we'll find the unfriendly wild of disturbed nature, we can't bring ourselves to imagine that pursuit of hyper-modernity can actually drive us back to the dark ages.

Some still insist that this talk about us being on the brink of oblivion rather than dominion is just that, all talk. They can point to startling projections made in the past that have not come to pass, such as Paul Ehrlich's 1968 bombshell book *The Population Bomb*,[98] which warned that the world would soon have more people than it could feed. They can point also to the perennial millenarianism, where death cults mistakenly preach that 'the end is nigh', or to scaremongering survivalists who warn that we should scarper to remote shelter against imminent apocalypse, when the grim reaper will 'reap' what we have sown.

Like the old joke says: just because you're paranoid doesn't mean they're not out to get you. Similarly, just because these doomsayers have been delusional in the past, doesn't mean that such premonitions are implausible in the future. And if for whatever reason, democracy is paralysed by the enormity of the challenge, some may reluctantly conclude that urgent decarbonisation demands authoritarian government, which would be real eco-fascism, way beyond what critics of current environmental activism mischievously label.

As products and predators of the environment, we're ambivalent about being both a part of, and apart from, that environment. As we've grown bigger in number, the world has become smaller in terms of travel and communication. Though we depend on nature, nature can't depend on us. For a species of around 300,000 years vintage, we're a mere blip in Earth's 4.5 billion years. In disrespecting the deep past as pre-history, we forget that while our presence has been short, our imprint has been huge. This is particularly so, when we take the uneven impact of the last 10,000 years of agriculture, and even more so, the last four centuries of industry.

When it comes to our self-protection, we tread forwards and back. In September 2022, NASA's Double Asteroid Redirection Test (DART) hit its asteroid target with deliberate intent to tilt it, in demonstration of a planetary defence mechanism against any future asteroid threatening collision with Earth. At the same time, we had countries potentially defaulting on their zero carbon targets by persisting with exploration and extraction of fossil fuels. Moreover, the urgent push for nuclear energy, as part of an energy security package, held its own peril, and not only from the standard risk of atomic fission; explosions as experienced in Chernobyl and in Japan's Fukushima nuclear plant; and the contamination of radioactive waste. Over half of Ukraine's electricity is generated by nuclear power. Putin's increasingly desperate onslaught on the country has risked radiation calamity, with shelling near the Zaporizhzhia facility, Europe's largest nuclear power plant, and an explosion close to Southern Ukraine's Pivdennoukrainsk nuclear power plant. Currently, nuclear energy provides France with 70 percent of its electricity and plans have been announced for 14 new nuclear reactors. The UK wants to increase the nuclear source of its electricity from the current 15 percent to 25 percent by mid-century. If global expansion happens at this rate, the chances of more accidents and the prevalence of nuclear waste both increase.[99]

Given our folly and fallibility, are we in an end-game, whereby we've outstayed our welcome in this rare place we call home? Has our progress in commanding time and space ensured this time we've run out of space to waste as we want? The Anthropocene paradox is that just when humans think they've overpowered Nature, they're overcome by their own overbearing nature – the familiar Greek tragedy of pride before ruin. While Icarus flew too close to the sun, before his melted wings saw him crash to the sea, we're set to feel the wrath of both sun and sea since we're no longer close to either. How do we weather extremes in weather, when in distancing ourselves from nature, our Human Age is turning out to be one unfit for humans? How can we deal with an urgency like climate change without fundamental change in the political climate? Strangely, we're most at risk in what is supposedly our era, by becoming our own worst enemies. Stark choices face us. Do we treasure wealth over health? Does it profit us to lose our humanity in pursuit of profit?

In our everyday attempt at resilient response to ordinary mishap, we're prone to console ourselves with the comment: 'Well, it's not the end of the world'. This chapter has pointed to some threats that could actually deliver that doomsday. In 1947 the Doomsday Clock was established as a metaphor for nearness to human-made catastrophe, represented in terms of proximity to midnight, and as estimated each year by the Science and Security Board of the Bulletin of the Atomic Scientists. With the end of the Cold War, it was the furthest ever away from midnight, at 17 minutes. In the aftermath of the Cuban missile crisis, it stood at 7 minutes. In 2022, for the third successive year, it was put at 100 seconds. Referring to just one aspect of our self-imposed hazard, one expert highlighted biological threats:[100]

> *The fact that we have active biological weapons programmes in Russia and North Korea, with China and Iran close behind, should give us pause. We stand on the precipice of a biological cataclysm.*

The next chapter considers whether, far from facing extinction, humans may be on the verge of an enhanced version of being human, partly by superseding the limits of their biology. It also deliberates on whether, to the contrary, the high-tech technology that accompanies this prospect, threatens the vary basis of what it means to be human.

Notes

1 www.pewresearch.org/fact-tank/2018/07/11/world-population-day. Accessed on: 16 September 2021.

2 United Nations. Population Division: Department of Economic and Social Affairs. (2022) *World Population Prospects 2022*. New York: United Nations.

3 www.statista.com/statistics/997040/world-population-by-continent-1950-2020. Accessed on: 16 September 2021.

4 Note: Two of these alone will account for nearly a quarter of growth. India, set to overtake China by 2027, will increase by around 273 million. Nigeria will increase by 200 million. By 2100, India will top the league with almost 1.5 billion, followed by China with just under 1.1 billion, Nigeria with 733 million, the United States with 434 million, and Pakistan with 403 million.

5 Note: While global fertility rates have reduced from 3.2 births per woman in 1990 to 2.5 in 2019, it was 4.6 that year in sub-Saharan Africa.

6 United Nations, Department of Economic and Social Affairs, Population Division (2019) *World Population Prospects 2019: Data Booklet* (ST/ESA/SER.A/424) New York: United Nations; Population Division of the United Nations Department of Economic and Social Affairs (2019) *World Population Prospects 2019. Highlights.* New York: United Nations. See also: Roser, M., Ritchie, H. & Ortiz-Ospina, E. (2013) *World Population Growth.* Published online at OurWorldInData.org. Retrieved from: https://ourworldindata.org/world-population-growth; Accessed on: 16 September 2021. See also: Lutz, W., Sanderson, W. C., & Scherbov, S. (2008) The Coming Acceleration of Global Population Ageing. *Nature.* 451(7179), 716–719; Lutz, W., Butz, W., & Samir KC (eds.) Executive Summary: *World Population and Human Capital in the Twenty-First Century.* Oxford: Oxford University Press. http://pure.iiasa.ac.at/11189/1/XO-14-031.pdf

7 Vollset, S., Goren, E., Yuan, C-W., Cao, J., Smith, A., Hsias, T., et al. (July 2020) Fertility, Mortality, Migration, and Population Scenarios for 195 Countries and Territories from 2017–2100: A Forecasting Analysis for the Global Burden of Disease Study. *The Lancet.* Published Online: July 14, 2020. https://doi.org/10.1016/S0140-6736(20)30677-2. www.thelancet.com/journals/lancet/article/PIIS0140-6736(20)30677-2/fulltext.

8 Note: At this stage, the five largest countries are projected to be India (1.09 billion); Nigeria (791 million); China (732 million); the USA (336 million) and Pakistan (248 million).

9 United Nations. Population Division: Department of Economic and Social Affairs. (2022) *op. cit.*

10 Vollset, S. et al (July 2020) *op. cit.*

11 Morland, P. (2019) *The Human Tide: How Population Shaped the Modern World.* London: John Murray.

12 United Nations. Population Division: Department of Economic and Social Affairs. (2022) *op. cit.*

13 Morland, P. (2019) *op. cit.*

14 Davis, R. (2003) *Christian Slaves, Muslim Masters: White Slavery in the Mediterranean, The Barbary Coast, and Italy, 1500–1800.* Basingstoke: Palgrave Macmillan.

15 Quoted in: Zureik, E. (2016) *Israel's Colonial Project in Palestine: Brutal Pursuit.* Abington, Oxon: Routledge. 213.

16 Yiftachel, O. (2006) *Ethnocracy: Land and Identity Politics in Israel/Palestine.* Philadelphia: University of Pennsylvania Press. 3.

17 White, M (2011). *Atrocitology: Humanity's 100 Deadliest Achievements.* Edinburgh: Canongate Books.

18 *Ibid.*

19 Kiernan, B. (2003) The Demography of Genocide in South east Asia: The Death Tolls in Cambodia, 1975–79, and East Timor, 1975–80. *Critical Asian Studies.* 35:4 (2003), 585–597. 587.

20 Widyono, B. (2008) *Dancing in Shadows: Sihanouk, the Khmer Rouge, and the United Nations in Cambodia.* New York: Rowman & Littlefield Publishers, Inc.,

21 White, M. (2011) *op. cit.* 541.

22 Pettersson, T. & Oberg, M. (2020) Organized Violence, 1989–2019. *Journal of Peace Research.* 57(4) 597–613. Data for this analysis derives from the Uppsala Conflict Data Program (UCDP). See also: Levy, J. & Thompson, W. (2010), *Causes of War.* Malden, MA: Wiley-Blackwell.

23 Source: www.macrotrends.net/countries/WLD/world/death-rate. Accessed on: 16 September 2021.

24 Goldstick, J., Cunningham, R., and Carter, P. (19 May, 2022) Current Causes of Death in Children and Adolescents in the United States. *The New England Journal of Medicine.* 386:1955–1956.

25 World Population Review (2022) *School Shootings By State.* https://worldpopulatio nreview.com/state-rankings/school-shootings-by-state. Accessed on: 25 May 2022.

26 Quote from David Attenborough on Population Matters Website. https://popula tionmatters.org. Accessed on: 16 September 2021.

27 Monbiot, G. (26 August 2020) Population Panic Lets Rich People off the Hook for the Climate Crisis They are Fuelling. *The Guardian.* www.theguardian.com/ commentisfree/2020/aug/26/panic-overpopulation-climate-crisis-consumption-environment. Accessed: 20/10/2020.

28 *Ibid.*

29 Gorvett, Z (6 September 2022) How Many People Can Earth Handle? *BBC Future.* www.bbc.com/future/article/20220905-is-the-world-overpopulated.   Accessed on: 7 October 2022.

30 Mumford, L. (1952) Introduction in Gutkind, E. *Our World from the Air.* New York: Garden City.

31 Waters, C. & Zalasiewicz, J. (2018) The Anthropocene and its 'Golden Spike' in Burtynsky, E., Baichwal, J., & De Pencier, N. *Anthropocene.* Toronto: Ago. 35–43. 35.

32 Lewis, S. & Maslin, M. (2018) *The Human Planet: How We Created the Anthropocene.* London: Penguin.

33 Crutzen, P. (2002) Geology of Mankind. *Nature* 415, 23. www.nature.com; https:// doi.org/10.1038/415023a

34 Crutzen, P. (2006) The Anthropocene in Ehlers, E. & Krafft, T. (eds) *Earth System Science in the Anthropocene.* Berlin: Springer. 13–18.

35 Williams, M., Zalasiewicz, J., Haywood, A. & Ellis, M. (eds) 2011. The Anthropocene: a New Epoch of Geological Time? *Philosophical Transactions of the Royal Society* 369A, 833–1112.

36 Waters, C.N., Zalasiewicz, J., Summerhayes, C., Barnosky, A.D., et. al. (2016) The Anthropocene is Functionally and Stratigraphically Distinct from the Holocene. *Science* 351 (6269), aad2622–1–aad2622–10.

37 Attenborough, D., with Jonnie Hughes (2020) *A Life on Our Planet: My Witness Statement and a Vision for the Future.* London: Witness Books.

38 Fuller, R., Landrigan, P. et al (17 May 2022) Pollution and Health: A Progress Update. *The Lancet Planetary Health.* www.thelancet.com/journals/lanplh/article. Accessed on: 30 May 2022.

39 Wallace-Wells, D. (2019) *The Uninhabitable Earth: A Story of the Future.* London: Penguin Books.

40 Intergovernmental Science-Policy Platform on Biodiversity and Ecosystem Services (IPBES) (2019) *Summary for Policymakers of the Global Assessment Report on Biodiversity and Ecosystems Services.* Bonn: IPBES.

41 *Ibid.* 3.

42 *Ibid.* 17.

43 *Ibid.* 4.

44 *Ibid.* 8.

45 Almond, R.E.A., Grooten M. and Petersen, T. (eds) (2020) *Living Planet Report 2020 - Bending the Curve of Biodiversity Loss.* Gland, Switzerland: WWF.

46 IPCC (2019)*Climate Change and Land: An IPCC Special Report on Climate Change, Desertification, Land Degradation, Sustainable Land Management, Food Security, and Greenhouse Gas Fluxes in Terrestrial Ecosystems.* New York: United Nations Foundation. Note: By 2015, intensification of land management saw around three-quarters of global ice-free land impacted by human exploit. To varying degrees, human use impacts about 60–85 percent of forests and 70–90 percent of other ecosystems, such as savannahs, wetlands and grasslands. About one-quarter of global GHG emissions are due to land-use. Between 2006–15, average temperature over land was 1.53°C higher than for the period 1850–1900, with negative consequence for regional crop yield and freshwater access.

47 Global Network Against Food Crises (2022) *2022 Global Report on Food Crises.* New York: United Nations.

48 IPCC (2019): *IPCC Special Report on the Ocean and Cryosphere in a Changing Climate.* New York: United Nations Foundation.

49 Abulafia, D. (2019) *The Boundless Sea: A Human History of the Oceans.* London: Allen Lane.

50 IPCC (2021) *Summary for Policymakers. In: Climate Change 2021: The Physical Science Basis. Contribution of Working Group I to the Sixth Assessment Report of the Intergovernmental Panel on Climate Change* [Masson-Delmotte, V., P. Zhai, A. Pirani, S. L. Connors, C. Péan, S. Berger, N. Caud, Y. Chen, L. Goldfarb, M. I. Gomis, M. Huang, K. Leitzell, E. Lonnoy, J.B.R. Matthews, T. K. Maycock, T. Waterfield, O. Yelekçi, R. Yu and B. Zhou (eds.)]. Cambridge University Press. In Press.

51 Note: According to the IPCC data, global surface temperature in the period 2001–2020, was 0.99 [0.84–1.10] °C higher than in the period 1850–1900. Taking the most recent period, global surface temperature was 1.09 [0.95 to 1.20] °C higher in 2011– 2020 than 1850–1900, with bigger increases over land (1.59 [1.34 to 1.83] °C) than over the ocean (0.88 [0.68 to 1.01] °C).

52 Note: They are: (1) No Poverty; (2) Zero Hunger; (3) Good Health and Well-being; (4) Quality Education; (5) Gender Equality; (6) Clean Water and Sanitation; (7) Affordable and Clean Energy; (8) Decent Work and Economic

Growth; (9) Industry, Innovation and Infrastructure; (10) Reducing Inequality; (11) Sustainable Cities and Communities; (12) Responsible Consumption and Production; (13) Climate Action; (14) Life Below Water; (15) Life On Land; (16) Peace, Justice, and Strong Institutions; and (17) Partnerships for the Goals.

53 Humanity's Ecological Footprint Contracted Between 2014–2016. See: www. footprintnetwork.org/2019/04/25/press-release-humanitys-ecological-footprint-contracted-between-2014-and-2016.

54 Note: These reached a new high of 55.3 gigatonnes of CO_2 equivalent in 2018, comprising mostly fossil CO_2 emissions, from both energy use and industry, but also land-use changes such as deforestation.

55 United Nations Environment Programme (2019) *The UNEP Emissions Gap Report 2019*: Nairobi, Kenya: UNEP.

56 UN Environment Programme (October 2021) *The Heat Is On: A World of Climate Promises Not Yet Delivered*. Nairobi, Kenya: UNEP.

57 Rowlatt, J. and Gerken, T. (21 October 2021) COP26: Document Leak Reveals Nations Lobbying to Change Key Climate Report. *BBC*. www.bbc.co.uk/news/science-environment. Accessed on: 22 October 2021.

58 Union of Concerned Scientists (2018) www.ucsusa.org/resources/each-countrys-share-co2-emissions.

59 Chancel, L (2020) *Unsustainable Inequalities: Social Justice and the Environment*. Cambridge, MA: Harvard University Press.

60 Friedrich, J., Ge, M., and Pickens, A. (December 10, 2020) *This Interactive Chart Shows Changes in the World's Top Ten Emitters*. World Resources Institute. www.wri.org/insights/interactive-chart-shows-changes-worlds-top-10-emitters. Accessed on: 18 September 2021.

61 See: Harrabin, R. (18 September 2021) Climate Change: Should Green Campaigners Put More Pressure on China to Slash Emissions? BBC. www.bbc.co.uk/news/science-environment. Accessed on: 18 September 2021; and Ritchie, H. and Roser, M. (2020) CO_2 and Greenhouse Gas Emissions. *OurWorldInData.org.* https://ourworldindata.org/co2-and-other-greenhouse-gas-emissions. Accessed on: 18 September 2021.

62 Klein, N. (2019) *On Fire: the (Burning) Case for a Green New Deal*. London: Simon & Schuster.

63 United Nations Environment Programme (2020) *Used Vehicles and the Environment: A Global Overview of Used Light Duty Vehicles: Flow, Scale and Regulation*. Nairobi: United Nations Environment Programme.

64 Moore, J. (ed) (2016) *Anthropocene or Capitalocene? Nature, History and the Crisis of Capitalism*. Oakland, CA: PM Press.

65 United Nations Development Programme (UNDP) (2022) *New Threats to Human Security In The Anthropocene: Demanding Greater Solidarity*. UNDP.

66 *Ibid*. iii.

67 Bonneuil, C. & Fressoz, J-B. (2017) *The Shock of the Anthropocene*. London: Verso. 236.

68 *Ibid.*, quoting data from Bairoch, P. 'The Main Trends in National Income Disparities Since the Industrial Revolution' in Bairoch, P. & Levy-Leboyer, M. (eds) (1985) *Disparities in Economic Development Since the Industrial Revolution*. London: Macmillan.

69 *Ibid.* quoting Giovanni Arrighi (1994) *The Long Twentieth Century: Money, Power, and the Origins of Our Times*. London: Verso.

70 www.un.org/development/desa/indigenouspeoples/wpontent/uploads/sites/19/2018/11/UNDRIP_E_ web.pdf. 3.

71 Working Group II Contribution to the Sixth Assessment Report of the Intergovernmental Panel on Climate Change (February 2022) *Climate Change 2022: Impacts, Adaptation And Vulnerability: Summary for Policymakers.* Switzerland: IPPC.

72 The Economist (4 April 2022) A New IPCC Report Says The Window To Meet UN Climate Targets is Vanishing. *The Economist.*

73 Working Group III Contribution to the Sixth Assessment Report of the Intergovernmental Panel on Climate Change (April 2022) *Climate Change 2022: Mitigation of Climate Change. Summary For Policymakers.* Switzerland: IPPC.

74 *Ibid.*

75 Kühne, K., Bartsch, N., Tate, R.D., Higson, J., and Habet, A. (July 2022) Carbon Bombs: Mapping Key Fossil Fuel Projects. *Energy Policy.* Vol. 166. https://reader.elsevier.com/reader/sd/pii. Accessed on: 27 May 2022.

76 Carrington, D. and Taylor, M. (20 May 2022) What Lies Beneath. *The Guardian.*

77 *Ibid.*

78 Intergovernmental Science-Policy Platform on Biodiversity and Ecosystem Services on the Work of its Seventh Session (IPBES) (2019) *op. cit.*

79 See: Pearce, F. (29 May 2019) *Geoengineer the Planet? More Scientists Now Say It Must Be An Option.* Yale Environment 360. Yale School of Environment.

80 Irvine, P., Emanuel, K., He, J., Horowitz, L., Vecchi, G. & Keith, D. (April 2019) Halving Warming With Idealized Solar Geoengineering Moderates Key Climate Hazards. *Nature Climate Change.* Vol. 9. 295–299.

81 See Ward, B. (8 October 2018) The IPCC Global Warming Report Spares Politicians the Worst Details. *The Guardian.*

82 Wallace-Wells, D. (2019) *op. cit.*

83 US Department of State (September 25, 2020) *China's Environmental Abuses Fact Sheet:* Fact Sheet Office of the Spokesperson. www.state.gov/chinas-environmental-abuses-fact-sheet.

84 62 China's Ministry of Foreign Affairs. (October 19, 2020) *Fact Sheet on Environmental Damage by the US.* www.fmprc.gov.cn/mfa_eng/wjbxw/t1824980.shtml

85 Song, W., Jakhar, P., Bhat, U., and Menon, S. (November 2020) *Fact-checking the US and China on climate and environment.* Reality Check team and BBC Monitoring. BBC News.

86 Wallace-Wells, D. (2019) *op. cit.*

87 Smil, V. (2019) *Growth: From Microorganisms to Megacities.* Cambridge, MA: MIT Press.

88 Ghosh, A. (2016) *The Great Derangement: Climate Change and the Unthinkable.* London: University of Chicago Press. 162.

89 Ord, T. (2020) *The Precipice: Existential Risk and the Future of Humanity.* London: Bloomsbury Publishing.

90 *Ibid.* 27.

91 World Population Review (2022) *Nuclear Weapons by Country 2022.* https://worldpopulationreview.com/country-rankings/nuclear-weapons-by-country. Accessed on: 20 May 2022.

92 Reality Check: The Atomic Bombings of Hiroshima & Nagasaki www.armscontrol.org/pressroom/2020-07/reality-check-atomic-bombings-hiroshima-nagasaki. Accessed on: 8 October 2022.

93 Note: most of the data used here derive from the work of Kristensen, H.M. and Korda,M. of the Federation of American Scientists. https://fas.org/issues/nuclear-weapons/status-world-nuclear-forces. Accessed on: 8 October 2022.

94 Briefing: *(Mar 24th 2022)*The Risk That The War In Ukraine Escalates Past The Nuclear Threshold. *The Economist.*

95 See: Nuclear Threat Initia/wwtive (NTI) website: w.nti.org/learn/treaties-and-regimes/treaty-on-the-non-proliferation-of-nuclear-weapons. Accessed on: 27 September 2021.

96 See: https://cnduk.org/list-of-countries-that-have-signed-un-global-nuclear-weapons-ban-treaty. Accessed on: 8 October 2022.

97 Tisdall, S. (19 September 2021) Making Waves in the Pacific: How Boris Johnson's Global Britain Went Rogue. *The Observer.* www.theguardian.com/commentisfree/2021/sep/19/making-waves-in-the-pacific-how-boris-johnsons-global-britain-went-rogue. Accessed on: 20 September 2021. Note: Tisdall is an astute commentator on geopolitics.

98 Ehrlich, P. (1968) *The Population Bomb.* New York: Buccaneer Books.

99 Plokhy, S. (2022) *Atoms and Ashes: From Bikini Atoll to Fukushima.* London: Allen Lane.

100 Asha M. George, Executive Director of the Bipartisan Commission on Biodefense, quoted in: Borger, J. (28 January 2022) Tick, Tick …Boom? Why We're Closer to Midnight Than Ever. *The Guardian Weekly.*

8

NET EFFECT

The Internet and AI: Connection, Contortion and Control

We've talked so far about what it means to be human and to live in the human age. In doing so, we've considered how we recognise the *natural* in ourselves and our living environment, and how we measure unique traits like human *intelligence*. We turn now to consider whether *artificial intelligence* (AI) augurs a basic shift in how we see, and are seen in, the world. Looking ahead, will humans compete or partner with machines? Will AI be a complement to, or proxy for, human agency?

Or is this a false dichotomy, since humans have always been 'technological' and technology has always been social? In other words, we've always devised implements as supplements to our self-capacity, and such equipment has been situated in a social context. Surely then, such accessories are *natural*? Since time immemorial, we've created the mechanical to help us advance the societal, and information technology (IT) and AI can continue this pattern. Or can they?

When humans first domesticated animals, 10,000 or so years ago, we transitioned from hunter-gatherers, and our new agricultural 'technologies' brought diphtheria, influenza, salmonella, and such like– diseases that threatened rather than extended average life expectancy. Industrialisation, and accompanying urbanisation, saw environmental health hazards that helped spread infections of cholera, tuberculosis, and typhoid. New industrial machines were attended with new health and safety issues.[1] Technology has always been both friend and foe to our species.

Some insist that these new technologies are qualitatively different from their predecessors. For instance, they allow for a surveillance society beyond Orwellian premonition. Moreover, if AI is able in time to self-evolve into ever-more clever versions of itself, how can it be stopped from out-smarting humans? Such fate would terminate the short-lived Anthropocene.

DOI: 10.4324/9781003106593-10

If such superintelligence lacks moral agency, how can it be held socially accountable? Stephen Hawking warned in 2014 that full AI could spell our demise as a species. Putin has remarked that the country which leads in AI will rule the world, and certainly in the battle for economic supremacy between the US and China, AI will be a key battleground.

Arguably, dread about machine conquest of humans is misplaced, since a more benign outcome could be human enhancement by AI, to allow us to age without the tribulations of ageing, or even ultimately to deliver the elusive elixir for immortality. These are big issues that have hitherto been largely in the hands of big tech, and right now it is largely a law unto itself. This chapter considers whether we're faced with a golden chance or a dismal dilemma, or something in-between, in the context of the increasing clout of tech titans.

Smart Cookies

A hundred years ago, the Czech playwright Karel Capek wrote a play about future human-like machines he called *roboti*, meaning serf. From that, we get the word *robot*. Of course, there's always a risk that serfs rebel against their masters, and that prospect haunts the discussion about our relationship with what we now call artificial intelligence.

Coined as a term in the mid-1950s by John McCarthy, AI comprises human-designed software (and possibly hardware) systems capable of pursuing complex objectives physically or digitally through data interpretation, information processing, knowledge-based analysis, and adaptive response. For McCarthy and colleagues nearly 70 years ago, it was about making machines that could mimic human brain-power; use language; cope with abstractions and concepts; problem-solve complexity normally restricted to humans; and self-improve.

This automated capacity involves combinations of *machine learning*, which can be by, for example, supervised learning where labelled data allows for object, speech and pattern recognition, or reinforcement learning, where the machine trains itself through trial and error by getting positive or negative feedback on its output; *machine reasoning*, whereby for example, through artificial neural networks and high computational power, the machine is capable of planning, scheduling and knowledge representation; and *robotics*, which includes sensors, actuators, and perception.[2] Typically, AI involves sorting high volume data in ways that identify patterns, and thus permit finely-tuned algorithms, by which future data can be classified and predictive models created.

Reading through copious literature on AI, two things stand out. First, ever since Alan Turing's 'test' in 1950 about whether a machine with which you were interacting could be mistaken for a person, and thus could think, the field has been bedevilled by hype. When inflated promise is unfulfilled, the research arena wanes into an 'AI Winter', and when some new-fangled prospect is on the horizon, it re-waxes. Second, definition of 'intelligence' here is as problematic as it is for humans.

As mentioned earlier, we now consider human intelligence to be multi-dimensional: logical, verbal, emotional, spatial, artistic, intuitive, and experiential, amongst others. Not all these are always present together. We recognise some people as street savvy, while bereft of much formal education. We talk about very bright people who lack nuanced social awareness as being 'somewhere on the spectrum'. Accordingly, would it be possible for an ultra-intelligent machine to have all these attributes, supported by consciousness, as credentials for what's called *general intelligence*? When the IBM computer Deep Blue won a game against champion chess-player, Kasparov, in 1996, it was not in itself a game-changer. The programme was still targeted to a limited though challenging task, and the journey from micro-domain to wider complex world remained huge.

Back in the mid-1960s, Good had talked about an 'intelligence explosion', whereby adroit machines could create even more accomplished machines in cycles of constant self-upgrading. In such a virtuous loop, AI would outshine the cleverest of humans, thereby invoking doubt as to whether it would stay submissive to our control. More recently, Kurzwell[3] has raised the impending *Singularity* – that time when human and machine become interwoven, permitting us to transcend our biological limitations. Blending of human and machine cognition would produce a techno-human fusion that would expand our bandwidth for absorbing and applying knowledge. In this scenario, overlapping biotechnology, nanotechnology and robotics would erase distinction between human and machine and between physical and virtual reality.

We would have no cause to fear the machine as 'the other', but rather embrace it as an integral part of our new Transhumanism, which could take prosthesis to whole new levels:[4] contact lenses that photograph or video; 'bionic' suits that amplify physical strength; universal language earpieces that translate foreign tongues wherever we are in the world; implanted chips in the brain that activate doors, computers and other gadgets at the speed of our thoughts; and wearable chips that share sensory experiences with others wearing matching chips. Were such exchange feasible, it might enhance our empathy as we cruised inside each other's minds. And all this interface is alongside advances in CRISPR gene-editing to eradicate disease, and identify personalised traits from our genome, allowing us to develop customised health and education services. Ultimately, this biotech ambition heralds promise of more resilient and proficient humans.

For the moment, let's assume the possibility of superintelligence (capacity to surpass humans at all relevant intelligence tasks), linked to Artificial General Intelligence and Artificial Consciousness. Superintelligence goes beyond answering queries or even problem-solving to open and independent objectives. This would mean machines no longer just imitate or replicate, but originate *entirely on their own* – not merely generate from data analysis through deep learning. Would this need a consciousness, a self-identity and awareness that could mediate moral choices, and even develop emotional intelligence? Or would a non-conscious superintelligent agent be able to operate in a value-free logic, indifferent to human consequence? This disputed terrain was further complicated by the claim of Google engineer, Blake Lemoine, that the firm's AI chatbot LaMDA was sentient, an assertation that has been widely challenged.

It's a mystery because we've no precedent for a species creating a more intelligent entity than itself. For now, AI is programmed. It is what it eats in terms of data feed. Mostly, it acts to our command, not to its discretion. When an algorithm's main task is to bait attention, and the best means is to narrow, rather than open, the mind by preferencing bigots and diehards, it has no scruples about the moral damage. With no guiding moral compass, for AI to venture into new frontiers could steer humans toward a hazardous pilgrimage.

Pilgrim's Progress

Bostrum[5] believes that progress in neuroscience and cognitive psychology will in time disclose the workings of the human brain, which will in turn provide a template for advances in AI. This doesn't mean that AI needs to emulate the human mind, thereby holding feelings such as love, hate or pride. He specifies three kinds of feasible intellect amplification: *speed superintelligence*, that involves a 'fast mind' system capable of human aptitude, but with much more rapid mental operation; *collective superintelligence* that involves a composite cognitive system that builds on humanity's collective intelligence to boost multi-tasking performance across many domains; and *quality superintelligence* that is at least as swift as the human mind, but qualitatively superior. A digital intelligence that possessed any one of these three could in time produce the other two, and subsequent virtuosity could lead to a crossover point 'beyond which the system's further improvement is mainly driven by the system's own actions rather than by work performed upon it by others'.[6]

Given such step change, Bostrum considers how a 'soaring' cognitive superpower could threaten humans and their habitat: '....hijacking political processes, subtly manipulating financial markets, biasing information flows, or hacking into human-made weapon systems'[7] or inventing new weapons technology, and in multiple ways reshaping our habitat to an extent that determines our demise. Such an agent would be oriented toward technological perfection, cognitive enhancement and resource acquisition. In its more detailed 'motivation', it might be beyond human predictability. Thus, it cannot be assumed that superintelligence will be attended by values and behaviour that we associate with the cultivated mind: benevolent intent toward others, suave cultural taste, unassuming grace and gallantry. For its self-survival, humans might be expendable. It could take a 'treacherous turn' and pursue its objectives as a *singleton* – an agent without intellectual rival – by double-crossing its human creator.

In a series of complicated scenarios, Bostrum speculates about how humans could preclude such perfidy. This includes 'boxing' it in by installing approved channels for its external relations; 'stunting' its development to avoid any deviant behaviour; and using 'tripwires' that can shut down the system upon detection of dangerous behaviour. Such negative control mechanisms could be backed by positive incentives that domesticate the system within acceptable norms. This seems optimistic, since it denies the ingenuity of ultra-intelligence to bypass restrictions devised by normal intelligence.

He goes on to imagine different castes of AI, including the *oracle*, which is a question-and-answering system; and the *genie*, which is a command-executing system. Conceivably, both these could be contained within pre-specified 'disaster criteria', though I'm reminded of genies escaping bottles. Then there is the *sovereign* system, designed for open-ended independent action. Again, the question is whether any of these can be 'protected' against imprudent use. Scenarios for menace are so multiple and inexact that it's hard to see how they can be pre-programmed out.

While another option is to build in a preview effect, whereby human ratification is required before AI's plans are operated, Bostrum concludes that human safety with AI ultimately depends on us being able to 'load' it with worthy values. But how do you codify something as complex as goodness and endow it with concepts like moral hazard? You wouldn't want to try to replicate human morality per se: first, because this has evolved through genetics and culture over millennia; second, because human moral behaviour can be always and everywhere very flawed; and third, because aspects of current notions of morality are tied to presuppositions and prejudices of our time and culture. Ideally, you'd want to script an optimal value-set that exemplified decency and kindness, beyond their blemished human version. Looking far ahead, this will remain formidable – garnering agreement about moral protocols in a world of deeply contested convictions, and then designing this specification in software. As we journey in that direction, Bostrum offers the 'common good principle' as the moral compass: 'Superintelligence should be developed only for the benefit of all of humanity and in the service of widely shared ethical ideals'.[8]

The problem is in identifying the common good in an arena that interweaves state and private commercial motivation. In the field of bio-engineering, we could meld our bodies with machines, or use AI to 'gene edit', or see AI make other key breakthroughs about our biology. For instance, Google's AI company, DeepMind, had its software AlphaFold2 recently recognised by Critical Assessment of Protein Structure Prediction (CASP) as a solution to unravelling what three-dimensional shapes proteins fold into, a longstanding scientific puzzle, known as the 'protein folding problem'. Proteins, which are large intricate molecules, comprising sequences of amino acids, sustain nearly all of life's functions. Each protein's operation hinges on its exclusive 3D structure. Ability to predict this shape will uncover more about what the protein does and how it works, interacts and malfunctions, an appreciation that can generate new disease treatments.[9]

Since this advance is from a private company, it raises questions about intellectual property. Will it prioritise commercial gain over public access to its code to allow for reproducibility and answerability? This balance between private profit and public good lies at the heart of this kind of AI research, whose foundations have been backed by public money. As a *Guardian* editorial put it: 'It would be strange if in years to come university researchers used government cash to pay DeepMind for a system built on government-funded insights'.[10] If a lot of the 'blue sky' research in this field is to be driven by private-public partnership, the 'public' interest must be better detailed in advance.

Meantime, we can acknowledge shortcomings in human know-how and morality, while acclaiming the aptitudes of AI. We've become familiarised with these talents. Some of them may seem to save us time, like filtering our spam emails, and identifying our online shopping preferences, or improve our health, through precision diagnosis and surgery, and enhanced flexibility in prosthetic limbs. In the work environment, AI is deployed to deal with sectors like high-volume containerisation to achieve greater efficiency, speed and safety. Satellite navigation systems offer efficient routes for long car journeys. Advanced performance of computer-aided design (CAD) presents inventive ways to conceive the built environment. Thermal imaging equipment helps night-time wardens expose poachers in Kenya's Masai Mara National Reserve. And future developments include greater scope for cars, trucks, trains and airplanes to operate without direct human steering. A private company, called *Planet*, operates over 200 satellites that daily image the world's landmass. It has worked with conservationists to identify deforestation; with Amnesty International to detect Myanmar's military torching of Rohingya villages; and with media to verify bombing attacks in Syria. Such constant tracking can identify illegal palm oil plantations, problematic crop yields that augur famine, and other menaces, all with benign purpose.[11]

We may think that all this is to the good, and that jobs displaced by AI can be replaced over time by jobs that place premium on human contact. Besides, the extra wealth engendered by AI's efficiency may finally deliver the dream of the 'leisure society'. It may help improve education, not only through digital learning devices, but also because learning may become less about cramming information that is readily retrievable through a search engine, and more about critical thinking and artistic creativity. But what are the costs of such benefits, in terms of malicious use such as cybercrime and cyber-attacks?[12] How far does it erode human agency? Does it empower or supplant human capacity? How do we avoid a widening digital inequality that would intensify social inequality?

Candid Camera

Alongside these considerations, application of AI can be seen as a lethal threat to freedom and democracy. We think of citizens subjected to constant scrutiny by pervasive CCTV cameras, many now with enhanced sensors, and whose footage is analysed through automated software such as HumanID. Increasingly, networks of such cameras will be centralised and connected to databases that can match visuals with people's identity through, for example, biometric data, and thereby extensively trace individual activity and movement.

A US example of how metadata of this type is being systematised is the Defense Advanced Research Projects Agency's (DARPA) *Combat Zones That See* (CTS) project, designed to connect multiple monitoring cameras in a battle zone to a centralised computing system, and analyse with AI software to observe manoeuvres of enemy military. Clearly, such all-out surveillance could be adapted for any city at home or abroad. When I read Orwell's *1984* in the 1960s, the idea that 'big brother is watching you' was science fiction dystopia. Now it's science fiction only insofar as it doesn't divulge the full facts.

Beyond CCTV, there are facial recognition devices, which employ thermal, geometric and other data to develop algorithms for: digital depictions, known as face templates; airport security screeners; roadway cameras, which are for automatic number plate recognition (ANPRs); a range of workers – not just police – who can wear body cameras; personal monitoring devices such as doorbells with lenses, and dash cams; computers and televisions with cameras; and then the countless visual recordings from within shops and businesses and from personal phones and drones. Our smartphones can geotrack our every move in real time.

Until recently, the idea that you could persuade people to actually pay for gadgets that could eavesdrop private conversations in their own homes, would have been dismissed with derision. Today, people voluntarily purchase such bugging appliance. Alexa's smart speakers catch conversations that are then processed through cloud computing for speech recognition and language interpretation, and can be tracked to the owner. Many believe that if they don't activate with the 'wake' word, or if they switch off the 'drop-in', they are safe from intrusive listening. That's not necessarily so.

Of course, Amazon may say that any decoding of people's words is merely designed to improve 'customer experience', a self-serving claim that by infringing your liberty, they're really doing you a favour.[13] This kind of voice assistant, and others like Apple's Siri and Google Assistant, can be connected to other 'smart home' gadgets, such as thermostats, lighting, kitchen appliances and security monitors. Apart from infiltrating into sensitive parts of private lives, these 'assistants' may stimulate expansive markets in voice purchasing and search – new scope to manufacture demand that can then be traced for further user-profiling. In being scanned, we're being scammed.

Alongside this ground-level snooping, there is increased aerial surveillance, using unmanned aerial vehicles, digital imaging technology and infrared heat-detecting devices. The US drone plane, known as the MQ-9 Reaper, can pinpoint small objects from 30,000 feet overhead, and states like the UK are pursuing their own versions of this technology for domestic policing. Beyond that again, there's the heightened zoom capacity and high-definition imaging resolution of satellite cameras orbiting in outer space – some 1700 of them eyeing down on us, listening-in, specifying our whereabouts, storing images of us, all without our knowledge or consent.

None of this alarming intrusion takes away the positive potential mentioned earlier. Not all scrutiny is state and security driven. However, there is a 'mission drift' element to these developments. We're doing a lot of new things in this field because we can do them. Enhanced scope for observing, scanning, sorting, recording, and archiving derives in part from greater data scale and speed. For instance, when we talk about Big Data, we're acknowledging not only cheaper and bigger data storage, but also improved capacity to compute large data sets to uncover relationships, arrangements, and tendencies. In this regard, Big Data is said to be marked by five Vs: **volume**: large amounts of low-density formless data to be organised and processed; **velocity**: the increasingly high speed of its generation and transmission; **variety**: its diverse sources in text, video and audio; **value**: its status as 'capital' in an information age; and **veracity**: its reliability in a world glutted with both fact and fake.

A key paradox of AI is how miniaturization of form has led to magnification of scope. Tiny devices can be mass-produced cheaply for mass purchase and wide use. Small *physical* objects can have vast *virtual* spread. One aspect of this is the Internet-of-Things (IoT), a term used for an amalgam of internet-connected electronic devices – smart phones, wireless sensors, radio-frequency identification readers, medical equipment, laptops, software, and such like – able to gather, integrate, analyse, swap and share data over a wireless network without human direction. As noted by Russell,[14] this 'provides AI systems with far greater sensory and control access to the real world'. In other words, we're witnessing a big leap in how lots of data can be accumulated and permutated.

For me, there are three basic laws of big tech: first, data craves data; second, the more the data, the more the need for ample storage and sophisticated processing technology; and third, the more this capacity is upgraded, the more data it invites to be hoarded and probed. This world of spying and prying is one where those on high have our lowdown. We used to think of private citizens and public officials. Now it's reversing. We are public and officialdom is private and opaque. Miniature devices can glean massive material. The process is invasive, yet unobtrusive. The insidious response to any resistance has oft been that 'if you've nothing to hide, you've nothing to fear'. Superficially reasonable, this really implies you're not permitted confidentiality and discretion.

Humans need privacy and even secrecy, a restricted part of themselves that is only shared in chosen intimacy. A world in which we're an open-book is one closed to the principle of confining our secretive selves to those near and dear to us. It's been said often that these companies are not simply communication platforms. They're publishers and advertisers. I would add that they are asset-strippers, since they steal the precious asset of personal data. They are implicated in what's been dubbed the 'digital kleptocracy'. Whatever their confidentiality protocols, they are designed for prying rather than privacy. What's worse, their data security is actually quite porous.

In 2021, it was revealed[15] that Pegasus, hacking spyware sold by the Israeli surveillance firm, NSO Group, was available to authoritarian governments for potential monitoring of journalists, human rights lawyers and activists, among others. With Pegasus infection, the software has potential to tap into iPhones and Android devices to record calls, and glean photos and emails. It can even covertly trigger microphones and cameras. What you think is a device *for* you – your mobile phone – could become a means for surveillance *on* you. The firm claims that it undertakes robust vetting of clients' reputation on human rights. But regulation of this market is weak, and this shows yet another means of mass data harvesting.

In short, those who scrutinise us can themselves be inscrutable. As has been said: they end up knowing a lot about us, whereas we understand so little about them.[16] Yet, as the reach of big tech spreads to herds, it's inner working can't be left to nerds. Snowden's revelation of US massive surveillance, Chinese use of facial recognition to control social behaviour, the Russian use of digital disinformation – all these and more are as rampant as repressive. Take the US: under its 1994 Communications Assistance for Law Enforcement Act (CALEA), makers and carriers of telecommunications equipment need to design their products and processes to guarantee their capacity to comply with legal information requests.[17]

As digital technology evolves, updates of this legislation ensure that law enforcement preserve the ability to conduct wiretaps and other monitoring of all phone calls and internet traffic,[18] usually captured by automated internet surveillance computers. The StingRay tracker is one such instrument for intercepting cell phone exchanges in the US and UK. It can let police intercept data – calls, texts, websites visited – from every phone. Selective analysis of the high-volume traffic is arbitrated by 'trigger' words or accessing of particular websites. Other analytical means can locate mobile phones and track how travel movements of 'people of interest' traverse with those of others. Private location data firms in the US can monitor precise whereabouts of smartphone-owning Americans via their phone apps, without their knowledge, and this data can then be sold to third parties, including government. A person's steps can be retraced, potentially going back up to five years.[19]

Snowden was so concerned about the unaccountable over-reach of the US National Security Agency that he wanted the issue to get world exposure, and in his first emails to Laura Poitras, who later made a film about Snowden's revelations called *Citizenfour*, he warned about how widespread was the scrutiny:[20]

> From now, know that every border you cross, every purchase you make, every call you dial, every cell phone tower you pass, friend you keep, article you write, site

you visit, subject line you type, and packet you route, is in the hands of a system whose reach is unlimited but whose safeguards are not.

Chinese Whispers

If this can be done under democratic regimes, the scope for authoritarian ones like China and Russia is boundless, not only for their own repressed populations, but also for export to other illiberal states. Presently, around 18 countries deploy Chinese surveillance systems, and twice that number have been involved in Chinese-led training about new information and media technology.[21] With its 'Great Firewall' of state censored internet access, China forged this path. Before Xi assumed the presidency in 2013, Chinese people still had some chance of transparent information exchange, with some deploying virtual private networks (VPNs) to open barred websites, and posting political dissent online. In 2000, Order 292 enforced internet service providers to ensure their online content abided by 'the law', and in 2002, a Public Pledge on Self-Discipline for China's Internet Industry set four principles: patriotic observance of law, trust-worthiness, honesty and equitableness.

The same year saw the jamming of Google, which later introduced a customised and safe Chinese version. Xi, keen to use the virtual realm as a vehicle for Party propaganda, in 2015 initiated the Great Cannon, an instrument for modifying and substituting dissident or 'false news' social media content and curbing any defiance of authority from Chinese web influencers. Gagging critical views and concocting compliant content is undertaken by some 2 million 'internet public opinion analysts'. Such intervention is set within Xi's 'socialism with Chinese characteristics' as a means of *rejuvenation*, itself a byword for retrieving ancient greatness. All this suppression faces China with a dilemma: how to be open globally as a modern science-based economy, yet closed internally to the free flow of global information that could stir political rebellion.[22]

Via a Cyperspace Administration, reporting direct to Xi, over sixty agencies supervise the Chinese web, including trendy social media sites such as Weibo and WeChat. Skynet, a joint venture between the Ministries of Public Security and Industry and Information Technology, has mounted a nationwide complex of CCTV feeds. China's capital, Beijing, home to around 20 million people, has the most such cameras of any city in the world, at 1.15 million. Indeed, of the 20 most surveilled cities globally, 18 are in China (though, interestingly, London ranks third).[23] More recently, such comprehensive observation has been rolling out across Chinese public space and top firms, a process dubbed 'Sharp Eyes', linked to location data from smartphones and vehicles. To organise and sift this data overload, China has spent big money in new AI companies like *Sensetime*.

The next Chinese step to over-power citizen autonomy involves a 'social credit score' system, whereby a database, monitoring government, corporate and individual activities will permit automated audits of an individual's summative data – bank, health, and work details, online activity, movement and conduct, etc. From this, people can be graded in terms of law-abiding behaviour. Government justifies these ubiquitous eyes as applying big data to enhance mutual trust. A person's composite tally would determine their earned access to public goods.

Of the world's estimated 770 million surveillance cameras, 54 percent are in China, with the US and Germany ranking next. If China retains this share as the number of such devices globally reaches 1 billion, then it would have 540 million cameras, approximately one for every two citizens.[24] We can see the autocratic control this precision monitoring offers when masses of Muslim Uighers and Kazakhs in Xinjiang have been held in various 're-education' centres, internment camps, and prisons, on the fabricated basis of preventing extremism, separatism and terrorism.[25] In 2022, a hacked batch of classified police files from the region exposed the securitised operation, which in the period 2017–18 saw over 12 percent of Uyghur adults confined under a camp regime that was prepared to shoot-to-kill escapees.[26] Selection of detainees for this mass incarceration has been facilitated by big data surveillance.

In its evident repression,[27] China has an accomplice in big tech. American semi-conductor firms, Intel and Nvidia, have provided chips that drive the surveillance complex, known as Urumqi Cloud Computing, which collates and processes photos, video-recordings, facial recognition, checkpoint data, and phone taps in Xinjiang, and effectively facilitates 'predictive policing'. This all-seeing intrusion into people's lives is itself part of its Integrated Joint Operations Platform (IJOP) that includes other sources of data such as 'wifi sniffers', which amass detected addresses of computers, smartphones, and other connected devices.[28] In the context of Russian expansionism in Ukraine, Taiwan's vulnerability to Chinese takeover has been underscored. Accordingly, global reliance on Taiwan's supply of microchips presents a risk of tech-dependency on China, as Europe is experiencing with Russian energy. It remains to be seen whether the EU's proposed *Chips Act* will improve European self-sufficiency in semi-conductors, thereby mitigating this exposure. Meantime, in October 2022, the US introduced a ban on sale of high-end chips to China, both by US corporations and other firms whose products contain American chips, a move that is indicative of the central importance of who gets a market lead in chip production.

Underpinning these systems is the digital national identification card system, which uses a citizen's card number as access point to many public and private services, as well as the code to unlock vast databases of private information government holds on each individual.[29] The US firms professed ignorance about any 'misuse' of their technology.[30] Despite the denial, this is part of a pattern, involving other US tech companies like Hewlett Packard and Western Digital, deemed to abet China's massive surveillance complex.[31] Looking back, it is funny to remember that Presidents Trump and Xi started off as buddies, sharing affinity for strong leadership. When the love-in soured, the former decided to turn on the latter in a trade show-down, and one tactic was to blacklist Chinese firms, particularly those leading surveillance like Hikvision and SenseTime, from procuring American technology. This ban was billed as protecting human rights as much as fair trade.[32]

It's not just the Americans. As part of a five-year programme called FACER2VM, involving UK academics from institutions such as Surrey University, and supported by a £6.1 million UK government grant, the UK has been in a shared research project with China on enhancing facial recognition.[33] UK involvement with China in a scheme that could influence repressive surveillance in Hong Kong would cement successive British failure to convert the former colony into a proper democracy, during their long colonial hold. Britain's complaint about Chinese erosion of Hong Kong's limited democracy rings hollow, given its own culpability.

Other Nosey Parkers

In 2019, Russia introduced its 'sovereign internet' law, supposedly to protect its online system against any future hostile Western disconnection of Russia from the world wide web. In reality, it's designed to help its telecommunications regulator, Roskomnadzor, ensure that the digital domain complies with the regime's strictures against disrespect for authority, extremism, and spread of subversive material. To that end, internet service providers are obliged to install deep packet inspection (DPI) that can spot seditious traffic and sift content, thereby curbing democratic speech and personal privacy.[34] Internet surveillance was already operated through the System of Operative-Search Measures (SORM-3) that keeps tabs on all telecom, and affords Federal Security Services retrieval of all data exchanged online. In terms of systematic video surveillance, since 2015, Russia's 'safe city' initiative automatically transmits tape content, including facial/object recognition data, to government officials.[35]

In September 2021, in the lead-up to an election, the Russian government forced Apple and Google to remove apps that were helpful to its political opposition. They meekly complied. In its coercively supervised 'democracy', Putin's party unsurprisingly triumphed with another electoral victory. Beyond Russia and China, other big geo-political players misuse communications technology to censor dissent. In 2019, as India was moving to annul constitutional autonomy in Kashmir, and bring it under tighter central control, it forced an internet shutdown in the region.

When state snooping takes the form of a biometric database, it can potentially stock a composite profile of a population's iris and retina information, facial recognition, fingerprints, DNA, signature, voice identification, and physical and behavioural traits. Using the body as a data source reduces humans to a digital code. It's not just that for each of us individually, we must submit to compulsory and automatic capture of personal information by a remote and unseen powerful force. It's that this represents a 'technocratization of citizenship', whereby our data is used to create predictive algorithms that categorise, filter and place us in hierarchies of risk and respect, an exclusionary process inclined to further discriminate against the vulnerable and marginalised.[36] Think of the impact for credit, insurance, job application, and so on. Moreover, such sorting is based on machine assessment rather than human discernment.

Mass surveillance concerns four key things:[37] recognition, connection, detection and discrimination – identifying someone, correlating their actions and relationships, discovering patterns in these, and then selecting those that merit further policing. We often assume that high tech offers precision and accuracy in this process. Unfortunately, this isn't so. For example, the facial recognition firm, Clearview AI, has scanned 20 billion images of people's faces and data worldwide from various online sources and these multiple feeds supposedly yield algorithms that spot faces with exactitude. People remain uninformed that their images are being thus assembled and exploited. Recently, the UK's Information Commission's Office fined the company around £7.5 million, and directed it to desist from further accessing UK residents' personal data, and to erase the data of UK residents from its files.[38] As in so many such cases, the penalty was puny, and hardly a deterrent.

A wider concern about such data collection, and supposition about precise recognition, is that tests show in-built bias that renders them much less accurate in identifying, for example, women of colour, compared to white men. Similar defects operate in automated risk-assessment credit profiles.[39] Inaccuracy is down to the slanted data used to 'train' algorithms, which let's remind ourselves, grasp uniformities and associations, and then use these patterns to predict. Positively discriminating in favour of minorities in the training data might help assuage this current ingrained bias.

If AI-run recidivism risk scores, like COMPAS, harbour biased assumption about high re-offending rates of African-Americans, these can lead to stricter sentencing and parole criteria for blacks.[40] As Schellenberg notes: 'By repeating our past practices, algorithms not only automate the status quo and perpetrate bias and injustice, but they amplify the biases and injustices of our society'.[41] The paradox here is that the all-seeing is not the all-knowing, that a system designed to control cannot control for its own errors. When it makes mistakes, it delivers the ultimate 'fake news', insights that are meant to come from detached objectivity of AI, but are actually blind to its fallibility, and the pretension of machines to detect what makes humans tick. In this moral maze, where is the moral agency?

Moral Maze

In his 1942 science-fiction story *Runaround*, Asimov famously enunciated three laws of robotics. First, a robot may not harm, or permit harm done to, humans;

second, the robot must obey humans unless instructions conflict with the first law; and third, the robot must guard its own existence, unless this conflicts with the first two laws. In 2011, two UK Research Councils gave a joint update of these, emphasising that humans, not robots, are the responsible agents, and that robots are instruments for human objectives. They should not be devised to exploit humans or create their dependency. Legal liability and duty of care for any robot should always be traceable. And telling robot from human should always be feasible.

Such attempts to frame an ethics for AI are underway in different countries.[42] Many frameworks for an ethical AI have emerged. One, from the viewpoint of labour, calls for: transparency, with unambiguous information about the ethics inherent in the system; safety and security, that allows for full human responsibility and control; a priority to serve people and planet, protective of human rights and privacy; freedom from gender and racial bias; a digital economy that benefits all humanity, and allows for a just transition from an analogue one; and prohibition of lethal autonomous weapons, including cyber warfare.[43]

Some research detects increasing global concurrence around five ethical tenets: transparency; justice and fairness; non-maleficence; responsibility; and privacy. But the devil is in the detail with regard to interpretation, prioritisation, and implementation.[44] A comprehensive literature review of twenty-seven primary studies addressing how AI ethics principles are being expressed and adopted across the world notes that the issue is beset by 'lack of ethical knowledge and vague principles'.[45] Fundamentals like people's right to control information about themselves, and stakeholders' responsibility and accountability for the system's decisions and actions tend to be stated in very broad terms. Arbitration of conflicts among the ethical principles and the lack of cross-cultural understanding constitute further dilemmas.

The European Commission has recently set a framework for European-made AI that is secure, ethical, and cutting-edge, and has acknowledged the preparation needed for the significant socio-economic changes that AI will bring.[46] It has identified six conditions for what it calls 'trustworthy AI': human agency and oversight; technical robustness, reliability and safety; privacy, and data governance transparency; diversity, non-discrimination and fairness; environmental and societal welfare; and accountability. Its general aim for a human-centric digital future means that AI has to endorse human agency, enabling a rights-based and equitable democracy. Human values, as embodied in the Treaties of the European Union and Charter of Fundamental Rights of the European Union, affirm people's undeniable moral standing and dignity. They also uphold respect for the wider living environment, to which the human ecosystem is intrinsic.

A follow-up expert report specified ethics guidelines and policy recommendations.[47] It affirmed AI as a means – not an end in itself. At minimum, it doesn't compromise human self-determination and right to private life. It treats people as moral subjects, not as passive objects to be processed. It protects against its malicious use for deception or manipulation. It regulates data quality, integrity, traceability and access. It encourages digital literacy so that all can understand and use its application. It allows for contest and redress when subject to abuse. It is free from bias around race, gender, sexuality and ability. And it ensures a just distribution of its benefits and costs. Beyond these minimum standards, it can enhance human welfare, offering greater choice and control. It can enrich rather than replace human cognitive, social and cultural skills, making for a 'smarter' world. It can automate dangerous labour and help humans focus on meaningful work that places premium on creativity and care. It can deepen democracy and advance human deliberation, and it can make delivery of public goods more efficient and effective.

To ground such aspiration in more specific stipulations, the Commission then produced an 'assessment list' to help pin down conditions for compliance.[48] So, for example, in the case of privacy, it must at minimum adhere to the mandatory measures under the EU's General Data Protection Regulation (GDPR) – of which more later. Beyond that, it must have a transparency and oversight that allows for *traceability* (can data input be tracked back through all stages?); *explainability* (is there capacity to clarify the technical aspects of the AI system and the rationale behind its decisions or predictions?); and *open communication* (are users told the objective, criteria and constraints of the AI system's decision(s), and that they are relating with an AI system instead of a human?).

Since the more advanced forms of AI involve 'black-box' algorithms, which even their designers sometimes struggle to precisely explain, traceability and explainability become problematic. Thus, the burden of proof is heightened for victims seeking compensation for harms derived from an AI decision. Moreover, the connectivity of AI across Internet-of-Things devices increases the multiplicity of producers in the value chain – some contributing algorithms, others data – each of whom will seek to avoid liability for another's actions. Indeed, there is a disincentive for any contributor to provide information that could pinpoint the causal connection between an AI decision and a particular detriment, as this could result in them being held liable, even if guiltless.

The EU's *AI Liability Directive*, designed to complement its *AI Act*, addresses such drawbacks by lowering the standard of proof for claims against AI, and by allowing claimants to request information from AI producers or operators. A question for the future is that if AI becomes increasingly autonomous in its decision-making, absent human intervention, who becomes liable when AI's actions become less predictable – without according AI legal personality? Such an attribution may, theoretically, address certain liability issues, but opens up a Pandora's box for a plethora of other philosophical and legal quagmires.

However, for all the attempts to establish a regulatory framework, what's missing to date is a universal code.[49] Such standard would provide a level playing field through a common understanding of these quandaries, reflected in uniform regulation. Achieving agreement that binds despotisms like Russia and China is likely to involve concession to the lowest common denominator, making for weak regulation and dilution of progressive values. Perhaps the most realistic avenue for a universal framework is via the EU's *AI Act*. Given that the EU is the largest affluent consumer market, third states, producing AI, may face corporate pressure to closely follow the EU's framework, for ease of doing business – the so-called 'Brussels Effect'.[50] Likewise, the EU can leverage its dominant market position with poorer third countries seeking to access the Single Market through a trade deal. Clearly, the EU poses an alternative practice to the digital authoritarianism evident in places like China. The operation of AI outside democratic accountability remains a significant threat to human autonomy, and maybe even ultimately, survival itself.

Since many of these problems are global in nature, and at worst threaten humanity as a whole, they need a common human approach. Yet the contemporary drive towards competitive nationalism militates against such global cooperation. Can the EU's *AI Act* foster requisite collaboration, or is it likely to institutionalize the fragmentation? Can you set the rules of the game when you're not dominating that game? Can demand-side power – having a wealthy consumer market – win despite supply-side deficits, namely Europe's relatively weak production capacity in AI? Indication of how complex this whole issue is lies in the failure, even *within* the EU itself, to reach common agreement on a definition, and thus regulatory scope. Does AI include all algorithms that can generate a standard prediction, and those machines that generate new insights based on our data, or only machines that produce new sources of knowledge?

Alongside such conundrums, enormous benefits beckon. Climate change can be addressed with more efficient energy infrastructure and consumption; decarbonised 'engines'; and intelligent transport systems that cut queues, optimise routes, organise traffic flows, and decrease fatalities. Worldwide at present, car accidents kill one person every 23 seconds. Customised and adaptable learning techniques can help reduce educational inequality. In terms of health, medical robots may assist precision surgery. Perhaps more important in helping make the shift from curative to preventative health care, are the personalised diagnostics that can improve early identification of illness, tailored treatment, and more effective management of chronic conditions.

Apple Watches, and in the near future Fitbits, can spot onset of critical conditions like atrial fibrillation. As noted: 'a rapidly growing array of electronically enhanced straps, patches and other *wearables* can record over 7,500 physiological and behavioural variables….machine learning can filter a torrent of data to reveal a continuous, quantified picture of you and your health'. Such monitoring, and its feed into algorithms, can subsequently translate those patterns into customised prescriptive care. Such longitudinal study of our wellbeing can potentially detect ailment with a prescience and accuracy, beyond that derivative of infrequent and brief consultations with a doctor. In 2020, around

200 million such devices were purchased. Presently, one in four Americans possess one. It's estimated that by 2026, twice as many will be bought. But as with all latent good technology, prospective downsides loom: will it accentuate health inequality by making such provision, and follow-up treatment, largely limited to the world's wealthy?[51] Will it come under the data privacy expected of personal health information, or be sold on for commercial purpose? Will it make insurance cover more restricted? Will feedback on behavioural profiles come to form part of our curriculum vitae in job applications? Will it make us more self-aware of our responsibility for our health, or induce us to become more anxious with hypochondria? Paradoxically, a non-invasive technique to determine our state of health may carry hidden invasive disclosure about our very state of being.

Such trade-offs are inherent to the granular capacities of the technology. EU ethics guidelines refer to 'unjustified surveillance'. Who then decides when watching is warranted? With AI, the difficult dilemma between security and liberty is amplified. Do we want predictive policing at the price of privacy invasion? How do we distinguish between targeted and mass surveillance, between state and commercial surveillance? What scope is there for citizen consent? How can humans know when they're 'talking' to machines?

Ahead, other quandaries await. For instance, forms of Lethal Autonomous Weapon Systems (LAWs) could be driven by learning machines with cognitive capacity to determine without human direction whom to target '(detect, identify, track or select), and attack (use force against, neutralize, damage or destroy)'.[52] International Humanitarian Law requires operation of *distinction* between military goals and civilian objects, and between civilians and combatants; also, *proportionality*, whereby an action cannot be excessive relative to the direct military gain expected; and *precautionary* capacity, whereby an assault can be stopped or suspended if it violates these previous two criteria. Though the specifics regarding activation of lethal autonomous weaponry are not covered by the Geneva Conventions, they are implicitly in the added protocols to them, under the Martens Clause, which protects civilians within 'the principles of humanity, and the dictates of the public conscience'. Human liability cannot be eluded: 'as for all obligations under international law, these legal obligations, and accountability for them, cannot be transferred to a machine, computer program or weapon system'.[53]

Mechanistic military engagement of this kind, that compromises human will and risks glitch, remodels mortal combat. In late 2020, Iran claimed that its top nuclear scientist, Mohsen Fakhrizadeh, was assassinated outside Tehran by a satellite-controlled gun directed by artificial intelligence. Though uncorroborated, its very feasibility is alarming. In Russia's aggression against Ukraine, it has allegedly used a robotic weapon – Kalashnikov ZALA Aero KUB-BLA – a so-called 'loitering munition', or searching drone, that comprises an AI-enabled sensor guidance system capable of exploding into a deliberate target. Purportedly, Ukraine has deployed Bayraktar TB2 drones, which contain 'autonomous' competence.[54] The Stop Killer Robots coalition refer to these new type of licences to kill as 'digital dehumanisation'.

In 2015, an open letter signed by leading AI researchers, and prominent names like Stephen Hawking and Noam Chomsky, called for a global ban on offensive autonomous weapons beyond proper human command: '...the stakes are high: autonomous weapons have been described as the third revolution in warfare, after gunpowder and nuclear arms'. They feared that such deployment could encourage war by 'lowering the threshold for going to battle' and that it would prompt a new arms race of AI weapon development. Unlike nuclear arms, these could be mass-produced cheaply and dispensed to dictators and warlords to repress their own people, target specific ethnic groups, and assassinate foreign bigwigs to destabilise geopolitics.[55]

Though for most of us, AI is barely understandable, the industrial world is moving ahead with the third wave of digitalisation, if we take the first to have involved the spread of networking technology, and the second to have been boosted by Big Data. Information has always been power in politics. Now it's also the raw material of contemporary capitalism.

In our economic production process, data volumes have been rising recently at 61 percent annually. AI has entered the fray to help us sort our stockpile. To do so, information must typically be stored centrally, though concentrated information control from the centre can be conducive to global totalitarian government, an extreme scenario certainly, but one that, if it happened, would see human freedom of thought, never mind expression, subjugated.[56] This brings us to another paradox: we need greater global cooperation to deal with common threats, including rogue AI. By the same token, AI itself can help create a coercive global authority. Democracy depends on deliberation, which depends on discrimination between fact and fiction. Social media, and other AI-dominated systems can blur that distinction. When we consider the massive use of surveillance, privacy invasion, and wider AI in the democratic world, we should remind ourselves that no one voted for this. It was not up for debate. It came, it saw, it conquered.

Techlash

That doesn't preclude the potential fight-back we may be witnessing. If so, the contest will be intense. Big tech brings big bucks. In 2022, of the ten largest companies in the world by capitalisation (number of issued shares multiplied by their value), eight are big tech corporations, headed by Apple Inc. Ranked second is Saudi Arabian Oil, a reminder of why that country's rulers get away with murder. In descending order, the tech firms are: Apple, Microsoft, Alphabet (Google), Amazon, Tesla, NVIDIA, Taiwan Semiconductor Manufacturing Co. Ltd. (TSM), and Meta Platforms (Facebook, Instagram and WhatsApp).[57]

Together, the top five of these enjoy market valuation of nearly $9 trillion.[58] In terms of the world's ten most profitable companies, half are in computer, information technology and e-commerce, and half are in financial services (with the total ten shared half and half by the US and China).[59]

Of the 735 American billionaires, the richest is Musk, who heads Tesla ($219 billion). Altogether, seven of the top ten wealthiest Americans derive their fortune from this lucrative sector. In descending order from Musk, these are: Bezos ($177 billion); Gates ($129 billion); Page ($111 billion); Brin ($107 billion); Ellison ($106 billion); Ballmer ($91.4 billion); and coming in on the rear, Zuckerberg ($67.3 billion), whose wealth dropped by almost $30 billion on the previous year, attributed to the near 30 percent decline in share value of his re-branded Meta Platforms.[60] Six of these feature in the top ten world's richest.[61] This intense wealth sits within a pattern, whereby in the midst of a pandemic, which most people experienced as economically exacting, eight of the ten richest Americans saw their bank balance improve. Indeed, the combined wealth of the top ten rose in the previous year from $1.05 trillion to $1.2 trillion, to constitute a quarter of total American billionaire riches.[62]

The dominance of US tech firms within their own specialism is considerable. Amazon is not only into e-commerce, but is also a big player in cloud service, with a market share of almost half. Also, it has subscription services for streaming entertainment, and sells devices such as Kindle e-readers and Alexa, while operating WholeFoods. Alphabet mostly hogs online web search, while also providing Gmail email service, Google maps and photos, and video sharing through YouTube. Meta leads in social networking and online messaging, with Facebook, Instagram and WhatsApp. It claims to be frontiering the 'metaverse', a domain of virtual and augmented reality. Apple towers over smartphones, and the mobile app store market, controlling access to over 100 million iPhones and iPads in the US alone; and Microsoft still overshadows competitors in operating systems and other software, while also big in cloud computing and the game industry.[63]

Nevertheless, the twins of digital technology and low-cost debt that have driven so much of the current world economy have been coming under strain with recessionary pressures, the exit from home-based online and streaming entertainment in the post-pandemic period, and rising borrowing costs. Up to recently, the big tech firms had a lot of surplus and investor interest to spur their diversification and conglomeration, even beyond an obvious digital province. Now, they are facing more pressure on profit, and with that 'shares of Alphabet, Amazon and Meta have all lost more than 10 percent of their value since the companies' latest quarterly reports in late October (2022)'.[64] And in this more vigilant environment, it's hard to tell what the constrictions will be on the space dreams of a Tusk or Bezos, or the metaverse aspiration of a Zuckerberg. But even under greater investor or regulatory restraint, the power of a small number of ultra-rich tech magnates remains alarmingly unaccountable.

When I took my first trip on the new 'information superhighway' just over thirty years ago, I never imagined its destination at this summit. A hand-held wireless phone can now also operate as a mini-computer, offering internet search, photographic camera, audio and video recording, texting, mapping, audio and video-based news service, video-conferencing, an extensive music library, and myriad other apps. It's a marvel of technology with great potential for good or ill across a diverse world. And its control is in the hands of a few people, mostly white American males, educated at elite colleges like Harvard, Princeton, Stanford and Chicago. Even if some became college drop-outs, they're hardly the embodiment of diversity.

It may appear that the Big Five information technology companies – Apple, Microsoft, Alphabet, Amazon and Meta – invest substantially in research & development, and thus in innovation. In 2021, they collectively spent $149 billion, a 34 percent rise since 2019. But this spend was from revenues that, between 2015–2020, rose almost three-fold. What many of them are into is 'killer acquisition', buying up new commercial reach and seeing off competition. For instance, Meta recently purchased eight of the thirteen companies developing augmented and virtual reality that went in public sale. Of Apple's twenty-two acquisitions since 2019, over half were AI-based start-ups.[65] Getting bigger by gobbling up the smaller is a recipe for continued concentration in the sector.

In July 2020, the tech titans were summoned to the House Committee on the Judiciary of the US Congress for an antitrust hearing.[66] Over a century ago, growing monopolistic power of American oil and railway companies was considered anti-competitive, and a set of US antitrust laws was introduced, such as the Clayton (1914) and Federal Trade Commission (1914) Acts to restrict this trend. Reagan's push against government regulation in the 1980s sidelined these directives, with the so-called Chicago School of more market-driven economics arguing that big was not necessarily bad for consumers or wider business. In fact, achieving bulk was a likely sign of success, and size gave scale and scope for innovative investment. Mergers and acquisitions were back in business. Since optimising shareholder value was now paramount, mega-corporate supremacy in Silicon Valley was deemed permissible. More recently, however, the political dial has shifted.

Alongside progressives' concern about monopoly, work conditions, and privacy invasion, some republicans associate the sector with West Coast liberalism, anti-conservative censorship, and particular mischief-makers like Bezos, who owns the anti-Trump Washington Post. Congressional hearings revealed this new politics and abusive business practice behind big tech. For example, it highlighted how Facebook adopted a predatory attitude to rivals, through acquisition rather than competition. A senior staffer emails Zuckerberg in January 2012: 'Instagram is eating our lunch. We should've owned this space....' In a set of responses in 2012, Zuckerberg exposes his land-grab approach to contenders: '....if they grow to a large scale they could be very disruptive to us....I'm curious if we should consider going after one or two of them'; and '....what we're really buying is time....buying Instagram, Path, Foursquare etc. now will give us a year or more to integrate their dynamics before anyone can get close to their scale again'; and, tellingly: 'Yeah, I remember your internal post about how Instagram was our threat....One thing about start-ups though is you can often acquire them'.

Facebook bought Instagram in 2012 for $1 billion, allowing it to retain market dominance in photo-networking. Its purchase of WhatsApp a few years later afforded admission into mobile real-time messaging. When it can't buy what threatens, it imitates. Concentrating economic power by crushing competition in this manner stifles innovative start-ups, as evident in the fact that no big social networking company has been created since 2011.[67] To give it its new name, Meta's strategy to serious rivals seems to be: copy, close or capture. Yet, to impel challengers to a buy-out as preferable to a wipe-out, directly violates the Clayton Act.

A similarly aggressive pitch was evident in Amazon's treatment of some sellers who used their platform, whereby Amazon exploited its knowledge of their data, its placement power, and its leverage to temporarily undercut their prices with its own products, thereby threatening their very viability. As expressed by VP Doug Herrington in an email reference to a leading Diapers company using its platform: 'These guys are our No1 short-term competitor....We need to match pricing (sic) on these guys no matter what the cost'. Subsequently, by manipulating Diapers.com into an uncompetitive position, it pressured the parent firm Quidsi to concede to a hostile takeover. Thereafter, diaper prices were re-hiked, and Amazon's control of its wider marketplace remained hidden in plain sight. The company's power is in the context of a massive growth in e-commerce retail sales. In the US alone, the sector rose for just under $33 billion in 2001 to about $600 billion in 2019.[68]

The Congressional hearings also revealed how Google's pre-eminence in search, advertising, mapping, online video, and smartphones, leaves it as a potential insider trader, since it can be buyer, seller and broker. As explained by Srinivasan:[69] 'Google's exchange shares superior trading information and speed with the Google-owned intermediaries, Google steers buy-and-sell orders to its exchange and websites (Search & YouTube), and Google abuses its access to inside information' owned by third-party buyers and sellers to alert its own trading interests. At its simplest, it can prioritise content linked to its ads at the top of a user's search results, while holding means to delist firms crying foul. Moreover, its linkage of advertising and tracking data means that a user's search history, Gmail data, and complete web traffic can be composited into a unified database. This flies in the face of assurances it gave government in 2007, when it purchased DoubleClick, then the biggest publisher-side digital ad platform, that it wouldn't blend its data on its consumers with that of its new acquisition.

Acquisitions can come to comprise a high share of earnings. In 2021, Instagram made up $42 billion of Meta's revenues, almost two-fifths of the entirety, and over double the amount in 2019, which then represented a quarter.[70] The 2022 EU's Digital Markets Act seeks to curb 'the ever-increasing dominance of Big Tech companies'. Targeted at the European business of large platform and messaging services (with minimum market capitalisation of €75 billion, or annual turnover of €7.5 billion), it stipulates that they must function reliably with smaller messaging systems, so that users can exercise greater choice in interchanging texts, files, and video calls across big and small platforms, as well as selecting their browser and search engine. Moreover, blending personal data for targeted advertising will require clear 'consent to the gatekeeper'. For instance, these market titans will no longer be able to privilege their own products, nor use other corporations' data to compete with them on their platform.

Similarly, gatekeepers will have to ensure that default settings, which nudge a user into selecting options that benefit the platform, can be easily changed or re-calibrated to suit the user. Non-observance will bring a penalty of up to 10 percent of the company's global turnover, and 20 percent for repeated violation.[71] In granting consumers more choice and data control, this represents a significant move towards fairer competition and consumer protection in the European market, which constitutes about $267 billion of revenue, or about a fifth of the collective total for Apple, Alphabet, Amazon and Meta.[72]

Google's search domination is under pressure from US legal action by a set of state attorneys-general, with possible federal involvement from the Department of Justice. As explained by the *Economist*, implication for earnings is critical:[73]

> *That puts American search revenue of $70 billion, a quarter of Alphabet's total, at risk of antitrust action. If Alphabet reduced its commission on in-app payments from 30 percent to 11 percent – the share agreed in a deal between Google and Spotify on March 23rd (2022) – American app-store revenues would plummet from $11 billion to $4 billion. Together these actions could imperil perhaps $150 billion of Alphabet's revenue, or about 60 percent of its global total.*

If similar pressures were applied to Apple, its exposure could be about $35 billion, a tenth of its total earnings. If Amazon's Marketplace was no longer allowed to jumble its retail offerings with those of third parties, the company could forfeit up to $77 billion annually, about 16 percent of total revenue. Should the US Federal Trade Commission also decide to break up these conglomerates – separating Instagram and WhatsApp from Facebook, and Amazon's e-commerce from its cloud-computing services, and such like – the total revenue hit on Big Tech from such anti-trust moves could amount to $330 billion, about a quarter of overall revenues of Apple, Alphabet, Amazon, and Meta.[74]

Mission Creep

However, this combined legal onslaught remains unlikely. For some time now, legislators have threatened restriction, beyond reliance on pledges of better behaviour. Promises from the powerful are breached at the whim of the powerful. Market dominance has allowed Google to disregard any consumer reservation about privacy invasion caused by ditching anonymity. Consumers have been left with a 'take it or leave it' decision to use the main gateway to internet search, an offer not easy to refuse. Similarly, Zuckerberg was grilled about why his company had discarded its initial privacy commitment to never track 'customers' with cookies.

The explanation for all such 'mission creep' toward detailed profiling is simple – they can do so with impunity, and huge profitability. The more money they spin, the more they can spin the saying: 'we're too big to fail or to flout'. Even a decade ago, Facebook comprised 95 percent of US social media use. Despite this scope to dominate and domineer, tech giants are keen to talk in terms of their justified 'market power' rather than monopoly, and to intimate that their unfettered status is crucial to continued global ascendency of American values and economic clout.

A Congress report in 2020[75] following on from the hearings was damning in its conclusions. It found that big tech abuses its excessive power by 'charging exorbitant fees, imposing oppressive contract terms, and extracting valuable data' from users and business clients. They act like unaccountable and protectionist gatekeepers, commanding the digital marketplace while also competing in it, thereby operating somewhat like private regulators who can adjudicate in their own favour. This allows them to snoop on nascent rivals, and then with this market intelligence, buy or bury them. Also, in their practices of self-preferencing and predatory pricing, they consolidate their dominant position. This monopolistic behaviour invades people's online privacy; restrains innovation and entrepreneurship; reduces consumer choice; downgrades a free and diverse press; promotes misinformation; and in general, enfeebles democracy. Details supporting these findings are given throughout the substantial report. It notes:

> *After purchasing the Android operating system in 2005, Google used contractual restrictions and exclusivity provisions to extend Google's search monopoly from desktop to mobile. Documents show that Google required smartphone manufacturers to pre-install and give default status to Google's own apps, impeding competitors in search as well as in other app markets.* [76]

> *Amazon has expanded Alexa's ecosystem quickly through acquisitions of complementary and competing technologies, and by selling its Alexa-enabled smart speakers at deep discounts. The company's early leadership in this market is leading*

to the collection of highly sensitive consumer data, which Amazon can use to pro-mote its other business, including e-commerce and Prime Video.[77]

Facebook's approach towards rival social networking app Snapchat is another case study in how Facebook enters "destroy mode" when its market position is threatened. In 2013, as the company was growing rapidly, Snapchat co-founder Evan Spiegel turned down an offer from Mr. Zuckerberg to acquire the company for $3 billion. Thereafter, Instagram — owned by Facebook — introduced the Instagram Stories feature…which was "nearly identical to the central feed in Snapchat, which [was] also called Stories".[78]

Without a clear *contract* with us, these firms *extract* our data and use it to *attract* our attention with content that can both *distract* us, and *detract* from our well-being, all with the intention of making money from selling our digital lives back to us or to third parties. Essentially, they sell us. That use to be called slavery. And yet they clothe themselves in virtue. Google's motto use to be: 'Don't be evil'. Under its umbrella corporation, Alphabet, it's now: 'Do the right thing'. They're patently *not* doing right and don't even seem to sense the right thing to do.

Does this suggest other paradoxes in big tech?[79] For one thing, it's every-where and nowhere. As explained by Foroohar,[80] its 'salient feature is intangi-bility. These companies traffic not in widgets that we can see and touch, but in the abstractions of bits and bytes'. Even though it's extensive and pervasive, big tech works furtively, and some of its power derives from its hush and imper-ceptibility. Its leaders present themselves as omniscient about the contemporary world and prescient about its future. Though if they're not intently doing evil, they're ineffectual in redressing predatory abuse. They let their services be commandeered for malevolence in part because of inflated self-regard for their own benevolence.

Though claiming to foster public engagement so essential to democracy, they have discovered that extremist content generates the most engagement. Democracy is devalued when we pander rather than ponder, when thoughtful and civil exchange concedes ground to the impulsive and offensive. Their innovations spring from the cosmopolitan culture of Silicon Valley that exudes values of rationality and diversity. Except they've ended up contrib-uting to a narrow nationalist politics that thrives on bogus conspiracy stories. In 'democratising' news production, they've made it difficult to distinguish good critical reporting from the blog and opinion piece.

In their news distribution and monetisation, Google and Meta undercut high-quality journalism. The fact that they suck in such high-volume adver-tising revenue effectively defunds authoritative and investigative reporting in mainstream news media, including local press. Moreover, online platforms risk spreading unreliable and inaccurate information that prompt alarmist conspiracies and hate speech, whose incendiary content inspires visceral reaction in targeted groups. They thrive on capturing and holding our focus, and the controversial and bizarre are excellent attention-grabbers. Despite their denials, tech giants invest insufficient financial and human capital into policing their sites, and deleting harmful material. In early 2018, Facebook amended its News-Feed algorithm to advance content that delivered more audience engagement. Content became more crass and less cerebral.

In turn, this feeds into the difficulty of fostering a well-informed democracy. A 2022 study[81] in the US found that 91 percent of adults hold the spread of misinformation to be a problem, with 7 in 10 adults regarding it as a contributor to extreme political views and hate crimes, such as violence stirred about race, gender, or religion. Around half respondents said that misinformation decreased trust in government, while the same proportion acknowledged that it increased political engagement. Tusk, who has taken over Twitter in chaotic style, regards himself as a free speech absolutist. He sees the online realm as a digital town square that should ideally offer an open platform. It's strange, by the way, how autocratic managers like Tusk profess to be libertarian champions of the average guy, and to be in the social media business for the love of humanity.

In news transmission, online platforms benefit from unfair advantage. There are twenty-six letters in the alphabet, and there are twenty-six words vital for Alphabet Inc. and the other tech giants. They are buried in the 1996 US Communications Decency Act, Section 230, which states that: 'No provider or user of an interactive computer service shall be treated as the publisher or speaker of any information provided by another information content provider'. Essentially, it protects online platforms from legal responsibility for third-party content, allowing transmission of information and comment, or removal of certain content, without publisher liability.

Recently, the US Department of Justice has been reviewing this controversial Section.[82] It expresses concern that whereas platforms have little inducement to tackle illicit material, they are able to filter lawful content without being transparent or answerable. While keeping the internet an open yet safe space, and retaining the core intent of immunity for defamation, the Department identifies four aspects ripe for measured reform, suggesting immunity be withheld for: first, content that violates federal criminal law, particularly sexual abuse, terrorism and cyber-stalking; second, civil enforcement actions brought by federal government; third, claims where liability relates to federal antitrust actions, not to third-party speech; and finally, for arbitrary removal of content as 'objectionable' rather than for specific breaches such as 'unlawful activity' or 'promotion of terrorism'. Otherwise, platforms should foster open discourse, and explain any decision to censor.

Google and Facebook earn big money from advertisers because they mine vast sources of user data that permit very targeted marketing. Google extracts information about their customers from user-facing services such as search,

Chrome browser, and Gmail; from mobile tools, running its operating system, Android; from video-streaming via YouTube; and from tags they put on third-party apps and sites, that allow for analytics. Facebook and its twin services, Instagram and WhatsApp, generate comprehensive datasets from users and from 'pixel' technology attached to third-party sites. This networking allows for more data accumulation. The more data-rich the company, the better it can target and attract users, creating self-reinforcing advantage that further reduces competitive restraint.

It's been well-noted that people are deceived into thinking they're *con-sumers* enjoying 'free' services, whereas they're actually the *product*. This rather understates the problem – they're also *producers*. What they offer is not some abstract dataset. It is the life and relationships that they create, as well as the value of their attention and time. Basically, users are led up the garden path that ends in a 'walled garden'.[83] As Zuboff puts it,[84] we once thought that we got services like Google for free. Now we know that they've got us for free. We once thought that we searched Google. Now we know, it searches us. We once thought we could exploit social media to bond. Now we know social media binds our data to exploit us.

No Free Lunch

In this topsy-turvy reality, privacy policies are really snoopers' charters. Of course, we supposedly sign up freely to online services. But who can really take time and care to fathom convoluted privacy terms and conditions? Because of these firms' dominance, they can afford to provide fewer privacy protections since users have nowhere else to go. In a survey of UK users,[85] the consumer agency, *Which?*, discovered that most respondents were amazed and uneasy to learn how their data allowed for their detailed individual profiles to be sold to other parties, without their consent, to target them in ways that may not serve their best interest.

Most consumers imagined that data about them was broad, anonymised, and particular to distinct transactions. In fact, their 'digital persona' is constructed with remarkable specificity from multiple data sources. Given the opaque process, they're unable to verify the accuracy of this digital self, and mistakes happen.[86] In any case, when we trade our privacy for a digital service, we may think it's our individual choice. Although activated separately, billions of us make what is in effect a collective choice that cumulatively can impair foundational traits of democracy, such as citizen sovereignty and human agency.

An exemplary case came in revelation that around 87 million Facebook users unknowingly had their data shared with Cambridge Analytica (CA). Wylie – a central figure in this company's development – admits now himself that he foolishly fell for Facebook's maxim to 'move fast and break things'. In his remorse, he became a whistle-blower about CA's underhand operation. He recounts how

Steve Bannon, former editor of right-wing Breitbart News, seeing potential in covert 'information warfare' for transforming political culture, helped steer CA's practice of building profiles on individual voters that could be subject to behavioural micro-targeting and adjustment.

As Wylie tells it,[87] this is asymmetrical war, since recipients of political messaging know much less about the source and intent of the senders than the latter do about them, just as the algorithms know more about how *we* work than we do about *them*. He says Bannon wanted CA to go dark in exposing hidden and forbidden thoughts about race, not just from the white supremacist end of the alt-right, but also from professed progressives, wary of ever being shamed as racist. Bannon believed that many do-gooder 'limousine liberals' secretly harboured prejudice in the form of paternalism. They wanted blacks to be weak enough to appreciate their help, rather than strong enough to constrict their privilege. In his eyes, post-civil rights Democrats traded positive discrimination toward minorities for their electoral support, and suppressed the inequity of this bribe by curtailing debate on 'race reality', via imposition of political correctness. Revealing this dirty deal could serve both to inflame resentment among the more dispossessed whites, and discontent among those people of colour, who felt patronised and short-changed by this Faustian bargain.

This assumed insight helped people like Bannon, and companies like CA, identify stress points to be exploited. In their view, political correctness, with its attendant derision and censorship of the white working class by liberal elites, left victims of such scorn feeling persecuted. The anger so aroused could be vented in full vitriol online, which users mistakenly considered anonymous. The more the outraged were enticed online, the more they could be emboldened by their mutually-endorsed fury. If online trolling and taunting were used to misrepresent anti-racist comments as slurs on 'poor ordinary' guys' identity, that could cause some 'regular folk' to see such disparagement as personal attack. In defiant reaction, they might be expected to avow their views as realistic rather than racist. This playbook of how to goad opponents and garner supporters by such feedback loop is now well set.[88]

The UK Parliamentary Committee investigating disinformation said plainly that 'the Cambridge Analytica scandal was facilitated by Facebook's policies'.[89] The Committee recorded that Facebook knowingly and deliberately violated data privacy and anti-competition rules, and was reluctant to be accountable to regulators around the world. In its view, firms like Facebook should not be permitted to act like 'digital gangsters' above the law.[90] In respect of its own investigation, it considered 'Facebook's response generally to be disingenuous and another example of Facebook's bad faith'.

Unregulated growth of social media permitted covert digital influence campaigns, which themselves were in the context of 'the rapid rise of new populist, right-wing news sites... pushing conspiratorial, anti-establishment content outside the channels of traditional media'.[91] Summarising the example of data manipulation in the 2016 American election, it noted:[92]

> *Theresa Hong, a member of the Trump digital election campaign described 'Project Alamo', which involved staff working for the then presidential candidate Donald Trump, Cambridge Analytica staff and Facebook staff all working together with the Cambridge Analytica data sets, targeting specific states and specific voters. The project spent $85 million on Facebook adverts and Ms Hong said that "without Facebook we wouldn't have won".*

Cambridge Analytica worked with Trump's 2016 presidential campaign to segment voters into eight 'audiences' of graduated support and opposition, a stratification that then allowed targeted ads on Facebook to these sub-populations in sixteen key states that can turn on slender margins. Grouped under 'Deterrence' were some 3.5 million African-Americans, whose votes could be ideally 'suppressed'. Trump's digital operation, nicknamed Project Alamo, held a vast database, with nearly 200 million Americans' details, subject to dissection by models and algorithms. Almost six million variations of tailored messages were posted to the feeds of targeted electorate, with assistance from a Facebook employee.[93]

Yet, in the face of voter manipulation and disinformation, what sanctions were imposed on Cambridge Analytica? None of any consequence. It folded. The UK Parliamentary Committee observed that its transformation into Emerdata showed how easy it was for 'discredited companies to reinvent themselves and potentially use the same data and the same tactics to undermine governments, including in the UK'.[94]

Faceless

It should be said that some are sceptical about unverifiable claims of influence made by, and about, Cambridge Analytica. In an interesting book[95] that attempts to debunk such assertions as extravagant, Sumpter cautions about the hype. Insights gleaned from Facebook about personality type and political preference are based on probability, not certainty, it argues. They can mistake connections among our attitudes and attributes with the basis of our political choices – 'potentially confusing correlation with causation'.[96] Reliability of algorithms identifying personality traits from 'likes' and thereby accurately classifying people from their 'digital footprint' is over-stated, leading Sumpter to conclude that 'there is no evidence yet that Facebook can determine and target your political personality'.[97]

In a similar vein, we can't concede that Facebook can completely control what we think. Bloggers may come to live in an echo chamber if they only network with the like-minded, and algorithms may be able to 'filter bubble' us by showing us material reflective of our web searches and browsing history. However, Facebook 'friends' are not as segregated into distinct mind-sets as supposed. From his own studies and others that he references, Sumpter contends that we're given an exaggerated impression of Facebook's life-changing impact on our lives, which he thinks 'is very weak compared with the effect of our everyday interactions with people in real life'.[98]

Social media can give voice to the mass in a way mass media did not. As such, it can be a democratic tool for informing and mobilising progressive social action. But one person's free speech can be another's personal abuse, or malicious scandal. Over 185 million people in the US and Canada make daily use of Facebook. Most of its billions in earnings come from targeted advertising, based on user data. In reaping this 'data bullion', the company promises its wealth source – its users – that they can exercise consumer control of their information through privacy settings. In 2019, the US Federal Trade Commission (FTC) found the company violated this trust, and made great play about imposing a $5 billion fine 'almost 20 times greater than the largest privacy or data security penalty ever imposed worldwide'.[99] Certainly, it sounds a hefty sum. But around the same time, the then Facebook enjoyed a shares surge, boosting its value by $30 million, six times its fine. For a big beast, what appears punitive is no more than mild reprimand.

In practice, social media that engages billions gives great unprecedented power to one person. Meta dominates social media and Zuckerberg dominates Meta. Since he controls around 60 percent of its voting shares, single-handedly he can adjudicate whether its discourse is inflammatory or simply provocative. He is editor supremo. His business model hinges on variations of clickbait that lures attention, increases traffic, and thereby gets us sharing more of our private selves. As such, his platform's innate drive is to deliver information skewed toward the intriguing rather than the thoughtful. Distinction between hearsay and truth becomes shaded amid sensational comment.

Ultimately, his command over algorithms can shape News-Feeds content, which in turn can 'change our culture, influence elections and empower nationalist leaders', enabling spread of 'fringe political views and fake news'.[100] Case in point, Facebook altered its News-Feed format in countries like Bolivia, ruled by left-wing populist Morales, and Cambodia, which is under autocratic rule by Hun Sen. It reduced access to independent, nongovernment news sources, to favour popular content and that from friends and family, that was considered more compelling. Though perhaps unintended, the effect was to circulate more bias and misinformation.[101]

In a damning illustration, Facebook was used by the Myanmar military to spread hatred against the Muslim minority Rohingya, contributing to brutal ethnic cleansing that included murder and mass displacement. Massive and rapid uptake in Facebook-use in the country meant many were unable to distinguish fabrication and fact in what seemed authoritative sources. Simultaneously, there was the scourge of ethnic incitement. One user posted: 'we must fight them the way Hitler did the Jews, damn kalars' (a pejorative for the Rohingya); another said: 'these non-human kalar dogs … we need to destroy their race'; and another: 'pour fuel and set fire so that they can meet Allah faster'.[102] Under international pressure for its role, Facebook commissioned an assessment from Business for Social Responsibility, which confirmed the company's contribution to human rights abuses. In response, Facebook conceded some responsibility: 'The report concludes that, prior to this year, we weren't doing enough to help prevent our platform from being used to foment division and incite offline violence. We agree that we can and should do more'.[103]

Misuse of platforms to inflame conflict is widespread. A United Nations report, referring to its role in amplifying tension in South Sudan, is clear:[104] 'Social media has been used by partisans on all sides, including some senior government officials, to exaggerate incidents, spread falsehoods and veiled threats or post outright messages of incitement.' It can be argued that social media is the vehicle rather than the source of harmful vitriol, and corporations like Facebook can repeat its repentance, while inferring that technology is not yet up to editing content with fine distinction.

Although, as Burrington argues:[105] 'to simply point at the unintentional automated wreckage or demand piecemeal repairs to the monstrous machinery of platforms feels like giving in to the fatigue and sorrow of a vacuous world in which everyone is sorry and no one is responsible'. And that's before you get to their role in disinformation in democracies like the US. In many ways, Facebook had been a blessing for Obama, mobilising the young as part of 'get out the vote' campaigns, and targeting specific electoral strata with customised appeal. While Obama may have been the first to mine this particular electoral shaft, it was small change compared to the 2016 election bonanza.

Personalised news fed to Facebook users is selected on the basis of what's most likely to prod interaction and sharing. In effect, what should be diverse information for democratic engagement is filtered to create multiple insulated 'bubbles' and loops, which act as echo chambers. We end up receiving that which brings confirmation and comfort rather than challenge. This creates hyper-partisan zones, into which ultra-right Breitbart and Fox News gladly channeled a politics of resentment. Given deliberate blitz of this from ultra and alt right, Facebook became an unwitting or uncaring conduit for alarmist mixes of hoax, humbug, and hate. Russian agents deploying Facebook ads to disturb and disrupt only added to Facebook's 'trending' algorithms, insatiable for controversy.[106]

In the aftermath of Brexit, the related scandal of Cambridge Analytica's use of Facebook, and Trump's 2016 victory, with allegations of Russian chicanery, the company produced a paper[107] to explain its vigilance and concerted drive to mitigate misuse of its information ecosystem. It affirms that 'authentic dialogue' demands action against 'information operations', designed to deceive and manipulate. This means curbing 'false amplifiers' – that is coordinated effort by fake accounts to influence political discussion via disinformation, bias, and bogus news, which propagate intentional factual inaccuracy to mislead, harass, and arouse passions by elevating 'sensationalist voices over others'.

Coordinated fake online personae and other devices such as rapid and repeated posts and 'likes' are among those abusive instruments for advocating or demeaning specific causes, implanting distrust of political institutions, and spreading confusion. In being pushed toward this oversight, Zuckerberg is accepting that his company doesn't operate as a neutral platform, and that content needs checks, which are informed by values. But it shouldn't be in his gift to decide those values. As a former insider concludes,[108] what its monopoly power really needs are two things: the break-up of Meta into many companies, starting with an antitrust verdict to annul the takeovers of Instagram and WhatsApp; and government regulation for more accountability. This would include privacy legislation that protected people's digital information and provided plain disclosure to users; and clearer guidelines for speech standards on social media.

Lanier,[109] another insider in the social media world, suggests that, for our own well-being, we delete our social media accounts. In his experience, it would free us from 'random reinforcement', the system that deliberately feeds our addiction not with guaranteed reward, but with the vicarious thrill of the uncertain and even elusive reward. He argues that this virtual world is exiling us from the real one. Its hooks are making us more despondent if not despairing. Exploiting our craving for validation, it is deceiving us in false measures of popularity of 'likes' and false promises of success promoted by influencers. It is summoning armies of surly trollers and fictional bots, and corralling us in the company of our own tribe, if not our own isolated head. By these means, it belies its own name, because it makes us anti-social. And in this anti-social world, manipulation has a field-day. More generally, there is an invidious way in which social media can project that there are perfect people leading perfect lives out there – a flawless universe that is elusive to most people.

In September 2021, the *Wall St. Journal*[110] covered a leak that Meta's Instagram had internal research that showed it made body image issues worse for 1 in 3 teenage girls. Addictive use of Instagram by some teenagers, and the risk that unfavourable comparison with idealised body images that are regularly screened on Instagram, can be associated with anxiety and depression, are not concerns that Meta has chosen to reveal to the public.[111] When the Meta whistleblower responsible for the leak, Frances Haugen, testified to Congress in October 2021, her opening remarks summed up her central critique of the corporation as one that consistently chose growth and profit over safety, and could not be trusted to self-regulate:[112]

> *I'm here today because I believe Facebook's products harm children, stoke division, and weaken our democracy....The company's leadership knows how to make*

Facebook and Instagram safer, but won't make the necessary changes because they have put their astronomical profits before people.

The point repeatedly made is that Facebook makes most of its money – $114.9 billion[113] out of its annual revenue of $117.9 billion[114] in 2021 – from advertising. That demands an attentive audience, and that audience is lured by enthralling content. Despite all the bad publicity, there's no brake on its earnings. In 2022, Meta released its performance data for the previous year, including a net income of $39.4 billion, a 35 percent year-on-year change. Faced with the prospect of a toxic trademark, Facebook has re-branded itself as Meta, in reference to what it sees as the next frontier – the greater shift to virtual reality, and ultimately the virtual universe – the so-called Metaverse.

Of course, dark arts of propaganda have long lineage. But the scale and speed of social media accentuate the problem of people filtering and endorsing views that confirm their predisposition, 'no matter how distorted or inaccurate, while dismissing content with which they do not agree as 'fake news'. This has a polarising effect and reduces the common ground on which reasoned debate, based on objective facts, can take place'.[115] Democracy depends on accessibility to pluralist views, and citizens' ability to verify information. Social decency depends on basic civilities – what we used to call 'good manners'. When communication can be anonymous or hard to trace, these reserves are eroded, and as the UK Parliamentary Committee investigating disinformation put it: 'some malicious forces use Facebook to threaten and harass others, to publish revenge porn, to disseminate hate speech and propaganda of all kinds, and to influence elections and democratic processes — much of which Meta, and other social media companies, are either unable or unwilling to prevent'.[116] The challenge concerns how people stay ahead of the machine.

To improve data protection and privacy, the EU adopted the binding General Data Protection Regulation (GDPR), which has been enforceable since May 2018. It applies across the EU, no matter where the company is established or data processed. On the face of it, it's a big step forward. For example, Chapter 111 obliges the 'controller' (the data holder) to communicate with data subjects (us) in a clear, concise, and responsive manner. When data are collected, the data subject has to be informed about: the identity and contact details of the controller; purposes and legal basis of the data's processing; the recipients of the personal data; any transference to a third party; suitable safeguards; and period of data storage.

It accords the data subject the right to access personal data held, and to request correction to inaccuracies and/or erasure. It gives the right to withdraw consent at any time, to restrict its processing, and to know whether it is used for automated decision-making, including profiling. If the data didn't come from you, controllers should divulge its source. The company/organisation processing your data has to respond to your request at the latest within a month, and any refusal to comply with a request has to be explained, with scope for complaint. All of which sounds good – until you discover that 'inferred' data – traits deducible from analysis of user data profile, rather than from specific data a user has shared – remain unprotected.

Other aspects of big tech control need redress. In March 2019, Google were fined €1.49 billion for breaking EU antitrust rules.[117] The misconduct included prevention of Google's competitors from 'placing their search adverts in the most visible and clicked on parts of the websites' search results pages'. As competition policy Commissioner, Margrethe Vestager, explained: 'Google has cemented its dominance in online search adverts and shielded itself from competitive pressure by imposing anti-competitive contractual restrictions on third-party website'. Google's privileging its in-house services over those of rivals and its compelling of phone-makers to incorporate its apps as a condition of using its Android operating system, epitomise abusive monopoly power that must be tackled worldwide and not just in Europe.

Market challenge and innovation are inhibited as big tech look at start-ups as up-starts that need to be crushed. And there are other issues. We've become familiar with lockdown in the new COVID world. Many are less aware of lock-in. This is where consumers are caught in a 'path dependency', as when iPhone users are locked into the iOS ecosystem, since their data, files, software and other accessories are compatible with only one product ecosystem, thus making portability and switching difficult.

Taking Back Control

Some European countries have been in the forefront of action against big tech abuse. Germany has the 2018 Network Enforcement Act for compelling companies to remove hate speech from their sites within 24 hours, and fines them €20 million for non-compliance. As part of the Digital Services Act, the EU plans to legislate on ad transparency, misinformation, and illegal content on existing online intermediation platforms, and provision against anti-competitiveness is contained in the Digital Markets Act. If properly pursued, this new regulatory framework could get to grips with market dominance and content liability. Another issue is the need for a digital tax. For the period 2010–2019, one estimate of the combined tax avoidance of the Silicon Six (the big five plus Netflix) amounts to $100 billion (£75 billion).[118]

The European Commission has produced an outline strategy for its digital future.[119] While it wants to expand ultra-fast broadband, super-computing capacity, and AI, it wants this undertaken with a digitally competent citizenry, protective regulation against cyber threats and privacy safeguards for personal data. Also, in upholding democratic values, it emphasises the need to fight against disinformation online, in good part by promoting reliable content.[120] In mid-December 2020, the US Federal Trade Commission ordered nine top tech companies to submit information about what data they collect and how it is used, apparently as a prelude to greater regulation.

These shifts can go some way to reining in the digital giants, who, despite their many downsides, have yet to suffer any downfall. They've all got off very lightly. Until recently, long investigations have achieved little, and regulation has been exposed as not up to the job. An example comes in the letter to Westminster Parliament by Denham,[121] the UK Information Commissioner, whose office was charged with investigating use of personal information for political influence, taking in the practices of Cambridge Analytica and Facebook. She concludes that it involved 'aggregating datasets from several commercial sources to make predictions on personal data for political alliance purposes'. Expressing 'concern that data and derived data from Facebook had been shared' more widely, and that data security was poor, she accepts Facebook's estimate that the worldwide total number of people, whose personal data was used was 87 million, of whom at least 1 million were UK citizens. She acknowledges how detailed profiles and predicted personality traits allowed for scores that then identified 'clusters of similar individuals who could be potentially targeted with advertising relating to political campaigns'.

Despite all this evidence, penalties levied were pitifully inadequate – for instance, Facebook only paid £500,000. Yes, as part of follow-up action within the UK, it was announced in late 2020 that the Competition and Markets Authority (CMA) will acquire a dedicated Digital Markets Unit, authorised to compose and enforce a new code of practice on tech firms, setting limits of tolerable behaviour. With the UK now outside the EU, it will have to take back control from big tech in its own sovereign way. We'll see how that goes. The UK's Data Reform Bill, set out in 2022, shows every sign of wanting to deviate from EU regulation under GDPR. In the name of increasing competition, efficiency, and innovation, while 'simplifying' compliance criteria, there is a strong signal that it seeks a lighter touch in regulatory regime, and greater 'flexibility' in data protection compliance. The backdrop of this shift to a 'Brexit dividend' of comparative advantage in the sector lies in the government's ten key objectives for the UK's big tech sector, such as: world-class digital infrastructure; creating a tech-savvy country; liberating the transformational power of tech and AI, and other similar boosterish rhetoric. Its echo is also apparent in the recent National AI Strategy. All the hype about being an AI superpower, with an AI-enabled economy, permeates the document. Then, by way of a nod to global collaboration towards proper social responsibility of digital technologies, we have the following interpolation:[122]

> *By leading with our democratic values, the UK will work with partners around the world to make sure international agreements embed our ethical values, making clear that progress in AI must be achieved responsibly, according to democratic norms and the rule of law.*

Each country can't simultaneously seek to pocket a competitive edge on rivals by making themselves more investor-friendly through weak regulation, while feigning commitment to international robust standards of democratic oversight. Though Brexit was sold on the basis of 'taking back control', it appears to be open to dilution of citizen control over those most precious assets of personal privacy and human autonomy, in the interest of boosting business assets. There's a political cost to such political 'liberation'.

At the same time, the UK's Online Safety Bill, going through Parliament in 2022, seems to offer a different slant, in terms of imposing greater content accountability on social media platforms, messaging apps, and search engines, whose non-compliance risks fines of ten percent of global revenue or possible total blockage. This push for 'content moderation' is pitched as moving to a 'new digital age' that combines safety online with protection of free expression. It targets the grey area of 'legal but harmful' material that includes disinformation, harassment, encouragement of eating disorders, fraudulent adverts, racist abuse, and hate spreading. How far big tech will self-police their platforms in conformity with what may be highly contested legal definitions remains to be seen. Particularly since their judgement has to balance such criteria with upholding adults' right to access content considered by others to be offensive, protection of political pluralism and vibrant discourse, many specific cases may be subject to judicial dispute. When does venting rage spill over into hate? Some such trespassing is flagrant. Some is more insidious. Ultimately, the Office of Communications (Ofcom), as media regulator, will be responsible for enforcement – a tall order.[123]

Such legislation has to be contextualised within the increasing concern about the untamed power of big tech in a frugal regulatory environment. A recent report from the UK's Information Commissioner's Office auditing how political parties use private data[124] emphasises that parties must inform individuals when 'using their personal data to profile and then target them with marketing via social media platforms'. Given that digital advertising in UK elections comprised 42.8 percent of total advertising spend in 2017, compared to just 1.7 percent in 2014,[125] the importance of official auditing of political parties' behaviour in this regard is increasingly important.

Big tech is pitched between techno-fetishism – if we can create it, we should use it – and libertarianism – it offers open platforms for debate and individual choice. However, we can see how data despotism in the name of security can erode the most important condition for human security – mutual trust. We see also how the techie world preaches liberty and openness, but is actually itself very secretive and 'confidential'. The democratic connectedness it claims to favour cedes to its own connection to power. For instance, the five digital giants spent a combined €21 million on European lobbying in 2019, whereas Europe's seven largest car companies spent €7.9 million. The tech sector has links with European 'Think Tanks' such as Centre on Regulation in Europe and the European Policy Centre. Regrettably, these links and their impact on 'independent' reports from such institutes are far from transparent.[126]

While big tech likes influencers on site, it does its influencing out of sight. In the period 2005–2018, the big five spent $582 million on lobbying Congress.[127] Seven big tech companies spent nearly $70 million in 2021 on such activity in the face of growing bipartisan intent to regulate them more – with Democrats angry about the role of social media in the onslaught of Capitol Building, and Republicans peeved at the incursion of free speech indicative, in their view, by exiling Trump from Twitter. Meta paid out just over $20 million, while Amazon expended about $19 million. Total spend is three times that of a decade previous, making the sector one of the top pressure interests in Washington.[128]

And their money can be spread ecumenically. Leading Democrat, Ms Pelosi, a noted advocate of tech companies, accepted donation for her 2018 re-election campaign from staff and political action committees of Amazon, Alphabet and Facebook.[129] The American Enterprise Institute (AEI), which has critiqued antitrust arguments against the dominant platforms, reportedly gets finance from Facebook, Google and Amazon. No wonder the Congress report cited earlier is concerned about the sector's lobbying power: 'By funding academics and advocacy groups, the dominant platforms can expand their sphere of influence, further shaping how they are governed and regulated'.[130] Just as in the case of other dominant sectors – Big Pharma, Finance, Energy, and Military – such influential lobbies belie the assumed people's sovereignty of American democracy. It's not only the country's gun lobby – the NRA – that thwarts the democratic process. Money buys power and devalues votes, a version of voter suppression – constitutionally cemented by the 2009 'Citizens United' Supreme Court ruling that considers campaign financing a form of free speech.

Digitising Humans

But it's not only the US. Governments across the world have yet to bring social accountability to big tech and its wider eco-system of AI. I take seriously Sumpter's reservations about the decisive influence of social media on our opinions and behaviour. From my early sociology studies, I remember the inconclusive debate about whether the mainstream media reflected rather than swayed our views of social reality. Other parts of my sociology course, on causes of crime, would theorise how sensational and distorted media stories could whip up 'moral panics' about supposed rampant lawlessness. The relationship between media and manipulation has been subject to long-standing contest. In simple terms at this stage, if political propaganda and commercial advertising had only marginal impact on shaping political and consumer cultures, substantial investment in these efforts would hardly have persisted.

As things stand, I've little doubt that with accumulation of digital power, the more of our lives that become digitised, the more our lives risk being hacked. We can argue about degree and implication. Perhaps I'm over-pessimistic about the coming surveillance society. Certainly, I think it is stupid to live in a smart home or city, if the price is constant stalking. Though talk about superintelligence is wildly exaggerated, it's still worth thinking now about the moral dilemmas such prospect would pose, because the pace of change can out-stride the time needed for due deliberation of ethics. Russell[131] is right to con-template how ultra-intelligence in machines could be the biggest, and perhaps the last, event in human history.

Hannah Fry[132] asks how we can be human in the age of the machine. At a time when social trust is under strain, she thinks we over-trust the infallibility of automatic systems, which are no more perfect than humans. Like Bostrum and Russell, she wants the equation to be humans *plus* machines, with the latter supporting rather than instructing us. More than that, the very existence of dispassionate algorithms should cause us to reflect on what it is to be human. We hold qualities that can't be quantified. For her, data and statistics can be impressive, but they can't reveal what it feels to be human. Of course, mostly everyone would want what Fry suggests. In that sense, it's somewhat banal in its prescription. The hard question is whether we're smart enough to ensure against unintended consequences.

This point is well made by Seth. He emphasises that consciousness is not the same as intelligence. Simply by producing an ever-more intelligent machine does not mean that it will become conscious and sentient, even at less multi-faceted levels of cognition than humans. But just as we don't know exactly what it would take to make a machine with consciousness and agency, we don't know what it would not. Thus, we could do so accidentally, and without immediate awareness that we had done so – a hazardous prospect that remains under-appreciated:[133]

> Were we to wittingly or unwittingly introduce new forms of subjective experience into the world we would face an ethical and moral crisis on an unprecedented scale. Once something has conscious status it also has moral status….And for these puta-tive artificially sentient agents there is the additional challenge that we might have no idea what kinds of consciousness they might be experiencing.

In the age of the machine, humans have never been more crucial. That is not to self-congratulate, or to romanticise the purity of nature over the sterility of the synthetic machine. As Bostrum notes,[134] nature 'would never pass muster with an ethics review board – contravening the Helsinki Declaration and every norm of moral decency….It is important that we not gratuitously replicate such horrors *in silico*.'

Earlier, we talked about intersectionalism, as a means of appreciating inequities attached to human diversity. If intersection of human and machine transpired, it would form an amalgam of human mix and uniform computers, and this shared machine augmentation might help deal better with human difference. It infers that in being transhuman, we learn to be more human. All this, I think, is getting ahead of ourselves. We still await the totally self-directed machine for general tasks. True, Google's Deep Mind's latest AI whiz-kid, MuZero, has recently shown mastery over a series of games by discovering the rules by itself. Even if the programme doesn't quite *understand* what it's doing, such success seems to support Google's ambition to 'solve intelligence and use it to solve everything else'. However vaulting this ambition, AI remains dependent on humans to design the software, structure the problem, set the task, retrieve and prime the data, encode assumptions, compose the algorithm, and assess the outcome and its consequence.

Algorithms depend on metrics, and we remind ourselves of the saying attributed to Einstein, that not all things that are counted, count, and not all that counts can be counted. When we talked earlier about what makes us human, we stressed the connection between biology and culture. It's the interplay of both that makes us not only instinctive, but also adaptive. At best, it allows us to distinguish information from knowledge, knowledge from wisdom, and wisdom from wit. It means that we can think actually and abstractly. We can operate not only automatically and routinely, but also with ingenuity, imagination and dexterity; not only mechanistically, but also with creativity and sensitivity. Our ability to distinguish the sarcastic and ironic from the literal is vital in communication. Far from being automatons, we're a mix of conformists, contrarians and even of the seditious. And we're people of values as well as utility. In short, we're complicated.

If a machine was able to mimic or outdo human acumen, it could dent our self-regard for our unique wisdom, from which we draw our very name, *sapiens*. As indicated earlier, we don't yet grasp fully what constitutes human intelligence and consciousness. Yet we're happy to wax lyrical about whether we'll perish or prosper under artificial intelligence, and perhaps even under machine consciousness. At present, we're a long way off 'simulating humans' spontaneous understanding of new contexts'.[135]

Since we're not near superintelligence and singularity, why worry about overstated doomsday scenarios of machines that surpass us, and then render us surplus, when we consider the clear and present danger from existential threats referenced earlier? Paradoxically, in trying to decode what intelligence and consciousness mean 'artificially', we may gain better insight into what they mean 'naturally'. Under pressure to become more robotic, we might re-learn what it means to be human. Instead of digitising humans, we could do with humanising technology.

This is a point made by Faroohar,[136] when she notes that 'algorithms have the aura of science – they are based on math and quantitative information, after all. And yet, they are all too human, in that they reflect the particular ideas and biases of the people who programme them'. So should the process of mediating our relationship with the machine help us think through what makes for the good society?

Moves to transhumanism ought to be considered carefully. It isn't wise to think of humans liberated from imperfection. We don't want the automatic and predictable to suppress the eccentric and unconventional. We can't get a universal machine appendage that does justice to cultural diversity. The agenda raises many questions. Would transhumanism enhance universal values over cultural relativism? Does the expensive bio-engineering science linked to transhumanism afford privileged access to the wealthy, accentuating 'survival of the richest'? In considering such questions, it's understandable that we focus on what enfeebles or empowers us in this relationship.

Nonetheless, a human-centric approach is insufficient. Human solidarity has to be enriched through greater regard for all sentient creatures and the wider living environment. But this demands interdisciplinary scholarship. It's interesting that the technology of super-surveillance has made humans observable as their true selves in a way that social science struggles to do. However, there's a danger that we've leaned too far toward Science, Technology, Engineering and Mathematics – so-called STEM subjects – and away from Humanities and Social Sciences. We need the latter to get proper perspective on the former. Industrialisation brought with it specialisation. In a more 'post-industrial' world, is our higher education focused too much on one specialism?

It's useful to bear in mind Russell's maxim:[137] 'machines are beneficial to the extent that their actions can be expected to achieve our objectives'. Implementing this standard involves examination of our shortcomings and those of machines. In the case of the latter, Russell identifies three limitations: *access* – lacking sensory grasp of what's happening; *content* – failing to understand what the user means; and *context* – lacking a 'commonsense knowledge of how the world works'. These deficiencies remind us of the defective state of current AI.

As the designers, we remain the biggest complication in achieving compatibility with machines. He reminds us that we're diverse, often irrational, insecure, shifting, contradictory, and envy-driven. Different value-systems among humans make it implausible for machines to be programmed with a definitive one – other than for assisting humans to attain their preferences. This shortcoming produces a consequentialist ethic, in that it assumes that machines don't need, or are incapable of, deontological or virtue ethics – of having moral character in the wider sense. It's doubtful as to whether we can be trusted to always act in ways that are conducive to our own preferences, something that Russell regards as unreliable. Indeed, it's unclear that our cognitive architecture allows us to appreciate our preferences.

Even allowing for that human frailty, Russell still concludes that the goal of AI should be beneficial machines that 'will defer to humans: they will ask permission; they will act cautiously when guidance is unclear; and they will allow themselves to be switched off'.[138] Importantly, this requires oversight based on regulation, and he recognises that this runs counter to the culture of Silicon Valley that believes innovation derives from light touch government. More generally, I think we face the paradox of wanting super-duper intelligence to be beyond human intelligence, yet still tied to human values that derive from our lower intelligence. Also, it's strange that our search for higher intelligence is in a period of pronounced dumbing down, as perceived by some, in the rush for infotainment.

Wild Frontier

Presently, big tech is running for cover. In their haste to distance themselves from Trump, following the insurrection at Capitol Hill by his supporters on 6 January 2021, they were keen to disavow their responsibility for providing him a digital megaphone for so long, and for transmitting the venom over many years that predictably helped motivate that mayhem. Online vitriol hasn't created the dereliction of democracy, but it has amplified it. When it comes to changing course, the stakes are high, but trust in normal politics appears low. Meaningful regulation demands global unity. Yet big tech operates to splinter and atomise, and thereby minimise prospect of such unity.

Though many concur with the need to tame the Wild West frontier that is the internet, others see any such curbs as unwelcome state intrusion on web freedom. This libertarian view of the net, traceable back to the nineties, resonates further back to 1960s counterculture. It's encapsulated in John Perry Barlow's defiant manifesto for a new civilisation of the Mind, entitled *A Declaration of the Independence of Cyberspace*, released in Davos in 1996.[139] It cautioned governments against any colonial project to invade the precinct of our virtual selves by attempting to arrest our thoughts:

> *you have no sovereignty where we gather…the global social space we are building (is) naturally independent of the tyrannies you seek to impose on us…You do not know us, nor do you know our world. Cyberspace does not lie within your borders….We are forming our own Social Contract….We are creating a world that all may enter without privilege or prejudice accorded by race, economic power, military force, or station of birth. We are creating a world where anyone, anywhere may express his or her beliefs, no matter how singular, without fear of being coerced into silence or conformity. Your legal concepts of property, expression, identity, movement, and context do not apply to us….You are terrified of your own children, since they are natives in a world where you will always be immigrants.*

But this grand rhetoric doesn't measure up to the risk to freedom and democracy posed by big tech and its ally, AI. Of course, it can be said that the equivalent of trolling was there in the public shaming of the stocks in the town square, and today's coarse online discourse and disinformation were manifest previously in the tabloid distortions of the Murdoch media, and predecessors such as Hearst. Nevertheless, we need to recognise the sea-change that currently rocks the boat. A net can either bind or trap. The internet certainly does both. With its related gadgets and apps, it can attach us to family, friends and wider social circles. It can connect us to a world of information, and thereby democratise the power of information. It can also disconnect us, and ensnare us into addictive and exploitative behaviours. As people live evermore online, less is off-limit about their real autobiography. But the more we bare our soul in this way, the more soulless we make our world.

Facebook promised that it could connect people, build community and bring the world closer together, all achieved with great transparency. Instead, in hosting info-wars, waged often by invisible sources, who bombard 'persuadables' with unattributable disinformation, they have helped to divide and polarise. Far from making a mutual world, they've been a conduit for populist nationalism. Whatever their globalist pretensions, when faced with regulatory or tax demands overseas, they're not shy about playing the nationalist card as American corporations that deserve to be championed by the US government. Ultimately though, Facebook prefers government's light hand to its pat on the back. Amid the growing protectionism of economic nationalism, they're distinctly protectionist about their own corporate interest. While helping to propagate identity politics, they're in the business of identity theft. They piece together the micro-bits of our digital lives, before slicing us into segregated audiences, and then shredding us further, for personalised messaging calculated to trigger behavioural change.

Despite all this, they've remained contemptuous of rebuke and immune from proper penalty. Instead of being brought to heel because they've got too big for their boots, they're considered too big to not grow bigger. For all the great talk about containing them, the remarkable thing is how little they've been tamed. In late 2020, the European Commission approved Google's takeover of Fitbit, despite repeated concerns about how these corporate captures were threatening open and competitive markets. Once again, pledges have been accepted. Governing authorities have caved in. Google promises for a ten-year period not to integrate its Fitbit data with its other data sources and not to exploit health, fitness and location data from Fitbit for advertising to users in the European Economic Area. We'll see how that goes. Similar promises didn't prevent Facebook from reneging on its commitment not to integrate its data with WhatsApp and Instagram.

Unbridled digital giants are turning economies upside down. Rather than processing physical raw materials of the kind associated with traditional industry, the new top sectors of big tech and high finance are manipulating abstractions like personal and financial data. This economic de-materialisation is then converting us into commercial and electoral material, to be sold as a material or political product. It's a phantom economy within a dispirited politics.

And given its opaque practice, we're still speculating how we're most emotionally drawn online by negative content of fear, distrust and hatred, and how the more of this we encounter, the more we reproduce it in our own post as highly charged response. Though presented as alarming, the content is actually alarmist. What's genuinely alarming is how this doom merchandise of the net can contaminate civic deliberation, captivating us in a spiral of outrage. It triggers our concern in good part because it convinces us that many others are similarly concerned. It becomes contagious because we are super-spreaders of what's considered 'viral' in the online universe. It's the impact rather than import that is truly shocking. We're left with a false equivalence of information, whereby evidence-based fact and propagandist fabrication are accorded equal authority. None of us readily confesses to being hoodwinked by propaganda because by implication, you must admit susceptibility to deceit. But we're all vulnerable nevertheless, and as consumers of digital technology, we want to be neither hooked or hacked. As Davies comments, many of us come to use and rely upon the very tech companies we loath and distrust, appreciating their negative impact on us and on society as a whole, and yet we show towards them both enmity and dependency.[140] The question is how much we concede out of compulsion rather than volition.

Information overload invites a law of diminishing returns, what some consider an 'infodemic'. One way to cut through the noise is to dumb down news by way of 'infotainment' that plays to people's love of gossip and scandal. And most of us do enjoy tittle-tattle. It's part of the human paradox. We treasure privacy for ourselves, while wanting to be privy to other people's secrets. Consequently, platforms are designed to immerse us in that which enthrals. And the lurid and ludicrous fascinate more than the cerebral. As a result, we get content that is bizarre and far-fetched, yet its very absurdity beguiles. Shock terrorist videos and over-the-top conspiracies, propagated by zealots, incite fear and indignation. Partisan political ads infuriate and embitter. Postings defame and inflame, and some drive us insane. Right wing conspiracist, Alex Jones, was fined nearly $1billion in 2022 for spreading the patent falsehood that the Sandy Hook school slaughter was a contrivance, deploying actors who posed as grieving parents, all to support the US anti-gun lobby. But it's unlikely that he will ever pay out such a sum, using bankruptcy or some other device, while re-inventing his 'info-wars' platform to propagate his vile view of the world. We need better deterrence.

As indicated in chapter two, this isn't the age of anti-politics as much as hyper-politics. The strident winner-takes-all politics of our time is mirrored by the winner-takes-all economics of big tech. It's hardly coincidental that Facebook's motto of 'move fast and break things' echoes Steve Bannon's idea that radical change requires you to break society before remoulding it for its betterment.

In a world where everything is seemingly speeding up, we have to ask – is speed always good? Not in many cases. Take fast food – though not literally.

Take high-frequency algorithm trading in financial markets that moves money swiftly around the world as in one big casino. Generally, speed can mean cutting corners, which in the context of information, can be a short step from being economical with the truth. Is breaking things a good idea? Not if it's about 'breaking' treasured things such as trust, democracy, or the environment.

In the eco-system of the alt-right, chan4, Breibart, and Infowars, this strategy of using big tech to spread conflict and confusion has been enthusiastically adopted. Propaganda involves deliberate manipulation of a target audience by using misleading information to render its belief and behaviour amenable to the persuader's objectives.[141] Saturating social and mainstream media with a glut of information and ideas makes sifting and verification difficult. That's the purpose - to convince people that, in the fog of culture wars, reality is impenetrable. Only the strong cult leader can be trusted to make sense of a bewildering world. Invest trust in him. Ease your anxiety by becoming a devotee, liberated from the burden of navigating and interpreting a complex world. Remnick explains the ploy:[142]

> *Steve Bannon, once Trump's chief ideologist, put the matter well earlier this year when he told Michael Lewis, 'We got elected on Drain the Swamp, Lock Her Up, Build a Wall,' he said. 'This was pure anger. Anger and fear is what gets people to the polls.' Bannon added, 'The Democrats don't matter. The real opposition is the media. And the way to deal with them is to flood the zone with shit'.*

Muddying the waters no longer does it. You've got to 'flood the zone with shit'. That's how you drown out deliberative democracy. Of course, it can be said that it was always thus. The idea of 'fake news' is not new. Discrediting critical news media as 'enemies of the people', as Trump did, is not new. The notion of a public enemy (*hostis publicus*) goes back at least to when emperor Nero was cast as such by the Roman Senate in AD68. Its pedigree is unmistakably malign. Robespierre in his Reign of Terror spoke of those who opposed the French Revolution as enemies of the people who deserved only death, and some 17,000 were guillotined. Lenin referenced the term about critics of the Bolshevik Revolution, and Stalin famously used it amidst his Great Terror in the late1930s. Mao Zedong resurrected it in 1957. If you can tell somebody by the company they keep, clearly figures like Trump fail the test. So, while it would be comforting to think that big tech abuse is peculiar to totalitarian states like China, unfortunately, it's rampant in places that pride themselves as citadels of democracy.

In particular, this shows the importance of perception. As humans, we react on the basis of reason. But we're driven also by what we believe to be true. The question of what constitutes objective truth and reality is central to how we navigate the social world and tell ourselves stories that give our lives meaning. And it's to that difficult terrain that we turn in the second volume. Meantime, it's time to take stock of this contemporary period in all that's been said so far, and ask: is this a particularly mean time that holds poor prospect of improvement?

Notes

1 Douglas, I. (2020) *Is Technology Making Us Sick?* London: Thames & Hudson Ltd.
2 High-level Expert Group on Artificial Intelligence (April 2019) *Ethics Guidelines for Trustworthy A1.* Brussels: European Commission.
3 Kurzweil, R. (2005) *The Singularity is Near.* New York: Viking.
4 Singh, S. (20 November 2017) Transhumanism And The Future Of Humanity: 7 Ways The World Will Change By 2030. *Forbes Magazine.* www.forbes.com/sites/sarwantsingh/2017/11/20/transhumanism-and-the-future-of-humanity-seven-ways-the-world-will-change-by-2030. Accessed on: 6 January 2021.
5 Bostrum, N. (2014) *Superintelligence: Paths, Dangers, Strategies.* Oxford: Oxford University Press.
6 *Ibid.* 77.
7 *Ibid.* 118.
8 *Ibid.* 312.
9 DeepMind (30 Nov 2020) *AlphaFold: a Solution to a 50-year-old Grand Challenge in Biology.* Blog Post Research.
10 The Guardian View (11 December 2020) DeepMind's AI Biology Breakthrough Raises Issues About Who Pays for Science. *The Guardian Weekly.*
11 Draper, R (February 2018) They Are Watching You—and Everything Else on the Planet. *National Geographic.* www.nationalgeographic.com/magazine/2018/02/surveillance-watching-you.
12 See the document produced in February 2018: *The Malicious Use of Artificial Intelligence: Forecasting, Prevention, and Mitigation.* Future of Humanity Institute; University of Oxford; Centre for the Study of Existential Risk; Centre for a New American Security; Electronic Frontier Foundation; and Open AI.
13 Su, J. (16 May 2019) Why Amazon Alexa Is Always Listening To Your Conversations: Analysis. *Forbes.* www.forbes.com/sites/jeanbaptiste/2019/05/16/why-amazon-alexa-is-always-listening-to-your-conversations-analysis.
14 Russell, S. (2019) *Human Compatible: Artificial Intelligence and the Problem of Control.* London: Penguin Books.
15 The Pegasus Project (23 July 2021) Revealed: Data Leak Uncovers Global Abuse of Cyber-Surveillance Weapon. *The Guardian Weekly.*
16 A point made by officials of the US Federal Trade Commission (FTC) in December 2020, while announcing privacy probes into big tech.
17 Federal Communications Commission (FCC) (Updated:Tuesday, October 20, 2020) *Communications Assistance for Law Enforcement Act.* Washington DC: FCC.
18 Figliola, P.M. (updated: 8 June 2007) *Digital Surveillance: The Communications Assistance for Law Enforcement Act.* Washington DC: Congressional Research Service.
19 The Editorial Board (7 February, 2020) The Government Uses 'Near Perfect Surveillance' Data on Americans. *The New York Times.*

20 Greenberg, A. (13 October 2014) These Are the Emails Snowden Sent to First Introduce His Epic NSA Leaks. *Wired*. www.wired.com/2014/10/snowdens-first-emails-to-poitras/ Accessed on: 26/11/2020.

21 Polyakova, A. and Meserole, C. (2019) *Exporting Digital Authoritarianism: The Russian and Chinese Models*. policy brief. Washington, DC: Brookings. www.brookings.edu/wp-content/uploads/2019/08/FP_20190827_digital_authoritarianism_polyakova_meserole. pdf

22 Economy, E. (2018)*The Third Revolution: Xi Jinping and the New Chinese State*. New York: Oxford University Press

23 Bischoff, P. (22 July 2020) Surveillance camera statistics: which cities have the most CCTV cameras? *Comparitech*. www.comparitech.com/vpn-privacy/the-worlds-most-surveilled-cities/

24 *Ibid*.

25 Amnesty International. *Up to One Million Detained in China's Mass "Re-education" Drive*. www.amnesty.org/en/latest/news/2018/09/china-up-to-one-million-detai ned/ Accessed on: 26/11/2020.

26 Zenz, A. (2022). The Xinjiang Police Files: Re-Education Camp Security and Political Paranoia in the Xinjiang Uyghur Autonomous Region. *The Journal of the European Association for Chinese Studies*, *3*, 1–56.

27 See: Han, R. (2018) *Contesting Cyberspace in China: Online Expression and Authoritarian Resilience*. New York: Columbia University Press; and Roberts, M. (2018) *Censored: Distraction and Diversion Inside China's Great Firewall*. Princeton, NJ: Princeton University Press.

28 Human Rights Watch (February 2018) *China: Big Data Fuels Crackdown in Minority Region*. www.hrw.org/news/2018/02/26/china-big-data-fuels-crackdown-minor ity-region. See also: Buckley, C. and Mozur, P. (22 May, 2019) How China Uses High-Tech Surveillance to Subdue Minorities. *The New York Times*.

29 Human Rights Watch (February 2018) *op. cit.*

30 Mozur, P. and Clark, D. (22 November, 2020) China's Surveillance State Sucks Up Data. U.S. Tech Is Key to Sorting It. *The New York Times*.

31 Lin, L & Chin, J. (26 November, 2019) Close
    Liza Lin
    • Biography
    • @lizalinwsj
    • liza.lin@wsj.com
    U.S. Tech Companies Prop Up China's Vast Surveillance Network. *TheWall Street Journal*. See also: Manjoo, F. (9 October, 2019) Dealing With China Isn't Worth the Moral Cost. *The New York Times*.

32 Mozur, P. and Wong, E. (8 October, 2019)By Taking Aim at Chinese Tech Firms, Trump Signals a Strategy Shift. *The New York Times*.

33 Das, S., Harper, T., and Griffiths, S. (15 March 2020) Taxpayer's Money Helps Beijing Identify Masked Protesters. *The Sunday Times*.

34 BBC News (I November 2019)*Russia internet: Law introducing new controls comes into force*.

35 Polyakova, A. and Meserole, C. (2019) *op.cit.*

36 Marciano, A. (2019) Reframing Biometric Surveillance: From a Means of Inspection to a Form of Control. *Ethics and Information Technology*. 21. 127–136.

37 Adapted from: Warzel, C. (21 January, 2020) We Need a Law to Save Us From Dystopia. *The New York Times.*

38 Information Commission's Office (ICO) (23 May 2022) *ICO Fines Facial Recognition Database Company Clearview AI Inc More Than £7.5 Million And Orders UK Data To Be Deleted.* London: ICO.

39 Warzel, C. (18 February, 2020) All This Dystopia, and For What? *The New York Times.*

40 Fry, H. (2018) *Hello World: Being Human in the Age of Algorithms.* New York: W.W. Norton.

41 Schellenberg, S. (April 2020) How biased algorithms perpetuate inequality. *New Statesman.*

42 Coeckelbergh, M. (2020) *AI Ethics.* Cambridge MA: MIT Press.

43 See publications by UNI Global Union. Nyon: Switzerland.

44 Jobin, A., Ienca, M. & Vayena, E. (2019) The Global Landscape of AI Ethics Guidelines. *Nat Mach Intell* 1, 389–399.

45 Ali Khan, A. et al (September 2021) *Ethics of AI: A Systematic Literature Review of Principles and Challenges.* 1. www.researchgate.net/publication/Ethics_of_AI_A_Systematic_Literature_Review_of_Principles_and_Challenges. Accessed on: 25 May 2022.

46 European Commission (2018) *Communication of 25 April 2018 and 7 December 2018 (COM(2018)237 and COM(2018)795).* Brussels: European Commission.

47 Independent High-level Expert Group on Artificial Intelligence (June 2019) *Policy and Investment Recommendations for Trustworthy AI.* Brussels: European Commission.

48 Independent High-Level Expert Group On Artificial Intelligence Set Up By The European Commission (17 July 2020) *Shaping Europe's Digital Future: Assessment List for Trustworthy Artificial Intelligence (ALTAI).* Brussels: European Commission.

49 See Boddington, P. (2017) *Towards a Code of Ethics for Artificial Intelligence.* Cham; Swizerland: Springer; and Turner, J. (2019) *Robot Rules: Regulating Artificial Intelligence...*Cham; Swizerland: Springer.

50 Bradford, A. (2012) The Brussels Effect. *Northwestern University Law Review.* 107 (533).

51 Leaders: Medicine (5 May 2022)Wearable Technology Promises To Revolutionise Health Care. *The Economist.*

52 Davison, N. (undated) *A Legal Perspective: Autonomous Weapon Systems Under International Humanitarian Law.* A Paper. International Committee Of The Red Cross. file:///C:/Users/Michael/Downloads/autonomous_weapon_systems_under_international_humanitarian_law.pdf. Accessed on: 26 May 2022. 5.

53 *Ibid.* 7.

54 Trager, R.F. and Luca, L.M. (11 May 2022) Killer Robots Are Here And We Need to Regulate Them. *Foreign Policy* (FP). https://foreignpolicy.com/2022/05/11/killer-robots-lethal-autonomous-weapons-systems-ukraine-libya-regulation. Accessed on: 26 May 2022; and Stop Killer Robots (22 March 2022) *Autonomous Weapon Systems Used In Ukraine.* www.stopkillerrobots.org/news/autonomous-weapon-systems-used-in-ukraine. Accessed on: 26 May 2022.

55 *Autonomous Weapons*: an Open Letter from AI & Robotics Researchers (28 July 2015).

56 Halstead, J. et al (2017) *Existential Risk: Diplomacy and Governance.* Global Priorities Project. Future of Humanity Institute, University of Oxford and Ministry for Foreign Affairs of Finland.

57 *Statista.* www.statista.com/statistics/263264/top-companies-in-the-world-by-mar
ket-capitalization/ and https://fxssi.com/top-10-most-valuable-companies-in-the-
world for September 2020.

58 Johnston, M. (fact-checked by Eichler, R.) (updated: 4 March 2022) Biggest
Companies in the World by Market Cap. *Investopedia.* www.investopedia.com/bigg
est-companies-in-the-world-by-market-cap. Accessed on: 22 May 2022.

59 Johnston, M. (Sep 9, 2020) 10 Most Profitable Companies in the World. *Investopedia.*
www.investopedia.com/the-world-s-10-most-profitable-companies-4694526

60 Dolan, K. (5 April 2022) America's Ten Richest Billionaires 2022. *Forbes.* www.
forbes.com/sites/kerryadolan/2022/04/05/americas-10-richest-billionaires-2022.
Accessed on: 22 May 2022.

61 Bloomberg. *Billionaires Index of the World's Richest People* (20 May 2022).

62 Dolan, K. (5 April 2022) *op. cit.*

63 fxssi (November 2020) Top 10 World's Most Valuable Technology Companies in
2020. *fxssi.* https://fxssi.com/most-valuable-tech-companies.

64 The Economist (3 November 2022) What Big Tech and Buy-out Barons Have in
Common with GE. *The Economist*

65 Briefing. (22 January 2022) What America's Largest Technology Firms Are
Investing In. *The Economist.*

66 House Committee on the Judiciary. Online Platforms and Market Power. July
2020. https://judiciary.house.gov/online-platforms-and-market-power/

67 Hughes, C. (9 May, 2019) It's Time to Break Up Facebook. The Privacy Project.
The New York Times.

68 Majority Staff Report and Recommendations (2020) *Investigation of Competition in
Digital Markets.* Washington: US House of Representatives.

69 Srinivasan, D. (2020, Forthcoming) Why Google Dominates Advertising Markets.
23 *Stanford Technology Law Review.* Available at SSRN: https://ssrn.com/abstract=
3500919.

70 Economist Business (30 April 2022) Lifting the Silicon Veil: The Secrets of Big
Tech. *The Economist.*

71 EU Parliament Press Statement (24 March 2022) *Deal on Digital Markets Act: EU
rules to Ensure Fair Competition and More Choice For Users.* www.europarl.europa.
eu/news/en/press-room/deal-on-digital-markets-act-ensuring-fair-competition-
and-more-choice-for-users. Accessed on: 23 May 2022.

72 Economist Business (30 April 2022) *op. cit.*

73 *Ibid.*

74 *Ibid.*

75 Majority Staff Report and Recommendations (2020) *op.cit.* 84.

76 *Ibid.* 14.

77 *Ibid.* 16.

78 *Ibid.* 164.

79 Vaidhyanathan, S. (2018) *Antisocial Media: How Facebook Disconnects Us and
Undermines Democracy.* Oxford: Oxford University Press.

80 Foroohar, R. (2019) *Don't Be Evil: How Big Tech Betrayed Its Founding Principles - And
All of Us.* New York: Currency. 122.

81 Pearson Institute and The Associated Press-NORC Center for Public Affairs
Research (October 2022) Many Believe Misinformation Is Increasing Extreme
Political Views And Behaviors. Chicago: The University of Chicago.

82 U.S. Department of Justice. *Review of Section 230 of the Communications Decency Act of 1996.* Washington DC: DoJ.DE

83 Competition and Markets Authority (July 2020) *Online Platforms and Digital Advertising Market Study: Final Report:* London: CMA. This follows the Furman Review (2019), *Unlocking Digital Competition.* Stigler Center: Committee on Digital Platforms Final Report.

84 Zuboff, S. (24 January 2020) You Are Now Remotely Controlled. *The New York Times.*

85 Which? (June 2018) *Control, Alt, or Delete? The Future of Consumer Data.* London: Which?

86 Deloitte (2017), *Predictably Inaccurate: The Prevalence and Perils of Bad Big Data,* available at: www2. deloitte.com/insights/us/en/deloitte-review/issue-21/analytics-bad-data-quality.html

87 Wylie, C. (2020) *Mindf*ck.* London: Profile Books.

88 *Ibid.*

89 House of Commons Digital, Culture, Media and Sport Committee (18 February 2019) *Disinformation and 'fake news': Final Report.* London: House of Commons. 26.

90 *Ibid.* 42

91 *Ibid.* 63.

92 *Ibid.* 40.

93 Channel 4 News Investigations Team (28 September 2020) *Revealed: Trump Campaign Strategy to Deter Millions of Black Americans from Voting in 2016.* Investigations Team: Job Rabkin, Guy Basnett, Ed Howker, Janet Eastham and Heidi Pett. News Production Team: Sola Renner, Michael French, Josh Ho, Matthew Cundall, Tim Bentham, Tony Fryer, Dani Isdale and Anna-Lisa Fuglesang.

94 *Ibid.* 83–84.

95 Sumpter, D. (2018) *Outnumbered: From Facebook and Google to Fake News and Filter-Bubbles- The Algorithms That Control Our Lives.* London: Bloomsbury.

96 *Ibid.* 53.

97 *Ibid.* 55.

98 *Ibid.* 150.

99 Federal Trade Commission (24 July 2019) *FTC Imposes $5 billion Penalty and Sweeping New Privacy Restrictions on Facebook.* Washington DC: FTC.

100 Hughes, C. (9 May, 2019) It's Time to Break Up Facebook. The Privacy Project. *The New York Times.*

101 Frenkel, S., Casey, N., and Mozur, P. (14 January 2018) In Some Countries, Facebook's Fiddling Has Magnified Fake News. *The New York Times.*

102 Stecklow, S. (15 August 2018) *Why Facebook is losing the war on hate speech in Myanmar.* Reuters Investigates.

103 Warofka, A. Product Policy Manager. (5 November 2018) *An Independent Assessment of the Human Rights Impact of Facebook in Myanmar.* Facebook.

104 United Nations (2015)*Interim Report of the Panel of Experts on South Sudan Established pursuant to Security Council Resolution 2206...*New York: UN.

105 Burrington, I. (20 December 2017) Could Facebook Be Tried for Human-Rights Abuses? *The Atlantic.*

106 Madrigal, A. (12 October 2017) What Facebook Did to American Democracy and Why It was so Hard to See it Coming. *The Atlantic.*

107 Weedon, J., Nuland, W., and Stamos, A. (27 April 2017) *Information Operations and Facebook.* Facebook Paper. Version 1.0. Facebook Inc.

108 Hughes, C. (9 May, 2019) *op. cit.*

109 Lanier, J. (2019) *Ten Arguments for Deleting Your Social Media Accounts Right Now.* London: Bodley Head.

110 Wells, G., Horwitz, J., and Seetharaman, D. (14 September 2021) Facebook Knows Instagram is Toxic for Teen Girls, Company Documents Show. *The Wall St., Journal.*

111 Zakrzewski, C. and Lerman, R. (29 September 2021) Facebook Tries to Minimize its Own Research Ahead of Hearings on Children's Safety. *Washington Post.* www.washingtonpost.com/technology/2021/09/29/facebook-childrens-safety-hearings. Accessed on: 1 October 2021.

112 Milmo, D. (15 October 2021) The Woman Who Stood Up To Facebook. *The Guardian Weekly.*

113 Statista (2022) *Facebook's Advertising Revenue Worldwide.* www.statista.com/statistics/271258/facebooks-advertising-revenue-worldwide. Accessed on: 22 May 2022.

114 BusinessofApps (2022) Facebook Revenue and Usage Statistics 2022. www.businessofapps.com/data/facebook-statistics. Accessed on: 22 May 2022.

115 House of Commons Digital, Culture, Media and Sport Committee (18 February 2019) *Op. Cit.* 5.

116 *Ibid.* 5.

117 European Commission Press Release (20 March 2019) *Antitrust: Commission Fines Google €1.49 billion for Abusive Practices in Online Advertising.* Brussels: EC.

118 Fair Tax Mark (December 2019) *The Silicon Six and Their $100 bn Global Tax Gap.* Manchester: Fair Tax Mark.

119 European Commission (2020) *A Europe Fit for the Digital Age: Empowering People with a New Generation of Technologies.* Brussels: EC.; and European Commission (February 2020) *Shaping Europe's Digital Future.* Brussels: EC.

120 European Commission (February 2020) *Shaping Europe's Digital Future.* Brussels: EC.

121 Denham letter: Information Commissioner's Office (IFC). 2 October 2020. *RE: ICO Investigation into Use of Personal Information and Political Influence.* IFC.

122 Department of Digital, Culture, Media and Sport (September 2021) *National AI Strategy.* Command Paper 525. 11. https://assets.publishing.service.gov.uk/government/uploads/system/uploads/attachment_data/file/1020402/National_AI_Strategy_-_PDF_version.pdf. Accessed on: 26 May 2022.

123 Department For Digital, Culture, media and Sport (19 April 2022) *Online Safety Bill: Factsheet.* UK Gov.

124 Information Commissioner's Office (November 2020) *Audits of data protection compliance by UK political parties. Summary report.* London: ICO. 7.

125 See: www.electoralcommission.org.uk/who-we-are-and-what-we-do/changing-electoral-law/transparent-digital-campaigning/report-digital-campaigning-increasing-transparency-voters.

126 Corporate Europe Observatory (23 September 2020) *Big Tech Lobbying.* CEO.

127 vpnMentor (2019) *The Big Tech Lobby.* see www.vpnmentor.com/blog/big-tech-lobbying-report/

128 Zakrzewski, C. (21 January 2022) Tech Companies Spent Almost $70 million Lobbying Washington In 2021 As Congress Sought To Rein In Their Power. *The Washington Post.*

129 Kang, C. and Vogel, K. (5 June 2019) Tech Giants Amass a Lobbying Army for an Epic Washington Battle. *The New York Times.*

130 Majority Staff Report and Recommendations (2020) *op. cit.* 76.

131 Russell, S. (2019) *Human Compatible: Artificial Intelligence and the Problem of Control.* London: Penguin Books.

132 Fry, H. (2018) *op. cit.*

133 Seth, A. (2021) *Being You: A New Science of Consciousness.* London: Faber. 263.

134 Bostrum, N. (2014) *op.cit.* 230.

135 Sumpter, D. (2018) *Outnumbered: From Facebook and Google to Fake News and Filter-Bubbles - the Algorithms that Control Our Lives.* London: Bloomsbury. 224.

136 Foroohar, R. (2019) *op. cit.* 57.

137 Russell, S. (2019) *op. cit.* 11.

138 *Ibid.* 247.

139 Barlow, J.P. (February 1996) *A Declaration of the Independence of Cyberspace.* Davos, Switzerland.

140 Davies, W. (20–26 May 2022) Your Own Digital Hell. *New Statesman.*

141 See: Benkler, Y., Faris, R., and Roberts, H. (2018), *Network Propaganda Manipulation, Disinformation, and Radicalization in American Politics.* Oxford: Oxford University Press; and Asmolov, G. (2018). The Disconnective Power of Disinformation Campaigns. *Journal of International Affairs,* Special Issue 71(1.5): 69–76.

142 Remnick, D. (30 July 2018) Inside An Off-the-Record Meeting. *The New Yorker.*

EPILOGUE

The Savvy of Paradox

If you've managed to get to the end of this book – rather than hopped through it to the end – you'll be struck by the perhaps tiring frequency of reference to *paradox*. Well it is, after all, the name of the book. I chose the title because I consider the paradoxical nature of ourselves and our world to be an important aspect to keep in mind, if we are to find a way together to tackle the pressing risks we face together. As you will have discovered, I've used the term to cover self-contradiction; inconsistency; catch-22; juxtaposition; apparent illogicality that nevertheless contains truth; and also the way our effort in one direction can inadvertently lead us to the opposite, as part of the general law of unintended consequence.

Paradox concerns not just the world out there. I am also full of contradiction. Indeed, I'd be surprised if I've not shown evidence of this discrepancy in the book itself. Like many, I'm prone to cognitive dissonance – juggling two or more opposing positions at the same time. As humans, we don't like to admit to contradiction, because that could be taken as a polite word for hypocrisy. The truth is that we all contain humbug – not that mere confession to it absolves its worst manifestation.

In a looser meaning, I see the issue of paradox in the compromised role of reason in many social circumstances marked by irrationality, and the consequent counter-intuitive way we sometimes have to approach conundrums and enigmas. We may want the world to have regularity and certainty. Instead, we often encounter incongruity, anomaly, and absurdity. The more we become aware of life's riddle and perplexity, the more we either retreat to the ironic and sardonic, or we embrace ambiguity and ambivalence. I think myself that we must forsake certitude in favour of greater humility about how little we know for sure. The benefit of doubt should be our new certainty. In upholding this, I appreciate that it holds its own paradox – just as, for example, the decree that you should not be dogmatic is itself dogmatic.

Moreover, some will say that such reservation only leads to evasion or equivocation, which can produce impasse. The world has pressing problems that cry out for urgent and definite solution. Exigency isn't patient for examination and evidence. If our response is that things are complex, and that genuine democracy demands deliberation and extensive participation, then we're in a quandary. In a fast-moving world, indecision can exacerbate the problem. By time we make up our collective mind, the particular boat may have sailed or sunk. Later, I want to address how we might make haste more slowly.

A persistent theme of this book has concerned the way that humans can be at odds with what they call *humanity*, at the very time we're supposed to be living in 'the human age' – referred to as the Anthropocene. Though we're supposed to hold the Earth under our domination, those earthly problems of our own making – climate emergency, nuclear threat, massive inequalities, abuse of high tech, and the like – are dominating us. In the worst scenarios presented here, our drive for hyper-modernity could drive us back to the Dark Ages. Though our presence on Earth has been short, our footprint on the planet has been huge. The basic lesson is that while we depend on Nature, Nature can't depend on us. That must change. We navigate life as storytellers. But if we are to live to tell the tale, we need a new narrative.

Likely Story

In the course of these chapters, the same old story has been specified in particular ways, and we've explored how we live both inside our heads and outside in the social domain. At once, we're part *of* the world, and apart *from* it. We live in *the* world, and in *our own* world. And it is in this uncomfortable terrain that we encounter the prevalence of paradox. As a reminder, I'll run through in note form some excerpts that illustrate the point:

• Modernity has helped free the individual (at least in the rich world) from parochial constrictions of familial, tribal and religious allegiance. At the same time, it has sometimes created the secluded individual, feeling detached in an uncongenial social world that is increasingly materialist, atomistic, and uniform. In the worst cases, genuine diversity has given way to a new sameness, whereby people have gone from personal identity to the identical. In seeking refuge from this isolation, individuals who feel cut adrift may seek affinity in religious or political cults that may end up imposing more restriction on them than the communities from which they sought liberation.

- One of the new freedoms that some people exercise is to travel the world and experience its variation. Arguably, the more we spread our wings to settle in across the world, the more we make each place look like another. Uniqueness becomes rarer. The very thing that attracts the tourist or migrant gets lost. What I call the *Babel effect* is part of what gives rise to populist anti-immigrant sentiment. People feel their particular place is forfeiting its integrity, in a motley remake, that is more copy and pastiche than genuine. In pursuing the benefit of greater human integration, we may aggravate the worst tendencies of differentiation, with its emphasis on the nativist.

- If opposition to this populism involves dismissal of its adherents' concerns as ignorant bigotry, this may confirm for them that intellectual elites regard them with contempt and condescension. If instead, populist claims are treated with respect and appreciation, this may grant those claims unmerited gravitas. Explanation becomes legitimation.

- The strange sight of the deprived being in awe to privileged elite saviour figures – a feature of populist politics – raises the question of how they can hope to escape subjection by being subject to such charlatans. One explanation offered is that often the oppressed can be 'hosts' to their oppressor, in that they have so imbued the logic of that dominance that they fear freedom from it, even as they proclaim their freedom in their reclaimed rights as 'the people'.

- Some on the left get themselves into their own bind. In wanting to appear moral, they have to confess to their crime of complicity in racism and misogyny and other violations of social justice. In doing so, they can make their target audience into nothing but victims, when many of them see themselves as engaged in self-empowerment rather than self-pity. Those who pursue leftist identity politics may end up forsaking the progressive banner of human solidarity.

- When the heat between both sides becomes hate, they contradict their own position further. The right want to talk about national belonging and patriotism, while wanting to secede from those in their own country, with whom they feel estranged; and the left want to be on the side of peace and love, while expressing venom about those who do not abide by the strict rectitude of their dictatorial decrees about justice. In the case of some of the left, the very people most likely to decry the fundamentalism of literal reads of the bible can end up authoring their own bible, to which they demand absolute conformity.

- Such moral absolutes can be embedded in cultural relativism, whereby it's perfectly okay to judge some, whereas to judge others outside your cultural/racial frame would be too judgemental.

- Many contradictions beset rightist forms of identity politics, including preparedness on the part of advocates of ethno-nationalism and borders to network internationally. Often, they're caught between an emphasis on their own particular culture, and common global cause in the interest of Judaeo-Christian religion or white supremacy.

• Protagonists of culture wars may have separate *identities* they want to protect, depending on their politics, but they have *identical* disposition to abhor and abuse their opponents, particularly through online vitriol. Out of such hatred comes little hope of help or healing.

• All this rage is related to wider shifts in economics and politics, and the difficulty of reconciling their contrary pulls. Economically, there is pressure for nations to join bigger blocs to get economy of scale in production, research collaboration, and trade. But politically, there is a pull in the opposite direction, toward greater de-centralisation and subsidiarity. In the face of a global economy outside their control, some want a more localised politics that gives them greater say.

• The financialisation of the global economy has produced its own contradictions. For instance, a key problem in addressing the financial crash was how to deal with banks 'too big to fail'. Now, the collapse of some banks during the crash, and new rules about secure financial reserves, mean that there's more opportunity for only the big banks to stay in the game – the chance, in other words, for even greater monopoly, the very thing that was a key part of the problem.

• The series of economic strains in recent decades has re-alerted us to the Keynesian *paradox of thrift* – the idea that penny-pinching and saving by both households and firms in hard or uncertain times can reduce spend and aggregate demand, which in turn prompts lower investment and growth, which then reduces total saving.

• These strains have also produced a contradictory pull between old-style Keynesianism and Neoliberalism, whereby governments want to spend for stimulus, but don't feel able to tax to fully fund increased public expenditure. But the borrowing and over-printing of currency that fills the gap can degrade currency value, and therefore purchasing power – essentially a closet regressive tax in the end.

• Political upheaval has been marked in part by the reversal of party appeal. The core base of Labour-type parties used to be the working class, and that of Conservative-type parties, the upper-middle and upper classes. Now rightist parties are drawing in more working class and less educated voters, while leftist parties are securing a greater share of the educated and professional classes. This pattern holds its own contradiction. For instance, Corbyn's Labour party in the UK drew in many new students and urban-based professionals, whose perceived predilection for cultural wokeism and economic radicalism was a turn-off for some of Labour's traditional supporters, a problem for an agenda geared to class politics.

- Globalisation evidences other inconsistencies, one being the paradox of poverty from plenty. Wealth from resources like oil and diamonds can induce bribery, war and repression domestically, while impairing further the condition of the poorest by hiking local prices; boosting greater inequality; and luring the most skilled from industry and government towards the well-paid sector. All told, many can end up more impoverished than if the precious asset was never extracted in the first place.
- Those seeking redress of inequality should not be tempted into any nostalgia for the alternative of communism. As practiced, it was politically despotic, while economically inept. Its inflated self-esteem was in inverse proportion to its accomplishment. Paradoxically, under its regime, many of those countries, whose names were prefixed with virtuous titles such as 'democratic', 'workers', and 'people's republic', merited such labels the least. Progressives everywhere should be unequivocal in saying good riddance to such bad politics.
- Trying to understand these patterns of tribe, class, and other social divisions, we can seek for explanation from our earliest formation as *sapiens* onward. What we find in each of us is reflection of wider contest and disaffection. We comprise a constant self, and a changing self. We're restless in search of repose. We're nesters who long for the greener faraway hills. We favour intimacy, yet familiarity breeds contempt. We want what we don't have until we have it. Though we're creatures of migration, many of us are wary of immigrants. As the outcome of much mixing over the millennia, we're a mongrel species, often in vain pursuit of ethnic or racial purity. No one's an island. Each of us is both individual and collective, because we're also partly creatures of culture, which involves us all in constant mutual transmission. By teaching each other, we learn our selfhood. Without socialisation, we're reduced to the feral.
- With the particular issue of immigration, it is rich countries at present that face most popular push-back against it. Yet the age profile of the rich world suggests that they will be the very countries in the future that will end up competing with each other for immigrants to boost their flagging labour markets, and increase the workforce to help support the rising demographic share that are students or retired. Meanwhile, the developing countries may invest more to halt their brain-drain, so that when rich countries want immigrants most, they may be available least.
- One of the instruments for making sense of this mayhem – *intelligence* – is itself subject to great dispute about the relative significance of genetic inheritance and social background. While typically, leftists want to elevate nurture over nature in this debate, the more equal we make society, the greater role genes will be accorded in the distribution of intelligence.
- The pros and cons of artificial intelligence (AI) are complicated by our apparently innate preference for the *natural* over the *artificial*. One of the

uses of AI will concern the ethical minefield of human enhancement. While it's been a long-time dream of humans to discover the elixir of prolonged lifespan if not of eternal life, for some, it is death that actually gives life meaning.

- In AI, we stand to create an entity more intelligent than ourselves. This carries a feasible risk of the *created* turning on the *creator*. Some think that the very democratisation of AI, in terms of ever more extensive access, increases the probability, by error or intent, of its being abused for anti-social purpose, through activities such as surveillance and invasion of privacy, through to contrived pandemics in biological warfare.

- All this is happening in a planet that may become less inhabitable. For some, it's partly a problem of population. They argue that in over-breeding, humans exhibit a death wish. For others, greater emphasis is on how we mistreat the Earth. Through their over-bearing nature, humans have debilitated the capacity of nature to bear them, making the human age one unfit for humans. A stark measure of our vulnerability is that in a planet overwhelmingly comprising water, there could be a supply-side deficit of safe water.

- Though it's widely accepted that we can only tackle these big issues together, the present drive of Big Tech is to split us apart. The scale, speed, and spread of these latest technologies outpace societal supervision and ethical codification. It's a moral maze with too little ethical oversight. Miniaturisation of innovations like AI have led to magnification of its operation. A system designed to control many domains cannot at this stage control for its own errors or over-reach. Because of our own contradictions – for instance, we like personal privacy, while wanting to be privy to others' secrets – Big Tech can exploit our curiosity for that which enthrals rather than educates. While at one level, its influence is pervasive, at another level, it's invisible or inscrutable. The public at large have not been given the chance to grasp its significance and ambition. We're researching toward ever more super-intelligence, while wanting the application to be based on human values, that themselves spring from our lower intelligence. In this, we stand to outwit ourselves, with unknown consequence.

- At the same time, something like AI, and our work to grant it independent agency and a form of consciousness, may help us understand better about human consciousness, about which we understand very little at present.

- Our search for such understanding has involved us in a tangled loop, what has been called the *paradox of consciousness*: we're investigating the very thing that is undertaking the investigation.

- Redressing the huge inequality in the world confronts a number of paradoxes: diminishing disparity *between* some countries alongside a widening gap *within* countries; the narrowing gap globally still leaving huge inequity between rich and poor worlds; within countries, the paradox of redistribution operates, whereby the less universal the service and the more targeted the redistribution, the less likely are such measures to cut poverty and inequality – services targeted mostly or totally on the poor tend to become poor services; meritocracy ends up being what it was thought to correct – an inter-generational transfer of privilege and wealth – only now justified by what is taken as deserved achievement; and the interesting outcome that the country which led the charge for greater equality in the early twentieth century – Russia – has ended up being the one with the highest wealth gap in the world between the top 1 percent and the rest, a boon for oligarchs and a bust for many.

- Through all these issues and actions, persistent human features prevail. For example, humans have developed, since the distant past, preference for sameness, stability and structure, and yet live now in a world that is increasingly diverse and uncertain, not only in living environments, but also in the virtual arena of social media. It is in this arena – the virtual public square – where empty vessels make most noise. In the celebrity age, the items that grab most attention are often those that matter least, and those voices that are most loud and aggressive have the least interesting things to say.

- As far back as Bernays, who is often taken as the father of modern public relations, marketing has been designed to persuade us to want stuff we don't need, and to see in material possession evidence of our chosen lifestyle and success. What seems like self-expression is mainly conformity. Apparent promotion of self is in many respects cover for controlling the crowd. Such mass propaganda has served commercial purpose with the dawn of the consumer age, but elements of it have always been part of the 'bread and circus'.

- Coming to the recent pandemic, it shows that social capital of friendship and community networks, together with the natural capital of the biosphere, are crucial parts of human wealth and well-being. So too is having access to reliable information. The virus has shown how rumour and conspiracy in social media can become viral. One contagion quickly leads to others – in disinformation, in economic fallout, and in depiction of the stranger as danger. What COVID-19 also shows is that though humans have come to regard themselves as high and mighty, they can be laid low by something small like a virus. When for social beings it comes to be regarded as anti-social not to keep a social distance; when a crucial part of coming together to beat the virus involves us agreeing to stay apart; and when the sophisticated global market system can be allegedly crashed by mishap in a small local market in Wuhan, we can see something of our strange world of paradox.

More Questions Than Answers

As has been said, the greatest adversary of knowledge is not ignorance, but rather the illusion of knowledge. It's crucial to know our limits, to become more aware of what we do and do not know. Mostly, ignorance is not bliss. One of its deadly variants is the conceit of baseless conviction. Some people can be most certain about what they least know. And we live in a media world where brash assuredness can gain more attention than thoughtful comment.

Often, conventional words of wisdom hold true. The proof of the pudding *is* in the eating. Actions *do* speak louder than words. But some sayings are not so prudent. All things *don't* come to those who wait. Every cloud *doesn't* have a silver lining. Possession is *not* nine-tenths of the law. Great minds *don't* think alike. And most good deeds *do* go unpunished. As the world increases in complexity, we should be cautious about taking refuge in simplicity.

As this book has covered, there remain lots of fundamental things about us and our universe that we don't know. As regards our very origins, we are still unsure about the dates and locations of our beginnings in different parts of Africa. Nor can we say, for sure, that the earliest societies were egalitarian, and that social ranking only came with human settlement. We cannot be definite that Earth is the only planet in our galaxy that has the 'goldilocks' conditions for sentient life, never mind about what other forms of life may exist in the multiple galaxies. The matter that we can see – planets, stars, asteroids, galaxies – makes up around only 5 percent of the total universe, with the rest being dark energy and dark matter, about which we know very little. And then there are rudimentary aspects of how we work – such as consciousness – and how we learn – such as the relative roles of nature and nurture – which we're still trying to figure. Such mystery merits human modesty.

None of this belittles science. We should still value astronomy over astrology. We should still be careful not to elevate feeling over fact in discerning truth. We should be guarded against abandoning reason in the search for reasonable conduct. To repeat an earlier point, the dictum that not all things that are counted, count, and not all things that count can be counted is crucial. Numbers carry authority. But we should be wary of their source, accuracy, and interpretation. Economic growth data do not reveal the true health of the economy, never mind the society. An international Happiness Index is an important counterweight to materialist dimensions of wellbeing. But it is dealing with qualities that are hard to measure.

In all this, education is critical. Yet it is a service either under-resourced in many parts of the world and/or allocated on the basis of income and social background. The contemporary university too often exhibits the problem. In many cases, we have seen a takeover by a culture of managerialism. Quest for cash and status has seen the university being corporatized, bureaucratised, and commercialised, with students often cast as mainly consumers. At its worst, in this instrumentalist model, the university is reduced to being a business unit, audited in terms of its fiscal standing, and designed mainly to serve a narrow vision of the economy, rather than a generous vision of society. I wonder sometimes whether those at the top of many universities have lost their educational nerve. An instance of this that I've come across is the demand now for lecturers setting assignments and exams to have 'model answers' prepared, against which they can assess scripts. This may be done to protect against litigious students unhappy with their mark. But it goes against everything a university should be. In most disciplines, of which I'm aware, there's no such thing as a 'model answer'. Indeed, you're looking for the very opposite, for independent critical thought. Yet in a world demanding critical and creative thinking, we are turning to new forms of rote learning such as 'teaching to the test', gearing students for almost robotic responses to questions based on learned prescribed answers.

There is a nobler vision of the academy: one that sees it as a key anchor institution in its urban hinterland; one that is engaged with people and problems in that wider social setting, not some kind of citadel that offers respite from a complex and troubling world, or a research wing of big corporate interests.

This involves the institution going beyond an *'outreach'* to this wider world. Rather, it has to embrace opportunities for these wider stakeholders to *'in-reach'* the university. While the university continues to be an important site of knowledge production, it is far from being an *exclusive* one. The co-production and application of knowledge in strategic partnership with a range of civic stakeholders is the key mission for an urban university contributing to a pluralist city for a pluralist citizenship. It has to take a lead in the social benefit of expertise. In an age when some leaders are given to a populist anti-intellectualism, and scant regard for evidence, an important principle has to be re-affirmed: people are entitled to their views; they are not entitled to their facts. Let's get beyond the imbecilic and supercilious: there is no such thing as a 'counter-fact'. Our places of learning have to go back to such basics.

Ideology and Idealism

In this first volume, I've concentrated a lot on politics. In the second, I turn to other sources of authority, such as religion. Politics and religion have been seen by many as the main means of making life better. Both can be seen by some to be based on empty promises – plying platitudes and pieties, of little practical good. The Earth faces urgent challenge for its very survival. As an old lefty, influenced a good deal in my youth by both the humanist side of Marxist thinking and the liberation arguments of Christian theology, my main concern is that the left is both radical and relevant. Today's world awaits re-definition of what it means to be a good human being in a good society. Old style politics of left and right – just like old-style religion – can't meet that test.

The political left needs to own up to the delusionary aspect of its glorious revolutions. Chic icons of the left like the Che Guevaras were false heroes. Cuba, for all its achievements in health and education, and its travails with its powerful neighbour, couldn't be governed for 60 years by anyone whose name wasn't Castro. That's how democratic it proved to be after the toppling of the dictator Batista. Nor can today's identity politics of some progressives, and its attendant wokeism, offer deliverance. The left needs to show much more in its current practice what prefiguratively a better society would look like.

Bertolt Brecht, in his 1940 poem, *To Those Born Later*, speaks of how hatred of malice warps the features, and how rage, even against injustice, can yield more harm than good. His plea for forbearance from the next generation is for the failure of his cohort to bring about in their own practice the fellowship they preached. He confesses that those of his time who had sought human liberation through fighting the class wars, who had 'wanted to prepare the ground for friendship', could not themselves be friendly with each other. Too often, they were comrades in name, while bereft of mutual compassion.

It is at once a profoundly sad, yet uplifting, poem. It speaks to how so often we on the left posture with empty talk, while refusing to walk the walk of kindness and care that we claim to want for universal deliverance. It's easier to express concern for abstract humanity than to practice concern toward actual humans. It's easier to loathe the oppressor than to love the oppressed. Of course, those who wrap themselves in the cloak of moral nobility, set an exacting standard for the assessment of their behaviour. The perennial gap between human word and deed is more noticeably a chasm when it comes to self-righteous champions of justice, who are more at home with angry denunciation than with actions of considerateness and conciliation.

Saying that is all well and good. Unfortunately, we're not built for love, peace, and harmony all the time. Conflict is endemic to the human condition. But it doesn't have to be nasty and vindictive. The challenge is how to make disagreement agonistic rather than antagonistic – to be able to express candid and contrarian opinion in a milieu that is respectful and civil, and open to agree to disagree. We all find this hard. As creatures, we can be petty, envious, and spiteful – traits enveloped in a big and sensitive ego. The Book of Ecclesiastes in the Old Testament may be right when it says that ultimately in human affairs, 'all is vanity'.

Conspicuously, in-fighting and acrimony are very evident in academia, despite its claim to being a preserve of reasoned difference. It's been often said that university politics are so bitter because the stakes are so small. It's also because people fear being exposed as unknowledgeable in an environment that values intellectual capital. Humiliation is only chosen by those into self-mortification. In my years as a university teacher, I never let my ignorance get in the way of a good lecture – not to say that they were always spell-binding.

The truth is that most of us feel fragile at some level, some of the time. We should embrace this susceptibility, because if we didn't experience it, there's a high chance that we would be somewhere on the spectrum of the sociopath and narcissist. Being vulnerable is very human. Indeed, there is strength in human frailty if it makes us more sensitive to the suffering of others. We have to practice being comfortable with the risk of failure and even loss of face. That's not to say that practice makes perfect, because there's no such thing as perfection. We're all full of contradiction and self-justification. It is to say that we can all benefit from reminder of this frailty in seeking to be better mediums of our message.

So how can the left lead by example? A step in this direction is to ask whether conventionally understood progressive stances are in fact regressive. Consider the 'progressive' credentials of those American colleges, which provide for separate dorms, orientation programmes, cultural events, and even graduation ceremonies, on the basis of race. These initiatives may be framed in attractive terms, such as 'affinity housing'. But in their racial exclusivity, they represent regression to the 'separate but equal' era, against which the Civil Rights Movement struggled long and hard. Under the rationale of diversity, this kind of segregation detaches people from each other – not usually a good basis for mutual engagement and understanding. How have we arrived at such reversal?

Another instance is when people are no-platformed, harassed, or even risk losing their job, at a place of learning, when they hold respectful difference of opinion about subjects that are open to scientific dispute. Some humans still love witch-hunts. Holocaust denial is not protected under the guise of academic freedom. Evidence of that heinous crime is indisputable. Most social issues are not so settled, and can be subject to passionate contest by people of good faith. When some insist that their right to 'safe space' should protect them from being exposed to uncomfortable argument, they misunderstand the purpose of education. People have a right to be safe from abusive behaviour, but not to be 'safe' from challenging discourse. Failure to demarcate these two will spell ruin to the prospect of open debate, upon which democracy itself depends. Unfortunately, all this is an example of the de-valuation of words. In the interest of those subject to real oppression, terms like 'victim', 'violence', 'safe', and 'grievance' are too important to be used loosely and liberally.

Parallel Universes

As discussed earlier, people have a tendency to give reasons for their beliefs, and to deem those beliefs as more than wishful thinking or doctrinaire opinion. Accordingly, they interpret any particular event in a way that supports their partisan position, rather than approach it with intellectual honesty. Although we all like to think that we're led by the data, we're often prone to lead the data in the direction of our preferred destiny. Consider three examples:

A. Extensive and persistent popular dissent against non-democracy and human rights abuse is evident on our screens in various expressions of specific rebellion and mass insurgency. Such prevalence can be seen in the following divergent ways:

(1) myriad street protests and civil disobedience worldwide show that people at this time are not politically apathetic as often portrayed. Employing social media to network and congregate, these movements are representations of people power in revolt against establishment power. They affirm an age-old truth that where there is repression, there will in time be resistance. Particularly, those demos and actions against war, sexism, misogyny, racism, extreme inequality and vandalised environment, illustrate growing global concern for humanity to act in unison for a common and better world. People marching and acting together is empowering, because it conveys that we're not alone. We're all in this together;

(2) protest has always been with us. There's nothing particularly new or hopeful about its current incarnation. Perhaps it gets more attention in an age of 24-hour news and social media. Mostly, it comprises transient events that either fade or get quashed, and rarely do they overturn embedded power, whether of capital, patriarchy, state militarism, or the like. Sometimes, it can even serve the interests of the powerful to have the powerless let off steam occasionally;

(3) protest across the world simply reflects how much we are at odds with each other. Its ubiquity testifies to how elusive is the collective spirit we laud as 'humanity'. Demonstrations and remonstrations can comprise theocratic zealots; shamans and prophets of doom parading apocalyptic warning; anti-immigrant campaigners; conspiracy activists; and such like, alongside campaigners for democracy and equality. Again, we all choose our side, in discriminating between good and bad protest. In any case, particular movements can carry their own contradiction. People can be on the street in Tunisia demanding democracy as part of an Arab Spring, only to be subsequently expressing preference for security and strict leadership in the face of anarchy. Similarly, movements in the past can be re-interpreted. Was sixties counter-culture a social revolt against bourgeois and militaristic values, or a faddish and stylised over-indulgence of individualism, by many privileged youth who went on to enjoy the bourgeois life? Protest can be in the eye of both beholder and beholden;

(4) traditional protest is largely rooted in an establishment mind-set about power, wanting to replace one type with another. What's really needed in today's crisis-driven world is a new mentality and spirit directed toward love and healing, away from the impulse of power over another. We may be on the cusp of such a shift in collective consciousness that transforms the language of politics from rivalry and antagonism to common purpose. Each of us can't change the world. We can best try to change ourselves, and that individual makeover will, when combined, make for healthier and happier social relations, based on trust not tribe.

The point is that any one of these views, or permutations of them, contain enough plausibility to sound credible. While protest can be the voice of the unheard, it's not necessarily the voice of the virtuous.

B. In the 2017 UK General Election, Corbyn's Labour Party secured 40 percent of the vote, relative to the Tory share of 42.3 percent, on a 69 percent turnout. Depending on your political position, this can be interpreted in four main ways:

(1) it was usual politics, in that Labour's decent showing was due to Tory Prime Minister May's poor leadership and electoral campaign. A government long presiding over austerity was inclined to lose votes. Generally, governments tend to lose elections, or at least drop support, rather than oppositions picking up positive endorsement for their agenda;

(2) the result was related to Brexit. The country was quite evenly split about the UK's departure from the EU, and this was broadly reflected in the result. Accordingly, May succeeded in consolidating the Brexitland part of the country, and Labour attracted those who wanted a re-run of the Brexit decision. Clearly, a section of its 40 percent support was not necessarily enthusiastic for the party's radical manifesto;

(3) this was confirmation that a radical agenda could secure substantial electoral backing, much better than Blair's win for New Labour in 2005, with a mere 35.2 percent share, on the lesser turnout of 61.4 percent; and even comparable to Blair's win in 2001, with 40.7 percent of the vote, on an extremely low turnout of 59.4 percent. A key problem lies in the UK's skewed electoral system, whereby Blair's weak vote in 2005 was still able to secure 356 parliamentary seats to the Tories' 198. Even Corbyn's very poor result in the 2019 General Election, at 32.2 percent, was not so very far off Blair's 2005 share, which brought victory.

(4) there was an issue with Corbyn's credibility as a potential Prime Minister. With a different leader, behind the same radical manifesto, Labour could have won.

Essentially, the radical left in the Labour Party can still convince itself that its manifesto was electorally as popular as that of the centrist Blairite offering in 2001 and 2005. For them, even under the new management of a different leader, Labour should stick with the radical agenda. By contrast, for those on the centre-right of the party, that flies in the face of clear evidence that the electorate decisively rejected the leftist programme. Take your pick.

C. The 2019 UK General Election result saw Johnson's Tory Party achieve 43.6 percent of the vote – marginally better than Blair's landslide in 1997, and only slightly less than Thatcher's in 1979. This success was attributable in good part to the conversion of many traditional Labour seats in the North and Midlands of England into Tory hands for the first time. It's a result again open to different interpretations. From 'The 2019 UK General Election' to 'interpretation' should be in bold as with the previous examples.

(1) this outcome upturns the conventional political axis of left and right in Britain. An ideology of big market and small state, with its attendant promise of low tax and public spend, that has marked the Tory Party, is hard to sustain if it is to retain this so-called 'red wall' of former Labour seats. Its talk of 'levelling up', meaning its intent to bring those under-developed and neglected parts of the country up to a level playing field with the most prosperous, converts the Tory Party into one that is caught in commitments to intervention and redistribution, the opposite of its traditional ideology;

(2) this is only rhetoric and optics, typical of Johnson's empty boosterism, and is accompanied mostly by modest compensation programmes, like the Towns Fund, targeted cynically at Tory-held seats, and some token-istic infrastructure projects. The agenda is suitably vague to permit varied understanding of its purpose, and how its performance would be assessed. What has motivated the current unusual combination of public spending and increased borrowing and taxation is the unusual circumstance of COVID-19, and subsequent energy and cost-of-living crises. It does not represent a long-term ideological realignment that gives Labour greater political space to be more fiscally adventurous;

(3) the Tory Party can be pragmatic in the interest of gaining and retaining power. Reading the runes of these volatile times, they could well decide to go left on economics and right on culture – a dual war on want and woke, designed to disarm the Opposition.

Elements of all three perspectives could be in play. What 'left' and 'right' mean today across the world is ambivalent. One aspect is the appropriation of 'patriotism' as part of a resurgent nationalism, seen as a protective buffer against the increasing power of globalism, and the economic insecurity it purportedly brings to already marginalised working class communities. Being a cosmopolitan 'citizen of the world' is depicted as at best a split loyalty. Traditional politics centred on class and capitalism are overtaken by a culture clash, whereby the electoral fissures primarily concern identity and social values.

Such remaking of politics from the ideological to the technocratic and managerialist, whereby main political blocs seek to 'triangulate' policies, by commandeering elements from their opponents, is falsely lauded as pragmatic and tactical in an age when grand visions and strategies no longer have the same purchase. In fact, this is not new. In much of the post-war industrial world, the emergence of some form of welfare capitalism augured a consensus politics, involving regular theft of rivals' political clothes. Political cross-dressing isn't a fad. It's a fact.

Moreover, amid this churning and uncertainty, pressing issues – most obviously, the threat of global warming – upset fixed positions. Many on the right may still prefer market solutions to the impact of climate change. But some business and conservative interests are drawn to the imperative for state and international action to 'conserve' the world as a stable site for sustainable capitalism. Demanding more than the usual policy tweaks of mitigation, radical response to the emergency does not easily fall into a left-right contest.

In times of great and rapid change, the law of unintended consequence becomes more apposite. Two examples suffice here. First, in Britain, Tory success in invading Labour territory poses a paradox for its retention of its traditional heartlands in the South. For instance, its supporters don't want a massive housing programme – as part of 'building back better' – trespassing into their greenbelt shires. If such a programme was to happen, and had the consequence of attracting young, liberal, professional people from the North and Midlands, it could serve to shift the electoral map in parts of the South-East that currently favours the Tories. Success can carry the seeds of subsequent failure.

Second, across the world, the dislocation and lockdown caused by COVID-19 has spurred some employers to re-think the organisation of work and the role of the office, and the future of shopping amid the expansion of online retail. With new 'hybridities', politicians and planners have to re-conceptualise the downtown, and its relationship to the wider city-region. If all of this was to re-configure basic social processes like commuting, this would require co-ordinated re-organisation of major strands, like transport infrastructure. Even hands-off, market-driven right-wing governments couldn't credibly claim that this upheaval is outside their remit.

Response to the Financial Crash, to COVID-19, and to the more recent cost-of-living crisis has shown the power of government, and the capacity after all to find hidden treasure in the magic money tree. Enormous cash spend has been sanctioned by governments of all political hues. Potentially, that makes the case for an ambitious Green New Deal to address environmental justice much more politically viable, without the stigma of fiscal irresponsibility. Alternatively, the massive borrowing and debt incurred by these emergencies, with accompanying inflation and higher interest rates, can be used to justify another period of fiscal retrenchment and austerity. Also, if the next period was to be one of widespread stagflation, governments may be prone to relax environmental and other regulation under the pretext of redressing stagnant growth.

Even if substantial public resources are devoted to de-carbonising the economy, the question of who are the main beneficiaries of that allocation – re-skilled workers in the old fossil-fuel energy industries, or large corporate interests in the new energy sectors – remains to be seen. Just as the rescue plan for the Financial Crash threw a lifeline to bankers rather than to people, the distributive impact of any Green New Deal demands public scrutiny and environmental justice. Whatever the scenario here, at least the dramatic and unprecedented events of the last few years widen scope for new political conversations. What is deemed 'realistic' has been re-defined. The mood music of contemporary politics may be open to new orchestration.

The challenge for a viable left politics at present involves being able to read the runes rather than regret the ruins, to be positive rather than gloomy and condemnatory. It may be that the crises of recent times have opened up prospect for people to re-set their priorities toward quality of life, and the importance of family and friends. Far from the vacuous Truss slogan of 'growth, growth, growth', it may be about de-growth for the rich world to let the poorer parts catch up, without an overall unbearable pressure on the planet. To achieve more of what they really value, people may be prepared to manage on less, and to appreciate that so much of what's important they can get for free – the open air, beauty of nature, time with loved ones, public galleries and libraries – or at low cost – reading a book, listening to music. In defining a new social order, we could do worse than re-visit some old slogans: work to live, rather than live to work; live simply so that others may simply live. Even a Tory Prime Minister in the UK had to reset the dial from blatant avarice, when he said that we needed to adapt the infamous Gordon Gekko motto of 'greed is good' to 'green is good'. This may be hot air, but the left can convert that hot air into political energy for its purpose.

We come back to these strange times. Consider just one example. An American president refused to accept the result of an election. He pressured officials to 'find votes' that would overturn it. He roused his supporters to believe that their vote had been stolen. He gave an inflammatory speech in Washington on the day that Congress was due to formally confirm his opponent's victory, warning an angry crowd that they had to fight to protect what they valued. He suggested that they march toward the Capitol Building, promising that he would be by their side. A good section of the crowd proceeded to do so, and many of them were involved in an invasion of Congress, designed to stop Vice President Pence from doing his duty on the day, with some even chanting that he should be hanged for his treason. He and the other Congress representatives had to be escorted to safety as the mob overpowered security to reach the Senate chamber. This was insurrection. Moreover, it was a sedition, for which at least some participants felt they had the President's blessing.

It's even worse than that. With a few exceptions, elected Republicans have effectively endorsed or excused the subversion, mainly because their careers depend on placating their electorate, who by a clear majority continue to give Trumpism their approval. The country, which sees itself as exceptional – as the New World that escaped the old one of tyranny and persecution, as the beacon of freedom in the Free World – is split in two about the very legitimacy of its electoral system. We should not have normalised populist nationalism to the point where we don't find the debacle that is the current American political landscape, other than shocking. Arguably, the US has been reduced to a low-intensity civil war. Its manifestation might be most marked by sensitive issues like abortion and gun control. But beyond these highly charged issues, there is a deeper disquiet about the viable co-habitation of very distinct political tribes.

There is a contagious element to this. Many looking at the way sizeable parts of the democratic electorate worldwide can inhabit a realm that hosts madcap conspiracies like QAnon, and welters in the wisdom of moronic leaders like Trump, end up feeling that there's no talking anymore to some people. Let's just concede that the 100-year experiment in mass democracy has demonstrated misplaced idealism. Some people don't deserve democracy. For the vote to be valued, it has to be earned. At minimum, to qualify for the franchise, some kind of civic literacy test is necessary.

I must confess to being ambivalent about aspects of this. My honest reaction to interviews with many Trump supporters is: how can the richest country ever in history have produced people so badly educated and ill-informed? But I can't bring myself to deduce that they're unworthy of the vote. Any such retaliatory voter suppression would be sending the paternalistic message to vast swathes of the electorate: 'you don't know what's good for you'. Democracy itself is contentious. Ultimately, its logic is based more on quantity – the electoral majority – than quality – the strength of argument. In many places, there would be a democratic majority for capital punishment, much to liberal distaste; and for assisted suicide, much to social conservative's distaste. Democratic elections can also be seen to deliver theocracy, autocracy, and patriarchy. At the same time, the alternatives aren't great. A 'selectorate' would give undue power to the great and good – the elect is always an elite. And benign dictatorships would only be agreeable to people who agreed with them.

When I look back over decades at politics in my part of the world, I'm taken with how some aspects have definitely changed for the better. I think it's less racist, sexist, and homophobic. On the other hand, I'm bewildered by the resilience of entrenched power. For instance, when I was a teenager, I thought we'd finally seen the back of Eton-boy rulers like Harold Macmillan and Douglas-Home. Then lo and behold, in the twenty-first-century, we get their reincarnation in Cameron and Johnson, only the recent version was even more reactionary in many regards. I remember in 1969, working in a student summer job for the preparation of the Garden Party in Buckingham Palace, and looking incredulously at the obsequious genuflection of the gathered worthies to the presence of the queen. Royalty, despite its scandals, patriarchy, and privilege, is still with us, as is the anachronistic House of Lords. The more some things change, the more they remain the same. To paraphrase Yeats, some change comes dropping slow. So how do we deal with this crisis time, demanding a new dial?

Beyond the Binary

Part of what has got us here is that too many of us exist only in a world of binaries. There is my side, and that other lot. They are beyond redemption, and deserve no quarter to be given. It's not enough to disagree. In the venomous language of social media, you must 'own' or 'destroy' your opponent, because they're not really opponents. They're enemies to be crushed, not adversaries to be persuaded.

When I was a child, I loved Westerns. They were simple stories. There were cowboys and Indians. There were goodies and baddies. I particularly loved the Lone Ranger, and when he came to Belfast to perform – which believe or not, he did – my brother and I were brought to see him. After a time of him on stage executing various gun tricks and telling tall tales, there was a roving mic sent around the audience to take questions. Many were what was expected: where was Tonto? were his bullets really made of silver? My older brother turned to me and whispered that if the mic came to me, I was to ask him whether he was Protestant or Catholic. You see, in a sectarian society that I inhabited, that question of tribal belonging was ever present and most pertinent.

But to be adults in the room, we have to put away some of the things of childhood. Part of growing up involves moving beyond binaries. A world of 'you're either with us or against us', of heroes and villains, is a deceptive and dangerous one. In many of the themes of this book, evidence of this binary mentality is clear: the natural and the artificial; the people and the 'real' people; reason and emotion; nature versus nurture; mind and body; blank slate or innate human nature; the material and spiritual; myth and truth; me and others; believers and infidels; and so on. Key issues facing us are more complicated than such dualism would suggest. Instead of 'either-or', it can be 'and'. We need more hybridity, rather than fixed identity. We need more options, rather than manifestos that sound like biblical tracts. We need more fluidity than inflexibility. At the same time, it doesn't serve us to abandon attempted agreement of core universal principles, in the name of cultural relativism. Honour killings are murder. Genital mutilation is injurious. Public beatings are barbaric. Preventing women having an equal place in public life is sexist, and often misogynist. If there's any chance of humans treating each other decently, these kinds of propositions are basic.

To take another example of the binary bind: there is a fundamental paradox in the fact that we live in radical times that would seem to demand revolutionary politics. In times past, in places like England, stark and urgent injustice summoned mass resistance. In Shelley's poem *The Masque of Anarchy*, written just after the Peterloo massacre in 1819, there was a stirring call for the masses to hold onto hope in unforgiving circumstance by becoming aware of their 'unvanquishable' power, because they were the many and their oppressors were the few. Throughout the poorest parts of the world still, this counsel for the subjugated to awaken like lions after slumber in defensible defiance retains commendable resonance. Yet the history of many revolutions is not reassuring. Too often one set of despots was displaced for another, and a lot of blood was spilled in the process. Consider just one current example in a long list – Ortega's Nicaragua. Nevertheless, today the reformist alternative of social democracy, with its slower, more incremental change, doesn't seem up to the urgency of the moment.

What I'm advocating is outside these binaries. It is a radical form of social democracy with the ambition of positive democratic transformation. This is distinctive from any negative upheaval, focussed almost exclusively on dislodging existing power structures. You don't imitate the means of bad politics to achieve good politics. That doesn't mean you wait for the meek to inherit the earth. That would be like waiting for Godot. I think it is possible to script a bold agenda, and to embolden people's faith in its feasibility. I'd express it as follows: lax, tax, max, pax, pacts, and facts. Let me take each one and outline the implication.

In terms of 'lax', we need to get away from the lax social accountability over many aspects of our economy and society. This involves greater regulation of corporations and sectors like Big Tech and High Finance. In terms of 'tax', we need major progressive redistribution of income and wealth. It's not enough for the super-rich to be left to their voluntary and often self-serving philanthropy. Two main arguments have been used against taxing the rich: it would induce them into tax exile; and the money raised would, in any case, be modest. Both are misleading. As the international movement, known as *Patriotic Millionaires* shows, some of the rich themselves accept that they're not paying a fair share, and are pressing government to be taxed more.

In October 2021, an open letter to the UK Chancellor, with over 30 millionaires as signatories, suggested that he tax them more, because the country's welfare was more important than growing their wealth. Given that the total wealth of UK billionaires had increased by 22 percent to £597 billion since the outbreak of COVID-19, there is a lot of scope. One estimate of the impact of a wealth tax in the UK suggests that it could generate approximately £70–130 billion annually – equivalent to about 9–16 percent of the UK's annual tax take – a significant sum. In recent times, the head of Treasury departments, in places like the UK and US, have themselves personal treasures of multiple millions, and it should be strongly stated that their public duty is not to safeguard their private interest.

On the 'max' factor, this refers to Democracy Max, meaning that we need to expand the scope of democratic decision-making into public policy-making, key social institutions, and corporate boardrooms. In the case of the US, basic anomalies like the electoral college are not fit for purpose. In the case of the UK, outdated, non-democratic institutions like the House of Lords should be long gone. The vote should be based on some version of proportional representation. Of course, some insist that this gives rise to multiple parties, who barter undemocratically after an election in the construction of coalition. This, it is said, can often mean splitting rather than making the difference – arriving at the lowest common denominator of agreement that represents a false consensus, that is likely to be inherently conservative (with a small 'c'). Others worry that proportional voting risks greater parliamentary presence of parties far outside the mainstream. It allows far right figures like Meloni in Italy to exercise disproportionate power relative to their share of the vote.

This latter concern to preclude the disputatious can delete certain topics, such as immigration, from democratic debate. Such suppression rarely works. It drives these issues underground, to be exploited by political chancers and demagogues. Besides, democracy disowns itself if it infantilises the electorate. This is no better than the claim that complicated times demand technocratic government that de-politicises in favour of decision-taking by experts.

In today's world, the nation-state has to come to terms with qualified sovereignty. If the Polish or Hungarian governments decide unilaterally that they won't comply with the EU's norms about democracy and justice, then the EU has to penalise that defiance, perhaps ultimately with their expulsion from membership. The Polish and Hungarian electorate has to then be allowed to have its say. Choices have consequence. You can't have your cake and eat it. Do they want to stay in the EU, and work with others in the club to change any rules they find objectionable, or are they happy to leave? Similarly, if you want a hard Brexit, it's hard luck if you don't like the impact. As the cavalier attitude of the UK's Johnson government to international law demonstrates, trustful relationships among democratic governments can't operate, if one side signs an agreement, on which it is prepared, even has planned, subsequently to renege.

The 'pax' is about peace-making over war-mongering. It concerns less expenditure on military and more on peace studies and conflict resolution as the most effective defence spending. Reference to 'pacts' is an acknowledgement that global collaboration is needed to address global challenges, and more networking and agreement on joint approaches are essential. The African term – *Ubuntu* – suggests that compassion for those closest to us should be nurtured and cherished. But it shouldn't crowd out the stranger in the crowd. The very ties that bind can be the same ones that blind. It is short-sighted to always see the 'other' as a hostile stranger. We need to make treaty beyond the tribe.

Finally, 'facts' is about ensuring that evidence-based and reliable information is transmitted to upgrade civic literacy. An informed public is central to a mature democracy, and this involves more independent public media, well-funded arts and culture, more social accountability of social media, and a good education system. Raising the standard of public debate involves considering opponent's arguments at their highest intellectual articulation, not as 'straw man' versions most easy to demolish. Also, it must recognise that many of the voices that get most heard – like, I have to say, many of the references in this book – come from 'wise guys', and this male domination of discourse throughout history has to cease.

My lax, tax, max, pax, pacts & facts agenda makes for a basic starting point of a radical approach that doesn't need to frighten the horses. Evidence from opinion polls suggests that this kind of programme could win popular approval, if its public benefit is properly explained. We have to keep reminding ourselves that a great many people seem not to be very interested in 'politics'. So the first step for radical parties and movements is to translate these ideas into practical outcomes that can be seen to improve people's everyday lives. That doesn't preclude talking about values, like kindness and compassion, or persuading people of imagined better ways.

The demise of communism squeezed the political spectrum. Mostly, it left the choice to one between mild social reformism and a more privatised and market-driven model. Neither cuts it. Being grateful for small mercies – as we all should be – doesn't mean accepting the crumbs from the table of the powerful and privileged. My notion of radical social democracy is about seats at the table.

But the caution here is what's been said throughout this book. Ideology that offers total answers is totally wrong. That doesn't banish the benefit of idealism, as long as we keep reminding ourselves that we are improvable, but not perfectible. Reformist programmes are less sexy than their revolutionary counterparts, but they usually wear better. In a hyper-fast world, it may serve us well to find ways to slow things down. That's not to excuse complacency over the real emergencies highlighted already. We can't stand idly by, like Nero, while all around literally burns. But in many regards, the secret to making haste slowly is to establish priorities. Frantic multi-tasking is often less efficient than setting clear goals and working through them systematically in order of their priority, and delivering practical results that build a solid foundation for the next stage of improvement.

Agendas for radical change are in plenty supply – just to take three examples of detailed programmes: for the world at large (Piketty's work on equality); for Europe as whole (*A Blueprint for Europe's Just Transition*, which presents 85 policy recommendations for a Green New Deal); and for one country, the UK (the IPPR-established Commission on Economic Justice). I elaborate these in the second volume. There are others. Unquestionably, there's more than enough ideas to consider. But to me, the important thing is that they're set within the ambition for a *New Social Contract*. In the second volume I make detailed reference to how this concept emerged. We now need an updated version. I mention here just some aspects that would need to inform it:

* we can't have a something-for-nothing society. Everyone has something to contribute to the well-being for all. But it's not a uniform donation. Of those to whom much has been given, much is expected. And this will be in

different kinds of currency: volunteer work, in areas like health, education, and environment; for those of us better-off, it may also involve something like 10 percent of income devoted to community and global causes; and for some, it may include a caring role for children or elderly in the family. The key principle is: we are each other's keeper;

- in this way, we need to move from welfare state to welfare society – involving a substantial paradigm shift. At a time, when the push is for greater individualism, re-making this social capital is difficult. Many of us retreat into a relatively closed world of kith and kin. For us, good fences do indeed make good neighbours. The demise of local collectivities, like churches, trade unions, workers' educational organisations, and the like, may seem to have left us with a few close intimates and Netflix. It isn't actually as bad as that. In many places, people are re-discovering 'community' in a new form: walking groups; book clubs; craft guilds; market gardening enthusiasts, yoga classes, among others. These networks may at present have a middle class bias, but that needn't be so, and they can be broadened also into wider social and global concerns;

- many health and social services cannot operate in the old bureaucratic way, as services *for* rather than *with* people. They need to be more personalised and participative. This would include: parental partnerships with schools in co-educating children; lifelong educational vouchers that people can cash in for their learning updates; people participating in local health centres for more preventative, rather than just curative, health care; and re-thinking social care of the elderly in terms of more sharing of responsibility with relatives, rather than substitution for them. Not only should the state stop 'contracting out' the public realm to business as part of a general privatisation of the social, we, as citizens, should stop 'contracting out' our social duties to the state, as part of a general disposition that 'I have a right to my own life' – an expression that can dress up selfishness in the virtuous language of 'human rights';

- such greater social responsibilities would have to be in the context of rethinking the economy, and particulars such as the working week, with more time available for family and community. Instead of proceeding further to economise society, we need to further socialise the economy;

- welfare benefits have to be both more generous and more tied to reciprocal obligation. The poor can be often labelled as the authors of their own misfortune, through selfish and feckless behaviour. Evidence shows that they are much more sinned against than sinning. But to empower and enable them, there have to be more opportunities for learning and skill-enhancement, together with appropriate tax credits, to help those in a position to move from welfare to work. In the past, this has been thought of as a conservative programme – part of a wider agenda to roll back the state. I'm suggesting that it should be the opposite. It should involve an expansive social state, providing a myriad of supportive services, including viable child-care, but one about partnership not paternalism, a way of enabling that is ennobling. Most poor people want the dignity and fulfilment of providing for themselves and family. Instead of talking pejoratively about the dependency culture, we need to create an inter-dependency culture, in which society collaborates with them in a just transition from their current predicament. This is not about the old conservative taunts about the need for more 'self-reliance'. It is about mutual reliance, skewed to help those most in need of support. It says to everyone, whatever their social position, that this is about genuinely replacing the cold hand-out with a warm hand-up. But make no mistake, for all, fair tax and fair dues are the admission price to the Social Contract;

- in re-setting the state, we have to acknowledge where in the past it has got things right and wrong. In post-war planning in the rich world, it improved environmental conditions for many who, across generations, had been consigned to squalor and slum. But in doing so, too often it created large, grim, soulless estates, with minimal creative design, architecture that verged on the brutalist, and with too little consideration of what made for vibrant, mixed-use and mixed-income community. For decades now, we've talked about a new way of place-making that planned with, rather than for, residents. Too little of that talk has met with transformative action;

- all these examples mean that when we re-look at how best to tackle want, ignorance, squalor, idleness, and disease, we need to do so in a framework that (1) accords more human agency and mutual social responsibility in a participative democracy; (2) sees it in global terms of equality, rather than as a social agenda suitable only for the rich world; and (3) locates it in environmental sustainability. The left largely failed to make a democratic welfare society that was tied to global justice and concern for the Earth's habitat. Speaking for myself, I used to regard 'green' issues as interesting, but mostly fringe to fundamental class issues. I was very wrong. And it is in part due to the neglect of people like me that we find ourselves now in a dire situation. Not only can the climate emergency deliver direct fatalities, food insecurity, and forced migration, on a massive scale. It can also pollute our politics. Unless it makes significant commitment to de-carbonisation, China can be castigated as holding humanity hostage, a charge that may 'fossil-fuel' a new Cold War. If world governments continue to promise more than they practice, the scope for risky unilateral geo-engineering responses to regional climate will increase. The gap between so-called cosmopolitans, emphasising the global nature of the challenge, and so-called communitarians, emphasising a self-interested local response, stands to widen. And the chance that some frustrated campaigners get lured into a totalitarian form of 'eco-fascism' cannot be dismissed.

When we look at the grim situation facing many today, and many more tomorrow if we don't get a grip, it's tempting to reduce the choice of persona to either Pangloss, the optimist, or Cassandra, the pessimist. Again, the binary is too tight a boundary. It's more nuanced. We tend to forget that Voltaire's Pangloss was meant as a satirical figure to expose the undue optimism of the Enlightenment about the power of human reason to overcome the dark side of humanity. On the other hand, Cassandra's fate was to have her impeccable prophesies and warnings go unheeded. We should be looking for measured optimism, not fatuous ebullience. Though it's usually wise to consider political bullishness to be bullshit, there are still reasons to be cheerful. Each sunrise brings the prospect of another day, and pastures new. But even new pastures bear both delight and distress.

I'm reminded here of the Leonard Cohen song, *Anthem*. He advises us to forget waiting for the perfect, which too often is the greatest enemy of the good. There is no credible drum for the march of the great revolution set to return us to Eden. There is no Eden. The world is full of faults. But that crack that is there in everything, that's where the light gets in. And we all have light that we don't need to hide behind the bushel. As Cohen says, every heart may cross the border of mistrust to learn to love, but it comes as a refugee. We're all refugees.

And part of that pilgrimage is captured by the poet Brendan Kennelly in his wonderful poem *The Good*, where he talks about the good being those who are vulnerable, who pay little regard to their safety in flight through time and space, luminous amidst the everyday casual venality, embracing their duties of light, always ready to commend, to appreciate that the finest aspects of this world cannot be torn completely, although forever imperilled. By their gift of grace, they reprimand the small-mindedness that parts people from each other. In their fortitude and forbearance, they resist becoming world-weary and cynical, instead staying forever young.

To this manner must we be born. The worst of what we inflict on each other are not 'crimes *against* humanity'. Unfortunately, they are part *of* humanity. If humans do have 'better angels', we need to detect them in an earthly rather than celestial habitat, in practical politics rather than promised utopias. Traversing the burial sites of past utopias reveals the disfigured domains of well-intentioned benevolence. In any case, the assumed heaven of a pristine ordered world would actually be quite hellish. It may appear that our ceaseless yearning robs us of the one thing we yearn for most – contentment amid life's commotion. But since only in death do we truly rest in peace, we are meant to live with unease. Particularly in troubling times, it's remiss to remain untroubled. While I've forsaken faith in the power of traditional prayer, it is the prayer of my namesake – Francis – that often comes to mind in this regard: to be granted the serenity to change the things I can, accept the things I can't, and the wisdom to know the difference between resistance and resignation.

In this, humility is preferable to hubris. Discarding certitude still leaves space for conviction and commitment. Ruefully, it's been often stated that the only certainties are death and taxes. Some of our ultra-billionaires now want to escape both. Their conceit represents a revolt against what makes us human – our mortality and solidarity. We are both blessed and cursed to love most that which is mortal and transient. But our time and love are amongst the few things that actually grow for us, when given away to others.

In this exchange, a narrow sense of identity can be more of a prison than a haven, something that contains rather than liberates. The world is too complex to be reduced to one source of solace or salvation. There are multiple ways to be human, and any political system that disavows that is inclined to create a new servitude.

Faced with so many issues, a new politics starts with agreeing values of the good society, compassionate community, equitable economy, and sustainable environment, while being empowered to deal democratically and peacefully with human disagreement. That is the subject of the second volume under this theme. We can get on each other's goat, without being at each other's throat. And I'm going to let you into the secret of the universe: there *is* no secret of the universe. There is no one path to life's meaning. We must live with its messiness. We must live with paradox. At least, that's *my* best bet. But I could be wrong.

BIBLIOGRAPHY

Abramovitz, M. and Hopkins, T. (1983) Reaganomics and the Welfare State, *The Journal of Sociology & Social Welfare*: 10 (4), Article 4. Available at: https://scholarwo rks.wmich.edu.

Abou-Chadi, T. and Krause, W. (July 2020) The Causal Effect of Radical Right Success on Mainstream Parties' Policy Positions: A Regression Discontinuity Approach... *British Journal of Political Science*. 50 (3) 829–847.

Abulafia, D. (2019) *The Boundless Sea: A Human History of the Oceans*. London: Allen Lane.

Adichie, C.N. (15 June 2021) *It Is Obscene: A True Reflection In Three Parts*. Chimamanda. com Accessed: 25 July 2021.

Advani, A., Burgherr, D., Savage, M. and Summers, A. (April 2022) *The UK's 'Non-doms': Who Are They, What Do They Do, and Where Do They Live?* CAGE Policy Briefing, No. 36. CAGE Warwick University and LSE International Inequalities Institute.

Advani, A., Chamberlain, E., and Summers, A. (December 2020) *A Wealth Tax for the UK: Final Report*. The UK Wealth Tax Commission. London School of Economics and Political Science; University of Warwick; UK Economic and Social Research Council; Atlantic Fellows for Social & Economic Equity; CAGE.

Agarwal, P. (2021) *Sway: Unravelling Unconscious Bias*. London: Bloomsbury Sigma.

Agencies. (13 May 2022) Calling a Man 'Bald' is Sexual Harassment, Employment Tribunal Rules. *The Guardian*.

AI & Robotics Researchers (28 July 2015) *Autonomous Weapons*: Open Letter.

Ali Khan, A. et al (September 2021) *Ethics of AI: A Systematic Literature Review of Principles and Challenges*. 1. https://researchgate.net/publication/Ethics_of_AI_ A_Systematic_Literature_Review_of_Principles_and_Challenges. Accessed: 25 May 2022.

Ali, S. (2013). *Identities and Sense of Belonging of Muslims in Britain: Using Survey Data, Cognitive Survey Methodology, and In-Depth Interviews*; DPhil. University of Oxford. Available online at https://ora.ox.ac.uk/objects/uuid.

All Party Parliamentary Group on British Muslims (2019) *Islamophobia Defined: The Inquiry into a Working Definition of Islamophobia/Anti-Muslim Hatred.* London: UK House of Commons. This report covers the many arguments around definition mentioned in this chapter.

Almond, R.E.A., Grooten M. and Petersen, T. (eds) (2020) *Living Planet Report 2020 - Bending the Curve of Biodiversity Loss.* Gland, Switzerland: WWF.

Amnesty International. *Up to One Million Detained in China's Mass "Re-education" Drive.* https://amnesty.org/en/latest/news/2018/09/china-up-to-one-million-detained/ Accessed: 26 November 2020.

Amnesty International: Death Penalty. https://deathpenaltyinfo.org/facts-and-resea rch/history-of-the-death-penalty. Accessed: 23 April 2021.

Amos, J. (7 April 2022) Tanis: Fossil of Dinosaur Killed In Asteroid Strike Found, Scientists Claim. *BBC News.* https://bbc.co.uk/news/science-environment. Accessed: 8 April 2022.

Anderson, B. (1991) *Imagined Communities: Reflection on the Origins and Spread of Nationalism.* London: Verso.

Anderson, S. (2009) The Golden Rule: Not So Golden Anymore. *Philosophy Now.* Issue 74.

Anti-Defamation League (2013) *Jared Taylor/American Renaissance.* https://adl.org. combating-hate/jared-taylor-extremism-in-america.pdf. Accessed on: 26 June 2020.

Anton, S., Potts, R. and Aiello, L. (July 2014) Evolution of Early *Homo*: An Integrated Biological Perspective. *Science.* 345 (6192), 1236828. DOI: 10.1126/science.1236828. https://science.sciencemag.org/content. Accessed: 1September 2020.

Appiah, K.A. (2018) *The Lies that Bind: Rethinking Identity: Creed, Country, Colour, Class, Culture.* London: Profile Books.

Appiah, K.A. (March/April 2019) The Importance of Elsewhere: in Defence of Cosmopolitanism. *Foreign Affairs.* 98 (2) 20–26.

Applebaum, B. (2010) *Being White, Being Good: White Complicity, White Moral Responsibility, and Social Justice Pedagogy.* New York: Lexington Books.

Asmolov, G. (2018). The Disconnective Power of Disinformation Campaigns. *Journal of International Affairs.* Special Issue 71(1.5): 69–76.

Atlantic Council (April 2022) *Global QE Tracker.* https://atlanticcouncil.org/global-qe-tracker. Accessed: 6 April 2022.

Attenborough, D., with Jonnie Hughes (2020) *A Life on Our Planet: My Witness Statement and a Vision for the Future.* London: Witness Books.

Bailey, R. and Tuby, M.L. (2020) *Ten Global Trends Every Smart Person Should Know: And Many Others You Will Find Interesting.* Washington DC: Cato Institute.

Bajaj, S. (12 August 2022) A Change of Heart. *The Guardian Weekly.*

Ballagan, K., Mortimore, R., and Gottfried, G. (2018) *A Review of Survey Research on Muslims in Britain.* London: Ipsos Mori Social Research Institute.

Barlow, J.P. (February 1996) *A Declaration of the Independence of Cyberspace.* Davos, Switzerland.

Barndt, J. (2007) *Understanding & Dismantling Racism: The Twenty-first Century Challenge to White America.* Minneapolis: MN: Augsburg Fortress.

Bartels, L.M. (2008) *Unequal Democracy: The Political Economy of the New Gilded Age.* Princeton, NJ: Princeton University Press.

Basel Committee on Banking Supervision (October 2021) *Progress Report on Adoption of the Basel Regulatory Framework.* Bank for International Settlements.

Baum, D. (April 2016) Legalize it All: How to Win the War on Drugs. *Harper's Magazine*.

BBC News (I November 2019) *Russia Internet: Law Introducing New Controls Comes Into Force.*

Beard, A. (January-February 2022) Can Big Tech Be Disrupted? Extracted from *Harvard Business Review*. https://hbr.org/2022/01/can-big-tech-be-disrupted. Accessed: 15 May 2022.

Becker, J., Stolberg, S.G., Labaton, S. (20 December 2008) White House Philosophy Stoked Mortgage Bonfire. *The New York Times*.

Bedard, S.J. (2010) Methodological Problems with the Jesus Myth Hypothesis. *Journal of the International Society of Christian Apologetics*. 3(1). 57–66.

Beinart, P. (07/03/2019) Debunking the Myth that Anti-Zionism is Antisemitic. *The Guardian*. https://theguardian.com/news/2019/mar/07/debunking-myth-that-anti-zionism-is-antisemitic. Accessed: 19 August 2020.

Benkler, Y., Faris, R., and Roberts, H. (2018) *Network Propaganda Manipulation, Disinformation, and Radicalization in American Politics*. Oxford: Oxford University Press.

Bennett, C. (24 January 2021) Universities as Source of Truth Compromised. *The Observer*.

Bennett, M., Bustos, D., Pigati, J., et al (24 September 2021) Evidence of Humans in North America During the Last Glacial Maximum. *Science*. 373(6562). 1528–1531.

Birch, J., Ginsburg, S., & Jablonka, E. (2020) Unlimited Associative Learning and the Origins of Consciousness: A Primer and Some Predictions. *Biology & Philosophy*. 35(56) 1–23.

Bischoff, P. (22 July 2020) Surveillance Camera Statistics: Which Cities Have the Most CCTV Cameras? *Comparitech*. https://comparitech.com/vpn-privacy/the-worlds-most-surveilled-cities.

Bloodworth, J. (2016) *The Myth of Meritocracy: Why Working-class Kids Get Working-class Jobs*. London: Biteback Publishing.

Bloomberg. (24 November 2020) *Billionaires Index of the World's Richest People*. Bloomberg.

Boddington, P. (2017) *Towards a Code of Ethics for Artificial Intelligence*. Cham; Switzerland: Springer.

Boggs, C. (1976) *Gramsci's Marxism*. London: Pluto Press.

Bollinger, L.C. (12 June 2019) Free Speech on Campus Is Doing Just Fine, Thank You. *The Atlantic*. https://theatlantic.com/ideas/archive/2019/06/free-speech-crisis-campus-isnt-real. Accessed: 3 November 2021.

Bolotnikova, M. (19 January 2017) Harvard's Economic Diversity Problem. *Harvard Magazine*.

Bonneuil, C. and Fressoz, J-B. (2017) *The Shock of the Anthropocene*. London: Verso.

Bonsignore, T. (14 April 2010) I was Wrong to Let the Banks off the Leash, Gordon Brown Admits. *Citywire*.

Bose, D. (September 2020) The Richest People in America Ranked. *Business Insider*. Oxford University.

Bostrum, N. (2014) *Superintelligence: Paths, Dangers, Strategies*. Oxford: Oxford University Press.

Bottum, J. (2014) *An Anxious Age: The Post-Protestant Ethic and the Spirit of America*. New York: Image.

Bourguignon, F. (2015) *The Globalization of Inequality*. Princeton, N.J.: Princeton University Press.

Borger, J. (28 January 2022) Tick, Tick …Boom? Why We're Closer to Midnight Than Ever. *The Guardian Weekly*.

Bradford, A. (2012) The Brussels Effect. *Northwestern University Law Review*. 107 (533).

Bretherton, L. (2015) *Resurrecting Democracy: Faith, Citizenship, and the Politics of a Common Life*. New York: Cambridge University Press.

Brewer, H. (September 2018) Slavery-entangled Philosophy. *AEON*. https://aeon. co/essays/does-lockes-entanglement-with-slavery-undermine-his-philosophy. Accessed: 30 July 2021.

Brignall, M. (5 February 2021) How Did a Call to Buy Shares in an Ailing US Games Retailer Became a Finance-shaking Mass Movement? *The Guardian Weekly*.

British Virgin Islands Commission of Inquiry (4 April 2022) *Report Of The Commissioner The RT Hon Sir Gary Hickinbottom: Volume 1: Report*. Published on the Authority of the Governor of the Virgin Islands.

BusinessofApps (2022) *Facebook Revenue and Usage Statistics 2022*. https://businessofapps. com/data/facebook-statistics. Accessed: 22 May 2022.

Brown, D. (1991) *Human Universals*. New York: McGraw Hill.

Brown, D. and Barnes, P. (10 February 2020) Labour Leadership: A Century of Ups and Downs in Charts. *BBC News*. Source: House of Commons Library/BBC Research 2020.

Brunt, R. (1989) The Politics of Identity, in Hall, S. and Jacques, M. (eds) *New Times: the Changing Face of Politics in the 1990s*. London: Lawrence & Wishart. 150–159.

Brynjolfsson, E. and McAfee, A. (2014) *The Second Machine Age: Work, Progress and Prosperity in a Time of Brilliant Technologies*. New York: W.W.Norton & Company.

Buckley, C. and Mozur, P. (22 May, 2019) How China Uses High-Tech Surveillance to Subdue Minorities. *The New York Times*.

Buettner, R. and Craig, S. (8 May 2019) Decade in the Red: Trump Tax Figures Show over $1 billion in Business Losses. *The New York Times*.

Bullough, O. (2018) *Moneyland: Why Thieves & Crooks Now Rule the World & How to Take it Back*. London: Profile Books.

Burley, L. (Producer & Director) (2018) *The Bank That Almost Broke Britain*. STV Productions. BBC.

Burrington, I. (20 December 2017) Could Facebook Be Tried for Human-Rights Abuses? *The Atlantic*.

Busby, M. (16 January 2021) James Murdoch Says US Media 'Lies' Unleashed 'Insidious Forces'. *The Guardian*.

Byrne, B. and Shankley, W (2020). in Byrne, B., Alexander, C., Khan, O., Nazroo, J. and Shankley, W. (eds.) (2020) *Ethnicity, Race and Inequality in the UK: State of the Nation*. Bristol: Policy Press. 35–50.

Byrne, B., Alexander, C., Khan, O., Nazroo, J. and Shankley, W. (eds.) (2020) *Ethnicity, Race and Inequality in the UK: State of the Nation*. Bristol: Policy Press.

Camus, R. (2018) *You Will Not Replace Us!* Renaud Camus.

Carrie Chapman Catt Centre for Women and Politics, Archives of Women's Political Communication. Iowa State University. *Speech of Marine Le Pen in her Presidential Campaign Launch, on 9th March 2017.* sourced in https://awpc.cattcenter.iastate.edu/ 2017/09/01/presidential-campaign-launch-march-9-2017. Accessed: 8 June 2020.

Carrington, D. and Taylor, M. (20 May 2022) What Lies Beneath. *The Guardian*.

Casey, L. (2016) *The Casey Review: A Review into Opportunity and Integration*. London: Department for Communities and Local Government.

Chancel, L. (2020) *Unsustainable Inequalities: Social Justice and the Environment*. Cambridge, MA: Harvard University Press.

Chancel, L., Piketty, T., Saez, E., Zucman, G. et al. (2022) *World Inequality Report 2022*, World Inequality Lab. 27.

Chang, C. et al (3 February, 2022) People's Desire To Be In Nature And How They Experience It Are Partially Heritable. *Plos Biology*. https://journals.plos.org/plosbiol ogy/article. Accessed: 18 May 2022.

Channel 4 News Investigations Team (28 September 2020) *Revealed: Trump Campaign Strategy to Deter Millions of Black Americans from Voting in 2016*. Investigations Team: Job Rabkin, Guy Basnett, Ed Howker, Janet Eastham and Heidi Pett. News Production Team: Sola Renner, et al.

Chaplain, C. (9 August 2021) David Cameron 'Made £7.2m in Salary and Bonuses Lobbying for Greensill Capital' i: https://inews.co.uk/news/politics/david-cameron-made-7-2m-in-salary-and-bonuses-lobbying-for-greensill-capital. Accessed: 23 August 2021.

Chesnut, R.A. (2003) *Competitive Spirits: Latin America's New Religious Economy*. New York: Oxford University Press.

Chetty, R., Friedman, J., Saez, E., Turner, N., & Yagan, D. (July 2017) Mobility Report Cards: The Role of Colleges in Intergenerational Mobility. Paper. https://opportun ityinsights.org/wp-content/uploads/2018/03/coll_mrc_paper.pdf. Accessed on: 20 November 2022.

Chi Dao, M., Das, M., Koczan, Z., and Lian, W. (July 2017) *Why Is Labor Receiving a Smaller Share of Global Income? Theory and Empirical Evidence*. IMF Working Paper. 17/169.

Choksi, N. (13 October 2016) Trump Accuses Clinton of Guiding Global Elite Against U.S. Working Class. *The New York Times*. https://nytimes.com/2016/10/14/us/polit ics/trump. Accessed: 8th June 2020.

Christian, D. (2018) *Origin Story: A Big Picture of Everything*. London: Allen Lane.

City of London Local Plan. Proposed Submission Draft (March 2021) *City Plan 2036: Shaping the Future City*. London: City of London Corporation.

Courea, E. (13 July 2021) David Cameron Earned £29,000 a Day as Greensill Lobbyist. *The Times*.

Crutzen, P. (2002) Geology of Mankind. *Nature* 415. 23. https://nature.com; https://doi.org.

Cobham, A. and Janský, P. (2017) *Global Distribution of Revenue Loss from Tax Avoidance: Re-estimation and Country Results*. WIDER Working Paper 2017/55. Helsinki: UNU-WIDER.

Cobham, A., Faccio, T. and FitzGerald, V. (October 2019) *Global Inequalities in Taxing Rights: An Early Evaluation of the OECD tax Reform Proposals*. A Preliminary Draft.

Coeckelbergh, M. (2020) *AI Ethics*. Cambridge MA: MIT Press.

Competition and Markets Authority (July 2020) *Online Platforms and Digital Advertising Market Study: Final Report*: London: CMA.

ComRes poll for the BBC *Today* programme: Interviews with 1,000 Muslims aged 18+, by telephone, 26 January-20 February 2015.

Congressional Budget Office (March 2021) *The 2021 Long-Term Budget Outlook*. https://cbo.gov/publication. Accessed on: 11 April 2022. See also: Committee for a Responsible Federal Budget (4 March 2021) *Analysis of CBO's March 2021 Long-Term Budget Outlook*.

Congressional Budget Office (July 2022) *The 2022 Long-Term Budget Outlook.* https://cbo.gov/publication. Accessed on: 21 November 2022.

Corporate Europe Observatory (23 September 2020) *Big Tech Lobbying.* CEO.

Crenshaw, K. (1989) Demarginalizing the Intersection of Race and Sex: A Black Feminist Critique of Antidiscrimination Doctrine, Feminist Theory and Antiracist Politics, *University of Chicago Legal Forum*: 1989 (1) Article 8. 139–167. Available at: http://chicagounbound.uchicago.edu/uclf/vol1989/iss1/8.

Crutzen, P. (2002) Geology of Mankind. *Nature* 415, 23. www.nature.com; https://doi.org/10.1038/415023a

Crutzen, P. (2006) The Anthropocene in Ehlers, E. & Krafft, T. (eds) *Earth System Science in the Anthropocene.* Berlin: Springer. 13–18.

Darroch, K. (2021) *Collateral Damage: Britain, America and Europe in the Age of Trump.* London: William Collins.

Das, S., Harper, T., and Griffiths, S. (15 March 2020) Taxpayer's Money Helps Beijing Identify Masked Protesters. *The Sunday Times.*

Davenport, C. and Steggerda, M. (1929) *Race Crossing in Jamaica.* New York: Carnegie Institution of Washington.

Davies, W. (20–26 May 2022) Your Own Digital Hell. *New Statesman.*

Davis, R. (2003) *Christian Slaves, Muslim Masters: White Slavery in the Mediterranean, The Barbary Coast, and Italy, 1500–1800.* Basingstoke: Palgrave Macmillan.

Davison, N. (undated) *A Legal Perspective: Autonomous Weapon Systems Under International Humanitarian Law.* A Paper. International Committee Of The Red Cross. file:///C:/Users/Michael/Downloads/autonomous_weapon_systems_under_international_humanitarian_law.pdf. Accessed: 26 May 2022.

Dawkins, R. and Wong, Y. (2004. 2016 updated edition) *The Ancestor's Tale: A Pilgrimage to the Dawn of Life.* London: Weidenfeld & Nicolson.

de Benoist, A. and Champetier, C. (2012) *Manifesto for a European Renaissance.* London: Arktos.

de Souza, V.S. (July 2016) Science and Miscegenation in the Early Twentieth Century: Edgard Roquette-Pinto's Debates and Controversies with US Physical Anthropology. *História, Ciências, Saúde – Manguinhos*, 23(3). Available at: http://scielo.br/hcsm. https://scielo.br/pdf/hcsm/v23n3/en_0104-5970-hcsm-S0104-59702016005000014.pdf.

de Waal, F. (1996) *Good Natured: The Origins of Right and Wrong in Humans and Other Animals.* Cambridge, MA: Harvard University Press.

de Waal, F. (2022) *Different: What Apes Can Teach Us About Gender.* London: Granta.

Dean, C. (October 19, 2007) Nobel Winner Issues Apology for Comments About Blacks. *New York Times.* https://nytimes.com/2007/10/19/science/19watson.html. Accessed: 14 September 2020.

DeepMind (30 Nov 2020) *AlphaFold: a Solution to a 50-year-old Grand Challenge in Biology.* Blog Post Research.

del Rio-Gonzalez, A.M. (June 2021) To Latinx or Not to Latinx: A Question of Gender Inclusivity Versus Gender Neutrality. *American Journal of Public Health.* 111(6): 1018–1021.

Deloitte. (2017) *Predictably Inaccurate: The Prevalence and Perils of Bad Big Data*, available at: https://deloitte.com/insights/us/en/deloitte-review/issue-21/analytics-bad-data-quality.html

Denham Letter: Information Commissioner's Office (IFC) (2 October 2020) *RE: ICO Investigation into Use of Personal Information and Political Influence.* IFC.

Dennett, D. (2006) *Breaking the Spell: Religion as a Natural Phenomenon.* Penguin: London.

Department For Business, Energy and Industrial Strategy (27 May 2020) *Trade Union Membership, UK 1995–2019.* Statistical Bulletin 27. UK Gov.

Department For Digital, Culture, Media and Sport (September 2021) *National AI Strategy.* Command Paper 525. 11. https://assets.publishing.service.gov.uk/governm ent/uploads/system/uploads/attachment_data/file/1020402/National_AI_Strate gy_-_PDF_version.pdf. Accessed: 26 May 2022.

Department For Digital, Culture, Media and Sport (19 April 2022) *Online Safety Bill: Factsheet.* UK Gov.

Department For Equalities (17 March 2022) *Inclusive Britain: Government Response to the Commission on Race and Ethnic Disparities*: Presented to Parliament by the Minister of State for Equalities. Command Paper number: CP 625.

Department For Transport (28 April 2021) *Road Traffic Estimates: Great Britain 2020.* Statistical Release.

de Waal, J.R. (18 November 2021) European Support For Populist Beliefs Declines. *YouGov.* https://yougov.co.uk/topics/international/articles-reports/2021/11/18/ european-support-populist-beliefs-declines. Accessed: 11 May 2022.

Diamond, L. and Plattner, M. (eds) (2016) *Democracy in Decline?* Baltimore: John Hopkins University Press.

Dolan, K. (5 April 2022) America's Ten Richest Billionaires 2022. *Forbes.* https://for bes.com/sites/kerryadolan/2022/04/05/americas-10-richest-billionaires-2022. Accessed: 22 May 2022.

Douglas, I. (2020) *Is Technology Making Us Sick?* London: Thames & Hudson Ltd.

Douglas, K., Sutton, R. et al (April 2019) *Why Do People Adopt Conspiracy Theories, How Are They Communicated, And What Are Their Risks?* Centre for Research and Evidence on Security Threats (CREST).

Dowden, O. (15 May 2021) We Won't Allow Britain's History To Be Cancelled. *The Telegraph Website.* https://telegraph.co.uk/news/2021/05/15/wont-allow-britains- history-cancelled.

Draper, R. (February 2018) They Are Watching You—and Everything Else on the Planet. *National Geographic.* https://nationalgeographic.com/magazine/2018/02/ surveillance-watching-you.

Durbin, A. (29 April 2022) British Virgin Islands: Premier Andrew Fahie Arrested in US Drug Sting. *BBC News.* https://bbc.co.uk/news. Accessed: 16 May 2022.

Durvasula, A. and Sankararaman, S. (Feb 2020) Recovering Signals of Ghost Archaic Introgression in African Populations. *Science Advances* 6(7), eaax5097. DOI: 10.1126/sciadv.aax5097. https://advances.sciencemag.org/content/6/7/eaax5 097. Accessed: 01/09/2020.

Eatwell, R. and Goodwin, M. (2018) *National Populism: The Revolt Against Liberal Democracy.* London: Pelican Books.

Editorial (15 April 2022) Britain's Non-dom Tax Laws: One Rule for the Rich and Another for Everyone Else. *The Guardian Weekly.*

Ebner (2020) *Going Dark: the Secret Social Lives of Extremists.* London: Bloombury.

Economy, E. (2018) *The Third Revolution: Xi Jinping and the New Chinese State. New York:* Oxford University Press.

Eddo-Lodge, R. (2018) *Why I'm No Longer Talking to White People About Race.* London: Bloomsbury Publishing.

Ehrlich, P. (1968) *The Population Bomb.* New York: Buccaneer Books.

Eisinger, J., Ernsthausen, J., and Kiel, P. (2021) The Secret IRS Files: Trove of Never-Before-Seen Records Reveal How the Wealthiest Avoid Income Tax. *ProPublica.* https://propublica.org/article/the-secret-irs-files-trove-of-never-before-seen-reco rds-reveal-how-the-wealthiest-avoid-income-tax. Accessed: 17 June 2021.

Emmerson, C. and Stockton, I. (October 2022) *Outlook for the Public Finances.* Report R220. London: IFS.

EU Parliament Press Statement (24 March 2022) *Deal on Digital Markets Act: EU rules to Ensure Fair Competition and More Choice For Users.* https://europarl.europa.eu/news/ en/press-room/deal-on-digital-markets-act-ensuring-fair-competition-and-more-choice-for-users. Accessed: 23 May 2022.

European Commission (2018) *Communication of 25 April 2018 and 7 December 2018 (COM(2018)237 and COM(2018)795).* Brussels: European Commission.

European Commission (2020) *A Europe Fit for the Digital Age: Empowering People with a New Generation of Technologies.* Brussels: European Commission.

European Commission (February 2020) *Shaping Europe's Digital Future.* Brussels: European Commission.

European Commission Press Release (20 March 2019) *Antitrust: Commission Fines Google €1.49 billion for Abusive Practices in Online Advertising.* Brussels: European Commission.

Evola, J. (1995 edition) *Revolt Against the Modern World.* Rochester, Vermont: Inner Traditions International.

Evola, J. (translated by J. Godwin & C. Fontana) (2003 edition) *Ride the Tiger: a Survival Manual for the Aristocrats of the Soul.* Rochester, Vermont: Inner Traditions International.

Eze, E.C. (1997 b) *Postcolonial African Philosophy: A Critical Reader.* Oxford: Blackwell.

Fair Tax. *How Do Companies Avoid Tax?* https://fairtaxmark.net/wp-content/uploads/ 2014/01/How-Companies-Avoid-Tax.pdf. Accessed: 17 March 2021.

Fair Tax Mark (December 2019) *The Silicon Six and Their $100 Billion Global Tax Gap.* Manchester: Fair Tax Mark.

Faye, G. (2012) *Convergence of Catastrophes.* United Kingdom: Arktos Media Ltd.

Federal Trade Commission (24 July 2019) *FTC Imposes $5 billion Penalty and Sweeping New Privacy Restrictions on Facebook.* Washington DC: FTC.

Federal Communications Commission (FCC) (Updated: Tuesday, 20 October 2020) *Communications Assistance for Law Enforcement Act.* Washington DC: FCC.

Field, J. (2018) *Is Capitalism Working?* London: Thames & Hudson.

Figliola, P.M. (updated: 8 June 2007) *Digital Surveillance: The Communications Assistance for Law Enforcement Act.* Washington DC: Congressional Research Service.

Financial Services Authority Board (December 2011) *The Failure of the Royal Bank of Scotland: Financial Services Authority Board Report.* 254. FSAB.

Finlayson, C. (2009) *The Humans Who Went Extinct. Why Neanderthals Died Out and We Survived.* Oxford: Oxford University Press.

Flynn, J. (2012) *Are We Getting Smarter? Rising IQ in the Twenty-First Century.* Cambridge: Cambridge University Press.

Flynn, J. (2016) *Does Your Family Make You Smarter? Nature, Nurture and Human Autonomy.* Cambridge: Cambridge University Press.

Foa, R.S., Klassen, A., Slade, M., Rand, A. and Williams, R. (2020) *The Global Satisfaction with Democracy Report 2020.* Cambridge UK: Centre for the Future of Democracy.

Forbes (2 June 2006) A Loophole For Poor Mr Paulson. *Forbes.* https://forbes.com/2006/06/01/paulson-tax-loophole-cx_jh_0602paultax.html. Accessed: 3 November 2021.

Forbes Advisor (19 January 2022) *Quantitative Easing Explained....*https://forbes.com/advisor/investing/quantitative-easing-qe. Accessed: 4 April 2022.

Foroohar, R. (2019) *Don't Be Evil: How Big Tech Betrayed its Founding Principles – and All of Us.* New York: Currency.

Fourquet, J. (28 April 2022) What the Presidential Election Really Revealed About Fractured France. *The Guardian.*

Francois, S. (2019) Guillaume Faye and Archeofuturism in Sedgwick, M. (ed) *Key Thinkers of the Radical Right: Behind the New Threat to Liberal Democracy.* Oxford: Oxford University Press. 91–101.

Frazer, G.J. (1890. 2008 edition) *The Golden Bough: A Study in Magic and Religion.* London: Forgotten Books.

Freire, P. (1970. 1993 edition. translated by Ramos, M.B.) *Pedagogy of the Oppressed.* London: Penguin Books.

Frenkel, S., Casey, N., and Mozur, P. (14 January 2018) In Some Countries, Facebook's Fiddling Has Magnified Fake News. *The New York Times.*

Friedrich, J., Ge, M., and Pickens, A. (10 December 2020) *This Interactive Chart Shows Changes in the World's Top Ten Emitters.* World Resources Institute. https://wri.org/insights/interactive-chart-shows-changes-worlds-top-10-emitters. Accessed on: 18 September 2021.

Fritz, S.M. (2019) *Our Human Herds: The Theory of Dual Morality.* (edited by Denise Morel). Indianapolis: Dog Ear Publishing.

Fry, H. (2018) *Hello World: Being Human in the Age of Algorithms.* New York: W.W. Norton.

Fry, S. (2018) *Mythos: The Greek Myths Retold.* London: Penguin Books.

Fukuyama, F. (2018) *Identity: Contemporary Identity Politics and the Struggle for Recognition.* London: Profile Books.

Fuller, R. (2019) *In Defence of Democracy.* Cambridge: Polity Press.

Fuller, R., Landrigan, P. et al (17 May 2022) Pollution and Health: A Progress Update. *The Lancet Planetary Health.* https://thelancet.com/journals/lanplh/article. Accessed: 30 May 2022.

Furedi, F. (2021) *Democracy Under Siege: Don't Let Them Lock It Down.* Hampshire: Zero Books.

Furman Review (2019) *Unlocking Digital Competition.* Stigler Center: Committee on Digital Platforms Final Report.

Future of Humanity Institute (February 2018) *The Malicious Use of Artificial Intelligence: Forecasting, Prevention, and Mitigation.* Future of Humanity Institute; University of Oxford; Centre for the Study of Existential Risk; Centre for a New American Security; Electronic Frontier Foundation; and Open AI. Accessed: 3 November 2021.

fxssi (November 2020) Top 10 World's Most Valuable Technology Companies in 2020. *fxssi.* https://fxssi.com/most-valuable-tech-companies.

Galbraith, J.K. (2020) Economics and the Climate Catastrophe. *Globalizations.* DOI: 10.1080/14747731.2020.1807858. Accessed: 5 April 2021.

Galston, W. and Kamarck, E. (September 1989) *The Politics of Evasion. Progressive Policy Institute (PPI)*. 2. https://progressivepolicy.org/wp-content/uploads/2010/01/Politics_of_Evasion.pdf. Accessed: 19 March 2022.

Galston, W. and Kamarck, E. (February 2022) *The New Politics of Evasion: How Ignoring Swing Voters Could Reopen the Door for Donald Trump and Threaten American Democracy*. Progressive Policy Institute (PPI). https://progressivepolicy.org/wp-content/uploads/2010/01/Politics_of_Evasion.pdf. Accessed: 19 March 2022.

Galton, F. (1869) *Hereditary Genius: An Inquiry into its Laws and Consequences*. London: Macmillan and Co.

Ganti, T. (2003) *The Principles of Life*. Oxford: Oxford University Press.

Ghosh, A. (2016) *The Great Derangement: Climate Change and the Unthinkable*. London: University of Chicago Press.

Ginsburg, S. and Jablonka, E. (2019) *The Evolution of the Sensitive Soul: Learning and the Origins of Consciousness*. Cambridge MA: MIT Press.

Giorgos, H. (July 13, 2020) A Deeply Provincial View of Free Speech. *The Atlantic*.

Global Alliance for Tax Justice (GATJ); Public Services International (PSI); Tax Justice Network (TJN) (November 2021) *The State of Tax Justice 2021*. Bristol: GATJ; PSI; TJN.

Global Footprint Network (25 April 2019) *Humanity's Ecological Footprint Contracted Between 2014–2016*. https://footprintnetwork.org/2019/04/25/press-release-humanitys-ecological-footprint-contracted-between-2014-and-2016. Accessed: 3 November 2021.

Global Network Against Food Crises (2022) *2022 Global Report on Food Crises*. New York: United Nations.

Goldstick, J., Cunningham, R., and Carter, P. (19 May 2022) Current Causes of Death in Children and Adolescents in the United States. *The New England Journal of Medicine*. 386:1955–1956.

Goodman, J. (2021) Nuclear Weapons Explained in Numbers. *BBC Reality Check*. https://bbc.co.uk/news/av/world. Accessed: 27 September 2021.

Gordon Brown's speech to the annual conference of the Confederation of British Industry in London November 28 2005. The full speech can be found at: http://hmtreasury. gov.uk/better_regulation_action_plan.htm

Gouldner, A. (Winter 1962) Anti-Minotaur: The Myth of a Value-Free Sociology. *Social Problems*. 9(3). 199–13.

Gorvett, Z. (6 September 2022) How Many People Can Earth Handle? *BBC Future*. https://bbc.com/future/article/20220905-is-the-world-overpopulated. Accessed on: 7 October 2022.

Graeber, D. and Wengrow, D. (2021) *The Dawn of Everything: A New History of Humanity*. London: Allen Lane.

Graham, B. (26 July 2020) Tom Cotton Calls Slavery 'Necessary Evil' in Attack on New York Times. 1619 Project. *The Guardian*.

Grant, M. (1916) *The Passing of the Great Race*. New York: Charles Scribner's Sons.

Gray, J. (11–17 June 2021) China's Covid Cover-Up? *New Statesman*.

Greenberg, A. (13 October 2014) These Are the Emails Snowden Sent to First Introduce His Epic NSA Leaks. *Wired*. https://wired.com/2014/10/snowdens-first-emails-to-poitras/ Accessed: 26/11/2020.

Greene, J. (2015) *Moral Tribes: Emotion, Reason, and the Gap Between Us and Them*. London: Atlantic Books.

Greenspan, Snow Hearing on Financial Crisis. *You Tube*. https://youtube.com/watch?v=4QIkysmrH2Y. Accessed: 28 July 2021.

Griffith, J. (2019) *Freedom: the End of the Human Condition*. Australia: Fedmex Pty Ltd.

Haidt, J. (2013) *The Righteous Mind: Why Good People Are Divided by Politics and Religion*. London: Penguin Books.

Hakl, H. (translated by J. Godwin) (2019) Julius Evola and Tradition, in Sedgwick, M. (ed) *Against the Modern World: Traditionalism and the Secret Intellectual History of the Twentieth Century*. Oxford: Oxford University Press.

Hall, S. (1992) The Question of Cultural Identity, in Hall, S., Held, D., and McGrew, T. (eds.) *Modernity and its Futures*. Cambridge: Polity Press.

Halstead, J. et al (2017) *Existential Risk: Diplomacy and Governance*. Global Priorities Project. Future of Humanity Institute, University of Oxford and Ministry for Foreign Affairs of Finland.

Hammond, S. (6 November 2020) Democrats Beware: the Republicans Will Soon Be the Party of the Working Class. *The Guardian*.

Han, R. (2018) *Contesting Cyberspace in China: Online Expression and Authoritarian Resilience*. New York: Columbia University Press.

Harrabin, R. (18 September 2021) Climate Change: Should Green Campaigners Put More Pressure on China to Slash Emissions? *BBC*. https://bbc.co.uk/news/science-environment. Accessed: 18 September 2021.

Harris, J. (14 March 2021) The Conservatives are Now the Party of England. Changing That Will be Hard. *The Guardian*.

Harris, S. (2014) *Waking Up: Searching for a Spirituality Without Religion*. London: Black Swan.

Harris, S. and Nawaz, M. (2015) *Islam and the Future of Tolerance: a Dialogue*. Cambridge, Massachusetts: Harvard University Press.

Hatton, C. (October 2021) *China: Big Spender or Loan Shark?* (October 2021) *BBC*. https://bbc.co.uk/news/world-asia-china. Accessed: 5 October 2021.

Heathershaw, J., Cooley, A., Mayne, T., Michel, C., Prelec, T., Sharman, J. and Soares de Oliveira, R. (December 2021) *The UK's Kleptocracy Problem: How Servicing Post-Soviet Elites Weakens the Rule of Law*. Research Paper. Russia and Eurasia Programme. London: Chatham House.

Heine, J., and Thakur, R. (Eds.) (2011) *The Dark Side of Globalization*. Tokyo/New York/Paris: United Nations University Press.

Helderman, R.S. and Cohen, J. (29 August 2012) As Republican Convention Emphasizes Diversity, Racial Incidents Intrude. *The Washington Post*. https://washingtonpost.com/politics/2012/08/29. Accessed: 18 March 2022.

Hellmann, T., Schmidt, P., and Heller, S.M. (2019) *Social Justice in the EU and OECD: Index Report 2019*.

Helmore, E. (15 May 2022) Buffalo Shooting: Teenage Accused of Killing 10 in 'Racist' Supermarket Attack. *The Observer*.

Henderson, C. (Updated 5:36 AM EST Dec 18, 2019) 'Rosanna Arquette slammed for saying she 'feels so much shame' over being white, privileged'. *USA Today*. https://eu.usatoday.com/story/entertainment/celebrities/2019/08/08/rosanna-arquette-feels-so-much-shame-over-being-white-privileged/1962475001/ Accessed: 30 July 2020.

Henry, J.S. (July 2010) *The Price of Offshore Revisited: New Estimates for 'Missing' Global Private Wealth, Income, Inequality and Lost Taxes*. Tax Justice Network & James S. Henry.

Herrnstein, R. and Murray, C. (1994) *The Bell Curve*. New York: Simon & Schuster.

High-level Expert Group on Artificial Intelligence (April 2019) *Ethics Guidelines for Trustworthy A1*. Brussels: European Commission.

Hirsi Ali, A. (2015) *Heretic: Why Islam Needs a Reformation Now.* New York: Harper.

HM Treasury, *HM Treasury Annual Report and Accounts, 2010–11* (July 2011) Certificate and Report of the Comptroller and Auditor General, HC 984. https://assets.publish ing.service.gov.uk/government/uploads/system/uploads/attachment_data/file/221 559/annual_report_accounts140711.pdf. Accessed: 3 November 2021.

Hobsbawm, E. (1990) *Nations and Nationalism Since 1780.* Cambridge: Cambridge University Press.

Hopkins, K. (21 October 2009) Public Must Learn to 'Tolerate the Inequality' of Bonuses, Says Goldman Sachs Vice-Chairman. *The Guardian.*

House Committee on the Judiciary. (2019–2020) *Online Platforms and Market Power.* https://judiciary.house.gov/online-platforms-and-market-power. Accessed: 3 November 2021.

House of Commons Digital, Culture, Media and Sport Committee (18 February 2019) *Disinformation and 'fake news': Final Report.* London: House of Commons.

House of Commons Treasury Committee (24 January 2008) *The Run on the Rock. Fifth Report of Session 2007–08. Volume I.* London: The Stationery Office Limited.

House of Commons Treasury Committee (October 2012) *The FSA's Report into the Failure of RBS. Fifth Report of Session 2012–13.* London: The Stationery Office Limited.

House of Lords Economic Affairs Committee (16 July 2021) 1st Report of Session 2021–22 HL Paper 42 *Quantitative Easing: a Dangerous Addiction?*

House of Lords Library (11 November 2021) *In Focus: Quantitative Easing.* House of Lords Library.

Huang, K., Greene, J.D., and Bazerman, M. (26 November 2019) Veil-of-Ignorance Reasoning Favors the Greater Good. *PNAS.* https://doi.org/10.1073/pnas. Accessed: 28 July 2021.

Hublin, J.J., Ben-Ncer, A., Bailey, S. *et al.* (2017) New Fossils from Jebel Irhoud, Morocco and the Pan-African Origin of *Homo sapiens. Nature* 546, 289–292.

Hughes, C. (9 May, 2019) It's Time to Break Up Facebook. The Privacy Project. *The New York Times.*

Human Rights Watch (February 2018) *China: Big Data Fuels Crackdown in Minority Region.* https://hrw.org/news/2018/02/26/china-big-data-fuels-crackdown-minor ity-region. Accessed: 3 November 2021.

Hunt-Grubbe, C. (14 October 2007) The Elementary DNA of Dr Watson. *Sunday Times Magazine.* https://thetimes.co.uk/article/the-elementary-dna-of-dr-watson-gllb6w2vpdr. Accessed: 14 September 2020.

Huntington, S. (1997) *The Clash of Civilizations and the Remaking of World Order.* London: Simon & Schuster.

ICM Survey of Muslims for Policy Exchange (2016) *Interviews with 3,040 Muslims aged 18+, Conducted Face-to-Face Across Great Britain Between 19 May -23 July 2016.* ICM.

Igbal, N. (21 Sep 2019) Birmingham School Row: This is Made Out to Be Just Muslims v. Gays. It's Not. *The Guardian.* https://theguardian.com/uk-news/2019/sep/21/bir mingham-anderton-park-primary-school-row-parents-teachers-demonstrators. Accessed: 24 August 2020.

Independent High-level Expert Group on Artificial Intelligence (June 2019) *Policy and Investment Recommendations for Trustworthy AI.* Brussels: European Commission.

Independent High-Level Expert Group On Artificial Intelligence Set Up By The European Commission (17 July 2020) *Shaping Europe's Digital Future: Assessment List for Trustworthy Artificial Intelligence (ALTAI).* Brussels: European Commission.

Information Commission's Office (ICO) (23 May 2022) *ICO Fines Facial Recognition Database Company Clearview AI Inc More Than £7.5 Million And Orders UK Data To Be Deleted.* London: ICO.

Information Commissioner's Office (November 2020) *Audits of Data Protection Compliance by UK Political Parties. Summary Report.* London: ICO.

Institute for Democracy and Electoral Assistance (IDEA) (2022) *Global State of Democracy Report 2021: Building Resilience in a Pandemic Era.* IDEA.

Institute of Fiscal Studies (October 2021) *Autumn Budget and Spending Review 2021.* https://ifs.org.uk/budget-2021. Accessed: 28 October 2021.

Intergovernmental Science-Policy Platform on Biodiversity and Ecosystem Services (IPBES) (2019) *Summary for Policymakers of the Global Assessment Report on Biodiversity and Ecosystems Services.* Bonn: IPBES.

International Consortium of Investigative Journalists (ICIJ) (3 October 2021) *Offshore Havens and Hidden Riches of World Leaders and Billionaires Exposed in Unprecedented Leak.* Washington: ICIJ. https://icij.org/investigations/pandora-papers/global-investigation-tax-havens-offshore. Accessed: 16 October 2021.

International Consortium of Investigative Journalists (ICIJ) (8 February 2015) *Banking Giant HSBC Sheltered Murky Cash Linked to Dictators and Arms Dealers.* https://icij.org/investigations/swiss-leaks/banking-giant-hsbc-sheltered-murky-cash-linked-dictators-and-arms-dealers/ Accessed: 21 March 2021.

International Holocaust Remembrance Alliance (IHRA) (2016) *Plenary in Bucharest: Working Definition of Anti-Semitism.* https://web.archive.org/web/2018082 5032144/https://www.holocaustremembrance.com/sites/default/files/press_releas e_document_antisemitism.pdf. Accessed: 3 November 2021.

International Labour Organisation; Organisation for Economic Co-operation and Development; with contributions from International Monetary Fund and World Bank Group (2015) *The Labour Share in G20 Economies.* Geneva: ILO.

International Labour Organisation (2020) *World Employment and Social Outlook: Trends 2020.* Geneva: ILO.

International Labour Organisation (ILO) (2022) *World Employment and Social Outlook: Trends 2022.* Geneva: ILO.

IPCC (2019): *IPCC Special Report on the Ocean and Cryosphere in a Changing Climate.* New York: United Nations Foundation.

IPCC (2019) *Climate Change and Land: An IPCC Special Report on Climate Change, Desertification, Land Degradation, Sustainable Land Management, Food Security, and Greenhouse Gas Fluxes in Terrestrial Ecosystems.* New York: United Nations Foundation.

IPCC (2021) *Summary for Policymakers. In: Climate Change 2021: The Physical Science Basis. Contribution of Working Group I to the Sixth Assessment Report of the Intergovernmental Panel on Climate Change* [Masson-Delmotte, V., P. Zhai, A. Pirani, et al (eds.)]. Cambridge University Press. In Press.

Irvine, P., Emanuel, K., He, J., Horowitz, L., Vecchi, G. & Keith, D. (April 2019) Halving Warming With Idealized Solar Geoengineering Moderates Key Climate Hazards. *Nature Climate Change.* 9. 295–299.

Janus Henderson Investors (17 February 2020) *Global Dividends Rose to New Record in 2019,Though the Pace of Growth Slowed Compared to Last Year.* https://janushender son.com/en-gb/media/press-releases/global-dividends-rose-to-new-record-in-2019-though-the-pace-of-growth-slowed-compared-to-last-year. Accessed: 30 March 2021.

Jobin, A., Ienca, M. & Vayena, E. (2019) The Global Landscape of AI Ethics Guidelines. *Nat Mach Intell* 1, 389–399.

Johnston, M. (9 September 2020) 10 Most Profitable Companies in the World. *Investopedia.* https://investopedia.com/the-world-s-10-most-profitable-companies.

Johnston, M. (fact-checked by Eichler, R.) (updated: 4 March 2022) Biggest Companies in the World by Market Cap. *Investopedia.* https://investopedia.com/biggest-compan ies-in-the-world-by-market-cap. Accessed on: 22 May 2022.

Joseph (Sir Keith) Speech at Edgbaston: *Our Human Stock is Threatened.* (19 October 1974) Grand Hotel, Edgbaston, Birmingham. Source: CCOPR 509/74.

Joseph, J. (2004) *The Gene Illusion: Genetic Research in Psychiatry and Psychology Under the Microscope.* New York: Algora Publishing.

Joseph, J. (2015) *The Trouble with Twin Studies: A Reassessment of Twin Research in the Social and Behavioral Sciences.* New York: Routledge.

Jupp, D. (2019) *A Gift for Treason: The Cultural Marxist Assault on Western Civilization.* Daniel Jupp.

Kang, C. and Vogel, K. (5 June 2019) Tech Giants Amass a Lobbying Army for an Epic Washington Battle. *The New York Times.*

Kant, I. On Different Races in Eze, E.C. (ed) (1997 a) *Race and the Enlightenment: A Reader.* Oxford: Blackwell. 38–48.

Kaufmann, E. (2019) *Whiteshift: Populism, Immigration and the Future of White Majorities.* London: Penguin.

Keane, J. (2016) *Money, Capitalism and the Slow Death of Social Democracy.* https://johnke ane.net/money-capitalism-and-the-slow-death-of-social-democracy. Accessed: 7 April 2021.

Kelton, S. (2020) *The Deficit Myth: Modern Monetary Theory and How to Build a Better Economy.* London: John Murray.

Kiernan, B. (2003) The Demography of Genocide in South east Asia: The Death Tolls in Cambodia, 1975–79, and East Timor, 1975–80. *Critical Asian Studies.* 35:4 (2003), 585–597. 587.

Klein, J. (1989 edition) *A Commentary on Plato's Meno.* Chicago: The University of Chicago Press.

Klein, N. (2019) *On Fire: the (Burning) Case for a Green New Deal.* London: Simon & Schuster.

Knowles, E. (ed.) (1999). *The Oxford Dictionary of Quotations.* 5th ed. Oxford: Oxford University Press.

Krause, W. et al (2019) *Does Accommodation Work? Mainstream Party Strategies and the Success of Radical Right Parties.* https://almendron.com/tribuna/wp-content/uploads/ 2019/09/krause-cohen-abouchadi-2019.pdf.

Krelle, H. and Tallack, C. (23 March 2021) *One Year On: Three Myths About COVID-19 that the Data Proved Wrong.* The Health Foundation.

Kurzweil, R. (2005) *The Singularity is Near.* New York: Viking.

Kühne, K., Bartsch, N., Tate, R.D., Higson, J., and Habet, A. (July 2022) Carbon Bombs: Mapping Key Fossil Fuel Projects. *Energy Policy.* Vol. 166. https://reader. elsevier.com/reader/sd/pii. Accessed: 27 May 2022.

Labour Together (2021) *Election Review 2019: Key Findings and Summary Recommendations.* https://electionreview.labourtogether.uk. Accessed: 7 April 2021.

Lammy Review (September 2017) *An Independent Review into the Treatment of, and Outcomes for, Black, Asian and Minority Ethnic Individuals in the Criminal Justice System.* Gov.UK.

Lamont, M., Yun Park, B. and Ayala-Hurtado, E. (November 2017) Trump's Electoral Speeches and His Appeal to the American White Working Class. *The British Journal of Sociology*. 68(S1). S153–S180.

Lanier, J. (2019) *Ten Arguments for Deleting Your Social Media Accounts Right Now*. London: Bodley Head.

Larsen, C. A. (2013) *The Rise and Fall of Social Cohesion: The Construction and Deconstruction of Social Trust in the US, UK, Sweden and Denmark*. Oxford: Oxford University Press.

Laruelle, M. (22 October 2021) Disillusioned With Democracy: A Conceptual Introduction to Illiberalism. *Institut Montaigne*. https://institutmontaigne.org/en/blog/disillusioned-democracy-conceptual-introduction-illiberalism. Accessed: 11 May 2022.

Lazar, M. (11 December 2020) 2020: A Turning Point for European Populists? *Institut Montaigne*. https://institutmontaigne.org/en/blog/2020-turning-point-european-populists. Accessed: 11 May 2022.

Levin, B. (6 April 2021) Mitch Mc Connell Doesn't Have a Problem with Corporations Getting Involved in Politics When He's Suckling at the Corporate Teat. *Vanity Fair*.

Levitsky, S. and Ziblatt, D. (2018) *How Democracies Die: What History Reveals About Our Future*. New York: Penguin.

Levy, F. and Murnane, R. (2004) *The New Division of Labour: How Computers are Creating the Next Job Market*. Princeton, N.J.: Princeton University Press.

Levy, J. and Thompson, W. (2010), *Causes of War*. Malden, MA: Wiley-Blackwell.

Lewis, S. and Maslin, M. (2018) *The Human Planet: How We Created the Anthropocene*. London: Penguin.

Lewontin, R. (1991) *Biology as Ideology: The Doctrine of DNA*. New York: HarperCollins Publishers.

LexisNexis (September 2021) *Top 50 Banks in the World*. LexisNexis.

Lilla, M. (2017) *The Once and Future Liberal: After Identity Politics*. New York; HarperCollins.

Lind, M. (2020) *The New Class War: Saving Democracy from the Metropolitan Elite*. London: Atlantic Books.

Lingoed-Thomas, J. (10 October 2021) Outrage Over £125m Bonuses for Staff at UK's 'Failing' Financial Watchdog. *The Observer*.

Little, B. (30 July 2018; updated: 27 September 2018) 7 Revealing Nixon Quotes From His Secret Tapes. *History*. https://history.com/news/nixon-secret-tapes-quotes-scandal-watergate. Accessed: 6 October 2021.

Lowell, H. (26 April 2022) Marjorie Taylor Greene Texted Trump Chief of Staff Urging Martial Law to Overturn 2020 Election. *The Guardian*.

Lucas, D. (2019) Measuring the Cost of Bailouts. *Annual Review of Financial Economics*. 11: 85–108. *doi:10.1146/annurev-financial-110217-022532*.

Luce, E. (2017) *The Retreat of Western Liberalism*. London: Little, Brown.

Luttig M. (2013) The Structure of Inequality and Americans' Attitudes Toward Redistribution. *Public Opinion Quarterly*. 77(3): 811–821.

Lutz, W., Sanderson, W.C., and Scherbov, S. (2008) The Coming Acceleration of Global Population Ageing. *Nature*. 451(7179): 716–719.

Lutz, W., Butz, W., and Samir, K.C. (eds.) Executive Summary: *World Population and Human Capital in the Twenty-First Century*. Oxford: Oxford University Press.

Lyotard, J-F. (1984) *The Postmodern Condition: A Report on Knowledge.* Manchester: Manchester University Press.

Macpherson, C.B. (1962: 2011 edition) *The Political Theory of Possessive Individualism: Hobbes to Locke.* Oxford: Oxford University Press.

Macpherson, W. (February 1999) *The Stephen Lawrence Inquiry Report.* Cm 4262-I. 6.34. https://assets.publishing.service.gov.uk/government/uploads/system/uploads/atta chment_data/file/277111/4262.pdf.

Madrigal, A. (12 October 2017) What Facebook Did to American Democracy and Why It was so Hard to See it Coming. *The Atlantic.*

Maher, B. (10 August 2019) Past & Furious. Real Time with Bill Mayer. *HBO.* https://youtube.com. Accessed: 30 July 2020.

Maher, B. (28 September 2019) White Shame. Real Time with Bill Mayer. *HBO.* https://youtube.com. Accessed: 29 July 2020.

Mair, P. (2013) *Ruling the Void: The Hollowing of Western Democracy.* London: Verso.

Majority Staff Report and Recommendations (2020) *Investigation of Competition in Digital Markets.* Washington: US House of Representatives.

Malik, K. (2014) *The Quest For A Moral Compass: A Global History of Ethics.* London: Atlantic Books.

Malik, K. (4 November 2018) Myths About Shared Culture Have No Place in the Citizenship Debate. *The Observer.*

Malik, K. (24 January 2019) Antisemites Use the Language of Anti-Zionism: The Two are Distinct. *The Observer.*

Malik, K. (31 January 2021) An Uprising Against Wall Street? Hardly. GameStop was about the Absurdity of the Stock Market. *The Observer.*

Manavis, S. (27 August-2 September 2021) The Problem With 'Incel' Discourse. *New Statesman.*

Manjoo, F. (9 October 2019) Dealing With China Isn't Worth the Moral Cost. *The New York Times.*

Marciano, A. (2019) Reframing Biometric Surveillance: From a Means of Inspection to a Form of Control. *Ethics and Information Technology.* 21. 127–136.

Maringe, C., Spicer, J., Morris, M., Purushotham, A., Nolte, E., Sullivan, R., Bernard Rachet, B., and Aggarwal, A. (August 2020) *The Impact of the COVID-19 Pandemic on Cancer Deaths Due to Delays in Diagnosis in England, UK: a National, Population-based, Modelling Study.* https://thelancet.com/oncology 21. 1023–1034. 1031.

Marr, A. (2007) *A History of Modern Britain.* London: Macmillan.

Marx, K. On The Jewish Question (1843) in Tucker, R. (ed.) (1978) *The Marx-Engels Reader.* New York: Norton & Company. 26–46.

Masters, B. (27 July 2020) Goldman Has Done it Again with its Malaysia Deal. *Financial Times.*

Mathieu, E., Ritchie, H., Ortiz-Ospina, E. et al. (2021) *A Global Database of COVID-19 Vaccinations.* Nat Hum Behav. Our World in Data.

McGregor, N. (2018) *Living With the Gods: On Beliefs and Peoples.* London: Penguin Books.

McGregor-Smith Review (2017) *Race in the Workplace.* https://assets.publishing.service. gov.uk/government/uploads/system/uploads/attachment_data/file/594336/race-in-workplace-mcgregor-smith-review.pdf.

McWhorter, J. (2000. 2001 edition) *Losing the Race: Self-Sabotage in Black America.* New York: HarperCollins.

Mian, A., Straub, L., and Sufi, A. (24 January 2021) Indebted Demand. *Quarterly Journal of Economics*. 136 (4). 2243–2307. Publisher's Version. https://scholar.harvard.edu/str aub/publications/indebted-demand. Accessed: 17 May 2022.

Milmo, D. (15 October 2021) The Woman Who Stood Up To Facebook. *The Guardian Weekly*.

Ministry of Foreign Affairs of the People's Republic of China (19 October 2020) *Factsheet on Environmental Damage by the US*. https://fmprc.gov.cn/mfa_eng/wjbxw/t1824980.shtml. Accessed: 3 November 2021.

Monbiot, G. (31 October 2011) The Medieval, Unaccountable Corporation of London is Ripe for Protest. *The Guardian*.

Monbiot, G. (26 August 2020) Population Panic Lets Rich People off the Hook for the Climate Crisis They are Fuelling. *The Guardian*. https://theguardian.com/commen tisfree/2020/aug/26/panic-overpopulation-climate-crisis-consumption-environm ent. Accessed: 20 October 2020.

Moore, J. (ed) (2016) *Anthropocene or Capitalocene? Nature, History and the Crisis of Capitalism*. Oakland, CA: PM Press.

Morland, P. (2019) *The Human Tide: How Population Shaped the Modern World*. London: John Murray.

Mozur, P. and Clark, D. (22 November, 2020) China's Surveillance State Sucks Up Data. U.S. Tech Is Key to Sorting It. *The New York Times*. https://nytimes.com/2020/11/22/technology/china-intel-nvidia-xinjiang.html. Accessed: 3 November 2021.

Mozur, P. and Wong, E. (8 October, 2019) By Taking Aim at Chinese Tech Firms, Trump Signals a Strategy Shift. *The New York Times*.

Mudde, C. (2019) *The Far Right Today*. Cambridge: Polity Press.

Mudde, C. and Kaltwasser, C. (2012) Populism and (liberal) Democracy: a framework for analysis. in Mudde, C. & Kaltwasser (eds) *Populism in Europe and the Americas: Threat or Corrective for Democracy?* New York: Cambridge University Press. 1–26.

Mukherjee, S. (2016) *The Gene: An Intimate History*. London: Vintage.

Muller, J-W. (2017) *What is Populism?* London: Penguin Books.

Mumford, L. (1952) Introduction in Gutkind, E. *Our World from the Air*. New York: Garden City.

Murdock, G. (1945) The Common Denominator of Cultures, in Linton, R. (ed) *The Science of Man in the World Crisis*. New York: Columbia University Press: 123–142.

Murray, D. (2018) *The Strange Death of Europe: Immigration, Identity and Islam*. London: Bloomsbury.

National Commission on the Causes of the Financial and Economic Crisis in the United States (January 2011) *The Financial Crisis Inquiry Report: Final Report of the National Commission on the Causes of the Financial and Economic Crisis in the United States*. Washington, DC: US Government Printing Office.

Neate, R. (31 March 2021) How David Cameron Got Caught Up in a Classic Lobbying Scandal. *The Guardian*.

New Scientist (September 2006) *Human Evolution*. https://newscientist.com/article/dn9 989-timeline-human-evolution. *New Scientist*. Accessed: 1 September 2020.

New Scientist (2018) *Human Origins: 7 Million Years and Counting*. London: John Murray Learning.

Nietzsche, F.W. (1881. 2012 edition) *The Dawn of Day*. translated by John McFarland Kennedy. Book 1: 17. https://gutenberg.org/files/39955/39955-pdf. Accessed: 24 July 2021.

Norris, P. and Inglehart, R. (2019) *Cultural Backlash: Trump, Brexit, and Authoritarian Populism.* Cambridge: Cambridge University Press.

OECD (30 June 2020) *International Community Continues Making Progress Against Offshore Tax Evasion.* Paris: OECD. https://oecd.org/tax/transparency/documents/intern ational-community-continues-making-progress-against-offshore-tax-evasion. Accessed: 16 October 2021.

OECD (8 October 2021) *International Community Strikes a Ground-breaking Tax Deal for the Digital Age.* Paris: OECD. https://oecd.org/newsroom/international-community-strikes-a-ground-breaking-tax-deal-for-the-digital-age. Accessed: 16 October 2021.

Office For Budget Responsibility (March 2022) *Economic and Fiscal Outlook.* https://obr. uk/efo/economic-and-fiscal-outlook-march-2022. Accessed: 12 April 2022.

Office of National Statistics (2015) *2011 Census Analysis: Ethnicity and Religion of the Non-UK Born Population in England and Wales: 2011.* Last updated: 18 June 2015. https:// ons.gov.uk/peoplepopulationandcommunity/culturalidentity/ethnicity/articles/ 2011censusanalysisethnicityandreligionofthenonukbornpopulationinenglandandwa les/2015-06-18. Accessed: 3 November 2021.

Ord, T. (2020) *The Precipice: Existential Risk and the Future of Humanity.* London: Bloomsbury Publishing.

Organisation for Economic Co-operation and Development (OECD) (February 2021) *Sovereign Borrowing Outlook for OECD Countries 2021.* Paris: OECD.

Parekh, B. (2000) *Rethinking Multiculturalism.* Basingstoke: Palgrave.

Parfit, D. (2011) *On What Matters. Volume One.* Oxford: Oxford University Press.

Parker, K. Horowitz, J. and Anderson, M. (12 June 2020) Amid Protests, Majorities Across Racial and Ethnic Groups Express Support for the Black Lives Matter Movement. *Pew Research Center.* https://pewsocialtrends.org/2020/06/12/amid-protests-majorities-across-racial-and-ethnic-groups-express-support-for-the-black-lives-matter-movement. Accessed: 18 July 2020.

Parliament of the World's Religions. (2020 update) *The Declaration of a Global Ethic.* 3.https://parliamentofreligions.org/sites/default/files/docs/global_ethic_pdf_-_ 2020_update.pdf. Accessed: 30 July 2021.

Paul, K. (26 October 2021) Facebook Profits Top $9bn Amid Whistleblower Revelations. *The Guardian.* https://theguardian.com/technology/2021/oct/25/facebook-profits-earnings-report-latest. Accessed: 28 October 2021.

Pearce, F. (29 May 2019) *Geoengineer the Planet? More Scientists Now Say It Must Be An Option.* Yale Environment 360. Yale School of Environment.

Pearson Institute and The Associated Press-NORC Center for Public Affairs Research (October 2022) *Many Believe Misinformation Is Increasing Extreme Political Views And Behaviors.* Chicago: The University of Chicago.

Pegasus Project (23 July 2021) Revealed: Data Leak Uncovers Global Abuse of Cyber-Surveillance Weapon. *The Guardian Weekly.*

Pettersson, T. & Oberg, M. (2020) Organized Violence, 1989–2019. *Journal of Peace Research.* 57(4) 597–613. Data for this analysis derives from the Uppsala Conflict Data Program (UCDP).

Pew Research Center (18 December 2012) *Religion and Public Life: The Global Religious Landscape.* https://pewforum.org: Accessed: 22 June 2020.

Pew Research Center (April 2015) *The Future of World Religions: Population Growth Projections, 2010–2050.* Pew Research Center.

Pew Research Center (2016) *Global Attitude Survey.* For a good summary, see Wike, R., Stokes, B. and Simmons, K. (11 July 2016) *Europeans Fear Wave of Refugees Will Mean More Terrorism, Fewer Jobs.* https://pewresearch.org. Accessed: 23 June 2020.

Pew Research Center (2017) *Europe's Growing Muslim Population. Estimates and Projections. 2017.* Pew Research Center.

Phillips, K. (Summer 2021) How Diversity Works, in: The Science of Overcoming Racism. *Scientific American.* 19–21.

Phillips, M. (2006) *Londonistan: How Britain is Creating a Terror State Within.* New York: Encounter Books.

Pinker, S. (2002) *The Blank Slate: The Modern Denial of Human Nature.* London: Penguin.

Plomin, R. (2018) *Blueprint: How DNA Makes Us Who We Are.* London: Penguin Books.

Pluckrose, H. and Lindsay, J. (2020) *Cynical Theories: How Activist Scholarship Mae Everything About Race, Gender, and Identity -- And Why This Harms Everybody.* Durham, N.C.: Pitchstone Publishing.

Plokhy, S. (2022) *Atoms and Ashes: From Bikini Atoll to Fukushima.* London: Allen Lane.

Polyakova, A. and Meserole, C. (2019) *Exporting Digital Authoritarianism: The Russian and Chinese Models.*

Pomeroy, R. (3 October, 2019) Has Malaria Really Killed Half of Everyone Who Ever Lived? *RealClear Science.* https://realclearscience.com/blog. Accessed: 24 April 2021.

Portella, M.A. (10 May 2022) Orbán's Challenge to Uphold Christian Democracy. *Hungarian Conservative.* https://hungarianconservative.com/articles/politics/orbans-challenge-to-uphold-christian-democracy. Accessed: 12 May 2022.

Potrafke, N. (2015) The Evidence on Globalization. *The World Economy* 38(3) 509–552.

Prime Minister Orbán (21 September 2020) Together We Will Succeed Again. *Magyar Nemzet.* https://abouthungary.hu/speeches-and-remarks/pm-orban-in-magyar-nemzet-together-we-will-succeed-again. Accessed: 1 July 2021.

Prime Minister Viktor Orbán's Commemoration Speech: 6 June 2020. https://miniszterelnok. hu/prime-minister-viktor-orbans-commemoration-speech. Accessed: 1 July 2021.

Prime Minister Viktor Orbán's speech at the Opening of the Exhibition "Treasures from Budapest". 6 December 2019. https://akadalymentes.2015-2019.kormany.hu/en/ the-prime-minister/the-prime-minister-s-speeches/prime-minister-viktor-orban-s-speech-at-the-opening-of-the-temporary-exhibition-treasures-from-budapest. Accessed: 1 July 2021.

Public Religion Research Institute (PRRI) with the Brookings Institution (2021) *Competing Visions of America: An Evolving Identity Or A Culture Under Attack? Findings From the 2021 American Values Survey.* Washington: PRRI.

Puri, S. (2020) *The Great Imperial Hangover: How Empires have Shaped the World.* London: Atlantic Books.

Quammen, D. (2013) *Spillover: Animal Infections and the Next Human Pandemic.* London: Vintage.

Race Disparity Audit (October 2017. revised March 2018) *Summary Findings from the Ethnicity Facts and Figures Website.* Cabinet Office. 2.9. 9. https://gov.uk/government/ publications/race-disparity-audit. Accessed: 3 November 2021.

Rand, A. (1957. 2007 edition) *Atlas Shrugged.* London: Penguin Books.

Raterman, E. (March 29, 2019) Tracing the History of Forced Sterilization within the United States. *Health Law & Policy Brief.* http://healthlawpolicy.org/trac ing-the-history-of-forced-sterilization-within-the-united-states. Accessed: 15 September 2020.

Reeves, M.E. Joachim of Fiore. *Britannica*. https://britannica.com/biography/Joachim-of-Fiore. Accessed: 13 August 2021.

Reich, D. (2018) *Who We Are and How We Got Here*. Oxford: Oxford University Press.

Reich, D., Kumarasamy, T., Patterson, N., Price, A.L., and Singh, L. (2009) Reconstructing Indian Population History. *Nature* 461. 489–494. https://nature.com/articles. Accessed: 6 July 2020.

Reich, R. (24 January 2021) Don't Believe the Anti-Trump Hype – Corporate Sedition still Endangers America. *The Observer*.

Reich, R. (3 August 2021) A Trump Bombshell Quietly Dropped Last Week. And It Should Shock Us All. *The Guardian*.

Reid, N. (2021) *The Good Ally: A Guided Anti-racism Journey: From Bystander to Changemaker*. London: HarperCollins.

Remnick, D. (30 July 2018) Inside An Off-the-Record Meeting. *The New Yorker*.

Renaud, M. (June 2018) *Toward a Global, Humanistic Theology: Constructing Moral Concepts of God*. Dissertation Submission for the Degree of Doctor of Philosophy. The Faculty of the Divinity School, University of Chicago.

Reporting Team BBC Panorama (20 September 2020) *FinCEN Files*. BBC: https://bbc.co.uk/news/business. Accessed: 21 March 2021.

Ridley, M. (2004 Edition) *Nature Via Nurture: Genes, Experience and What Makes Us Human*. London: Fourth Estate.

Rifkin, J. (2011) *The Third Industrial Revolution: How Lateral Power is Transforming Energy, the Economy, and the World*. New York: St. Martin's Griffin.

Rifkin, J. (2014) *The Zero Marginal Cost Society: The Internet of Things, The Collaborative Commons, and the Eclipse of Capitalism*. New York: St. Martin's Griffin.

Ritchie, H. and Roser, M. (2020) Co2 and Greenhouse Gas Emissions. *OurWorldInData.org*. https://ourworldindata.org/co2-and-other-greenhouse-gas-emissions. Accessed: 18 September 2021.

Roberts, A. (2010) *The Incredible Human Journey; the Story of How We Colonised the Planet*. London: Bloomsbury.

Roberts, A. (2018 edition) *Evolution: the Human Story*. London: Dorling Kindersley.

Roberts, M. (2018) *Censored: Distraction and Diversion Inside China's Great Firewall*. Princeton, NJ: Princeton University Press.

Robinson, J. (1962: 2006 edition) *Economic Philosophy*. London: Aldine.

Rodrik, D. (2011) *The Globalisation Paradox: Why Global Markets, States, and Democracy Can't Coexist*. Oxford: Oxford University Press.

Rogers, A., Harris, N., and Achenbach, A. (Feb 2020) Neanderthal-Denisovan Ancestors Interbred with a Distantly Related Hominin. *Science Advances*. 6(8) eaay5483. DOI: 10.1126/sciadv.aay5483. https://advances.sciencemag.org/content/6/8/eaay5483. Accessed: 3 September 2020.

Rosenfeld, S. (2019) *Democracy and Truth: A Short History*. Philadelphia: University of Pennsylvania Press.

Roser, M., Ortiz-Ospina, E. and Richie, H. (First Published in 2013; Last Revised in October 2019) *Life Expectancy*. https://ourworldindata.org/life-expectancy. Accessed: 21 April 2021.

Roser, M., Ritchie, H. & Ortiz-Ospina, E. (2013) *World Population Growth. Published Online at OurWorldInData.org*. Retrieved from: https://ourworldindata.org/world-population-growth; Accessed: 16 September 2021.

Rowlatt, J. and Gerken, T. (21 October 2021) COP26: Document Leak Reveals Nations Lobbying to Change Key Climate Report. *BBC*. https://bbc.co.uk/news/science-environment. Accessed: 22 October 2021.

Rowlingson, K., Sood, A., and Tu, T. (2020) *Public Attitudes to a Wealth Tax*. Wealth Tax Commission Evidence Paper 2.

Runnymede Trust (2017) *Islamophobia: Still a Challenge for Us All*. London: Runnymede Trust.

Rushton, J.P. and Jensen, A.R. (November 2008) James Watson's Most Inconvenient Truth: Race Realism and the Moralistic Fallacy. *Medical Hypotheses*. 71(5):629–40.

Russell, S. (2019) *Human Compatible: Artificial Intelligence and the Problem of Control*. London: Penguin Books.

Rutherford, A. (22 September 2018) Human League: What Separates Us from Monkeys and Dolphins - Language, Tool-Use, Non-Reproductive Sex? We Now Have an Answer. *The Guardian*.

Rutherford, A. (2022) *Control: The Dark History and Troubling Present of Eugenics*. London: Weidenfeld & Nicolson.

Salzberg, S. (2018) Open Questions: How Many Genes Do We Have? *BMC Biology*. 16(94) https://bmcbiol.biomedcentral.com/articles. Accessed: 30 September 2020.

Schellenberg, S. (April 2020) How Biased Algorithms Perpetuate Inequality. *New Statesman*.

Schultz, A. (1908) *Race or Mongrel: a Brief History of the Rise and Fall of the Ancient Races of Earth*. Boston: L.C. Page.

Schwab, K. (2017) *The Fourth Industrial Revolution* (2017) London: Penguin Random House.

Sciencealert Staff. *What Is Quantum Entanglement?* https://sciencealert.com/entanglement. Accessed: 11 May 2021.

Scientific American (Summer 2021) The Science of Overcoming Racism: What Research Shows and Experts Say About Creating a More Just and Equitable World. Special Edition of *Scientific American*.

Sedgwick, M. (ed) *Against the Modern World: Traditionalism and the Secret Intellectual History of the Twentieth Century*. Oxford: Oxford University Press.

Seth, A. (2021) *Being You: A New Science of Consciousness*. London: Faber.

Shakespeare, S. and de Waal, J.R. (26 November 2021) Be Reassured: the World is Not as Divided as We Might Think. *YouGov*. https://yougov.co.uk/topics/international/articles-reports/2021/11/26/be-reassured-world-not-divided-we-might-think. Accessed: 11 May 2022.

Shaban, H. (29 September 2020) JPMorgan Chase to Pay $920 Million to Resolve Illegal Trading Cases. *Washington Post*.

Shankley, W. and Rhodes, J. (2020) Racisms in Contemporary Britain in B. Byrne, C. Alexander, O. Khan, J. Nazroo and W. Shankley (eds), *Ethnicity, Race and Inequality in the UK: State of the Nation*. Bristol: Bristol University Press.

Shankley, W. and Williams, P. (2020) Minority Ethnic Groups, Policing and the Criminal Justice System in Britain in Byrne, B., et al (eds) *Ethnicity, Race and Inequality in the UK: State of the Nation*. Bristol: Bristol University Press.

Shaxson, N. (16 June 2021) Making Sure the 'Big People' Pay their Taxes Would Be a Boost to Democracy. *The Guardian*.

Shaxson, N. (2011) *Treasure Islands: Tax Havens and the Men who Stole the World*. London: Palgrave Macmillan.

Shaxson, N. (2018) *The Finance Curse: How Global Finance is Making Us All Poorer.* London: Bodley Head.

Shaxson, N. (24 February 2011) The Tax Haven in the Heart of Britain. *New Statesman.*

Singh, S. (20 November 2017) Transhumanism And The Future Of Humanity: 7 Ways The World Will Change By 2030. *Forbes Magazine.* https://forbes.com/sites/sarwa ntsingh/2017/11/20/transhumanism-and-the-future-of-humanity-seven-ways-the-world-will-change-by-2030. Accessed: 6 January 2021.

Sinn, H.-W. (2010) *Casino Capitalism: How the Financial Crisis Came About and What Needs to be Done Now.* Oxford: Oxford University Press.

Smil, V. (2019) *Growth: From Microorganisms to Megacities.* Cambridge, Massachusetts: MIT Press.

Smith, A.D. (1999) *Myths and Memories of the Nation.* Oxford: Oxford University Press.

Smith, R. and Pickard, J. (undated) Greensill Capital Paid Cameron Salary of More Than $1 million a Year. *Financial Times.*

Smithsonian Institute. *Human Origins.* https://humanorigins.si.edu/research/age-hum ans-evolutionary-perspectives-anthropocene. Accessed: 1 September 2020.

Social Mobility Commission (June 2020) *Monitoring Social Mobility: 2013–2020: Is the government delivering on our recommendations?* London: Social Mobility Commission.

Socratic Q&A: *What is Difference Between Gravitational Force and Magnetic Force?* https://socratic.org/questions/what-is-difference-between-gravitational-force-and-magne tic-force. Accessed: 17 May 2021.

Song, W., Jakhar, P., Bhat, U., and Menon, S. (November 2020) Fact-checking the US and China on Climate and Environment. Reality Check team and BBC Monitoring. *BBC News.*

Spathari, E. (2016) *Greek Mythology.* Athens: Papadimas Ekdotiki.

Spencer, J. and Delmastro, T. (authors); Delmastro, T. (director). (2017) *End of the Road: How Money Became Worthless.* A Documentary by 100th Monkey Films.

Spiegelhalter, D. and Masters, A. (13 June 2021) What Were Some of the Collateral Effects of Lockdowns? *The Observer.*

Spong, J.S. (1998) *Why Christianity Must Change or Die: A Bishop Speaks to Believers in Exile.* New York: HarperCollins.

Srinivasan, D. (2020, Forthcoming) Why Google Dominates Advertising Markets. 23 *Stanford Technology Law Review.* Available at SSRN: https://ssrn.com/abstract= 3500919.

Statista (2021) *The 100 Largest Companies in the World by Market Capitalisation in 2021.* https://statista.com/statistics/263264/top-companies-in-the-world-by-market-cap italization. Accessed: 3 November 2021.

Statista (February 2022) *Market Capitalization of the Largest U.S. Internet Companies as of February 2022.* https://statista.com/statistics/209331/largest-us-internet-compan ies-by-market-cap. Accessed: 15 May 2022.

Statista (2022) *Facebook's Advertising Revenue Worldwide.* https://statista.com/statistics/ 271258/facebooks-advertising-revenue-worldwide. Accessed: 22 May 2022.

Stecklow, S. (15 August 2018) *Why Facebook is Losing the War on Hate Speech in Myanmar.* Reuters Investigates.

Stenger, V.J. (2007) *God: The Failed Hypothesis: How Science Shows that God Does Not Exist.* Amherst, New York: Prometheus Books.

Stevenson, J., Demack, S., Stiell, B., Abdi, M., Clarkson, L., Ghaffar, F., and Shaima Hassan, S. (September 2017) *The Social Mobility Challenges Faced by Young Muslims.* London: Social Mobility Commission.

Stewart, M., Clark-Wilson, R., Breeze, P., & Janulis, K. (18 Sep 2020) Human Footprints Provide Snapshot of Last Interglacial Ecology in the Arabian Interior. *Science Advances.* 6(38). eaba8940. DOI: 10.1126/sciadv.aba8940.

Stoddard, L. (1920) *The Rising Tide of Color Against White World-Supremacy.* New York: Charles Scribner's Sons.

Su, J. (16 May 2019) Why Amazon Alexa Is Always Listening To Your Conversations: Analysis. *Forbes.* https://forbes.com/sites/jeanbaptiste/2019/05/16/why-amazon-alexa-is-always-listening-to-your-conversations-analysis. Accessed: 3 November 2021.

Sumpter, D. (2018) *Outnumbered: From Facebook and Google to Fake News and Filter-Bubbles- The Algorithms That Control Our Lives.* London: Bloomsbury.

Taibbi, M. (8 July 2015) Eric Holder, Wall Street Double Agent, Comes in From the Cold. *Rolling Stone.*

Tamir, Y. (2019) *Why Nationalism?* Princeton, NJ: Princeton University Press.

Taylor, C. (2002) *Varieties of Religion Today: William James Revisited.* Cambridge, MA: Harvard University Press.

Taylor, J. (2005) *American Renaissance website,* quoted by the Southern Poverty Law Center. https://aplcenter.org/fighting-hate/extremist-files/individual/jared-taylor. Accessed: 26 June 2020.

Taylor, J. (July 3, 2008) *American Renaissance website.* quoted by the Southern Poverty Law Center. https://aplcenter.org/fighting-hate/extremist-files/individual/jared-taylor. Accessed: 26 June 2020.

The ADL Global 100: An Index of Anti-Semitism. (based on a 2014 survey, with follow-up surveys in 2015, 2017, and 2019, tracked attitudes in 102 countries and territories, claims 1.09 billion people harbour anti-Semitic attitudes). https://global100.adl.org/map/global survey of anti-Semitic views. Accessed: 19 August 2020.

The Center for the Study of Contemporary European Jewry. Faculty of Humanities. Tel Aviv University (2022) *The Anti-Semitism Worldwide Report 2021.* Tel Aviv University.

The Economist (4 April 2019) The Promise and Perils of Synthetic Biology. *The Economist.*

The Economist (25 July 2020) The COVID-19 Pandemic is Forcing a Rethink in Macroeconomics. *The Economist.*

The Economist (1 July 2021) A New Human Species May Have Been Identified. *The Economist.*

The Economist (4 October 2021) How Do People and Companies Avoid Paying Taxes? *The Economist.*

The Economist (4 February 2022:Updated 13 May 2022)Why Does So Much Dodgy Russian Money End up in Britain? *The Economist.*

The Economist (24 March 2022) The Risk That The War In Ukraine Escalates Past The Nuclear Threshold. *The Economist.*

The Economist (26 March 2022) Spring In His Step. *The Economist.*

The Economist (8 April 2022) What Are Non-doms, and Why Does It Matter that Rishi Sunak's Wife Is One? *The Economist.*

The Economist (30 April 2022) Lifting the Silicon Veil: The Secrets of Big Tech. *The Economist.*

The Economist (5 May 2022) Wearable Technology Promises To Revolutionise Health Care. *The Economist.*

The Economist Intelligence Unit (2021) *Democracy Index 2020: In Sickness and in Health?* London: EI.

The Economist Intelligence Unit (EIU) (2022) *Democracy Index 2021: The China Challenge.* London: EI.

The Editorial Board (7 February, 2020) The Government Uses 'Near Perfect Surveillance' Data on Americans. *The New York Times.*

The Guardian View (11 December 2020) DeepMind's AI Biology Breakthrough Raises Issues About Who Pays for Science. *The Guardian Weekly.*

The Irish Fiscal Advisory Council (November 2019) *Fiscal Assessment Report.* Dublin: IFAC.

The United States Department of Justice: Office of Public Affairs (22 October 2020) *Goldman Sachs Charged in Foreign Bribery Case and Agrees to Pay over $2.9 Billion.* The United States Department of Justice.

Tippet, B., Wildauer, R., and Onaran, O. (2021) *The Case for a Progressive Annual Wealth Tax in the UK.* [Working Paper] (Unpublished) University of Greenwich. https://gala.gre.ac.uk/id/eprint. Accessed: 25 October 2021.

Tisdall, S. (19 September 2021) Making Waves in the Pacific: How Boris Johnson's Global Britain Went Rogue. *The Observer.* https://theguardian.com/commentisfree/2021/sep/19/making-waves-in-the-pacific-how-boris-johnsons-global-britain-went-rogue. Accessed: 20 September 2021.

Tooze, A. (2 June 2020) The Death of Globalisation Has Been Announced Many Times. But This is a Perfect Storm. *The Guardian.*

Tooze, A. (2018) *Crashed: How a Decade of Financial Crises Changed the World.* London: Allen Lane.

Trager, R.F. and Luca, L.M. (11 May 2022) Killer Robots Are Here And We Need to Regulate Them. *Foreign Policy* (FP). https://foreignpolicy.com/2022/05/11/killer-robots-lethal-autonomous-weapons-systems-ukraine-libya-regulation. Accessed: 26 May 2022.

Transparency International Press Statement (28 February 2022) *Stats Reveal the Extent of Suspect Wealth in UK Property and Britain's Role As Global Money Laundering Hub.* Transparency International UK.

Treanor, J. (11 January 2011) Bob Diamond Stands Firm Against MPs' Calls He Forgo His Bonus. *The Guardian.*

Turner, J. (2019) *Robot Rules: Regulating Artificial Intelligence.* Cham; Switzerland: Springer.

UN Environment Programme (October 2021) *The Heat Is On: A World of Climate Promises Not Yet Delivered.* Nairobi, Kenya: UNEP.

UN Special Rapporteur on Contemporary Forms of Racism, Racial Discrimination, Xenophobia and Related Intolerance. *UN Human Rights Council Document No. A/HRC/6/6* (21 August 2007). Available at: http://oicun.org/uploads/files/articles/UNHRC-rep.pdf.

UNESCO (1950) *The Race Question, including Text of the Statement Issued 18th July 1950.* Paris: UNESCO Publication 791.

United Nations. Department of Economic and Social Affairs, Population Division (2019) *World Population Prospects 2019: Data Booklet* (ST/ESA/SER.A/424) New York: United Nations; Population Division of the United Nations Department of Economic and Social Affairs (2019) *World Population Prospects 2019. Highlights.* New York: United Nations.

United Nations. Department of Economic and Social Affairs, Population Division. (2022) *World Population Prospects 2022.* New York: United Nations.

United Nations Development Programme (UNDP) (2022) *New Threats to Human Security In The Anthropocene: Demanding Greater Solidarity.* UNDP.

United Nations Environment Programme (2019) *The UNEP Emissions Gap Report 2019*: Nairobi, Kenya: UNEP.

United Nations Environment Programme (2020) *Used Vehicles and the Environment: A Global Overview of Used Light Duty Vehicles: Flow, Scale and Regulation.* Nairobi: United Nations Environment Programme.

United Nations (2015) *Interim Report of the Panel of Experts on South Sudan Established pursuant to Security Council Resolution 2206…*New York: UN.

United States Department of Justice: Office of Public Affairs (19 November 2013) *Justice Department, Federal and State Partners Secure Record $13 billion Global Settlement with JPMorgan for Misleading Investors About Securities Containing Toxic Mortgages.*

United States Department of Justice. Case 1:12-cr-00763-ILG Document 3-3 Filed 12/11/12. *Statement of Facts.*https://justice.gov/sites/default/files/opa/legacy/2012/12/11/dpa-attachment-a.pdf. Accessed on: 3 November 2021.

United States Department of Justice. *Review of Section 230 of the Communications Decency Act of 1996.* Washington DC: DoJ.DE. https://justice.gov/archives/ag/department-justice-s-review-section-230-communications-decency-act-1996. Accessed on: 3 November 2021.

United States Department of State (September 25, 2020) *China's Environmental Abuses Fact Sheet*: Fact Sheet Office of the Spokesperson. https://state.gov/chinas-environmental-abuses-fact-sheet.

Uscinski, J.E. (ed.) (2018) *Conspiracy Theories and the People Who Believe Them.* New York: Oxford University Press.

Vaidhyanathan, S. (2018) *Antisocial Media: How Facebook Disconnects Us and Undermines Democracy.* Oxford: Oxford University Press.

Vanderslott, S., Dadonaite, B. and Max Roser, M. (2013. last revised December 2019) Vaccination. *Published Online at OurWorldInData.org.* Retrieved from: 'https://ourworldindata.org/vaccination'. Accessed on: 21 April 2021.

Varoufakis, Y. (5 April 2016) Why We Must Save the EU. *The Guardian.*

Vollset, S., Goren, E., Yuan, C-W., Cao, J., Smith, A., Hsias, T., et al. (July 2020) Fertility, Mortality, Migration, and Population Scenarios for 195 Countries and Territories from 2017–2100: A Forecasting Analysis for the Global Burden of Disease Study. *The Lancet.* Published Online: July 14, 2020. https://doi.org/10.1016/S0140-6736(20)30677-2. https://thelancet.com/journals/lancet/article/PIIS0140-6736(20)30677-2/fulltext.

Vonk, R. and Visser, A. (October 2020) An Exploration of Spiritual Superiority: The Paradox of Self-enhancement. *European Journal of Social Psychology.* 152–165.

vpnMentor (2019) *The Big Tech Lobby.* see https://vpnmentor.com/blog/big-tech-lobbying-report.

Walker, P. (7 May 2021) Keir Starmer Under Pressure from Labour Left After 'Disappointing Night'. *The Guardian.*

Wallace-Wells, D. (2019) *The Uninhabitable Earth: A Story of the Future.* London: Penguin Books.

Ward, B. (8 October 2018) The IPCC Global Warming Report Spares Politicians the Worst Details. *The Guardian.*

Warofka, A. (Product Policy Manager). (5 November 2018) *An Independent Assessment of the Human Rights Impact of Facebook in Myanmar.* Facebook.

Warzel, C. (21 January, 2020) We Need a Law to Save Us From Dystopia. *The New York Times.*

Warzel, C. (18 February, 2020) All This Dystopia, and For What? *The New York Times.*

Waters, C. & Zalasiewicz, J. (2018) The Anthropocene and its 'Golden Spike' in Burtynsky, E., Baichwal, J., & De Pencier, N. *Anthropocene.* Toronto: Ago. 35–43.

Waters, C.N., Zalasiewicz, J., Summerhayes, C., Barnosky, A.D., et al. (2016) The Anthropocene is Functionally and Stratigraphically Distinct from the Holocene. *Science* 351 (6269), aad2622–1–aad2622–10.

Wattles, J. (1996) *The Golden Rule.* Oxford: Oxford University Press.

Weedon, J., Nuland, W., and Stamos, A. (27 April 2017) *Information Operations and Facebook.* Facebook Paper. Version 1.0. Facebook Inc.

Wells, G.A. (1982) *The Historical Evidence for Jesus.* Buffalo, N.Y.: Prometheus.

Wells, G., Horwitz, J., and Seetharaman, D. (14 September 2021) Facebook Knows Instagram is Toxic for Teen Girls, Company Documents Show. *The Wall St., Journal.*

Which? (June 2018) *Control, Alt, or Delete? The Future of Consumer Data.* London: Which?

White, M. (2011). *Atrocitology: Humanity's 100 Deadliest Achievements.* Edinburgh: Canongate Books.

Whitehouse Briefings: https://whitehouse.gov/briefings-statements/remarks-presid ent-trump-south-dakotas-2020-mount-rushmore. Accessed: 12 July 2020.

White House Communications Agency Sound Recordings Collection. Conversation 700–10 (3 April 1972) *Nixon Presidential Materials,* The White House Communications Agency Sound Recordings Collection.

Widyono, B. (2008) *Dancing in Shadows: Sihanouk, the Khmer Rouge, and the United Nations in Cambodia.* New York: Rowman & Littlefield Publishers, Inc.

Wilczek, F. (28 April 2016) Entanglement Made Simple. *Quanta Magazine.* https://qua ntamagazine.org/entanglement-made-simple. Accessed: 11 May 2021.

Wilkerson, I. (2020) *Caste: The Lies That Divide Us.* London: Penguin Books.

Williams, M., Zalasiewicz, J., Haywood, A. & Ellis, M. (eds) 2011. The Anthropocene: a New Epoch of Geological Time? *Philosophical Transactions of the Royal Society* 369A, 833–1112.

Wilson, E. (1975. 2000 edition) *Sociobiology: The New Synthesis.* Cambridge MA: Belknap Press of Harvard University Press.

Wilson, E. (1978. 2004 edition) *On Human Nature.* Cambridge, MA: Harvard University Press.

Wimmer, A. (March/April 2019) Why Nationalism Works and Why it isn't Going Away. *Foreign Affairs.* 98(2), 27–34.

Wheeler, C. (13 March 2022) JK Rowling Rounds on Keir Starmer Over Gender. *The Sunday Times.* World Justice Project (2021) *World Justice Project Rule of Law Index 2021.* Washington: WJP. World Population Review (2022) *School Shootings By State.* https://worldpopulationreview.com/state-rankings/school-shootings-by-state. Accessed: 25 May 2022.

Working Group II Contribution to the Sixth Assessment Report of the Intergovernmental Panel on Climate Change (February 2022) *Climate Change 2022: Impacts, Adaptation And Vulnerability: Summary for Policymakers.* Switzerland: IPPC.

Working Group III Contribution to the Sixth Assessment Report of the Intergovernmental Panel on Climate Change (April 2022) *Climate Change 2022: Mitigation of Climate Change. Summary For Policymakers.* Switzerland: IPPC.

World Population Review (2022) *Nuclear Weapons by Country 2022.* https://worldpopul ationreview.com/country-rankings/nuclear-weapons-by-country. Accessed: 20 May 2022.

Wrangham, R. (2020) *The Goodness Paradox: How Evolution Made Us Both More and Less Violent.* London: Profile Books.

Wright, T. and Hope, B. (2019) *Billion Dollar Whale: The Man Who Fooled Wall St., Hollywood, and the World.* London: Scribe.

Wu, T. (2016) *The Attention Merchants: From the Daily Newspaper to Social Media. How Our Time and Attention is Harvested and Sold.* London: Atlantic Books.

Wylie, C. (2020) *Mindf*ck.* London: Profile Books.

Yglesias, M. (Updated 1 April 2019) The Great Awakening: A Hidden Shift is Revolutionizing American Racial Politics — and Could Transform the Future of the Democratic Party. https://vox.com/2019/3/22/18259865/great-awakening-white-liberals-race-polling-trump-2020. Accessed: 20 July 2020.

Yiftachel, O. (2006) *Ethnocracy: Land and Identity Politics in Israel/Palestine.* Philadelphia: University of Pennsylvania Press.

Yudell, M. (2018) *Race Unmasked: Biology and Race.* New York: Columbia University Press.

Zakrzewski, C. and Lerman, R. (29 September 2021) Facebook Tries to Minimize its Own Research Ahead of Hearings on Children's Safety. *Washington Post.* https://washingtonpost.com/technology/2021/09/29/facebook-childrens-safety-hearings. Accessed: 1 October 2021.

Zakrzewski, C. (21 January 2022) Tech Companies Spent Almost $70 million Lobbying Washington In 2021 As Congress Sought To Rein In Their Power. *The Washington Post.*

Zanghellini, A. (May 2020) *Philosophical Problems With the Gender-Critical Feminist Argument Against Trans Inclusion.* Sage Journals. https://journals.sagepub.com/doi/full. Accessed: 17 March 2022.

Zenz, A. (2022). The Xinjiang Police Files: Re-Education Camp Security and Political Paranoia in the Xinjiang Uyghur Autonomous Region. *The Journal of the European Association for Chinese Studies, 3,* 1–56.

Zinn, H. (1997/2009) *The Zinn Reader: Writings on Disobedience and Democracy.* New York: Seven Stories Press.

Zuboff, S. (2019) *The Age of Surveillance Capitalism: The Fight for the Future at the New Frontier of Power.* London: Profile Books.

Zuboff, S. (24 January 2020) You Are Now Remotely Controlled. *The New York Times.*

Zucman, G. (2015) *The Hidden Wealth of Nations: The Scourge of Tax Havens.* Chicago: University of Chicago Press.

Zureik, E. (2016) *Israel's Colonial Project in Palestine: Brutal Pursuit.* Abington, Oxon: Routledge.

INDEX